GW00392117

"A remarkable book. I know of no embraces and illuminates the relationship. E. Graham Howe ph oversimplification. He is clearly a but in the ways they intertwine. What is most remarkable is the clarity and ease of presentation, a mark of someone who knows his subject. He addresses the general reader, but especially the psychotherapist. It is wonderful to have his work in print."

—NATHAN SCHWARTZ-SALANT, PhD
author of *The Mystery of Human Relationship:
Alchemy and the Transformation of the Self*

"This is an extraordinary labor of love that finally makes the teachings of E. Graham Howe brilliantly available to a wide audience, including psychotherapists of all persuasions. Howe is singular in his ability to integrate the wisdom of the East with humanistic elements of psychoanalysis in a way that is unique and intuitively accessible to clinicians who do not have a background in either tradition. William Stranger is to be commended for his ability to gather the many pearls of wisdom from Howe's varied publications into a format that is faithful to the original sources while making them even more illuminating. Destined to become a classic."

—M. GUY THOMPSON, PhD
Personal and Supervising Analyst at the Psychoanalytic Institute
of Northern California, and author of *The Ethic of Honesty:
The Fundamental Rule of Psychoanalysis*

"This book is a tour de force that under one cover that includes selections from all of Howe's writings. Howe illuminates the causes of human suffering by using the language of psychoanalysis to help us understand the mystery of human experience. It is a wonderful book for both psychotherapists and the general reader to gain greater understanding of what it means to be human."

—JOHN M. HEATON, MD
author of *The Talking Cure: Wittgenstein's
Therapeutic Method for Psychotherapy*

"An exciting, challenging work that helps us look beyond our smaller attitudes and seek a broader, fuller path. Uplifting and therapeutic."

—MICHAEL EIGEN, PhD
Associate Clinical Professor of Psychology at New York University,
editor emeritus at *The Psychoanalytic Review*,
and author of *Contact with the Depths*

"Sooner or later, each and every one of us who presumes to follow a spiritual path must endure the difficult, humbling revelation and purification of his or her own deep-seated neurotic patterns of thought and action. Because psychoanalysis, psychotherapy, and psychiatry came of age in a secularized world, these are typically regarded as a matter unto themselves, both generated and cured without reference to our spiritual nature. In this landmark and vitally necessary book, the great English psychiatrist E. Graham Howe not only disproves that presumption but provides us with our era's first truly esoteric and integral psychology. Graciously written, profoundly wise, *The Druid of Harley Street* is itself an instructive, healing, and liberating meditation that should be in the hands of every psychotherapist—and by the bedsides of the rest of us."

—ANDREW HARVEY
author of *The Direct Path: Creating a Journey to
the Divine Through the World's Mystical Traditions*

The Druid
of Harley Street

The Druid
of Harley Street

The Spiritual Psychology of
E. Graham Howe

EDITED BY
WILLIAM STRANGER

DHARMACAFÉ BOOKS
COBB, CALIFORNIA

NORTH ATLANTIC BOOKS
BERKELEY, CALIFORNIA

Published by
DharmaCafé Books   and   North Atlantic Books
P.O. Box 1289   P.O. Box 12327
Cobb, California 95426   Berkeley, California 94712

Photo on cover and page 26 courtesy of Carolyn Whitaker
Cover design by Steve Alexander
Book design by Matt Barna
Illustrations by E. Graham Howe
Printed in the United States of America

The Druid of Harley Street: The Spiritual Psychology of E. Graham Howe is sponsored by the Society for the Study of Native Arts and Sciences, a nonprofit educational corporation whose goals are to develop an educational and cross-cultural perspective linking various scientific, social, and artistic fields; to nurture a holistic view of arts, sciences, humanities, and healing; and to publish and distribute literature on the relationship of mind, body, and nature.

DharmaCafé Books' publications are available through most bookstores. For further information, visit our website at www.dharmacafebooks.com.

North Atlantic Books' publications are available through most bookstores. For further information, visit our website at www.northatlanticbooks.com or call 800-733-3000.

Library of Congress Cataloging-in-Publication Data

Howe, Eric Graham, 1897–
  The druid of Harley Street : selected writings of E. Graham Howe / E. Graham Howe.
    p. cm.
  ISBN 978-1-55643-774-8
  1. Psychology. I. Title.
  BF173.A25H69 2009
  150—dc22
                              2009031815

1 2 3 4 5 6 7 8 9 Sheridan 17 16 15 14 13 12

Printed on recycled paper.

TABLE OF CONTENTS

LIST OF FIGURES

FOREWORD

The history of thought can be fleeting, and the thinkers who made vital thoughts accessible to us can consequently vanish in the mist as one generation passes to another, until we are hardly aware of their legacy and indirect influence upon our contemporary mindset. We are all too familiar with the names of those who managed to survive the unpredictable (mis)fortunes of time and history or the fickle fate of fame and notoriety. But for every Aristotle or Freud there are perhaps dozens if not hundreds of equally remarkable thinkers who were just as important to the era in which they lived but whose impact faded following their death. They left no followers or disciples to perpetuate their contribution and transmit their teaching to us. Fortunately, these names do not necessarily disappear altogether, because occasionally there remains a select few who continue to speak of them and remember what made them so remarkable in the first place.

E. Graham Howe is one such individual, and it is because of William Stranger that we are privileged to become acquainted—many of us for the first time—with this extraordinary sage. Though Howe's name has not been forgotten by some contemporary psychiatrists and psychoanalysts in Great Britain, his fame did not stretch all the way to the United States, and his many books and other publications, which never made their way over here, are now completely out of print in both lands.

I first learned of Howe's work when I had moved to London from San Francisco in the 1970s to study with R. D. Laing, whose work I had followed for some years. I lived in Great Britain for nearly a decade, during which time I trained as a psychoanalyst and enjoyed the rare opportunity to live in one of Laing's post–Kingsley Hall community households, Portland Road. It was Laing who first told me about Howe and who encouraged me to read his work.

Laing told me that he had met Howe in 1960, soon after he had published his first book, *The Divided Self.* He had been sought out by one of Howe's students, John Heaton, who did his psychotherapy training with Howe and his group, The Open Way. Heaton had read Laing's book and, after putting Howe onto it, arranged to meet the author. Laing and Heaton hit it off immediately when they realized they shared many common interests, including a passionate devotion to phenomenology, Eastern religions, and varied spiritual practices. Heaton soon introduced Laing to Howe and they, too, became immediate friends.

It was a very fortunate meeting for Laing. He had recently completed his psychoanalytic training at the British Psychoanalytic Society, a bitter and disappointing experience that left him with no desire to pursue further involvement with the society. Though Laing had got on just fine with his analyst, Charles Rycroft, and two supervisors, D. W. Winnicott and Marian Milner, other members of the society, including some of his teachers, took a disliking to this young Scottish psychiatrist who could never suffer fools gladly and couldn't resist the opportunity to one-up anyone he came into contact with who he believed was ill-informed, or just plain stupid. Moreover, Laing's interest in philosophy and the psychoanalytic treatment of schizophrenia fell on deaf ears at the Tavistock Clinic, where he was employed during his training.

There is an irony here, because Howe was one of a group of iconoclastic psychotherapists who became involved with the Tavistock starting in the late 1920s and continuing through the Second World War. These included Eric Trist, Maxwell Jones, and others, who all shared in common a passionate interest in Buddhism and other Asian spiritual traditions. As the Tavistock evolved, it became a center for developing a variety of therapeutic practices, including but not exclusively psychoanalysis. These included Maxwell Jones's "therapeutic community," Wilfried Bion's pioneering group process, and Howe's singular integration of Eastern and Western psychological traditions.

By the time Laing began his psychoanalytic training there in 1956, however, the Tavistock had become more or less inseparable from the British Psychoanalytic Society and all vestiges of Eastern traditions had vanished. Howe had long since departed along with the other iconoclastic practitioners who found a narrowly psycho-analytic perspective constraining. Having already extensively stud-ied psychoanalysis, phenomenology and existential philosophy, and Buddhism before moving from Glasgow to London to pursue analytic training, Laing was in no mood to be reduced to the new order there. Upon graduating from the British Psychoanalytic Society, then, he was at loose ends when Heaton made the fortu-nate introduction to Howe. Laing soon made himself at home in The Open Way, and Howe made him the director of the Langam Clinic, a reduced-fee psychotherapy center under the auspices of The Open Way. Although Laing eventually left The Open Way to start his own organization, the Philadelphia Association, for the purpose of developing treatment methods for alleviating schizo-phrenia, Howe's mentorship had left an indelible mark.

With the exception of his first book, *Motives and Mechanisms of the Mind*, none of Howe's works had won favor with the psychiatric establishment. Although several sold fairly well to the general pub-lic, by the time I arrived in London all his books were out of print. It required many visits to London's famed Watkins Bookshop on Cecil Court, which specialized in esoteric and mystical publica-tions, for me to find the six or seven secondhand copies of Howe's books I was able to get my hands on. They had an enormous impact on me. I was mildly interested in Eastern practices, but I had been turned off by Jung's efforts to integrate Eastern and Western traditions in a manner that didn't, in my opinion, capture the essence of the Eastern sensibility. In contrast, I found Howe's efforts to effect this integration far more interesting and fruitful. I saw in his writings all the elements of Buddhist philosophy fleshed out in his views about neurosis as well as the aims and practices of psychotherapy. Previously I had seen psychoanalysis and Buddhist meditation practices as two completely separate, even incompati-ble, belief systems that spoke such different languages that it was impossible to find the common thread between them. What sur-prised me about Howe was his easy and seemingly effortless way of inserting all of the wisdom of the East into the ostensibly banal "relief of psychopathology." The need to develop compassion for others, to overcome the crippling power of the ego, to embrace hardship with benign acceptance, and to feel connected to something much larger than our own self-interest were all themes brought brilliantly to life in Howe's depiction of the psychotherapeutic process as he understood it. Whereas previously I had assumed that the only way for a psychoanalyst to include an Eastern sensibility in his practice was to engage in his own personal pursuit of meditation practices, I now understood that psychotherapy practice is *itself* a kind of meditation, but one that uses listening and speaking as the basic tools of meditative practice.

After reading Howe I realized the impact that he had also had on Laing. How much of this Laing already knew from his own journey and how much came from his association with E. Graham Howe I do not know. But I could see what a superb moment of recognition must have passed between them upon meeting and working together. Both men had that uncanny knack of slipping the wisdom of the East into their own therapeutic genius. And both were also gifted with the ability to befriend severely disturbed people, including some long since written off as hopeless schizophrenics—not a skill ordinarily divined from the psychoanalytic sensibility. The key to this sensibility can only be found in the East, or in those Western travelers who have journeyed there and brought it home. And it is this same sensibility that comes through loud and clear in the writings of E. Graham Howe, the first sage I know of to ply his serving trade on Harley Street.

Now, due to William Stranger's brilliant and painstaking compilation of Howe's writings—a true labor of love—you too have the privilege of becoming acquainted with this rare thinker and gifted healer of troubled souls.

M. Guy Thompson
San Francisco

SPIRAL SYMBOL

This spiral symbol is copied from the design of those at New Grange in Ireland, dated variously between 2000 and 1000 BC. It is an ideogram suggesting continuous movement, the twin base spirals never meeting, always opposed, interwoven, inseparable and interdependent, contained within the closed but endless single spiral.

Whether or not this was a key to Celtic religious thought, the need of the two opposites for each other, their containment within the evolutionary third, and the unity of the system makes good modern sense of an age-old pattern.

E. Graham Howe's
Psychology of Incarnation

by William Stranger

*It is my belief that any psychological system must be unsatisfactory
and misleading, both in theory and practice, until it does admit
our essentially spiritual nature.*

—E. GRAHAM HOWE

Psychiatry and religion are of necessity wary bedfellows. However insultingly one-sided Sigmund Freud's psychoanalytic critique of religion (as little more than a sublimation of sexual impulses enacted through the projection of both protective and threatening parental imagos), who can doubt that our conventional religious sentiments are riddled with precisely the unconscious motivations he observed? Of course Freud was passionate about establishing psychoanalysis as a legitimate science, and, after Marx, Darwin and three centuries of triumphant scientific discovery and technological invention, both God and the paranormal were faring poorly in the very academy he was trying to impress. Nevertheless, in a conversation about the spiritual factor in healing with Ludwig Binswanger, a key founder of existential psychology with whom he sustained a lifelong friendship, Freud conceded, "Yes, the spirit is everything." He went on to say, "Mankind has always known that it possesses spirit. I had to show that there are also instincts." But of course the notion that there is a living spiritual reality plays no role whatsoever in Freud's psychoanalysis. In every effective sense he willingly embraced the dogmas of scientific materialism.

1

Freud, Jung and Adler were the preeminent psychiatrists of the first half of the twentieth century. Despite their estimable respective contributions—Freud's revelation of the grammar of repressed desire; Adler's taxonomy of human social competitiveness; and Jung's complex vision of a gendered psyche that, fed by the numinosum (or "spirit"), spontaneously unfolds a higher and integrated human wholeness—none of the three truly integrated the spiritual dimension of existence *per se* into his own psychological system.

Enter Eric Graham Howe, born on February 3, 1897, and thus a member of the first generation of modern psychiatric thinkers. In his last book, *She and Me: A New Statement of an Old Problem*, published just a year before his death, Howe bluntly asserts:

> In 1949 Erich Neumann, who had studied under C. G. Jung, published a book entitled *The Origins and History of Consciousness*. But, like Dr. Jung himself, he did not specifically believe in THAT, so that his studies refer only the development of "little c" [that is, egoic self-consciousness], which is still dependent on "the unconsciousness," [sic] and not on the NON-DUALITY of original CONSCIOUSNESS. In fact, no book has yet been written for doctors and psychologists on the importance of THAT.

Of course Howe had to know that this was a gross overstatement. During his long professional career he had himself written more than a dozen books on precisely that subject.

Howe strode upon the scene of British psychology in high style, while still in his early thirties, when Great Britain's premier medical journal, *The Lancet*, published a series of twelve articles he wrote on medical psychology—the first writings on the subject they had ever put into print. These were subsequently republished under the title *Motives and Mechanisms of the Mind*, a book that became required study for physicians seeking a diploma in medical psychology. Moreover, because of its lucidity, common sense, and practical usefulness, the book sat on the desks of a generation of the United Kingdom's general practice doctors, who found it of great help in understanding their patients' emotional difficulties.

The first of Howe's thirteen published works, *Motives and Mechanisms of the Mind* was no doubt also his most conservative—appropriately so given its purpose. In some ways the book can be regarded as an inspired synthesis of the ideas of Freud, Jung, and Adler. Yet it is even more an original essay by an original thinker within which we see prefigured key themes that would be vastly more developed in his subsequent writings (the central influence of parental imagos, growth beyond competitive egocentricity, the complementarity of the sexes, etc.), along with several unguarded statements opining the reality of paranormal phenomena and the existence of God (however undefined he left the Deity). The latter two presaged a psychiatric career that would consistently challenge not only scientific materialist presumptions in themselves but also psychiatry's capitulation to such dogmas.

Howe did so in the most direct and uncompromising manner possible. In the twelve additional books that would be published before his death, from which this anthology draws, he built a coherent and integrated system of psychology explicitly rooted in the proposition that the transcendent, egoless Consciousness, or living spirit (which he defined using language from both Eastern and Western religions), is the source of our physical well-being and emotional healing and growth, as well as of our ordinary human happiness and higher cultural achievements. Further, he jettisoned Jung's coyness about paranormal phenomena and the materialist myth they disproved, along with his reductive approach to Asian spirituality. Instead, Howe freely drew from the lexicon of Indian esotericism (especially its description of the *chakras,* or spinal energy plexuses), as well as the Western revisions of that esotericism found in Rudolf Steiner's anthroposophical writings, to create a truly psychophysical psychology that he also related to the anatomy of the human nervous system.

Nevertheless, Howe was cognizant of the psychological theories and case studies of his time. His writings address the same character disorders, psychoneuroses, and psychoses found in the standard literature, albeit without the condescension that too often lurks behind their technical jargon. He was a superb writer, with a novelist's eye for character, circumstance and destiny. His deftly drawn case studies, which are often graced with a revealing wit, leave us with no doubt that he related to his patients as living, breathing presences, not mere clinical entities. I had to omit most such descriptions from this anthology, but before proceeding further here, the reader deserves some small exposure to Howe's style of clinical portraiture. This passage was excerpted from *Mysterious Marriage: A Study of the Morality of Personal Relationships and Individual Obsessions*:

> Pat's mother was the village Lady Bountiful. She was most admired by those who knew her least—the vicar, for instance. To those who knew her best—her family—she was a constant source of irritation or worse, an insoluble problem and a crushing bore. Her finger was in every pie, directing those who did the detailed work she never did herself. She was extremely generous in giving away what cost her nothing, especially if she gained thereby what she wanted. Her energy was boundless, especially for benevolent interference. Her charm was natural. It was woven round her like another skin, to be admired by all, which was her only end. Beneath that skin there lurked an octopus who lived on what it held from which it sucked the rich warm blood of other people's lives. In fact, she was a parasite disguised as providence.

Critique of Scientism

Howe was the last man to indulge escapist delusions, whether presented under "spiritual" cover or not. By identifying the underlying developmental failures and spiritual faults associated with our common neurotic syndromes, however, he provided his patients (as well as us, his students) a more inclusive framework for understanding their specific disturbance and their path to healing. It is precisely because of the greater explanatory power afforded by his inclusive perspective that Howe very deliberately refused to grant the dominant schools of psychiatry powers of comprehension and explanation he did not believe they deserved. He could be devastatingly insightful when he turned the tools of psychoanalysis upon the cultic behavior he saw rampant within the profession.

> Psychology has its limitations. The structure of "scientific" psychology is only a matter of form, an abstraction from a limiting point of view. However accurate it may be, psychology does not reveal to us the whole truth about the person of the patient. In fact, it must obscure it, unless we can see through psychology to the spiritual problem. We have to learn to see through psychology, as we must learn to see through all words to find their latent meanings, and through the labels on the bottles, to discover by experience what they actually contain. Illness, whether mental or physical, is not a label, and diagnosis is not enough. Illness is maladjustment in relationships occurring to a person. *It is not the person.* The illness is obscuring the person. It is preventing him from seeing through himself, and being seen. To identify the person with his disease, or life with psychology, is again to be the victim of compulsion neurosis.
>
> But present day psychology, as a matter of form or structure, is not even good form. Freud, Jung, Adler and the rest have not yet developed a sound, complete and wholesome structure of their findings and beliefs. Psychology is a clumsy, contradictory jargon. It is patchy, partial and incomplete. Yet there are many psychologists today who are identified with the particular teaching of their own approved Master, often exceeding him in their zealous overemphasis on certain articles of his all-too-rigid "faith."
>
> In this matter, psychologists need to be reminded that they are now behaving as the Churches did before them. Psychologists thought that they had seen through the compulsive schizophrenia of the Churches. Yet they have themselves fallen victims to the same disruptive and schismatic disease of disagreeably competing partial-"isms," each seeking to be recognized as not only right, but best.

Of course Howe's penetrating critique of scientism was in no way meant to discount science's virtues. He was a rigorous empiricist, and he would not have endorsed any excuse for failing to do science well. Indeed, it is likely that he was the first psychiatrist to closely observe the profound correlation between our emotional disorders and the now famous fight-or-flight response of the autonomic nervous system (enacted via its parasympathetic and sympathetic branches). Heading his list of "Things We Want to Know" near the end of *Motives and Mechanisms of the Mind*, Howe poses critical questions that only recently, in what some describe as our ongoing "golden age" of neuroendocrinological research, have begun to receive detailed answers. But he called for the "extension of the scientific method, to include the intangible and the subjective," arguing that the ethic of free and unfettered scientific inquiry into all things is precisely what is violated by a dogmatic scientism that refuses to fairly evaluate evidence that may contradict its own premises.

Yet Howe refused to hide behind the laboratory coat he wore on rounds when he was in medical school. In his introduction to Howe's *Cure or Heal? A Study of Therapeutic Experience*, the Scottish psychiatrist R. D. Laing, another brilliant, iconoclastic, spirit-affirming psychotherapist, pronounced him "a master psychologist" and explained why his writings were destined to be neglected by both their professional peers and the religious establishment:

These books differed from any others by psychiatrists in this country during that period, in that they brought to bear on empirical issues an understanding that derived from spiritual experience. Since they were written in a clear and simple way, unimpeded by psychiatric jargon, the psychiatric profession evaded giving them serious attention, and since they exhibited spiritual authority anchored to flesh and blood reality, drawing on Eastern as well as Western images and symbols, organized Christianity has also not given Howe the recognition he deserves.

The Meaning of Relationship

Howe's own marriage of experience and intuition bears a likeness to the presuppositionless "science" (or method) of phenomenology that was launched by the philosopher Edmund Husserl at the beginning of the twentieth century and that quickly became central to the development of existential psychology. Although he was not trained in philosophy and surely had greater sympathy for the writings of Plotinus than Jean-Paul Sartre, Howe could be said to both a natural phenomenologist and a natural existentialist. It was through his intuitive examination of his own bare, psychophysically felt experience that he had the breakthrough insight that I believe places him in the forefront of modern psychiatric thinkers. That insight is that the experience of *relationship* itself is the master key to human growth, maturity, and self-transcendence, and thus it is also the key to understanding and healing human neurosis and psychosis.

With the entirety of this book to understand all of what E. Graham Howe means by the term, we can proceed for now with his own pithy definition of relationship as "the interior unexpressed experience of meeting between self and other." This is very different from what psychologists normally intend by the term *relationship*, by which they actually mean what Howe calls "communication," or "the exterior expressed experience of meeting" between individuals. Relationship viewed as communication is usually understood in terms of its symbolic meaning to the individual— his or her social recognition, sense of belonging, of being protected, and the like.

Of course the theme of relationship itself—especially as it is lived in the therapeutic encounter—has long since become central to psychology and psychotherapy. It was brought squarely into clinical theory and practice through the allied revolutions wrought by gestalt and existential psychology. The gestalt experience of the "contact boundary" and the existential-phenomenological analysis of "inter-subjectivity" (especially as explicated in terms of Maurice Merleau-Ponty's description of "the intertwining," defined by the philosopher David Michael Kleinberg-Levin as "the symbol of our rootedness, the weave of feminine wisdom, the interrelatedness of all beings, the interdependency of self and other, the interactional co-emergence of subject and object,"[1] and so on) certainly carry much of Howe's meaning here. But by no means all of it.

While Howe's conception of relationship carries all the meanings mentioned above, it goes further. Most fundamentally, it is his term for the meeting place between the non-conceptual, non-dual, unconditioned Consciousness (which on various occasions he also terms the "whole self," "big C" the "Void," "Spirit," the "Infinite," the "Eternal," "Self," "THAT," "I Am," "Wholeness," "CONSCIOUSNESS" and "PERSON" in the upper case, "the Wheel," "that other ground," "A," or, most simply, "I") and our every kind of ordinary or mundane daily experience (likewise variously termed "egoic man," "little c," "consciousness" or "person" in the lower case, "the Road," "this familiar field," "B," and, perhaps most simply and frequently, just little old "me"). In themselves, "A" and "B" are irreconcilable opposites:

> At some time or another, sooner or later, we shall be turned out to face our crisis; for we are ourselves children of this two-ness, divided within, if not against, ourselves. We are destined to have one foot in Eternity and the other in space-time, to be constantly in danger of falling between two stools, and always to be faced with the horns of a dilemma in a seemingly vital choice. We have the devil on one side for our father and the deep sea on the other for our mother, and, to use a flippancy quite seriously, we have one foot in, or beyond, the grave, and the other on, or very near, a banana skin. It is the problem of mankind, thus to be torn between the ecstasy of eternity and the space-time prison bars of our material conflict.

Who or what connects, mediates, and is caught between the two fundamental but inextricably related opposites of the Heavenly "A" or "I" and the earthly "B" or "me," somehow separating and uniting them at the same time?[2] Howe notes that religion and spirituality call it the "soul," and indeed on occasion he elaborates their relationship in terms of his own revision of Christianity's doctrine of the Trinity, the Athanasian Creed. In his formulation, "A," the Unconditional "I" as "father," and "B," the mortal "me" as "mother," give birth to "C," "the traveler" or "the soul," their "child." In his later works Howe sometimes employs the word *experience* as the mediator between the subjective and objective worlds: "I"–*experience*–it. (In his bestselling book *The Politics of Experience*, R. D. Laing employs *experience* in much the same way, pointing out that "experience used to be called the Soul.") Our life of experience, or relationship, then, is a process of human and spiritual growth in which we learn to fully accept and embrace both horns of our dilemma. Although this inevitably involves a trial or travail of the soul that is the undoing of our egoity, it is the only way we can ultimately come to realize the underlying unity of all things. Howe summarizes the process this way: "The only hope for the fullness of our sanity is that we should be prepared to recognize the two-ness of A and B and the third-ness of C; and the one-ness of the A and the B and the C." It takes a while to understand how these categories constitute a non-dual psychology, but what Howe means by them will become increasingly clear as you read this book.

In line with tradition, mostly Eastern but also found in the West, Howe's non-dualism is manifested as a complementary play of polarized, gendered opposites. These begin with our own personal settlement of the tension between the great categories of A or "I" and B or "me," but it is also operative as the polarized play between individuals and between the individual and society as a whole. Given the recent wars over gender, power and social mystification, it is important to understand that although Howe assigns the Heavenly function of spirit-awakening intuition to the masculine and the earthly function of soul-quickening feeling and suffering to the female, theirs is a play in which there is no superior. In fact, it is their fulcrum, the "child"—C, relationship itself—who unifies the two and whom they both therefore are always obligated to serve. As ever with Howe, far from being abstract, this vision of our polarized being is expressed very concretely via our natural body-mind.

As the union or interpenetration of the two most basic realities— timeless, non-dual Consciousness and time-bound, conditional objects of all kinds—relationship itself is a paradox, since each of the two poles it conjoins must always appear together (and thus are "true"), yet each of the two, when considered by itself, appears to contradict the other. This is why Howe greatly stresses the untenability of the old fixed absolutes, whether couched in sacred or secular language. Although it rarely comes to full consciousness in us, the paradox of our inherent relatedness is the essence of everyone's moment-to-moment experience.

In any case, he was not interested in offering a philosophical theology. By this vision of life as a tension of irreducible but inherently related (or necessarily polarized) opposites, he is identifying the fundamental *problematique* that will yield a powerful basis for understanding human psychology. For the basic problem of the maturing human being is to develop the ability to accept the tension created by the apparent contradiction between the two opposed terms without attempting to reduce one to the other. Are we mortal? Are we Divine? Do we know? Are we ignorant? Howe affirms the paradox that both are always true, simultaneously. The British psychiatrist John Heaton, who was first Howe's patient and then later his trainee, summarizes his approach this way:

His principal concern was to use the language of modern psychology, especially psychoanalysis, to show that the problems of human suffering lie principally in confusions about the relationship between the unknowable and knowledge. He develops his thought by using the verbal structure of the dialectic between related pairs of opposites such as "whole self" and "egoic man," "I" and "me," center and periphery, "inner" and "outer," male and female. Our modern tendency is to put our weight on the known, on "me," on the part rather than the whole; these we feel we can control. However if we do this the dialectic movement between the opposites is broken; we lose control and sooner or later suffer pain and distress and may become ill.

So psychotherapy should involve paying close attention to relationships, not only between therapist and patient but also between the patient and his illness. This attention may heal the broken dialectic and is the common denominator of every practice of therapy.[3]

Since most psychological problems are based upon our failure to achieve a viable personal autonomy, the psychotherapist's first order of business is to reconcile the patient to his functional separateness and independence. By presenting his psychology in a context of paradox, however, Howe is able to introduce healing distinctions in the course of psychotherapy without creating rigid, mutually exclusive categories that deny us the healing power of relationship itself. He advises us:

> If we are ever to be really as one, then we must be content to begin as two and bear the burden of our yoke. If we are ever to find our unity, then we must first accept our separatedness. We must learn to move always in this order, for it is so easy to go the wrong way round and, from our false beginning in impatience, to be in the end on the wrong side of the paradox, finding ourselves indeed separated from the object of our love. If we assume in our anxious benevolence that we are one, when this is not in fact the case, then we shall most certainly end by being divided into two, when after all we might have been as one.

While such an approach would seem to exacerbate aggressive individualism, in reality such analysis liberates us from the confusing identifications that foster it. The key separation is between the "I" or A and the "me" or B:

> The B self will always tend to refer to life in terms of absolutes and compulsive competitiveness, striving by its defensive aggressiveness to maintain both its mask of apparent courage and the defenses with which it hides the lack of it. Before it can find its A again, it must go back to the anxiety of the original two-ness from which it fled and never lose sight of the relationship and difference of "this" and "that," self and not-self. There it will find that burning is not so bad as being burned, and that correct analysis provides the key to courage and also sows the seed of action.

Analysis does not separate the whole into its thousand parts: it only separates a confusion into its related two-ness, self from not-self, you from me, I from me, this from that, the A-ness from the B-ness, each instant now from every other upon the pendulum swing of time. When this is done, Analysis is complete, though such finality is never possible within the rhythmic, moving curves of life.

Far from being abstract and hard to understand, Howe's notion of relationship itself is a great simplicity, albeit one that is almost impossible to define. As the bridge, link, or means of connection between the invisible spirit and manifest reality, it is intuited and felt rather than conceived. In chapter 5 of this book Howe likens it to touch. And yet he also says it resembles nothing so much as the element of water:

> What is between us, what is the medium of our mysterious communication? What flows. The creative medium through which life flows, the truly creative medium, is "water." But the inverted commas must serve to indicate that this mysterious bridge, or medium, is only "analogous" to water. As Jung might say, this is "archetypal" water. But these are only words, and to appreciate the reality of this medium it is necessary to experience it.

Most basically, we know relationship as the truly mutual exchange of life and awareness that is, in its depth, why we seek out one another's company. Yet it is also precisely the thing we avoid. As D. H. Lawrence wrote in his testamentary book, *Apocalypse*, "We *cannot bear connection*. That is our malady." Howe would be in complete agreement. He regards the dissociative avoidance or refusal of relationship as the essence of our suffering—which is to say our neurotic and even psychotic patterns. Therapy is the difficult process wherein our ambivalence is explored and its healing secrets allowed to do their work:

> [A] great mystery exists between the essential light that "I am," and the relative darkness, which is egoic "me." From this . . . state we derive all our energy for life, as well as all our

resistance against the privilege of living. From it we derive all our healing as well as all our resistance against being healed, and our persistence in preferring to remain ill.

The Mechanism of Neurosis

The word *neurosis,* which was adopted by clinical psychiatry in 1923, can be defined as "the functional derangement arising from disorders of the nervous system." It comes from a combination of the Greek *neuron,* or "nerve," and the Latin *–osis,* meaning an abnormal condition. In chapter 6, "The War of Nerves," we begin to see the profoundly psychophysical nature of Howe's psychology:

> What are these nerves of ours, and what is their proper function in the living organism? They are our *instruments of relationship.* They are the living links between one organ and another, as they are also links between the organism as a whole and that other outer world in which it has to live and strive for life. They are instruments of information, which tell us what is going on in other parts. They keep us in touch with one another and make contact over the distances which separate the parts that together make up the whole. They are bridges upon which the lives of many separate parts can meet. As organs of relationship, they are our most precious means of making friends and fighting enemies: of planning and of deliberate response to the many problems of experience by which we are so constantly beset. Thus they become the living root of our philosophy or attitude to life. As our nerves respond, so will our conduct be determined. If our nerves are rightly "relative" and timely in their manner of response, so shall we be balanced and temperate in our way of life. As men and women, for better or for worse we are all instruments of relationship, and so upon our "nerves" we must depend.

Most remarkably, Howe goes on to identify the mechanism behind all emotional (neurotic, perverse, psychotic, etc.) disorders: *contraction.*

Two things may first strike us about the problems of our nerves: the first is their complexity and the multiplicity of symptoms from which nervous patients suffer. The second fact however, as so often happens, is the reverse: namely, that all our symptoms seem to be variations of the single habit of *contraction*. Like flowers, we can open and we can shut. Our nervous habit is to shut.

On a number of occasions he illustrates this typically unwitting act of contraction through the simile of a hand that meets the world either as "an open palm or a closed fist." It was that most physical simile that first drew my attention to Howe's work. But I did not read the phrase just quoted in one of his books, which were not available in the United States. I read it in Henry Miller's title essay on Howe's work, which I happened across while perusing his collection *The Wisdom of the Heart*, a book I found in the well-heated library at the Mountain Of Attention Sanctuary one wintry afternoon. I could not have been more impressed. My spiritual master, the Western-born Avatar Adi Da Samraj, whose own writings are widely regarded to be "the most creatively original literature on radical nonduality currently available in the English language,"[4] demonstrated the fundamental mechanism of egoity through precisely the same simile on the cover of his first book, *The Knee of Listening*, which is his autobiography.

Adi Da came to this insight through a different route than Howe. While contemplating his own hand one day in his early twenties, Adi Da suddenly grasped the implications of its design: the hand, like the body and all manifest things, is made not for self-enclosure (like a closed fist) but for relationship (like an open hand). In Adi Da's case, this insight was a critically important moment in a spiritual process, already underway at his birth, which ultimately resulted in the complete dissolution of his ego-soul illusion, and thus the transcendence of "the illusion of relatedness"— a development beyond the compass of Howe's own work. What they have in common, however, is a recognition of the simplicity and singularity of the action that is human egoity and a deep appreciation of the rhythmic polarity of intake and outflow essential to health and well-being.

Howe and Jung

Spiritual ideas entered modern psychiatry through the work of C. G. Jung. Nevertheless, Jung, a product of European Romanticism if ever there was one, often camouflaged his overwhelming interest in the esoteric, the occult and the paranormal. It was not until 1952 that he would write his famous essay "Synchronicity: An Acausal Connecting Principle," which began with this confession: "In writing this paper I have, so to speak, made good a promise which for many years I lacked the courage to fulfill." He had no doubt long observed how furiously the scientific establishment reacted to investigations that dared trespass against its root presumptions. In the 1870s, the eminent chemist and inventor William Crookes agreed to investigate the capabilities of a famous medium, Daniel D. Home, purely with the intention of debunking the reality of paranormal experience and capabilities. After publishing a report of his own well-controlled experiment on Home that appeared to validate such phenomena, Crookes was quickly and harshly anathematized by the very same Royal Society (then, as today, the world's foremost scientific association) that only a few years before had unanimously elected him to its membership. It should be understandable why it was only very late in his life, after he had already achieved the status of sage, that Jung consistently and openly dared challenge scientistic presumptions.

But Jung's caution in this area reflects more than a desire to protect his career. He had his own prejudices against key aspects of humankind's reported esoteric and spiritual experience—prejudices that continue to challenge the analytical psychologists who have built upon his work. We see this most clearly in his response to Asian spirituality's core critique of human egoity as both unnecessary and unreal and its corresponding affirmation of a transcendent non-egoic Consciousness. ("I cannot imagine a conscious mental state that does not relate to a subject, that is to an ego," he writes in his "Psychological Commentary on *The Tibetan*

Book of the Great Liberation.") Indeed, Jung never renounced his view that full ego-transcendence is an impossibility for Westerners.

Likewise, although he expressed the greatest respect for Indian yogic spirituality and was led to his inspired investigations of Renaissance alchemy by reading Richard Wilhelm's translation of a classic Taoist alchemical text, *The Secret of the Golden Flower,* Jung felt that it was inappropriate for Westerners to actually engage in Asian esoteric practices. He considered the Western psyche too rigid, too self-conscious, too in need of first being loosened up by contact with the unconscious to be capable of surviving a direct plunge into Eastern springs. Westerners, he believed, would have to await the future appearance of specifically Western yoga produced "on the basis laid down by Christianity."

As we might expect from this, Jung's several introductions to Indian, Tibetan and Chinese esoteric texts consistently subjected them to rather reductive psychological interpretations. He viewed the alchemical processes, subtle anatomical diagrams, and maps of postmortem journeys found in those texts as merely symbolic expressions of archetypal psychological processes. Nowhere in his introduction to or commentary on *The Secret of the Golden Flower,* for example, does he admit that its depictions of the circulation of subtle energy might be literally true. While his interpretations were not without value—Jung's psychological judgment was always acute, and he was rightly alert to how the introvertive tendency of some schools of Asian spirituality encourages our dissociation from the relational play of life—those particular writings often did as much to obscure as they did to clarify their subjects. Thus, although Jung and his successors acknowledged the creative power of the spirit, they thought we can access it only in mediated form, via the images thrown up by the deep psyche.

In his doctoral dissertation on Howe's psychology, Ian C. Edwards narrates portions of two dialogues between Howe and C. G. Jung that took place during the first two of the five lectures that Jung delivered at the Tavistock Clinic in the fall of 1935.[5] In those dialogues Howe persistently engaged Jung in a discussion of intuition, the fourth dimension, and his schema of the four faculties. As Edwards explains, Jung was very reluctant to publicly accede to the obvious mystical implications of Howe's identification of intuition with the fourth dimension because doing so might threaten his own credentials as a strict empiricist and otherwise endow his analytical psychology with a dynamism that would confuse ordinary people. In his commitment to likewise publicly validating the vertical dimension that is our transcendent spirituality, however, Howe could not accept a psychology confined to the ego's three familiar dimensions. Moreover, he had already learned that the paradoxes of the fourth dimension, which are epitomized by the mathematical symbol i (the square root of minus one or $\sqrt{-1}$), are an undeniable implication of the process that goes on in psychotherapy:

> I found very early in my professional experience that something happened after the first 12–14 minutes which made the remainder of the interview quite different. I can only describe it as being "switched on" or "the penny dropping." From then on, I feel I know what is going on with "a feeling of certainty that is not derived from experience." It is almost as if I know this patient's mother or husband better than she knows them herself. It is this capacity for "insight" which I believe to be of the utmost value in psychological medicine and it is lost rather than gained by much reading. It can be developed only in the field of experience, with a willingness to suffer and endure all persons patiently, respectfully and without prejudice, thus learning all the time from what is always new.

Esoteric Anatomy

Howe recognized that emotional healing is an unavoidably psychophysical and psychospiritual process. His esoteric anatomy is a brilliant appropriation of Jung's theory of the four ego-functions—intuition, thinking, feeling, and sensation—which, by connecting them to our functional anatomy, endows them with greater scope and power. He does this by first recasting Jung's "intuition," which the latter viewed as a faculty of psychic or "gut" knowledge, as the primary instrument wherein and whereby we gain "direct knowledge of wholeness not derived from experience." Most importantly, he maps the four functions onto the extended human body-mind, which he explicates via both our functional anatomy and the ancient theory of the four elements: *fire, air, water,* and *earth.*

In Howe's esoteric anatomy, which is presented in part II of this book, *fire,* or gnostic *intuition,* is at the top of the body, making it the first to receive the Light that descends from above. Below it is *air,* the *thinking* mind, followed by *water,* our *feeling* psyche (which Howe says also relates to the "astral" or psychic dimension). At the bottom of course is the *earth,* the vehicle of *sensation. Intuition* and *feeling* are the introverted functions; *thinking* and *sensations* are the extroverted functions. All four together, then, make up a polarized, rhythmic whole that sings the unity of Howe's non-egoic whole man (or whole person). Our business with these functions or faculties, says Howe, is that of incarnation of the Lighted spirit. This requires us to receive both the Light from above and the healing force of all earthly powers—the power of Life itself—rising from beneath our feet. These two great currents, of Light and Life, signed male and female respectively, meet and are integrated at the center of our being, literally in the region of the human heart, which is where we receive the spirit's fullness and are thereby enabled to live the great and ongoing sacrifice that is Love.

By understanding the process of human maturation in this expanded context, we can better appreciate why Howe refuses to grant psychotherapy the franchise when it comes to psychological growth. Innumerable individuals have managed to move beyond the all-but-inevitable neurotic maladaptations of our early life without the benefit of professional psychotherapy. Howe's "invisible anatomy" gives us a means to understand something about how this comes about. For those who make genuine contact with it, the living spirit is a power of relationship that drives insight, produces understanding, and yields powerful emotional healing of deep-seated neuroses and even psychoses. Nevertheless, there are also many who, despite having been granted substantial access to spiritual guidance and blessing, yet evade the ordeal of their own transformation and growth. E. Graham Howe has done all of us great service in outlining the characteristic patterns of such avoidance.

It should never be forgotten that by grounding his observation in our living anatomy Howe was brilliantly fulfilling his scientific calling. In this regard, his insight was most extraordinary. Howe recognized that the physical locus of our common, reactive suffering is in the abdomen, literally at and around the navel—what he called "our ancient belly-mind." (That squares with Adi Da's own description of "vital shock," the persistent, self-created background abdominal contraction that rules almost everyone's subconscious and unconscious mind.) A number of people have pointed out that this "belly-mind" constitutes a semi-autonomous mode of functioning that could well be called "the abdominal brain." This is that critical underpinning of our emotional life that recent neuroscience has been exploring as our "limbic brain." I believe that every great psychotherapist is tacitly aware of how this "belly-mind" epitomizes the suffering and striving of his or her patients.

Howe describes how the reactive contraction operates through the two branches (parasympathetic and sympathetic) of the autonomic nervous system—open in the case of the former, shut in the case of the latter. These are the two dispositions that Howe describes as protopathic and epicritic. Understanding the complementarity of these two modes is crucial to grasping his work altogether.

> If only it were possible to accept the <u>breathing principle</u> as essential to all our experience of life, we could realize more clearly how all the Yins and Yangs of our reciprocal polarity come to play their rhythmic parts: in the systole and diastole of the heart; in the anabolism and katabolism of metabolism; in the spring and autumn of the year; and in the life and death of all creation. Perhaps, if we made a simple sign to represent this principle of open ☾ and shut ﹥ we could see how much they need to come together to complete ⪥ our dance of life, including death.

Viewed in terms of our esoteric anatomy, real maturity arrives only after our chronic, wayward emotional reactivity has been brought under the control of the central nervous system, the access point of the spirit above. But to put it that way would make the process of psychotherapy appear to be a technical process. It is in fact something more—a decidedly non-moralistic "moral conversion" that can only come about through that acceptance of the suffering of born existence necessary to gain true access to the source of regeneration and renewal. Such requires a purifying ascesis, or "burning," that is always a soul-shaking ordeal.

Howe's Relevance to Spiritual Practitioners

As I began to acquire and read his books, I could only marvel at the enormous relevance of E. Graham Howe's distinctive marriage of psychological insight and spiritual intuition to the very difficult beginning stages of spiritual practice with which I and so many of my friends were still struggling. He was a genius about the ways of the ego, with an instinctive grasp of the essential tasks, trials, and lessons encountered on the road to human emotional maturity— which he summarized as "unweaning." These included the vital importance of contact with the spiritual dimension of existence (however this may be experienced or defined) in achieving a non-neurotic human autonomy; the necessary complementarity of masculine (fatherly) challenge and feminine (motherly) love in early-life development; the classic authoritarian (childish) and rebelliousness (adolescent) modes of avoiding the ordeal of growth; the centrality of identification and dissociation to our complex reactive patterns; the esoteric anatomy underlying our emotional and spiritual development in the humanizing stages of life; the inevitable "burning" experienced in the purification of one's own egoic willfulness; the healing power of faith, rest, sleep, and death; and the sovereignty of the regenerative Law of sacrifice. These are the necessary elements and understandings of our growth.

At the same time, Howe's work only sharpens the distinction between genuine spiritual practice and even a psychotherapy well-informed by Eastern notions. While we may be indeed greatly served by engaging the therapeutic process before we take up the rigors of a spiritual path, the two are not the same thing.

As Adi Da has explained in *The Lion Sutra*, "The ego-'I' is a Paradox of relatedness and separateness." Which is to say, it alternates between two motions, toward life and relationship ("open") and withdrawing from them ("shut"). Psychotherapy permits us to investigate the complex pattern of ambivalences that repetitively drive us from one to the other and thereby relax and relinquish our reactive struggle within dualistic dilemma.

Real spiritual practice, by contrast, purifies, concentrates, and utterly refines every kind of dilemma of opposites (ego and world, doubt and faith, life and death, etc.) until there is a breakthrough in which the discriminating mind that is "me" utterly vanishes, leaving only the egoless Self that is "I," or, better, "I Am," behind. Intelligence is certainly one of the virtues this process requires, but the process itself is far from an intellectual matter. To the contrary, it involves an undoing of all that we presume and cling to, which breaks our heart as much as it does our mind. In Korean Buddhism, the word for enlightenment is *kkaech'im*, which means "brokenness." Sung Bae Park explains:

> Why is the enlightenment experience of *kkaech'im*, or "brokenness," so difficult to achieve? In order for this breaking to occur, the polar conflict between affirmation and negation, faith and doubt, or "I am Buddha" ["I"] and "I am an ignorant sentient being" ["me"], must be brought to its extreme. There must be 100 percent reverence for the teacher's words and 100 percent honesty toward one's own degree of attainment. If even 1 percent of either reverence and honesty or faith and doubt is lacking, then although the polar tension might be great, the breaking experience of *kkaech'im* cannot occur, since the limit of these poles has not yet been reached. If only faith and reverence are present one's practice declines into blind fundamentalism, whereas if only doubt and honesty are present one's practice declines into negativism or skepticism. It is therefore only with complete reverence and honesty or faith and doubt that the dynamics of questioning meditation can ignite the explosive enlightenment experience of *kkaech'im*, which as Wu-men wrote, is simply the "casting away of discriminating mind," in "a moment of yes-and-no."[6]

Surely such awakening is what is being touched on what Howe tells us, in his great chapter 35 essay, "The Spirit," that "'a broken and a contrite heart' can never break, nor be broken, for the simple reason that it has been broken once already—and has accepted it."

Howe's Influences

Although Howe's entire approach to psychological understanding was one of great inclusiveness, it would be a mistake to see his work as a synthesis of eclectic borrowings from all manner of sources. He was a *sui generis* genius who wrote from his own experience and intuition and simply felt free to utilize whatever concepts and language he thought best illustrated his own observations. In his introduction to his third book, *I and Me: A Study of the Self,* he advises us:

> I have again greatly dared to formulate my ideas and opinions without reference to authorities, past or present. For a work in which the word "scientific" occurs with almost irritating frequency, this may seem unusual, but it has certain advantages for the reader and certain points of interest for the observer. To the writer it offers freedom from a responsibility that is too great. If we are to read at all from the authorities we must read enough, and they are many. Therefore better, perhaps, not to rely on them, but to draw from life instead. Indeed it would seem to be a tragedy to rely upon meanings learnt at second hand, when the book of Life itself is open. It seems certain that there has never been so awe-inspiring an opportunity for seeing within the lives of others, to watch and understand the movements of men's minds, as that which is open to the psychotherapist of these days. These lessons of experience must be my authorities, for which my patients are not to be held responsible, other than by having been to some extent instrumental in creating this responsiveness.

This holds true even regarding his employment of Eastern religious concepts:

> It would not be fair, however, to offer acknowledgments to Buddhism and Tao, because I feel sure that I have not gleaned my knowledge from the literature of such sources. For instance, I read Waley's *The Way and Its Power* after and not before I gave these lectures. I am well aware of the similarity of pattern between the teaching expressed in them

and that presented so many years ago in the philosophic system of Tao. I am quite sure, however, that the source of the one is not to be found in the other: but rather that both owe their origin to a common source, namely, Life, the essential verities of which transcend both time and place.

I do not wish to claim originality for these pages, as I fully realize that they are only part of a tide of similar ideas, moving in many places and in many forms. Each observer can recognize this movement from his own viewpoint and within his own experience. It is certainly interesting to see similar patterns showing themselves from the different angles of many minds, apparently uninfluenced by each other: and all repeating a similar pattern provoked 2500 years ago, when Relativity's sweeping curves again broke the ordered bounds of Absolutism.

The only bibliography that Howe ever published, which appears in *Cure or Heal? A Study of Therapeutic Experience*, was prepared not by Howe but by Geoffrey Watkins, the owner of London's famed metaphysical bookstore of the same name. References to other psychiatric thinkers and their theories are rare in Howe's books. I recall Freud, Jung, and Adler each getting several mentions, Melanie Klein and R. D. Laing just one apiece, and that's about it for his fellow professionals.

Rightly or wrongly, I have always regarded much reading as dangerous for students of psychiatry, because I believe we are all inclined to have "too much room at the top." The brain is like a vacuum, and is easily over-filled at the heart's expense. The psychiatrist who has read all of Freud or Jung or both is bound to overlook his patient, because he will not see what is there, but only what he expects to see according to the textbook.

For me, a very little reading on any subject goes a very long way. I regard one or two books a year at most as providing valuable reading in the sense of a <u>creative</u> <u>experience</u>. Otherwise, every patient is a new textbook, to read which it is necessary to forget all the others if we are not to be prejudiced by the false assumption that "this is another of those."

Not surprisingly, Howe's manner of expression was highly original. He illustrates his ideas through both a novel linguistic scheme of polarities and a series of graphic symbols and schematic drawings of his own design. He had no choice in the matter. Once he took the giant, decisive step beyond the existing psychiatric schools of his day, whether rooted in the instinctual materialism of Freud or in the creative archetypal psyche described by Jung, he could not rightly be confined to their terms of discourse.

Howe's Significance for Our Time

I do not want to minimize the profound cultural importance of the ongoing challenge to the still-dominant Cartesian cultural paradigm (of the abstract, separate, independent, power-obsessed, and other-controlling ego) now being brought to bear by psychologists who draw inspiration from not only gestalt psychology and existential phenomenology, but also critical theory, feminist theory, process philosophy, and other approaches. Most of them rightly assert and celebrate the primacy of embodied feeling, empathy, honest communication, cooperation, and other virtues of a truly human relatedness. And since the 1960s, when large numbers of Westerners began to be exposed to Eastern spirituality, many psychologists have come to leaven their work with concepts taken from not only the ever-popular Buddhism but also from Taoism, Hinduism, Samkhya Yoga, and the various indigenous shamanisms. This has led to the development of what is sometimes called "transpersonal" or "integral" psychology. Yet too often what falls out of these syntheses is both the expanded psyche and the living spirit itself. There is perhaps no better sign of this than the common reluctance to admit to the actuality of psychic experience in the therapeutic process, with all the attendant philosophical implications such bring with them.

Therefore, despite language about "embodied feeling" and an "embodied spirituality" in such psychologies, which are often presented as an extension or elaboration of the ego-transcending non-dualist propositions characteristic of Eastern (but also some-times Western) spirituality, "body" and "spirit" are often thinly sketched characters in what is otherwise the usual pursuit of a mortal, egoic fulfillment. But the illusion of egoic fulfillment is precisely what all great spiritual traditions—East and West alike—tell us must be clearly comprehended and thereby renounced *before* we can begin serious spiritual practice. Which is to say that despite their best intentions, these hybrid, ostensibly spiritual psychologies too often remain in thrall to the utopian humanism that yet dominates the modern world. This is why so many lack traditional spirituality's existential seriousness, its vibrant, demanding esotericism, and, when most profound, the shattering, consummating magic and mystery without which we cannot truly be acquired by the realizable divinity that truly is beyond birth and death.

E. Graham Howe, then, should be a wonder to us. He was modern psychiatry's first great psychospiritual phenomenologist. Unquestionably born before his time, it is perhaps only now, after several decades of increasing cultural commerce with Asian spiritual ideas and practices, that we in the West are ready to receive and incorporate his wisdom. To do so, we will have to stop making compromises with the soul-deadening scientific materialism that more mature cultures have always recognized as little more than a sign of human inexperience and immaturity. Now that our civilization is reaping the whirlwind of what the French psychoanalyst Jacque Lacan called "the ego's era," there is no time to lose in correcting our mistaken views. Howe's unique body of work offers everyone, including psychiatrists and psychotherapists, new arms for the task.

NOTE: This anthology is drawn from twelve of the thirteen books Howe wrote and published during his lifetime and the pamphlet-sized summary essay, *Consciousness: A Western Treatment of Tibetan Yoga*, that was privately printed and circulated to a few friends after his death. Howe's use of capitalization throughout these works is inconsistent. In general, he capitalized words to indicate their reference to the non-egoic or spiritual reality. However, sometimes he capitalized words simply for emphasis. In his later works he frequently wrote the same word in two different ways to contrast their non-egoic or spiritual meaning with their egoic or conventional meaning. Thus, CONSCIOUSNESS (in small capital letters) and consciousness refer to the ultimate reality and ego, respectively. Since Howe's meaning is always evident from the context, I felt it best to preserve his choices in the matter rather than impose my own regime merely for the sake of consistency.

E. GRAHAM HOWE

E. Graham Howe:
A Brief Biography

by William Stranger

Eric Graham Howe was born in London on February 3, 1897, the twelfth child of John Foster Howe, an idealistic, liberal-minded but repressed Protestant drawn to Swedenborg and England's Nonconformist sects, and his loving, sweet tempered but overworked wife, Caroline. There is a small sibling dispute about his parents' age at the time of his birth—Howe himself thought his mother forty-eight and his father a decade older, while one of his brothers maintains they were about three years younger—but in any case both parents were well into middle age when their last child arrived. Of the twelve children to whom Caroline gave birth, only one, Dora, was a girl. Four of her sons were already dead before young Eric's arrival, a "not unusually disastrous state of affairs in those dark days," he notes in his unpublished autobiography, "The Autobiography of an Unwanted Man," which his daughter Carolyn Whitaker found in his papers. Two more of Howe's brothers would perish in the killing fields of Flanders during World War I. Those who survived appear to have led successful lives.

With his father most often out following his own interests, and a raft of brothers to otherwise absorb his parents' attention (Arthur, the eldest, was some twenty years Eric's senior), Howe found himself attended to principally by Tim, the family terrier, and a migraine-afflicted girl named Clara (who he called "Auntie Tobba"), one of several young people adopted into the burgeoning Howe household. (Howe's father occasionally succumbed to the entreaties of dying parishioners to "look after" one or another of their soon-to-be-orphaned children.) It was the available Clara, and not his beloved but overburdened mother, who received the lion's share of Eric's earliest affections.

While Howe offers us a compelling portrait of the influences and events framing his own emotional development, what strikes us most about his autobiography is the degree to which he was both undeterred and undetermined by the contrary pressures upon him. His narrative reveals a man bearing a destiny not quite of his time, a conclusion reinforced by the fact the book was dedicated to the Chinese. "Even as a child," Eric Graham Howe tells us, "I have always wanted to know <u>what</u> it <u>was</u> <u>that</u> I <u>knew</u> <u>when</u> I <u>was</u> <u>born</u>." Indeed, his constitutional disposition bears a distinct likeness to the Taoist way of *wu wei*, or non-action, which explains the deeply meditative quality of both his life and his writings. (R. D. Laing explained, "Howe does not write *about* anything, existentialism or Zen for instance. His writing *is* existential and *is* Zen.")

> [I] have been able to capitalize on my two assets which have stood me remarkable well in stead. One of these is my "forgettery": I can and do forget everything which is irrelevant to the occasion. This can be very useful in my profession, and is indeed indispensable for the all-important experience of <u>concentration</u>. My other asset is my "I-function" of intuition, insight, inspiration and much else: of which I shall be having more to say, as being basic to my life's experience.

Concentration and intuition, or insight, are the two primary virtues cultivated by all meditation schools. That they appear, at least in nascent form, to have been available to Howe from birth helps us to understand how he could himself give birth to a total system of spiritually based psychology with virtually no encouragement from within his own profession.

Given the size of his family, the agony of their losses, and the age of his burdened parents, it was inevitable that parental attention, if not affection, would be at a premium. He was clearly more exercised upset, however, by the fact that he was largely ignored by his many older brothers as well:

> I experienced great loneliness and longed inordinately for the comfort of companionship, for which I believe I was somewhat gifted, but from which I was almost entirely

either debarred or deterred. My brothers gave me none. They were all too busy with their own concerns to notice my belated arrival, other than with the indifference of suppressed resentment: Not another!

The schools where he received his primary and secondary education were, Howe tells us, mediocre. In a pattern that would be repeated throughout his life, young Eric found himself quickly promoted level by level and was on the verge of a scholarship to study mathematics, a subject for which he displayed an extraordinary aptitude, when an untimely case of scarlet fever combined with his family's stretched finances to bring his scholastic career to an end.

None of the incidents in his childhood, even the most embarrassing, appear to have left a lasting mark on his psyche. It being the Victorian era and his parents being rather typical Nonconformists, he found himself burdened with that era's usual sex negativity.

> The only instruction I ever received from my father on the "facts of life" was when I was about 12, when in the deepest embarrassment and a propos of nothing, he suddenly said, "Never touch yourself down there", and turned and walked away.

The sexually suppressive atmosphere around Howe began to lift only in his later adolescence when he and his friends enjoyed petting parties with the local girls. These were followed by several adolescent homosexual experiences that, then as perhaps also now, were more common to an English upbringing than they were in the United States. Although Howe's professional judgment was that adult homosexuality is most often a case of arrested emotional development, his own tolerance and compassion are without question. Certainly no one could describe Howe, who felt his own adolescent homosexual experiences were a benign transitional moment in the process of his own maturation, as homophobic:

> For me, homosexuality while it lasted was an intense emotional relief and the physical side of it hardly mattered at all. By the time I joined the army at 17 ½, it had disappeared, and other matters had occupied my attention.

Throughout this period, Howe judged himself afflicted with "Sir Galahad complex," a tendency that "was emphasized and exaggerated by both my family upbringing and their Nonconformist morality," and which disappeared in his fifteenth year. "As I recollect my early life," he tells us, "I can see how falsely easy it was for me to be unselfish. If I wanted anything, that in itself was a good enough reason for giving it to someone else." It was not until his divorce, when he was fifty-four years old, that he felt himself truly free of the need to subordinate his own desires to those of others.

While he writes that his adolescent personality bore many signs of a "Messianic complex"—"a protective over-compensation for my guilt and insecurity" that, "in its simplest and most exaggerated form . . . is the other half of a paranoid state of mind"—later on in his autobiography he also gently mocks the very same self-diagnosis. By any honest measure, Howe was a classic Aquarian personality. The Aquarian is the leader of the Zodiac because he or she can envision a future that few in the present can see. In his case, it took the form of "the most general and forthright urge of the Missionary spirit: realizing as profoundly as I do how wrong the world is, I want to put it right." Before his fourteenth year he was teaching at his Sunday school, for which he on occasion wrote and delivered sermons that display an astonishingly mature religious sensibility. And if Howe remembers himself as somewhat dissociated and wary in relationships, this manifested itself in the form of increased, rather than diminished, care and sensitivity to others.

Children grew up quickly in those days. When his father moved out of London, Howe took it upon himself to find a job in the great metropolis. Landing at a London accountancy firm, he left home for lodging nearer to work. He was just fourteen and a half years old. There his education took another turn:

> The only thing that I really learned was the filthiest language that I've ever come across since. An encyclopedia of filth was nothing compared to what went on amongst the article clerks.
>
> As I recollect, in self-defense I went into "shock." Since my training and after nearly forty years of experience as a psychiatrist, I do not believe I have heard of any item of the

30

varied psychopathology of sex with which my tender care had not been regaled before I was fifteen.

Two years later, on July 28, 1914, Europe was tossed into the catastrophe that was World War I. Howe, then just seventeen and a half, must have been caught up in the patriotic fervor because a week later he lied about his age and enlisted in the Artists Rifles. His life pattern of apparently effortless promotions continued. After six months training as a private, he was suddenly offered a commission in another regiment and soon thereafter posted to India. Now an officer, he found himself tasked with training combat veterans, orderly room sergeants, and men twice his age in subjects about which he knew nothing. By the time he was twenty years old he held the rank of major. Just as the war was coming to an end, his regiment was sent to Vladivostock, Russia, ostensibly to liaise with Czechoslovakian troops in the area. It was a dangerous, revolutionary environment, and other British troops had taken losses. Howe, who learned Russian and served as an acting major in the Anglo-Russian brigade, saw to it that his own troops evaded harm. Although the war ended on November 18, 1918, it wasn't until early in 1920 that he and his men finally arrived back in England. The young major had been in uniform for nearly six years.

Howe immediately took a job in his brother Arthur's shipping office where he worked for two years until, "almost as dramatically as St. Paul on the road to Damascus, I was knocked for six and experienced my conversion." He had stumbled upon Freud's *Collected Papers* and was immediately seized with the desire to become a medical psychologist: "There was no option—I was going to follow Freud." Although he hadn't completed his secondary education, the Dean of St. Thomas' Hospital accepted the impressive young veteran as a student. His continuing attendance, however, was contingent upon him passing a formidable array of tests on some sixteen different subjects, a feat he accomplished by working and studying day and night, seven days a week. In 1927, after just four years of medical training, Howe received both his M.B.B.S. (the British equivalent of an M.D.) *and* a diploma in psychological medicine—an extraordinary feat. The very same year he married Norah Blaxill, the sister of his best friend at medical school.

By then he was undergoing his own psychoanalysis while also serving as house physician at Bethlem Royal Hospital (the place that gave us the word "bedlam"). Without hesitation he dove right into the deep end of his profession. In order to develop "insight into insanity, which you really need if you're going to be a psychotherapist," he tells us:

> I used to lock myself into the padded cells with the worst ones, and possibly spend hour and hour locked into a padded cell with various kinds of raging lunatics to see what it was like. Nobody else did that. They also gave me permission to practice psychotherapy on anybody else that I chose to practice on, and nobody else on the staff did that.

That Howe was a large man with a military background no doubt afforded him significant protection. Nevertheless, only the most gifted therapists are able to so readily win the trust of such profoundly disturbed people.

As if all this weren't enough, in 1928 Howe also helped found the highly experimental Tavistock Clinic, in those storied early years (as we learned in M. Guy Thompson's engaging foreword to this book) a mecca for the kind of iconoclastic psychotherapist that he exemplified. Meanwhile, Howe and Norah had started a family. There would be two daughters: Gillian, born the same year, and Carolyn, who arrived eight years later. But tragedy would befall this next generation of Howes as well. Both of his sons, born between the two daughters, died in infancy. A third, much beloved, adopted son was killed while testing an experimental jet for the Royal Air Force near the end of the Second World War.

The publication of *Motives and Mechanisms of the Mind* in 1931 made the thirty-four-year-old Howe one of the most sought-after psychiatrists in the United Kingdom. With the strong book sales and a full clinical practice, his family enjoyed sudden prosperity. However, while the old pattern of ready advancement would bring him offers of marquee positions at prestigious hospitals and clinics, he would pass them by if he felt they would constrict his professional freedom. When he lunched with Ernest Jones in 1933, Howe dared to decline the enormously influential Freudian's invitation to join the British Psychoanalytical Society, of which Jones was then president. Jones was Freud's first biographer and also president of the Institute of Psychoanalysis, so Howe must have known he would pay a price for offending him. It was one he was willing to pay. Likewise, as the Tavistock Clinic eventually came under the sway of Melanie Klein's object relations school in the 1940s, Howe and his fellow free spirits migrated elsewhere.

In 1937, with the war clouds gathering over Europe, Howe published *War Dance: A Study of the Psychology of War*, the best reviewed of all his books, as well as his personal favorite. When Henry Miller read it in Paris in 1939, he was so impressed that he immediately traveled to London where he greeted Howe on the steps of his Harley Street office when the psychiatrist arrived for work the next day. Miller's essay on Howe, "The Wisdom of the Heart" (the title essay in his anthology of the same name), brought Howe's name to the United States but seemingly did little to garner him a substantially wider audience. Though Miller gladly fulfilled Howe's requests to petition various publishers in the United States, the novelist was never able to persuade any of them to give serious consideration to Howe's books.

If Howe's East-West synthesis of psychology and spirituality rendered him somewhat suspect within his own profession, and his straddling of the divide between clinic couch and church pew likewise failed to sway most churchmen who encountered his work, none of this precluded Howe from playing a prominent public role in wartime England. During the Second World War Howe functioned as the country's unofficial national psychologist and was called upon to deliver to the traumatized population, over BBC radio, a series of four popular but controversial lectures on how to cope with the enormous stresses of the time. He was an extraordinarily gifted speaker, whose strong but calmly reassuring personal presence enabled him to challenge his listeners in ways that few others were willing to risk. Those lectures, published in 1941 under the title *Where This War Hits You*, became a best seller. Howe's two other wartime books, *The Triumphant Spirit: A Study of Depression* and *Invisible Anatomy: A Study of "Nerves," Hysteria and Sex*, also sold well. Meanwhile, he contributed articles to the *Picture Post*, a large

circulation British magazine. During and immediately after the
war, Howe put great energy into writing *Mysterious Marriage: A Study
of the Morality of Personal Relationships and Individuals Obsessions*,
which formed a trilogy with the previous two works. Published in
1949, it sold poorly despite receiving positive reviews, leading
Howe to wonder if he should bother to continue to write at all.

Howe, the would-be world-changing idealist, and Norah, a
most practical woman, turned out to be incompatible partners.
The family never really understood their father, who was a good
provider but deeply committed to his work. By 1952, with their
daughters grown, he concluded that their marriage was effectively
over. Seeing a major transition in his life, Howe relinquished his
clinical practice and traveled alone to Sri Lanka (then Ceylon),
Myanmar (then Burma), and finally northern India, to study meditation. During those three months he was instructed by some of
the most notable Theravada Buddhist meditation masters of the
time, including the German-born Nyanoponika Thera and the
famed Burmese teacher Mahasi Sayadaw, as well as the Hindu yogis
Vishnudevanda and Swami Sivananda. He concluded his retreat in
the company of the latter two, who resided next to the Ganges
River, near Rishikesh. Seated by the river in meditation one
evening, a chance encounter with a Hindu sadhu produced the
initiation that, he felt, revealed "the Ultimate."

Penniless upon his return to England, Howe remarried almost
immediately. Nevertheless, his repeated promise to his family that
"the good Lord would provide" always turned out to be true.
Whenever things got difficult, an attractive new opportunity or an
admirer bearing funds would suddenly appear.

Howe and his new wife, Doris, soon started "The Open Way,"
an educational society and eventually also a mental health clinic
purposed "to bring together psychiatrists and clergy in their common study of the 'spiritual nature of man'." With their combined
energies and the support of ardent friends, it soon attracted lec-
turers such as D. T. Suzuki and Jiddu Krishnamurti, as well as
developing a well-engaged membership. Howe also continued his
deep interest in psychical phenomena by maintaining an association with both the Society for Psychical Research and the College

of Psychic Studies. Although he occasionally appeared on radio and television, after the Second World War his public influence began to fade. Never truly accepted within establishment psychiatry, it became accepted wisdom that he was a bit mad. On more than one occasion, he learned that a fellow psychiatrist had refused to appear in the same venue with him.

Howe was an early friend and advocate of R. D. Laing and secured his appointment as the head of the Langham Clinic. But as the sixties cultural revolution unfolded, Howe found Laing's employment of LSD in therapy unacceptable and, in 1965, had him relieved of the same position. Of Howe's final three published works, *Cure or Heal? A Study of Therapeutic Experience, The Mind of the Druid,* and *She and Me: A New Statement of an Old Problem,* only the first received much attention. In the early 1970s a blood clot led to the amputation of one leg. Nevertheless, he fulfilled his longstanding desire to reside in Wales, the site of ancient Druidic culture that he felt exemplified many of his principles about life and spirit. Howe and Doris lived for a while in a small stone house near Bala, but eventually the situation became too difficult for them and they returned to London. As his health and finances began to fail, providence again intervened and new friends arrived to help. Despite his rapidly waning energy, he was able to write a final, pamphlet-sized summary of his thinking, *Consciousness: A Western Treatment of Tibetan Yoga.* Eric Graham Howe died on July 8, 1975, the day after he completed the manuscript.

Howe was perhaps the first true apostle of wholeness and transcendence in a profession that all too often finds its truth in dilemma and disease. These appear to be the fruit of gifts provided for him at birth and called upon throughout his life:

> Neither depression nor ill-health have I ever suffered from. I am never out of mood on waking in the morning and often, when turning over in the night, I find myself, for no apparent reason, declaring "Hooray! Hooray! Hooray!" The fact that I have this experience of direct access to the forces of vitality and the goodwill of the Infinite Benevolence must, I believe, be included in all fairness in their evidence by any students of my Messianic complex.

PROLOGUE

If my reader will now perform an experiment, he will see what I mean. Make of your left hand a tightly enclosed fist, and squeeze it as tightly as you can. Hold it. Now very gradually begin to open it, just the slightest. Hold it again. Now pause and make your choice, experiencing exactly what you are doing, and paying attention to the two alternatives from which you make your choice. You can either SHUT: then you will be safe, holding all you have and certainly amassing more. In the immortal words of Kipling "You will be an (egoic) man, my son!" Or OPEN: you will then indeed become more vulnerable, with your exposed underbelly open to attack from both sides. Beware, for you will have your past as well as your future to contend with. Your enemy will not only be the other, but your SELF also. You will be between two fires and must decide for yourself whether it is really worth it. Surely it is better to shut up?

This is our choice. And I for one would be the first to shut up and contract out of this uncertain and painful engagement, if my experience of life did not believe in another factor entering into my otherwise meaningless situation. It is a tragic fact that this reality has been spoiled by egoic man's habit of giving it names, in order to lessen his anxiety. This REALITY has been effectively denigrated by every name by which egoic man has ever attempted to catch and tame it, whether it be God: Christ: Our Lord: Jehovah: THAT: *vis medicatrix naturae* or what not.

"I" am so much more than "me" will ever see, but blindness is not forever. It is very temporal, as even death must prove. One day, I will see, not as through a glass darkly, but simply and clearly, the true psychology of life and what my neighbor means to me.

From *Cure or Heal? A Study of Therapeutic Experience*

PART I

Relationship—
The Meeting Between
Heaven and Earth

CHAPTER 1

What Is Reality?

"There was something, undefined and incomplete, coming into existence before Heaven and Earth. How still it was and formless, standing alone and undergoing no change, reaching everywhere and in no danger of being exhausted. It may be regarded as the mother of all things."
—LAO-TZU, *Tao Teh Ching* XXV

"I am the beginning, the middle, and the end of all beings."
—KRISHNA, Bhagavad Gita

But the reader should not assume from these quotations that this book has an oriental or esoteric trend. By its persistent reference to the "son of man," and the central position of the Christ upon the experiential cross of reality, dependent upon his "Father," Christians will, I hope, feel themselves to be at home.

Yet, oddly enough, by its insistence upon the importance of form, attention and applied consciousness, the book may seem to some to have a rightly scientific, and even existential, trend.

Reality Is a Secret: At Least, Partly So

If reality is a relationship between the unknowable and the knowable, then it follows that reality is essentially a mystery and, in its entirety, unknowable. This of course also applies to persons, who all share in their entirety the nature of reality.

Important as this assumption is in itself, it becomes still more important in its application to human beliefs and consequent behavior. It is as if we cannot bear this barrier beyond which all is not only unknown at present, but even unknowable forever. If we

From *Cure or Heal? A Study of Therapeutic Experience*

are ever apt to experience anxiety, then surely this is the very situation to induce it, and the compulsive behavior which is aimed to end it.

The claims of humanism are not as obviously a threat to mankind as are the claims of science, which proclaims that if not today at least tomorrow or one day, there will be no barriers to human knowledge and no limit to our know-how.

Perhaps, however, it is in our more intimate domestic behavior that we are most endangered by the existence of the unknowable in the very heart of the family, in the ones we love. Surely it is here that the question of power over the other or not, gives rise to the most compulsive behavior in order to make plain that the answer is in the affirmative. Human nature, essentially curious, becomes doubly so under the compulsive pressure of our paranoid anxiety: "What is going on over there behind that screen of invisibility? I MUST KNOW!" So love, which is a mystery, becomes reduced to sex, which at least seems as if it need not be.

It is always women and children who suffer most from this attack upon their privacy, because they hold the secret answer to the question, "What is reality?" Only they can experience it, which is hard to bear for those others who cannot, or will not, dare to do so much themselves.

Perhaps the most important effect of the unknowable aspect of our selves upon our behavior, however, is the fear which the knowable aspect of our selves, feels towards that which is beyond itself. It seems to me as if there is an aspect of myself which is in no sense mine, nor on my side. It appears to be my enemy. It appears to me as if "I" am not only impossible to handle, but in fact that "I" provide within myself a dread threat to my existence. The finite perhaps rightly fears the infinite, and my potential omnipotence may well seem to me to be experientially too dangerous.

For this is a matter of dreadful experience, in the very marrow of our bones as it were, and not a question of theory or belief. For "me" either has to live with "I," or else get rid of "I's" larger part and so live with "me" alone. In practice this seems apparently to be the lesser threat, in spite of the fact that all "me" feared from "I" is now projected onto everybody else, so that "they" must become my enemies. With so many enemies surrounding me, it seems clear that I am going to be kept very busy trying to make my world even tolerable to live in, unless I can make them into friends. And all this effort must be without the benefit of help from "I," whom "me" has preferred to disavow as being an even greater threat to my security than all my outward enemies could ever be.

By making use of the verbal structure of related pairs of opposites, I hope to set up a series of simple dualities which have some actual correspondence with one another, besides being apt to my theme; and then to confine our consideration of the therapeutic problem firmly within these verbal limits. The particular duality of "self" which I shall use may be called many names; the simplest analysis into "I" and "me" is a very useful one, but leads to grammatical difficulties. In terms of the notation of the sphere, the analysis is between centre and periphery; in teleological or end-seeking terms, the distinction is between "causal" and "effective," "original" and "dependent," "restorative" and "distributive." These words all serve to build up the idea of two selves, operating respectively in "inner" and "outer" worlds. At one point, I shall be referring specifically to an analysis between "space" and "lines" to make my meaning more clear. But for general purposes, I have settled for two rather clumsy terms; that of "whole SELF" and "egoic man." This should enable us, in the course of the development of my argument, to discover not only what I intend each term of the analysis to mean by itself, but also how they are related to one another.

Briefly, I shall claim that egoic man is a three dimensional abstraction from whole SELF, from whom he is derived. Being only an abstracted part of the whole SELF, he can abstract only a part of total reality, of which however he makes his real world, in which he lives and moves. I shall further claim that egoic man, in his effort to solve his problems and achieve success in his own world, produces his own diseases. He can therefore "cure," but never "heal" them. Healing is the sole prerogative of "I"; but it is "me" who makes me ill. Therefore "me" can do no more than reap some temporary benefit of "cure" which falls far short of "healing," and uses an entirely different and opposite method to achieve its end.

This is not in any way to diminish "me," but simply to limit me, which is my need. Whole SELF, by definition, must be cut off from the experiential world of egoic man. It is the parts, the instruments, the machinery, the fingers, the brain and the "know-how" of egoic man, which the whole SELF needs, by means of which to get on in a difficult and obstructive world. All this egoic man provides.

To this end egoic man needs to be a hero, born as he is into a very troublesome and terrifying world. The state of paranoia, or persecution, is our normal lot, in a frequently depressing and hostile world. Indeed, we must recognize "hope" as one of egoic man's most fond illusions; and projection of his wishful thinking against the evidence of contradictory facts, as one of his most normal habits. How else could he live? No one should blame him for his skill in developing means by which he is able to do what we all praise so much, which we often call "making the best of it."

Our Hero Meets—and Defeats—His Troubles

Let us face it, therefore, that to be born is to face a hostile world. Surely the paranoiac was not wrong in his opinion that some unfriendly "they" were after him. But he was wrong in thinking in his resentful fancy that "they" ought to love him, or that he should be able to change his evil case in some way by improving it. In our wiser moments, we know that "they" are not really much concerned with us at all, being too much bothered by the compelling needs of their own problems and devices. They neither love nor hate us, in spite of our would be omnipotence blindly hoping otherwise. Indeed, in most instances "we" are but "they," reflected back upon our selves.

Fortunately for our hero (which of course is you and me), he is endowed with a great wealth and variety of instinctive artillery, with which to defend and assert himself. Living in his own real world, his only aim is his self-preservation and his self-increase. He means to obtain security, and more of it, preserved against all loss. Above all, he means to avoid the ultimate imminence of (alas, always so untimely!) death.

Therefore our hero's egoic personality starts off upon his journey through life determined that success will avoid failure, life avoid death, hope rescue him from his despair and light finally disperse the dark, until all questions can be answered in the assured belief that our hero will be supremely right. Such is our/his private world: and so he hopes, by means of his convenient abstractions (called good ideas) to fix it so. And, fortunately for him, he is far from being unsupported in his intentions. They are shared by the great majority of his fellow men, who are equally determined to stick together and make their world the success which they know it ought to be.

Thus every force within the egoic personality is fighting for his egoic self-preservation, a fact which should show us the immense importance of this function in the biological scale of values. Physically, our hero is equipped with a complex and very efficient system of resistance and attack against the dangerous invasions of unsuitable food, or improper conditions of living. If he is given the wrong food his stomach will reject it, or the white cells of his blood will mass to destroy or repel the toxic enemy. If an adverse environment should cause him to experience chill, his temperature will rise and he will cough and sneeze himself back to better health. Break his bones and they will mend themselves—if only the surgeon will but clean and bandage the injured limb, and give it time in which to heal itself. On the physical level, it is quite clear that unconsciously and automatically, given the opportunity and time enough, a healing process is doing its best, and only requires our cooperation and support. Too often, however, we try to stop our therapeutic reactions, regarding what is going on as the disease itself, when in fact it is only our natural attempt to cure it.

But if we are to be fair to our hero and see him as he really is, we must admit that his conduct is not as conscious as he thinks it is. Here, on the level of his so-called consciousness, which is considered to be particularly characteristic of egoic man, his defense mechanisms are just as automatic, blind and only partially successful, as they are on the physical level. On the conscious level, he is still identified with his own habits of thinking. He is therefore incapable of using thought as the efficient instrument of attention that it well might be. On the level of what he believes to be his conscious behavior, he is curiously compelled (but unconsciously) to take such good care of himself (but even then only of "me") that it can happen that in the end he finds himself stuck with the end-products of his own success. Then, in his dis-ease, he finds that he may still be compulsively defending himself against the dangers of a situation which ended thirty, forty, fifty years ago! However "bad" our symptoms may now appear to be, we should accept the fact that at least the original intention behind them was always "good."

More often than we realize, clinical problems and behavior disorders have been determined by defense mechanisms, called out by situations in the dim and distant past, probably during the first five years of life; often before there can even be memory of the disaster which occurred. Such situations are of course only too familiar, but I would like to mention a few in order that we can see more clearly the dilemma within which egoic man finds himself bound. He only did his best, unconsciously: to find that in the end his best was not so good, because it was ambivalent.

Very briefly, let us consider the defense reactions which operate, for instance, in anxiety, compulsive behavior, delinquency and schizophrenia. I suggest that in everyone of these we shall discover a brilliant tactical operation for the defense and safe establishment of our friend—and enemy!—egoic man. At the time of its origin, we find that this apparently abnormal behavior was actually needed, in order to protect "me" from "them." (And I would remind you that "they" are only egoic-individuals too; so that in fact the blind are always misleading the blind, to our social detriment, as too frequently occurs in the protective-aggressive lunacy of war.)

Anxiety is the attempt to hold on to some "thing," some "idea," and some "hope"; or even on to "me" myself, when "they" did not sufficiently protect me by caring for my needs. So now I must care for my "self" by doing something about everything, especially if it cannot be done. *Compulsive behavior* arises when it becomes necessary in self-defense for me to hand over my responsibility either to "them" or "it," so that a compulsive ritual takes the place of personal responsibility and choice. *Delinquency* is a protest and a self-assertion of impotence against a provocative society. The other day a bewildered mother said to me, "But why did he need to steal? He had plenty of pocket money. We always gave him all he wanted!" So what he needed was to assert himself in such a way that mother's watchful eye could *not* see what he did. What he needed most was that "they" should be deceived; he never needed the objects which he stole. The *schizophrenic* way of rescuing his threatened egoic personality from the impossible emotional dilemma, such as: "You must love me and do as I say, darling, or else I won't love you any more," is by extricating himself out of life altogether, thus preserving his egoic omnipotence unimpaired. (Which is why the schizoid have such negatively strong personalities. They are all "there," but never all "here.")

The point which I have wished to make by these very brief references to our commonplace disorders of behavior is that egoic man, who is so expert at taking care of himself and others (whom he assumes all too readily to be like himself) is left with the by-products of his own success. Having consistently regarded death as his enemy all his life, he may even find it hard to die when his time comes. Meanwhile, he has made his world after his own image and takes care of it, as of himself, according to his own ideas. He preserves it all from loss or failure, with fitted-in scapegoats all complete.

Egoic man, living in this "real" world of his own invention, is after all only everyday man, ordinary man, wise or foolish, success or failure. In fact, he is our neighbor and our selves. He is determined to do good, according to his lights; and furthermore to stop others from doing evil, according to the same. Thus in politics his aim is peace, his enemy to be destroyed is anyone who disagrees with him. In education, it is good to know and be at the top of the class: it is bad to be wrong and anywhere other than where you are expected to be. In religion, identification with the good is best, and bad should be put out of life and mind altogether. In law, society is right and the criminal, or the juvenile delinquent, must somehow be changed to fit in with it. And finally in medicine, the enemy who is to be stopped and destroyed is all too plain to see. He is ill-health, suffering, pain and death; but especially, of course, that ever-present scapegoat, BACTERIA, BACCILLI, the VIRUS, for these are the apparent causes of all our troubles, as egoic man most scientifically proves. Obviously to egoic man, if only all our enemies could be destroyed, how happy, peaceful and healthy we always should be.

Briefly, then, we realize that egoic man is naturally exclusive and apt to pick a quarrel, although always in a good cause. He easily becomes dissociated, with resultant signs of hysteria when he is frustrated. And, in spite of his claim to consciousness, he actually behaves compulsively, blindly and destructively, albeit benevolently, in almost every aspect of his life. Indeed, egoic man certainly does his best; but sometimes, alas, he does it all too well. Himself, invented by himself; his world, also invented by him, must by him be sustained. Being our hero, he certainly makes a very good job of it.

But—is it enough to be a hero? If, for all his good intentions he is blind, and so only partially effective in a partial world, is it possible that he may have left something out of his life and calculations? What threat, or even maybe what help, is there to be expected from beyond his ken?

Reality Changes at Different Times in History

Over the thousands of years of man's evolutionary development, his experience of reality has been constantly changing as his state of mind, or consciousness, developed. It was a common error of our earlier anthropologists to project their state of mind upon the object of their studies, thinking that a primitive savage could behave as he did for reasons that would appear reasonable, or unreasonable, only to the anthropologist himself. We know better nowadays. We know, for instance, that a man's state of mind, or consciousness, can be not only different from, but reciprocal or even opposite to, that of a woman's. The minds of men and women work on different wavelengths, or dimensions. They should therefore only be expected to meet in so far as both sexes realize that they are ambivalent, sharing similar instruments, even if they do not always know equally well how to use them. Similarly, children are not only on a different wavelength from their parents. Their wavelengths vary even for themselves as they grow from year to year and sometimes almost from day to day.

The Great Divide

It is certainly safe to claim that the state of mind of ordinary men after the scientific or industrial revolution, or after the invention of printing, or after his conversion to Christianity, must have differed from the state of mind which preceded it. There is a constant interweaving process between mind, on the one hand, and the world in which man lives, upon the other. Mind changes matter: but matter also changes mind. It is thus that all things flow, as Heraclitus said. But some hundreds of years after his death, Plato and Aristotle were of a different state of mind, and saw reality differently.

For Lao-Tzu, Buddha, Aeschylus, Heraclitus and Sophocles perhaps, the world was still whole, and was experienced in terms of its relationships of part with part and part with whole. Then man still moved with nature in an experiential process of rhythm and of law. He was then more concerned with what was wholly true and less with what was partly good. But perhaps somewhere about 300 B.C., a great divide of consciousness was crossed which prepared the way for the scientific revolution on the one hand, but also for a dangerous state of social and personal schizophrenia on the other. Socrates, Plato, Aristotle: the Jewish Church: certainly the Christian Church under the Emperor Constantine after the Councils of Nicea in 300 A.D. (but perhaps not the original teachings of Christ, before they became politically useful to the Roman Empire), all these were concerned to discover an abstracted reality of things-by-themselves, objective not subjective, static not moving. On these terms science could proceed and did; but the more general concern was towards what seemed to be good, rather than what could be proven to be true. On these terms, the conceptualized rather than the experiential viewpoint of reality was founded. Our subsequent state of consciousness has dangerously divided self from other, soul from body, good from bad, science from religion, until now we are divided into separate parts and systems, races, religions and persons. In spite of all the progress of egoic man's scientific discovery in the world of atomic physics and modern medicine, something has been lost, which has to do with the experiential value of his personal relationships.

At least, this was so until recently. But science and physics have now rediscovered the reality of relativity, so that we are in process of developing a new state of mind, a new consciousness, in which we can know again an undivided world. The great divide which was crossed from left to right somewhere about 300 B.C. is once again being retraversed in the opposite direction, as we move from the divisions of abstract science towards the mystery of relationship, between part and part and part with whole. This could well mean the beginning of another stage for Man upon his time-track journey, with a new development of consciousness and the birth of a new age.

Reality today is known to be very different to what it was thought to be in the nineteenth century. Our state of consciousness has changed and so have our ideas about the world in which we live. Whether we are considering the macrocosm of the stellar universe or the microcosm of the intricate structure of a single cell, we know that in its essence, in itself apart from our personal approach to it, all form is energy-in-relationship. In fact the mind of modern man, even of the man-in-the-street, knows that the old idea of form is as much an illusion as the Buddhists knew it to be 2,500 years ago, when they called it Maya, which meant illusion. However solid any structured form may seem to be in our similarly structured mind and senses, in itself reality is energy in relationship. However reliable the performance of our machines may be when they are launched on the almost infinitely complex operation of a flight through outer space, in the end it all amounts to the behavior of certain constellations of energy, in varying relationship with one another. Energy must be thus contained in images, things or persons: but it is the relationship which counts.

What Is Existential, or Experiential, Reality?

Reality being an emergent process, life in its experiential aspect may be properly regarded as a constant state of emergency. Egoic man, however, being also anxious man, has done his best to make life as safe and sure as possible. By intellectualizing instead of experiencing, by thinking and talking about life, by giving names to things-by-themselves and describing them in detail as men do, egoic man has almost brought about an end to the insecurity of our personal experience of the ever-changing relationships of life.

Both Buddhism and original Christianity were concerned with the meaning of experience. Zen Buddhism (which was founded in about 600 A.D.) more particularly emphasized experience as the way, or middle way, of life, and produced in different forms many miracles of artistic beauty. Kierkegaard, at the end of the nineteenth century, Jean-Paul Sartre during and after the Second World War, and certain modern philosophers like Heidegger, have seen the point, and by restating it have been in danger of losing it by not losing it. It would seem, however, that the problem of *experienced relationships* is in the air today, as an essential product of the wind of change. It belongs particularly to modern psychotherapy, but otherwise, like truth itself, it can belong to no man, except in so far as he can experience it.

What then can we regard as the salient features of existential or experiential reality? I would suggest the following:

(1) It is an experience of a relationship which comprises four parts, in the four terms of I-experience-it-now. The experiencer may or may not contain a transcendental element, which was certainly present in Buddhism (including Zen), in original Christianity and in Kierkegaard, but is not necessarily found in the opinions of Sartre and his followers.

(2) It is non-conceptual and free from any defensive preoccupation, either with aim or origin. Traditionally, the Chinese called it "wu-wei," the aimless or wayless way. For the early Celtic and Druidic traditions, experience was what "hap-pened" or "happed" to you, and that was life. There was no more to say about it, and nothing must ever be written down.

(3) Egoic man is therefore the antithesis of existential or experiential man. The present trend in the wind of change is a necessary swing-back of the pendulum from periphery to centre, from objective to subjective, and from thinking-about-it as an intellectual abstraction of things-by-themselves, to a more simple, direct, personal experience of an exact relationship.

(4) Although so much discussed by men, existential or experiential reality is really only the normal life of women and children. When they are permitted to be as they are, women and children just *are* and *know*. But this naturally annoys egoic men very much, which is perhaps why women and children are so rarely permitted to be what they are.

Meanwhile, egoic man is clearly self-satisfied with his position as a real person in a real world. He is down to earth, he says, and no nonsense. He knows he knows he knows: and all he knows is in his textbooks, filed for reference, accurate, objective and complete. To be "subjective," for him, is to be very wrong indeed. To be "enthusiastic" is only to be still more subjective, and so more wrong than ever. He is the perfect civil servant, identified with the rightness of the establishment, the same yesterday, today and tomorrow. He is in a very strong position. He keeps his world safe from the uncompromising threat of life, or experiential reality, by which it is constantly—but fortunately for him always unsuccessfully—assailed.

But experiential reality implies uncertain undefendedness, and non-conceptual readiness to confront, not only the unexpected, but also the unknown and the undesired. This is what lies, as the next development for Man-the-traveler, in the mysterious movement of his experience of consciousness from one state to another, upon this side of the Great Divide. So it is no wonder that our new image of new man has few friends, but many enemies.

Meanwhile, our most effective contraceptive against change will always be the preconceptions of egoic man.

To What Is Our Experience of Reality Relative?

Obviously existential reality is not so easy to experience as it first might seem to be. Tied as we are to memories of past experience, too often with the compulsion to avoid them, and the desire to achieve the security of gaining some future aim, we are no longer free to experience life apart from the conditions in which it happens. However, we must start from where we are, now. So let us try to set out a list of the conditions to which our experience of reality is actually relative and by which our behavior is either partially influenced or wholly determined:

(1) Our experience of reality "now" is largely determined by some past experience, either of a similar or dissimilar, pleasant or unpleasant, nature: e.g. "I know all about that, it is only an X." This will of course absolve us from the necessity of ever experiencing X at all.

Most of us, most of the time, are more under the influence of our undigested past experience, as something to be avoided, rather than being related to the present opportunity. Most of us have experienced too much, too often, and too soon, of something unpleasant, even if it was only the pressure of numbers of other people, or the need to accumulate information for the purpose of passing exams. It became for most of us a primary necessity to avoid being hurt, or being criticized. Therefore every subsequent moment of our experience is regarded as offering another threat to our security. The injunctions of childhood, which were so often SHUT UP! STOP IT! YOU OUGHT TO BE ASHAMED! have achieved their aim. Thus the defenses against the past remain intact, to stand between us and the not-so-dangerous "now."

Our motivation, therefore, is only partially the positive one of "I want it *now*." We are more frequently motivated by "I want to avoid what happened *then*," when I was made to feel unbearably frightened, insecure, ashamed, or inferior. Thus we all have a chip, or picture, on our shoulder, derived from the past which may be long forgotten, but in regard to which our day-to-day behavior is still relatively determined.

(2) Our experience of reality is relative to *what we desire*. I do not experience rain if I wish it to be fine. What I do experience is resentment or disappointment. If I want you to love me, I do not experience the justice of your critical remarks; I only feel hurt and offended by what you have said.

(3) Our experience of reality is relative to an idea, myth, or mental picture, of which we are usually totally "unconscious," in the sense of being blind to its existence. We have such pictures, whether derived from inner archetypes or outer experience, of good and bad parent figures. Our behavior may be completely determined also by the picture which we hold of ourselves, whether as a success or a failure.

(4) Our experience of reality is relative to the instruments we use, be it heart or brain, eye or ear, intuition or "extrasensory perception." Our experience of reality may indeed sometimes be of someone else's reality, and not our own at all. The differences in information derived from our different instruments may be as great as those between a telephone and a micrometer, but they all afford us some different communication with total REALITY.

(5) Our experience of reality may be actually determined by the object of experience itself, as something which is in fact distinct-in-itself from our relationship with it. This is certainly possible, although it is improbable. It is wiser for us to enjoy our own experience for what it is worth, rather than to regard it as obligatory on anyone else to do the same. This warning particularly applies to parents' experience of their children. They do not see them as they are, but only relatively, against the determinism of their own personal background of desire and fear.

That reality is always a medium of communication may seem at first to be a strange idea, but further consideration will prove that any experience of reality is always some kind of communication. We communicate with the world outside ourselves by means of the senses, or between one another by means of speech. But our experience of beauty or of love, of horror or of wonder, is also due to a communication on a different level, using a different medium or instrument. Any communication must always be somewhat mysterious, and we have needlessly restricted it by thinking that it is limited to words and meanings which can be fixed in a dictionary, or measured by scientific (egoic) man.

Reality Is like a Game with Mirrors

Our inner world is projected outwards on the screen of appearances, in much the same way as a cinematographic film appears to have its own illusion of reality in the world we see upon the screen. We see the present in terms of the past, the actual in terms of the feared or the desired. Those who fear death see death in all they fear. Those who desire to be loved, see love, or more often the lack of it, in all they see. Few see what is of itself, when all that is real-in-itself is obscured by the projection on to it of what is only real-to-us, which is usually some past experience of reality to be avoided.

The parents whom we have *not* had are sometimes more important than the ones we have experienced. In contradiction to the determinism of the psychoanalysts, we live IN SPITE, and not BECAUSE, of our conditioning; which is a verdict most rightly upheld by our judiciary.

The task of our outer father and mother is to represent, and so to affirm and give reality to, our inner "father" and "mother," who hold in our inner world the images of our potential bisexuality. We need both parents, because we are originally both, within ourselves. Hence, in the absence or misbehavior of either, the need to find a parent substitute, or else to find in phantasy what we have lost in fact. Fortunately for us, our hidden reserves within each inner world include a hierarchy of antecedents, from our grandparents back into the mists of time and history. Between these real inner and outer worlds, each one of us must stand, somewhat confused and not a little afraid until, by one means or another, we can each find our own personal standpoint. It is to be hoped, however, that this will not require the total defeat of our inner real resources.

Thus the mirror traffic between the inner and the outer world flows both ways, to and fro. "I am a camera" is dangerously true. Even in the womb, the embryo is being impressed "photographically" by its environment; the more so because at this stage there is no mental filter to protect the recipient from the impact of an experience, which must therefore be "all or nothing."

These pictures which are printed earliest upon the sensitivity of our minds, or lack of them, can be so disastrous because, although they may be real to us, they are completely destructive of the experiential reality which may subsequently be presented to us. The imprinted photographs may be of good-mum or bad-mum, of good-little-boy or bad-little-boy, of unwanted child or spoiled child. They will all recur projected again and again, as destroyers of the real in the reversing and distorting mirrors of experience.

The idealized picture of romantic love, whether between mother and child, or between lovers who will "marry and live happily ever after," can also be only an invention to avoid experience, by reference to which the ability to experience real love can be destroyed. Similarly, a picture of being a good-little-boy, or a bad-little-girl, makes it increasingly difficult ever to be a real person. Thus the "good" must be seen only too often as the destroyer of the "true," as the half-life in a half-reality is the destroyer of the possibility of the fuller life-in-reality.

The Reality of Myths and Dreams

From what has been said already, it is apparent that, whether we are awake or asleep, we are the victims of a wonderful mixture of images, which somehow sort themselves out to make a world of apparent sense and continuity. This is not very different from our world of dreams, except that in sleep we are contained within our inner world, with all its past conditioning. The point which I shall be making later, however, is that in sleep we are more under the influence of the forces of the inmost "I," which is the healer. There is no doubt that sleep is an intense period of repair and of healing activity. It frames a reality of its own, and the experiences which occur to us in dreams are as real and as respectable as they are under any other condition, as long as we are attentive to the limiting nature of these conditions.

Incredible as it may seem to egoic man, myths and dreams are communications of significant reality, as long as we are prepared to admit that Heaven and earth, Gods and men, I and me, centre and circumference, are equally real: and that relationship and communication does exist between them, independently of the expectations of egoic man.

Myths are dreams of a people, as dreams are the myths of a person. Both assume the reality of origin, of the ultimate. Of the PERSON and of the GODS: both assume the reality of time in history: both use the common everyday techniques of drama, art and imagination: and both form the link or bridge between the unknowable BEYOND, and that little which is known of egoic man, here-and-now.

The Reality of Illness

It is the thesis of this book that even illness is respectable, and requires our attention if we are ever to experience the healing of egoic man.

Given one of any pair of opposites, it is the instinctive habit of egoic man to grasp the better and avoid the worse. But why should he not do just that, because egoic man is preeminently reasonable, according to his lights? The idea of health being achieved by destroying disease is basic to scientific medicine. But the danger which we shall be discussing in the next chapter is that a valid half-truth becomes untrue, unless it is kept in constant confrontation with its contradictory other part.

Egoic man experiences his opposites of "sick" and "well." But the great divide with which this book is concerned is: what is to be the relationship between them? And, in particular, what is to be our relationship with this other, this shadow on our lives, this sickness, this symptom or dis-ease?

It is our thesis that egoic man has brought his disease into being by his avoidance of his dis-ease, or capacity for suffering, in his attempt to cure himself. By committing surgery on this shadow of his other side, he has fastened it the more securely upon himself. Ultimately power over the other can only be obtained by killing our enemy, whoever he may be: but, being dead and still tied to us, he only threatens us the more. By killing him again and again, we only aggravate the severity of our troubles.

However, our thesis will be that there is indeed a way of healing, or of making whole, by accepting REALITY, in terms of personal experience, just as it presents itself. As such, it is not to be approved or avoided, but to be strictly accepted according to the discipline imposed upon our experience by the way of Life on the other side of the "great divide," where all is to be personally suffered, endured or enjoyed, in time.

Reality Is Tragic

Egoic man is apt to make the best of his experiences and lives hopefully frowning on those who would be less cheerful than himself. All will be well, he hopes, if not today, one day. Love will make all things right. Therefore, we have been exhorted to love one another, but we must admit that such benevolent exhortations have never really met with much success. By insisting so strongly that we ought to love one another, Christianity has in effect not only interfered with our normal sexual development, which is not like romantic love at all, but also with certain innate trends of cruelty and hatred which are necessary aspects of our reality, at least during our early experience of Life.

If we are willing to face the facts of history, especially during our own lifetime, we must surely admit that all is not so well as egoic man likes to pretend. It is as if, in his avoidance of the impending evil day, he is hoping to avoid even death itself. But it is not only the ultimate experience of death which comes for all of us that makes life tragic. Surely, to admit the reality of the VOID, the reality of the trafficking between Gods and men in imagination, myth and dreams, and the reality of the warring relationships between men and women, is to declare the necessity for our experience of tragedy. On our journey from Heaven to earth, from PERSON to person, from INFINITY to measured space and time, from SELF-at-birth to self in our alleged maturity, all must be lost not once, but many times. In order that the Self must be born, the SELF must die; and, reciprocally just, in order that the self may be born, the Self must also die. There can be no birth without the loss and pain of previous, unwilling, death. But, again reciprocally just, this death is not the end but the beginning of a new and different reality, under different conditions, with a fresh chance of finding the freedom to enjoy it better than we have done before.

Therefore, viewed as a whole, as it were from the side or wings of the stage of life, this experience of tragedy is all for our better entertainment. As the hero struggles with the monster, we realize that there is in the end neither victor nor victim. It is the fulfillment of our life which should be our aim: not avoidance of defeat, nor victory, but only traveling on.

If life has its tragic element, it is only part of reality, as we know from our experience of Music Hall, which at its best has always been very near the heart of the matter. If there is comedy in tragedy and tragedy in comedy, there must always be laughter somewhere at the heart of things.

But Is Reality Actually Sometimes Insufferable?

However, if we are to face our truth experientially and as it affects us personally, is life in fact sometimes insufferable? Is our personal experience of reality sometimes beyond our limited capacity for acceptance and suffering? Is this what our egoic activities are all about—not for getting somewhere, but for getting away from the intolerable fact of insufferable pain?

Is life perhaps not for getting something from it that we want in the future, but only for forgetting what has already happened to us in the past? Is optimism for some of us only a protective front of cheerfulness to cover a reality of endless pain?

It is not for nothing that the Christians hold their Son of Man upon His cross, in order that he may bear the load of suffering for our sins. This is no pretty picture of a congenial world in which egoic man can enjoy the random appetites of his flesh. Christian theology has always taken the pessimistic view of matter, flesh and human appetite for happiness. As things-by-themselves, they must all be redeemed by loss, death and suffering, before the TRUTH of "I" can be borne in upon resentful and resistant "me."

It is an interesting confirmation of the more pessimistic view of egoic reality that Freud, as taken over and redeveloped subsequently by the work of Melanie Klein, should have come to believe that our earliest experiences of infancy are those of deprivation and assault. According to their views the primal experience of the infant in regard to mother must inevitably be of *separation*, and this is now regarded as having been in fact *experientially intolerable*. This is called the *depressive position* of the infant, which he does all he can to avoid, at the expense of a subsequent development of neurosis, physical illness, psychosis or delinquency. Worse immediately follows, however, because, according to the same opinion, even in the first few weeks of his experience and certainly in the course of months, the infant is confronted experientially by the intolerable fact that THEY not only do not care to support, but are actively concerned to frustrate and deny him. This is called the *paranoid position* and it is compulsively escaping from it that is believed to cause the development of every subsequent attempt to obtain power over the other, by one means or another.

What is certainly agreed, however, by the great majority of therapists is that, although our human ills of every kind may seem to be temporarily alleviated by having what we want, even to the extent of seeming "cure," a true healing in the sense of a lasting result and return to a full enjoyment of life, can only be obtained by those who are able to bear the tension, and experience the insufferable strain, of living through the depressive and the paranoid reality of experience without any kind of escape whatever. Only thus can egoic man be truly healed.

What Is Meant by "Total Man," or "Whole Self"?

The picture which has been drawn of partial, egoic, three dimensional man—just "me" if you like—now needs to be set in contrast with our ideas of total, or multi-dimensional, man. It has been suggested by others who put more faith in these words than I do, that "conscious" is to "unconscious" as that part of an iceberg which appears above the water is to the rest which is submerged. Certainly, for total man, the invisible part of him is much more than, and much more important than, the visible.

There are various ways of considering total man. First, let us include him in his time-dimension, so that his total self is seen as a time-continuum from birth to death, with the possibility of a still further extension into "before" and "after." Then we can realize that his past is able to influence his present, because it is actually operative (or present within us) "now." The anatomy of the time-body is at least as real as that of the physical body, but of course it is not so visible. (We should perhaps add that the "now" is not only under the influence of the past, especially if it has been rejected, but also sometimes of the future, as we can prove by study of our dreams and other kinds of prophetic experience.)

In our time-picture of total man, the state of consciousness known to his egoic personality exists BETWEEN his experienced past and his not-yet-experienced future, and is under the constant influence of both. Therefore, without his knowing, it is this very state of egoic consciousness which cuts him off from knowledge of his larger, other self, the very existence of which egoic man must be protectively anxious to deny. Today, it is only in our sleep that we are set free to wander, or wonder, in more spacious realms.

Another way of describing total man is in terms of his four functions, which divide him into experiential compartments. These are intuition, thought, feeling and sensation (corresponding with the four "elements" of fire, air, water and earth). In only one of these, in thought or "air," can egoic man be said to have consciousness of his own existence. (Descartes' statement "I think therefore I am" only applies, if at all, to this abstracted "me" of egoic consciousness. "Me thinks therefore me is," in our grammatical terms, is true enough. But only if we realize that, by definition, "me" is not "I.") The total self must include all these functions or instruments of experience, as well as the experiencer himself, who uses them. Truly, "In my Father's house are many mansions." So also in the psychic house of our mysterious tenant "I," there are many different dimensions of experience, and many and various states of consciousness to be enjoyed.

The simplest framework of all, however, which I wish to use to illustrate this concept of the total SELF, is an arrangement of lines and spaces. The lines enclose adjoining squares, of which only one is occupied by egoic consciousness. The other squares stand for other dimensions of experience, other states of consciousness and other "rooms" in our psychic house:

Here "total MAN" is space plus lines. The lines are here to limit space, which is unlimited without them. The space is there to "cause" the lines, or to inform them. In a certain special sense, we can claim that it is "space" which really "matters"; but matter matters too, as long as it recognizes and admits its dependence upon "space."

It is this concept of SPACE (spirit, void or plenum) which enables us to include the "spiritual nature of man" as a primary

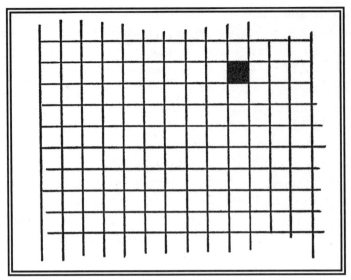

Figure 1 Grid

postulate in the inclusive being of total man. It is out of this apparently negative background that our experiential world is derived: thing from no-thing, self from not-self, personality from person, me from "I," and man from God. From this metaphysical dilemma, however, we can all escape, either in one direction or the other. Some of us prefer to escape into matter, others into space or spirit: but it is the balanced relationship between both which brings him into health and wholeness.

To egoic man, this concept of space, void, plenum, spirit, relative emptiness, may seem to be either unscientific, or too metaphysical. I would claim for it, however, several practical advantages. First, it is obvious that our knowledge of space is certainly experiential. We live and breathe in it. In fact, our body owes its life to the way in which it uses holes in space. Second, why should it be more scientific to speak of "thing" than "no-thing"? Surely, a thing is only what it is by reason of its relationship with what it is not? In fact, it will be found that no-thing is the medium of all relationship, without which we are in a fix. Thirdly, it has always been traditional, and a working premise, of every system of ideas concerned with MAN as a total person, to provide him with a capacity for experiencing total REALITY, including death. This has been done by means of a concept of a medium called "spirit," which precedes the "matter" which it transcends and leaves after death. And finally, what is most important for us, the plenum, void or not-self is the foundation principle of all experience of faith, hope and courage which are the only means of dispelling the appalling doubt and anxiety which are the inevitable lot of egoic man. In the end, all form must fail: but space, or spirit, never. Such is the wisdom of experience which is unfortunately denied to egoic man.

The Psychological Breakthrough

As a result of the practice of psychotherapy (in which I include all forms of analysis), a revolution in the art of healing has happened during the present century which, although strongly influenced by the work of Freud, Jung and others, seems not so much to be due to the ideas of anyone in particular, as to the participation of many therapists over the years in a new and practical, more experienced, approach to the patient as a living, growing person, with a history and a context. In this therapy, the vital word is *relationship*. I mean not only a relationship between the therapist and the patient, but also between the patient and his illness. By means of this relationship with, instead of dissociation from, the items of the illness, it has been found that healing does take place automatically, in course of time, without any effort or interference on the part of either the therapist or the patient. In this sense, the therapist is claimed to be no more than a catalyst, without whose inert presence the healing change could not take place.

It has been found that it is not only unnecessary, but that it is in fact bad practice, to expect any effort on the part of the patient. To say "You must pull yourself together! No one can help you but yourself! Only your willpower can pull you through!" should by now be completely out of fashion. The victim of all such well-meaning advice only succeeded in pulling himself to pieces in his efforts to pull himself together. Our modern psychotherapy is indeed the very opposite of such a practice of "power over the other." Indeed it has now been proved in fact that the opposite is the case. In effect, we now say to our patients: "Yes, look and see but do not touch the exhibits. Relax, rest, sleep, if you can. But the less you do to help yourself the better. Wait—and see! And then let's face it all—in time, and in minutest detail, together."

So now, in this new therapy, the therapist and patient work together on the same level. In the result, we are able to make a certain claim, which must be of some importance; namely, that there is demonstrably a benevolent healing influence which can be seen in the actual process of its operation, and that its beneficial results can be observed in detail. Given the conditions, anyone can now prove this fact for themselves, if they will but obey the rules. This healing influence is found to operate in sleep, through dreams. It also operates, however, in a state of normal consciousness, provided there is an occasional chink of empty space through which the healing, guiding force can move. It therefore appears that there is something (or someone?) within each one of us who wills us well. This is no longer wishful thinking, because it is true, as experience has proved.

I have mentioned the rules, which I believe to be essential for success. I believe these must be obeyed exactly if this healing work is to be carried out successfully. It is not for nothing that the word "patient" implies both time and suffering. The essence of the rule for healing is *"Acceptance* of *the rejected other."* All the instinctive habits of egoic-self-defense must now become reversed; from hang-on, to let-go: from attachment to detachment: from effort to rest: from rejection and avoidance, to acceptance and relationship. Egoic man's favorite method of instinctively solving every problem, like the ostrich, by dissociation and pretending it is not there; may cure us for a time, or pass the burden to someone else to carry. But it is certain that this can never heal us of our real ills.

Healing requires us, at least to start with, to be as ill as we are. It requires the digestion of the undigested experience from the past; but, first, it requires the acceptance of the pain it caused, and of our instinctive desire to be rid of it. In the end (but this only comes later), healing requires the full acceptance of the rejected other, who is originally part of ourselves: and acceptance of the "shadow," who presents every opposite aspect of the character we want to appear to be. Whatever it was which caused us to say "I cannot bear it!" must gradually be defined, met and accepted. It must be "suffered," in fact, in the sense of "Suffer those little devils to come unto me."

But we should remember that all the instinctive efforts of the egoic personality have previously been directed towards exactly the opposite purpose, of avoiding suffering. Indeed, the medical profession is bound by its Hippocratic oath to "alleviate suffering." This is only wise, however, if it is not carried too far, as the all-too-frequent use of tranquilizers today suggests that it may be. The universal dread of death would no longer lead either to our premature relief by suicide or to its compulsive postponement, if it was realized that timely death is our ultimate healer, and part of the will of the great benevolence. Therapeutically speaking, death is our last and greatest friend.

Some are inclined to think that psychotherapy began with Freud's researches at the beginning of the present century, or that there is something essentially different in its practice from the principles of healing which have always operated in successful medicine. I suggest, however, that the breakthrough to which I am referring is not a sudden eruption of new light, but rather the rediscovery of a very old one, now used over a much wider field of experience in mental illness. In its essence, psychotherapy is as old as man, and always has been taught as the way of wisdom. Acceptance means "Love thy neighbor as thyself"; "live and let live; love and let be." It is in line with the simplest teaching of the Christian gospel. It is also interesting to note, however, that, without knowingly having learnt from that source, it is also in full agreement with the basic doctrines of Buddhism, which are ANATTA (not-self), and SATI PATANA (bare attention). And, even more particularly, with ZEN, which is at present a great focal point of intellectual attention, both in this country and in America.

What is of more importance, however, to our day and state of mind, is that the psychological technique of detached objective observation, without preconception or interference with the evidence, is in full accord with the highest requirements of the scientific method. Indeed we may even claim to be at the growing point of the scientific methods, because we realize, as do the best modern scientists, that it is not enough to study things-by-themselves, or people-in-test-tubes. Reality requires movement, in context and relationship, with a proper study of our place in history.

Moreover, the practice of psychotherapy, as I have defined it, does not divide any particular psychological school of thought from any other. What I have described is, I believe, the common denominator of every successful technique in psychotherapy that there has ever been or, indeed, can ever be.

Let me say again that we who practice psychotherapy have been able to prove on the anvil of our own experience that, given the right attitude on the part of both, patient and therapist and a sufficiency of time, our old friend the *vis medicatrix naturae*, which mends our broken bones and heals the common ailments of our bodies (with some help maybe, but also sometimes in spite of more than a little hindrance from the doctor), works on every level, and all the time, to heal us of our ills. Mysteriously, we find that both our inner and our outer worlds conspire, against our belief or hope, to make us whole. And yet I fear that this healing process must always come about somewhat at the expense of egoic man.

CHAPTER 2

The Selves

B y what words can we define Life? What is to be our idiom, and what form, what frame, what manner of speech, is to do justice to the wholeness of experience? Surely the answer is that there is no form, no frame, no idiom, no words with which *in themselves* we can do justice to our experience of life. Within this hollow shell of words there must be something else, some hidden fire, some inner end which uses them as means. Our verbal tools are good enough if we can but make the most of them: although insufficient in themselves, they are adequate enough when used only as agents or as means to an end. Words are for this service, and, to the end of better describing our experience, we can choose our own form as it seems to be convenient. Therefore to some extent at least I am going to invent and use my own idiom, which must then be allowed by the reader to become the frame of reference by which we agree to exchange our ideas. This frame of reference is the circle, the wheel or the sphere; let it be whichever we like for our convenience, but only let it move, for it is about this circle that we are to spin together.

I have chosen the circle because it is a figure of movement. Nature abhors straight lines and will not be forced into a square frame, however mankind may strive to effect this fixed imprisonment. It is no use talking about "dynamic psychology," which is the psychology of motive and of movement, unless we are prepared to spin with it, moving both with and within a moving idiom. This wheel of fate, this geometric circle, is a moving system within the limits of which we can also serve the Law with moving minds.

Let us take the circle and, using it as an abstract form or image, look into it to see how much we can get out of it. The first

---

From *I and Me: A Study of the Self*

thing that we can see is that it has two parts or aspects, an outer and an inner, which for our convenience we will label "A" for the center and "B" for the circumference. We notice how big is B and how small is A; for the circumference is obviously much larger than the comparatively tiny spot in the middle. This distinction between the outer and the inner aspects of our circle we may also correlate with another pair of opposites, namely the superficial and the deep.

Next let us think of our circle as a sphere. Then further consideration of its two-ness suggests that there is that part which we can sense, seeing it with our eyes or touching it with our fingers; but there is also that other part which we cannot sense at all, and which is thus, for us, our non-sense. But do not let us, for so slight a cause, lose sight of its existence, which is objectively quite as real, in spite of the fact that subjectively we may have no sense with which to understand it.

So far we have seen that there is this big, external, able-to-be-sensed aspect of our circular form which we have agreed to call for brevity B, and this smaller, non-sensed part within, which we call A with a warning in case, being unseen, we may forget it altogether. So far the balance seems to be weighted very heavily on the side of the external, superficial B. But if we agree to allow our abstract sphere to represent an orange and enlarge our still unseen center to include the pulp (for why shouldn't we?), then the skin is B, and the fruit is A. This may suggest a note of warning, that, even though it is less obvious, the inside may yet be more important than the outside, the unseen as real as the seen, and the "non-sensed" as much all-there as anything dignified, as worthy of acceptance by the most matter-of-fact and plain-speaking of materially minded critics.

But now let us take a plunge into the mid-stream of philosophical metaphysics (without being unduly alarmed, however, for it is only common sense), by noticing that the center of our sphere has no extension either in space or time. It is a non-sense and no-space point in Eternity or No-time; and yet, in spite of that dubious designation, it is the center of the whole affair. The circumference, on the other hand, is in a condition of extension in time and space. What does this mean? It may sound difficult to talk about this central no-point in no-time, but if we imagine ourselves moving upon a moving wheel it becomes quite simple. Let us spin the wheel, and imagine ourselves turning on the rim. Then we shall find that we are travelling relatively fast; but as we climb down one of the spokes of our spinning wheel until we get to the center of the hub, we shall then find that we have stopped moving altogether, while our private universe obligingly spins round us. Thus by moving from the circumference to the center we have moved from movement to no-movement, which suggests that our B stands relatively for "action" and our central A for "repose".

If now we regard our circle as a cross-section through a glass vessel, then the circumference (B) is the vessel and the part in the middle (A) is the fluid content. Here we have another idea: namely, that B is of hard material and that A is relatively soft and fluid (or why should we not use the word that belongs opposite to "material," namely "spiritual"?). If we imagine this central fluid as a reservoir, then we can see that the container, or surface part, has a definitive and distributive function. This introduces yet another idea, that the central part, A, is storing, and the outer part, B, is using. This central part we can call "essential", and we can call the outer part "definitive" because it defines and gives the limit to all that is inside it.

To use a Platonic idiom, we can call the central part the "idea" and the outer part the "form." This is important, because if we try to fit the wrong form on the right idea, or the right form on the wrong idea, then something happens which is both uncomfortable and confusing. For instance, a child is A to the form B of its parents' discipline: each may be right, but what is important is that they should be relatively right to one another.

There are still several more of these related couples that we can discover within the unity of this phenomenon, the circle. The central A is the undifferentiated beginning, the creative fluid, the "water" which is of so much importance to those interested in the understanding of dreams. The outer part B is the material aspect, earth: so A and B stand for the relationship of water and earth, spiritual and material, creative and created. From another point of view, the central "section" is the female (A) and the outer "section" is relatively the male (B), which serves to suggest that most fundamental example of all opposed couples, the two sexes. Then again we may regard A as the positive and B as the negative pole of our related couple, responsible between them for movement by reference to each other's "slope." Whatever the language that we use by which to make clear this distinction: whether we regard A and B as nucleus and protoplasm respectively of the living cell, or as "spirit incarnate," or quite abstractly, as "content defined," I do not wish to use such words as these with any limited biological, religious or philosophic significance, but only to describe as best I can the meaning of this relationship of many forms between these two factors, A and B. These simple letters do less harm to the movement of ideas than do many more weighty words, which unfortunately seem to have a morbid effect upon our understanding. As tolerant observers of the "facts of Life," we must learn to see beyond the convenient illusions of labels, and to do without such abusive epithets as "mystical," "metaphysical," "spiritual" or "supernatural." With less shouting, the facts may the more easily be allowed to speak for themselves.

Having gone so far, we can now summarize these and many other aspects of this partnership, arranging the A's and B's in two columns for comparison:

A	B
Center	Circumference
Little (apparently)	Big
Deep	Superficial
Unseen	Seen
Non-sense	Sense
Unimportant?	Important?
Fruit	Skin
A point in eternity	Extension in space-time
Repose	Action
Content	Vessel
Reservoir	Distribution
Intact	Contact

Nucleus	Protoplasm
"Cause"	"Effect"
Essential	Definitive
Idea	Form
Fluid, formless, spirit	Solid, matter
Water	Earth
Female	Male
Positive	Negative

But in order that fire may perhaps be set to other trains of thought, and that we should be encouraged to create and work out the details of our own ideas in more familiar and comfortable language for ourselves, here are a few more provoking suggestions as to these coupled bedfellows:

Virgin	Fruitful
Blue	Red
Question	Answer
Sleeping	Waking
Awareness	Consciousness
Inspiration	Discipline
Freedom	Servitude
Heart	Head
Command	Orderliness
Pride	Humility

Perhaps it may seem that I have taken unwarrantable liberties with my circle, sphere, wheel or orange, before it is possible to deduce so much information from them, and from their intrinsic relationships. But I hope that in the course of my illustrations I have not done great injury to what is true. The point which I have wished to make more plain is that there is this fundamental dualism of relationship between the seen and the unseen, where B is the obvious, outer view of reality, and A is the inner, hidden aspect, which is something just as real, although by some realists it is liable to be forgotten, because it is dutifully ignored. It may shake our certainties, but in all things there is this relationship of the two-ness, the A and the B.

What is more important to us as students of the mind is that this same principle of relative two-ness applies to Self. Whether we are thinking of yourself, myself, or himself, there are always at least two of them. Since these two selves are related as subject and object, observer and instrument, they may be conveniently referred to as inner "I" and outer "me."[7] Since we agree to agree about it, we may then ask ourselves the question: Which of these two selves is Reality? But then let us be warned not to take sides, and not to join the ranks of those who would exalt one of those aspects of self at the expense of the other. There are those who prefer one half-truth, and who stand at B, saying "Only B is real. This is Reality and all else is Illusion." They are most respectable people, their knowledge is extensive and their experience may be vast: but if they stand with both feet and both eyes firmly fixed at B, we shall always have the advantage of knowing where to find them. We shall know much about them and their opinions, and amongst other things we know that they will be, within our definition, idolaters. (They prefer to describe themselves, however, as hard-headed, matter-of-fact, plain-spoken simple realists.)

Then there is the other group who stand at A and say of those who stand at B: "They think they know, but they are living in a world of illusion, for their reality is not reality at all! What we have here at A is real and what those poor people have at B, and think so important, is only shadow and illusion." We know of those who stand at A that they are liable to get "illuminated," and that they may then become difficult to understand because they are too far above the common herd of humanity to make themselves intelligible. Sometimes the protagonists of these two sides are rudely outspoken to each other, because each cannot understand that the other is entitled to his opinion, for there must always be these two points of view, each true at least to a half-truth. A feels sure that B is "bad," and B retorts with equal certainty that A is "mad." We have all met members of these opposite camps and I hope that we can sympathize with them. But why should we attach ourselves to one side or the other, thus to become involved in this moral but unscientific atmosphere of misunderstanding and vituperation? Let us keep strictly to scientific principles and say quietly and firmly: "Reality, you are both, and between you both I stand."

But now we are faced by the difficulty of language, for we must learn to speak a strange tongue. It is one that no one likes to use, for it is the language of Paradox. There have been those whose reputation for wisdom has depended upon their skill with this language, and others whose names will yet rise to fame for the same reason: for paradox is the Law, both of Today and Yesterday, and it must become the Language of Tomorrow. Whether we like it or not, it is the only way by which we can measure both sides of the wholeness of life's experience, so that if we are to be accurate in our description, we must learn to talk that way. The dualism of the dilemma of paradox is hard enough to manage, but our problem is made even more difficult because, besides being a Law of life, paradox is also a moving Law, which we cannot fix anywhere for our anxious convenience. But there is no other way in which we can accurately move: as observers by the scientific method we must be prepared to let go everything and see what happens as we swing and spin with Life.

We can call this circle anything we like for our convenience, so long as we are prepared to burn our symbolic boats as we go. Then let us call it an orange, so that we can the more easily divide it into sections, and let us separate one, which we will call AB. Then let us be possessive and say, "This is my bit." But there are two aspects of it, A and B, pulp and skin, as there are of the whole sphere of the orange. This single section, AB, which we have cut out, is a part of the whole and it also contains the same parts as does the whole. However many times we may take this two-ness out from between its neighbors, it will always be a two-ness, AB. But again there are also two neighbors, one on either side; for there is always the same two-ness in everything.

In this relationship of the one and the two we can understand the genesis of all creation. Out of one, nothing can ever happen: there is no making or movement until it has been divided into its two-ness. Only out of two can there be born a child. That is why it is so important to become used to the language of paradox, the two-ness, because only out of that two-ness can anything ever be created. Only as a consequence of the union of those two parts of the dualism can there be born the third factor of the living child. He is important, so let us call him C.

We will put C in the middle way, between Heaven and Earth. Poor little C, no wonder that he doesn't know where he is, suspended thus between the twin horns of his dilemma! A is somewhere and so is B, but where, crying in what unseen wilderness, is C? Where has he come from, where does he belong, where is he going to, where shall we put him, what can we do with him? The answer, for the better discipline of our too insistent anxiety, will be: "Nothing, at present; leave him alone, but don't forget that he is there."

CHAPTER 3

Incarnation

If I speak of "I" and mean to speak of the plane where a man is indeed like a god, how shall I distinguish that "I" from this very mortal creature "me," the child of space and time, half-beast, half-angel, wholly confused, who is also entitled to speak of himself in terms of the first person singular? If we could keep his separate selves as far apart as subject and object, cause and effect, or "I" and "me," then we should at least have some logical framework within which to indicate this elementary distinction. But as grammar does not allow us to do so, we must plod on as best we can without its aid, yet warned of this incipient confusion.

In order to keep my two opposing categories clothed in as good and simple English garb as possible, I am going to refer to them as "that other ground" and "this familiar field" respectively. Then my idea of their relationship can be at least partially stated within these terms: *"That other ground is constantly projected into and manifest within and through this familiar field."* An alternative statement of the same basic idea in personal terms would be: "I is constantly projected into and manifest within and through me." I shall also sometimes choose to express the same idea in abstract terms, according to the general formula, "A is constantly projected into and manifest through B." Finally, but meaning exactly the same idea, I shall draw it as a simple design of two lines at right angles to one another, thus ——|.

I believe that all life is a consequence of this pregnant relationship, which is its elementary principle. It is this relationship with a mystery in which we are all engaged. It's this most intimate creative partnership with an unknown factor, that I have called "mysterious marriage."

From *Mysterious Marriage: A Study of the Morality of Personal Relationships and Individual Obsessions*

That Other Ground

Whatever we may say about that other ground, it is certain to be inadequate and in some degree false, because it is by definition totally incomprehensible and utterly indescribable. It is open to experience but not to reason; nor can it be described by the experiencer. It therefore appears to reason to be at best paradoxical and contradictory, at least confusing, but at worst as infuriating as a wasp that will not leave you alone. But reason has a weapon which is strong enough to satisfy reason at least of its sufficiency, *for reason can prove that there is nothing there:* there is no wasp, but none the less, the wasp of death still stings.

I would willingly accept the negative verdict of the rationalist, and yet stand firmly on the ground which he declares is not there. That other ground is indeed nothing; it is neither here nor there, nor anywhere in space or time. In the beginning, Zero, a blank, an empty space, a void, with nothing to see, touch, hear, taste or smell, nothing sensible, nothing to measure, nothing to understand—and—most important of all—nothing that can be conceptualized, pictured, formulated or defined. All that I give you in definition mark you and it is my deepest hope and wish that the rationalists and everyone else who approaches that other ground would first accept this utterly negative definition of all that they could expect to find there. That other ground, if it is ever to be realized at all, must be left utterly and totally open and undefined, because that is what it is.

Why, then, should we bother about it? Why all this fuss about "nothing"? The answer is very simple, but it must be stated dogmatically, as an idea or pattern that can be seen in universal operation: *That other ground is the cause of which this familiar field is the effect: it is the constant source of our renewal: it is the medium in which we are suspended; it is like water to the fish, in which the fish swims, and which at the same time flows through him: it interpenetrates everything, everywhere, so that all doors are open to it, irrespective of size and density: it is the ocean from which all existence comes into being, and to which all must in time return: it is the tideless, timeless, sea: its essence is eternity.*

A few words about its paradoxical qualities will perhaps serve to make plain some of our conceptual difficulties in regard to that other ground. It is nothing, yet it is in everything; it is nowhere, yet in everywhere: it is indefinable, yet constantly defined within the framework of creation: it is eternal, yet manifest in time: it is the whole, the All, and the One, yet it is ever in each part of the Many: it is abstract, inconceivable, and utterly apart, yet it is personal, most intimately experienced and perpetually present: it is parental towards our familiar world, and we are its beloved child, yet at the same time the relationship is also that of "husband" and "wife," mysteriously wedded.

That other ground is capable of being experienced more or less directly by those who are called "mystics," but we might also loosely include within this term all children, all lovers and all those who use their imagination to realize the meaning which is partly hidden beneath revealing form. Mystics are, as it were, professional or especially devoted, lovers. They are apt to regard the ecstasy of love as it is experienced on that other ground as something directly given, as worth more than life itself, and certainly they may find it more precious than the love experienced by them in the familiar field of human relationships. But our more human lovers are neither as wrong nor as mad as they sometimes seem in their illusions and delusions about the worth of the beloved. They are not wrong in what they "know" and "see." They are only wrong if they attribute this immeasurable worth to B and not to A, to "me" and not to "I," to the familiar field of experience instead of to that other more-than-mortal ground.

That other ground is also responsible for what is called *intuition*, that universal golden guesswork, which is direct knowledge of wholeness not derived from experience. (In this sense it must be remembered that intuition is categorically opposed to instinct, which is of the familiar field, earthy, a predisposition in certain circumstances to behave after a certain fashion.)

Man is the only full projection of the A category within the B level. Man himself therefore is utterly paradoxical, split, confused and self-contradictory, unless he can find the key which opens the door between his two opposing selves. He is both "over there" and "in here," as he meets that other ground both directly in himself, and as it is reflected back to him from within this familiar field.

A is absolute, perfect and total; but B is relative, imperfect and partial. In A, all is one, now; but in B there is conflict and confusion. In every sense, therefore, A is more and B is less. There is a fall, a separation and a self-diminishing from I to me, and from that other ground, which is as the pure snow-clad vastness of a Himalayan peak, to this familiar field in its enshadowed valley. It is the fault of man, not that he should fall from A to B, but that having done so he should fail to recognize its supreme significance, seeing instead only the tactical advantages of increasing his given powers in B to improve his earthly situation. He is all too apt to regard progress as the reward of his own efforts, and the evidence of his superior ability. He therefore regards a fall as something to be ashamed of and, feeling exceedingly guilty about it, pretends it is not there by assuming that it never happened.

It should be noted that science and scientific psychology can have nothing to do with A, which is not a scientific (measurable) category. Science is not at fault when it applies its methods to the measurable world, the familiar field. Science is not at fault when it admits it has no means whatever of measuring A, as it has also no means of measuring love or freewill, which are also by definition immeasurable. But science, and particularly scientific psychology, are hopelessly at fault if they claim that, because they cannot measure A, therefore A does not exist. They are equally at fault if they insist on judging and interpreting A's manifestations by B's familiar yardstick. All I ask is that the two categories A and B should be allowed to differ—like male and female for instance—and that neither should suffer tyranny at the hands of any moral or scientific cult which claims that they ought to be in any way other than they are. Such is my hypothesis which even Science must allow.

What, then, is the clear essence of that other ground? It is, of course, whatever we may mean by the word Spirit, but I have hesitated to use that word because I did not wish to invite the reader to approach that other ground with a familiar preconception as to what he might find there. Rather, I would suggest that its nature is that of *Will*, which is, however, only substituting another word of which we do not know the meaning. Essentially, that other ground is creative, seeking the form in which to clothe and implement its will. It is therefore *Love*, which is longing to generate its own response from the body of its beloved, this familiar field. Thus *I Will* . . . vibrates itself into existence across the abyss that divides, into the very heart and body of our world.

It is in the same manner, surely, that an author creates a book, intensely vibrating his *Will* through his *Idea*, projecting it, sending it forth, into his reader's world. And this reminds us, too, of the need for some measure of willingness on the part of his recipient: a state of attentiveness, a paying attention, a receptiveness, alert, ready, listening, watching, waiting for the word.

This Familiar Field

I need say very little about this, as it is all a matter of our common knowledge. It is the world of science which can be proven by repeated tests. I would emphasize, however, that the common reality of this familiar field is not in itself either a primary or a final reality. Although we can measure it and stand on it, we cannot so simply trust it, because it is never wholly tamed nor wholly known. It provides its own surprises, not the least of which are birth and death which bound it on either hand, and put all reasonable and scientific men most firmly in their proper places.

Science knows that our work-a-day world, solid as it seems to be, is comprised of energy in whirling movement. Nothing is as simple as it seems to be, and we are commonly deceived by the simple information of the senses. It is not that we are wrong in thinking that we can sit upon a chair: we are not actually deceived by its apparent solidity. It is solid, and we can sit on it. But the other fact is also true, that its actual solidity is comprised of minute particles of latent energy in whirling movement. The two opposing facts are proven, parallel and contradictory, so again let no moral tyranny burst in with "Nonsense, it cannot be!" It may be inconvenient to tidy minds, but such is the most extraordinary case. We sit solidly enough upon this real chair, in spite of its being made of energy in ceaseless enterprise.

If we look through the other end of a telescope, the field of experience is apparently changed. We see things differently in different lights and circumstances. In fact, our senses are well known to be instruments of limited value. They tell us what they can, each in its own language, but we should realize that, like all other reporters, they also tell us something of themselves and who they are. No sense can claim to tell the whole truth, not even all the senses together, nor with all the functions of the mind thrown in to work in perfect harmony. The whole truth is all the parts, *plus*: and reality is all the parts, *plus*. Do you think that anyone could ever tell you *all* about that *plus*?

What that "plus" means is that there is always something queer and unforeseen when the living element comes into play. If I kick a brick, a scientist who takes the trouble to collect all the relevant data can calculate exactly how and when the brick will fall. But no scientist, however accurate and painstaking he may be, can tell me where it will finish if I kick a cat! A pure scientist is like another brick in a world of bricks, and as such he can only tell you about cats in so far as they are also bricks. He is—or should be, if he is honest—impotent and silent when in face of the category *plus*. (We shall consider later whether psychology is a pure science or not.)

Time, as we measure it by our convenient clocks, is a peculiarity of category B. It is particularly suspect, being a by-product of the "brick," rather than of the "cat," mentality. It is certainly not a primary or final philosophic term. It is a conventional method of measuring the relative velocity of objects in category B. Time is therefore an abstraction from an abstraction, a convenient myth, and too much attention should not be paid to it by those who are willing to make a world for themselves. Time is measured by "bricks" for "cats" to keep them in their places: or by the relatively dead for those who are more living. The more bound by time we are, the more dead we prove to be.

I want to say that once again, because it is important. The B world is the time-bound, dead, resistant world of habit and convention. Of itself, it never changes, except to fall into decay: it goes on and on, to settle down in its accumulated rings of time-encrusted age until it dies, departing drearily back into itself. Into these time-binding rings of category B, like an arrow shot from a bow to the center of the target, or like a beam of light flashed from a lantern in the dark, there comes the mysterious messenger from A, bringing his eternal refreshment of mysterious seed from that other ground.

It is as if an opponent and more positive TIME springs, as it were, across the gap between the two worlds of Eternity and space-time, bringing new life as it becomes embedded in our world, thus supporting and reviving it. Thus, indeed, the biological process of fertility constantly recurs, as the TIME-seed is thrust forward from the special seedbed of one generation to the next. But the summation of this endless continuity of time, as it is revealed in recurrent and interminable life, is not eternity as it exists in category A. In the two "worlds" of categories A and B it will be found that all our common words, such as Life, Will, Love, Time and Personality, have very different meanings. We must develop a new mental elasticity, as we learn to span the gulf which separates our higher and lower natures.

There is one more warning I should like to issue for the reader to consider at his leisure. It is that we should not be content to believe in the logic of cause and effect, as if both are complete within themselves in the watertight enclosure of this familiar field. Belief in an inevitable consequence of *because . . . therefore* is the most dangerous breeding ground of human disease, and of all misfortunes which are worse-than-death. From this important fallacy springs its logical and most unpleasant child "if only", by which we mean that the only way to alter the effect is to alter the (apparent, material) cause. Such an assumption would let everyone out, as a responsible person, a creator of worlds; and would let in instead a world governed by castrated mechanics, psychopathic politicians and neurotic Marxists. For such an assumption does, in fact, deny the essential freedom of the personal Will.

I am not wishing to imply that cause and effect are not in fact related to one another. I only wish to state what is commonly known to be true and constantly proved, but often forgotten, that cause-and-effect as we know it is only partly true. All effects are actually achieved by many causes, not by one: and when all the known causes are added together, there is still some factor of uncertainty, some mystery of relationship, some unknown, perhaps unknowable, element beyond our comprehension, which I have called simply *plus*, that remains unaccounted for. The human will is such a factor.

I only ask that these other factors, which also play their parts, should not be omitted in our would-be-scientific, but not yet reasonable enough, world. I also claim that the true banner of the latent Godhead in mankind is expressed not in the words "if only!"—but in these terms: "In spite of . . . nevertheless, I will. . . ." That mysterious element of the WILL is the unpredictable and the essentially human factor. With that left out, we are much less than men.

Reminding ourselves again of the pattern ——| with which we first set out, we can now make it more dynamic by adding arrowheads, to show the conflict which exists in category B between opposing forces. Thus the will ⟶ is confronted by the frustration of a variably resistant barrier ⟶|. It is not free in the sense that it is unopposed, nor can it choose in any way the degree of resistance; it is only *free to choose what it will do about the resistance.* But the resistant world is also divided against itself.

It should be very plain to us all that category B, this familiar field or "me myself," is founded and framed on a system of "pull Devil, pull baker,"[8] and that we are precariously balanced on an invisible razor-edge, which is the fulcrum of these opposing forces, thus →⇅. We cannot ever rightly hope to dismiss the other of any opposing pair, such as lower, backward, inner, evil or unknown, merely because we may choose to associate ourselves with the apparent better of them, such as higher, forward, outer, good or known. The other, rejected or not, is always there to balance, oppose, correct, frustrate and bring us down to earth again. There is always this seeming conflict between opposites, and therefore an apparent choice between alternatives. It should be clear however that, whichever alternative we may choose, the opposite is not thereby so easily escaped.

If there is always this critical situation of conflict between our human will and the opposing currents in category B, we must not forget the further complication which arises from our relation with category A. If self and situation, or will and that which opposes it, are related thus  in category B, the same relationship is also true of B's relationship with A. The complete pattern of the human problem may therefore, be expressed by 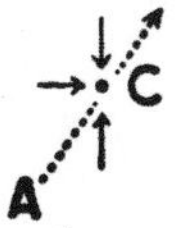 where the dotted line represents the emergent WILL from that other ground. The point of impact and relationship, C, is therefore doubly critical, and we may well say that the human problem is a crucial one.

The question that is vital to the theme of this book is, What is in fact one's personal attitude towards these opposing "others," these seeming enemies, seen or unseen, tangible or intangible? What is to be my relationship with that other if—as seems to be the case, proven by experience often enough—it is impossible for anyone totally to rid me of the plague of it? Indeed, what happens at "C"?

We must now consider what we mean by this word, relationship.

The Relationship Between

This is our third category, C, which stands between A and B, so: , or as the point of critical impact, so  is obviously a variable: how does it vary in practice, for instance, when A stands for an author and B stands for his book?

The author had an idea, and the author and the idea were on the same plane, and the idea was crystal clear. At this point the author and his idea are one. The idea has not yet started on its process of projection and is still on the same plane as the author. It has not yet been born, but it is ready to be conceived. The author is suitably struck, the time is ripe and so the idea is conceived. I will write a book: but how does that book become born?

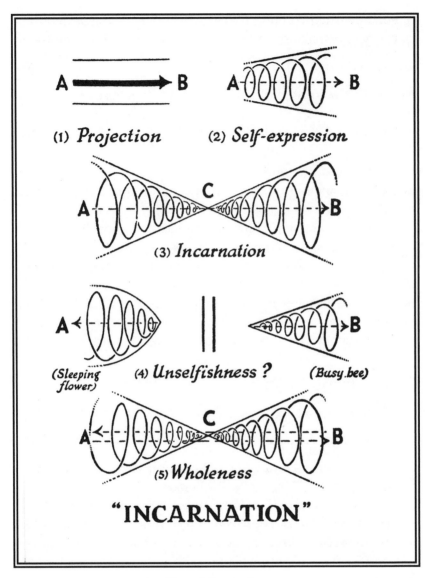

Figure 2 Incarnation

The answer is startlingly simple. I put my pen to paper, and "will" that my book should become extended in the material world (category B). Every word—100,000 of them maybe, and every one rewritten time and again, probably—has been pressed through this minute point, where my pen impinges upon the plane of the paper. This book has passed—but literally!—through a point no larger than a needle's eye, before the author, like a rich man upon his ideal camel, could enter into his kingdom, his land of promise, the eye and mind of his reader. The hole of entry, through which this book must pass in its entirety, was no bigger than this!

But when we come to consider the actual fact, have not you and I passed through much the same experience? Life uses such small points as means for its emergence into the plane of B. We are always being thus pressed through the doorway that opens into life, and often feel too large to fit the door. Sometimes it is a tight squeeze and we are in a "jam"; but if we put our ears back, if we are folded very small, and if mother pushes from behind, projecting us on . . . we emerge, in time, much as a book does that is now engaged in the process of being written. (Who writes the book of my experience? Who is the author of my self?)

Oak trees and elephants, saints and sinners, kings and cuckoos, they must all submit thus once to the gross indignity of birth. They must pass through an even smaller hole than that . when first conceived, which is their microscopic birthday. After that, the hole becomes a little larger through which they emerge as separated seeds, eggs or babies. Then again, there are many other doors of varying sizes through which we humans have to pass, some larger and some smaller, as we swell and shrink through the varying phases of our mixed experience. But for any *complete* experience of rebirth at any time, it is essential for the personal self to go back to the very beginning, to Zero, as it were, back to the dotted line of the stripped emergent Will itself as it passes through the abyss A—C—B (see figure 2, "Incarnation," opposite), where it must be for a moment at least, utterly alone and perfectly emptied of all that self has ever held.

The diagram INCARNATION on page 84 shows this process of progressive *self-diminishing* on the A level as the essential preliminary to *self-expansion* on the B level. If the baby—or the book—has passed through the point C completely, then both the author and the book, or the mother and the child, are free, because they are completely cut off from one another except for the possibility of a renewed "C" relationship (figure 2) in the meeting place between them.

Unfortunately, such a complete release at birth, whether for book or baby, is all too rarely the case. Both author and mother know from experience how closely they are identified with the advantage of their precious child. If you hurt or blame my child, it is I who feel it, I who leap forward to protect—no, not my child—my self. The unweaned author sees his *self* expand in the progress of his book. Author, mother and hen have much in common in their attitude towards their chicks! They do not want to let them go, to set them really free.

But consider the perpetual frustration and annoyance of having to put pen to paper. Why should I bother? The idea itself is very wonderful, and the author enjoys contemplating its beauty perpetually within the guarded enclosure of his own mind. Try as he will, his efforts to project it fail. He simply cannot do it justice. In any case he feels—perhaps quite rightly—that his idea would not be appreciated, that the critics would not understand it, and that the public would not even recognize a masterpiece if it were pushed under their noses. Pearls before swine—why bother? So perhaps our author's efforts at creation, never very strongly willed, remain abortive, and his child never reaches the bookshelf. Yet, in his mind, it swells and swells, uncomfortably: for it can only rot or burst, atrophy or petrify, in the arid regions of the unborn, unwilled, unwilling, ghosts.

Unweaned, the separation comes, if it comes at all, too late; abortive, the separation comes, if there has ever been any relationship at all, too soon. The creative enterprise requires a persistent continuity of relation with the other, with moments of ecstasy strung as rare jewels upon the long string of patient endeavor. Meanwhile, the author, with willed projection of the idea held constantly in view, waits for the process of creation to mature within the womb of the familiar field, until the child is ready to be born. And when the book is written and the child is out, the author knows how little has been in fact the outcome of his willed idea. All the endeavor and attention, all the will and waiting, all the willingness on the part of the other, yes, all these are necessary for the creative act to bear its proper fruit in time within the field. And yet, in fact, there is always that mysterious element "*plus*," the effect of which can never be foretold or entirely circumvented. Indeed, every birth is so much a "virgin birth" that every author should accept his lesser part with fine humility.

The Pattern

Having now dealt with the three categories as far as is essential for my purpose, and in order to make plain to the reader what follows, it only remains to establish the idea of this relationship in terms of pattern, thus ——|, of two planes or systems at right angles to one another. I have carried out the idea in the cover design in a more abstract form, where I have represented a sphere being shot through by an arrow from another plane. What I have tried to indicate is that, whether that sphere is you and I or the world in which we live, we are indeed shot through by a mysterious influence, which we call *Life*, and some believe is *Love*. In each case, the sphere stands for a resistant and confining world (B), a world of form and matter, or what we call "body." Its work is to nourish the seed of life within the "body," so that it may grow. It is "mother earth," and its function is maternal. The arrow (A) is the "father principle," the bringer of the energy of life, the fertilizing force which meets the resistant-responsive form of its "beloved" and enters into it, becoming incarnate there. What I wish to convey, therefore, in this seed pattern, is that principle of life, as it exists in itself, and also as it is manifest in the relationship between the two sexes, male and female, as we know them. Each sex, whether male or female, contains the whole pattern, and is a complex of A, B and C, but each sex is also mainly, as male and female, engaged on one side or the other of this profound experience of "mating." Ours is the pattern of creation, in which we live and move and have our being. We are partners, not only with one another, but also in a creative scheme that is greater than we can ever know.

Simple as our pattern may seem to be in its oft-repeated essence, it is, of course, immensely complex in the infinitely various ways in which it is worked out. One of the most important lessons I want to draw from it is the overall importance of personal responsibility, which is the hallmark of our recognition of the primacy of the spirit. There is too much involved and invested in each one of us for anyone to need to feel unworthy or incapable of standing up for themselves. The corollary to this important recognition of the value of the person is that we need never feel responsible for saving either ourselves or one another, because the principle of salvation is in THAT which is given. Our "salvation" is in A, not in B. We are responsible, not for "saving" one another, but for sustaining the relationship ("C") with one another, through which the spirit of goodwill and the creative principle may work.

The pattern may also remind us of something about love that too often slips our memory. Love is not always kind, nor easily to be understood: it does not only give in gentle self-surrender: the face and manner of the beloved is not always the expected friendly and familiar one. There is also a quality in love, especially as it strikes its peak, that may seem hard, ruthless, inconsiderate of the other in the flash of untameable passion and of indomitable will. The ecstasy of love is sometimes more than half destructive. To leave out that aspect of affection, which seems indeed to be too often absent in our relationships nowadays, is to despoil not only God, but man. Love tends to be flattened out by the sentimentalists to a dead level of respectability which is neither life nor death, until some apparently destructive blow from that other dimension shatters complacency and life is thus—perhaps—renewed.

The pattern in love, as in life, is like breathing, and implies a rise and fall, a rhythm and a dance. Like the act of conception itself, it implies the breaking of a covering skin, the vibration of a diaphragm. It implies a mysterious relation between "will" and "willingness," or between energy principle and a resistant but responding principle. It is also like speech, as the word issues forth, projected across the intervening air, to enter and strike a chord within the other's ear and mind.

The pattern also serves to make plain an important fact about C, the focal point of the relationship. Here and here alone, unique, alive and ever changing, is the whole point and simplest truth of the matter, perpetually revealed. Metaphysical, mysterious and indefinable as it may seem to be, it is yet the proof or actual meaning of the relation. In that sense it is *reality as we know it now in our experience.* Moral qualities are not attributable, if we are honest with ourselves, to either A or B. They exist in our attitude towards, or relationship with, them (i.e. the use we propose to make of them). We are always inclined at first to think of mother or religion, we will say, as "good," or of failure or alcohol as "bad." The point I wish to make is not really arguable, although it is so often forgotten; namely, that it is up to me to prove by my relationship with the "other," whether it is good, or just how bad it is for me. The moral quality is not in you or me: it is in our experience of our relationship with one another. It is not A, nor B, but C that matters, morally. Or, to say the same thing in a different way, it is not quantity, but quality, that counts.

Finally, there is the matter of control. If there is to be a relationship between A and B, or you and me, then, if we are to be true to our pattern, the result must spring, spontaneously and in its own right, from the conditions of our meeting. If we are really meeting in this free relationship, then we must not attempt to control either ourselves, each other, or the effect of our meeting (i.e. A, B or C). We are not things to be under control. We are complex organisms in a vital setting, dynamically thrown together. It is the height of folly on our part to attempt to know the answer or control the final issue.

It cannot be done, because it is at this point, certainly but incomprehensibly, that "plus" comes into the picture, to provide us with our human stature. Control, if successful, leaves out "plus" (which, however, comes back in our misfortunes!) and lowers us to the level of mere things.

Three in One and One in Three

Having made that as clear as I can, and as simple as A B C, it is with no intention of being unkind or awkward that I must now upset this simple system but not, I hope, my reader. For the truth is not simple, and our words, as often happens, need some contradiction.

What we need to add to our analysis of the subject-object relationship is that there is a common factor present in all three, which in a way simplifies, as it also complicates, our problems of relationship.

To begin at the beginning. Light entered darkness and the world began. Again, "God so loved the world that he sent His only begotten Son . . . who did not abhor the virgin's womb," and the world continued in fresh hope and with a new power, for good or ill. To come nearer to the point of our own experience, our parents "met" and we were "born." In each case, A "met" B and C "happened." *We were in both our parents, as both our parents are also in us.*

This is what must be added to our analysis, therefore, because it is very important for our experience of relationship. *We all have something in common.* In a certain mysterious way, we are neither apart from, nor outside, one another, as we seem to be. I am in you, as you are also in me; and we are both together in our relationship. "The Yin is in the Yang, and the Yang is in the Yin," as the Chinese say, speaking of their opposing principles of female (resting-resistant-responsive) and male (active-moving-willing) respectively. It makes all the difference to our "understanding" if we know that we have this part of ourselves constantly inside one another. It means that we cannot cut off any other, without also cutting off part of ourselves. (So also life is in death and death in life; and both are in us now as problems for our equal interest.)

This common denominator is also called "love." It is a very mysterious element, and we shall never get to the bottom of it. But there—and here—it is.

I do not claim to have said anything new, nor to have said it very well. I have only attempted to restate the ancient wisdom of the Trinity in terms suited to the purpose which I have in hand. It is far better stated in the Gospel of St. John 14:20, "I am in my Father, and ye in me, and I in you." If that is true, it is obviously most important for our understanding of any human problems of relationship.

The Nature of Reality

What is the nature of Reality, the reality of the world in which we live and the objects that comprise it? Of what kind is our own personal reality, and how is our reality to be related to the other, within which we are both incarnate and engaged? To what extent is it our responsibility to improve or change reality as we find it, one another as we meet, and our own selves, with whom we sometimes seem to be such strangers that we never meet at all?

My reader, I hope, will now realize that many good questions are spoiled by the way in which they are asked. Such questions as I have asked assume that subject and object, I and reality, can be regarded as separable from one another, and are therefore capable of being defined as events-in-themselves. It is my point, however, that although such definitions may sometimes be convenient, as a label is convenient to state the contents of a bottle, they are in fact dangerous unless their limitations are clearly understood. Definitions, even the simple use of ordinary words and names for things and people, set them apart in a most arbitrary way. But it is the relationship between us which is always the all-important, although most indefinable fact, in our perpetually changing reality.

All objects, and still more, all persons, owe their reality to their relationships with other objects or persons. No one can live alone, i.e. without any relationship. Actually, therefore, being thus the derivative of an "idea," reality itself is metaphysical, not physical. Reality is a "C" factor, a middle term of a series, and not a "B," or end term. That is to say, reality is functional and derivative; it is an effect of a preexistent partnership, and must therefore always be dependent on other factors beyond itself. Reality of any kind cannot stand by itself, alone. There is no thing or person which can exist apart from its relationship, either with some other thing or person. It is always the relationship, and not the object itself, which "matters."

Objects which appear to our senses to have a continuous reality in space and time, i.e. to "endure," may nevertheless actually have a state of continuity and endurance which is only apparent and illusory. Reality may be as discontinuous, evanescent, flashed up out of its flow of ever-changing relationships, as it were, as are those discontinuous images which appear to us continuous when we see them projected on to a cinema screen.

In fact, I think, we should be prepared to go further in our recognition of the metaphysical nature of reality. We should regard it as a personal variable, which is different for you and me, as you and I are different. It has been the habit of Buddhist philosophy to describe our familiar field as maya, or illusion. This somewhat derogatory attitude towards our everyday world is also shared by Western mystics, who regard A as Reality with a capital R. They call it Absolute Reality, and some have regarded our world as only being real, in so far as it is really a snare and a delusion.

But again, it should be remembered that reality is a by-product of relationship. It therefore cannot be sought or made as something by itself. *Men are like gods.* They also make their worlds and make them real. We are each one of us living at the center of a real world, which we are constantly making out of our own projected inward patterns or ideas. Inwardly and outwardly, we are rooted and imprisoned both in what we are and what we have made from what we are. That is why it is so very hard to change. First, we must change the ideas and patterns from which we have made our present world. Then, in time, our next world will emerge, and as we have changed, so it also will be different.

Meanwhile, we make two serious mistakes in our relationships with one another. The first is to assume that we all live in the same world, experiencing the same reality. It simply is not true to assume that your world and mine are the same. But we shall never realize how different they are, until we make some intelligent inquiry. The second is to assume that I can change my world, or you, without first experiencing some needed change within myself.

Mysterious Right Angles

At this point I do not want to scare those of my readers who feel that the subject of mathematics is not within their real world; nor, indeed, to cause hope to spring in the breasts of those for whom it is a happier subject. I only want for a moment to refer to the fact that human progress has in the past been associated with certain experiences of rotation through right angles. Once upon a time, a long time ago, and it may have taken him a very long time to do it, the monkey's pelvis rotated through a right angle and he was able to stand upon his ground, so __|__ . At about the same time, the monkey's thumb also swung through a right angle, enabling him to oppose thumb to fingers, and thus to grasp, manipulate and use his world. But something also happened to his mind, of immeasurable but related importance. He no longer had to stay close bound inside his world, for one day he realized a new relationship. He said, "Hullo, monkey!" and recognized himself as man. His mind had stretched to comprehend a new dimension of experience. He had risen above the plane of earth, which is flat like that _____ to look back upon it, so __↓__ . And that is how our experience of relationships began.

And man, in spite of his clipped wings of angels, is still based on monkey. We are still in the world of flesh that we have also gone beyond. We are variously placed, each one of us, upon the pattern of our dual experience. Some are still firmly held within the monkey's world. In spite of their new powers gained from countless centuries of man's experience, their monkey's world is still the only one which matters to them, because it is the only one that is real. Their paws, with the added strength of machinery and atom bombs, are still as apprehensive as they are acquisitive.

Others see life differently, which determines different behavior. Some are the "back-room boys" of scientific research, who live only through their microscopes and formulae, or their philosophic systems and political fanaticisms. When it comes to the point, with all that knowledge which is power, they may prove that the monkey is not far behind. Others use their wings in still more ambitious flight, and who would say that our aerial adventurers see our world in the same fashion as those who are still limited to more pedestrian accomplishments? Some see and do: some think: some meditate: some feel their way through life. But some miss every bus and fall off every stool, with their right angles confused and their patterns in a sorry mess. But even such a misbegotten world is real to those who dwell in its confusion.

The Meaning of Value

"That is good," we say, evaluating an object for its worth to us; or "I love her!" bestowing upon the beloved a value which may or may not be more than even she deserves. Whence comes this sense of worth, this measurement of wealth?

It may, of course, come from the other. It may be derived actually from the good thing, or from the person herself. For instance, it may be a good car, a Rolls Royce. And she may be as good as she seems. But that is not where "worth" usually comes from. It usually comes from inside us, by projection. It is, therefore, necessary for us to know what is inside us, and how it may come out.

Inside "me" is "*I*." How much is that worth? Inside B is A. To what extent is B's value determined by A's projection or reflection? Can we see through B to A, mistaking B for A? Indeed, is that what "love" is? Perhaps we are more mystic with our inner sight than we are apt to admit.

The answer to the question, "How much are you worth to me?" depends not only upon you, but also upon how much of myself you can reflect back to me. If you reflect back to me a portion of myself of which I disapprove, I shall disapprove of you: if I hate it, I shall hate you: and if I want to hurt it, I shall also want to hurt you. If within myself are many discarded parts, then outside myself there will be many rejected people. If my world is in dissociated pieces, it is because I am in disconnected bits, myself. If I feel you ought to change, it is probably because you remind me of myself, but without my knowing it. If I have large areas of myself of which I am totally unconscious, then there will be much about others that I do not understand.

So do not be surprised if you suddenly find that my feelings for you have changed. Yes, you have really changed to me, although in yourself you may seem to be the same. You have caught the projection of a different pattern from my ever-running cinema. There is more within the concealed patterns of my "karmic" celluloid than can ever reach the currency of known "ideas."

Centralization and Decentralization

When I say that "I" am the center of my world, if I paid more attention to the truth, what I should say is that "me" is there. "Me" seems to be the center of my real world, and it is from "me" that I shall conduct my operations. It is "me" who thinks he knows, not "I." And "me" does not know "I," nor ever wholly can.

From this unacknowledged slip from "I" to "me," from A to B, much else inevitably befalls. The authority has been transferred from "author" to "agent", and from first to final term. The "fall" from "I" to "me" has been avoided or misplaced, if "me" takes pride of place and rules instead of "I." "Me" gathers to itself the reins of power, and, ignoring alike both "I" and the guidance of the Godhead, takes upon itself responsibility for enforcing change upon an awkward and resistant world. Surely that was Lucifer's mistake?

"Me" sees what's wrong, which is easy enough, and then proceeds to plan to put it right, with mighty powers engaged to do so. "Me" is a very powerful, although falsely central, point from which to engineer the world's salvation. "Me" has a mass of information, and gives benevolent orders that others may implement "me's" good advice. "Me's" world is centralized about me. Thus "me" accumulates more power, as it is drawn parasitically from "me's" periphery.

All such centralization of authority must increase B's importance at A's expense. It treats persons as things and ignores the primary values of the truly causal world. It creates its own reality, which is dependent on "me's" successful interference with the passage of events. To remove "me," and cause me suddenly to cease my efforts, would be to provoke the downfall of my real world, with all its dependent subordinate realities, and with all its complexity of relations. The responsibility cannot be justified. Nor, if it could be justified, could it be carried out, for you cannot change me as easily as that. Nor can "me" change myself

What we can recognize, however, with crystal clarity, is that as centralization leads to A's decrease, so decentralization leads to increasing opportunity for its creative emergence. Decentralization allows maximum opportunity for those on the periphery, and in subordinate positions, to exercise their own autonomy, by making their own free choices and exercising to the full their own responsibility within their special fields.

Thus were we born, decentralized, sent forth to be ourselves and find our way without any map or guidance. When we are born, we must at first experience a false centralization, as we must confuse "I" with "me," A with B. It is only when we are born again, with wisdom learnt from experience, that we can see the real point of practising decentralization.

CHAPTER 4

What Is Relationship?

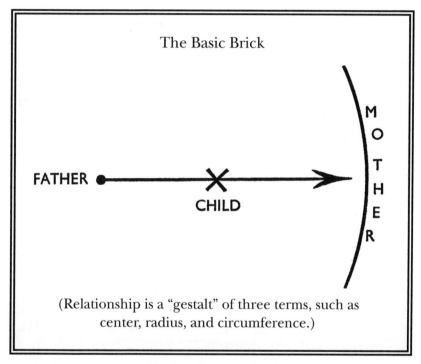

The Basic Brick

FATHER

CHILD

M
O
T
H
E
R

(Relationship is a "gestalt" of three terms, such as center, radius, and circumference.)

Figure 3 The Basic Brick

Relationship Is Polarized

It used to be enough to believe that we, in our relationship could–indeed should–be united together. In fact we should "love" one another: just like that, and everyone seemed to know what it meant. It was better still if we could be found together in a group or community, a church or a political party of like-minded people, who all thought in the same way about the same thing. Thus our link was a massive and undifferentiated one of which we agreed to agree.

From *Cure or Heal? A Study of Therapeutic Experience*

The new idea of relationship, however, first of all introduces the idea of *polarity*: i.e. that we are all in some degree opposed to one another, which is what makes us tick. To live is therefore not to love one another, but to recognize, admit and accept one another, each as we are *now*. It is this small word "*now*," however, which makes the greatest change in the meaning of our experience of relationship. Our experience is changing all the time; however small this change may be, it requires our constant attention, because even the smallest change may sometimes prove to be of the greatest importance. Therefore the communication which is involved in an experience of relationship requires to be most subtly exchanged on all levels. To be in touch with one another in an ever-changing relationship, it is impossible for anyone ever to pay sufficient attention to the other, who still remains of necessity to a great extent beyond our ken.

Experience Is Personal

The basic brick, of which life is compounded, is this statement: "I-experience-it." This is a gestalt-of-three, or statement of potential change, due to energy being opposed to energy, but each in relationship with the other. Of the three parts of the whole, it is possible to interfere by removing any one, or all.

Removing both "I" and "experience," then only "it" is all. With this we are already too familiar, as the habit of homo scientificus. It is a state of compulsive virtue doing compulsive work, because "it" must be done, well or better. This state of mind is normal to egoic man, but for him it is also normal to rebel against his own compulsions. His will is contradicted by his will-not, and his obedience to the establishment is reversed by his determination to contract out of it. So mechanically must the pendulum swing to and fro, within its compulsively limited orbit of contradiction.

But surely, there can be no experience of value, unless I-experience-it? It is this gestalt of three, or experience of wholeness, which is essential, if we are concerned with the personal experience of life, which is our truth.

If we are to establish the importance of persons as our basic general principle, then we must be willing to bring ourselves, as persons, into everything, and especially into the hinge-point of relationship. Reality is personal: experience is personal: communication is personal: even "it" is personal to me, in so far as I-experience-it. The truth is personal to me. Indeed there can be no other, unless I can experience it, and so make it my own. We can go even further and claim that a God, over there by Himself, is of no meaning to me whatsoever. It is only in so far as I can experience Him, making Him my own, personally, that He can be of any value or meaning to me. It must then be clearly recognized as a necessary limitation of Him, that I-experience-Him. My experience of course has no evidential value to anyone else. For them also, the only evidence which matters to them must be derived from their own experience.

In every sense, therefore, reality is only personal experience. You may have been told of it, you may have read of it, you may even have thought of it. But it cannot become real to you until you have experienced it. And then it has only become real to you personally, according to the exact nature of your relationship with it.

Relationship Is the Source of Life and Energy, and of the Renewal of Personal Being

Relationship is the experience of polarity between self and other. It is the cause of what flows, or happens, or eventuates, between us. I am over here. You are over there. But what is between us? A certain experience happens, a certain force flows, and expresses the truth, even miraculously, certainly non-conceptionally, of our relationship. Whatever we may have thought or hoped or feared, if we are able to appreciate this new event in spite of our hopes and fears, we find that it is something quite different, new, true-in-itself, now for a moment, and personally—mine, and yours.

What is between us, what is the medium of our mysterious communication? What flows. The creative medium through which life flows, the truly creative medium, is "water." But the inverted commas must serve to indicate that this mysterious bridge, or medium, is only "analogous" to water. As Jung might say, this is "archetypal" water. But these are only words, and to appreciate the reality of this medium it is necessary to experience it.

Let it be enough then for the time being to state that life needs apartness, separation, division and polarity, in order that energy may flow, experience may be realized and growth may happen. To close this vital gap, for the sake of comfort or security, is to find neither life nor death, but only depression and inertia. Apartness from the object of desire is the means of our life and renewal, and satisfaction is most salutary when soonest dissatisfied. The heart of life is like the wound of Amfortas, in the story of Parsifal. It is at its strongest when broken, provided that it claims no need for being mended.

Relationship Is a Way of Self-Diminishing

The instinctive, or natural, habit of egoic man is to ask and seek for MORE. His is a motivation of (real or imaginary) NEED. He needs, or thinks he needs, more safety, more power, more love, more attention, more learning and even more of the virtues which he happens to fancy, such as unselfishness, or kindness—or just a general quality of goodness. These are all good things in themselves, be it noted: but they are all seen by egoic man as a means of acquiring more power. In any cyclical motion, "more" is on the side of ascent or increase. Therefore decrease, loss, death or any degree of self-diminishing, are its *bete noir* or shadow, to be avoided at all costs by egoic man.

Yet it must be fully appreciated that, although it is in many ways contrary to instinctive egoic self-defense and aggression, self-diminishing is not actually so unnatural or unusual as at first sight it might appear. For instance, it is of the essence of all receptive or passive experience such as looking, listening or paying attention. Self-surrender is the nature of the feminine principle. Therefore it may have suffered contempt during the passing of centuries, as being evidence of weakness. The feminine principle has always suffered the risk of shame, contempt and destruction, and it has always been unsafe to be a woman.

Let us consider the nature of receptor mechanisms, such as the eye or ear, in their open, passively receptive or feminine aspect. In shape, they are very like the modern radar receptor apparatus, which stand on our airfields, guide our ships, and bring us information from the stars.

Figure 4 Receptor Mechanisms

They are flattened cups with a focal center which catch, collect and correlate appropriate stimuli; sound for the ear, sight for the eye, or "feelings" for the "feelers," each experience is appropriately differentiated by our different instruments of sensitivity.

Experience, Now

One characteristic of the new orientation which requires especial emphasis is that it refers to an event NOW, as personally observed and experienced: whereas previously it was something to be *thought about*, either in retrospect or anticipation. It was considered right to think about a world of events as Aristotelian abstractions, as "things-by-themselves." We could then do more or less what we chose with them, at least by fixing them in thoughtful and convenient order. This certainly produced a world of a certain reality, but one which could also be highly confusing, because different systems of thought appealed to different people. Each system could as well be proven as any other, by those who happened to be their partisans or adherents.

Limiting ourselves to ATTENTION NOW, however, requires a change of dimension. To *think about* something may be described thus, but to *pay attention* to it requires a new detachment, a fresh orientation and a new dimension in which the time factor is changed from

"before" ———> "during" ———> "after," to

I-EXPERIENCE-IT-NOW

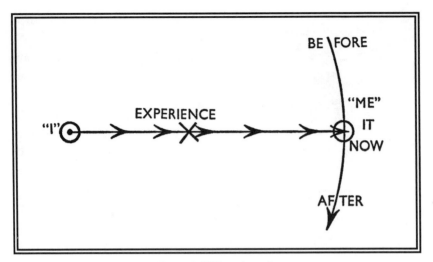

Figure 5 "I" Experience It

The Basic Brick

This introduces the concept of what I call the "basic brick," which can be built in infinite variety into the complex structure of all our human relationships. It can be regarded either as a gestalt of three or as a unitary complex. Although it is apparently intellectually divisible into three, experientially it cannot be so divided.

This diagram represents the basic structure of a relationship, whether between self and other, between two aspects of self, between subject and object, ear and source of sound, or eye and source of sight. Some effect or communication is passing BETWEEN a pair of opposites, which realizes, manifests, or "experiences" the "meaning" of the relation. This median factor behaves just as does the verb in the grammar of a sentence: it animates and brings life to the meaning of our communication.

In this sense we may regard this median factor, which we call the experience, as "X the unknown." It is something apart from any preconception, whether of your own or another's imagination. For instance, in the simple case of the sentence "I love you," I cannot know in advance what my experience of loving you may actually mean to me or to you at any given moment, now. In spite, or perhaps because, of the fact that X is our only actual experience of reality, it is not a constant, but a variable from moment to

102

moment. In spite of the difficulty in which this may seem to involve the lovers of fixed meanings, academic accuracy, and dictionary definitions, we know that "ALL THINGS FLOW." This aphorism was as much a commonplace of understanding among the early Greek philosophers, as it was at the same period for the Buddhists. It is the combination of Christianity, education and scientific development which, in the most ultimate extension of the Aristotelian error, has placed us today in the moralized illusion of being fixed persons in a fixed world, with the power to fix things, including ourselves and one another, as we choose: or not, as we may discover by our failure to do so. But we shall then still be hoping to fix tomorrow what we have been unable to fix today.

It is for this reason that reality for egoic man can only be determined by his idea of what he thinks it ought to be. The facts of life are far from self-evident to egoic man, if they happen to differ from his familiar expectation of what is "good" for him. For instance, a state of rest in emptiness, or a process of self-diminishing towards that end, can never seem so good to egoic man as an activity directed to improving it by filling it with something which he thinks he needs. Egoic man is allergic both to emptiness and to peace. But he is addicted to the good idea of filling space with good things and also of getting rid of his enemies, whether these are in himself, or in his illnesses and dis-eases, or amongst his acquaintances, or on the battlefield. In every case his well-meaning actions are limited in their results by the limitation of his state of mind. But in his determination to put reality "right," egoic man must eventually find himself to be in the "wrong," simply because he has avoided it.

What Are Our Instruments of Relationship?

The senses are all instruments of relationship. They are means of knowing "What, now?," so that a person can experience "IT," whatever it may be, which is at the end of our particular instrument, be it telescope or microscope, eye or ear, "heart" or "brain." These are all means of telling us "What's up, now?" According to what our senses tell us, just like the amoeba, the sea anemone, or the favored rat of the experimental psychologists, we shall read accordingly. Stimulus provokes response, in reflex action: or so say our experimental psychologists, who are scientifically trained to think only in terms of "because, therefore," which is also found in the determinism of Freud. This can only be true, however, if, like the rat, we are only motivated by need.

But persons are not amoeboid jellyfish, or even rats. They have another power not possessed by lesser creatures, or at least not to the same extent, which is called "WILL" or "CHOICE." It operates IN SPITE of the laws of reflex action, as well as "because" of them. For this reason, PERSONS defeat all scientific investigation, because they operate in a dimension which is beyond that of egoic man.

All instruments of relationship function BEWTEEN self and other, as a means of denoting experience. I see it: I hear it: I feel it: I know it. In general, the formula is I———X———it, and it is this X which is the determinant of motivation. It is derived from the relationship *between* I and it, and not from "it" alone, which would be reflex or deterministic causality. In certain circumstances and with some training, I can interfere with, or defeat, all the common sense of reflex or deterministic behavior, just as long as "I" am not defeated, or simply ignored, or brainwashed out of my state of being.

Although no philosopher or psychologist in Western or scientific thought has so far been able to define or describe the origin or motivation of behavior. There has, however, been a very old Eastern or Hindu tradition to describe these engines, or mediators of energy in human behavior. They were called CHAKRA (sing. CHAKRAM), meaning "wheels" or "flowers." Spirally, they spun.

The Chakra Belong to a Cyclical, Not a Serial, Order of Experience

Western thought, developing "serially" in a system of things-by-themselves, existing in a time order of before and after, was unable to appreciate the meaning of the CHAKRA, which belong to a previous or "cyclical" system of wholeness, balance or rhythmical harmony. The abstract symbol of this system is the MANDALA, which is said to be actually older than man-made wheels, and to have been drawn on Mayan caves to represent man crucified against the sun. Like the Chinese "YIN-YANG," the Mandala "holds together" not only the mystery of creation that 1+1=3, but also the still nobler and more vital statement that 2+2=5. Any system of relationship on one level needs to be "crossed" by another system of relationship, on another level, if life is to be satisfied. The person, as well as the world of reality in which he lives, is multi-dimensional, and the whole system of the unfolding of life, through time and through the CHAKRA, may be seen as a spiral, each rotation being carried a stage forward from the previous phase.

As in the Christian tradition it was said that "the WORD was made flesh," so the Hindu system of the Chakra was also claimed to have been created as "form" out of "sound," as Krishna played upon his lute and danced us into life. So the Chakra occur together to form an "octave" in the spine, developing in terms of time, both racially and individually, from below upwards, each one completing the fulfillment of its phase before passing over to the next.

The Chakra have strange-sounding names to us in the science of Hindu metaphysics, but these need not concern us here. For us, they are facts of experience-in-time, and as such have their place both in racial and individual history, and both in experience and in physical form. These parallels are shown in figure 6 on p. 106. Interesting speculations are raised by seeing each Chakram as representing a 7-year period of individual growth, the watershed or breakthrough of maturity occurring at the diaphragm at 21; the historic "breakthrough" occurring at the demarcation line BC/AD, with perhaps 1,500 year periods of racial growth. In the latter case, if the watershed is placed at BC/AD, our present disposition is to explore the heart Chakram, which is the experiential area of personal relationship.

Time and timing is the LAW behind the Chakra: they represent the experiential reality of time as a function of relationship. Each lower center requires to be fulfilled completely in its turn before it hands over to the next above, itself dying down to form the root from which in turn the next phase draws its life. Impatience destroys the balance of the whole, and egoic man has long since lost his sense of time, rhythm and relationship. Egoic man is not

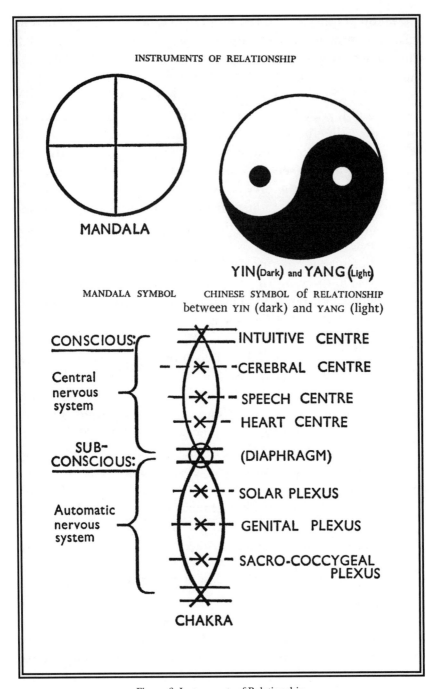

Figure 6 Instruments of Relationship

necessarily "aggressive." He is a violently anxious and impatient man, and scientific man is swiftly approaching his ideal of being no-time man. The effect of such emphasis upon the upper levels of consciousness is to turn the human shape into that of a tadpole, with a much enlarged head and a very attenuated tail or heart.

Growth and Progress

If we stay with the pattern of the Eastern system of the development of the CHAKRA a little longer, we are able to keep some check on the Western ideas of growth and progress. The pattern of development of the Chakra is pyramidal $\triangle$ and therefore stable; but the pattern of Western morality and educational progress tends to the pattern of the inverted triangle ∇, and therefore to be unstable. On the other hand, the Eastern aim for the effective develop-ment of a person, the "work," as it has been called by the Alchemists, of changing lead into gold, earth into Heaven, or the "raising of the Son of Man," was referred to by the Hindus as the raising of the snake called KUNDALINI. (Moses was also said to have lifted up the serpent in the wilderness.) The snake was the symbol of basic energy, and the process of human progress was conceived as the timely development of each level of "consciousness," or of experience, until the whole potential nature inherent in the Divine origin of man could be fulfilled, as it were, pyramidally. This was also sometimes referred to as climbing "The Holy Mountain."

According to this oriental view of Reality, the Western concept of evolution according to Darwin was unbalanced, because biological progress could not possibly mount continuously up $\uparrow$ without a Divine incarnation balancing and feeding it, by falling sympathetically down $\downarrow$.

Communication

Communication is an application of the same principle of the basic brick; it is an *experience of relationship*. Communication is not only an act of talking, writing or signaling, to another person. It should also be an experience of relationship.

However, it is only necessary to listen attentively to any conversation between two people, to realize that this is not always so. It soon becomes obvious that we are talking to ourselves, and not to one another; and that this is the case not only in the desultory circumstances of being at a cocktail party. In any ordinary conversation we are not listening to one another more than is necessary.

In general, when we are engaged in such uncommunicative conversations, we might as well be fish ogling one another from inside our respective fish bowls, or birds fluttering behind glass cages. Perhaps we think we can see a real world over there, where you are. We even think we can interest you in us, or even change you more to our liking. But too often if the world over there is different from what we expect it to be, we do not see it at all. If it answers back, we do not listen. Usually we are too busy in our egoic selves, protecting our selves from our selves and others, to pay attention to what is really going on over there. We are the more blind because we think we see. We are the more deaf because we think we hear.

But communication, if it is to be alive and effective, must be an experience of a relationship. This requires a self-diminishing towards the point of self-emptying, a letting go of the egoic self, undefended, in a state of self-surrender, which is called "paying attention to the other." It also requires the use of a suitable symbol, or mediator, which may be described as "speaking to the other in the language which is familiar to the other." To find out the language or idiom of the other it is necessary to listen and wait for quite some time. This is, of course, the practice of the psychotherapist, who finds the language of the other in the symbolism of the illness and its symptoms, but particularly in his patient's dreams, and also in terms of his experience, past and present.

CHAPTER 5

Relationship, Touch, and Meditation

Relationship with any other implies a kind of *touch* at a meeting-point, so A→C. There is a common point of impact, C, where A meets B. It would be interesting to know, if we could find out, what goes on at this vital focal point of all our most intimate personal experience, C.

As you touch the back of one hand with the finger of the other, you are relating the two hands, A and B, at the common point of touch, C. As you draw your finger across, you make a continuous line of experience, C C C C C. Life itself is such a continuity of experience. In compulsion neurosis it is the continuity of experience, the C-line, which has been fractured, so that an interrupting force, the compulsion, must take the place of spontaneous growth. Relationship by the tyranny of compulsion, or what is called "identification" and "dissociation," is a denial of the freedom of the experiencer, the subject, a proof of disorder and a sign of ill health.

The dividing line between "right-relationship" and "shock tactics," or between "touch" and "force," is obtained by asking the question, "Is there any intention to control the other, by exercising power over the other, in order to change the other?" If so, this is not truly a love-relationship in the sense in which I have been defining it. It is a compulsion because the consideration is not bilateral.

The C-point of shared experience is not, therefore, a fulcrum at which the pressure of a lever is applied to the life of another person, in order to obtain a certain response. The event at C cannot be predetermined, because it springs out of the given conditions. It is a mystery, an adventure. In fact, it is an experience, subjective,

---

From *Mysterious Marriage: A Study of the Morality of Personal Relationships and Individual Obsessions*

personal, unrepeatable, unique, alive. Such might be the impact of a sound upon the ear, a sight upon the eye, or the presence of the beloved upon the "heart"—but we are all too well-guarded, too defended and encrusted, to allow so much freedom to uncertain visitors. We prefer to shut the door, to keep all strangers out, and then to contemplate our mental pictures of what the other ought to be and do, until such time as we can force or bribe, threaten or seduce him, to do so. Disappointment in our plans is then attributed to a moral failure in the other, who was not "good."

But if relationship is only to have this accidental quality of touch, what is to be the dynamic, the incentive? Obviously, if I believed in force and that I knew what you ought to do, and if I wanted you to do something for me, I would push you and pull you, bribe you and threaten you, until I had got you where I wanted you. ("But, my dear, if I did not do that nothing would ever get done. It is only for your own good!") This worked excellently as long as it was successful, i.e. as long as you were "good" enough to obey me; but in personal relationships of greater quality of strength and opportunity, it led inevitably to nagging. In prayer, where God was the "other" who did not get busy on my behalf, it led, inevitably but erroneously, to disbelief in God. Now, putting force on one side, just as between you and me, if we meet—will anything happen? When A meets B—will there be any C?

I do not know. If that uncertainty is intolerable to either of us, then there can be no meeting, for an indeterminate, unprejudiced approach of simple expectancy or wonder is the only prerequisite to a meeting. Who can tell what will happen, what mystery may be unveiled, what miracle may be revealed, what adventure started, or empty nothingness disclosed? But shall we fling a bridge across this separate chasm and, opening our doors at either end, approach and see?

It is like plugging in to an unknown power circuit. What lamps will light, what wheels will whirl? Something comes in to this side, as something else goes over to that. We talk and listen to one another, as we show and see. For the time of the meeting, you are somewhat in my circulation and I in yours. In exchanging experience, we are exchanging blood. This is very exciting. I am indeed enjoying meeting you. (In fact, I am quite surprised. I never thought I could have enjoyed meeting you so much.) But please be sure to let me go; when I want to leave you, as I certainly shall, please don't hold on to me, or I shall be afraid to risk my life again *with anyone.* It is a terrible thing to be caught, and taken advantage of, in this unguarded mood of sharing one's circulation with another.

This, therefore, is the second incentive: that in sharing our experience, you and I are each entirely free to choose what we will do about it. Our meeting has not affected either your freedom or mine, nor our responsibility for minding our own business and considering one another. Experience is enriched by meeting. But we must not say that, because we meet, therefore such and such must inevitably follow. There are to be no strings, neither in your hand nor in mine. You are not "cause" to predispose any "effect" in me. Our bridge is tenuous, and if it will not hold the weight of a house, it most certainly will not stand for a succession of bulldozers to pass over it.

But does not its very lightness suit the simple traffic of our love?

Hands

From touch to hands, for hands are the instruments of all relationship. They are the wingtips of the angel and the front paws of the monkey, modified by the molding influence of contact with the ground. It was when the monkey rotated his thumb through a right angle that he was able to mold things to his fancy. And now the whole world, and all that is in it, is in men's hands. A man's hand is like a mirror, a bridge and a magnet. It reveals what it draws to itself, and, between finger and thumb, man holds his universe intact.

Hands can control things, but they should not try to control people. There is so much power today centered in a man's hands that he can now almost destroy his world in one gigantic release of atomic energy. He can control the forces of nature and bring all things to obey him. One touch from his finger-tip and the effect is felt on the other side of the world. Naturally, he is very proud of this and, rather like a child, he enjoys showing off what he can do, the marvelous tricks he can perform. Being so good at making things, he naturally tries to do the same with people. Inevitably, he fails, unless he can induce people to behave like things. To control another person successfully, whether that person is worker, voter or slave, husband, wife or child, is to rob them of that essential virtue by which they are their true, their personal, selves. Whatever the meaning of the spirit is, its life depends on a man's right to choose what matters to him. If he has lost that, his spirit soon follows, for it cannot live under compulsion. When a man has lost his spirit, he has not only lost all that matters to him, but he has lost his life also, for he has nothing with which to meet it. The spirit is that with which we meet one another, our lot and situation, Life.

If I say that power has emerged from monkeys' paws, but love from angels' wings, I do not mean to imply that there must be any final and indissoluble dichotomy in man's nature, but only that power is a rising force and love a falling one. Such familiar pairs of opposites always need wedding. Fortunately, the wedding is not impossible, for there is love in power, as the saw loves the very wood it cuts, and there is power in love, as all good healing proves. But man will only come to understand his dual nature when he allows for its two sides, unseen and seen, falling and rising, love and power, and does not get them wrongly mixed. As he understands them both, meeting them on either hand, so he must wed them in himself.

The breath of the spirit, the quality of heaven, the touch of an angel, is still present in men's and women's hands. I keep on harping on the reality of heaven, because it is so plainly true, in the daily commonplace events of your experience and mine. It is heaven to be touched by the firm yet gentle hand of love. And it is hell to be pushed around, pinched, poked and shoved, exploited and misused, as if you were some *thing* to be possessed or thrown away—by "love."

In mastering and gaining the things of the world, the monkey's paw has travelled a long way. The angel's wing, the all-penetrating breath of the spirit, the quality of heaven, is also a great traveler. It travels so far and so fast, it does not need to move at all. Always, it has arrived. Always, it is given. Always, it is everywhere.

Poor Lucifer! Confronted by a world which needed love, he gave it power and nearly burnt it, and himself, to death.

Poor Christ! Confronted by a world which needed love, He gave it love and they crucified Him.

Poor man! Confronted by a woman, he tries to hold her in his power and, exploiting her apparent willingness, loses her.

Poor woman! Confronted by a man, she tries to hold him by her love and, apparently pleasing him, she loses him.

And yet the secret of life and death, of love and power, of you and me, and of the relationship between, is all within the span of any one man's hands. In a man's hand, fortunes are made and lost; worlds of beauty are disclosed or broken; life is received or destroyed; and love is honored or betrayed. Here, in the hand of man, is where macrocosm and microcosm, heaven and earth, angel and monkey, you and I, can meet.

Meditation

I pass from "touch" to "meditation," because I believe that these two are fundamentally the same, and that we have the same opportunity to learn from both of them. It is, indeed, a most valuable example of the "similarity of opposites," because we might think that touch was only material, tangible and sensible, whereas meditation should only refer to supersensible experience. In fact, I think it is not so.

Elsewhere, I have defined love as a way of keeping touch with the other, without intent to change. Love, therefore, is a common denominator between touch and meditation, and all are equal means for the working of the spirit.

I suggest that all good work is the outcome of a previous "meditation," which was no more than a prolonged experience of "touch without intent to change," or study. I once watched a farmer milking his cow. His eyes were shut and his expression one of rapt content, as a smile lurked round the corners of his mouth. He turned to me, not even knowing that I was interested in the subject, and said, "This is how I do my meditation." So all craftsmen meditate upon the substance of their craft; but it is less easy to meditate upon machinery, though not impossible where the engineer can love his greased and glossy instrument. So the teacher must meditate, not only on the subject which he teaches, but also upon each pupil whose face, whether blank or bright, conceals those unknown depths of appetite or resistance; but it is not easy to meditate on a dull subject, or a class of forty unruly children. So the psychologist must meditate upon his case and his material of dreams and phantasies, of idiosyncrasies and disorders of behavior; but it is not so easy if he relies on diagnosis for a snap judgment, or the psychological textbooks for an answer. Each one keeps touch, with finger, eye, ear, mind and heart. Each one must "love" the object of his prolonged and continuous attention. This is surely meditation, wherein we meet all that the other gives.

But, unfortunately, the word meditation has been applied too exclusively to its higher use, of meeting the divine other, as an exercise of the spirit towards the supersensible, or an excursion of the Will upon the mysterious perpendicular path of that other dimension. Indeed, I believe this to be a most important exercise, and a most worthy discipline. Yet, if this were the only use of meditation, I would think it most dangerous, as tending to cut off "that other ground" from "this familiar field." It leads to what we have heard of as the Indian rope trick, in which a rope shoots up into the air supported only by itself, while a boy climbs up and disappears into thin air. Of course, that would never be done in fact, unless our "facts" include this actual danger of a mystical disappearance into union with the divine ground. In that sense, the trick can be learnt and practiced. I am not saying that it is a "bad" trick. Indeed, I believe it to be a very "good" one. But I think it immensely important that we should not forget that exactly the same trick of disappearing into the "other" can also be performed in this familiar field, where it is perhaps of more value, as it is also less dangerous.

In either case, let us agree that to keep in touch with the other is an excellent habit, whoever that "other" may be.

PART II

The Anatomy of Incarnation

CHAPTER 6

The War of Nerves

The Meaning of Nerves

What are these nerves of ours, and what is their proper function in the living organism? They are our *instruments of relationship*. They are the living links between one organ and another, as they are also links between the organism as a whole and that other outer world in which it has to live and strive for life. They are instruments of information, which tell us what is going on in other parts. They keep us in touch with one another and make contact over the distances which separate the parts that together make up the whole. They are bridges upon which the lives of many separate parts can meet. As organs of relationship, they are our most precious means of making friends and fighting enemies: of planning and of deliberate response to the many problems of experience by which we are so constantly beset. Thus they become the living root of our philosophy or attitude to life. As our nerves respond, so will our conduct be determined. If our nerves are rightly "relative" and timely in their manner of response, so shall we be balanced and temperate in our way of life. As men and women, for better or for worse we are all instruments of relationship, and so upon our "nerves" we must depend.

Instruments of Relationship

"Nervousness" (or "nerves") implies a breakdown of our capacity for relationship. That is to say, the nervous state is one in which, for some reason or another, relationship in certain conditions cannot be tolerated. There are, or seem to be, only two alternatives: one of us must go, to be dismissed immediately, out of relationship into

From *Mysterious Marriage: A Study of the Morality of*
Personal Relationships and Individual Obsessions

an "absolute" or unrelated state. It is either *fight*, and you must be destroyed: or *flight* and I am not in your vicinity any more, which is as good as proving that you don't exist for me and so you cannot trouble me. Where *nerves* are relative, the difference which our inverted commas make is that "nerves" are absolute. Even time itself must be cut out, since time is relative. There be no suspense or space of time where "nerves" are on the wing. Duration cannot be endured. The only two alternatives are "fight" or "flight," or so it seems to us as we feel that we must react according to our instinctive judgment. But, as I shall hope to show, we need not act instinctively. There is another alternative if we can employ the higher function of our consciousness, and learn to reconstruct another bridge of right relationship. Meanwhile, however, we can simply state that all nervous disorders are a breakdown of relationships, the impulse being towards a timeless solution of a problem of relationship by the instantaneous dismissal both of the problem and its apparent cause. Some of us are born with this unfortunate tendency: and some of us acquire it for various reasons which I shall shortly show.

"Nerves" are a social—or sometimes anti-social—disorder or disease, because they are due to a disorder of relationship.

Rhythm

Let us go back within ourselves, and study for a while the more formal states of our activity and rest. Here is a rhythm, a tidal full-swung breath of life, that flows from deepest in, at rest, to furthest out, at work. In fact, we swing or breathe from that near-death which we know as sleep, to waking life. In the former we are inside ourselves, central: in the latter, we are concerned with those exterior matters that keep us busy in the world outside. In order to sleep we must actually shut out the exterior evidence and the demands which it makes upon us: the darkness falls, causing in effect a diminution of external stimuli: we draw the blinds over our windows and, with similar intent, the eyelid's curtain falls over our tired eyes. We enter into the bedroom, we enter into the bed, which closes like a warm cave around our tired limbs: we turn off the inner light, our minds grow empty, dark, and so we fall asleep, becoming mysterious travelers on an uncharted sea. Here is no effort of the will, only an effortless peace—if we can feel that way and comfortably relax. Dreaming or dreamless, according to our depth and custom, Time passes in immeasurable hours. When morning comes, our traveler returns from his mysterious adventuring; we say that we return to "consciousness," meaning that we return to the external world as focal point of our attention, which has wandered, who knows where, within the dark of night. We open our eyes to signify our sight's return; we clamber out of bed, to pull the curtains back: our cave disgorges us, and we go forth to face the sun (if there is any) and work. For we have breathed again, as we expired and travelled deep within the well of sleep.

Here is our rhythm, then, manifest, as in so many other ways, in waking and in sleeping. Down to sleep, falling: rising, up to waking life again: these waves proceed, continuously. As we relax to sleep, so on waking we must clench our wills and grit our teeth somewhat in necessary tension with which to face the daily combat of our lives. The pattern is repeated everywhere: the open palm, the closed fist: the bent, and then extended, arm: the beating heart, systole and diastole: the breathing lungs: from all these opposite dualities, there springs a third mysterious visitor, the ebb and flow of Life. Missing either one we cannot be alive. We throb and pulse: and all our throbbing pulses are in some mysterious way harmonized and unified, as but a single clock. In spite of all our whirring wheels, our rising up and falling down, one person remains wrapped up within our outer skins: *I* am, *I* want, *I* can, *I* will. "I": that is the one, the man, woman, child or babe in arms. *I AM.*

It seems to me unfortunate that we can have no fine anatomy of sleep. It cannot be dissected out, and shown within its proper place. The surgeon with his sensitive exploring hand can never find it in your stomach or your chest. Nor, still more remarkable, can he find the one that we call "I." The will, important agent in our lives, is missing, too. Where are they all, these invisible and all-important facts—for facts they are, although they are invisible? We know our visible anatomy: that is plain, and the textbooks will tell you what you cannot see, with colored pictures to explain your more obscure geography. But here is the truth: really, *you are not like that.* You are not your limbs, nor your liver, nor the sum total of your nerves' complexities. You are not the convoluted marvels of your brain, nor all its cells. They are visible to the prying eye of the microscope, but *you are not.* And yet, indubitably although invisibly, you *are* you, and I *am* I. Can this invisibility become apparent: can we make our invisible anatomy become visible, without again defrauding truth?

I think we can, but two conditions are necessary. First, we must disabuse our minds of the limited forms and structures of our visible anatomy. We must face ourselves in the mirror and say, very firmly, to the form we see there, "No, I am not that, I am not even like that (although possibly that is a little bit like me, as it is one of many aspects of me)." Then if we set out to portray our invisible anatomy within insulting diagrams, we must be careful to admit that these are only diagrams; they are motionless snapshots of moving forces, and must be changed as soon as they are seen from other angles. With these two warnings, with due humility, I hope we may set out to depict the invisible. (The Truth, invisible, is also inaudible, perhaps—and yet we do not hesitate to speak.)

The Flower

Two things may first strike us about the problems of our nerves: the first is their complexity and the multiplicity of symptoms from which nervous patients suffer. The second fact however, as so often happens, is the reverse: namely, that all our symptoms seem to be variations of the single habit of *contraction.* Like flowers, we can open and we can shut. Our nervous habit is to shut. Therefore, true to an old tradition to which I shall be referring later, we shall begin simply and, according to Biblical injunction, "consider the lily of the field;" or, more simply still, the flower.

The first of my charts of invisible anatomy is shown in figure 7, "All-round Me," p. 121. It shows a central point within an outer ring: the center is I AM, who is the invisible one in the middle of it all. The ring is the skin, or margin, between the two worlds of inside me and outside me. The petal-shaped curves represent our many parts and instruments, each one within itself a breathing whole: they suggest the breath of life itself and also, in a certain sense, the presence of a traveler or go-between, who journeys round between the many aspects of ourselves, experiencing relationship.

Figure 7 All-round Me

Like all my patterns, this one must now be made to work. What is it meant to show? First of all, it indicates the balanced, breathing state which is the living essence of our normal health. This is the way we are incarnate, restful, poised within ourselves and yet in constant touch, through the many sensitive doorways in our skin, with what is going on outside us in that other world. But are we always so quietly and comfortably installed inside ourselves? To this question we must often answer, "No, we are not". Since childhood days, the outer world has made its own demands on us, with offers of rewards and punishments: "Do this at once! Don't do that ever! Be quick! How stupid and how slow you are!" (These exclamation marks all imply impatient violence.) Sometimes the arbiters of outer time have scant respect for childhood's inner clocks. In consequence, we are inclined to be pulled out of our inner quietude of growth, becoming attached to the outward emphasis of pleasure, duty, work, as if compelled to leave ourselves behind, unselfishly. Then we can only grow as parasites upon some support derived from outward strength, because we have lost the source of life that springs and swells from our own deep-hidden roots within ourselves. Thus our two worlds are forced to separate, with inner push and outward pull at variance. The more we lose our inner selves, the more we must become identified with outward people and the things that seem to matter most to them.

The opposite, however, is also true and we must always watch the two extremes. Some go out too much and gather all their energies around their outer rims, but some throw their balance back the other way, leaving the outer active world behind their backs, they turn too much within themselves, refusing to come out and face demands that they resent. Lazy, they only want to sleep within themselves: they don't want to get up in the morning, they "moon" around and lounge about, uninterested in that restless, working world outside themselves. Those who of their own free will are normally more concerned with the outer world and its activities are called "extraverts": those who are normally more concerned with the inner world and its more restful state are called "introverts:" those who are *abnormally* concerned with the outer world, i.e. as a refuge from their inner selves, are called "nervy:" those who are *abnormally* concerned with the inner world, i.e. as a refuge from exterior demands, are called "moody."

Organism and Personality

We shall be considering our inner and outer worlds in detail, but we must build up our psychic structure as we go. The inner world is an ancient *organism*, which reacts to its outer problem as a whole, just as a limpet on a rock, or a hedgehog in a ditch, or a sensitive plant in a greenhouse, would do. They open or shut, expand or contract, with the whole organism mechanically tuned together in its different parts, for fight or flight. The inner world is *protopathic* in its reactions, meaning "all-or-nothing," which is its organic characteristic. The outer aspect of the psyche, however, derived from skin and brain and characterized by consciousness, shows the evidence of true personality, namely, conscious choice and discriminative (*epicritic*) behavior. Although still founded on organic and instinctive levels, the conscious man has evolved and grown beyond these old organic roots and is capable, at times at least, of intelligent and critical behavior. The nervous man is less able to rely on his conscious and exterior powers, because he is more influenced by his old organic, all-or-nothing and unconscious life. He is the unconscious victim of his inner world, although he usually blames the outer one for his misfortunes.

In our exterior relationships, that is to say in our attitude to life in that exterior world and all the claims it makes upon us, we may feel "positively" or "negatively" disposed towards it. If we are in good heart, with full confidence in ourselves and in our ability to cope with life, we feel that we can enter into it with zest and gusto, with eagerness and hearty appetite. Then the petals of the flower are open wide to life, expanding to meet experience with enjoyment and goodwill. But we do not always feel like that. Sometimes we feel inferior and shy, unequal to the task of facing life, and then the petals of the flower recede as we unconsciously withdraw inside ourselves. Those who are exceptionally sensitive are more liable to experience shyness, because they have a greater capacity for making contacts with the outer world and are therefore more easily overwhelmed by its apparently teeming confusion. It is as if they must experience first the negative aspect of their instrument of sensitivity, before they can learn to use it positively as an enduring instrument of relationship.

Unconsciously, deep inside ourselves in our invisible anatomy, we respond to shocks of every kind at first by this instinctive protective gesture of withdrawal. We shrink internally from harsh looks or angry words, and children especially must respond instinctively to this protective interior call for self-withdrawal. Thus our inmost "hearts," or unconscious nervous reactions, are actually formed by the experiences of our early years. Insecurity of any kind leads to the heart's withdrawal. Security, affection, encouragement, however, lead to the heart's expansion as the petals of the flower unfold.

Later in life, a shock may have the same effect. Then we are suddenly withdrawn into our heart's core and it is as if the flower is locked into a bud, clamped tightly down within the overwhelming grip of darkness and of fear. Then for a time it is as if the light of life goes out. We may collapse or faint, and the feelings that we experience have the quality of death, as the light within the flower is forcibly blown out against its will.

Anxiety can also be referred to the unconscious movements of the petals of the "flower." We react at first inwardly, unconsciously, and as a whole to our problems of relationship. Anxiety causes a quiver of uncertainty as the petals prepare to withdraw: unconsciously, fear sets up a protective movement in response to danger on the part of the whole interior organism, of gathering itself together for immediate escape.

Our nervous system responds instinctively and as a whole, in terms of fight or flight. The movements which occur within the "flower" are felt and described as experiences of the "heart"; such as "my heart failed me," "my heart stood still" or "my heart jumped out of my mouth." Of course this does not refer to the physical blood-pump that beats beneath the ribs, although that is affected too, as I shall describe later. For the moment, we must allow poetic license and keep our inverted commas for "nerves," "heart," and "flower," to help us realize that our emotions are indeed indications of an *interior experience of change.* Our flower can open and our flower can shut: between these two extremes or opposite poles, our flower breathes. In every "nervous" state, our flower contracts and, as we say, we feel anxious, disturbed or upset. Let us now consider further the nature of this interior polarity that can be so shaken at its core.

Polarity

It is as if there is a center of positive energy, expanding, which is opposed by a negative ring of energy, contracting: these two energies in rhythmic alternation comprise the "breath" of life. Symbolically, they may be regarded as the forces of "light" and "darkness": but it depends upon which one you are yourself identified with, whether you will call it positive or negative, light or dark. I prefer to call the inner central force "positive," because it is pushing out, extending: and dark, because its "light" is invisible to us, being so far beneath the surface of our lives. The external, marginal energy I call "negative," because it is compressive, resistant to the expanding force: and "light" because it seems to be in the light, to us who are conscious of it. I would be quite willing, however, for anyone else to have their plus and minus, light and dark, the other way round if they prefer. These two energies are opposed and combined, to form a third which is their child, a living traveler in time. They are also related to one another as male (outer, active, negative, "light" world) and female (inner, quiet, positive, "dark" world). We are therefore both female and male, whether we may be man or woman; and we must be both to live.

Dr. Rudolf Steiner has drawn attention to an interesting comparison in regard to the bony structure of our skeleton. He points out something which is obvious, and perhaps for that very reason we have not realized its true significance: namely, that whereas the body is built softly round the hardness of the bony structure of the spine and typical limb bones, in the head the reverse condition is the case, and the soft structures of the brain are surrounded by a bony skull. To put it in another way: although in the body we are built as *vertebrates,* in the head our bony structure is *crustacean.* Dr. Steiner suggests, and I agree, that this is due to an effect of reversed polarity between the body and the head. In the body, we have the "positive" state expressed, of energy expanding outwards from a center. In the head, however, we have the opposite "negative" condition of contracting energy, confined within a closing ring. The head, therefore, is as it were an intensification of the function of the skin. Related thus to the outer world, its function is to keep us well confined within our place. Relative to the expanding forces of our hearts' desires, the function of the brain is to act as brake upon our swiftly whirring wheels. This seems good sense, and it is interesting that the truth should thus be represented in the living poetry of our body's form.

Incarnation

Our pattern of the psychic flower may also serve to remind us, because we are sometimes liable to forget it, that we are the victims, whether we like it or not, of the principle of incarnation. We are spirits boxed in flesh; we are the prisoners, not only of our body's earthly chains, but also of those conditions in which we have to live. Light in lantern, sap in flower, organism in personality or soul in body, we are unlimited yet confined within the limited, and thus is our problem set. We are children of two worlds, spiritual and material, with a problem of conflict with, and adaptability towards, our material conditions. Some seem to fit into their places more willingly than others, and some find it irksome to fit in at all. Thus ringed round or boxed in by our material instruments and conditions, we are like a seed or bomb or jack-in-the-box, according to the way in which we behave. Seeds grow, expanding according to their proper form in time, bearing flowers and fruit in due season. In this they are lucky: they neither have to toil nor spin for it, as we must do. Bombs burst—and so do we sometimes. Jack pops out of the box and sometimes he cannot get back into his skin again. As we say, "his heart jumps out of his mouth." Sometimes, if he gets a "shock," he may get stuck outside his box and have to be assisted back again.

We therefore have to consider "Jack's" two main problems of relationship: namely, his relationship with his "boxes," which are his outward aspects or "bodies," physical, emotional and mental, in successive rings; and his relationship with the outer world which lies out there beyond himself, in which he has to live and make his way.

We may define "right relationship" as the state of being well incarnate within the ring, whichever that may be; or being "well in with" the other, whoever that may be. It is a state of restful balance, with potential energy contained, disciplined and ready for appropriate action when the time is ripe. It is a state of willingness to be confined, willingness to experience change, and finally, willingness to act, thus causing change, as change may be required.

Normally, therefore, when we are in this condition of right relationship with reality, we are in a state of what we may describe as *dynamic acceptance* of the ring, or of the resistance of the limiting principle by which we are both balanced and beset. We are then content to be held in by the problem, as we work gradually through its resistance towards its solution. In the state of "nerves," however, there is always a tendency to *jump out* of the ring, to refuse relation-ship and to dismiss the cause of the resistance. We are therefore in a state of tension, with energy negatively and protectively released, in order instantaneously to escape from the problem of relationship, by fight or flight. In hysteria, as I shall be describing later in "Hyste-ria: The Great Reversal," the protective trick is to *become identified* with the resistance imposed by the limiting principle.

Claustrophobia

No, right relationship is not the condition of the "nervy" man. He cannot bide within his boxes, because, he feels, he must be free. This condition is known as *claustrophobia*, which is a state of "nerves" that shows an unbearable objection to being shut in. *Jack cannot stay inside any box whatever.* He must get out, driven by an inward terror that he cannot control. Put him in prison and he will commit suicide if he can: he would rather be a gypsy or a tramp, and often is. He cannot go to a cinema or church, unless he sits on the outside seat, near the exit: he cannot travel in a train: he can-not enter a restaurant or face company at table: he is terrified of death for fear of being shut in his coffin, and leaves a clause in his will that two doctors must open his arteries in order to make sure that he is dead. But there are other kinds of confinement than those that exist between four walls. There is the marriage ring: for women there is pregnancy: and for all of us there is the discipline of work itself. Some people who have this affliction of their "nerves" cannot face the altar, but must flit round, lovers as free to come and go as birds in the air: some cannot have babies: some cannot stick at any job. They say: "I must feel free; I cannot bear people prying into my affairs. I always seem to be up against it, people will not leave me alone!" In greater or in less degree, the sufferer from claustrophobia *must get out.* He cannot stop inside a ring of any kind, and so he must refuse relationship.

Jack is suffering from a fundamental error of judgment, because he is confused between what is inside and what is outside himself. His inward energy is in fact exploding outwardly, refusing incarnation in his bodies' rings; therefore he feels that he must get out, wherever he may be. As far as this symptom is concerned, he is deeply deceived. He does not know the "fault" is in himself; but blames instead the outer ring by which he happens to be confined at any moment—the barber's shop, the crowd, the church or cinema, the job or marriage bond.

Now let us see why this should be so. I suggest we apply the axiom of ancient wisdom: "As above, so below: *as it is outside, so it is inside.*" Although the trouble to the "nervy" man always seems to be due to some external cause or situation, in fact that is only an excuse and an error of his judgment. He is seeing himself projected in the mirror of his external world. Really, the cause of his trouble is not out there, so why should he try to alter that? His trouble is within himself and there also is his only hope of cure, although he does not see it so. The exterior problem, which seems to him to be so terribly important that it must be solved immediately, is in fact only an illusion. To solve it by swift successful flight leaves the problem still unsolved. He may escape a thousand times from "it," but from himself he cannot fly away successfully—and that is where his deeper problem dwells. There is the source and center of his restlessness: the cause of all his fearful bother is his "nerves." There is deep-seated trouble in his organs of relationship. It feels to Jack as if he must fly out of his box: center out of circle, "I" out of "me," "she" out of "him," the positive pole out of its relationship with the restrictive negative ring by which it is opposed. It is as if the incarnate state itself is intolerable to the claustrophobic sufferer. He must get out, even of himself.

Having succeeded in doing so, he suffers again from an extreme anxiety, because, being bereft of all his prison guards, he now must find some place or person to hold and fix him firmly, as a sheet anchor in a constant storm. Therefore the need for mother or for home, and all the difficulty that he experiences in movement, change or travelling. There is no peace for Jack except at home. But home, like the Kingdom of Heaven, is inside us, in the heart of the "flower." No other outward home can take the place of this, our inner state of self-abiding confidence. Our outer home can represent it for us: as children, it can nourish us: but the aim and purpose of the outward home is to enable us to find and strongly build our source of central peace, where "I" can dwell in faith and in security. In claustrophobia, "I" am not at home. The bird has flown and the body-cage is restless, terrified. Meanwhile, the world is our scapegoat, as usual, and on it we feel that we must swiftly vent our blame.

It is very rare to find a case of claustrophobia that has been caused by some experience of compulsory confinement, such as being shut in a chest or caught in a dark passage. Although such cases have been reported, an experience of terror is not necessary in the causation of claustrophobia. It is a potential problem which is inherent in our invisible anatomy, and many conditions may produce it. One of the more common causes, especially in war-time, is *shock*, such as occurs from the blast of a near explosion. Claustrophobia is therefore one of the common symptoms in the condition known as shell-shock. What happens? Bang goes the bomb and bursts. Very naturally and understandably, Jack bursts too. With no moral implication of cowardice whatsoever, his inward energy explodes and runs away. Explaining what he feels like afterwards, the patient often says: "I feel that I am inside out," or, "I seemed to turn over inside." It is not literally true, of course; but in terms of invisible anatomy and the patterns of our inward energy, it is very true indeed. The shell-shock patient feels that he is a raw surface open to the world—and so he is. From the standpoint of energy, claustrophobia is an unbalanced state of *compulsively reversed polarity*: the interior command, as well as the subsequent effect, is *inside out*. In order to cure his uncomfortable state, he must be folded back inside himself again, invisibly.

We go by opposites. Where some cannot stay within a ring, others cannot bear to be without one. They cannot bear the space of empty streets: they cannot face the world at all, for fear of everything (*Agoraphobia:Panphobia*). Being so locked up within themselves, they symbolize their inner state by fixed attachment to familiar objects of their outer world. Some, who may not need to be so firmly fixed within their homes, must ever be surrounded in their minds by an iron ring of fixed ideas that never change. They are terrified if you suggest anything new and unfamiliar to them, and fling your new ideas away in utmost fright.

Old and New Nervous Systems

Yes, we have many boxes. We are boxed in our bodies (physical level); boxed in our hearts (emotional level); and boxed in our heads (mental level). Some hate them and some hate to let them go. Our boxes set us many problems of relationship. But now I want to divide our boxes into "square" and "round." The square box signifies the brain, which links us with the outer world that we know as three-dimensional space and time; the round box signifies the inner world that we do not know, but somewhat *feel*, without the benefits of consciousness. These two boxes, square and round, have two different nervous systems, new and old, or brain ("conscious") and belly-brain ("unconscious"). These are the *cerebrospinal nervous system* and *autonomic nervous system*, respectively.

And so in figure 8 (opposite), a single flower no more, we see our "nervy" man within two boxes, a square one for his head and a round one for his belly. The square box represents the external world and is therefore the central station for all the messages from his senses and his skin. It is the "brain." It is actually derived in its first origin, morphologically, from an infolding of the skin, with which it therefore shares the task of making contact with the outer world. The brain is, in fact, a very highly specialized sort of skin, and so it links within its complicated folds the messages from all those other specialized areas of skin which we call the "senses," such as touch, taste and smell, hearing and sight. The brain connects and contains all this information in regard to the outer world within its box, using it to build up a coordinated impression of what is going on, now, in our external world. Thus, when the moment comes for action, we can act appropriately.

Normally, the relationship between these two worlds that we can roughly designate as "heart" and "head" is a balanced one. Either the head expresses and fulfils the heart's desire in time; or else, since this is only rarely possible in the world in which we live, the head applies some reasonable brake upon the flying wheels of our desires. The head is, or should be, a strictly matter-of-fact organ: consciousness is a valuable bridge between the interior world on the one hand (I feel I want . . .) and the exterior world (but the fact is that . . .) on the other. In our heads, we are related

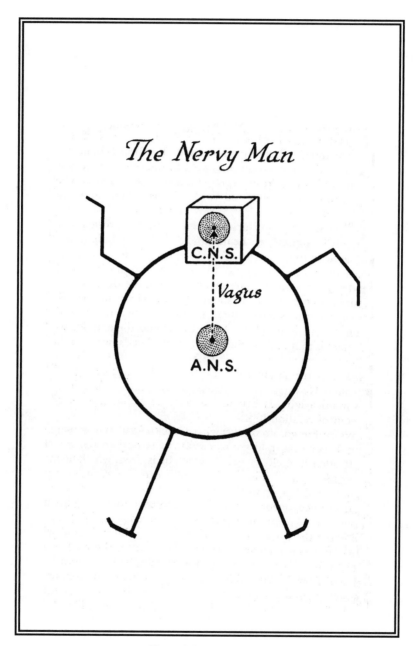

Figure 8 The Nervy Man

to that exterior world; but in our hearts, we are free. It is that longing for his freedom which is the ever doubtful advantage of the "nervy" man. He must have freedom *from*, and therefore does not use his mind aright. It becomes a *means of escape*, instead of an instrument of relationship.

Always on the go, no matter where, the "nervy" man is inclined to mental worrying and over-activity in regard to the exterior world. Restless himself (especially when he is tired, which he must soon become with all this excess expenditure of nervous energy), he cannot let the poor world rest, or anybody in it. All must be changed at once, according to the compulsive dictate of his unconscious state of deep unwillingness. When really nothing can be done because the time is not yet ripe, he does things in and with his mind that never go any further. He is full of the restlessness of his ideas that never give him peace. In fact, he hides both from himself and from his life within the cover of his brain-box, as an over-active mental refugee. He lives to think, but does not think to live. He becomes the victim of his own ideas, obsessed by them, because they are more real to him than is that outer world in which he lives and by which he is beset. He is withdrawn from circulation, petrified in his mental world of fixed ideas. His mind is his cocoon, another self-protective womb. Sometimes he stays inside and simply thinks, becoming too "introverted." But more often he escapes again (too much "extraverted"), into a stream of endless speech and then we call him "chatterbox." He, or perhaps more often she (but it is as characteristic of children as it is of those who suffer from their "nerves"), cannot keep still inside the limits of this mental box. They chatter on, these "nervy" folk, in a continuous spate of verbal flux about anything, everything or nothing. They never get anywhere, because their only purpose is to escape, as "Jack" bursts through the bounds of his intolerable box. You cannot get at or into these people, because they are covered by this moving barrage, this endless screen of self-protective words. Words can become both the means of escape and the ever-present refuge of the nervous man. Within his verbal cocoon, he is untouchable.

Ideas, therefore, have a curious and noteworthy quality for the "nervy" man, which they do not possess for those who do not suffer the same disability in regard to their relationships. They tend to be held in an absolute and unrelated way, fixed, tyrannical, autonomous and unarguable. The ideas of the "nervy" man are not susceptible to reasonable proof. They are too fixed for that. As a source of fear, they are therefore terrifying in their intensity, the more so because they are quite irrational. For instance, one of my patients had decided that he was suffering from cancer of the throat and no competent examination would convince him otherwise. Another, a young girl with no experience to justify such a conclusion, allowed the thought to enter her mind that she might be going to have a baby. It became a fixed idea that lasted for a week, and terrified her while it lasted, *although she knew it was not true.* Such "absolute" ideas can be a source of endless terror to the "nervy" man.

Anxiety and Imagination

Anxiety implies that we are anxious to escape from a problem, to be off out of the box in which we are, for fear of what might happen to us if we stayed there. It is important to notice that our reason for so acting is always fear of what *might* happen, and the cause of our behavior is therefore always, to some extent, imaginary. When imagination has thus become a source of fear and flight, we call it "morbid" and the "nervy" man is always the terrified victim of his own morbid imagination.

In right relationship, the safeguard of the normal man is that both he and his imaginative powers are directed towards the world in which he lives, accepting whatever may comprise his reality now, with all his creative energies confined within that box, through which they will express themselves in time, perhaps. With his attention thus narrowed within the focus of here and now, his fears, if fear he has, are necessarily limited, because reality must be limited, and "now" is so small a point in time that it is always relatively safe. From this limited situation however, anxiety must escape, and imagination offers limitless scope for escape into a world of endless opportunity for make-believe.

Where their opportunities for relationship are either lacking or difficult, lonely or unhappy children, and sometimes adults too, tend to live in an imaginary world of recompense for all they lack, in order to escape from boredom or from danger. There is greater danger, however, in this apparently innocent escape, than any which might exist within their real world, because imagination thus misused may soon become an unlimited source of terror in itself. The unlimited must always be more terrifying than the limited, because it is impossible to do anything about it. The time-track may be a nuisance with its endless train of little dots in time which we call "now": but the agonies of anticipation which are experienced by those who have lost their simple touch with reality are far worse than those discomforts and hindrances which reality may impose upon our over-hasty lives. When once the focus of attention to reality "now" has been lost, and expanded to include the limitless extent of our imagination, we are in a poor way, for we are the victims of powers with which it is no longer possible to contend, because they are not real. Hence, we experience more anxiety and still further motive for escape, in a vicious circle that carries us ever further from the facts that together make our real world.

Morbid imagination of this unlimited escapist kind plays a very serious part in causing the disorders of the "nervy" man. Although the cause of all his troubles may be, and usually is, imaginary, the effects, in terms of his interior disturbance, are very real. In order to do justice to the "nervy" man we must realize, once and for all, that although his imagination is at fault, his symptoms are not imaginary. They, at least, are real.

We will now discuss some aspects of this inner world, from which the material for our imaginative use or misuse is mysteriously drawn.

The Inner World

However much he may be disposed to believe the contrary and find his scapegoat in the outer world, it is in fact *always* the inner world which provides the main problem of the "nervy" man. We need not wonder that it should be so, for here indeed is a source of great complexity, which the wisest mind might well find to be a cause of unlimited confusion. I will first state some aspects of this inner world, and then do my best to sort it out as simply as I can, although I must admit that no one knows the truth of it. This inner world is partly non-material: that is to say it is not exposed to our three-dimensional examination. *It does not exist extended either in space or time.* These non-material contents of our hidden unconscious world are numerous, important, extremely complex and difficult to understand. First of all, there is our own *essential personal nature*, the arrangement of our true and inward seed, our private "pattern," as it were. As the oak tree emerges from the acorn and the chicken from the egg, so we must also emerge in time from this invisible womb which conceals and contains the inward and potential constellation of the self. Next in importance in our non-spatial inner world is the energy that causes our unfolding through the activity of appetite, desire and will. Here is our engine-house and boiler-room concealed. Thirdly, our inner world contains impressions recorded from our past experience: it is the womb of Time, wherein there lies not only unconscious material derived from our own past experience, but also much garnered wisdom from times that stretch far back into our most ancient history, before even the human race was born. Here is great wealth for our imagination's use, as it is discovered and unfolded within the space-time framework of experience. Fourthly, here is a mysterious *organ of sensitivity*, by means of which we are in touch with subtler movements than the senses can describe. Here feelings dwell, as we experience change; here information is recorded in the heart, below the level of our consciousness. Here also is the source of psychic powers, called "paranormal" now, that have been more useful to us in the distant past but still exist today: such as telepathy, prevision, and the phenomena induced in trance and mediumistic states. While in chaos, here is a source confused enough for every kind of lunacy. When in order, here is material enough to feed the mind of genius and formulate every aspect of perfection in creative art.

This inner world does not exist extended in three-dimensional space or time, as I have said. That may seem to set an unanswerable poser to our anxious seekers after scientific truth, who say: "Where is it, then?" Let them not dismiss the evidence too lightly, in the absence of what they would regard as a scientific explanation, because it is quite probable that some other branch of science may know more than they do. There is another kind of space, which we may call 4-space, that is different from the 3-space of the exterior world. It is a state of movement and it includes Time. We can, as a tentative hypothesis, regard the space of our interior world as 4-space, to which the 3-space conventions of the exterior world (time and consciousness) do not apply. The whole, that consciousness may seek and sometimes dimly see but never find, is here within this inner world. "The Kingdom of Heaven is within you." The whole of time, including past and future, is within us. The whole, all that has ever been, will be, and is now, is within us. *All that power of which we are not yet master, remains our master in this inner world.* It waits there for our experience *in consciousness*, that it may one day be wrestled with, mastered and redeemed, before it can take its place in right relationship. Each one must experience his own share of this interior world and feel his way through it, in time, with fear.

So much for that part of our inner world, our source of dreams or "belly-mind," which has no material form that we can see. There are also two aspects of it which are possessed of material form; that is to say, which are extended in space and time. These are the *physical organs* which are enclosed within the body's wall; and the *autonomic nervous system* of ganglia and fibers by means of which the organs are related and controlled. As far as possible, I will limit my discussion of these various aspects of the inner world to such points as may throw some light upon the problems of the "nervy" man.

The Nature of the Self

"Know thyself!" "To thine own self be true!" How easy it is to command, and yet how hard to obey! Each child is different from every other, unique yet changing all the while as its own life unfolds and as it grows. It is emerging out of darkness into light, out of the unlimited into the limitations of space and time, out of "chaos" into "order," out of the invisible into the visible, out of the whole into the separated and differentiated part. This emergence of the human spirit into space and time, from bud to flower, is growth. It is an effort in the face of resistance: it is an adventure against the danger of disaster: it is a test of endurance and a proof of willingness

136

to go to any length, even to Death itself, for Life's sake. The problem of any single life, in failure or success, is worth our limitless respect. There is no end to individual worth or to the vast potentialities of our secret inner world. But there are many pitfalls and obstructions on the path and not the least of these are made by the well-meaning ignorance of our responsible advisers. Do parents and teachers do all they can to assist at this miraculous birth of individual life? Or do they impatiently demand short cuts to swift material success, superimposing their idea of what they think is good upon a child's slow mysterious unfolding? Do doctors seek deeply enough in their pursuit of cause, or are they satisfied to cut off the patient's problem with a timeless knife? Amidst the constant clatter of exterior demands from home and school and business life, what chances have we of growing up—ourselves? The task of fitting in our delicate emerging cogs to the grasping teeth of the time-track on the road is fearfully difficult and dangerous for the delicate points of slow-emerging life. We should not be surprised at sensitivity's fear of suffering too much, and folding back in desperate escape into itself, while it covers itself as best it can with a fixed protection of conventional facade. This inner world, from which he springs with so much pain and suffering, so much initial goodwill and willingness, so much ingenious equipment and imaginative wealth, too often becomes the refuge of the "nervy" man as, "scared to death," he returns in swift escape from all that seems too difficult, back into this inward mother's womb.

Energy and Desire

It was with the intention of using it again that I introduced in figure 7 the pattern of the flower. In the wise tradition of the East, this is the customary device for describing that living energy which is the invisible cause of all material form. According to traditional Eastern physiology, energy is located at various centers which, however, are not extended in 3-space, although they are most important elements in our invisible anatomy. These centers are called CHAKRA (a Sanskrit word, singular CHAKRAM, meaning "wheels" or "flowers"), and their extension is in 4-space. They are spiral whorls or nebula that spin, silently balanced, generating in relationship with one another the energy which we use in life, as well as the organs of our visible anatomy through which this energy is expressed. When we describe illness as organic, these instruments are at fault: but when we describe it as functional, the fault is on the deeper level of unbalanced energy and disturbed relationship.

All disease must, of course, be a disturbance or modification of normal function. Normally, our 4-space spirals "breathe" outwards and inwards, expanding and contracting, rhythmically complete and balanced, with their energy directed in action out towards the world. In nervous disorder the direction of the flow is reversed: it is back towards the self, where it is caught and held as in a prison or a vice. In terms of flow, the center is normally at a higher potential than the periphery, and so the flow of energy is outwards. But in nervous disorder the periphery is at a higher potential than the center, and so the flow is reversed (reversed polarity). Thus, as regards the sum-total of his invisible anatomy, the "nervy" man is self-centered: and many of his specific energy centers may have become self-centered also, either through shock or some disturbance of his timely growth. In extreme cases, the chakra may become inverted, or blown inside out. Then it is as if our electrical fuses have been "blown," so that the instruments with which they are connected cannot work. Sometimes, if excessive strain is thrown upon one chakram, its function is temporarily destroyed and the energy may be suddenly transferred elsewhere, e.g. from the belly to the brain. A tightly contracted chakram may be a source of pain, and disturbance on the level of energy is the primary cause of fainting, collapse, shock and brainstorms.

I have described the process dogmatically for the sake of simplicity, but unfortunately we know very little about this mysterious level of our invisible anatomy. We have, however, several sources of information: e.g. Eastern tradition, clairvoyant inspection, intuition and the patients' descriptions of their own experiences. It is common, for instance, to hear of patients feeling "as if they are inside out," "they have turned over inside," "something suddenly snapped," "my inside feels exposed like a raw wound, instead of being properly tucked away." Their energies are self-centered, turned backwards against the normal course of radiant life. We can regard this as only a hypothesis, but it does provide a reasonable explanation for clinical events which are otherwise inexplicable.

I will briefly describe two cases to illustrate some of these points. The first was a boy of fourteen, shy, sensitive and idealistic, prone to be easily upset, who had a secret love affair with a housemaid. On his side, the relationship was idealistic, sentimental, romantic and always unfulfilled. Sexual intercourse did not take place, although his physical desires were continually stimulated and inflated. Although his love affair was never discovered, the girl was indiscreet and got the sack. She suddenly disappeared, with no explanation given. With nothing to sustain or to release his pent-up energies, the boy collapsed and had a nervous breakdown. He said he felt "turned inside out." He could not face anyone and could not leave the house or travel in a train. His heart raced in terrifying panic and he felt that he must die. He was sent to live on a farm where he partially recovered, but much of his nervousness remained with him. He still felt liable to panic and about to die when I saw him thirty years later.

He described his fear of impending collapse, as if he were about to faint or to die. A terrifying pressure gripped his heart, a convulsion caught him in his belly and his energy was drained from him. It was much worse than death, he said, as this constant threat prevented him from ever forgetting himself or enjoying life. He was swept with compulsive and intolerable force away from life, back into himself and out the other side, into some indescribable limbo of lost souls. That was his panic fear.

He also described the mirror phenomenon, which is another experience of reversal often reported by such nervous folk. He could not bear to see himself in a mirror; he felt he was not over here inside himself, but over there, the other side of the mirror, outside himself. There was nobody on this side, inside his body: he felt unbearably reversed, literally "beside himself" and not inside himself at all. I have been told, too, after a panic period of this kind, of the indescribable joy of looking at yourself in the mirror and feeling for a change that you are really here, inside yourself again. Perhaps only those who have known it can realize the depth of this experience. By others, who know it not, it is all too readily dismissed as "only nerves." To be told this and that they must pull themselves together, adds insult to their deepest sense of inward injury. They would if they could, but how?

Another patient, a married woman of twenty-five, came to me suffering from loss of memory and violent headache, which she described as battering and boring through her head. The nearer she came to recollecting this lost episode which she had obliterated defensively from her memory, the worse the headache became. She said the banging was as if someone was hammering nails into a door inside her head, with every bang an agony of pain, until she felt that she would lose all consciousness. I advised her to let her consciousness depart, but she said that if she did she would fall to bits and die, never to come back again. However, she risked it: she relaxed and fell into an hypnotic sleep in which she talked of her husband's infidelity. The pain was then in her stomach, ripping and violent, and not in her head. After a while she woke and remembered not a word that she had said, but the pain was in her head again. After about five interviews of this kind the memory was recovered into consciousness and the headache completely disappeared, as the problem was re-experienced more positively and the pain "suffered" on the emotional level. I asked her about those belly pains: had she had them before she lost her memory? Yes, she said, there had been terrible quarrels with her husband, when it felt as if there was a red hot cone vibrating in her stomach, with its sharp end pushing out in front, and as if great pulsing kicks were pushing it outwards from the region of her spine. It was a hateful sensation and ended with complete loss of consciousness, in a dead faint. One morning, after one of these attacks the previous night, she had woken with her memory swept clean, her heart at peace again, and a frightful headache. Her problem had been solved by an unconscious defense mechanism of dissociation and repression, but, apparently, the abounding energy had been transferred from the belly to the brain, with an inversion of polarity, or change of direction, at both levels: hence the banging headache. After the treatment which I described above, her memory returned in four weeks to the day, and both belly and brain were quiet and still. Her hidden forces were in their proper place again, as her invisible anatomy had been manipulated into right relationship.

Daemonic Powers, Dreams and Imagination

The inner world is large and very old, with secret wisdom of its own. It is as old as the hills and in it there still roam our ancient ancestors, from wild animals through barbaric man, reaching up towards ourselves—and possibly, dimly foreshadowed, far beyond. We are, here and now, the apex of a pyramid of living history. The crust of consciousness is very thin and we are like volcanoes waiting to erupt in nervous outbursts of uncontrolled emotion, destructively released. Our recent wars have proved how close we are, even in our intellectual and scientific pride, to our unseemly origins. Our nervous tempers prove the thinness of the fabric of our lives and the violence of these inward fires. Our dreams— amongst many other things—are nightly messengers from those mysterious caverns of the past. Imagination also springs from this interior wealth and all creative artists owe their talents, as well as the worst of their birth pains, to its uncomfortable store. The origins of genius and insanity, imagination and delusions, dreams and visions, are never far apart.

A young artist of wild views and disturbed conduct dreamt that he was standing on a rock, surrounded by the turbulent sea. Beneath him was a giant jellyfish "going on forever" (the exact wording of the dreamer) and it was coming up to strangle him. Near genius himself, he was in some danger from these prehistoric energies of his inner world by which he was being invaded. For here is energy, undisciplined, primitive, "all-or-nothing," and if these forces overwhelm us it may mean insanity. This energy must be wrestled with until it is harnessed and controlled: it must be ridden, mastered, used, or it will drive us where we do not want to go, overwhelming us with the adversity of our excessive life. Dreams are the key to, and messengers from, this mysterious unconscious life. They speak a language of their own which can never be exactly learnt, because it is not precise. It is pictorial, symbolic, slang. The boy is "on the rocks," in danger of his mortal bankruptcy. He said it was only a silly dream. He was a very clever boy: but which was the sillier, the dream or he?

Here is the source of those powers which are called psychic, mediumistic, sensitive or paranormal. Here is a kind of direct knowledge that escapes the barriers of time, for these are ancient powers that were once more common than they are today. The past and future are open to it, and it can see beyond the limits of the now, to prophecy with pre-vision. But there are several catches to this process, or we could spot the winner of the Derby more often than we do. Just as we have to interpret dreams, so also this inward knowledge of our ancient "belly-mind" must be interpreted, and that requires a very sensitive intelligence. Furthermore, we must remember that this is the engine of desire itself, and it is therefore most sensitive to wishful and hopeful misinterpretation. We are always in danger of seeing what we want to see, or what someone else wants us to see. There is no filter, no check, no discipline imposed upon this occult sensitivity from within itself: it is a hoary old jellyfish, as old as Time and as knowing—but how hard to catch within the teaspoon of our little consciousness! Yet there it is, still very much alive today, in spite of all that the outer box can do to cover it with education's ordered world. Children have access to it and lose it as they grow: women have access to it more than men, because they are nearer to it—sometimes much to the annoyance of the more logical male. Artists derive their strength from it, poets speak of it, and all must draw their imaginative wealth from its mysterious unplumbed depths. We are all afraid of it, and rightly so. It is possessed of fearful powers that can destroy us as with a giant's blow. And yet, in right relationship, it can be our strongest aid and surest friend.

In fact—like the Female Psyche which it is—it contains the very limits of all our opposites. It is the moon, and it may lead us to our lunacy. Yet it reflects the sun and may show us the face of wisdom's light reflected, cool and clear. It is the heart of love, the warmth of beauty's life, and it is the frozen horror of more than mortal hate that can destroy the very love that it contains. It can let loose a very awful power, this primordial, mysterious, unconscious jellyfish that looms beneath the rocks on which our feet seem to be so securely placed.

It is no wonder that we should prefer the new square box we keep within our heads, so brightly lit with consciousness, and so attached to familiar objects and the simpler time that Greenwich clocks can tell. But the jellyfish is not so lightly to be ignored or forgotten. He pursues us from below and the man who chooses to forget him is a "nervy," frightened, bedeviled and unbalanced man, because his security is constantly threatened by rumblings from below. He must be faced, this Ancient One, or we shall be "hysterical."

A word of warning is needed here, in case we should be tempted to regard this curious wisdom as "Intuitive." It is often, perhaps usually, miscalled Intuition, but it is unnecessarily confusing to call it so, for this is Moon not Sun, reflector not original source of light. The inner world is a very mixed and curious bag of ancient mystery and it is not the primary source of light. It is all most untrustworthy stuff, because here are earth and water mixed in much disorder, with ancient wisdom interwoven with one's own desire. There is much work to be done on this very dirty mixture, which is dangerous, explosive and often exceedingly corrupt. It needs a sieve or filter to make it anything like pure. Its guidance in important affairs of daily life is never to be lightly trusted, because it requires our constant watchful wrestling.

Intuition, however, is very different: it is the pure, unguarded, single source of light. Its wisdom is universal, unvarying, the same in every time and place. It is more abstract, mathematically pure, with a certain absolute quality of essential clarity. It is pure Fire and, like the fire, it can be dangerous. A little light goes a long way: to be too close to the central fire burns and destroys us. As intuition is "fire," so in symbolism this unconscious ancient wisdom is "water": that is to say, dreams often refer to it as water. Water is what fire needs to make our energy. They are not the same, but opposite. That is why it is important to distinguish between the "unconscious" or "subconscious" field (but what unworthy words these are!) which is a level of lower psychic sensitivity, and intuition which is a level of higher wisdom (see quadrants 1 and 3 on figure 13, p. 179).

It was the custom in the past to speak of certain nervous and emotionally unbalanced states as "daemonic possession" or "possession by the devil." Although such a description may seem to be out of date as a result of modern progress, it is not really so and we can often learn something by a re-examination of such disused terminology. Under certain circumstances, even today, we are possessed by evil powers and we can state an axiom for further consideration: In the end we are always possessed by any power we use possessively. The power genie, when released from the unconscious bottle, may seem at first to be a very promising servant—but he soon becomes our threatening master, and he is the very devil to get back inside the bottle again. This rule applies to every kind of self-indulgence, from alcohol to oratory, and from women to wishful thinking and angelic sentiments. Either our powers run us, and we seem to be privileged to use them cheaply for a while, until they run amok and threaten to destroy us: or else we must first wrestle with such powers and talents as we may possess, until we have finally proved our mastery over them. Then both the powers and our selves will have been rightly disciplined and we can play our proper parts in our community.

Sensibility

I propose to deal briefly with this aspect of our inner world, although it is perhaps the most important thing to understand about the "nervy" man. The inner world functions as a whole, instinctively, in an "all-or-nothing" way. It either expands towards the outer world, experiencing *pleasure*; or it contracts away from it, back towards the self, experiencing *anxiety*. Our sensitivity functions normally as a breathing spiral, but it can be caught at one extreme, as it "catches its breath" in violent contraction, instinctively withdrawn. To be *normal* is to be fully expanded and many-tentacled in our differentiated feeling antennae, with innumerable subtle points of enduring contact with the world, however adverse that may seem to be; the other half of the psychic "breath," or the return journey, is expressed in normal sleep as we withdraw within the privacy of our interior world and dream. To be *nervy* is to be compulsively withdrawn and self-centered, grasping material safety first. "*Nerves*" *are not due to fear*; they are due to the protective tension which is instinctively set up *in order to reject the experience of fear.*

Instinctively, therefore, when we are threatened, we contract our bodies on the physical, emotional and mental levels, and withdraw the inner Will in an effort to escape. This is the way of "nerves." To become cured or normal, it is necessary to reverse the process. Namely, we have to learn to relax our bodies on the physical, emotional and mental levels, at the same time intensifying the interior Will as willingness to reenter the world, returning into the bodies, into the instruments, into the job and, in the last resort, into the enemy. This is rebirth.

We vary in our psychic texture, as we are "tough" or "tender" types. Some are fine and sensitive in their secret texture; some are tough and dense, incapable of finer feeling. Some have a quality of "give" and "bounce" that enables them to act as shock-absorbers when life is hard and difficult. But some, who are sensitive without endurance, break down more easily when they experience strain. I speak of texture, therefore, to describe this psychic stuff of which we are composed, because I want to describe this quality which differs in the weave. We should be surprised, perhaps, if we could realize how many different kinds of this material, how many different grades of elasticity and degrees of sensitivity there are, besides our own. Some of us tear and break more easily, while others have more resistance in the stuff of which they are made. The word "hypersensitive" implies the more tender, less resistant stuff: but when applied to the nervous subject, it also means more than that. It means protective tension, as if the stuff is always under extra strain.

These qualities are those of our inborn differences, but they are also modified by our experience when we are young. This is living tissue and it responds best to nourishment by love, which makes it both sensitive and strong; and worst to fear, which makes it either deadly hard, or, in more sensitive natures, fragile, brittle, and withdrawn. If we snap at children, they become "snappy" in return: if we overload them with responsibility or with anxiety, they may break under the strain: if we praise them one minute and blame them the next, this invisible texture becomes distorted and twisted. In fact, for better or worse, it is being modified by our reactions to experience all our lives. In alcoholics, drug addicts and after repeated anesthetics, some of this invisible psychic texture may be destroyed altogether. Its condition has much to do with our "nerves."

The Autonomic Nervous System

Now we can consider something more tangible and gather up the complex threads of the autonomic nervous system (A.N.S.). This is the "belly-mind," which coordinates the working of our inner world, in contrast with the brain and central nervous system (C.N.S.), whose task it is to coordinate our impressions from and actions in the exterior world. The A.N.S. is below the level of consciousness and therefore largely beyond the control of the conscious will. It is not entirely beyond our control, however.

On the material level of the visible autonomic nervous system, we have central nerve groups or "ganglia," which are a fine meshwork of nerve fibers gathered in certain places, such as the coccygeal plexus, sacral plexus, solar plexus, etc., which occur at various spinal levels in that order from below upwards. These are then connected by a pair of nervous "reins" to different organs in the body (e.g. genital area, stomach, heart, lungs, skin, etc.—almost everywhere in fact). I use the word "reins" to suggest the idea of guidance, because these nerve fibers can affect each organ either one way or the other, to make them breathe in or out as the case may be. These nerve fibers convey impulses that are either positive and expanding or negative and contracting: they are called "parasympathetic" and "sympathetic" fibers respectively. We must, therefore, complicate our over-simplified triangulation of figure 9, "Triangulation" (opposite), because each system within itself is similarly built, as related opposites plus link or bridge. That is to say, the autonomic nervous system has A (+) B (—) and C (linking) fibers. In figure 9, I have pictured these "triangulated" systems as existing on four levels, namely, (1) within the autonomic system, (2) between the A.N.S. and C.N.S. linked by the vagus nerve ("vagus" means "wanderer"), (3) within the central nervous system, and (4) between the two "worlds" of self and circumstance. Each of these systems is to be regarded as polarized (or triangulated, if you prefer) within itself, as well as in regard to each of the others.

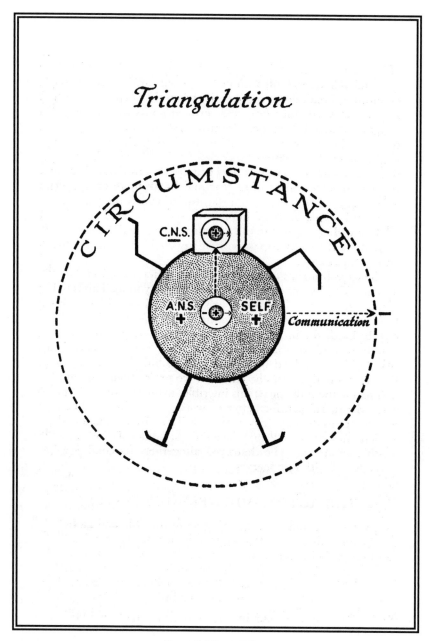

Figure 9 Triangulation

It must be realized, however, that as we shift in our relationship, so we may experience a change of sign or flow. For instance, the C.N.S. is relatively — to the A.N.S.+: but the outer world is relatively — to the C.N.S.+. "All things flow" and the significance of slope changes with a change in relationship. In this, our invisible anatomy of force is more mobile and fluctuating than our visible anatomy of form, but that is as it should be. If we understand the mobility of the "idea," we shall be less confused by the necessary fixity and inadequacy of anatomical labels. Here is the point about it all. The normal man is balanced and breathing between his positive and negative forces and is elastically bridged. The "nervy" man, however, is not bridged, and is in each case disposed to be upset by a preponderance of energy operating on the negative and contracting side. Normally, we feel self-confident, i.e. as if our voltage of energy is sufficient to overcome the resistance of the work to be done in the exterior world. The nervous man, however, experiences otherwise. His voltage is insufficient, and the slope of the flow of energy is thereby reversed. To put it briefly: "nerves" are "no's."

The distribution of the nerves of the autonomic system is very complex, but it may be understood in general that the sympathetic fibers serve the purpose of the protective withdrawal of the whole organism, while the parasympathetic fibers serve the purpose of advance and expansion. Stimulation of the sympathetic fibers is associated with our experience of *anxiety*; although it relaxes the muscles of the bronchi to increase the intake of air, it dilates the pupil, stimulates the secretion of adrenalin, contracts the peripheral arteries, the stomach and glands of digestion, and also the heart muscle, causing the common symptom of palpitation. Taken together, these all serve the same purpose of defense by fight or flight. On the other hand the parasympathetic fibers all invite co-operation with the exterior world, with expansion and *pleasure feeling* throughout the organism as a whole; the muscles of the bronchi contract (expiration and relaxation), the pupil narrows, the peripheral arteries expand (warmth), the stomach and salivary glands are stimulated and the heart beats slowly and quietly. On the whole, therefore, in the unbalanced oscillation between the two systems, the sympathetic extreme is towards anxiety, shrinking

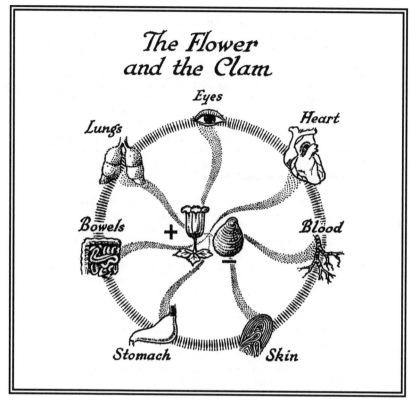

The Flower and the Clam

Eyes
Lungs
Heart
Bowels
Blood
Stomach
Skin

Figure 10 The Flower and the Clam

and closing up; but the parasympathetic fibers favor opening up and streaming out in pleasure towards the exterior world.

In figure 10, "The Flower and the Clam," I have drawn a simple pictorial representation of what is going on in the inner world of the autonomic system. Our "flowers" can open or our "flowers" can shut: that is to say, energy centers can either open or close, expand or contract, soften or harden, go slower or quicker, advance or retire, according to the needs of the organism as a whole. We are not concerned with a protective impulse of withdrawal on the part of any single organ, such as heart or lungs. It is not the organ itself which is in danger, but the whole organism. The reaction, therefore, is total, massive and general, although it may be particularly evident in regard to some special part, for reasons which I shall be discussing later (see Chapter 24, "Hysteria: The Great Reversal").

In the interior changes which take place in the A.N.S., we are either like open flowers or closed clams. We either open out or close up: and that is what and how we experience when we "feel." We experience these moves or changes of the rhythmic breath of inward life. We feel in the belly, as our nervous energies change their rhythm and routine. The solar plexus (I mean the chakram or "flower" which is invisibly situated there) is stirred: and we feel warm or cold, contented or disturbed, angry or afraid. We can feel very much disturbed inside and then, instead of being afraid of our exterior conditions, we are liable to be still more terrified by the interior disturbance of this primordial jellyfish, which we feel moving deep inside ourselves. We are then reminded of our long-forgotten inner world: our solid and familiar earth is rocked; we quake inside. This seems to be more dangerous than anything we know, because we know it not. So we set up a vicious circle, by escaping from our own escaping selves. This is panic; it is nervous energy gone mad, tormented by its own tactless efforts to escape.

When the flower or chakram of the solar plexus closes and withdraws, the nervous impulse is transmitted on all the negative (sympathetic) lines: ESCAPE: WITHDRAW: CONTRACT. If the heart gets the message, it rushes off in palpitations: if the stomach gets it, its reaction is lack of appetite (anorexia), nausea or vomiting: if the lungs get it, we catch our breath, feel choked and cannot breathe: in the throat a lump arises and we feel we cannot swallow (globus hystericus): the pupils dilate: blood is withdrawn from the skin, we go pale and break out in a cold sweat. All this is characteristic of the "sympatheticotonia," or spasmodic negative withdrawal, of the "nervy" man.

It is the evidence of our unconscious flight, as the fearful situation is inwardly escaped, rejected, and refused. Psychologically, this acutely negative state throws us off our balance, over to the male, exterior, active, contracting and destructive side. It should be noticed that our "nerves" are saboteurs, traitors both to ourselves and to the cause of more abundant life. *Physiologically*, the nervous reaction sets up the response which is called "allergic": by which we mean a state of compulsive protective spasm, with sudden discharge of energy. Examples of these allergic states are hay fever and acute catarrh, migraine and certain other kinds of headache, urticaria (a rash of the skin), asthma and what is called "acidosis" in children, which is a nervous condition of hypersensitivity, with symptoms of gastric disturbance and raised temperature. These are all due to a state of nervous irritability or hypersensitivity, as if the gun is fired by the merest inimical touch upon the nervous trigger. Resistance at the nervous bridge or "synapse" is diminished and relationships, both on the physical and emotional levels, are at fault. Chemically, the balance of the acid-base system is disturbed towards the acid-forming side.

The complex fibers of the A.N.S. are the visible "roads" and "bridges" on which our invisible "wheels" of energy must travel. If we can control the wheels, the roads will take care of themselves. In order to control our wheels, however, we must first control our fears.

Fears and Phobias

We must now consider the experience of fear in further detail. Fear is an interior emotional reaction, involving physical and chemical changes in the body, to an exterior situation which appears to threaten loss or danger. Fear is therefore a reaction to an experience of inadequacy. It is by no means the simple and unchangeable reaction that it sometimes seems to be, because the nature of the experience, the degree and quality of fear, depends upon both interior (subjective) and exterior (objective) factors, some of which are within the scope of our control, while others are not. For instance, fear is always fear of losing something. The more you have to lose and the less you are willing to lose it, the more you have to fear. With nothing that you are not prepared to lose, your life included, you have in fact no cause for fear at all. The measure of your experience of fear is therefore actually determined by your attitude to life or personal philosophy. Again, if your attitude to life permits misfortune without protest, you react the less fearfully when misfortune comes. The more you hope for easy peace and privilege, the more you have to fear. Moreover, if your attitude towards yourself permits that you should feel afraid, experiencing the full force of fear without being afraid of it, your fear will actually be less, because you are accepting it for what it is. Fear is not wrong: fear is a kind of truth for our experience on the emotional level. Flight is not necessarily wrong: it is sometimes wise. But our self-protective instinct does not fulfill our human needs, when it demands protection compulsively, unconsciously, and instantaneously.

Anxiety is experienced as we try compulsively to remove the cause of fear. There are so many causes, inside and out: how can they be removed? Anxiety is always a symptom of the nervous state, because it claims the right to overcome all threatening powers by resort to overwhelming power. The danger must depart, the problem must be solved: immediately, here and now. Anxiety is therefore an "attack," and we speak rightly of an "acute attack of anxiety." The symptoms may be any of these I have described: the cause is primitive escape from fear by magic use of power: the cure is to forgo power altogether and to let the experience resolve itself in time with deeper understanding of what it is all about.

Sometimes the anxiety attack is so extreme as to assume the intensity of what is called a "brainstorm." The release of energy is then like a bursting bomb and rushes through the brain as if the skull itself must burst. The victim wants to rush around and scream, in desperate fear that sanity is lost. It ends as a rule with numbness and coldness of the limbs, temporary collapse and sometimes loss of consciousness. Terrifying as such an experience must always be, it is never in fact as dangerous as it seems to the sufferer. It is not evidence of insanity, and rest and quiet will always restore complete recovery.

We can now trace the pattern of our frights and flights on various levels, to show more clearly the different unconscious subterfuges of the nervy man. On the autonomic level, his energy is withdrawn in various ways and may lead to fainting and collapse, or to any disturbances on the organic level through the stimulation of the sympathetic nerve supply to the affected part. This interior disturbance, being itself so provocative of fear, will lead to further fright and flight, in panic's vicious circle, setting up various "negative" responses within the instruments connected to this part of the nervous system, which I have already detailed, and of which we are again afraid.

On the mental level, there are certain irrational ideas, very highly charged with emotion, which are known as "phobias," or "fear-complexes." The object of fear is usually innocuous, but symbolic of some deeper source of fear. Common examples of such phobias are the fear of mice, which are harmless enough, but they serve to hide a deeper underlying sexual fear: of snakes, which are not so harmless in themselves, but again the fear is irrational and is related to deeper unsolved interior problems of potentially creative energy: the very common fear of spiders seems to indicate a deeper fear of our inward psychic sensitivity: and the fear of heights, in which there is usually an underlying feeling of insecurity, caused by some excessive claim on personal success that has been grasped instead of grown. All such phobias indicate an escape from the real underlying source of fear. They are protective in so far as they evade the point, by directing an unwieldy mass of emotion into a pigeonhole of comparative safety. Such unconscious devices for our mortal safety are far from being satisfactory, but they are as near to wisdom as our Ancient One can get.

In the relationship of the "nervy" man with the exterior world, there is a negative attitude of fear and flight again. Feeling so inwardly insecure and lacking in self-confidence, it feels to him as if there is some cause in the outer world which is to blame. It is all too much for him and he is overwhelmed by it. The responsibility of life is more than he can bear. He cannot face people or what they think of him. The burden is too heavy and the danger is too great. When we cannot face our overwhelming "relatives," the Ancient One arranges our escape, protectively.

Where to? There are two answers, for we may escape in either of two directions. Either we may go towards the amorphous and earlier state of our unconsciousness, returning, as it were, into that womb of "mother" from which we have emerged. This is a regressive direction, backwards out of life to a state of more complete dependence. The resort to invalidism provides a neat escape, because we are not to be blamed if we are ill. There is no malingering about it, because our defense is unconsciously provided by the Ancient One. We do not see the way in which our desire for power and privilege can exploit our weakness and our ills, as we demand relief and medical attention. The real source of fear must always be disguised, while some scapegoat or symptom is offensively pursued instead. That is why "nerves" are always resistant to treatment unless they are more clearly understood.

On the other hand, we may escape the other way, into the realm of consciousness itself, which should have been our willing bridge with life. Then we slip easily into the freedom of our thinking world, as refugees. We live within our mind's imaginings ("wishful thinking" escapes the problems which we dare not face), or else we become immersed in the study of knowledge, hoping thus to acquire a nice extension to our powers (but thinking does not add a cubit to our stature): or yet again we become busybodies, nagging incessantly in restless weakness against the problems that we cannot solve. None of these tricks uses consciousness as the means for our enlightenment, or as the organ of relationships and the living bridge with life which it should be. Instead, they make of it a bunkhole or a bludgeon. It is our human tragedy that we are allowed this personal freedom to misuse the marvels of our instruments.

In either case, "nerves" are a refusal to face reality, a rejection of relationship. That is why we can say that "nerves" are "no's." They are our inward, protective response to the unconscious demands for self-defense. They are evidence of the very ancient rule of the body over the body's needs: as ancient animals, surely we must protect ourselves? Of course we must, up to a point. But are we merely animals any longer? No, we are not: we are also human, angels with feet of clay, born of both worlds, conscious and unconscious, with an indomitable spirit incarnate in the weakness of our material flesh. We are like the Grecian centaur: animal below, but with human chest and head. The dictates of the body's scares in self-defense are no longer wise enough to rule the problems of our waking work. In fact, exactly the opposite is the case, and we must learn another, more sacrificial attitude to life. "Greater love hath no man than this, that he lay down his life for his friend." The lamb that has been slaughtered since the beginning of the world must learn in consciousness and in the most matter-of-fact way, the daily need for death and sacrifice. In life, we die to live: and others, too, must sometimes die that we may live. So what becomes of nature's ancient devices to provide our animal cowardice with all the mechanisms which unconsciously dominate the actions of the "nervy" man?

It is a nice problem and we must solve it if we can. There are several false solutions, which I will summarize. First, there is the ancient law of safety first, catch-as-catch-can; I'll keep out of danger and the devil take the hindmost. That attitude to life is still too common, but it will not work, because however hard we try to escape danger, we still take our pursuer with us, now firmly fixed inside ourselves. Second, there is a way of living in our heads alone, as reasonable men in a planned and conscious world. But that is no good either, because it is not true. We are not reasonable men; we are "nervy" men, slung within a dual rein of friend and foe. The world in which we live cannot be reasonably planned; it is too old and wise for that. "The best-laid plans of mice and men gang aft agley," because there are other forces in our world besides those we know. A wiser realism will allow for the invisible and mysterious elements. Third, there is a way of life called "humanism," which asserts that kindness and service towards our fellow men will solve the many problems of our lives. That is better, but it is only partly true. It is not true enough, because we are not gods and should not undertake so willingly a god's responsibilities. If we are partly gods, we are not only or entirely divine. Angels, with feet of clay: what about that lesser item, clay? That is going to need some patience and some other guidance than our own, before it can be redeemed. We must be very humble still, and wait upon some other, deeper wisdom than our own. Our hearts are not enough, however kindly they may be disposed. We need a deeper, wider willingness: a larger gift of life than we think reasonable. Life, for our human solution and salvation, demands all of us, not less. The price of our humanity is human sacrifice: the ancient wisdom said the price was Death.

So what becomes of the "Nervy" Man? Poor man, he is on the horns of his own dilemma. Sentimentalist and cynic, realist and dreamer, too—his problem is his life, his life is his problem. Escape as he may try to do and will, there is no final escape. So, in despair, he gives the problem up and faces it, at last. And in that simple gesture of his despair, his solution lies. He faces all his facts, accepting them as they occur. That is the proper attitude to life. That is our human sacrifice, and it will cure the "nervy" man of all his nervous state.

In case acceptance might seem to some too negative, I hasten to add that, whatever else it may be, our attitude to life must not be that. It is the positive aspect of our willingness, by facing life's adventures and misadventures with goodwill, which is the whole point of the healthy, wholesome life. The Chinese say that the greatest virtue in a woman is her willingness. Now, if we interpret that in terms of our invisible anatomy, we are all "woman" in a certain sense, within our hearts. Our greatest virtue, also, is in our willingness to suffer our experience exactly as it comes to us, and as it is. Only after that is done, can we as "men" (invisible anatomy again), do the best we can to change experience according to our light.

This method of tackling our experience would be the end, not only of our defensiveness, but also our offensiveness. It would be the end of all our fussiness, of anxiety and fear, of cruelty and all self-centeredness. But it would not be the end of our desire and effort for better things.

Healing Time

The healing of the "nervy" man requires the use of healing Time. We are the "nervy" man. We are the "city slicker" on his hurried way through life, acquiring what we can. Teachers, nurses, writers, readers, and doctors too, they all rush along their horizontal lines, harried themselves and harrying their charges towards some urgent goal. The healing light is not so fast as they are: it always shines, as we rush past it on our urgent way, but it is very slow. The vital rhythms and slowly moving tides of growth do not necessarily chime in time with clocks. Their pulses are their own and we must learn to wait awhile for them. So don't let us be so hurried in our haste to catch the morning train, or to finish the book we are reading, or to push the child through that exam, or that patient to recovery, or the confused and warring world into our plan. Ours is not the only hand that moves these complicated works. We who pride ourselves upon the quickness of our thoughts may reach the end before we have properly begun. All things must grow if we would have them in their rightful harmony: to be alive, the good must always grow.

We must learn to see ourselves as "cause" more often than we do. "IT" does not matter so much as we believe: "IT" is not the only bogeyman: "IT" is not the cause of all the trouble. We may be sure that we can only very rarely change IT, however hard we try; but, fortunately for our "nervy" state, we can always do quite a bit towards changing this unruly and mysterious "I." Perhaps that is what "Mind your own business" means. The cause of all our woes and fears is here, inside, in our invisible anatomy. For others a true philosophy of life may be a luxury; but it is a necessity for the "nervy" man. He must find faith or suffer worse than death. He can do either as he wills.

CHAPTER 7

The Holy Mountain

It is my own belief that any philosophy which is not based upon the essential recognition of the "Spirit" is inadequate, either for the description or for the practice of human life. As to the meaning of this word "Spirit," I shall have more to say in the chapters that follow, but it seems to me to be such an essential ingredient of life itself, that life is dead without it. I claim, therefore, that all "cause" is to be found on the level of the Spirit, and that all that is not Spirit rightly belongs to the level of "effects."

Although the concept of "Spirit" must be vague, yet there is one analogy that is traditionally used to make its meaning plain. It is a very near analogy to describe Spirit in terms of Light; as Light emerging and manifesting from a central source, and penetrating through the darkness that surrounds it.

Picture, therefore, a central light which is the creative Source, with rays radiant in all directions. Follow one ray until it lights up some object on its path, lighting within it, as it were, a little separate light or lantern. This new light then itself becomes another creative source, and it can repeat the same process from within itself, sending forth its rays, and giving birth again to other little lights. The living process is therefore one of extension in manifestation from a basic hierarchy, with each light capable, as it is created, of being a free and independent Creator in its turn, different and separate, yet also holding in its heart the image of its parent source.

In this simple story of Creation, the point to notice especially is the freedom that is given to each separate child to go forth and illuminate its own especial darkness in its own different way. But we as individuals do otherwise. We pour our life and light into certain

From *The Triumphant Spirit: A Study of Depression*

159

objects, whether they be written or spoken words, children or animals, facts or fantasies, and, having lit their lanterns with our own creative force, we do not send them forth. We like to keep them on a string instead, or locked within a ring for their imprisonment. We are not only attached to them, but we are also even identified with them. And so, when the time comes for us to lose them, as come it must, we mourn their loss the more, as if, by losing them, it is ourselves that die. So we are wise to watch this point and to realize that what our Light or Life or Love creates has, as its own free gift, its own separate way to follow, independent of ourselves.

Here is another point that I should like to emphasize, while using this analogy of Light. Although we may shine into the darkness, penetrating it with our rays and touching objects other than ourselves with light, we must not throw our Light itself into the darkness, or into objects other than ourselves. That is to say, we can work only through the emerging ray. The Light itself must be held, central and still, within the heart of our own lantern. We must not throw the fire away. We must not throw our own central fire at others, to force them to comply with our own wishes. Otherwise, although the darkness may be lit and others may have been forced to change for fear of being burnt, we shall have lost our light. We shall be dead, and it will not have profited us although we try to gain the whole world within the compass of our shooting star. To lose our central light is to collapse, and we must guard it within the lantern of our lives, or die.

This pattern can also be expressed by another earthly image. The flower, emerging through its stem from hidden roots, obeys a similar law and presents a similar pattern. From a single source, invisible, there emerge the many flowers, and each one in its heart holds the seed of another generation of creative life. So "Many" can spring from the heart of every single "One," in limitless extension of created life.

I suggest, therefore, that we can now make a picture with which to represent tentatively a philosophy of our creation. The human being is a child of two worlds, and must be represented in our picture as both descending from above as Light, and ascending from below, as living flowers do. It is as if a luminous bulb, within its ornamental shade, is suspended from above by an invisible flex, and falls to meet a rising flower emerging from its roots, themselves invisible within the heart of the Earth. We draw our nourishment from higher and from lower worlds. Each one is real and they are opposite: and at least half of each remains invisible.

And now I want to draw another picture in the reader's mind, which I will call "The Holy Mountain." First, as an abstract, it is a simple triangle, with its apex joined by a dotted perpendicular line to the middle of its base. That perpendicular is divided by three lines parallel to the base of the triangle into four equal parts. Now clothing the abstract pattern with a concrete form, the triangle becomes the Holy Mountain. At the apex shines a Light and the perpendicular becomes a tortuous path down which the Traveler descends towards the earthly valley at the base below. His way is barred four times as he descends, until his journey is complete and he is born, a human child, on earth below. The path he has to travel is his "fall," from Heaven to Earth, before he is born as an individual sinner, free to rise and fall some more as he continues on his earthly path. He starts as "spirit," or as an undifferentiated sexless angel: he arrives below, incarnate, sexually and personally differentiated and equipped as a child ready to become man or woman.

Emerging and arriving on Earth, he has four garments on his back, or instruments at hand. His earthly incarnation now complete, he has no heavenly powers at all. He is born a baby now, and has to grow within the strangeness of his earthly frame. Before going any further with his story, I must explain the four garments or instruments, which he has acquired by paying for each their proper price. The first was his "spiritual body," the function of which is knowing. The second was his "mental body," the function of which is thinking. The third was his "emotional body," the function of which is feeling. The fourth was his "physical body," the function of which is doing. (Of these divisions of the self, more will be said later.) Now composed, as it were, of the four "elements," fire, air, water and earth, he is born—a woman or a man. But he is born a baby first and from this small beginning he must grow until the end. He is still a traveler and although he has already fallen so

Figure 11 The Holy Mountain

far from his angelic source, he must go on falling, again and again, to grow in stature as he lives on Earth.

His entry into life is marked by someone's tragic and unavoidable pain before he can be born. His mother must buy his earthly ticket for him, and make her willing sacrifice. Although no one can doubt the blessings of anesthesia, with which the mother may reduce to some extent the price that she must pay, yet no one should hope that any skill can take away altogether the price of suffering that Life exacts. The symbolism of birth is fearfully true in its presentation of the obstructing wall, and of the Stranger at the Gate, and of the price that must be paid for Life.

Having arrived on Earth, a mortal and incarnate "self," our traveler proceeds upon his own especial path. Let us hope that he has forgotten his one-time heavenly powers and left his clouds of glory far behind, because if he remembers them he may be tempted to rattle too much upon his prison bars. His box is very small, his energies are weak, and only the obstructing walls are strong. His falls continue. He falls from the protective comfort of his mother's knee, and bumps into the nursery. He falls from the protective comfort of the nursery, and bumps into his schoolfellows. He falls asleep and falls in love. With falls and bumps he grows, and buys his tickets as he grows until he is mature, a Man; but still the falls and bumps continue, for the obstructing wall is always there, with other Strangers at the Gate, and always new tickets to be bought as the price of his experience.

We can observe his "goodwill" or "willingness" upon the one hand, and his ardent "will" upon the other. These are related and inseparable, like the two halves of any living breath. With willingness and all goodwill he enters into things, and enjoys the very heart of them, sensitive, receptive, observant and intelligent, using all his instruments each in its proper way, to tell him partial truth at least about the obstructing elements that beset his path. He is a very sensible man, as well as sensitive, and he burrows his way along with least resistance, like a cheese mite through cheese. He is willing to be very accurate and judges all things for what they are and not for what they ought to be. In fact, he is "scientific," as long as we remember that he has more instruments with which to make contact with life than Science yet admits. But watch his finely tempered will. As well as his "goodwill" or "willingness," he has a living backbone ($0-1-2-3-4-5$, the perpendicular) that must be kept tempered, straight and true. It must not kink or twist, nor ever break as a softer wishbone would. Neither appetite nor desire nor imagination must ever become separated from the wholeness of this persistent instrument, this boring flame, this brightest diamond-thread, the Will.

Of course, there is no reason why our willing traveler should not enjoy himself as he travels along the time-track of his earthly road. He has desires and appetites, and life can be very good to him. After all, it is in his own image and it is rightly part of him for his enjoyment, in experiment and discovery. But he must keep his light burning brightly in himself, and keep his spirits up, because life is not always good. Indeed, it can be very bad for him. Then he must keep his temper true, his courage right, and his Will burning with the essential hardness of its high bright flame. Then he must face his brick walls with a minimum of personal resistance, and a maximum of willing goodwill. He must lighten himself of some of his load, laying back his wing tips, as it were, the better to get the arrowhead through the little holes in the target. Sharp-pointed, straight, he will get through all right, if he is not overloaded by his attachment to good things. Nothing in our experience is too bad, if we tackle it in the right spirit. That is to say, if we approach it "lightly." The only sin that matters is the sin of separation, wherein we lose the wholeness of ourselves by sticking too heavily to our separate parts and pieces.

In life, we must work and we must pay to work. The kind of work we have to do is rather like Alice getting through the keyhole into her Wonderland, or the rich man getting into heaven. We must get down to it, and get into it, before we can get through it. It is as if life is pouring through little holes, the whole through the holes, the one through the many.

Because I think that it is very important to understand this process, I am going to try once again to illustrate the significance of it. Life can be so "thrilling." What does "thrilling" mean? The origin and construction of the word is interesting, because it illustrates the same idea of force being blown through the keyhole. The Oxford English Dictionary defines a thrill as "a penetrating influx of emotion." The meaning is more plain, however, when we consider the cognate words of similar origin, "thirl" (nostril) and "thrall." A "thirl" is a small aperture; a "thrall" is a slave. The idea, therefore, which is in the word "thrill" is that someone has to go through something, or something has to go through someone. The thrill of Life is experienced when we are going through it, or when it is going through us. To get the thrill of it, we must be prisoners, enslaved, because large forces can only operate through such small focal points.

"Resistance is a good thing" (figure 12, p. 166) places the meaning in pattern form, and illustrates the process of a thrill. As "persons" we are located at such focal points. We are the blowholes of the spirit, and into personality is focused the creative power of life. (N.B. Personare-to sound through.) Life is made manifest through us and we are the instruments for its re-focusing. It is impossible, therefore, to over-emphasize the importance of personality, by which I mean the unique quality of everyone, which must be different from that of every other person. Every one of these focal points is in its essential nature apart from all others. Human life never repeats itself and we must either find ourselves, or else he is always somewhat lost. No one else can find us, and no one else can lead us. We must find the way ourselves.

In the process of self-discovery I hope that I have by now made plain that what we experience as resistance (the wall) is not a "bad" thing, but a good one. It is the stuff that personality is made of, and it is also the stuff that makes personality. The creative energy is released by that which can contain and obstruct it, and without resistance it cannot do its work. The vital flow in which we live is not a simple fall, like rain or dew from Heaven. It is driven through a great resistance, before it can be made sufficiently tame and disciplined for us to handle such a fiery steed.

This is the meaning of Jacob's wrestling with the angel (Genesis 32:24). We must all wrestle with Life, not only with such problems as may beset us, but also with such forces and talents as we may be so fortunate as to possess. They must be tamed and

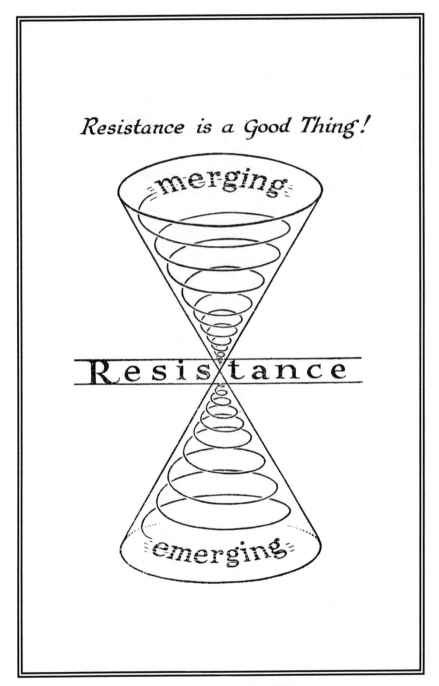

Figure 12 Resistance Is a Good Thing!

overcome, or we shall be either destroyed or inflated by them. The greatest danger to our personal well-being comes from the powerful "angels" who emerge from sources deep within ourselves. Tamed and aptly fitted to their little tasks, and passed through the sieve of many little holes, they can make life thrill with creative joy. Untamed, undisciplined, and flying loose in their angelic freedom, they are very devils, because they have not been properly caught as spirits incarnate within the prison of our human flesh. Then they possess and will continue to destroy us, until we have wrestled them into place, as disciplined and willing prisoners, with patience inexhaustible.

Thus the human problem must always be a double one, as we stand between two fires, from above and from below, from without and from within. This is no easy, peaceful part to play, and the human battlefront requires all the virtues of the earthly battlefield, with more patience, more courage, and infinite goodwill. In fact I have never been able to detect any evidence of a "Heavenly Father" wishing us to have an easy time, while he prepares a still more comfortable place for us. As I see God's mind in action, He is working very hard to secure our intelligent cooperation with His plan, to which end we are developing our Consciousness, or spiritual insight. Heaven knows, He must be patient, because we are taking a very long time to recognize the part that we are being so carefully "groomed" to play, as partners cooperative in a great creative design.

The kind of freedom that the spirit needs is the freedom to find its own right keyhole when it needs, and to blow through it just that kind of noise that it requires to make. Each one must be free to find his own keyholes and to make his own contribution to the fullness of Life. Freedom from bondage we can never have, but freedom to build our own prisons, and work within them (without rattling the bars!) according to the guidance of our inner light— that freedom we can and we must rightly claim. For freedom of the spirit, we must be free to choose.

Out of Light into Darkness, the positive energy of the emerging Spirit becomes incarnate in the negative framework of the space-time world. Thus matter and life are compounded out of Yin and Yang, Light and Darkness, Positive and Negative, or Good and Evil, which still remain their two indwelling, opposite, and embattled elements. In the absence of the positive, expanding, emerging and radiant light of the Spirit, we are left in the dark, uninspired, dead, evil and ill. We are lost without this Light to guide us.

Into our earthly bodies, with their four "elements" of fire, air, water, and earth, the Spirit, already implicitly dwelling, is still being poured. We are actually using it, living on it and living in it, whether we know it or not. Without it, we become dispirited, and it is therefore of great importance to our health to know how we lost this precious "Heavenly Fire," and, having lost it, how we may safely get it back. This light or spirit is our Healer. That material dust, or dark layer, in which we are enshrouded, as spirits in a tomb, or as prisoners in a prison, is not evil in itself. It only becomes evil in so far as we become one with it, losing our unity with the source of light in doing so; and we had better know how strongly and deeply those dark bits of us resent and resist the light! There is no welcome waiting here to embrace the other half. The Puritans, the Calvinists, and the old Evangelists were right. "The world, the flesh and the Devil" are all wrong if they are by themselves, or if they have turned successfully against the spirit which is in the midst of them. But, being wrong, they must not then be avoided or escaped. Rather they become the goal and purpose of the Spirit, as darkness is the goal of dispelling light. The problem of the Spirit, however, is always to discover how it may enter into those who churlishly refuse it, without having resort to force or battery. That is the external and mechanical way of darkness and dictators. It cannot therefore be the way of the indwelling Light.

The indwelling Light, or Healer, effortlessly holds the tension within the actual constellation of defined events. This is the spiritual or heavenly way of Love, fighting and striving in this way only to enter into the heart of the enemy. This is also the vital way, which is the way of Health. It is the way of Christ, as it is of the Chinese "TAO." It is the mysterious way of Life.

But Lucifer, whose is the way of mechanized external power, attacks all problems by force as from outside (space-time side) and cuts out all that he regards as evil, in no-time if he can. He also collects "good," assuming that it exists thus by itself, in the largest quantities he can. His is the earthly way of unenlightened human effort, glamorized, identified, confused and always fighting to be rid of the encumbering resistance of some imagined enemy. This is the mechanical and "evil" way of the destroyer. It is as typical of an "attack" by Hitler as it is of an attack by a disease.

Saint and sinner, friend and enemy, inanimate and animate, animal and man, to say that all things are glowing with the living God is literally true. But such an "animistic" or pantheistic philosophy betrays us, for as human dwellers on this earth we are not as all things are. We have a job of work to do, which is, in conscious cooperation with the Law behind the scenes, through consciousness in Mind, to effect the movement forward into consciousness not only of the unenlightened remainder of ourselves, but of all others too. We are the vanguards of a certain process of expanding Mind. It is our privilege to lead the way, and meanwhile to act as scouts, reporting our discoveries to others wiser than ourselves.

CHAPTER 8

The Psychic Compass

The story of creation which I told in the previous chapter, with its moving pattern, may remind us of the angels who ascended and descended the ladder, which stretched from Heaven to Earth in Jacob's dream. Like the angels in the dream, we are also moving up and down within a certain range, each of us occupying a different place in the cycle of experience. Comparisons are odious, if they imply that any of us should be other than we are. In fact, at any moment of our existence, we cannot be other than we are; and where we are, now, is where the work needs to be done. There is room for all upon the ladder of experience, and all can play their parts, by working where they are. It is no use envying the higher place which someone else may occupy. Height, as a standard of measurement in personal affairs, is always false, and the best work is often done below. In any case, each must depend on others differently placed, and it is the unity and wholeness of the team, and not merely height above a certain base line, that counts for moral quality.

To change the illustration, and thereby perhaps to make more plain the way of working in a team, we can think of how a candle burns. That, I think, is very much like life. At the base, or lowest level, we have the solid wax. Next comes the liquid molten wax, and then the unburned gas, and finally the flame. In reverse order, we have Fire (combustion), Air (gas), Water (liquid) and Earth (solid), which are the four familiar "elements," corresponding to the four "levels" which I described in the previous chapter, "The Holy Mountain". Together, united in a team, but not always joined in harmony, those four different elements comprise the wholeness of our Selves. We are like candles, burning with the fire of Life.

From *The Triumphant Spirit: A Study of Depression*

The energy of life works through those four levels, in four different ways. Starting from the top, we recognize the "Will," as the central fire within our lives. Then comes "Imagination," which is "in the air," too free unless it is linked with, and imprisoned in, the levels lower down. Next comes "Desire," in which the first free Will is caught within the bonds of personality. And finally, our "Appetites" speak of the many needs within our hungry, and always unsatisfied, physical bodies. These four aspects of the vital force set us a nice problem in alignment and relationship, if we are to live as one efficient whole.

How is that to be done? The first clue to understanding how life works this miracle in its own way, is to understand that we are TUBES. Whether we are flowing through life, or whether life is flowing through us, does not matter much, because it seems that both are true. The tube is the instrument through which life breathes, and each single personality is the trumpet through which the spirit sounds.

So let us get down to tubes. We *are* tubes, when we come to think of it! We are made up of a complicated system of tubes, always with something flowing through. Our body as a whole is tubular: arms and legs, toes and fingers, are all tubes. Our eyes, our skin, our ears are tubes. Our food canal, our blood vessels, our lungs and our nerves—all these are tubes as well. Life is a very tubular business and, crosscut it where we will, we find a simple circle in ourselves. And if we lay these circles side by side, we find a tube again. With inner and with outer circles, we are travelers—by tube!

Let us take TIME. Is not that tubular, too? The only Time we really know is NOW, and that is circular. At any moment, NOW, we are ringed round by our conditions, circumstantially. The NOW encircles us, and if we lay these circles side by side in a long line, from birth to death, we are long tubes, like sausages, with every moment, NOW, cutting off a single slice. Again, we are travelers by tube.

But all these tubes are clocks as well, and this is a very important part of the Law we know as TIME. Traveling takes Time, and all our travelers experience Duration, in varying terms. Some travel fast, some slow, but somehow all our different travelers, within the

172

living system of our bodies, are miraculously coordinated together in such a way as to make them fit in with each other, so that the many parts that make up the whole can work as one. We might well admire this clever trick, and wish that all the members of our human society could work together as smoothly and efficiently! But alas, free will makes havoc of our social clocks! We're all too busy beating time to stop and watch it beat. And so it beats us in the end, in sorrow and confusion.

Ladders, candles, tubes and clocks! If that seems too much of a medley, it is not more so than we are ourselves. But we are getting down to something. What happens when we try to stop the steady flow of circulating life? What happens when we try to push back the hands of the clock, or to push them on a bit faster, with impatient hands, to suit our own convenience? The consequence will certainly be up to us, and we shall be responsible for damage done. With tubes blocked, clocks broken and rungs missing in the ladder, the candle will go out. And then is the proper time for us to learn from Life how to get it all going again. But, let us remember well, that "constipation" or "fixation" or ill temper or untimeliness all lead to our ill health. They mean the end of life!

To learn from life: there's the rub! However much we may be willing and able to learn from our experience, the lessons which we learn must still depend upon our attitude to life, because it is ultimately our philosophy that will decide the value and meaning of our experience. If we should chance to run away, with our backs turned towards experience, how can life teach us anything? Yet to escape from suffering is the chief motive in some folks' philosophy. Others have such definite ideas about what life *ought* to be, that they can never stop to notice what life *is*.

So let us get down to a working philosophy. Let us draw a plan, and see if it will work. Let us call it Psychic Compass, (Figure 13, p. 175) because it shows the way. Its construction is quite simple. First, we draw a circle, because that is the proper pattern in which to enclose the all-round self. Then we divide it by a horizontal line, to show that there are upper and lower elements in our all-round man. Part angel and part animal (HUM-AN-IMAL), he has not one nature, but two, and they are enemies. Therefore he can find no

sanction for his conduct in either of his worlds, by simple accla-
mation that "It's only natural!" Part of himself is still up at the top
of the hill, and part is down below. That is his problem.

But there is more to it than that. He is not simply divided into
two parts, but into four. And so we draw another line, vertical this
time, to divide his left side from his right, and his inside from his
outside. These two parts are also enemies, and each cannot tell
what the other part is doing. All his parts are strangers to each
other, yet each one has a proper part to play within the whole.

We now have four quarters in our psychic compass, and number
them off, as we did the stages on the Holy Mountain. "Nought" is at
the center, the starting point. "One" is at the top left corner, "two" is
at the top right, "three" is at the bottom left, and "four" is at the bottom right-hand corner of the circle. "Five" sees the finish where we
began, but a spiral higher on Life's endless circuit. These numbers
(0)–1–2–3–4–(5) represent the same four stages on the journey
from Heaven to Earth as we have seen before, and they correspond
with the four "elements" of "Fire," "Air," "Water" and "Earth",
respectively. Our ladder will look a bit twisted, but the dotted line
down the Holy Mountain, which was our traveler's path, must now
wind to and fro. To complete the cycle of his journey, he goes
(0)–1–2–3–4–(5), and crosses his Rubicons, meets his barriers and
buys his tickets as he goes, just as he did before.

So far we have his four instruments only numbered; but they
are also related to each other, as No. 1–upper, inner; No. 2–upper,
outer; No. 3–lower, inner; No. 4–lower, outer. Our Psychic Compass,
properly set, must BREATHE. This it does by alternately swinging
from one opposite to the other, and from one level to the other:
inner (one)–outer (two)–inner (three)–outer (four), and so on,
to and fro and down and up. It is thus the principle of alternation
and opposition implied by the "odd" and "even" numbers that is
of importance, rather than the serial order or the numerical values of the numbers by which we are referring to them here. The
swing from "odd" to "even" and back again, represents this breathing movement between the inner and outer, upper and lower. So
life flows and breathes. So also it grows, obeying each in turn the
orders of its tubes and clocks.

174

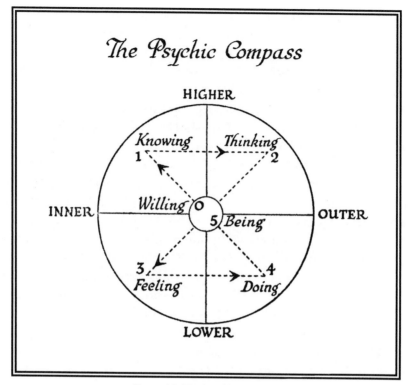

Figure 13 The Psychic Compass

Each instrument is related to its special task, and is equipped to work only on its own level. Each has to learn to mind its own business, and to get on with it, in proper time and place. Each belongs to its own place and level, and knows no other. It never does to mix them up, at will.

The quality of the upper half is "universal," but the lower is "personal"; that is, the act of incarnation is developed on the lower level to a further stage. The quality of the upper half is on the level of ideals and ideas, but in the lower we are dealing with personal desires, feelings and activities.

The quality of the "left" or "inner" side of the psychic compass is dark, passive, "unconscious" and essentially feminine. But let me say at once that it is not negative, so that negative definitions will not suffice. We do not describe a woman by saying that she is "not a man." Such negative definitions are always not only unjust, but rude. They simply cannot be true. To call any part of the self "unconscious" is both unjust and rude, because it sets up the opposite state of "consciousness" as if it were the right and proper, and indeed the only, judge. Each part of the whole, if left to itself, will always regard the other parts as negative, unfriendly and inferior. But no part is better than the rest, because it cannot do its work without the others to assist. The whole is good: the parts are only good in so far as they can serve the whole.

The "outer" or "right" side of the psychic compass is the easier to describe, because it deals in measurable quantities. It is adapted to the familiar outer and external world. It is concerned with the world of "objects," which we are able to discern and describe, because we are outside them. In our relationship to all these external objects, we are, or should be, "objective." That is to say, we can know of their existence only in so far as we can stand apart from them. The preposition which belongs to this external world of measurable quantities is "AT." It is this kind of experience that we are always "at," actively, but we can do so only if we stay outside it.

There is also quite another kind of "knowledge," which belongs to the other, inner, aspect of the "self." The preposition that belongs here is not "AT," but "IN." We are always IN this inner world, and from it we can gain "insight" into the inside aspect of events, if only we can open passively to receive impressions, as they flow into us, invisibly.

So far, I have only tried to show the meanings of our various psychic parts. Surely there must be familiar words to convey these meanings in our daily lives? Of course there are, not once, but many times.

The advantage of our psychic compass is that it will tell us not only what words mean, but also how these functions work and what their limits are. It will allow other words to fit, too, such as (1) insight, the higher psychic faculty, inspiration; (2) conceptual imagination; (3) sensitivity, suffering, pathos and the psychic powers that go with mediumship on the lower level; (4) physical science, measurable data within the field of normal perception. The first level is mystical; the second, philosophical; the third, artistic; the fourth, practical or scientific. Each is "true" and "real," within its proper limits; but each requires the others, to fulfill the balanced whole. In a rough and ready "journalistic" way, we speak of "mind" (2) and "body" (4), to express our recognition of the upper and lower halves. We speak also of "spirit" (1) and "matter" (2, 4); or of "heart" (3) and "head" (2). Our psychic compass, however, sets each one of these loosely used names into a certain place, order and relationship: i.e. spirit (1); mind (2); heart (3); body (4).

C. G. Jung has offered a classification and analysis of the psychic parts that make up our larger whole by describing "intuition," "thought," "feeling" and "sensation" as the four functions of the psyche. Although these terms correspond in general with my meanings, they have certain disadvantages which make them unsuitable to fulfill the basic purpose for which I am using the psychic compass. For instance, there is no verb in common use by which to describe our exercise of the faculty of intuition, though the word "to intuit" is sometimes used. I propose, therefore, to use the simpler verb "to know," and to accept the noun "knowledge" as being significant of the contribution of intuition, at least at the beginning. It is by intuition that we receive immediate knowledge, not arrived at by a process of reasoning. So WILLING starts us on the course of birth, from zero at the center, and proceeds to KNOWING, at (1). Thence we proceed through THINKING, at (2), to FEELING, at (3), and at last arrive at DOING, or ACTION, at (4), which brings us into BEING, and so through (5) to (0) again, to start another round. I have abandoned the use of the word "sensation" for the fourth corner as being commonly confused with "feeling" in the sense of "affect," as for instance when we describe the "feeling" of pleasure or pain as having a certain pleasant or painful "sensation." "Sensation," in the stricter sense of sensory experience leading to perception, is included in the wider term "action." Our senses are the instrument through which we make our contact with the external world in which we act.

Inevitably, I am afraid, there must be some confusion in our use of the word "consciousness." I can see no way out of it, other than to realize that it must mean different things according to its place in our experience, for which we have, as yet, no different words. I would like, therefore, if I can, to make plain at this point how this word "consciousness" fits into the psychic compass. I have already said that I do not approve of the word "unconscious," because all negative definitions are bound to be unsatisfactory and improperly biased. We might, for instance, invent the word "in-conscious" for the left-hand side of the compass, and then "ex-conscious" would do for the objective and external side. It then becomes apparent that the whole of the psychic compass, and each one of its separate functions, is conscious, *but in a different way.* What we usually call "consciousness," and associate with "thought" at the second corner of the compass, is really better called "self-consciousness" or human consciousness. It is at this point that the human race has stepped off the animal level and acquired something more in its mysterious evolution that the animals so far had never had. *We can get outside ourselves, and see ourselves objectively, at least to some extent,* but I can find no word with which to describe this experience satisfactorily. When man turned through that strange right-angle and experienced the vertical instead of the horizontal dimension, he saw something that no animal had ever seen before, not even a monkey in a mirror: man saw *himself as his own self.* He said, "This is me." We cannot claim yet to have progressed very far in our capacity to make use of this mysterious advantage. I think that we are only beginners yet, but that meanwhile we have much to learn about how not to misuse the powers that are invested in our psychic instruments. Of this I shall have more to say; but I want to make quite plain at this point that I believe it to be important to recognize that all life is "conscious" within certain limits and that there are many grades of "consciousness." It is this "consciousness" which is the life-force, and it is growing and extending, as it works its way forwards and outwards, expanding its frontiers and increasing its powers as it goes. In our human consciousness we have one of its most advanced front lines. We are in the trenches not merely for ourselves, but also as witnesses and combatants in this most important and mysterious battle. There are many names for the Traveler, for we are all such travelers. But one of the general names for him is Consciousness, and as such he travels everywhere.

Working and sleeping, we "breathe" between our outer and our inner worlds and their appropriate instruments. In sleep, we shut off the activities of the external world, and close our "2/4" instruments, to enter passively into the "1/3" level of experience. The world of dreams is "real" enough, because it is real to us, and yet it is not real to the 2/4 side of ourselves. In insanity, we lose our contact with, and our adaptability in regard to, the 2/4 world; we have become submerged and lost in 1 and 3. In death, we are divested of all our instruments like outworn garments; but in sleep we are very near to death, in closest similarity with that mysterious state. The great difference is that from sleep we can awake, but from our journey into death no such assured continuous return to consciousness is possible.

For those who like their definitions clearly in front of them, I offer the following, for which I am indebted to the Oxford English Dictionary:

(1) *Intuition: General*: Direct or immediate insight.

Scholastic philosophy: The spiritual perception of immediate knowledge, ascribed to angelic and spiritual beings, with whom vision and knowledge are identical.

Modern philosophy: The immediate apprehension of an object by the mind without the intervention of any reasoning process.

(2) *Thought*: Formation and arrangement of ideas in the mind.

(3) *Feelings*: Passive experience of an object, through having experienced its effects.

(4) *Action*: Process or condition of acting or doing; the exertion of energy or influence; working, agency, operation. The way in which an instrument acts; also, the mechanism by which this is effected.

Sensation: Perception by means of the senses (sight, hearing, smell, taste, touch).

But again I would emphasize that these functions do not rightly exist apart, and that they can only be understood in their relationship with each other. Seen alone, our understanding of them must always be somewhat at fault. Seen together, they may be seen whole, but then they may not be seen at all. That is one of our difficulties.

Although the proper working of our Psychic Compass requires that we should travel through each corner of the psychic field in turn, breathing rhythmically to and fro according to the tides of life, we can gain some knowledge of the different corners if we consider each one separately. We must not forget, however, that the parts comprise the whole, and that we shall still be left with the more important problem of their right relationship.

The first corner. Here we are still very close to the source and origin of life, and to the place of ecstasy, immortal, timeless and alone. It is immaculate, because it is the place of all that has not yet started on Life's journey. Its angels are still unborn, and they dwell in Heaven, as one united choir. It is therefore very tempting as a resting place, or as a haven to which to return, but once we have started out, we must not try to hurry back. There is so much work to do. We must get down to it and do the job that lies below.

Having emerged from the center and turned this corner, the traveler takes "0" with him, and through it he maintains his original contact with the hidden, obscure, invisible center of himself. It remains with him, as his guiding star and undying, although invisible, light. It is the channel through which he is nourished from the center of original life; it is never to be satisfied, and yet should be unquenched, no matter what happens to the traveler upon his journey through experience. Here is a source of universal knowledge, timeless and unvarying. Here is the seed of all wisdom and truth, the "creative" from which all life must grow, the precious, priceless stone, mysterious beyond all other mysteries.

Here is intuition, insight, inspiration. But, undisciplined and misinformed, here is the royal road to vanity, impatience and inefficiency. And here is energy, the quality of fire, the source of the living ray of light. It is very hot up here and very dangerous for mortal minds to have too much of it. Our safeguards here must be infinite patience and uttermost restraint. It is safe for priests, perhaps, if they are very wise, but not for others less well-disciplined. For the rest, it is better down below.

The soldier-priest, or savior-destroyer, finds that this corner is the very Devil. Alas, poor Lucifer. He jumped from "one" to "four," and burned the fuses of the world, with lightning flashing from his sword of perfect Truth. We were not ready then. We are not ready now. Indeed, we never shall be ready for such a sudden overdose of Truth. The sword needs tempering. The spirit is omnipotent, it is true, but only if it takes an eternity of time to do its work and to achieve its ends. These timeless folk are ill-tempered, and so very cross when they are crossed. They do not know the meaning of the cross, and make of it instead a Nazi, a crooked thing, bent to the cross-less purpose of intolerant and arrogant self-will. Of course, they always know that they are right, these arrogant ones. But Heaven knows that to be merely right is not enough! It causes most of the wrongs that the poor suffering world has ever known; because it is no better than self-righteousness.

The second corner gives us a bird's eye view of life. It is the corner in which "mind" reigns supreme, with all the power that knowledge gives. Here are philosophers, teachers, scientists, the learned professions and the leaders of all the blind and murmuring crowds below. Here is a great responsibility. Those who dwell here are our modern "magicians," whose work is either "black" or "white," according to whether their powers are used for the welfare of the many, or to serve the privileges of the selected few. Their responsibility is the more, because there are always so many who depend upon their leadership, without ever knowing whither they are going, or how they should be led.

There is another danger here. Having a bird's eye view of life, why bother to live at all? Why not stay up in the air, and merely think about it all? Why not design good plans for living, and then just leave it at that? So here is the happy hunting ground of all the refugees from life, who would rather live in their imaginations than face the facts and come down to earth. Living in the air, we are not hurt so much. We say that it is better so. We are idealists, we think. Yet if we do not get down to it and face the facts within our own experience, we are only refugees, more anxious to escape from suffering than to live. We are very privileged, up here. Let us not forget that we are mostly leaders and teachers, too; and if we are only refugees at heart, how can we teach those others to be any different from ourselves?

The third corner. I must be content to fail in my description of this corner, falling into error with enough humility. Here is, in fact, the lower aspect of the "indescribable." It is a confusing corner, in more ways than one! The reader must be content with such scanty information as I can give, and add to it himself from his own imagination and experience.

Here is a creative and mysterious source of energy wrapped in primordial darkness, seeking for employment, but in itself undifferentiated and so far unemployed, until it finds its expression or manifestation at "2" or "4." It is unharnessed "chaos," but it is intensely dynamic. It is like the boiler-room or power-house of a ship or factory, from which energy is drawn for living work. As a source of steam, it needs a piston and a cylinder to give it proper incarnation, or it just "blows off" or "blows up."

It is the heart of life and in it the "impersonal" can become very "personal," especially through our experience of, and attitude towards, suffering. It is the heart of all creative life, and the artist in us all depends upon its fertilizing stream for his inspiration. It contains a sort of primitive stuff of which we must make good use, and master it, or it may master us. It is the source of personal desire and so of all self-will. It is our special driving force and needs proper and continuous employment. We sometimes call it "guts." We know it as a source of strength, of endurance and of the will to live. It is therefore a very important part of our psychic "backbone," and as such it can enable us to stand up against such difficulties as may beset us.

As the organ of personal sensitiveness, it is the instrument of the aesthetic function. It is the source of what we call "feeling," or what the Greeks called "pathos." It gives us a personal measurement of the quality or meaning of experience. We say "It feels to me as if . . .," and in this way we report what this aesthetic instrument has registered in regard to a certain aspect of reality. Unfortunately, however, few of us can let this instrument of suffering work without interference. In this corner of our psychic field, we must always experience conflict and find ourselves divided against ourselves. Desire steps in and falsifies the movement of the needle of our psychic galvanometer, because we wish it to register only "pleasure." We will not let it register "pain" or "loss," if we can help it. The two aspects of "desire" and "suffering" become confused, which is a pity for several reasons. For good work, they must be kept apart, so that on the one hand we can go on wanting, and on the other hand we can go on suffering because we have not what we want. Otherwise, we suffer more in the end and do not gain the full advantage of our suffering.

Ruskin, in *Modern Painters*, refers to the "pathetic fallacy," and his observation and description fits exactly into our customary misuse of this aesthetic faculty. He says, "All violent feelings produce a falseness in impressions of external things, which I would generally characterize as the 'pathetic fallacy'." We are all guilty at times of this protopathic emotional overloading of our epicritic judgment. Even the most careful observers allow such words as "always," "never" and "only" to take the place of the calmer "sometimes," "rarely" and "on this occasion."

There is no doubt that proper suffering, or sensitive acceptance of experience, is a great teacher, as well as a builder of our psychic character. Endurance is good for the soul's growth. It is as if we have here a kind of stomach in which experience is absorbed and digested, thus building up the structure of our whole psychic body. All experience is nourishing, if it can only be passed fairly through this sensitive filter. Thus both we and it finally become purified and purged of our personal habits of fixation. This, I think, is where the Christian teaching comes to earth. It shows how the state of sin (separation) can be redeemed (paid for) through suffering (acceptance), so that each one in his own way, and through his own experience, may in time be made whole again.

There are certain other aspects of this third corner of our psychic field which need to be mentioned. It is a lower psychic field of experience, chaotic, primitive, instinctive, undeveloped. Its nature is savage and animal in quality, and in deep need of fine development. It is a " protopathic continuum," by which I mean to imply that it is like a ball of many colored wool that needs to be sorted, unraveled, and woven into a fitting garment.

It is the source of all those lower primitive types of what is known as "mediumship." It is the organ of psychic sensitivity in paranormal phenomena, from poltergeist to prophecy. It is used by people who are said to be "psychic," as indeed we all are to some extent and in different degrees. It is, however, not necessarily a laudable or desirable gift to possess. It is highly dangerous and a grave responsibility to the possessor. In general, children have more of it than adults, because we lose it as we grow more into the real external world. Women have it more than men, because in them as a rule the "1/3" is stronger than the "2/4" side. For the same reason, all artistic natures are also somewhat more psychically sensitive. It is more prevalent in simple than in cultivated races, because it is characteristically and essentially undeveloped, and immature. It is the beginning out of which the end is still to be made.

This function is used in fortune telling, in witchcraft and, somewhat less, in magic. There are people who can tell fortunes, though they do not always succeed in doing so accurately, because desire is usually stronger in them than is pure insight (so-called "second sight"). Witchcraft may be no longer recognized as a profession, but witches still exist in our society. They are people who possess certain powers, because they have let themselves be possessed by them. Witchcraft is therefore always evil, because the self has lost its own integrity. It has lost its soul for the sake of certain powers possessed, and this is a criticism that applies to many of us. Although we may not believe at all in witchcraft, we are often used by powers that we enjoy but are not able to control. In magic, on the other hand, the magician is in control of the power which he uses. He works from the first or second corner of the psychic compass, rather than the third, and is traditionally known as "White" or "Black," according to whether he uses his powers for good or evil ends. Witches are therefore always bad, because they have sold themselves for what they have received, and they are therefore soulless (or relatively so). Magicians (usually they are scientists, today) maybe good or bad, according to the way in which their powers are used.

Another term used by some for this continuum is the "astral plane." We enter it in sleep and experience it in dreams. That is why dreams can never be brought clearly into consciousness, and why they cannot make sense to reasonable folk. Yet dreams speak a language of their own, using the symbols that belong in their own special field. The dream material is primitive and symbolic: its nature is that of a fluid continuum: its sex is feminine: and its espe-cial guardian deity is the "moon." It reflects the original source of light, which is the "sun" at the first corner of the psychic compass, but it is not strictly speaking original in itself. It has a derivative, secondary and reflective kind of life, and owes its life to sources other than its own.

The moon may lead us on to "lunacy." When we are absorbed and sunk beneath the surface of this mysterious world, "merged" instead of "emerging," having lost our hold upon the surface level of experience at 2 and 4, we are wholly "lunatic." We are held in the grip of all the powers which we cannot use, possessed by their demonic energy, and, for all practical purposes, lost to life. If we are only partly submerged, retaining partial contacts with the real external world, we are what is called "neurotic." We are then sub-ject to symbolism, partly activated by these daemonic forces, and only partly "real." But the pink rats and purple elephants of *delir-ium tremens* are real denizens of the world of the astral continuum, falsely described by the senses as belonging to the real external world. The terrors, the illusions, and the daemonic energy are all only too real. But they are realities of the "3" world, not of the "4" world. There are different realities, according to the measure of our different instruments, on different levels of experience.

Before we move on to consider the nature of the fourth level of psychic reality, let us confer upon this third corner the impres-sive title of "Dangerous Corner." It is the source of fear. Here we are soft and fluid, and here, therefore, fear dwells. The origin of fear is not in that ordinary exterior world, but deep within our-selves. We are not really as much afraid of that familiar external stuff, people, or things, as sometimes we think we are. We are afraid, however, of what we feel within ourselves, provoked some-times by those exterior events. The immediate experience of fear is always within us, and the utmost that we have to fear is our own experience of fear. We are afraid of fear and of the inward devas-tation that our fear can cause. We are therefore very glad to locate the source of fear in some innocent cause such as mice, or death. Anything seems preferable to this awful state of inward emotional uncertainty. We are glad to project the dignity of "cause" on to some, or any, ready exterior scapegoat—and, of course, there are always plenty standing ready for our heart to blame. "That is the cause!" we say, glad to find an explanation for the unexplained distress. We feel relieved by our deceit, and go on more happily for being self-deceived. "The fault is *there!*" We are glad indeed to pretend that it is not *here.* Sometimes the inward horror is indeed out there, exposed to open gaze. When the inward nudity is exposed to outward view, the word we use to describe it is "obscene." So much that is real is really better covered up! Nudists should dress themselves in fitting garments and avoid exposure of their obscene absurdities and absurd obscenities. The occult was properly intended to remain unseen, although it may be invisibly detected by the proper instruments, used with discrimination.

By contrast, *the fourth corner* of our psychic field is a sensible, tangible, measurable world, in which we have to live and work, against resistances, in time. It is the place where things are done, in which efforts are completed more or less efficiently, but in which nothing lasts for long. All things are clocks, and all are running down, in everlasting entropy. Yet craftsmen and technicians use their tools, farmers sow and reap, gardeners dig, and families grow up and die. Millions are led by few, usually without much wisdom. Many are exploited and few will understand. In spite of all the light and energy, in spite of all the effort and hard work, in spite of all the beauty and all the pleasant things, this fourth corner needs a lot more light.

Reality is therefore a most complex affair, more complex than any of us can fully realize. Yet it is our task to realize this wholeness, through our various instruments, as abundantly as we can. Of course, we must all be somewhat limited in our realization of life's infinite variety. We realize, instead, only a part broken from the whole, unbalanced, immature. But what we realize is real for us, because we made it so. Many of us live in a broken world of illusory fragments of experience that we believe to be the "real" world. Well, at least it is real for us. And many of us create a world of our own, out of our illusions, and it becomes so real to us that no evidence can convince us that there are other worlds than ours. That second corner is the tempting one, so there we set imaginary course, to live in the air, imagining that the substance of our thoughts is all reality. We think of life and talk of life and teach of life. We decide just how it ought to be if it were better than it is, an ordered world constructed according to our thoughtful plan. We bend experience to suit our wills and view it with one eye, the other blind, to satisfy our ready-made conclusions. Experience is thus prejudged, for we are prejudiced, and nothing can be new and true. It must be according to our fixed conclusions, or else there is something wrong with it. Sitting in our chosen corner, judging life from outside, we may seem to be very clever, but unfortunately for our ordered plans, Life has some other cards to play, and there are surprising aces up its sleeve for our discomfiture. All is well for a time, and nothing can touch these elevated folk, it seems—until Life wins another trick, and they are brought to earth, at last. We call this state of affairs a "breakdown," and find it hard to realize that the movement, uncomfortable as it always must be, is nevertheless not only in the right direction, but also long overdue.

We have all seen plenty of examples of one-sided lives and one-track, limping, minds. On the first level, we have seen people on fire with inspiration, always impatient, usually self-important, often hot-tempered, sometimes epileptic. They find life hard themselves and often make it hard for others, because they find it hot. Hence they have a nasty and impatient trick of trying to burn all others cooler than themselves. Strangely, they are babies in many ways in spite of all their inner "knowledge." They have never been quite born and usually need a woman's goodness or guile to lead and nourish them. They make bad companions, because they have not learnt to share. They are sometimes parsons, often demagogues, and always eccentric.

On the second level, we have all the "airy" ones, whose cleverness is far from earth. They are detached, living in righteous and important worlds. Often, they are professors and teachers, but in spite of their vast knowledge they cannot always find their spectacles or feed themselves. They do not know much about life in any personal sense, but much about ideas. It is an airy diet that they feed on, and they are usually great talkers. They are liable to be quarrelsome with anyone who differs from their own ideas. They usually require someone more earthly wise than they are to look after them, but in spite of that they are often given jobs as teachers of the young in important seats of learning.

At the third level, we find the passions seated. Here is desire, and all the suffering that love ensures. Here we experience life's cruelest surgery, without an anesthetic, unless we provide it for ourselves. But even in their passions, there is something friendly and touching about these people. They are close at hand, although they are often violent. They are more advanced, in their earthly journey, than many of their would-be teachers who have stayed aloft in their superior airs. Of course they do not always talk sense, but they are always expressive. Their hearts are in the right place, and, in spite of their complaints, they are "getting down" to it.

But this is "dangerous corner," and perhaps many of us are more prone to avoid it than we know. We'd rather stay at "2," and think about life, than dive into its darkness and deep waters at "3." Or we can try to leave this corner out of our experience, enjoying what we can that satisfies our appetites amidst the glamour and bright lights at "4." There is no doubt that "3" is the level of suffering and of redemption, where personality must pay its price by being "proved." The question asked by the Stranger at the Gate, as we approach this Rubicon within ourselves, is "Can you endure?" And our soul's echo usually answers "No!"

This is the zone of conflict most insoluble. It is a mistake indeed to try to solve life's problems here. They are not to be escaped by being solved, but to be lived through, proved by experience. For Life is the child of these opposing forces in deep conflict joined. Solve the problem too speedily by successfully avoiding it, and you kill the child. Your life is dead.

And so to the fourth level, and we have arrived on Earth at last. Finally we have got down to it, and life is a job of work for those who have brought their instruments with them, bought at the proper price. But we must not expect to see "important people" here! Those great important ones are still probably up aloft somewhere, as leaders and teachers talking volubly. Those travelers who have really arrived at this stage of their journey are probably only the more simple ones, who scrub floors, drive buses and dig soil. These are the ones who have arrived at last. We hardly notice them, because they fit so well into the landscape and are without complaint.

But there are many more besides these, who are knocking about the earth. They know nothing of the other levels; caring even less, except perhaps to prove that they do not exist. There are many earthly ones who have never yet really grown to man's estate. They are the playboys (and girls, too), who are out for fun, with healthy appetites that can be enjoyed, because there's plenty here to eat. They believe that fun is all, and that their happiness is simply to be satisfied. Or they may be students, working hard in their belief that all things may be known to them in time. These have a lot to learn, and much more to forget. They pride themselves on being matter-of-fact, but they are not really, because they miss out half the facts. They fancy they are old and tough, some of these really "earthy" people, but they have hardly started yet on life's mysterious journey.

We have so many instruments and each is capable of limitless development. So why should anyone of us despise another for what he has not got? Let us live and let live! Let us live and learn! Let us live and grow! But what is most important for our healthy growth, let us *flow*! Fertility needs irrigation, fields need water, cold needs warmth, and men need women, as women need men, to round each other off. So does the upper need the lower, and the outer need the inner, if we are to fulfill the object of our lives. So let us set our psychic compass, and walk on! There is more in life, for all of us, than what we may at present know.

Whichever way we set our psychic compass, we can see that we must link the opposites, if we are to be balanced, whole. The problem of relationship is involved in this mysterious "link" or "yoke." (Compare Hindu *yoga* and Christian *love*.) Somehow, the opposites must woo and wed each other, if this psychic family, which dwells within us, is to become united, whole. We are like male and female in ourselves, and these two must make their mysterious marriage, before they can give birth to the healthy child of Life.

Darkness must marry light: passive must be wedded to active: female and male must throw in their lot with each other, and make themselves at home within the familiar compass of the self. Higher must enter into lower: the great must suffer the bondage of the small: goodness must redeem evil: and knowledge illumine ignorance, all as light penetrates darkness.

Does this seem difficult? Actually, I think it is a very simple process, although it may not be easy either to describe or to fulfill. To put it negatively at first, there are certain things that "right relationship" does not allow. It does not allow either "Nuts in May" or "King of the Castle," by which I mean that we must not try to win the other to our side, nor must we try to get rid of our opponents. In fact, *we must not try to win at all.* Life is an endless game, with neither side victorious, but each continually and dynamically opposed.

But let us see if we can give right relationship, or mysterious marriage, a more positive description. There are, I think, four main points to emphasize. First, each party must be content to be himself, not envying the advantage that the other seems to have. Secondly, each must accept the other, making such contact as they can without seeking any private gain; for all that this experience may be worth. Thirdly, neither must try to decide the issue for himself. That will always be somewhat beyond control, mysterious, as children always are. And, lastly, there will always be some price to pay in suffering or loss.

The woman in this partnership has certain qualities that words can do a little service to describe, but not much, because by her nature she is dark, mysterious and beyond description. She is implicit, unformed, unmanifest—and yet she is the great creative urge, seeking expression and needing to become informed. She is passive, but not negatively so, because she is receptive. She is an urgent void, asking silently to be fulfilled. She is the guardian of the fire, the keeper of life's oil, the source of life and inspiration of the psychic home. She is the tender one, but she is no angel. She is demonic and must never be set free, or the powers that are hers, and her sublime attraction, may be used destructively.

The man is her counterpart, actively opposed. He is the hunter in the field of life, and his weapons must be keen and subtle, plastic and strong. He forms a ring round her, to keep her in her place at home, and bring back to her the spoils of his hunting, that she may prepare the dish for him to eat. He thinks of tomorrow, comparing it with today and yesterday, but she is more the realist, today. Together, they are reciprocal and in their wedding each can provide all that the other lacks. Yet he is also a dual nature in himself, as so is she, because the whole was divided into four opposing parts, and each part is subdivided also, against and within itself. Such is the Law of Life, that makes the wheels go round. Energy is always at its highest potential where there is the greatest difference between the opposites: least opposed to greatest, highest to lowest, man to woman, as darkness is opposed to light. *The reason why all difference is to be respected and not eliminated is that it makes for energy.* Equality means inertia, and fixation means the end of breathing, dancing, Life. Dictatorship is only foolishness. It will learn its lesson in the end, if it can learn at all, for Life must always win. As we learn to obey Life's Laws, so we learn its secret mysteries, and so acquire some at any rate of its creative powers.

So what is to be our philosophy of Life? Let us try to define it, because we are our own philosophy. We are the product of a scheme, wise or unwise, explicit or implicit, for better or for worse, as it may be.

There is a plan behind the scheme of things, however muddled it may seem to be, and we are required to cooperate with others who know more, as workers in the field of our experience. Each one is different, and each has different work to do. Each must refine his special instruments, and make the best of them, whatever they may be, not envying others for their different aptitudes. Life is our teacher, and whatever is, although it may not be "right," it must be what it is, because it cannot be otherwise. *The proper attitude towards Reality is one of intelligent acceptance, wedded to goodwill.* We are not here for fun, but to get on with a job of work, which is, in part and at least to start with, concerned with ourselves and the growth of our own natures at the hands of experience accepted. We are growing in obedience to Law, and the proper use of our free will is to learn as best we can from Law. This is the purpose of experience. We can enjoy all that can be enjoyed, but we must understand that all such satisfactions, however good they may be, are only temporary. We must lose them in the end, and even losing has its value, too. Relationship is a difficult art and not a business deal. It is often better to be worse, and we may be worse off when we think we are better. We cannot receive with fists clenched hard, but must keep open hands and open house to Life. The criterion of virtue, progress and growth is *wholeness,* and that is cyclical or spiral. We must learn to travel on the roundabouts, as well as on the swings, for all comprise a necessary part of Life's adventure.

Through all, and in all, and all the time, the Will is the thing that counts. It is the living spirit of our lives, the force that lies behind our Life's philosophy. It is intangible, invisible, unprovable, a mystery. It is like the creative Source itself; the first and last, the furthest and the nearest aspect of our complex selves. It is the light that must be kept burning bright, within the darkness of our daily lives. We are up against it, and our job is to go through with it, whatever "it" may be. Whatever we may choose to do or to escape, the price of Life adds up, and we must pay up in the end. So let that be part of our philosophy of Life, and let us buy our tickets, willingly. In all things, let us be as intelligent as we can. We never can be intelligent enough, and there is always more to learn, with all our instruments. There is no end to Life, or Death either. It is all for our adventure. It is all a battle, and requires courageous and obedient soldiers who are inspired artists—and accurate as scientists, as well. There is so much to learn; and room for all, in Life. We travel further, as we travel light.

If we are to be thus willing to be knocked about by life, surely we must be willing, too, to knock life about a bit. Although we have to treat life with respect, it pays us to be rough with it, to take a chance at times and live adventurously. Life cannot be tender towards us, so we must be tough about it. Life is no meal for sensitive or queasy stomachs, and we must strengthen our "guts," the better to endure.

We are like children who must learn their lessons, and their manners, too. Or like unbroken colts who must learn to be disciplined with collar and harness, before they can be used to pull a cart to market. We must also be "collated," caught in the prison ring of truth's encirclement, before we can become mature as men and women. There is a price to pay for that, a price of freedom lost, hope broken, and desire sacrificed upon the altar of experience. But it is not too bad if once we realize that this is the way of Life. It is the Law, and it requires our obedience and our cooperation with it. It is a matter-of-fact way of living with good humor. There is really nothing strange or mysterious about it. It means being strictly scientific in our use of instruments, knowing their purpose and their limits, keeping them in good condition and using them properly for the purpose for which each one has been designed, as skillful carpenters keep and use their tools. We have still to learn how good our tools can be, and how skillfully they have been fashioned to suit them for the work they have to do.

Our Psychic Compass is a marvelous thing, more wonderful in its complex subtleties than anyone has yet discovered, or ever even dreamed. It cannot be described or analyzed, because words are only one of its many instruments. It must be used on many of our journeys, with courage and goodwill, each one for himself, before we can begin to realize the many wonders that its living heart contains. In it there is no proper stopping-place, no "best," no final goal. The breathing to and fro, the cyclic rhythm, 0–1–2–3–4–5–0, is like the turning of a wheel. Progress depends, firstly, upon the skill which we acquire in the use of all our instruments; and, secondly, upon the degree to which we use our skill in willing cooperation with the present needs of the emerging Law.

.

CHAPTER 9

The Wheel and the Road

Truth is not a plain tale. It cannot be told simply, as if it were in a straight line, with a beginning and an end, word for word, once and for all. It is too subtle, too manifold and too self-contradictory for that. Like hunters after our prey, we can have a shot at it with a quick-fire of words, and when we miss, shoot at it again from a different direction. Then, either all our shots must miss, or, even if we hit it, we shall do injury to truth, merely wounding it by our injustice. Then we must try again, but more as poets do, to catch it in a picture, and see a fleeting glimpse of it as it disappears like water through a sieve. In truth, the truth cannot be caught nor held nor simply told, because it is more subtle than the mind can see.

Of course, we can make certain observations of limited accuracy, such as that today is Tuesday and it is half-past four in the afternoon, or that I owe the baker four and threepence, or that the distance to the moon is 238,860 miles. Such accuracy in small matters is important, and Science has done much by the accuracy of its observations and its measurements to build for us the framework of an ordered lucid world. But in the end its data only become more and more complex and, instead of coming nearer, the truth moves further off as a result of our patient observations in the material world of space and time. It is necessary, therefore, to accept our conclusion at the beginning and to admit that truth is something subtle and contradictory. It is indeed a paradox, and with that assumption I propose to start.

Since we cannot escape from the awkward opposites, let us begin with them and state as a preliminary axiom that the truth must always be a compound, self-contradictory subtlety, derived from a certain relationship between two opposite orders of experience.

From *The Triumphant Spirit: A Study of Depression*

195

Spirit and matter, dark and light, immeasurable and measurable, truth has at least these two aspects, and seeing that both are present, neither must be omitted if we are to tell the truth.

It is sometimes easier to convey this basic concept by means of a pattern or a diagram, and I call the one that I am going to use "The Wheel and the Road," (see figure 14, opposite). Geometrically, it is a circle with a tangent; but I want this pattern to represent a picture of a wheel rotating as it travels down a road. There are four different categories: namely, the Axis of the wheel, which represents a potential "hierarchy" of coexistent centers in the background; the Wheel, which represents the invisible order (subjective or "1/3"); the Road, which represents the visible order (objective or "2/4"); and the point of contact between the Wheel and the Road, which represents neither Wheel nor Road, but a complex category involving the relationship Wheel-and-Road.

I now propose to put forward an experimental postulate, not as "truth," but as a useful working guess. I suggest that all the material and familiar forms in what we call the "real" world of space and time are but abstractions, or fractions, caught by a tangent at a point upon the rim of a whirling wheel. (In two dimensions it is a wheel, but in three dimensions it is a spiral vortex turning about its axis.) Reality in the external world as we know it, according to this hypothesis, is the visible and measurable fraction cut out, as it were, from this invisible, moving matrix. The whirling vortex turns and spins upon its spiral course and all that we can ever know or sense of it is just that point where the Wheel touches the Road. The Wheel stands for the invisible matrix, and the Road stands for the external world of the material space-time order of experience. As the Wheel turns and travels down the Road, the "now" emerges in the historical and geographical reality of the three-dimensional order. The past lies behind (B–C), and the future, still invisible, is stretched out in front down the Road (C–D). But it is important to realize that the emergence of the external order is not dependent on itself. This emergence of what we know as "Reality" is an effect of prior causes, that are latent within the turning of the Wheel. That is to say, a future event is not preexistent on the Road (C–D), but is somewhere in the unmanifest order of the Wheel itself, emerging as an event in history only when the Wheel has turned so far.

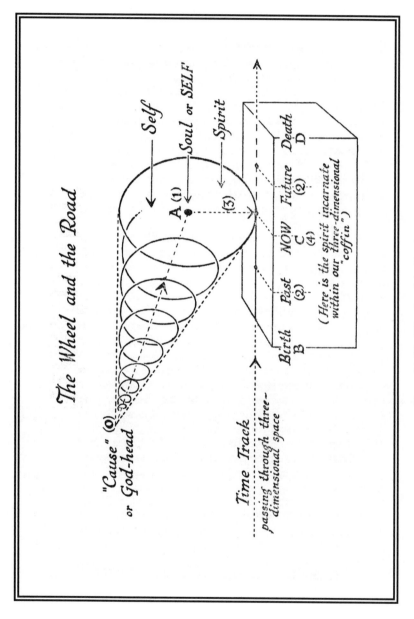

Figure 14 The Wheel and the Road

The best analogy to suggest what I mean is the cinema. As we see the screen from our seat, it might appear as if both "cause" and "effect" were on the screen, with nothing beyond or behind the picture that we see, to interfere with it. Actually we know the "cause" to be in the operator's box with his light, his roll of film and his projector. For the purpose of my analogy, therefore, the "road," B–C–D, is the unfolding of the story on the screen, with the picture at any moment "now" at the point C. The path of light from the projector is A–C, and the projecting mechanism is the "wheel." (Plato was on the same problem with his shadows moving on the wall of a cave, but he did not have the cinema to help him with an illustration.) What it means, in practice, is that what we call the "phenomenal" world, or the "real" external world of science and physics, with its measurements in three dimensions and in clock-time, is actually a system of apparent effects, a secondary and derivative world of appearances, which are continually emerging out of an invisible primary system which is its true cause. The Buddhists call the "apparent" world Maya, or "illusion." The "intrinsic" world, Sangsara, they prefer to call the "real" one. I do not think that we are helped to understand our experience by any such suggestion of preference or derogatory comparison. As I see them, both are equally "real," but quite different.

Let us continue with the analogy of the film projected on the screen in the cinema. In our "real" external world B–C–D, we have a sufficient degree of "free will" to be able to behave on the screen as if we were free agents, or as if we were writing the script as we went. We behave as if we were free to choose and to create our own future according to our conscious choice; and free also to interfere with the lives of other people, either for better or for worse. Yet, in fact, I am sure that we must all realize that we are indeed much more tied than that. Without our being labeled "fatalists," our common sense itself must see that there is something in each one of us that is unfolding during the course of our often unwilling history. That which is "in the bag" is coming out, even if we try to dodge it and to grasp something we like better in exchange. We are to this extent like the living things that emerge from seeds or eggs, that we also are unfolding from the invisible source of mystery within ourselves. The fun is to see what the bag contains and to be alert in the living moment now, so that we are able to catch opportunity as it emerges and make the best of it. Far from being a fatalist in any fixed or pre-determined sense, I believe that if we can but stand alert at this point C, on the road of external reality as it is now, and use our intelligences as they can be used, creatively, then we can play a fitting part in the unfolding of the plan. (This is what the Buddhists have always aimed at, too, by seeking freedom from the Wheel.)

Axiomatically, *whatever is on the road is also in the wheel.* All "forms" are the reflections of their antecedent "forces." Wheel and road are therefore similar, in that the forms which appear on the road must have been produced from the force-patterns or dynamic images (cf. Platonic "ideas") which are latent within the wheel. Thus the patterns of our bodies repeat the patterns in the wheel. Thus all history, as it emerges on the road of our time-track, is the outcome of the wheel's rotation. All "truth" is the manifestation within the real external world of the Truth that is its parent source within the wheel, unmanifest, invisible, unproven, and yet forever being proved. Nothing can originate, either of good or evil, in this real external world. It is all emerging, caused, derivative, dependent. To undertake to be the "cause" of what occurs, therefore, in this secondary world, is to undertake a great deal too much. A man can bear this burden for a certain time, but must find himself overwhelmed by these emerging inward forces in the end.

It is clear, I think, that according to this pattern of life, the truth must be constantly renewed, as it emerges out of the wheel's rotating womb of time. There can be no last word, no final truth, no historic point, no psychological moment nor particular person, that is not capable of being repeated at some other point of time, with suitable modification. At all times, in all places, and through the infinite variety of all its voices, in fact, *Life is always saying the same thing.* We do not listen in to hear it as we might; but that, too, is part of our necessity, because I believe that we are all engaged very busily in the most important business of being ourselves.

Now I wish to extend the use of this basic philosophy, or hypothetical pattern, in order to study from it some further problems of the nature of the psyche and its relationship with the inner world of the Wheel, on the one hand, and with the outer world of the Road, on the other. In the previous chapter on the "Psychic Compass," I suggested that there were four categories or instruments within our psychic field, two of which were related to the inner world (1, Knowing and 3, Feeling), and two to the outer world (2, Thinking and 4, Doing). To start with 4 first, we can realize that the only way in which we know the "now" is through our common use of the five senses. We can only see-now, touch-now, and hear-now, and it is through our senses that we are brought into direct contact with the real existence of this external world. Here we are, therefore, now, at C, continually going off at a tangent upon a series of adventures as the Road emerges at our feet and at our fingertips. From the data thus derived from sensory experience, however, we can build up in our minds a conceptual order which is the mental stock of the more independent traveler on the Road. The thoughtful traveler can remember what has gone before and furthermore he can deduce what is likely to lie ahead. We can therefore place number 4 at C to show our traveler's "sense" relationship, and number 2 between B and C, and C and D, to show his "thought" relationship.

For present purposes, we are using the system to represent the dynamic mechanism of a single psyche, and the Wheel as the whole "Self." The center or axle of the wheel at A, then, is the soul, and at the far end of the axis of the spiral there is a still deeper source upon which this soul depends, connecting it, as it were, with a continuous hierarchy evolving in extension. The single individual soul of each one of us, however, has its own essential meaning, worth or pattern, and its own different "quality." The soul, therefore, from which the "self" is emerging into "personality" is a private thing, my own, different from all other souls. In terms of light, it is a shining thing that draws its essential quality of light from a deeper source within and behind itself. From it another ray emerges down the line A–C, to vitalize the living personality at C on the time-track in the real external world B–C–D. This emerging light, which exists on either side of the soul and ultimately manifests itself in personality, is what is known traditionally as the "spirit." It is the same as the "divine messenger," or the "Holy Ghost."

In this vast scheme, we can realize that our "minds" in the second corner are only little things, minute abstractions from the whole. They are well suited to deal with other minute abstractions, and if they boggle at the vast complexity, it is because they are of necessity blinded to the implications of the whole, of which they are only a small, though not unimportant, part. Life is emerging from dark deep central sources, and, important as the real external world may be, it is but an abstraction, a vision seen inverted in a mirror and ultimately an illusion, as the Buddhists and the mystics knew. In all this complex process of life manifesting and emerging, two things must happen which give rise to the appearance of conflict and self-contradiction. As the ray from deeper sources emerges through A, the soul, further into outlying personality, the essential purity and unity of the Godhead must be present at the heart of all created things. On the other hand, as manifestation takes place, the opposites are created, and unity thus becomes mirrored in the inverted images of diversity. From this the struggle of life ensues, and the Wheel must wrestle with the Road, and religion and science, art and philosophy, mystery and the knowledge of technique, female and male, be not friends but enemies.

With "knowing" (1) we are closest to the heart of the mystery and on the line A–C nearest to A. Intuitive knowledge therefore is not personal, nor derived from experience upon the Road of life. It is universal and hardly varies at any point in time. All who have known the inward truth have the same inward knowledge, and must then prove it in their lives through their experience upon the Road. This leads us to (3), and it is through our "feelings" that we emerge into the often unwelcome reality of personal experience. This is the battlefield of personal struggle and conflict, where the real clash occurs between the "Odd" (1/3) and "Even" (2/4) worlds. It can be seen how men have tried to formulate the "Even" world in such a way that they could control it and organize within it the fulfillment of their own desires, without necessity for suffering. But always they experience defeat, because the world of the Road is the servant, the effect of the causes which are hidden within the mysterious mastery of the Wheel's rotation. This is what is meant in Eastern terms by the word "karma," which implies the unfolding of the inexorable, mysterious inward Law.

The whole is emerging through the part, as life itself becomes manifest in a complex variety of material forms. The source, invisible, is becoming actual in the space-time world, and life's children are growing into adult men and women as they emerge in space and time upon the outward level of experience. As I have said, we are all cardinally represented through the four points of our "psychic compass" in both worlds, but some of us are more in one than in the other. For instance, all beginners belong more to the ideal world of the continuum, or Wheel, and are more "over there" than "over here." Children have this subjective protopathic awareness of the nature of the internal world, with their forces still latent and waiting to emerge in actuality. Women also belong here, as well as creative artists, religious mystics and psychic sensitives or mediums. They all have this deep and mysterious inward knowledge, coupled with some resentment against the material bars that form their cage in the actual world in which they have to live. Undeveloped and unproved up to now, they need to grow, emerging through confinement as seeds do into flowers, until their latent potentialities are ultimately fulfilled through their wrestling with that unfriendly world beyond themselves. The bars which form their cages become the instrument which they themselves must ultimately forge for their success. And side by side with these, with no disparagement intended, are all those lunatics who have failed to make the grade on the external Road, and have lost themselves within the mysterious and powerful forces of the psychic wheel. Although "lunatic" has come to be a rude word, it was not always so, because in medieval days it was believed that lunatics were very close to God. We can see how the idea may have arisen; but, having failed in adaptation and relationship, they cannot really qualify as saints. But we should not give too much praise either to those whose successful adaptation on the Road has brought them their prosperity, at the expense of losing their awareness of the greater life within the Wheel. The Wheel may lose touch with the Road in lunacy, or the Road may lose touch with the Wheel in great material success. These two are opposites, and neither justifies praise or condemnation from the other. But obviously it is not fair that lunatics should be treated by "scientists" who, however much they know about the Road, have long forgotten and lost all knowledge of the real importance of the Wheel.

From what I have said it should be plain that the Wheel is very close to all of us, and that it is, in fact, a normal part of the everyday experience of all our lives. In sleep, for instance, we are travelers in its mysterious depth, having lost the attachment which our senses give us to the real external world. As we close our eyes when darkness falls, we leave the Road and merge into the mysterious continuum of the Wheel, to emerge again with breaking day as wakeful, working men and women, restored to our senses, and our duties, too. In our sleep we are dreamers, and our dreams may vary as much in meaning and in value as our ordinary conduct does, from the extreme of the trivial on the one hand to matters of the deepest consequence on the other. We all, I think, realize that our dreams do not actually occur in the same way or in the same sequence as that in which we subsequently remember or report them. When we tell the story, if we can remember it after we are awake, we have pulled the thread out of the hall of wool and arranged the data "on the Road" in a linear sequence. But in the dream itself as we dreamt it, the data were not linear in sequence at all, but were merged instead in the dimensional wholeness of the ball of wool.

All dreams are not by any means of value, but sometimes we dream "big" dreams and touch in sleep upon the mysteries of life itself, merging ourselves then in those myths and dramas within which our forefathers caught their occult wisdom, and expressed their inner knowledge of the Wheel. The dream is essentially a picture language and it can be understood, I think, that pictures bear the same relationship to analytic verbal description, as the Wheel bears to the Road, or symbols to matters of fact. The composition of the protopathic "mind" is a pictorial one and it is through symbols and pictures that we must understand the mysterious movements of the Wheel. Dreams are not unreasonable, any more than women are un-men. Nor, for the same reason, is it wise to speak of life within the Wheel as being "unconscious." As I have said before, all negative definitions are bound to be derogatory, because they imply the superiority of the positive form; as here, for example, of "consciousness." But the Road is not better than the Wheel, because it is created out of it, and "consciousness" is not better than "unconsciousness" for the same reason. The Wheel, and all our dreams within it, form the sources of all creative urge of life which is destined to emerge ultimately in our work upon the Road. Dreams, daydreams and the experiences of trance and ecstasy, imply that we have been traveling within the Wheel. The height of ecstasy means that we have entered very close to the height and source of life within it. In anesthetics, too, the Road is taken from us by the force of drugs and our connections with it are temporarily severed. But whereas in sleep and trance and anesthesia the silver cord A–C remains intact, in death that cord is cut, and, traveling still, our path is otherwise, and we are seen no more by familiar travelers along the space-time Road.

It is interesting to consider the process by means of which it is possible to rotate ourselves, as it were, about a right-angle, and enter into the other-dimensional world of the Wheel. Essentially, it is a process of de-focusing, relaxation, or expansion. By effort we cannot arrive there, but only in rest can we experience it. The rule of the Road is *attention*, but the Law of the Wheel is *relax*. By closing our eyes we shut out the details of sensory experience in the real external world; we relax our attention and, as we say, we "fall" asleep. It is hard to say, however, whether we really rise or fall, and neither word seems precisely adequate. What is quite certain is that as we *expand* and open out, we withdraw at the same time, emptying ourselves of our attachments, loosening our hold upon things and losing all as we let ourselves go. The process, therefore, by which we enter into this mysterious kingdom is one of giving up; whatever "it" may be, we cannot take "it" with us. We cannot even take our "selves" if we are to let our "selves" go. The wealth of the rich man must be left in the real external world, and only in poverty can we find the indwelling wealth that is within the Wheel. We sleep as children in our innocence; we leave behind us all our worldly wealth when we must die. As we grow older and become less innocent, we sometimes find in sleep that we have more to face and more to fear.

Let us now see if we can more clearly understand what is happening, and how we can best play our personal parts in this mysterious creative process. In its rhythmic fashion, life is always working out a plan, and, however little we may understand its subtlety, so must we. From its hidden creative source, life is manifesting and emerging in the same way that light manifests and emerges from the flame within a lantern. Just as light picks out different objects in its path, so life itself is always manifesting as a variety of forms. In the "Holy Mountain" I suggested that the Word which launched us on the road to existence was "Go forth and be my light." Into each one of us, therefore, is poured the creative principle, and we must go and make it manifest within ourselves upon the Road. We are the messengers of light, we are its carriers, yet dependent on our secret source, as any flower must depend upon its earthly roots for nourishment.

We must go forth and then we must return again, obedient to the breathing rhythm. The line A–C is therefore to be used as a kind of umbilical cord, through which the living circulation passes, with a double line of traffic up and down. In the language of the East, this is the cord of Shiva, and in the language of dreams it is Jacob's Ladder, on which angels are seen ascending and descending. In the language of our religion, God the Father in Heaven sends forth His Son, the Christ, to dwell upon the earthly Road amongst men. This is the meaning of the Fall, and the process of incarnation as described in traditional Christianity. Paradise Lost is a profound story, mysteriously wise and more deeply true than most of us have yet been able to realize. The experience of Pentecost, when men were touched with the mystic fire of the angelic visitor from on high, the Holy Ghost, is the deepest essence of human experience, the living truth. So, too, the Virgin Mary, the immaculate eternal feminine principle, the mystery at the heart of all religion, is to be found at the same central source, creative, emerging, and self-manifest. This is the meaning of the mystery of the Virgin Birth, and, far from being a ridiculous statement, it is as near the truth as human poetry can be.

Judas, and the Quislings who without difficulty accompany him, is also found on Life's revolving stage, a regular turn, invariably playing the same part. He is cast to play it and, to the last word and coin obedient, he always does. His crime is a simple and well-meaning one, or he would not be so easily convinced that he ought to play it.

He never seems to seek the fault that he commits. He pursues what seems to him a reasonable goal. He sells his Master for reward in gold; he betrays the inner mystery of the Wheel for some advantage on the Road. He does deny the Christ, but always to avoid some needless suffering. He provides the easy way out and arranges an escape. You simply change the color of your shirt, or make a different gesture with your hand to salute your Conqueror. It is all the same; what does it matter as long as we get enough to eat? He is quite a friendly fellow after all and means no harm. Besides, just think of all the needless suffering if you do not acknowledge him as master: not yours alone—that does not matter—but think of the unnecessary suffering of those you love!

Although I have said that the Christian story is so near the truth, students of Oriental teaching will recognize that my use of the Wheel as an analogy is even closer to the Buddhist than to the Christian doctrine. The great teacher Gautama was not deceived by the illusions of the real external world. With inner vision clear, he saw the Wheel and knew it for what it was, a living and mysterious fact. He taught us how human consciousness might learn to cooperate with it creatively without being bound to it as its enslaved victim. Some Buddhists and some Christians too have taught and practiced an escapist doctrine that the Wheel was better than the Road, and that the highest purpose was that each of us should find Nirvana in the center of the Wheel. There, in the highest ecstasy, we were to prove our vast superiority over the rest of the world by turning our spiritual backs upon the Road and all its evil works. But others, both Buddhists and Christians too, have neither taught nor practiced such an escapist version of the Indian rope trick, in which the boy climbs up the rope to disappear forever in the Heavenly blue. We were not born to turn our backs on life, but rather to bring life to earth and use it there according to a plan, getting down to it with all the intelligence and goodwill that we possess. According to this view, the Fall was not a fault or sin, but part of a God-directed plan to enable us all to act as partners in creative life.

Having discussed some of the more normal aspects of the problems which derive from the relationship of our two worlds of experience, let us now consider very briefly its pathology, or some of its abnormal aspects. These come under the headings of infla-tion, invasion, elation, dissociation and depression. The Wheel is a source of wealth of immense value and it sets us all a great prob-lem what to do with it. The whole is worth much more than any part can be. Yet somehow the whole must be filtered through the smallest part, in time. Some find it easy, some hard, and some find it impossible to perform this trick of passing more-than-camels through less-than-needles' eyes. Some are composed of more mal-leable and elastic psychic stuff, and some are full of undigested lumps that stick and bump our wheels upon the road. Yet whatever it is made of, this wheel of stuff that we call "Personality," at any moment "now" is experiencing a focal point where immense forces are being directed through relatively minute channels. All the people I have mentioned as dwellers within the (1 / 3) world of the Wheel are liable by nature to experience *inflation*, and even to be destroyed by this inward psychic *invasion*. Thus inwardly enriched, they are liable to become too "blown up," as they are increasingly invaded by the ever-expanding pressure of their interior psychic forces. Hence the danger of inflation, and hence the importance of getting down to it and building personality solidly and well in a continuous sequence of slow and normal growth. These inner winds of the emerging spirits can blow at gale force. Their force must be canalized and directed with intelligence, if we are to avoid the lunacy of undirected and explosive effort.

The purpose of these mysterious forces is not for our personal elevation into mystic heights, in order that we may forever avoid the necessity of a fall. In spite of all the evidence to the contrary, those are not better off who are the highest up. They may have the further height from which to fall. It is true that the mystics can enjoy pleasures superior to earthly ones. Certain drugs and sexual ecstasy, certain forms of madness in which euphoria and elation occur, are the merest foreshadowings of what such unearthly joys can be. But let us be warned that that way madness lies. Such time-less and *elated* joys are not for us. We are but earthly folk, and needs must turn our backs on Heavenly memories, while we put our shoulders to earthly tasks. The job is the thing and we are bet-ter off who keep our noses in the "now."

Happiness as a human goal is most deceptive. It is far better to get down to the job and get on with it, than to hope for a happier state, either here or elsewhere. It is no use, in fact, avoiding anything if anything be true, and the world of the Road is as true as that of the Wheel; and it is also true that it means for all members of mankind a fair share of the work that befell Adam when he was forced from Eden's Garden. Attached as we are to earthly things, they are our spiritual enemies for us to wrestle with, and we must not permit *dissociation* to occur merely because things do not fall into our ordered plan for happiness. It is as wrong on the one hand to try to split the Wheel from the Road and bounce it up on high, as it is on the other to say that the Road is all, and that the Wheel does not exist. The philosophy of rationalism and the final claims of materialistic science are but inverted lunacy, and neither can solve the problem that is life. Escapism of any kind leads but to *depression* in the end. Fallen we are and fallen we must be, or else the dose will come when we shall have to be depressed. It is better to accept as soon as possible the fact from which there is in the end no escape. There is no virtue in any over-simplification that denies the truth, because finally the truth must win.

Before concluding this chapter, I want to make use of an illustration drawn from dreams. There is a bicycle, with someone riding it. To connect this with the illustration of the Wheel and the Road, we have to imagine that besides the large Wheel itself, there is also a small wheel at C, connected by an endless chain with the central driving forces at A. The bicycle is therefore of the old "penny-farthing" type, except that the wheels are the other way round, with a large driving wheel behind and a very small one in front. Now for the illustration. If we forget the large wheel and sit only on the little one in front, trying to drive only that one, as it were, with our own hands and feet, we not only assume a very heavy responsibility, but we also feel pursued from behind by the mysterious forces from which we are always trying to escape. I have found variations of this dream very common, and it seems to me to represent something that has happened to many of us. We have lost touch with the real motive power of spiritual forces, and we are traveling either self-propelled or with no more powerful motor than a self-starter. However important personality may be, and however near men may be to gods, they cannot ignore their motive engines with impunity for long. If they do so, they will find in the end that they have in their hands only the negative end, the brakes of the mechanism, and that the real motive power is pursuing them ruthlessly, uncontrolled and overwhelming. Then they must link up again, or fall broken into the ditch, which is a different and a further fall from that which life itself intended.

With the help of various illustrations I have tried to make plain that the special problem with which we are all faced as human beings, is that we are dwellers in two worlds. Both worlds are real, for each is opposite to the other. Therefore, if we are to be worthy to be called "realist," we must realize the nature of each of these two worlds. We are Wheels and we are Roads. But what is more, we are also the Riders, who must join the two, and provide a living bridge with which to span the gulf that lies between them.

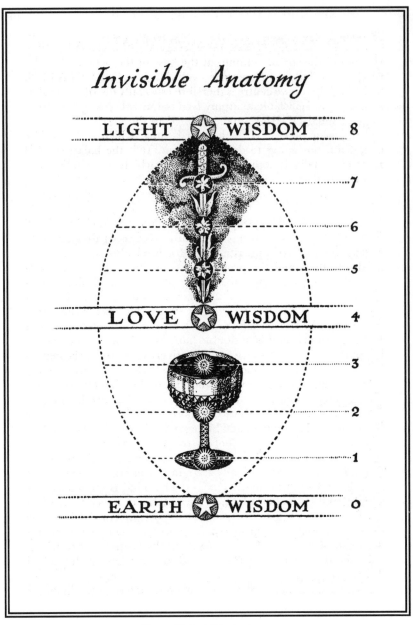

Figure 15 Invisible Anatomy

CHAPTER 10

Anatomy of the Invisible

Broadly speaking, we first have three levels which are pictured in figure 15, "Invisible Anatomy" (opposite). The lowest one, which I call "Earth-wisdom," is sub-human, and there our roots begin. The middle one, called "Love-wisdom," is the axle of our total human wheel, round which the whole rotates. This is our human problem, and it involves a right relationship, not only between our upper and our lower worlds; but also between their various parts and functions, which need a proper balancing. Thirdly, at the top there is a superhuman or spiritual level, which I call "Light-wisdom," which is our highest human crown, that can only be attained as and when our lower problems have been rightly solved.

The lower triangle or trinity contains the stuff of our animal natures: by which I mean, it does not know anything other than itself or its own immediate desires. It does not possess self-consciousness: its "mind" is only in itself, submerged, subconscious. In terms of form, this lowest level is represented in dreams by *wild animals*, especially the snake and elephant. (The snake is the root of the tree, and means creative life, which is the healer, when properly in relationship; but obviously its healing virtue is lost when it breaks out and assumes the rights of higher deity. Then it becomes the tempter and the destroyer, as in the Garden of Eden story.) At the next level, after evolving and becoming more particularly applied within a proper discipline, the creative energy is represented (in dreams again, but also in Eastern thought and myth) as *domesticated animals*, such as the cow or horse, cat or dog, which are more useful, and friendly-disposed to our humanity. At the top of this lower triangle (now stand by for a shock!) we have *woman*.

From *Invisible Anatomy: A Study of "Nerves," Hysteria and Sex*

Why on earth must she occupy this invidiously Oriental position, amongst the lower animals? Restrain your rage a moment please, and I will explain as soon as possible.

In the higher triangle we have the entry of a different element, which we call "self-consciousness." Above this physical diaphragm of our human visible anatomy we have now entered into another, lighter and more spiritual world, in which we are able, not only to see ourselves a little as others see us, but also, and even more usefully, to see others a little as they see (and feel) themselves. Here, therefore, is the beginning of ethics and altruism, of service and responsibility, and of true "personality," as distinguished from "organic" life. Here man emerges in creative role, a little bit like God, yet still burdened by those earthly roots from which he draws his energy. At the apex of this triangle, high up in the head, stands man. (And if, as a woman, you feel inclined to say: "What cheek! Of course, he would say that: the writer is a man!", I must ask you to wait a little while. I know how you feel, and this is coming out all right for you, if you are prepared to suffer my intrusion and be patient.)

In symbolism again, the lower triangle is the *cup*, or female principle of "mother earth," which must be redeemed by the intrusion of the "sword," or impregnating principle of the spiritual will, which is relatively male. That is to say, the higher principle must descend into the lower principle, as the male "sword" impregnates and diffuses life within the female "cup." The spirit is incarnate within the earthly garments, and the Christ-child is born within the virgin's womb. The woman's function is to occupy the role of the redeemer, to be the meeting-place within herself of higher and of lower life, in order that the earth may be fertilized and so show forth the glory of the "Father." In her heart (or womb), she bears the seed of Life brought to her by a male messenger from the gods above, and she must nurture it, bringing it forth in due time to its own independent life. *The woman does the work*: she always did. *The woman makes the home*: she always did. The man takes the credit and makes a lot of fuss; he always did! (Now are you satisfied?)

The woman is the "sufferer": that is her role. She permits the seed to enter into her and holds it in her "heart," its loving guardian. She brings forth the child and cares for it. Life is in her hands, and the next generation owes its being to the fact that its roots are ever nurtured by this mother's earth. She makes her sacrifice, continually. She gives, willingly, and sends forth her children into Life, to pass on the torch and seed again. Because she is what love in action means, she loves her work. She does not need to understand, because she is a realist. But men are different and they are not such simple realists; they try to order life about and so become the victims of their vanity.

Perhaps the easiest and shortest way to make my women readers more content is to remind them again of what I have said already: namely, that whether we happen to be men or women, we are both bisexual. Men have to feed and develop their female, sensitive and receptive side, but women have to develop their abstract powers of reasonable thought. In fact, whichever we are best at and whichever comes most naturally to us, we must not only develop that, but also the other side which is its opposite.

The lower triangle is an expanding principle or "positive pole." The upper one, its higher center in the brain, is a contracting, limiting principle, or "negative" pole. Thus the role of the male partner in the sexual relationship is to put a limit to his wife's unlimited desires, to "put a ring round her finger," to make her "obedient" and to guard the altar of her sacred fire within the sanctity of their domestic hearth. I have suggested already that Rudolf Steiner had fine insight when he detected that the truth of this principle was reflected even in our visible anatomy, whereby bones are central (vertebrate) in the lower half of the body and become increasingly externalized (crustacean) as we approach the head. The nervous core of the lower triangle is the autonomic (old) nervous system, which is the "belly-mind." The nervous core of the higher triangle is the central (new) nervous system, the head ganglion of which is in the brain.

Before going on to consider other things, I would like to say something more about the snake. This is not really a phallic (sexual) symbol in itself, although it may have a certain phallic aspect or significance, especially in deteriorated minds and their religious practices. It stands for energy, as something prior to genital reproduction, and therefore may be made to serve specifically sexual ends, if we are so disposed. Actually, it is both more and less, because it is an earlier force than sex. It is the earthly source of energy, for any purpose, creative or otherwise. When the opposites are rightly polarized or set to partners, the answer is the "snake," which is frequently seen in symbolism as the emblem of the third between two opposites. Then it is the healer and so we use it in the cap badge of the Royal Army Medical Corps, whose interests are not especially concerned with sex.

This earthly source of energy is perhaps best likened to the sap within the stem of the tree, and the seven levels which I have indicated in our invisible anatomy are then like branches or flowers that each evolve in turn, as the energy is raised to higher levels of expansion. One quality which occurs increasingly as the energy evolves is *differentiation*: that is to say, energy which is massive and lacking in fine definition at the root, becomes increasingly refined or subdivided as the tree grows. This is also true of our human development. In fact, what we mean by development is that crude powers are increasingly refined, so that they can be applied to a wider and more various range of usefulness. One becomes many, one becomes many, is repeated at every level. Energy evolves and living forms emerge in increasing particularity. They would tend to dissipate, with loss of energy, were it not for a certain cohesive integrating power in consciousness which tends to keep the many parts and functions related to a central focal point, which is I AM.

Time is the essence of all living growth. Life is extension in time. The normal growth of any child therefore depends upon its development in time, *in its own time.* Unfortunately for our normality, that happy state of timely growth occurs to few of us. Parents and teachers are such impatient folk and vanity enjoys the signs of prematurity.

Children are angels, yes: but they are also savages! That is their dual nature, and time, with a little luck, will find a fitting harness for such opposing energies. The first stage of a child's development requires to be well-founded in direct experience of the tangible, as they experiment with their bodily powers and movements and their senses' aptitudes. They need to get the sense of life on the physical level first, fitting their emerging powers within the limits of more physical tasks. Then they can begin to develop their feelings about things and people, finding out what they mean and how their sensitiveness can be stirred. They discover an aesthetic sense of what they like and what they dislike, of what they want and what fills them with disgust. Thus they experiment within their private, inner world. Thus they realize experience and make it real to themselves. This inner sense of life's reality is a very precious thing and it takes some time, and some mistakes, before it can be built. Only in the third stage can they begin to rise above the "diaphragm," and start to use the more objective detached powers of reason and self-consciousness. This new ability must be built upon a strongly developed base of slow extension, until finally each one can rise and as high as he can realize the aspirations of the higher man. There is an apex to our human triangle or pyramid, but it requires a sound sufficient base. The fruit cannot be plentiful in due season unless the roots are secure and well-nourished, deep-tucked within the soil from which they grow.

That would be normal growth, but it does not always seem to us to be convenient simply to let our children grow within those limits which best suit their tender years. The idea of what is good imposes its impatient tyranny. "Come on . . . you ought . . .": and so in untimely fashion we push and pull the growing plant, forcing it to assume a premature advantage. We do not see the rings of their invisible anatomy and therefore we do not let them dwell long enough within their limited scope. By introducing urgent and impatient power, we sow the seeds of their hysteria. We pull them on and yet a part hangs back; and so we may destroy the bridge that links their opposites. A part advances, while a part recedes. The part that we succeed in pushing on is "good," and the part that remains invisible is still further pushed out of the picture by being labeled "bad," and morally condemned. Alas, poor tree, whose fruits are prematurely plucked, even as it is cut off from its roots! If men are "like trees walking," this is most ignorant gardening.

The mistake that we most often make is that we do not "triangulate," or make a right relationship with growing life. We want the child to grow? Then that is one point of our base. The child has not grown yet? Then there is the other point. Time is the patient go-between, who travels to and fro as we provide the proper nourishment within the ring, until the growing life evolves as from within itself, by its own powers which have been held within a proper discipline. We must be balanced in ourselves and balanced also in our relationship, if we are to help those who are learning to gain a better balance in their lives.

Besides this process of our upward growth in time, there is also time required for the growth of our interior relationships. Normally, we should pass through four phases, corresponding with certain intrapsychic shifts of our centers of gravity. In the first phase, the center is in the lower triangle (organic unself-conscious selfishness). In the second phase, the center is shifted to the upper triangle (personal ethical consciousness), which is in opposition with the still persistent center in the lower triangle. In the third phase, we experience synthesis (harmony) at the level of Love-wisdom (4). At the fourth phase, however, we experience a higher illumination of consciousness, as the lower mental level at (7) becomes shifted into the higher synthesis of Light-wisdom (8), which corresponds with the lower level of Love-wisdom at (4). This process is proceeding gradually as the race grows older and as we all evolve. We are at different psychic ages, and so we differ in the degree that we have grown.

Emotional Development

We are like clocks, and all things living grow in time. In the beginning, mother and child are one; that is near enough to Paradise, but Paradise is lost as we are weaned. Slowly, gradually and in course of time, we learn to stand alone, as separated individual selves. The object of our being born is that we may become ourselves, mature, whole and independent; yet capable of a right relationship and possessed of full capacity for making our communications across the gulf which separates us from those with whom we live. As we grow ourselves, the growth of all our complex instruments takes time and they are also clocks. Our hands must not be pushed or pulled by interfering other hands, however

216

well-meaning they may be, or we shall perforce become hysterical. Prematurity is one high road to hysteria: dependence upon another's helping hand is just another.

The order of events in our emotional development is first, I love my mother; second, I love myself—how else can I discover who I am, and what I have to play and work with? Third, I begin to recognize similarity and difference, and turn away from "me" to those who are most like me. Fourth, I become attracted to the opposite sex, as I become "polarized" or sexually mature. Fifth, I make a home and hold my children in a larger ring of family affection. The first phase is "mother" or "cupboard" love, the second is self-love, the third phase is homosexual, the fourth is heterosexual, and the last phase is parental love. As "love" matures, it becomes more effective and inclusive in its relationships. At first, it is all within the lower nature of instinctive and animal appetite. As it grows and extends, it climbs the ancient ladder of human growth and evolution, and recognizes more and more the nature of those who are other and opposite, until at last emotional maturity can see the endless possibilities of love.

The organ of desire and the instrument of the emotional life within the lower triangle of the psychic ladder must suffer much change as it experiences growth. It starts as a single and unwieldy mass of "protopathic" force, untimely, all-or-nothing and intensely blind. As it grows, it is as if it gradually differentiates into myriad sensitive threads or tentacles, each one capable of being separately applied within a different interest, and each one acting as a little bridge between the central "I" and the external "it." Thus in our emotional development there is increasing capacity for diversity in extension. As we grow, our eggs are wisely not kept in one basket but in many, so that if one is lost or broken, there are always others to hold us in interested contact with the real world. Life being so insecure, it is important to have many of these feelers or contacting threads, in case some should be broken. They multiply, extend, strengthen and become more sensitive, as experience is increasingly studied by the faculty of consciousness and digested in the solvent space of time. Emotional development depends upon increase of right relationships, both within our own invisible anatomy and also within the exterior framework of the conditions in which we live.

I have shown what I believe to be the right relationship within our invisible anatomy, by linking the opposites and by means of the synthesis of bridge-making (Western, "love"; Eastern, "Yoga"). The integrity of the system as a whole depends upon the opposites being *balanced*, in order that they may *evolve*. As I explained in the previous chapter, the opposite energies must "triangulate," in order to achieve and keep this state of balance. When they do so, we are healthy, happy "all-rounders." When they do not, we are kept balanced internally by our symptoms (our "complaints"), which we automatically produce, and externally (also our complaints!) by the disturbances that we create in our surroundings.

So let us make our pattern work again, and see what it can tell us of what happens when our balancing goes wrong and we develop a disordered state. I will refer to four mistakes that can occur in the balancing mechanism, with more or less disastrous results. The first and commonest I have already mentioned, but I will do so again. I have called this aggressive extirpatory morality "Cutting off the other end of the stick." We hope for victory by the short cut of getting rid of our opposite number. It is the simple surgery of hopeless war. It keeps us very busy, because it simply cannot be done; however hard we try, the other half always must come back, pursuing and bedeviling us until we let him in, and succeed in achieving a more positive and patient relationship with this beloved enemy. The aggressive surgical short cut of instantaneous power is tempting, because it feeds our vanity. Yes, it is only natural: I mean exactly what I say, that it is the simplest by-product of our single unselfconscious (undeveloped) lower nature. In that lowest triangle most of us are still deeply confounded.

The second error is that of trying to "sublimate," or lift the lower bodily energies at one fell swoop up to the higher levels, holding them there by force of personal will. By doing so we misunderstand the meaning of the word "redemption." The redeemer does not so push or pull us up by force. He enters into the heart of the lower level, but still leaves it the moral independence of free will and choice. He says, "Do as you please, but I am here. Use me if you will, but you must come my way with me, or I shall be your enemy." This may seem at first sight difficult to understand, but again we may remind ourselves of the Chinese saying, "The Yin is in the Yang, and the Yang is in the Yin. The opposites are always represented in each other. The Highest is in the lowest, and the lowest is in the Highest. The top is at the bottom and the bottom is at the top. The female is in the male and the male is in the female. The child is in the man and the man is in the child. This is axiomatic within the law of our invisible anatomy. It is true and it is paradox. Therefore it is wrong to try to pull the lower up or the higher down. *It is not necessary, because it has been done already.* Yet many of us are still engaged in this morally exhausting and fruitless pastime. We must learn that top and bottom are each all right where they are. They do not need our urgent interference. They do need right relationship, or triangulation. They need to be redeemed, reciprocally. But that is not natural; it is supernatural.

The third error is Hysteria, pure and simple. This error lies in folding the pattern over on itself, turning the whole thing upside down and inside out, and equating or identifying the opposites with one another. This is that! Surface is center! Woman is man! Man in God! Nicely moralized, this looks good. Is it not obvious that this is as we ought to be? Yes, it is. But we are not. So, being so near the truth, Hysteria is all the more untrue.

The fourth error is to run amok and, drawing timeless rage from its abiding-place at the bottom of the ladder, to smash the whole outfit for Heaven's sake. What is the use of it all, anyway? We may then either become mental aggressors projecting the timeless tyranny of our ideas upon others who are usually more patient in their suffering than we are ourselves; or else we may go a stage further, folding our timeless tyranny of unexpressed rage back into ourselves, repressing it. Then, as we are so swiftly changed in spite of being the same beneath, we have asserted the opposite negative tyranny of an absolute pacifism. With power repressed, there now must be no display of power at all. Yet even so we are dictators still, and even in negation we display our impatient tyranny.

PART III

Separating the Opposites

CHAPTER 11

Yes and No

The relationship of the individual or organism to its environment may be expressed as a problem within the idiom of Yes and No, for self and not-self are part of the language of dualism, expressed within the circular frame of movement. The organism is circumscribed by circumstance in such a way that it is "positive" to the definitive "negative" of that by which it is surrounded. "*I am*": that is my central circle: *not* is where I finish, and where my circumstance begins. Here is the same dualism to which we are becoming accustomed, the polarity of positive and negative, "I am" and "I am *not*." The same polarity of "yes" and "no" occurs in the relationship between what I am and what you are, as between what I am and what I am not, or between me and my surroundings. Again we can see the language of the onion skin, the picture of the concentric circles, the one round the other, circumstance round each individual, of Yes to No, of positive to negative, of "I am" to "I am not." It is from this picture of the relationship of two forces that we may draw the meaning of all movement. It must always take two forces to make any movement. *I am not*: and that is why I want to be. *I have not*: and that is why I want to have. It is that *not* which makes me move. Give me what I want and I am finished. Take it away from me—but not too far—and you will have done your share to make me move.

When we are clear about the significance of this negative, we can understand more of the meaning of our dis-ease. If the negative of circumstance is more than I can positively bear; if the problem with which life presents me is too much; if, in other words, I cannot say "Yes" to that inexorable negative, which, therefore becomes intolerable, then I am in a state of some dis-ease. If I cannot say "Yes" to this negative, whatever it may be, then I must say "No," for

From *I and Me: A Study of the Self*

the no alternative. But by treating the negative defensively by thus saying "No" to it, that is, by identification with it, unfortunately for me I have myself become negative by becoming one with it. That is the beginning of my diseased state, because now I am divided against myself and I am become with my supposed enemy. We are in a state of "nervousness" or "nerves," for our attitude towards life is that of defensive negativism. In some way or another, whether more or less, our "nerves" are simply "no's."

If the problems, the negatives, the frustrations and disappointments of life are presented prematurely, as beefsteak to the baby's stomach, then there is only one possible answer and that is "No!" When once it has been so initiated into the way of rejection, from then onwards in time through life, even in spite of its more fortunate experience, inevitably and continually as a pattern of habit, the baby's stomach feels as if it were being presented constantly with more of the same kind of intolerable and indigestible beefsteak. "This makes me sick," it says, and the sick feeling represents the defensive rejective phase, both of body and of mind. Thus if we cannot cope with the Goliath of Reality, we shall make our negative gesture of self-defense; either we shall run away, going to bed in some way "for a rest," or else we shall copy him in defensive identification and pretend that we are Goliath. Somehow or another, either by action or inaction, we shall say "no."

Now although it is quite possible for us to say "no," since we have that choice, it is not always wise for us to do so. It is part of the law of life that every day we should go to bed and sleep, or that we should escape from our responsibilities if we are so lucky once in every year by going on holiday, or finally to find a deeper phase of sleep in death. But these intermittent arrangements for our occasional recuperation should be enough to enable all of us to deal with the problems of our existence. We are allowed this amount of rope with which to play, so much flight and so much rest from the labor of more strenuous living. But there are some whose experience of living has made them feel disposed to take advantage of it, adopting the permanent attitude of flight, the repeated "No, no, I cannot bear it!" These escapologists try the battle of life through evasion of existence, instead of taking life in the rhythm of Yes and No, they can only answer "No!" to experience, as if it were all beefsteak to the baby's stomach. But treated in this way their digestive systems can never improve, and they become martyrs to their own defensive indigestion.

CHAPTER 12

Anxiety

L ife is a situation of anxiety. Anxiety and fear are as inescapable, in fact, as are any other of the facts of life, except through the fallacy of flight; but we shall continue to believe in the actuality of our freedom and independence as long as we can. "I am afraid; and so, in my anxiety, what shall I do? I am small, it is large; what is good for it is bad for me, what is good for me is bad for it; it won't like that, it is bigger than I am, so whatever shall I do? It would be a marvelous solution, tempting in the might of its magic, if I could but pretend and feel that I were it, and that subject and object were united without unfriendly difference!"

This act of identification, this false assumption of defensive unity, is the armor that each of us can put on against the threat of fearful circumstance, so that "I" may assume that "I am it" and "It is me." By doing so we certainly make a oneness, but it is the wrong kind of oneness. It is a oneness of confusion, which reaches the semblance of comforting achievement by jumping to a false conclusion, instead of the more valid oneness of a real fusion. But the miserable consequence of paradox unrealized is that, when acceptance of anxiety would lead to real fusion between two separated and apparently conflicting parts, rejection of it and replacement of reality by false assumption serves only to bind these enemies more securely in unfriendly grips with one another. In my anxiety, of course, I would like to feel that I am one with you and with your steamroller—but, alas for me, it is not true, for I am not.

It is here that the feeling of anxiety rises to a crisis, to answer the question "What shall I do: stay or run, and thus prove true or false?" At this point of our reckoning we are engaged in an act of analysis. As we hold up self and not-self, I and me, we see the two

From *I and Me: A Study of the Self*

related parts of the two-ness of life. This two-ness remains truly inevitable, although by the false assumption of our unity we can be so deceived as to seem to ourselves to have escaped this conflict. That is why we have to watch so carefully, because if we let them do so, these two parts of self and not-self, which belong separated, will run together when we are not looking, to resolve our pain into an apparently real and inseparable confusion. It is quite easy, and seems to me quite right, that I should feel that I am you and you are me. But by acceding to the temptation of this false assumption I shall have lost both my sense of logic and my sense of humor, in a mushy sentimentality that seems so true to me because it suits my convenience. But in fact it is not true at all.

It is so easy for the mother's love to make her feel that the child is part of herself and that this identity is as it really should be. She feels so sure that they are one: surely, if not they ought to be. But no, they are not one, for they are two. The word "love" requires a dictionary to define its many meanings and it is easy to confuse two different kinds of love. One, which is not truly love in any better sense, is a false identification or utter possessiveness, the desired goal having been achieved "immediately," through flight from anxiety (I love you as if you were me). The other is love in truth, where the pain and anxiety of love for an uncertain object is held for its own sake (I love you as if you were yourself). However, since in reality these two kinds of "love" are poles apart, under the law of what is good for A is bad for B, it is best that we should recognize it and keep them so. It is always a hard matter, but this analysis must be made and kept if any relationship is to be a real one. We want so much to have this sense of utter oneness, and we do not like the truth of paradox, which claims that separatedness, not one but two, is the inviolable law.

If we are ever to be really as one, then we must be content to begin as two and bear the burden of our yoke. If we are ever to find our unity, then we must first accept our separatedness. We must learn to move always in this order, for it is so easy to go the wrong way round and, from our false beginning in impatience, to be in the end on the wrong side of the paradox, finding ourselves indeed separated from the object of our love. If we assume in our anxious benevolence that we are one, when this is not in fact the case, then we shall most certainly end by being divided into two, when after all we might have been as one. This is the fate of parents in so many families where the good intention was to be as one, and yet in which the divisible elements failed to recognize that they must accept this fact of their dividedness. The fact remains, however, that we are all agreed in our desire for unity. This is no rare virtue, for in this we are as one. It is only in our method that we differ, and wisdom knows the winning way of paradox, where those more ignorant prefer the more tempting fallacy of direct attack.

In this situation of anxiety which we all must share, it is interesting to consider the attitude that is generally adopted by those who are in authority. The father, the mother, the teacher, the parson: they all can look upon this fearful problem of the little child and clearly recognize a situation of dangerous uncertainty. Their anxiety seems justified, for what have we here, what is this dark, uncertain, mysterious and intangible object, this child?

To some of us there is something very frightening about this experience of looking at a child. We do not find that our more personal contacts with grown-ups are so bad: they are not so frightening, because they seem more firm and fixed. With grown-ups we can feel that we do know more or less where we are, even if we are not there; but it is the sense of uncertainty and formlessness that makes contact with a child so deeply disturbing to those who prefer to surround themselves with reasonable fixtures.

There is something so fluid, so moving, so unlike ourselves about a child: something so formless and undefined, so unlike the familiar B of our more comforting idolatries. We feel that we would like to give a child something to do and then we shall know what it is doing, for we shall have fixed it somewhere. Let us make it better and then we shall at least know that the child is being "good." So in one way or another, by our good intentions, we shall set up our defensive dogmas to make more comfortable the anxiety and dis-ease of our own discontent. We shall paint upon these children pretty coats of many colors, we shall give them some good defensive B's, because we are terrified of what they would be and do if we left them alone with their own A's, to take care of themselves and develop their own B's in their own space and time.

Anxiety will always try to create a false idea of unity, by fixing some false assumption upon the moving state of growth. But we must remember that the child also is anxious, and of the two, perhaps, has even more cause for fear, because the grown-up has at least the advantage of the support of the big battalions. It is not that something is being forced upon the child against its will, for it will like this benevolent offer of a good B, because it will see the illusion of apparent safety within its narrow walls, and will feel good by being accepted on the same side as authority. Because I am so very small, my A seems very small to me; my biscuits are so easily broken, but it seems that nothing can shake the magnificent certainty of your steamroller.

Because we want it thus to soothe our fears, therefore, we develop that smothering, external "me," to become, through its grave parasitism, the greater of our two selves and, so often, the grave of all our greatness. This crustacean instead of vertebrate form of character leaves insignificant and relatively unvalued and undeveloped the other more essential but non-material self of the "I." When we have once begun our flight from fear in this inflated material shell of self-consciousness, we become competitive, and this is heartily encouraged by all our anxious relatives. "Yes, you must be better: you must get on; your place is at the top"; so we are urged upward and ever onward in the great competitive arena of school and home, as well as in the moral circus of the churches. We must climb until we become afraid to fall, always compelled by panic from behind, with the false inference that our rightful place is somewhere above the rest of less-favored humanity. If we are not there, then we are agreed we ought to be. But that is no more than a B-idolatry of self, and is the false value of an exaggerated and isolated half-truth.

Of all the evidences of the predominance of this outer and more superficial part, the B aspect of the self, the most fundamental sign is this competitive insistence upon superior and inferior values: "Because I cannot bear to be what I am, therefore I must be better and have more than you." Competitiveness aims at false isolation, so that at the top we may each be one alone; but, like the aggressive act of war itself, it is as much a rejection of reality as any coward's flight from danger. It differs from flight in that it is a more positive form of cowardice, but it is nevertheless a way of escape from an unbearable anxiety.

What is good for competitiveness (B) must be bad for cooperation (A). The self that thrives upon it becomes easily parasitic, and anxiety is transferred to maintaining the welfare of the host upon whom it feeds. Parasite and host, self and society: in their false assumption of identity, the competitive self will always assume that they are one. David makes his defensive false assumption of being (no, having) Goliath, because he has lost sight of the inner security of his other half of self. The B self will always tend to refer to life in terms of absolutes and compulsive competitiveness, striving by its defensive aggressiveness to maintain both its mask of apparent courage and the defenses with which it hides the lack of it. Before it can find its A again, it must go back to the anxiety of the original two-ness from which it fled and never lose sight of the relationship and difference of "this" and "that," self and not-self. There it will find that burning is not so bad as being burned, and that correct analysis provides the key to courage and also sows the seed of action.

Analysis does not separate the whole into its thousand parts: it only separates a confusion into its related two-ness, self from not-self, you from me, I from me, this from that, the A-ness from the B-ness, each instant now from every other upon the pendulum swing of time. When this is done, Analysis is complete, though such finality is never possible within the rhythmic, moving curves of life.

A patient once said to me: "Surely the root of all our trouble is Fear." I disagreed with him, because we can never have any balanced expression of the problems of life, while we ascribe the status of being the cause of all the trouble to any oneness of a thing by itself, such as fear. Fear is all right; there is nothing wrong with fear. There is no solution to our troubles by this blaming any external "it" whatsoever. The problem exists, not in the fear itself, but always in our attitude towards it. We can either stop and see this fearful matter through, or we can run away, in one way or another.

So here is the two-ness once again, which might be overlooked by those who missed the point. Is our attitude towards fear to be one of "yes" or "no"? Do we run away from fear; are we afraid of being afraid, or do we accept the reality of fear? No, there is nothing wrong with fear. The problem is whether the fear is being unwisely fled.

Let us examine this feeling of fear more closely and we shall find within it a very important two-ness, for it includes within itself two opposites. At one extreme, to flee from fear is to generate panic and terror. But at the other, fear accepted is nothing that we would recognize as fear at all. In the ordinary affairs of life, under different circumstances the entire gamut of emotion can be expressed within the one word "fear," as it can be within the other word "love," which also contains a dictionary of meaning. Each comprises its own antithesis, this fear and that fear, this love and that love. We are accustomed to use these small words as if they meant something definite, but they do not, for each of them can mean almost anything between the poles of its own antithesis. We cannot escape from an act of definition as easily and clumsily as that, for fear has two antitheses within itself. There is the fear to which we say, "Yes, I am afraid," and this is what we are accustomed to recognize as courage. On the other hand, there is the fear to which we say, "I cannot bear to be afraid," which we call cowardice, panic or terror.

This act of separation, "I" from "me," and "it" from "what I feel about it," may set going in our minds many other analyzes of a similar kind. For instance, we can make the same distinction in regard to feelings of inferiority and disappointment, for it is the attitude of "yes" or "no" which we feel towards them that determines their meaning to us. Inferiority accepted is a feeling of content, that "I am what I am"; but when it is not accepted it is a feeling of humiliation. It is very important not to lose such vital distinctions by missing the two antitheses included within the implied confusion of a single word. Again there are some who feel that they ought never to be disappointed; these, when disappointment inevitably occurs, are desolated. They feel sure that such a thing should not happen in the order of their lives, because they cannot bear it. But there are others who are ready to accept disappointment because they have anticipated it; it is part of their idea of the very nature of existence. These, when disappointment occurs, are not even surprised. It all depends upon the degree of our weaning whether we feel desolated or undisturbed.

CHAPTER 13

Instinct and Intuition

"I did it instinctively. It seemed the natural thing to do." What is to be our point of view in regard to instinctive behavior? Can we afford to be "natural?" Is instinct some brilliant and trustworthy light from the unconsciousness within us which can solve all our external problems; or are we to be suspicious of our instincts, or possibly even more than suspicious?

Instincts are an unconscious and automatic behavior pattern, and the characteristic of instinctive behavior is its invariability. Instincts do not "grow," and their behavior patterns go on repeating in spite of any change of outward circumstance. For instance, as an example of instinctive behavior, we may imagine the kitten on the tiled floor of the kitchen from which it cannot get out. It behaves on the tiled floor in exactly the same way as it would have done out in the garden. Every movement and gesture is the same, in spite of the fact that it is quite pointless on a tiled floor. Instincts are thus adapted to jungle days and jungle ways, but not to the modifications of social requirements. They treat "now" as if now were the same as "then"; but it is not.

Think of the instinctive reaction to danger. Instinctive self-preservation is the gesture of the closed fist, with the protective purpose of keeping me intact. If I am frightened of you, instinctively I shall hate you as you seem to threaten to hate me, and if I must fight I hope to get my blow in first. If I do not choose to fight, instinctively I may run away. Instinctively, David would fly from Goliath. Instinctively, if he were cornered he would fight him if he must: but equally instinctively David might identify himself with Goliath, feeling as if he were himself Goliath and find his self-defense that way.

From *Time and the Child: A Study of Morality and Reality* and
War Dance: A Study of the Psychology of War

But is such instinctive behavior always wise? True, it is some-times wise to fly from danger, or to put up a bluff. I would not sug-gest that flight is always wrong, but I would suggest that an invari-able attitude (which is what you get from an instinctive reaction) is often wrong, for instincts do not pick and choose; they react in general according to a fundamental pattern that may be quite inappropriate to this particular circumstance. For instance, the dentist sometimes says to us, with or without an apology, when we sit in his chair, "This is going to hurt a little." Then we hold on to those padded arms, we dig our fingers into the velvet or the leather, we grit our teeth until we are forced to open them and everything is held as tight as possible. We are in a state of tension, and that is instinctive self-defense. But is it common sense, or is it wisdom? Next time anybody threatens to hurt us, let us try another way and see which hurts most—to be in a state of tightness and tension, or to be as limp and relaxed as we can. If ever we are going to fall, it is wise to fall loosely, because if we tighten up we shall probably crack somewhere. But that is something which we have to learn to do, because our self-defensive instinct will always tend to try to keep us intact, in a state of tension. For self-defense we cannot afford to rely on instinct, because it is often better exactly to reverse instinctive tendencies.

In everything we do, we have to learn to overcome instinctive habits. They are generally wrong because they are not adapted to serve the requirements of higher levels of behavior. We have to learn, for instance, to overcome the instinctive tensions that are characteristic of anxiety, both in body and in mind. The compli-cated machinery for living cannot possibly work efficiently that way. The public speaker has to learn this lesson: he must relax his mind, as well as the muscles of his chest and vocal chords, or he will lose the thread of his argument, his breath, and the control of his voice as it gets higher and higher. The swimmer has to learn to accept the water, to give himself easily to it: and when he dives he must relax or he will experience a most painful impact. The dancer cannot dance well until he has learnt to let himself go into the rhythm. The footballer is taught how to fall limply, so as to avoid injury. In jumping a horse over a fence, tension of mind or body is the worst mistake, and is also very easily transmitted from the rider to the horse. In fact, in every case the chief thing that we have to learn is to "let ourselves go," to relax, and consciously to overcome the bad unconscious habits of instinctive self-defense. It is strange but true, that for body, mind and spirit, if we are to be saved, our *instincts must sometimes be exactly reversed.*

Similarly, the maternal instinct, to use a label for a group of feelings associated with maternal behavior, is often dangerous both for the mother and the child. No mother should trust her maternal instinct, because it will be inclined to lavish most inappropriate feelings, at most awkward moments, upon a child who is too young to be able to act other than instinctively in response. As to the sex instinct, who would suggest that it were wise to rely upon an unguarded sex instinct? It would be fatal not only to society, but also to ourselves, if we were to live "naturally." In fact there is not one of these instinctive behavior patterns which is trustworthy or appropriate for behavior under social conditions and modern circumstances.

But it is not only the cruder types of instinctive behavior that are the cause of trouble. In more subtle ways than that, unconscious defensive behavior patterns interfere with our more successful adaptation to our circumstances. Suppose that we have a certain task "X" to do and that we do not feel quite happy about doing it. In fact, we do not want to do it, but there it is, a job of work to do. Defensively, instinctively, we get busy with everything else that comes to hand and mind. We start at the other end of the alphabet and do A, then B, C, D, which have nothing to do with X at all. But at least we are busy and getting busier and busier every moment, instinctively, unconsciously and automatically defending ourselves against the task which is really there in front of us to do. There are a great many of these busy people who are doing, doing, doing, instinctively and self-defensively, in order to avoid doing anything which is worth while, because it is dangerous.

Most subtly also, instinct may affect the very process of our thinking. Fear offers a great opportunity for intellectual fussing, so-called mental reason. In thinking (worrying in fact), we find something to do, something to shout about in our minds, instead of settling down and "staying put" in a real adaptation to a real situation. Thus mental aggressiveness may take the place of emotional deficiency. All such nervous worrying about a problem is instinctive. It may be quite natural in the circumstances, too, but it is not the better for that.

Morality also is tainted with this facile instinctive reaction of self-defense against a problem which we are afraid to face. There is reality, and it is something of which we are afraid. We feel it ought (meaning we would like it) to be different; so we try to fix it as we would like it with consciousness and conscience, when it would really move and we might move in cooperation with it.

This conscience of ours is all very well up to a point, but is it something that we shall always need to rely on as a guide? In fact, ought we to have a conscience? In the end, I believe that the answer is "No": for a conscience, like all authority, is there for our service only for a while, to be got rid of as soon as possible when its task is done. The holy man, who is complete in his development, has one mind, not two. He feels no dependence upon his conscience, because he no longer needs it any more than he needs help from any other external dictatorship or authority. His wishes are as much at one with the Law, as he is with himself. He has no need for conscience to act as makeweight in his moral balance. But for us who have not yet fully grown, it may serve its purpose still, as long as we do not too blindly rely upon it according to the demands of our instinct of self-defense.

I suggest therefore that instinct is something to be watched very carefully, and never to be relied upon, because we have grown beyond our jungle ways and also beyond our instinctive adaptation to them. As civilization is beyond the jungle, so is common sense or wisdom beyond the instinctive method of adaptation to the problems of living an organized society. If we are to react instinctively, it will be in the direction of keeping intact by flight or fight. But if on the other hand we choose in terms of common sense and wisdom, we shall sometimes react in the very different way of acceptance, making closer contact by moving *towards* the fearful object (i.e. loving our enemies) instead of running away. "Well," we shall say, "lets see!"

It is very important to recognize that this great reversal is in our power, by which our attitude toward experience becomes exactly opposite, according to whether we react instinctively or by the light of this other wisdom. If we are to live in the light of the latter, then something has to be not only changed but actually reversed (or, if you like, we have to be converted). What I am suggesting is that in fact there must be this great reversal in our behavior before we can find our true adaptation towards, and acceptance of, not only the reality of ourselves but also of the outside world in which we live and have our "being."

I think that the real reason for our mistakes about instinct is that we have confused it with quite another word and meaning, namely intuition. To the lay mind, in novels and in the Press, the words are used as synonyms. Even the dictionary has this same confusion, for it says that instinctive reaction is "internally compelled" as the result of "innate prompting" (O.E.D.). Yet so is intuitive behavior "internally compelled." "I feel intuitively that I must, because I know it to be true," says intuition.

The distinction between instinct and intuition is an important one for practical purposes. The reason why intuition ("the immediate apprehension of an object by the mind without the intervention of any reasoning process") is more reliable than instinct is because intuition is a source of information, but instinct is a habit of behavior. The difference between the meanings of the two words, therefore, is in fact a difference of opposites. Intuition is "incoming" (information) and instinct is "outgoing" (behavior). We can regard intuition as a virtue because in the highest degree it is illuminative: but instinct is not so trustworthy, because it is in the lowest degree (i.e. materially), self-protective.

There is a rhythm in the curve of life which finds at about the age of forty a deeper need to change towards this inward path. It is as if the earlier half of life must learn first how to live, before it can learn the larger truth of how to die. Material progress has reached its height, the family seed has been planted, position is assured and success can only look forward to eventual decline. This is the period of threatening depression, as advancing years offer no other hope than that of losing what has been so hardly gained.

This then is the period of potential rebirth, when the depth thrusts out its needs again, demanding a return to deeper things. Now is the time for successful aggressiveness to learn the deeper truth, as the other half of life comes forward for completeness, changing material progress to spiritual depth, instinct to intuition, male to female way of living, and death to rebirth. The change requires courage, but not that of aggressiveness. The instinct of aggressiveness is a man's cowardice, but intuition is a child's fact and a woman's courage, for a man to learn again as he becomes older.

It is the female aspect of the psyche which thus requires to be fulfilled in the rhythm of developing experience. First male, then female: first the experience of the seen, then of the unseen: first waking, then sleeping: first having and doing, then becoming a being: first life, then death. It is as if we need the re-creative effect of some deeper inward dip, a way sleep, peace and letting go the tension of our fierce attachments, to be overwhelmed by our abandonment into this reality of the unseen, which has been so long neglected and so fearfully escaped. The change may seem like death, where habits of living have been most arbitrarily fixed: but this death is to be heartily embraced, this depression of the self is to be willingly encouraged, forced even further down. The depression which we experience with so much evidence of grief is the outward proof of unwillingness to be depressed. This is what in fact we need: to go down into the depth of the unseen within ourselves, falling, abandoned, overwhelmed—until we can be reborn, to wake, as if to a new day. This is the time for change of attitude, but so much past habit and poor teaching still bids us to hold on.

From intellect to intuition: from storing to circulating: from personal to universal: from holding on to letting go: from climbing to falling: from living to dying: this is the crisis of life, and the crisis particularly of our times. Can we let go, falling willingly or must we be shattered by the law of life, which demands inexorable obedience, soon or late? Delay makes matters worse, and the role of healer is not to support this falling structure, crying some panacea of cure, but to play the part of gynecologist to death.

Intuition is the term which best describes this greater wisdom, but it is a definable technique which requires some understanding of its laws. It is not only mystery and miracle; it is an experience of that reality which is very near the heart of life. It is not the privilege of some rare mystic few; it is the need and primary process of us all.

Children are intuitive: this is their key to the kingdom to which grown men may thus eventually return, sadder and wiser for their experience of the fruits of knowledge. The process and method of intuition are not new, but they do require the framework of a new metaphysic within which to take respected place. Sleep, trance, death: the ecstasy of life: guesswork and the flash of instant vision: the birth of a new idea: wonder and an inexpressible joy: these are for all, if the bias of unbalanced education in bitter competition with the truth has not entirely eliminated from experience the reality of the unseen.

Intuition is the direct method of experience, whereas that derived from sense and consciousness is not only indirect, but also limited, illusory and inaccurate. Consciously we live in part, within the limits of our senses, through the medium of "space" and "time," believing the measures of our senses to be true. Yet there is more in life than either sense or that which seems to be non-sense. Immediate experience is not negative, nor is it only illusory experience of the non-existent. Intuition is an unlimited insight into that mystery of self and life, which consciousness can only partly scan.

CHAPTER 14

Feeling and Emotion

In regard to the next item for analysis, however, even the dictionary itself fails to help us. It is as if in this, as well as in many other ways, our understanding has to travel beyond the limits of habitual language and conventional meaning. In the case of the process of thought itself, we found no words to make clear the distinction between its cognitive and conative aspects. In general, however, language is kinder to us and there are usually two words in common usage to distinguish between two such different meanings, although very often the ignorant and careless may use them both as synonyms, so that even the dictionary must loosely follow current usage.

Confusion is always significant if we regard it from the angle of potential purpose. It is the common habit of both layman and expert to use the words "Instinct" and "Intuition" as if they meant the same, from which we may infer an instinctive preference for the former, and doubt in regard to the latter. Yet Instinct is as low as Intuition is high: the one is heat, the other light. Instinct is a tendency to action, but Intuition is a sensitiveness to judgment from experience; the former is partial and the latter total; in all respects of our analysis, these two are opposites, and yet they are confused as one. Our ignorance of Intuition is in fact so great, that we may infer it must be purposive, in order to protect us from this feared faculty of experiencing the reality of the unseen. Here is a flight from fact, expressed in words of common usage.

We are at peace through Intuition, but at war by Instinct. The same applies between Feeling and Emotion, for here also the same confusion commonly occurs. Yet Feeling is cognitive (incoming) and Emotion is conative (outgoing), and they are poles apart. Feeling,

From *War Dance: A Study of the Psychology of War*

like intuition, is a state of sensitiveness, but emotion is a tendency (instinctively, aggressively, urgently) to do something about it. Seeing that sensitiveness is usually related to a state of painful suspense, it is easy to understand our bias in favor of uneasy action, so that emotion is instinctively preferred. Although there can be no peace in our emotions, yet we can feel peaceful, in spite of the external threat of War.

Although the distinction between these two words is as important as that which exists between Income and Expenditure (which surely should not be confused) and is essential for an accurate analysis of Peace and War, yet in *The Oxford English Dictionary* Feeling is defined as "the state of being emotionally affected: emotional attitude." Emotion, however, is defined as "a state of stirring, agitation, or passion: psychologically, a feeling, e.g. of desire." It seems strange that so little account should be paid in common usage to our state of peace in regard to reality, as distinct from the warlike tendency to do something about it, prompted by our own desire for wish fulfillment. There is surely something here which needs some deeper understanding, and clear "cognitive" thinking. That which we lack, namely, broadmindedness and toleration, such as is exemplified by the scientific method, depends upon this peaceful capacity to evaluate without interference, to be sensitive without doing anything about it. Perhaps we are gradually in process of learning a new attitude towards life, which involves this accurate analysis between feeling and emotion. But it seems we have not learnt it yet, either in our public habits, or in the common usage of our language.

Our learning is an uphill task, however, because we are instinctively intolerant of that state of suspense in which the sensitiveness of our feelings must always involve us. This instinctive tendency to resolve suspense by means of flight from feeling has resulted in a habit of defensive "taboo" upon feeling. It is something to be despised, because we feel sure that feeling ought not to exist (but note the contradiction), and that its place should be taken by superior reason. The fallacy goes further, and we judge that, because women feel more and men think more, therefore men must be the superior sex. The morally defensive bargain which we have made with an offensive reality has thereby become conveniently rationalized; that which we chose for safety's sake has now also become morally recognized as best. It is noteworthy how often this automatic process of burglar becoming policeman is successful, as a solution of our possible discomfiture.

Figure 16 (p. 210) is drawn to show the point of tension which exists, where this analysis between feeling and emotion is fairly made. Above the horizontal line is "Not-self," separate from Self; to the left of the vertical line is Income (cognition), to the right Expenditure (conation), which is the second necessary analysis. On the left-hand side (1) external stimulus (2) arouses sensation, which is then distributed in the psyche in such a way as to create (3) a "feeling" or "judgment" about the external situation. On the right-hand side the outgoing path of the nervous impulse is traced from (5) emotion, through (6) impulse, until there is (7) some eventual response either physically, inside the body, or externally, through behavior in regard to the environment. It is at (4), the bridge or "synapse," that the condition of strain is felt.

It is important to relate the psychological with the neurological aspect of this problem. It seems as if the nervous system of some people finds it extremely difficult to maintain a state of strain at this nerve junction or synapse, without overflowing from one side of the bridge to the other. These are the ill-balanced people whom we are accustomed to call "hypersensitive" or "highly strung"; or if we judge them by their defensive activities, "emotional" or "hysterical." In fact there is no doubt that our judgment is never in favor of these emotional people, but it is always in favor of those who are restrained, balanced, self-contained, and deep instead of superficial. It proves the poverty of later psychological development, however, that of recent years the only alternative to this ill-balanced emotional overflow has been generally considered to be the equal error of emotional repression.

It is true that these two, emotional expression and repression, are opposite to one another. But there is another psychological attitude which is in itself opposite to them both: namely, instead of impulse being allowed to travel unchecked without resistance across the bridge or synapse, something may happen on the left-hand side

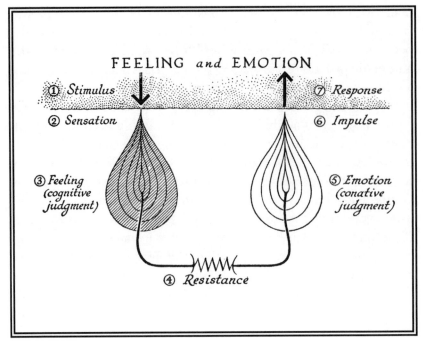

Figure 16 Feeling and Emotion

of the diagram, which enables balance to be maintained without calling upon the emotional response at all. Through an attitude of positive relaxation, the "onion skin" of sensitive self may grow. Thus the sensitiveness of feeling or awareness may be intensified by a process of inward expansion, for which the proper description seems to be "suffering" or "acceptance." In other words, it is possible to want something very much and yet not to make a fuss if we do not get it, although we still want it. Also it is possible to suffer a great disturbance of feeling, either of pain or pleasure, without bursting into tears or laughter or doing anything whatsoever about it in order to change the strain either of inward or outward state. It is not that we require to preserve the impassivity of poker-face, but merely that good manners and good sense realize that feeling (like many other things) should most frequently be preserved *in situ* and in silence. The outbreak into emotion belongs to a world of sentimentalism and sensationalism, which does not believe in the essential probity of the unseen, but would have all things undressed in the public eye and served up to breakfast with a kipper. But thus to insist that the unseen should be seen is to make it seem obscene, which it need not be if it is allowed to dwell in its proper place.

The emphasis upon emotion must of course inevitably lead to a degree of intolerant interference, which is the early phase of war. If we feel that which is true for us, then it is within our own selves that we suffer, and no one else is involved thereby. But if we become emotional about it, then experience is being externalized and someone else must share the privilege of our suffering. Sensationalism, sentimentalism, emotionalism, lack of self-control, a habit of blaming others and of most unphilosophical emphasis upon external cause, all go together to induce a final state of war. We balance our inward instability by insisting upon some external change.

It is instructive that this whole aftermath of consequent war has developed out of a situation the original purpose of which was self-defense. Because we could not bear the strain, this war-like process was first set in being; it then must grow as vicious circles do, because the end result is larger strain than that which first initiated it. If we could only learn to bear the beginning of these troubles sensitively within ourselves, there would be less argument and our external troubles would decrease instead of grow upon us as they do. This idolatry of external cause and change, devised instinctively as it was for safety's sake, has propagated that very danger which it was planned to avoid. But being so sick of war, physicians are now trying to heal us by a double dose of our disease.

CHAPTER 15

Aggressiveness

"**A**ggressiveness is energy applied to reduce time and/or space between subject and desired objective." This definition includes growth, which is movement step by step in natural time, and introduces the simplest derivation of the word "aggressiveness" (Lat. *ad*, towards; *gradior*, I step). This cannot be all, however, that is meant by aggressiveness, for it is not from such graceful growth that we have ever suffered. As desire is more hasty, beating time anxiously, so aggressiveness increases in its pathology until, when time is altogether eliminated, it has reached its maximum.

It is important to notice that through a continuous process of time elimination, the significant value of aggressiveness has changed from positive on the one hand to negative on its opposite extreme, and from contructiveness in growth to destructiveness when time has been eliminated. The seed is the symbol of all that grows in time, but the bomb is the symbol of all that timelessness destroys.

Normal growth occurs in space-time by means of a relationship between the positive and the negative, or between desire and resistance. Thus the negative resistance is first "accepted," and then in time grown through. By this process of growth we are always involved within a discipline, facing an unknown, and active in a state of suspense (see figure 17, p. 250). There is something that we want which is beyond us: life is like an open question, the unknown answer to which involves anxiety, which for our normality in this experience requires most positive acceptance. Contrasted with this is the abnormal state of anxious urgency: "I-must-have-it-NOW," which is the condition illustrated in figure 17 (b). In this, the strain of anxious suspense is felt to be intolerable and both space and time are jumped by means of a false assumption, which can the more readily be believed within the facile screen of consciousness, because it can be so easily moralized by conscience

---

From *War Dance: A Study of the Psychology of War*

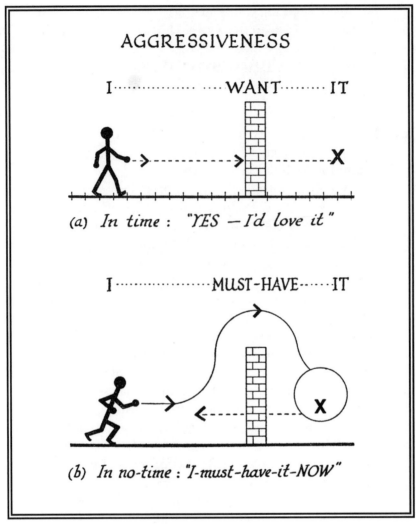

Figure 17 Aggressiveness

into a sense of duty. "I want it; I must have it now; I ought to have it now because it is good; it ought to be mine now; in fact it is mine now, and who denies that is my hateful enemy." Upon the screen of consciousness we can draw so many pictures of our own reality, which are the more intensely held as belief, because they represent desire achieved. No wonder, then, that we are anxious not to have opinions changed or prejudices cured. We hold to what we have, from fear of that unseen which would rob us of our fond illusion.

"Do not tell me the truth, for I am precariously balanced by my own beliefs."

Figure 18 on p. 252 illustrates (c) the possibility of relationship between two moving systems, connected as it were by cogs, fitting one into the other each in time. The normal process of growth is that the motive power from each of these two systems should operate within itself in spite of this relationship. Watch, however, what happens if the larger system on the left-hand side of the page becomes over-active in its sense of duty, and starts to rotate the smaller system to which it is related. The motive power is then external and not internal, and the actor has in this sense become a puppet of the audience, or the child a movement of its parents' motor.

This problem may be further illustrated from diagram (d) in which a moving system (X) is met by a resistance, or more slowly moving system (Y). Growth will then be a process of expansion of X within Y, in which Y is moved outwards in time. This process may be continuous, as X gradually overcomes the resistance of Y, so that its movement may gradually extend to cover the whole of Y's system; or on the other hand, the relationship of these two systems may be an alternating rhythm, such as occurs in the piston and cylinder, in which X rises and falls as the resistance of Y diminishes or relatively increases. As a third alternative, the force of X may be less than that of the resistance which it meets from Y, so that Y may gradually overwhelm its lesser neighbor. These three alternatives may again be referred to diagram (e) in which on the left-hand side there is a movement from X to Y, as Y's resistance is gradually resolved (positive phase), whereas the next diagram shows what happens when the resistance of Y is too great and the system is therefore moving in a negative phase. In the third diagram the two forces are in conflict, and altogether out of time relationship or harmony. (This problem is worth special consideration in regard to the movements of partners in ballroom dancing.)

To return to the earlier illustration, figure 17 gives a more personal flavor to the problem, where the "Little man" walking along the time-track of experience is faced by the resistance of some obstruction in his path, between him and the desired objective. On the one hand (a) his attitude is graceful, tolerant and disciplined,

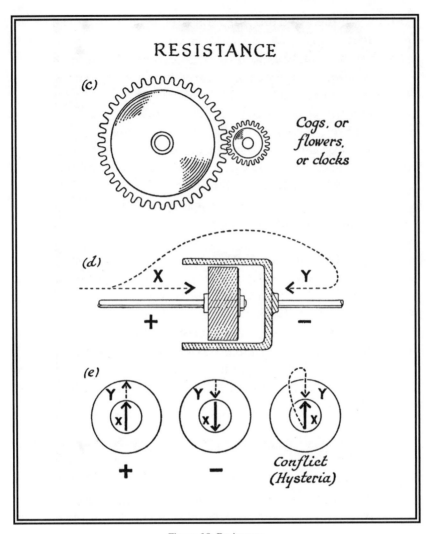

Figure 18 Resistance

so that feeling "Yes, I'd love it," he still retains his place in space and time, moving gracefully towards his desired objective if he can. Compared with him, his more urgent neighbor (b) in the lower part of the diagram finds morality more activating than reality and phantasy than fact. He feels so sure that he ought to have it and therefore assumes that it is his now, jumps the wall, possesses himself of it and finds that he has thus gained a dubious advantage. He must now adopt a negative attitude, because he has thus identified himself with that which was so negative to him. The arrows of direction have become reversed, through an intolerance of this fundamental fact of time. This will always be found to be the case, for although growth (in time) is positive, timeless aggressiveness is negative. There is so much instruction to be gained from this fact, that it is surprising that the significance of time should be omitted from our philosophy. Yet if we look at the methods of our education, whether in nurseries, schools, religion or politics, there is still too little known of the deep discipline of time.

There is so much moral virtue to be easily acquired by beating the clock, that it is difficult to realize that such ardent endeavor is evidence only of the unweaned state of egotistic insistence upon the right to have timelessly, hastily, securely, NOW. Such aggressiveness will be the very enemy of truth and peace, yet it is only time that separates it from the natural process of growth in grace. It is dangerously easy to transfer the values that belong to system A (i.e. four-dimensional reality, eternity, spirit or the whole) from A to system B (three-dimensional reality, space, time, the material part), where they do not belong. "Me" assumes the quality and value of "I," and Me's egotism thus enjoys a universal importance, which is the prerogative not of Me but of I. (This is vanity, idolatry, neurosis or untruth.)

"I want it now!" These desired objectives seem to assume so much external value in their own right, but we must learn to regard them as meaningless and valueless in themselves, being only mirrors projecting some deeper value upon our vision. That deeper value is not external but internal, and is derived not from external B but from internal A. "It" is the means to the end that I should be that which I am: which is not Me. Yet anxiety will always persuade us otherwise, offering us trick solutions, showing us vain causes, asserting moral compulsion to achieve some impossible promise in the name of some mythical respectability. Here is our problem, and it is a matter of Time.

It is this same matter of an attitude towards Time that makes all the difference between the behavior of two passengers in the same bus. They may both be late for an appointment, yet one is jumping up and down in his seat, as if by so doing he thinks that his activity will be transmitted to the driver and the engine. His state of mind, aggressively pushing within the slowly moving bus, makes no more difference to the time at which it arrives at its destination, however, than does the mood of his more relaxed and easy-going companion, who is able to enjoy the passing scene in spite of the fact that he cannot make it move any faster. If this restless one is only a passenger, he is less likely to do harm than if, as is unfortunately too often the case, he is the driver of the vehicle. In that case, being more independent, he is more free to "step on it," causing his presumptuous over-activity to collide disastrously with less impatient travelers upon the way of life. "Beating the clock" is not really to be regarded as a virtue because, under whatever guise it travels, its destructiveness will account for the slaughter of mankind, which is left as tragic litter upon the path of this impatient self-assertive Juggernaut.

To summarize before leaving this very important question of the nature of aggressiveness, we may divide it into two kinds:

1. Normal, e.g. timely growth; the seed lives gracefully.

2. Abnormal, e.g. timeless bursting of the bonds of discipline; the bomb.

The latter may again be subdivided into

(a) Timeless defensive identification with the feared object.

(b) Timeless offensive identification with the desired objective.

We may also note that as between these two kinds of aggressiveness:

1. The Time factor is decisive in diagnosis.

2. The two kinds are opposite in sign and value.

3. "Fitness" in Time is the essential virtue, both for growth and grace.

Aggressiveness even unto death itself is an attitude towards life which can best be expressed by the metaphysical diagnosis of the "infinite regress." There are thus two ways even of dying; and two deaths, negative and positive. Acceptance, on the other hand, which is the development of a positive attitude towards experience, an ingratiation of the self into its necessary discipline, fulfils the creative law symbolized in the growth of the tree of life, the mating of female and male to create the child; and makes manifest that uprising of the dragon, which is akin to rising sap or the development in time of the fullest energy which abides within the self.

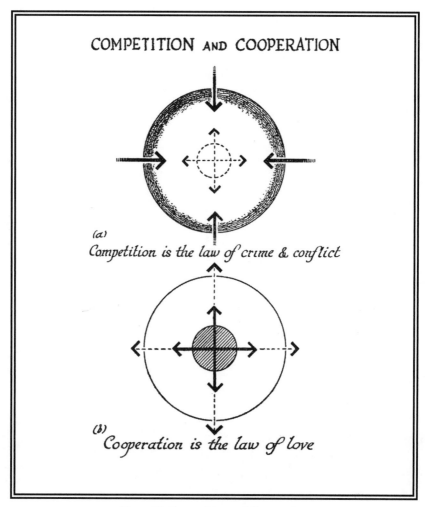

COMPETITION AND COOPERATION

(a)
Competition is the law of crime & conflict

(b)
Cooperation is the law of love

Figure 19 Competition and Cooperation

Then death is no longer to be regarded only as a bad thing, a punishment, but can be seen in due proportion as the true fulfillment of the greater law of life. Only the criminal (impatient one) need fear the punishment of law, and only he who has not learnt to live need fear to die.

The urge of aggressive competition is illustrated in figure 19 (a), where the forces within the psyche, or between self and circumstance, are set in opposition one against the other, aggressiveness always being associated with the predominant negative of a destructive attitude towards life. Diagram 19 (b), however, illustrates the law of love working in cooperation from the center outwards as the sap rising in the tree, or as the development of the serpent force, the uprising dragon, within the self.

CHAPTER 16

Repression

We have dealt with many of the external aggressors, but it is now necessary to turn our attention to that inward aggressor, who is the inward image of his external manifestation. Repression is aggressiveness aggressively treated by its elimination. Reality repeats itself, and the same problem exists within the psyche as outside it. Our inward order of "opposing tensions" is also unfortunately lacking in harmony. Seeing that we are within ourselves not one but two, the same question arises, Which One? There is the same tendency to eliminate one member of this opposing group. As to which is to be the chosen one between ourselves, there is little difficulty in providing the answer. The one we want to be is that which represents the seen aspect of the self, operating in terms of the physical body and its conscious and conscientious (male aggressive) function. We therefore impose a taboo on all that is within the unseen, which includes the inward spirit, the serpent-force, as the source of movement. Thus space, darkness and death; feeling and the female aspect of the psyche; magic and witchcraft, are all included within the same taboo. All these are to be numbered amongst the bad things, because of their vitally disturbing nature to the world of the seen, of which they hold both the key and the roots. In this battle to eliminate the unseen enemy, victory is assumed by morality and reason, by thinking and fixing, by having and doing, and by all that the materially possessive male can hope for in his urgent demand for safety, possessiveness and privilege.

In the name of peace of mind, by means of repression, intolerant of suspense, we provide a false facade of unity, approval and self-righteousness. Behind this, however, there is always lurking the

From *War Dance: A Study of the Psychology of War*

unseen enemy, which contains the seeds of life itself. Thus the negative forces in the psyche hope to have gained a victory over the positive, and the aggressor rules blandly above the submerged head of his own aggressiveness.

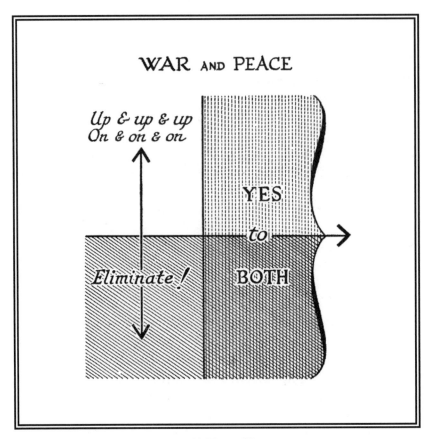

Figure 20 War and Peace

The answer to such a process is best described in terms of infinite regress, and leads to that state of psychic unrest in which so many of us find ourselves at the present day. The situation is illustrated in figure 20 above. On the left-hand side of figure 20, the two aspects of the psyche are divided horizontally in terms of opposition between the seen and the unseen. The same bilateral condition is seen on the right-hand side of the diagram with, however, the difference that where on the left the two are held to be in conflict, on the right they are allowed to be in harmony. On the left it was a case of Either/*Or*, on the right it is This *and* That. On the left, one must be maintained in superiority over the other (repression); but on the right, both are regarded as the very elements of life itself, to be related in abundant harmony. These two attitudes towards life are negative and positive, but it is towards the former that we are most reasonably prone.

If we make a list of the variety of our aggressive mannerisms, which determine the details of this negative attitude, it is impressive in its length:

Fixation	Men
Repression	Mechanization
Conscience	Missionaries
Morals	Idealists and Progressives
Honor	Faddists
Loyalty	Amusement, (B-musement?)
Action	Invalidism
Organization	Pacifism
Efficiency	Humor
Freedom	Teasing
Rights	Reason

Of course it is not intended in any way to belittle such activities of the spirit as are prepared to flower within the discipline of accepted limitations, and thus to grow. The above list may be added to indefinitely, because in all things it is possible to adopt the aggressive attitude, but in themselves there need not be anything wrong with any item. For example, a sense of humor is inserted because so much of humor is unkind, being engaged largely in laughing aggressively at something, instead of smiling tolerantly with it (i.e. the laugh is external and negative, instead of internal and positive). Jokes of a sexual kind supply the material for so much of what is loosely called a sense of humor, but they are in fact the strongest indication of the lack of it in the deepest sense. Wherever humor is forced in any way, it may be suspected that it is behaving as a function of aggressiveness, rather than according to the laws of kindlier growth.

If the reader should feel that any one of the items listed above has been unfairly placed, the covering grace of inverted commas will show more clearly that it is only the aggressive aspect of this virtue which is being selected for our disapproval. (There is of course no doubt that we may disapprove. The point is that we may not force change upon the objects of our disapproval. We may change them, but not by force: all true change is an emanation of growth through fertilization by love.)

CHAPTER 17

Willpower

What should we do when things are not what we want, and when they are not what we feel they ought to be? The answer seems simple: if things "ought" to be different, surely we "ought" to try to change them, and we should use our willpower to change them as we wish. For instance, we have some child in our charge, who is to be educated in the way we think it should go. This child has its own life, its own volition, its own experience, and uses its will-to-live in a way of which we disapprove. In fact, for us, this child is bad: what should we do? Are we to use our willpower to make it do as we think fit? Or if we are not to be so willful ourselves, are we at least to encourage the child to use its own willpower? We have often heard the good advice: "If at first you don't succeed, try, try, try again!" This willpower is the idol of the Spartan as well as of the sentimental nursery, as long as it is only exercised in a negative sense of not being annoying: it is not so "good" when it appears under the trying guise of willfulness. It is advice which we offer more freely to others than take ourselves; as, for instance, when we advise those who try us: "Do, for goodness sake, use your willpower and pull yourself together!" But it usually sounds more like a threat than a promise, and it is quite time we asked the question: What is willpower? It is more than probable that most of those who are so ready with their advice do not know what it is.

In our understanding of this and other matters we are handicapped by language. Perhaps I have sometimes made matters seem even harder than need be the case, by insisting on the right to make an unfamiliar language of my own, keeping a two-ness working all the time, and making it even more complicated by having a third party present. It was, however, with the idea that, having

---

From *I and Me: A Study of the Self*

made it, this language might be of some practical use, and a better guide in time of trouble than the false simplicity of a oneness in confusion. So let us see if we can make any use of this circular terminology of A, B and C, to learn something about willpower. There may be a latent confusion in the word; perhaps there are two willpowers, or even three. If there are, it is no wonder that we are all somewhat confused when people insist on using the word "willpower," as if, so simply, it meant something that we might understand. Perhaps it is a word like *Self,* or *Love,* or *Fear,* that needs further analysis? Undoubtedly it is a most important word, but it seems very confusing as we loosely use it and it does not seem to mean what we are apt to believe. We are not tidy enough in our thoughts; and indeed it is very difficult to be an accurate thinker amidst the wild confusion of our experience, which becomes so readily cluttered up with the meanings and values with which other people have found it convenient to obscure reality.

The trouble about this clumsy use of willpower is that it won't work; or, if it does, only at the price of conflict and confusion. If we use our willpower we soon discover something else, namely, that we have a "won't-power" too. Coué recognized that our "won't-power" was stronger than our so-called "willpower," and described it as the "law of reversed effort." Therefore, he said, if we wanted results from self-suggestion we must not use our willpower, because this paradoxical effort would defeat our own ends by introducing an opposite factor, the negative of "Won't-power," which would be stronger than the positive with which we hopefully opposed it.

Such unorthodox advice as this, although it has been found often enough to be excellent in practice, should be disconcerting to members of the "Try, try, try again" and "Pull yourself together" schools. Such strange advice as "Don't use your willpower if you want results" should have surprised our nursery moralists and taught them something, but we are still confused. Yet what could be more important than that we should know the most efficient way to obtain what we want? If willpower works, let us use it: but if it does not, let us know what would better take its place. It is strange that there should be this confusion, both in our language and our principles, about so important a point.

For instance, to give up smoking by means of willpower costs a great deal of unnecessary effort, if it succeeds at all. We try very hard, with grim determination—"I will be master of my own habits!" "I will not be beaten" "I will *not* smoke!"—and we feel a swelling sense of pride from this exercise of our moral grandeur. But as we watch the virtue of our efforts we may notice a curious thing. As we say, "I will *not* smoke, I will not smoke," using our willpower as hard as we can, before we have gone very far we find that it has turned round on us and changed into won't-power. The great effort of willpower, which we had put at the disposal of not smoking, is now the measure of our desire for a cigarette, and we seem to have been stoking up the fires of desire instead of damping them down. The trouble about willpower is that it is a sword which is liable to turn in the hand against its user, or a boomerang that returns against the thrower. In the strength of will that is divided against itself by the effort of desire, we find in practical experience that effort suggests laziness. Yes is balanced by No, and willpower by won't-power.

If we wish either to achieve anything or to give up something, we must take care how we use this very doubtful asset of our willpower, for there are these two of them, the Yes and the No, and they are in conflict. "Yes, I will: No, I won't," impulse and inhibition, is the essence of the two-ness of mind. It is a power system of plus and minus, and it is built like all other power systems upon a plan of that same two-ness, the law of which is that what is good for A is bad for B. Yet these two parts or force-systems of the mind, for perfect functioning, must learn to cooperate and act as friends. This is the conflict implied within the very nature of all desire, and it is responsible for much wasted effort and ultimate disappointment, in which we sometimes say: "But I tried so hard!" Yes, and meant well too; but, unfortunately for us, we happened to be backing the wrong horse. It did look good, but Willpower (by Desire out of Effort) is a very disappointing runner, because we can never be sure that he will not turn round and run in the opposite direction when the critical moment occurs.

There is too much of this clumsy fallacy of willpower and conflict taught both in the family and in the school. "I want my son to be a parson": "I want my daughter to be good": "I wish she were a boy." This is all desire, desire, desire, and implies a certain use of willpower. But is it good, and does it achieve what it sets out to get, or does it defeat its own ends by making enemies where it most needed friends? It does not succeed as a method if it raises resistance or creates false standards. It seems to be part of the law in regard to the use of all power systems that, for all we may wish, either for ourselves or for anyone else, we are faced by a negative against which, since it is there, it is no use indiscriminately fighting. Since this negative (I want and have not) is part of the Law, it is something to be accepted and not rejected, to be "eaten" and not fought against. This acceptance of the facts of life, in spite of disappointment, involves an act of submission, a passivity of effort and a limitation of desire. It may seem to be a shameful giving in, a miserable betrayal of our post of personal responsibility, but that is not quite the case, for things are not what they seem.

When we first recognize the harm that willpower can do, it may come as a startling surprise. It is quite a commonplace experience, however, to doctors who are engaged in psychotherapy. We do not want willpower from our patients, for we know that what has caused their illness will not help their cure. We want them to stop trying to pull themselves together, in fact we want them to do exactly the opposite, which is to relax and let things go. But this is just what they are afraid to do, feeling that they ought not: for in their illness they have done, with best intentions, what they thought was well.

In the work of a psychotherapist, the fact that the patient wants to get better and that the doctor wants to effect a cure is from one point of view a chief obstacle to progress and success. The process of healing is not aided but inhibited by such desire. This at first may seem surprising, because we are so used to hearing the virtues of hope extolled. Yes, but we must watch the two-ness: for all hopes are not to be so simply trusted. It is better to give up hope sometimes, for it is wiser to lay down our arms when we cannot stand the strain of battle any longer. We cannot have calm seas all the way and it is no use being buoyed up by false hopes to the contrary. We must be willing sometimes to accept the storm and take it lying down, setting on one side both willpower and desire, which are always in opposition to the negative aspect of the will, the other side of the power system. We must be very careful of our desires, because they are always creating for us the balance that will frustrate them, and wishing is the parent of its own disappointment.

So far we have only considered the two willpowers of power (Yes and No), which always seem to be defeating their own ends in clumsy fashion because they are thus engaged in conflict. This kind of willpower does not seem to hold the key to a technique of efficiency. For that we must find the third willpower, the "C" which is neither A nor B, but related child of both. This is the willpower of wisdom, which is the principle of unity that leads to the "peace that passeth understanding" (see figure 21, p. 266).

The willpower of wisdom is related to the willpower of power as an antithesis, and they are opposites; for the most important characteristic of the willpower of wisdom is that it knows no conflict because it knows no desire. It is, in fact, the willpower of desirelessness. But that is only a negative definition, and since there seems to be no special word to hold our meaning, we must try to define more positively what it means. The chief characteristics of the willpower of power are two: one is competitiveness and the other is revulsion. Where we find any attitude of competitiveness or of revulsion, then we can feel sure that we are dealing with the willpower of power, with its conflict within the limits of self-will. The willpower of power is the willpower of conflict, the alternating dualism of "yes . . . no, yes . . . no," which are the two aspects of desire. But the willpower of wisdom has nothing to do with such competitiveness; in fact it behaves in quite the opposite way. Its manners are perfect; it is never rude, because it feels no revulsion; it never says "No" and is never offensive. The willpower of wisdom is the willpower of a single motive of acceptance—Yes, yes, yes. It therefore has all the technical efficiency of single-mindedness and effortless concentration upon a single far-off goal.

This willpower of wisdom is something with which we are quite familiar, and which we all know from our own experience to succeed. It is strange that there is no word with which we may more readily distinguish it from confusion with its opposite, but there

Figure 21 Will Wisdom and the Two Willpowers

does not seem to be one in the English language. Nevertheless, if we think clearly in the terms of the one, two and three, even without the aid of any special word for it, we can recognize the distinction between these "wills" in our everyday behavior. There is nothing unusual or surprising about this third quality of willpower, except perhaps the absence of a word for it. The willpower of wisdom is what is meant by "love," using that word in the rather special sense of that quality which is to be trusted and admired whenever and wherever it is met.

The exercise of this function of love, which is the willpower of wisdom and forbearance, is not an easy matter, for we are easily prompted by the urgent voice of conscience to action in a contrary fashion. We feel so sure that by our constant efforts we can achieve more desirable results, so that we ought to try to make things better, to try to make these children good. Yes, of course we should: but it is a very vital question as to which is the best way to the desired result. The direct method of force is doomed to failure in the long run, however attractive it may seem to be at first sight as a short cut. There would be nothing wrong about this method if it worked, but it does not, because it omits the law of paradox. The ready success which it sometimes seems to offer proves disappointing when the urgent force flags from its own fatigue, and then a natural and inevitable reaction follows, to upset all our pretty plans to the contrary. The trouble about this policy of "trying" is that it soon becomes "too trying": it is the restless over-active way of strain and tension which is known as "living on our nerves." It is the way of conflict and of neurosis: it is the way of self-will and exploitation of others: it is the way of willpower versus won't-power, of endless argument in terms of "Yes, I will: No, you won't." The alternative policy to any such display of active force is the method of relaxation, which is the "female" path in, contrast with the "male." This other way of relaxation is the "Yes" way; it is the opposite of the "Yes—No" way, as female is the opposite of male.

However, it is very difficult to see any virtue in a policy of acceptance which seems so like taking our troubles lying down, and we feel that surely we ought to fight to take care of ourselves: but now we are in trouble over this word fighting and its turn has come for the inevitable analysis.

There are two ways of fighting: again these are the "Yes" way and the "No" way. The former says "yes" to everything and so loves the enemy (but still as enemy, and not as friend). This is in fact the way of love, or of acceptance, that keeps contact undefended against truth. The way is difficult: Yes. The pain is bad: Yes. The time is short: Yes—or long: Yes. The child is dead: Yes. Here is a battle indeed that needs no guns or drums to emphasize the conflict. The other way of fighting is as aggressive as it is sure of its own moral righteousness; as dogmatically instructive to others as it has faith in its own power to answer every question; and as determined to alter the march of events in its own favor as any self-willed child. It is not an acceptance of reality but as surely an evasion of it as any coward's panic-stricken flight: only the method of evasion differs, and there are these two ways, by fight (positive) and flight (negative).

Yet if this fact of which we disapprove is true, what else is to be done but accept it, unless we run away from what is true? We fall so easily into the cheaper idolatry of competitiveness and prefer to have things and people neatly ordered on a scale of marks. There is something comforting about all idolatry, it is so pleasing to be fixed good. And since it so appeals to all of us, there is no doubt that our salesmanship will pass it on to children in such a way that it will not only appeal to them, but also appear to them to be both natural and inevitable. Yet this is not the case, for there is this other way, though it sometimes requires much courage (which is itself the policy of an accepted fear) to stand back and do nothing. The way of forbearance, however, achieves wholeness through the accepted two-ness, by saying "yes" to the dualism of Life's experience. It means, to some extent at least, living above our personal desires and so learning to overcome all revulsion. That may be difficult, but then our task in Life must always be difficult, and we can only make it more so by our willful efforts to have it otherwise.

The fact that the willpower of wisdom does not use revulsion, when looked at from the willpower of power, sometimes looks both very mad and very bad. But it is a fact that when looked at from the willpower of power, the way of wisdom does look mad and bad, except in regard to the results which it achieves. In fact, posed upon a pedestal in moral and rejective mood, at least half the world looks mad and bad to the willpower of power, as if it ought to be something quite different from what it is. But the willpower of wisdom has the courage of a little madness and is able to see deeper and more clearly by that inner light which enables it always to say "yes."

In the struggle and conflict of our lives, we feel that we have the "right" to liberty, claiming it as something which is ours that ought not to be taken away from us. This is certainly more true to our wishes, however, than to our experience, for liberty we surely have never had, although we may relatively have stolen too much of it. For liberty is like a poison bottle, on which "Not to be taken" should be written. We feel so sure, however, to the contrary. Of course we ought to have our "rights," and so of course we ought to fight in their defense.

But have we any right to interfere? The answer will depend upon whether we really have any rights. These rights that we expect as something due to us, these liberties we claim as ours and sometimes even nobly die for, are they not privileges that put someone else in prison or in pawn? These selective-rejective people who claim the right to choose by saying "yes" to this but "no" to that, claiming their right to take such liberties, are putting someone else, if not themselves, at a disadvantage. All wars, whether domestic or national, are fought in just such a good cause, for right and against wrong, in the name of liberty and for the sake of peace. This moral attitude is at the opposite pole from the other kind of fighting, through acceptance and by the way of peace. By this other way, those who accept experience may find that by saying "Yes" to the two-ness of both this and that, they have gained a real liberty both for themselves and others. For them there is no price to pay in prison, because there is no desire. Nor can they be disappointed, for they have felt no anticipation of their righteous harvest.

There should be no moral persuasion in the use of any personal law, which is unjustifiable interference except in so far as it can mediate and represent the impersonal law of external reality. The characteristic of this impersonal law of life is its desirelessness, its impartiality and profound indifference to you and me and what we want. It is not possible to raise a family well, or in fact to rule or organize efficiently any group or institution whatever, without the practical elimination of the forces of egotism and personal desire. Desire exploits advantage at the expense of another. It causes trouble because it makes conflict both within the self and beyond, in ever-widening circles. It does not matter that the desires are good, such as desiring to get on, to improve, or to be good. We must still learn to curb them under the yoke of accepted facts.

We need to be far more impersonal in all our dealings with one another. Since there must be a ruler in a household, it may well be the clock, which has no desire and whose impartiality can therefore be better trusted not to operate unfairly to anyone's disadvantage. Therefore the clock is a good ruler and children are prepared to obey clocks (if they have not been unjustly exploited) when they are not prepared to obey the desires of parental authority, which are not by any means so impartial.

In order to make more clear the alternative policies of desire and desirelessness, we can refer to them respectively as heat and light, horsepower and candlepower, or as the lifeboat and the lighthouse. In a world in which worship of the policy of action is swift to class inaction with laziness, it is sometimes difficult to act as lighthouse, when the dictatorship of moral temptation is all in favor of acting as lifeboat, with a spectacular dash to someone's rescue. Our hearts are instinctively prepared to prefer heroic rescues and the policy of the lifeboat to that of the lighthouse, power to wisdom, action to rest. We are all possessed of this yearning for power, that must always be doing something, this urgent anxiety to take steps to get somewhere, to be anywhere but where we are. That is why it is so important to set up this other way of the lighthouse as an alternative to the moralized impatience of self-will.

This is not merely a matter of abstract and unimportant theory, but one of most vital importance in everyday practice. For good results in the long run it is much better to keep desire out of the domestic atmosphere and to develop in its place a law that is as impartial as it is impersonal, after the manner of the lighthouse that does not move but neither does it go out. This lighthouse is to be regarded as the symbol of security and of silent warning; as the eye that sees all, but, whether approving or not, retains the same unremitting affection and kindly tolerance, always saying "yes," even though it does disapprove when little ships threaten to pile themselves upon the rocks of harsh experience.

Of course I do not mean that we should never offer help or that we should always refuse to lend the lifeboat's aid. I do mean, however, that we are apt to forget that lifeboats can be very dangerous things if they give the impression that there really is no danger, for then foolhardiness may go hard on the rocks with its eyes shut. As always, there is this twoness; we must keep our balance between horsepower and candlepower, lighthouse and lifeboat, repose and action, desire and desirelessness. But it is better that we should know beforehand the bias with which we are prone to lean. The solution of our problems is not to be found in idolatry of either side of life's antitheses, but, remembering the inseparable relationship of each, in the balanced use of both. We must not try to ease the tension of dis-ease by cutting off either horn of our dilemma.

It may be objected that the lighthouse way is the way of the Saint, through the wisdom of his deeper understanding, and that therefore it is not the way for us, whose interest lies in smaller things. But psychotherapists are not saints, although in their limited way they use the same technique with their patients. The fact is that it is a sound working method in spite of our instinctive bias against it. It is the way that works best in practice, whether in home or school. It is the way of a softened image of Reality, in which impartiality has been humanized by the influence of understanding Love.

PART IV

The Holy Family

CHAPTER 18

In the Beginning, . . .
CONSCIOUSNESS

It is important to emphasize one outstanding fact, which is universal and axiomatic to our understanding of our experience of relationships and communication. Of any pair of opposites, such as X and Y, *X is in Y* and *Y in X* because they are both the by-products of NON-DUALITY, which is in both. It is in this manner that the Godhead is within us, as we are represented within the Godhead from which we have sprung. Similarly, light is inherent in its opponent darkness, and vice versa: as man is essentially part of woman, so woman is also of her partner man. We are in fact in a brotherly-sisterly relationship with one another, however young or old we may be, and to whatever generation we may belong, as FATHER are all children of one FATHER, who is always present within us, although beyond our ken. Thus our hope of wholeness depends as much or more upon our enemies as upon our friends.

Having stated our FIRST CAUSE and origin as CONSCIOUS PERSONS, and the opponent duality by which we must ever be confronted if we are to achieve our "wholeness" (Anglo-Saxon "halig" = "health"), it is now necessary to see how our relationship with the opponent other can be achieved.

At first sight, it may seem that we need power over the other, as it were to add the second part to the first, in order that everything can be neatly under control. Humanly speaking this is what we often try to do, but it is our all-too-common error. For life, in its mysterious way, performs its miracles by dying into life; and death into rebirth, not power over the other, is the secret of life's mystery.

From *She and Me: A New Statement of an Old Problem*

How can INFINITY diminish itself, except by "dying down to nothing," which is how the elephant got into the bottle in the Zen Koan, as well as the simple manner in which our consciousness is able to concentrate at the point of its attention? At the heart of all creation there is a cross, which means that death is so much a part of life that without it we cannot live. From point to circle, from circle to sphere, from sphere to spiral, when once life is emergent from the VOID, duality proclaims that although LIFE may be eternal, death is the lot of all that moves upon the ascending and descending curves of space and time.

We can now realize that we are concerned with two systems of "duality." The first has to do with the relationship between NON-DUALITY and duality, SPIRIT and matter, Godhead and manhood, or "I" and "me." Here is our original area of experience between CREATOR and creature; this is our lifeline and radial link with SOURCE, from expanding periphery to contracting center. The second system of duality is within the area of experience of duality itself. The moment of departure from the source in the VOID (FATHER) requires a splitting in the "son," who must hereafter forever be divided within and against himself, as male and female, higher and lower, light and dark, inner and outer, life and death. Once these were only ONE, in NON-DUALITY: now as many in their diversity have become the mediators and dispensers of all that energy and personal motivation, which we experience as "life."

Re-thinking John Donne, we can say that in this world we are all "islands," united only in and by the INFINITE BEYOND. Mistaking the facts, however, we have tried to turn "here" into THERE, and "this" into THAT, preferring to ignore the fact that all pairs of opposites are polarized against each other in their degree of difference. However much we may enjoy our experience of "togetherness," the fact remains that we are born apart; heart from head, self from other, man from woman, and left hand from right. This is the truth of "sex," that although love may grow between a man and a woman, it is not "natural." Greed and the longing for power over the other with which to quell anxiety *are* "natural": misunderstanding, sickness and unbalance *are* "natural": violence and war *are* "natural." But LOVE, like life and health, is supernatural, because both are gifts only of the Divine "Grace."

It was "natural" for man to choose the lesser light, rather than the greater dark: security rather than danger: success rather than suffering: life rather than death, and to be the victor rather than the victim. But it was not wise to deprive the tree of its roots and to ignore the invisible anatomy of his cave. Choosing to use his right hand at the expense of his left, he not only tortured CONSCIOUSNESS. He also put at terrible risk the truth regarding his woman and his child, which were the other, inner, weaker aspects of himself. After thousands of years of this right-handed moral bias, he has still to learn the error of his ways.

The "light" side may seem to have the advantage of more power over the other: but, especially if it seems to be for their good, this can prove a very dubious policy, by progressively depriving them of their divine right to be and choose for themselves. But there is great virtue also in our darker side. So we are born to die. So lovers kiss and meet—to part again. So communication occurs by "letting go," if it occurs at all. Given the two alternatives of acceptance of our lot as it is given to us, or improving it by managing for ourselves, by choosing the latter we are caught in the vice of our rejected paradox and find ourselves pursued by all that we have previously rejected.

I AM like an island in the sea: I AM like a candle burning in the dark: I AM like a tree growing from its roots in the soil: I AM like a stream flowing down the mountain side into the valley below. More mechanically, I AM like a pendulum, swinging to and fro: and I AM like a toy train rushing backwards and forwards, operated compulsively by a simple trip-switch mechanism. More personally, I AM the experiencer, both nourished and opposed by every circumstance I meet. Very much to the point, but almost ridiculous in its simplicity, I AM like a hot-cross bun in a bath full of water, by which I am both permeated and surrounded. Each of these illustrations has fulfilled the necessary condition of verifying my duality, both within and outside my "self": and of establishing my relationship with the ETERNAL GROUND.

One of our first experiences of duality is that of time and space. At the moment of birth (time), I am born into my household (space), like a center in a circle which will eventually become the central line of a spiral, as in course of "time" I come to move through ever-changing "space."

By expanding the diameter of our circles-in-space, we allow for growth, progress and evolution; but by keeping the continuous concentration of our points upon the time-track, which we call "now," we keep within the heart of the matter, which is that we are moving in time through space. Thus the experiential self is a traveler in a space-time "continuum," and past, present and future should never be considered as abstractions on their own. It is by using all our instruments of experience, or states of consciousness, that we are tuned to life and one another, if we are ever to function as a whole, and not as mere cerebral abstractions.

Like sound itself, our lives vibrate in rising and falling cadences as we respond in time to what we experience in space, from near or far. Our images, which are the imprinted stuff of our imagination, are stirred and we move in appropriate behavior. Life could be such a dance, if we were orchestrated in harmony within ourselves, with one another and with the universe (or in "CHI," as the Chinese used to call it long ago when they were more in CHI themselves than they are today). But there are so many good reasons nowadays why this should not be so.

The "balance" in our relationships depends upon a "cross," or "dying" one into the other, and a "mediator" between us. The function of mediator is fulfilled by the "female principle" in general, or by "women" in particular. She is the "watery element" in which the miracle of life takes place. Just as the holy Ganges of India flows from the high Himalayas to the plains below, thus joining Heaven and earth and bringing the possibility of fertility and growth, so woman in all mythology throughout the ages has preserved the flame of life, and served her purpose at the altar of our human mystery. Whether as one of the innumerable fertility goddesses who crop up everywhere, or as Shakti who was the wife of Shiva, or the Virgin Mary, who was the chosen one of God, the INFINITE can only function through the obedient body of a woman, who is like water in HIS hands. She is the recipient, HE the donor, and we receive our gift of life through her, from HIM.

There is a movement on the face of the waters, a stirring of the blood, a vibration of the tissues, an experience of fear, awe and wonder at the miracle of it all—and the "little wriggler" is born. So

CONSCIOUSNESS has been brought from THERE to here, and incarnation becomes a fact of experience in human consciousness as little c, who is born in the same image as his CREATOR, who is big C.

All that we have and are we owe to consciousness, which we share (but on different levels of experience) with the whole created universe, and all the manifold variety of creatures in it. It is important to realize that consciousness on every level is always non-dual: it is a point to point affair, and is therefore not in itself possessed of energy. It has to be motivated by other means and the images which underlie that motivation will determine how it will be used.

It is in the nature of consciousness to grow extensively, which it has done as we have seen over the many years of its development, but with increasing rapidity in our more recent history. It has always been the growing point of the scientific method, which represents the antennae of lowlier creatures, and the ciliated sensitivity of much earlier, more simply biological, days. ("Let's see!") Mathematics, motorcars and the health and wealth of teeming millions, all depend on consciousness, as it has become extended by our progressive use of the scientific method.

But how is our present knowledge to be used, and how can it be misused? There are three dangers, all of which are our especially human temptations, motivated by our insecurity, anxiety and greed. The first is that it can be used *exclusively and partially*, as a means of obtaining power over the other. The second is that it can be used as a *"mother substitute,"* by means of which to obtain especial privilege for her favorite "son." The third is that big C will be forgotten and FATHER denied, as little c becomes convinced that he is now fully capable of traveling on his own.

Little c is particularly liable to experience dissociation because it is dependent for its function on separation and discrimination. So it gets carried away by a morality of expediency and convenience, always seeking for the "more" and the "better" which are ever round the corner, tempting, just ahead.

It is sadly obvious that, in spite of all its potentiality for more abundant life, little c is ambivalent and also has another, reversed, face. Having no sense of time, and no "heart" either, little c can easily become a monster, bestriding the earth like an insolent Colossus, ignorant of everything except its own *all-compelling* intentions.

Our task, then, is to find the "middle term," the third, the mediator, the catalyst, who can stand the strain of being between the opposites, this being always in danger from both sides. This was the goal of Hindu Yoga, the "Middle Way" of Buddhism, the fulfilled "now" of Zen, and the experienced truth of the Druids. This was the place of Christ upon the Cross, nailed to the Tree of LIFE which grows between the opposites of death and resurrection.

The problem of our day and age is to experience this median position, which is at the heart of all relationship and communication. This is our meeting point, wherein we join and circulate, as we "give in" to one another even with a little death, "paying attention" as we say, and listening to the other more carefully than we often do.

This is the journey of the soul, or experiential body, of man the traveler through time. But the linguistic difficulty which makes it sound as if "I" am "me," also makes it sound as if "woman" is less than "man," when most essentially she includes him within her total self. Man and woman, each is both; but it is only woman who can lead us back to the ground where we belong, which we have left so long, so far, behind us. It is only woman, and the woman in each one of us, who can suffer the strain of all experience and bear the child of truth which tomorrow always needs, in order to solve the many unsolved problems of today.

It is about the role of woman in her own right, without reference either to her sexual qualifications or her justification by motherhood, that this book is written. She may be cast in the role of the "Mother of God," perhaps as virgin undefiled: the Guardian of the flame of life she always is, most certainly: but she is most important to us all in the role of ordinary woman, just woman. For she is then in her proper place as the bridge-maker or enabler of experience, and is our noblest teacher of the truth about the way of life.

CHAPTER 19

Sex: A Problem of Relationship

S ex is not a subject that can be adequately studied by itself, for the good reason that it is a function of relationship and it must therefore always be considered in relationship with those other parts of our experience which together make up our very complex whole. Isolated, sex becomes morbid if not meaningless. Against a suitable background, framed in our greater reality, sex takes its place and plays its part, in right relationship.

Love

Life and love can be shared and related, but they cannot be possessed. The precious wealth of the emerging, self-expressing soul is not for any gangster's capturing and putting in his bag, however benevolent he or she may claim to be. Therefore husbands must not try to catch or capture wives, as if they can thus become their property. Nor is there any proper power by which wives can control their husbands' willful vagaries. Parents have no rights over their children's lives, neither as to what they are, nor what they should become; nor can children rightly claim what anyone must give them. Wherever rings are set, love can flow in to fill the space with love. As to what happens after that, love can but wait and see, and go on making love with which to solve each problem as it comes.

A man's love is different in quality from a woman's, because a woman is different from a man. Love goes beyond itself, outwards into life. A woman stands, if our definition is correct, within, behind, her man and so her love flows out from her to him as her beloved object. It is as if he is standing within her light, and so she loves him there. But he is placed differently, as his light shines

From *Invisible Anatomy: A Study of "Nerves," Hysteria and Sex*

forth beyond the circle of his responsibilities, out there. His love and life are spent, partly at least, in passing on the flame that his wife and home feed into him, from behind and from within. She is his "subject;" he is her "object." His object is to work in that more distant field which is beyond the home. He has his work to do and she must not object! When work is done, then he returns, to be subjected to the softer rule of wife and home. He must not stay, however, within that ring of tenderness. Home is his resting-place, but she must not keep him there for longer than the time that rest requires. He must go out and catch his train, leaving her behind where she belongs. Home ties are not for any tightening by anxious love. These lovers must be free to behave according to their rules and natures, each within their proper ring, differently reciprocal.

If this seems too strict a rule for these more modern times and liberated days of emancipated womanhood, it remains symbolically true. If you are a woman, with exterior responsibilities, manlike, so that you must be living in your head and working in the world, do not forget the claims that tie you to your softer, tender side. There is your home within your heart, to which you must return. Because both sexes are bisexual, therefore we have our inner loves that must be recognized and used, according to the same law of love's reciprocal division. By understanding how we can love and work together, we can also see more clearly how we must love and work within ourselves.

Love may vary in direction, back or forth, and still be love: yet one is right and the other must be wrong. True love, "good" love, creative love, is always sending forth. False love, destructive love, which therefore must be "bad," is pulling the beloved back, possessively. "Darling, come back to me!" These are ordinarily harmless words enough between lovers. But between mother and child they are more than dangerous, because they mean a sin against emerging life.

Love's Opposites

Now let us consider some of love's other opposites. The first of these is glamour, which is true beauty's tinsel sister. Glamour is love's inverted empty opposite, but it takes a well-trained and suspicious eye always to detect the difference. Glamour is clever in deception, but it is the evidence of Power, and not of Love. Then what is Power? Here is another opposite of love, because it has cast its lot upon the material side, for which it always claims advantage. Love is of the spirit, making new forms: but power claims its right over these forms, to augment or to diminish them, to arrange or to destroy them, according to power's advantage. Power is always adding to itself, and would add love also if it could. Power often pretends to use itself to love's advantage, and deceiving love by so doing, transmutes love into power. True love never uses power and only by avoiding power's use can it transmute power, to bring it back within the spirit's path again.

I set Love and Power, therefore, as positive and negative energies, or Light and Darkness, opposite to one another. Ranged against Love's spirit are the powers of darkness, the principalities and powers, the energies and inertias of the earth side, which only love can change. These earthly powers are not to be despised or denied. They do most certainly exist and they are not merely to be destroyed. They are, in the end, to be transmuted by love's endless energy. That is Love's work within the material field. Love is the light within the seed, the sap within the tree, the courage in the heart of a man, the enduring sacrifice of womanhood; it is the hope of victory that makes us all fight on, in spite of our defeat and bitterness. Love is up against it all the time as soon as it enters into material existence. That is why love must always be renewed, remade, by the loving sacrifice of every one of us; or else love dies and then only power can claim its morbid victory.

Anger (ill-temper) is impatient love and therefore must be opposite to love's patience. But hatred is another opposite to love, and this time it is opposite in direction. Anger is not love's destroyer on purpose, as hatred is. Hatred is a powerful purpose, on the part of love's greatest enemy, to kill love. As a human impulse, it means that we have joined ourselves with love's deepest, deadliest enemy. Hatred is ill-will, the spirit's enemy. Love is goodwill, and therefore it is in conflict with every other aspect of the will, but especially the will-to-power.

Love is better incomplete, because it is thus less exacting. That first unweaned estate of love's perfection can bear with nothing less than itself. It finds so much unbearable, because it has not yet been born. It is very hard to live with, until it is somewhat diminished by being spent or given. As love grows up, it is a spending, giving force. The more it grows, the more it spends and gives. Yet spending, it is never spent, but thrives on what it gives, for thus love grows.

Love is a means of contact and the master of all separating space. There is no need for lovers to be together in the flesh, for love can always fill the space between with love. There is no need for physical proximity: but in their physical proximity, all lovers feel the pleasure of that nearness which is the sign of love. Therefore the kiss is love's true symbol of approach: closer than the skin's barrier of separation, the lips can feel, warm ring applied to ring, the pleasure of an intimate relationship. Thus lovers meet and meeting there or anywhere, on any level, is love's true pleasure. In love's experience, we prove the greater joy which comes when experience is shared by meeting the beloved. In love, there are innumerable ways of meeting which are not limited by either space or time. The meeting-place of love is always, everywhere.

The Origin of Sex

Sex itself is not original but consequential. Biologically, it is not the "first cause" of our existence, as some psychologists have been inclined to claim. Sex is an effect of that duality which is behind and within the whole created world. Sex is but one proof of our "sectioning," by which the wholeness of the coin was divided into its opposing quarters. The division into sexes is but one of many "Mandalas," or quartered circles. The human family is such a Mandala, with its two generations and two sexes making four opposites within the single ring of "home." The Mandala is the original pattern in our invisible anatomy. For instance, flowers, trees and even human bodies are modified Mandalas; but so are all the opposites in their abstract and metaphysical conjunctions, such as Light and Darkness, Healer and Destroyer, Good and Evil, call them what you will. These are not aspects of Sex, nor are they derived from sex. They all reflect, in different ways, the same original pattern of the Mandala, which is behind and within the form of everything we know. The Mandala manifests the wholeness of the universal plan, and thus we must all submit to being cast in the Divine image. The Mandala portrays the universal common root of our invisible anatomy. Self-evident in all things, it is also self-evident in sex, which is only one aspect of the Law's epitome.

In sex, we have our quartered natures crucified, and therefore in sex we find the significant problem of suffering, which exists in all relationships. Being so opposed within ourselves and amongst each other, we may well ask what is the right relationship that can unite these warring and discordant elements? That is our human problem. We dismiss the matter too easily by saying simply, "Love." The more practical answer is not love, but our whole conception of life in all its fullness and variety, which is a very different matter. Only by living in our own experience of many battles, can we find out what love is, and what it cannot be.

Of course, biologically, sex is creative. All such Mandalas are, and sex is no different in this from all the rest. In it is expressed the Divine plan on the material and physical level. Therefore sex is both Divine and material, as it is also both yours and mine. Thus it is quartered. It is not only Divine, nor is it only physical: it is not only yours, nor only mine. It is, in its complex nature, essentially ours. In fact, it is our bridge and meeting-place. In each one of us, it also has four elements or roots, one in each corner of our Psychic Compass. Inner and outer, higher and lower man, we are sustained within ourselves in a creative "sexual" relationship, and our opposing elements require to be wooed and wedded in mysterious marriage. Here are our various natures, animal, human and divine. Sex is our experience of this complex relationship and, rightly regarded, it concerns the unity of the whole, through the coming together of our opposing parts.

The sexual organs of either sex are not complete within themselves. As organs of relationship, they are as reciprocal in their opposing functions as the piston and the cylinder. Two things are true, which, if they are borne in mind, will always guide us in the way of right relationship. Firstly, sex must always be the concern, not only of two of us, but also of two generations, past and future. Children come into it, as part of the full responsibility of the creative act. Secondly, sex is a relationship between the opposites. It is an experience not of pleasure and of play only, but also of war and work. As a whole, sex is at least concerned with all these opposites: pleasure, play, war and work. To cut off any one of these is to omit an essential part of sex. In order to be whole, we need the whole of it. To leave out any part of it is to cut off the corresponding part of ourselves, which we can ill afford to do, because our health depends upon our wholeness in all things.

Sex is a reflection on our human, physical and material plane, of something which in itself is not any of these things. What we experience here as sex is therefore a symbolic act, which has higher meaning "over there," upon another, higher, plane. Therefore sex is essentially a sacrament, because it expresses a spiritual significance in a material way. There is something inherently religious about sex, in the sense that it has this spiritual significance behind the material form. To fail to recognize this hidden element in sex is to lose something that belongs to this experience of life. We must become idolators when our most important acts lose meaning and significance. All idolatry leads to deterioration, as surely as life must always deteriorate when it is cut off from its roots.

Sex and Guilt

The very word SEX implies a sectional or bisected state, as if the wholeness of the coin of our intrinsic wealth has been cut by some unseen hand into two or four opposing parts. Separated and opposed, therefore, as we must be, we must not feel too "cut-up" about it. Sex is not, and cannot be, an altogether clean and wholesome business, because it is a relationship of opposed component parts. It is the art of linking our opposites, which are all contained within the completeness of our sexual experience. In sex we meet our opposites, in every sense. Sex is for that, and so our opposites are neither to be blamed nor avoided. They are for right relationship and not for surgical exclusion or hygienic elimination. A conscience which blames the part for not being whole is surely somewhat of a sinner in stupidity. How can the lesser be the greater, too? We need them both, in order that the greatest may enter into the least, and the virtue of the whole may become manifest within the lesser part. Only hysteria, which cannot accept the fact of separation at all, would claim that sex must be, or ought to be, "nice," "good," "clean," "right" or "perfect." It is all these things, certainly, but it is also all their opposites. It is obvious, therefore, that hysteria must find in sex its utmost confusion, and in a morbid conscience its pathological assumption of a false salvation. If "nerves" are "no's" and "liars," then this morbid state of self-destructive conscience is the most negative deceiver of them all. Alas for all our hopes of a successful short cut, we cannot so simply dismiss the problem. The condition of a morbid conscience must be cured.

There is expressed in sex a double fact of separation: firstly, between the spiritual and material, or divine and physical levels, and secondly, the separation or opposition between the male and female forms and energies. These opposites are polarized like an electric battery. The ensuing energy is creative sex. Complex in origin, it is also complex in function. It is not only for the gratification of our animal desires, nor is it a supernatural power to be enjoyed in some personal achievement. It is always both, and more. It is for God and Life, for man and woman, for pleasure and for power, for suffering and for comfort, for satisfaction and for self-denial. It is neither good nor evil in itself, but it easily becomes a source of sin. "Original sin" describes our separated state. We are born that way. Our further "sin" is tickled, however, as we take from sex (or any other privilege or power) something only for ourselves, excluding other aspects which belong within the whole experience. To exclude, disparage or deprive the other of that which by right belongs to him is therefore "sin." To exclude the essential fact of the spirit's presence in the act is sin. To enjoy the act without a full sense of responsibility in regard to the future generation is also sin. Of course, we are all somewhat sinners in all these respects, because we are only human. That does not matter, however, as long as we are able and willing and wanting to grow in wholeness, as we face the larger facts of life.

The origin of our sense of guilt is always a very complex matter. To understand that, we must understand the nature of hysteria, because most guilt is hysterical in origin. We have already defined hysteria as a compulsive state of assumed identification with the beloved object. We assume in hysteria that whatever seems "good" to our judgment is ours already, and put within the bag: "I am that!" Therefore, when hysteria assumes the perfection of achievement where there is none, guilt is the intolerable measure of apparent failure. We are familiar with many common examples of this morbid and destructive process. For instance, if a mother is identified with her child, and the child shows some individuality or separation of which the mother does not approve, then the child seems to be wrong or "guilty." If the woman is identified with the man and he does something against her will, then he seems to her to be "guilty." If a man is identified with his own conception of what he thinks ought to be a good picture of himself and he does not come up to his own ideal standard, then he feels "guilty." If a woman is identified with her ideal of the good life, and does not keep to it, then she is "guilty." The compulsion of hysteria in all cases is that the beloved state or person must be regained at once. It cannot be lost for an instant. Therefore hysterical guilt is never truly a recognition or admission of a state of sin. It is the very opposite of true repentance. It is an urgent, incessant and compulsive drive to regain at once the sinless state. Really, therefore, hysterical guilt is in itself a very sinful attitude, because it must steal in no time something which is not at present true. It excludes the truth, the sinner and the sin, in order to steal a total and unseparated state, that never has been true in this world and therefore was assumed. It is a further example of what I have called the great reversal, that in hysteria the sense of guilt is really another sin, because a proper admission of the state of sin or separation from the beloved is quite impossible for the hysteric. The term we use for the feeling of guilt may be the same, but every word we use can thus contain within itself an exactly opposite meaning. Therefore we must watch our words most patiently and never be content with mere appearances. If words can so deceive us, how much more easily can we be deceived by other people and especially by ourselves?

Hysteria is apprehensive and therefore does not grow. It jumps, excitably. Identified with those good outer forms which it strives to but cannot control, it jumps back again to ring itself around with all the completeness that can be found inside the self. The mind, which should have been a bridge with the external world, becomes instead the timeless source of satisfaction for desire. The mind is misused subjectively, for phantasy and wishful thinking, instead of being used objectively as an accurate measure of outstanding truth. Thus the hysteric self aims to become self-satisfied through being self-centered. All it requires is contained within its own ring and if it is not there, then mind supplies it by the magic process of imagination's phantasy. Now all is one and self is all-enclosed, self-satisfied. That is the would-be attitude to life of all hysteria.

It should be plain, from what I have said of guilt, that redemption is an act of reparation. It requires acceptance of the fact of sin, i.e. of the truth about oneself. It also requires acceptance of the facts that are outside our selves, in other people and in the external world. It requires surrender of all our false assumptions, in order that we may face the whole truth, simply and honestly. Thus properly incarnate in the truth, we acquire our change of heart and our new birth. Redemption is then a gift of grace, but first we must be willing to put our house in order and strive to keep it so. Confession helps because it provides us with another, clearer, eye which is more objective than our own: like analysis, which is the doctor's way, it enables us to separate our selves from all that is not truly ours. In any case, we have to pay the proper price that suffering requires, if redemption is to prove effective.

CHAPTER 20

This Woman Business

Can one generalize about women with any justice or must they be left mysterious, enigmatic and utterly, eternally, unknowable? That is to say, have women an "invisible anatomy" which is different from the male, or are they formless and void, as empty and meaningless as any vacuum? If that were so, I think Nature would abhor them, which Nature, human and otherwise, certainly does not. In fact, women are very natural, far more so than men. They get on very well with nature, better than men do. A woman knows what she wants and, naturally, she gets it. If reason or conscience come into her argument, they are used as means by which to gain her end. But for a man reason and conscience are an end in themselves. Oh yes: he must be right! But she must have her way!

Now, can we go on in that kind of way, asserting that woman-in-general, all women collectively, have certain characteristic qualities and attributes which distinguish them from men, or is it wrong to generalize? I claim that "woman," or the "female psyche" to be more precise, has a certain definite pattern of her own, and that all women are variants of this common theme, with infinite subtleties and modifications so that no two of them are exactly alike. But, basically, they have their clear-cut pattern, too. The pattern may not seem "reasonable," but it is not true to declare that women are therefore "unreasonable." They are themselves, accurately cut to their pattern. One way of defining the difference between the sexes might be put in the form of a Chinese proverb: "When a woman says 'How hot it is!,' a man takes his coat off." If that is too subtle, I only mean to imply that the female psyche is concerned with the generation of appropriate *feeling* (willingness),

---

From *Invisible Anatomy: A Study of "Nerves," Hysteria and Sex*

whereas the male psyche is concerned with the generation of appropriate *action* (will). Together, they are reciprocal in this as in all other matters. They are not similar: they are "round the corner" to each other. They are related thus ⸺⎤. He cannot pattern her according to his way of life, nor can she hope to hold him by her apron strings, if either is to be a right and proper "self." But I do not think that either should give up hope of ever understanding the other, merely because of this fundamental difference of viewpoint. Besides, she has her male side to help her to understand him, as he has his female side to link him with her unknown qualities.

The female psyche contains within itself every conceivable opposite, and so we rightly say that, in her ability to surprise us, woman is a mystery: but that does not mean that she is a muddle or that she must be unknowable. A mystery requires our initiation into it, through the experience of something which has a real but hidden meaning. Life, women, and religion have all this same occult quality of a hidden inner meaning, into which we are gradually initiated by experience. It is a great mistake to think that we could ever "know" any of these three merely by some act of "thinking." They can only be appreciated by this deeper quality of understanding which is partly intuition and partly instinct: partly feeling and partly desire: but wholly experience and wholly immersion in the act of becoming initiated. Such understanding is something that reason must be prepared to die to gain. To know a woman, therefore, a man must let himself go and be a little mad.

Hysteria is terrified of this woman business. It insists on being a man, or two men if necessary, but not a man and a woman. There must not be a woman in the case! Rather than feel hot (or feel anything) the hysteric must for ever be taking another coat off. That is why the nervous subject never can keep still. "Nerves" and hysteria are illnesses of compulsive over-activity with all the stress thrown over on to the side of the male psyche, in order to repress or obliterate this informal and eternal "SHE," who is the source of so much fear and trouble. (Indeed, she is: but must we be hysterical?)

The pattern of our invisible anatomy has already been laid down and on that pattern we shall work. Oversimplified, the sexual relationship is a derivative of our bipolar duality, as we are constituted of positive (unlimited) and negative (limiting) principles. The first is "female" and the second "male." They are related as central expanding, and peripheral contracting forces, reciprocally alternating in the rhythmic "dance of life." As woman and as man, we represent these elemental forces, which are in us as we are also in them.

Now let us consider again, then, the simple pattern of center and circumference, and see what we can learn from that of these two balanced roles of opposite sex. She would expand, unlimited: but she has no instruments with which to work. She is all "heart" and needs to be "headed off," kept in a ring, supplied with discipline and instruments of technical efficiency. She is inspired, but needs to be related to that real external world which is her daily round, her common task. She is a bird who needs a cage, or else she flies away in dissipated ecstasies of unfocused light. She must be caught and held, brought down to earth and made to work, as her limitless energy is applied within the domestic circle by which she is hemmed in. She longs for freedom; sometimes she calls it happiness, and sees it somewhere over there, round the corner or outside the ring. She is easily tempted to exceed herself and claim that she ought to be allowed to be unlimited. But no: if our hypothesis is correct, she belongs inside a ring that holds her tightly in, but not too tightly. Hers the energy, his the brakes: hers the piston, his the cylinder: hers the inspiration, his the technique: hers the task of keeping bright the fire at home, and his the work of keeping all secure within the ring and bringing home the bacon. Thus they dance as rhythmic opposites; as he steps forward, she steps back: as she advances, he retires: as his left foot moves, it is matched by the opposite movement of her right. This should make it plain, as all must learn, that agreement between man and woman is not agreement to be similar, or in mutual extension one to the other. On the contrary, it is agreement to differ, in reciprocally related opposition. Harmony is not a Siamese-twin relationship of identical similars, but a rhythmical relationship of timely opposition. In marriage we learn that, if we can live and learn.

She is the earth, as he is the plough that furrows through it, letting in the fertilizing light of sun. Thus she is the passive target, receptive of the arrow's flashing light. The "heart" receives the "head's" enlightenment, as reciprocally the head fulfills the heart's desire, in real achievement if it can, and not merely in the minds imagining. As earth, she is the guardian womb of all maternity. She is the darkness of the resistant material world which needs to be redeemed by the infiltration of the spirit's light. She is the cup, receptive, and into the darkness, in the deepest heart of it, is thrust the sharp point of the flaming sword, the spiritual will, the fertilizing principle, the male force. She is the seed, the egg, the ovum, of which he seeks and finds the central heart, into which the spermatozoon pokes his flashing vibrant head. Hers the darkness, his the light: so hers the moon and his the sun.

If she is "earth," then she is "water," too, and both are fertilized by the opposing principles of masculine "fire" and "air." He is, to push a dubious claim to justify his masculine pride, a Heavenly visitant, sent to redeem the darkness of her earthly state. He is a shaft of light, Thor's thunderbolt, a flashing sword; her waiting waters long for his releasing touch, and she is stirred to life, as life did once emerge, evolving from the primordial water's depth. His is the strength and hers the weakness as she waits. His sword is hard, her flesh is soft. He overwhelms her with his thrusting passion's weight. She is "Old Adam" and still older "Eve": he is the star that prophesies her newer birth, redeemed. She is the casket of mysterious wealth, in waiting beauty hushed: he is the imperious pirate, who is out to loot the swag and satisfy his greedy appetite. She is destroyed and he is her Destroyer. But, to even matters up, he is destroyed by her and she is his Destroyer, too. Therefore each has much to fear about the other, before the miracle of life can issue forth from this mysterious partnership.

So far we have dealt with this problem of the relationship between the sexes in the over-simplified form of a duality, as if there is only one of each, opposed against the other. This introduces too many paradoxes and contradictions, however, because it is not true enough. Classification into such a simple dichotomy of male and female, or good and evil, is never accurate enough, because it does not allow for the deeper subdivisions and contradictions that exist. We must divide each one again into another duality. That is to say, there are always two of her, whichever way we look at her: she also has her male and female sides, in regard to each of which all that we have said applies. But there are also two different aspects of her femininity (and of his, for he has them as well), which we will call, to give them simple names, "Dark Woman" and "Fair Lady" respectively.

"Fair Lady" is her front facade, her outer form and sweet beguiling way of offering all her beauty's charm (and guile!), as if it were the fruit of innocent simplicity, which never could mean harm. This one looks easy, as indeed she would be if it were not for the lurking shadow of her other opposite, the Dark Woman, who is not far behind but has not yet appeared. Fair Lady baits the trap, it seems, the better to admit the unsuspicious fly for the Dark Woman to consume him at her infinite leisure. Fair Lady is as good as she is beautiful: Dark Woman has her beauty too, the beauty of the moonlit night, but she is not good at all. Fair Lady is possessed of innocent simplicity and every willing charm: she gives her sympathy and interest to most unlikely and uninspiring subjects, but things have a way of suffering curious and unsuspected change when the Dark Woman turns her face. We sometimes say she is the very devil then, and we should know that all women have it in them, somewhere, to be that at times. They are not what they seem, by at least a hidden half!

The Dark Woman is somewhat of a shadow side for all of us. She lurks within the darkness of our psychic hinterland, unborn, amoral and unrealized, a source of power, a temptress, and yet of great potential creativity. She is all that might ever be, as well as all that always was. She is the Future and the Past. She is our mystery. She is, in fact, our dream, and in our dreams she sometimes shows herself, but never clear and always with an element of mystery. She is never in the open, but she is always there. If she is never clearly seen, how can she be remembered? Yet if she is forgotten, she will turn up when she is least expected, to contradict and upset the simpler order of our hopeful plans.

Dark Woman can play Fair Lady as a most deceptive front with infinite skill and patience, until she has got her man. Then she can manifest a degree of cruelty that reminds us of the greedy spider and the poor fly. She can be a formidable fury, a calculating humbug or a skilful actress, varying her roles as she plays the many parts within her repertoire. In none should she be trusted, because this is a game of "catch-as-catch-can." Either he catches her and tames her to his will, redeeming her: or else she catches him and sucks him very dry! So clever and infinitely subtle can she be, that he may never know and even quite enjoy the way she has him on her string. As cat and mouse, this woman plays her man, but not to his advantage, nor ultimately to hers.

The Dark Woman is a witch. She has her broomstick and her cat with all the rest of her ancient paraphernalia, as she exploits her lunar powers. She is as possessive as she is possessed. She is as old as the hills and as young as tomorrow. She never dies and never lets herself be born. She is a problem for us all to wrestle with, because she represents the ancient fallacy of power without responsibility, of exploited privilege and utter selfishness. The only way to tame her and redeem her is to know her for the hopeless phantom that she is, and not to believe in her gently whispered offerings. She is not the easy extension of our hopes that she pretends to be. She is the shadow on our lives and not the sun. She is a temptress and she is not Providence. Mother of us all she may be, but we should have left her womb long since, and now be wiser in the way we set about our work. Of course, she can be useful to us still, but only if we wrestle and fight with her, with every grain of sense that we possess and for every little thing we want to make or do. If we do not fight against her, it is quite certain that she will overshadow us. If we avoid her, she pursues us. If we are beguiled by her, hoping to possess her, she possesses us and we shall be to that extent consumed and spiritually lost.

By which I mean to say that a woman is not to be properly considered as a plaything for a man, as a thing of beauty to be kept on the mantelpiece until some convenient moment when she can be taken down and handled with enjoyment, or eaten off a gilded plate. That is a dangerous error, a specious laziness and a great stupidity. Woman is energy invisible and uncontrolled, as amoral as a bomb with an unknown time-fuse set to explode we know not when. She is an enemy, a job of work, a great game for a man and not a soft and harmless plaything for a silly boy.

A woman is a woman twice, a cup with double rim and double lips. She is a living pledge to paradox. On the one hand, she is receptive to the plunging Spirit's sword, and thus immaculate. As eternal virgin, she is the prepared recipient of the divine messenger, the holy seed of life. But on the other hand, she is the recipient of the human seed of her adoring male. She is angel to his animal, and animal to his angel. Whichever half of herself she shows, she always must retain invisible the other half of her dual nature.

The power which she seems to have is also paradoxical. Hers is not the Spirit's power by right, although she sometimes shows it forth as if it were her own. She is the moon which reflects again the primary rays of the sun, and so in her own right she only seems to shine. Viewed as her own, her light is only the glamour of illusion's scintillating worth. She must be proved in actual experience as being truly good in heart and will, or else her promises are only worthless fraud and dangerous deception. She is a transmitter of powers that she does not rightly own and should not rightly keep. Loving, she passes her powers on to those whom she loves, keeping none back for herself, and so she feeds and nourishes her husband and her children with the life they need. She is a catalyst, whose presence is required to work a miracle of change. She is a messenger who brings good news, but whose work is not connected with the news she brings. For her to claim any power or "rights" for what she does is for her to prove herself to that extent at fault. "Because I love you, therefore you must . . ." is not for her a valid argument. She need impose no conditions of security for herself, as she passes on her power and wisdom to the ones she loves. As she nourishes and protects them unconditionally, so can each and all go forth to do their proper work. To be a power herself is not her rightful role. To claim reward or praise as due, such as "Because I did this, therefore I am good," would spoil her willing sacrifice. She must not fertilize nor praise herself: she must not hold the sword nor plan the use of power: she need not interfere. The sword of power belongs in the hands of her man. Of course, she needs his nourishment with constant praise and offerings of flowers! Hers is a life of willing, happy, natural, spending sacrifice. The less she makes demands for power, the more she has. She need not ever worry that she seems so powerless. The power is really in her all the time, but she must remember that she is the other half of paradox. "She stoops to conquer": yes, she conquers, never fear!

The Chinese say that the greatest virtue in a woman is her willingness, and one can imagine that if men were the judges of a woman's greatest "virtue," they might well decide that it was so out of mere laziness and greed. But I think perhaps there may be more wisdom in the Chinese view than that. There usually is! It suits my view very well that, if the female psyche is the source of energy, it should be willing to be harnessed, used and disciplined. The woman is a source of flow; a flow of nourishment, of energy and love. We need this tap to run unceasingly, but not, of course, to overflow. She must be willing even to be turned off, sometimes, regarding her own inaction and passivity as part of her need for greater discipline. In a very practical way, without meaning any disrespect, we need a willing woman as we need a willing horse or motorcar. Ease in regard to discipline is the greatest expression of goodwill. The earth itself is such an example of goodwillingness. She spends herself to give her children life, dust as a willing woman does.

All that I have said so far I have intended to apply in general. Of course, I have not meant it to be applied to any woman in particular and especially not to the personal affairs of any female reader of this book. Every woman has her male side also to consider and if I seem to have been unfair to one side, giving undue advantage to the other, she, being both sides herself, is of course entitled to the advantages (and disadvantages!) of both. Being a "mere man," I am sure I must have been unfair, although I have tried to be as objectively balanced in my judgment as a man could be.

Now let me try to be more practical. If we accept the hypothesis of our duality, there can be no proper argument about sexual equality. In our education, for instance, it has been our recent custom to model girls' schools on the assumption that girls are, or should be, just like boys. I claim that they are not and that they should not be. I think we have not yet devised a system of education that is entirely suitable for girls, and that we have also dangerously neglected to develop, or even to recognize, the existence of the emotional life or creative sensitivity of boys. We have gone too strictly on the assumption that this is a weakness that should be knocked out of them and a danger that is best abolished by ignoring it altogether, or smothering it with a constant succession of more morally praiseworthy activities.

I would like to consider, therefore, some of the ways in which the "female psyche" can be trained and developed in either sex. My first requirement is a sufficient amount of time, space, emptiness or rest, which is the prerequisite of all such early growth. The female psyche is a fallow field and should not be ploughed up or trampled over all the time by the din and discipline of marching feet. It needs a certain waiting upon its emptiness, for time to grow that which it contains of its own essential nature. It needs quiet and darkness, and more encouragement for doing nothing, or "spare time," than most schools have the courage and good sense to provide. (Incidentally, this would cure a lot of laziness, which is often nature's self-protective cure for the constant pressure of the urge to overwork.)

I do not mean that children should be left idly to lounge around, because they are often very bad at finding their own proper outlets for themselves. Such leisure should be spent constructively, in finding out the sort of things we like to make and can. It demands more individual attention than mass-production methods can ever afford to give. It therefore requires more teachers and also that they should be more sensitive themselves in their ability to discover individual differences and various aptitudes.

Education must recognize, I think, the narrow limits of its own task of "nourishment." We cannot be eating knowledge all the time, if we are ever to absorb it into ourselves, building up our "bodies" with it as we go. Nor is it possible to build a balanced "self," unless all that is thus absorbed is ultimately brought back again as something that I saw and felt and did, myself. Shakespeare is all very well: but I am not Shakespeare and I never shall be. I cannot even hope to copy him. So what about me and all that I have got inside myself, waiting to come out and be expressed? It is no advantage to me, surely, to have a smattering of Shakespeare in my head if the doors of my own creative heart are all securely locked, and I have lost the keys. The development of the female psyche requires that it should be nourished (a little, not too much, please!) and then encouraged to grow of itself, finding in course of time its aptitudes and proper discipline. Otherwise, education is merely a fraud, with false facade and camouflage on top, but underneath a flaming, threatening pit of undeveloped energy. We really cannot afford to risk the prolongation of such a harmful system of deception, while we miscall it education and regard it as a virtue, which it most certainly is not.

I see no reason to object to competition as long as it is kept in its proper place, and comes after full confidence in self has been established. We must respect the different clocks that children are and the different times in which they grow. To set their clocks too fast is to rob them of self-confidence, which may never be regained. The fable of the Tortoise and the Hare is very true for children's growth, and the one who is allowed to start more slowly may well exceed his swifter brother in the end. Each child must be established in his own time, with his roots firmly settled in his own earth; that is to say, in his own female psyche, which is his source of inner nourishment, as well as of his faith and confidence. Without it, he can never feel "at home," or sure of himself. Without it, he is a cripple needing crutches, greedy for power and security from outer things, because he lacks this "jewel" of inner worth. It is no good forcing him to do the things he cannot do, setting him in competition against those who have the strength that he does not possess. That breeds a tortured race of greedy cripples seeking some compensation from a secure position of despotic tyranny. It is no use giving him someone else's well-praised worth with which to clutter up and cover the confusions of his mind. That makes it even harder for him to find himself. The harvest of the tree springs from its roots in time, but our roots are in the female psyche and there is no other source of living worth. The proof of a sound all-round education is that it keeps its eye upon these hidden roots, guarding them well against intrusion or premature exploitation. They are the source of life.

But of course we do interfere too much. Our fingers itch to pull the plums from every pie. We cannot wait and even our impatience is moralized as a virtue, as if time spent in growth is merely wasted unless we interfere. Children suffer excessively from the benevolent activities of those who fill them to the mental brim with the fruit of other people's well-spent lives, so that they can never grow their own. How can they grow if they are overfed at the same time that they are undernourished, because they are not allowed the time which their bodies require for food's digestion, let alone the time required to create some original contribution of their own?

The result of such misspent energies on the part of our educational authorities is to set up a state of hysteria, or unbalanced power. It is the woman who suffers: the woman in us all, the true creative urge, the source of individual life. She has no time or chance to grow. Instead, restless we stand on our impatient heads. The stable pyramid of our anatomy is turned upside down, so that we are more in need of support from external things than we ever need to be. We are inside-out to life and wrong way round, because we have been taught to start at the wrong end. We are more easily "fed up," because we have no hearty appetite for life. In any case, we are again the more unstable, because we are only half alive. The male half of "mind" and "consciousness" is overdone, without, however, having its proper relationship with the female half of "heart," feeling and the deeper unconscious drives. We thus become engrossed in a greedy and quarrelsome jitter of unnecessary but highly moralized activities, without knowing right from wrong, or being able to distinguish what we really need from what is pure excess. We have not sufficient sense of right relationship with our fellow men (or women), because we have not this right relationship within our dual selves. Our sexual affairs are desperately confused and ridiculously muddled for the same reason. Fortunately, life allows for an enormous margin of error and so we manage to grub along fairly well.

"The place of the woman is in the home," says old simplicity and is accused of anti-feminist bias. Yes, of course it is true. The place of the woman is at home and it is a pity that some of our old women in the front rank of politics have not been content to stay there. But in case I too should be accused of anti-feminine bias, let me remind you again that women are very busily (too busily?)

301

developing their male sides. So let them go out and take their place where they can find it, in the forefront of the battle if they can get there. I would like to see them holding every position of responsibility. They could not make a greater mess than men have done. But let them not lose their women's hearts, or they will be no more good to us as heads than men have been.

Women have always been the most tireless workers at the dullest jobs. They are our realists and on them we all depend. They are our roots and deepest source of nourishment. Invisibly, we still draw our life-force through an umbilical cord that links us with this source of life. Invisibly, we are still within the universal womb of Time, emerging from our Mother. Invisible anatomy retains the old familiar design and we are still as children, and more dependent than we sometimes like to realize.

"Emerging from our Mother." Who is she, this broody hen who sits so patiently (sometimes too patiently, too heavily?) upon her chicks and keeps them safe and warm? She is a universal principle shown forth in human motherhood. She is the source, eternal and immaculate, the limitless creative universal One, called Woman in her role of Motherhood. So deep in her this task persists that it is perhaps easiest of all for her to be a Mother, instinct-wise: harder to be a woman, experienced in suffering: hardest of all to be a wife, who has to keep the peace amongst her husband and her children in her home, working with love in daily sacrifice.

In the beginning, Mother: in the beginning, all within the home. And in the end, we are all out and away, far-flung as seeds distributed by the wind, or birds flown far from the nest. In the beginning, all in: but in the end, all out. Mother must lose her chickens, every one. Therefore her only solution of this deep-set problem of her life is by willing sacrifice. It may seem to be a hard law, but it is harder still for mother and for her children, too, if she resists it. The direction of emerging life is onward, outward, forth: towards adventure, independence and new birth. So she must let her children go and grow and send them willingly upon their several ways. That is her job. It is a simple act of sacrifice that runs throughout a mother's life. Actually, she need not fear, because she is on the right side of Paradox. The more she gives, the more she gains: the more she sends them out, the more they will come back to cherish her. Her love well spent will always be her best investment.

The direction in which we and our energies flow determines our state of psychic health. The right direction is towards the world beyond us; that is, away from mother and away from self, shining outwards from a steady center, like rays from a lighted lantern. The wrong direction is to be self-centered, which is always mother-centered, too, as if mother and self are still united, indivisible, absolutely One. Our mother's job therefore, is to feed us well and send us out, on and away to find ourselves in independent life. To reverse the arrows of direction and to hold her children in or to pull them back is to make her children cowards and to betray her role of fine encouragement. If mother is right, we are all right: if mother is wrong, we are all wrong. If she is wrong, she is the first and deepest cause of "nerves" and of hysteria. So what is right mothering?

First, to provide security. The child must feel safe in childhood or he will have a craving for security ever afterwards. The child who felt safe when he needed safety will not need it later on. The presence of the mother's love means safety and the courage for adventure in the child. Secondly, she provides food: she is the source of nourishment: she is the earth in which the child's invisible roots are growing, until he can be fine and strong himself. Love is our most important early nourishment, without which we cannot find our deepest roots, nor really thrive in happiness or health. Thirdly, she is the source of our encouragement. "That's fine!" she says. "That's jolly good! Go on and try some more!" She is the living source of our goodwill and lights the lamps that we can later turn on life. Thus sheds our Creator and makes us Creators; as she was herself creative, so we shall find it easy to become creative too. She is our great example. As she is, so will our hearts and spirits be. She is the most important woman in the world, and no-one, nothing, else can ever take her place. It is every man's business to care for her and to protect her, and to provide for her the comfort and the home she needs. The happy home is the beginning of the healthy life: and the heart of the home is the mother.

The heart of the tree is in the root: the heart of the self is in the female psyche. When our hearts jump into our mouths, or on to our sleeves: when fruit is dragged carelessly from overloaded branches and roots are never fed: when questions are answered before they can be asked, and things are given before they can be needed or desired: when men only think and women show off or play at being men: or, as the Greeks had it, when the womb floats: then the verdict is—HYSTERIA.

.

CHAPTER 21

Where Has Father Gone?

Where, in our time, has father gone? Why has all stature been diminished, all worth defiled, all difference smoothed over until even genius itself is fast becoming mechanized? In our world today, mother has everything; and she has either given it to the child too soon, too often and too much, or else taken it away, so that the child has too little, too seldom and too late. The world is an entanglement of fussy mothers and restrictive governments, with spoiled and angry children quarrelling everywhere.

If manhood means independence and free choice, loyalty unto death for a principle, the joy and adventure of creation and more abundant life, then where has manhood gone? Everywhere it is threatened more and more, so that even hope falls gutless to the ground. It is as if manhood has a knife at its vitals. Is it "because" a man might be dangerous? The fuss of spinsters groping in the dark has entered the very precincts and principles of government. The psychoneurosis of father-resentment and father-destruction, of mother-fixation and self-centeredness, has come to rule the world. Now all is expediency, material reward and material security, with an old hen over all to cluck her chickens home.

But where has our manhood gone? And where in heaven's name is Father?

"Our Father . . ."

Manhood is a quality of the spirit. When the spirit has gone, the quality of manhood has departed. No spirit, no man. It is as simple as that. Our age is an age in which the spirit has been lost, denied, betrayed. Its place has been taken, by material things. So

---

from *Mysterious Marriage: A Study of the Morality of Personal Relationships and Individual Obsessions*

father has been sacrificed for mother, which is exceedingly bad for the child, who is upset. We are the upset children, you and I. We are surrounded by offers of salvation, or we are told that we can only save ourselves. But speaking for myself, I do not wish to employ a savior. But nor do I intend to save myself, because I do not believe that I can do so by my own efforts, any more than I believe that I can pull myself up by my own ears. I believe that salvation is given, but that we must make sure that we really have received it, before we go prancing off in an abortive ecstasy of premature enchantment.

"Our Father which art in Heaven" is a phrase that we have all heard and repeated times without number. It has become meaningless with countless repetition, so that many of us do not even repeat it any more. But, if only we do believe in the reality of heaven as a fact in our experience, and also an integral part of our own selves, I believe it holds the clue. As the center is in the heart of a circle, so heaven is within us; and our Father, who is the clue to our essential manhood, is in THAT. The extensive circle, the material framework, the world of cause and effect, the world of Caesar, the body and the womb, are the world of the mother and they belong to her. The source, the center and the fire, the adventure and the creative impulse, the knock on the door and the kick where it hurts, the spiritual principle and the order to obey, the accident and the surprise which breaks the resistant rock, the word spoken for the first time, "lo!"—and here comes Father! But we have lost the sound of his voice, so that we hardly hear it any more. Now mother has our world in hand instead, and a lot of little ungrown megalomaniacs are robbing us of our personal meaning and values, by persuading us that we live in a world of cold accountancy.

The mother whom I have learnt to regard with so much suspicion is the "mother" in inverted commas, the one who represents this material world and its comforts, the mechanical world of cause and effects, the cold world of accountancy and planning, and the constant physical claims of my own body for "more" of something for itself. It is the world of safety first, of "if only," of plausible deceptions, multiple excuses and much humbug.

It seems that men have a surprise value which is liable to be resented, but little of that superiority which they claim so constantly. It does not seem that men have any right to rule the world. In any case, as we have seen, it is the old women of both sexes who assume that great responsibility.

To date the octopus has won. The tentacles of the "old woman" have closed on the collective mass of human inertia, fear and greed all over the world, dividing it against itself, and destroying it. The "old woman" is everywhere in male disguise, saving and destroying, protecting and discarding, planning and rejecting plans, busy, benevolent and moral to the tips of her last tentacle. "Take this, it will be good for you." "Do this, it will be good for someone else." But the result is always the same. The life of the spirit is exploited, endangered and destroyed.

She is everywhere, this old woman who has it in her heart to destroy her man. She is like his shadow, of which he is afraid. In fact, she is his shadow, but she has convinced him, to his greater downfall, that she is his light. She is the one who covets her child to his destruction, as the Church of every religion has always coveted power over its children, to their destruction and its own.

The hope of the world is that the "man" should come again into his world, dwelling in it and not abhorring it. The "old woman" must take a lesser place within the trinity, becoming submissive to the incalculable will of her Lord, so that she may be the mother of his child, whose servant both, in fact, must be. For in our human trinity, it is the child who must ever be our leader.

To restore the male element to its own place is to restore the element of surprise, of rebirth and adventure, which is the freedom of the spirit. It is not to restore the superior or ruling element, because within the subtle trinity of the family there can be no such rank as higher or lower, better or worse, first or last, leader or led. In this most human family, where each one does his proper task, there is no measurement of virtue. Each member lives and works in his or her own way. This whole and "holy" family is within each one of us, in you and me.

CHAPTER 22

Marriage

As we are within ourselves, so we shall discover our experience to be. The cinema of life unfolds within us, and all that comes to us upon the outer screen has been already there within the inner film, or else it could not come. Our conditions must always be determined by what we are ourselves and so it is no use grumbling. If we change ourselves, our conditions must also change. To agitate for change in circumstance alone is to prove ourselves hysterical. Especially, our experience of sex is a reflection of our inner attitude to life and, in all our matrimonial troubles we had better look within. In waking life, in nightmare or in dream, both "he" and "she" are hidden somewhere there. We wed our hidden problems when we wed the one we love.

Obviously, the beloved attracts us by the charm and beauty that she shows, and that is why we want to marry her. At first, we do not see the shadow side, the opposite to love, which lurks invisibly behind the beloved mask of beauty and of charm. Yet here is the problem of all love and marriage: *we must also wed the opposite of what we see and love.* In the end, this is true in regard to exterior marriage, as we sooner or later discover. It is particularly true, however, of that mysterious marriage which is also taking place *within ourselves,* where we are faced with the exact opposites of all that we would choose to be, yet we must "marry" that. That is to say, although marriage is partly an experience of fulfillment and comfort, it is also a plunge into the forbidding waters of frustration and adversity. Our advantage is not only measured here by what we receive as gain: it is also finally proved by what we can afford to give and lose, willingly. Marriage, like Death, takes all we have to give. It is a killing business, too, unless we can discover a way of

From *Invisible Anatomy: A Study of "Nerves," Hysteria and Sex*

dying into, and for, the beloved. On its light side, marriage is for our comfort, security and well-being; but on its darker, hidden side, it is also another occult initiation, into the sacrament of Death.

Awake and sane, as masters of our selves, which one of us would ever choose to marry trouble as we do? We are hoodwinked into it; blind, drunk, crazy, off our heads and out of our minds, as we are led up the garden by those blind forces which nature has left so mysteriously active in the hidden depths of our invisible anatomy. To fall in love is never a reasonable performance. It is a supreme example of Ruskin's "pathetic fallacy," or the tragedy of emotional judgment. Good Heavens, she is not like that! She is not what she seems to be, as you regard her with your blinded love's apparently all-seeing eyes. She is not a perfect angel, nor is she the promise of effortless fulfillment of your urgent heart's desires. She does not really understand you in the least. She does not know who you are, nor what you mean by what you say. In fact, she hardly cares. You are both sharing in a miracle, bewildered by a divine ecstasy. You are not yet responsible; but you will be one day. Thus love is born in beginning, whole, in a blinding, rending, self-destroying flash. But lovers, from now on, you are each other's enemies! You may not like it, but you will find it true. Continue patiently and you will find that it is good as well, and may be beautiful, if love is made that way.

Meanwhile, woo her, win her and wed her. May good luck and Heaven's blessing attend the day, for you both will need it all! Having overcome her resistance and led her to the altar (if you are wise, for marriage is a sacrament in which the spirit of goodwill is very much concerned), you will place the ring upon her finger and she is yours for better or for worse, for richer or for poorer, until Death parts you, as they say.

Why that ring? I have heard many addresses at the altar to the bridal couple on their wedding day, when the parson has referred to the significance of the ring. It is hard indeed to do it justice, because this ring is everything. It is the binding or limiting principle. It is the home, the prison and the castle wall. It is the enclosure of protected love and the limit of love's effort. It is the man in his strength, and the woman in her softness. It is the womb that will contain the child. We all should live within a ring, but most of us spend much time in trying to get out of it, compelled to escape by a sort of claustrophobia. The voice of freedom calls, "You are not free! Surely you should be free? Is it not for freedom that you have been fighting all this while." The call is false, because you are not, and never will be, free. You are love's prisoner. Behind that, you are the prisoner of your living form. Yes, the spirit is free; but are you only Spirit? In any case, the freedom of the Spirit is best expressed as it accepts its prison in the ring of the body, willingly. No, you are not free when you are married, and the man must put a ring around his wife: to prove she is not free. That is her home, her boundary, her case and her condition. She is a bird in a cage and now must cease to be a fluttering butterfly. Love does not say, if it is wise, "Of course, my dear, you are absolutely free to take another lover if you choose. I'd never bind you to your marriage vows!" That has been a modern way of entering marriage, but it is not wisdom and it is not law-abiding love. It is impotence and claustrophobia disguised as charity and consideration. Love is a battle which each must fight for dear life and for dearer love. Creative love is very tough. It is no easy sentiment.

Love is a battle, because the sexes are opposite in all respects. When he is hard, she is soft: when he is over, she is under: when he expands, she contracts: when he rises, she falls. She stoops to conquer, which is most disconcerting for her would-be conqueror. And of course, the law of love's relationship is intimately revealed within the drama of the sexual act. Like all occult secrets, the act and its instruments must be kept concealed. This is a deep religious mystery, performed behind a veil. It is not meant for tawdry play by irresponsible youngsters. It is not meant for nudist exhibition. It is designed to be private, central, intimately shared within the enclosure of love's ring. It is meant to involve the wholeness of two beings in creative ecstasy. It is meant to work a miracle, creating life within the ring of home. It is not meant only for pleasure, however pleasant it may be. The pleasure is life's gift to love and together they belong.

In dreams, the sexual act is often represented as a stairway. He rises as she falls, and each must find the special moment of the other's time when their clocks both unite as one in throbbing peak of ecstasy. The full crisis of orgasm is the central point of love's combining rings. It is the mystic height of fire which dwells upon the Holy Mountain's peak. It is one proof of our divinity, as we catch fire and fall again in flame to earth, exhausted, by our flight. It is a delicate operation and a fine art, because love must indeed be "made," not sought, nor aught, nor bought.

In this, our evolution has set us a very pretty problem, because the further we have grown beyond our earthly roots, the more difficult does it become to manage the sexual act successfully. Education is inclined to develop the head's activity, and the head is the negative pole of sexuality: that is to say, it tends to bring the sexual act to premature conclusion, or to stop it altogether, or to make of it a superficial matter, by losing the lower aspect of the body's deeper drive. It is as if a man is halfway up the hill already and therefore, having not so far to go, he reaches the end too soon. Woman, on the other hand, by her higher education, suffers the same dissociation from her more earthly roots, and therefore, having all the further to fall, she is more slow to reach her goal. As men become more quick and women slower by their head's increased activity, therefore the timing of this ritual dance is liable to become more confused and less satisfactory. The problems and unhappiness that arise therefrom are far beyond our computation, but surely it would be wise to see this matter clear and whole within the ring of some fairly reasonable philosophy? The problem must be clearly recognized before it can be solved.

The competition of women with men, "to be as good as they," can only lead to disaster and a sort of homosexual state in which the fundamental differences and polarities of the sexes have been lost. There should be no question of being "as good as" or "as powerful as" or "as privileged as." Women are women and men are men: as such they need to mind their own business, and to be reciprocal to one another. In all things they are limited and opposite: but, in terms of the triangle, being opposite at the base, they can share the apex in which they are unlimited, in so far as this state can be made and realized by love.

She must not try to rise, or she will upset the timing of her clock. She must relax, to fall asleep most willingly and die, before she can experience love's all-embracing sea of more than mortal flame. That is her way, as he climbs slowly, very slowly, up and up, until he catches fire and bursts in that same flame. Then the seed springs forth as Heavenly messenger of earthly fire, to find—or not!—its earthly incarnation in a mother's womb. As an arrow it seeks its target, to bury itself if can within the ovum's ring. Life is very generous and does not mind a million, million misses for a single hit. That, too, might be a lesson to us all.

Satisfaction is as important for one party to this living contract as it is for the other, and each should feel complete by reaching their goal of emotional crisis in their own time, if it cannot be achieved together. Success in this matter is a matter of practice and patient experiment. Nothing is wrong within the ring of love, if it is for love's reciprocal enjoyment. Each one should find and give that which the other one likes best and give it with all the art of love's complete surrender. Where love is, conscience need never be. The art of love, with all its intimacy shared and fulfilled in goodwill and mutual sympathy, is just another play of Everyman, dramatized and enjoyed the more as it is understood. The more that we can make of this love-play, the more can our experience of life's joys and wonders be fulfilled, so that each can gain by what the other gives.

In visible anatomy, our bisexuality is proved by the fact that the woman's body contains the embryonic vestige of the male organ (the "clitoris"). In the male, the vaginal opening is closed and undeveloped. In the woman, the clitoris remains a very sensitive point, appreciative of manual stimulation, and for this purpose it may be used as an instrument of love's expression. There is nothing wrong about gaining satisfaction for love in this way, but its significance may perhaps be understood more clearly with advantage. Relatively, it is a "male" way of enjoyment, and therefore it is indicative of a somewhat male or active emotional psychology. In extreme cases, its use is associated with the development of power phantasies, or alternatively with the opposite phantasy of morbid and impotent slavery. It is better, therefore, in general for a woman to learn to acquire the more feminine way of sexual experience if she can. For those who care to study it, I have made a "Mandala" diagram, called "Bale Out." It shows the various alternatives of our related opposites, and repeats a pattern of invisible anatomy that I have used before. The way down from the "Mountain of Gold" (the clitoris) to the "Dark Valley" (the vagina) is by casting yourself loose and letting yourself go. That is why I call the diagram (figure 22) in aerial terms, "Bale Out." It requires courage to take the plunge, but in the end it proves to be a gain for our emotional experience, as such a "dying" gesture often does.

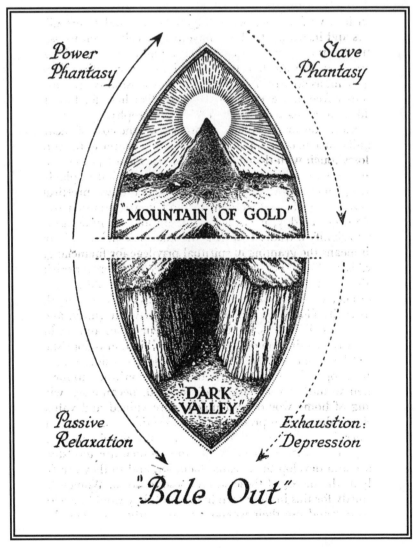

Figure 22 "Bale Out"

CHAPTER 23

The Meaning of Time:
Time, Tide, and Rhythm

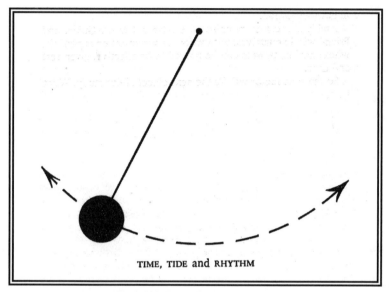

TIME, TIDE and RHYTHM

Figure 23 Time, Tide and Rhythm

Time Is Not Clocks

We have clocks. We also have, or have not, time. Clock time may tell us, for instance, that we have an hour to spare before we catch our train. But we have an hour of what? Well, an hour maybe in which to have a good time—or perhaps only to be bored, kicking our heels. On the contrary, the clock may tell us that we have no time to spare; we must make haste or we shall miss that train. Impatiently, we wave desperately at taxis which ignore us, driving past. Caught in a traffic block, we fume and fret—we are going to miss the train! How much of joy or sorrow can one suffer in an hour, as it ticks itself away inexorably, regardless of our mood, upon the face of any clock? We know that

From *Cure or Heal? A Study of Therapeutic Experience*

time is experience, to be patiently endured or impatiently escaped in a mad rush of unnecessary activity, repeating restlessness; or sometimes (but how rarely) it is ecstasy which then passes in a flash. Alas, it is grounds indeed for a pessimistic view of life, to realize that joy flies most rapidly knowing eternity now; but sorrow drags on leaden feet, only knowing the dry tedium of what seems to last for ever.

We are told by those who ought to know, such as mathematicians and philosophers, that time is the fourth dimension, which goes beyond the familiar three of space. If this is so, then time is certainly outside the capacity of egoic man to comprehend it, for he is devised to dwell consciously in space, but not in time. Time, being outside and beyond his conscious mind, requires clocks to tell him of its existence. Of time itself, of experiential time, egoic man knows nothing. Not knowing that time is experience, and experience is time, it is not surprising that, as he constantly watches his clocks, saving time whenever he can, he has little time for experience, now.

Our concern in this chapter, therefore, will not be with egoic man and his ingenious clocks, but with our own personal variants of experiential time.

Time Is Relative

Our first discovery will not surprise us. Time is not some thing-by-itself. Clocks hang on a wall or stand on a shelf, by themselves, isolated. But time is always relative. In fact, time is a function of movement-in-relationship. It is a gestalt-of-three, its items indivisible other than by the bridge of the relationship which joins them. This bridge, or link, is relatively the "time" of this particular constellation, be it of stars in the sky relative to one another, sun and moon relative to earth, cars on the road relative to one another, or personally as it happens between us as we enjoy communicating with one another, having a good time—or perhaps just being bored.

Time is relative—but to what coordinates? It is essential to know what our relatives are, if we are to reckon with the relationship between them. If space is space, we can consciously determine the three dimensional coordinates of space and reckon with them.

But if time is not in space, but beyond space, what shall we say are its coordinates?

According to the assumptions of this book, of which the basic dogma is always the same and plainly stated, our personal coordinates are analogous to the center and circumference of a circle, which Goethe called respectively counter-space (expanding) and space (contracting). Our personal system therefore comprises three terms or coordinates, which we call PERSON, central "I," or expanding CONSCIOUSNESS: Person, which is mediate, radial, relative and experiential; and person, which is peripheral consciousness, egoic, contracting and concerned with what can be done and known in three-dimensional space. To these are added time, which is space's inevitable addendum to make up our full gestalt-of-three. These coordinates and their relationship comprise the total reality of time, with its two coordinates of center and periphery, eternity or no-time and egoic or objective clock-time; and its mediate reality of radial Time, which is experiential, personal and subjective.

The Space-Time Continuum

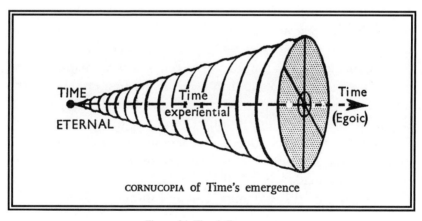

CORNUCOPIA of Time's emergence

Figure 24 Time's Emergence

If we repeat our basic diagram of the emergent spiral, we are able to "see" the meaning of the term "time-space-continuum." This is total time as it is already actually co-existent, apart from the abstractions which belong to its different coordinates or component parts. The whole spiral is the whole person, TOTAL MAN, you or me, including past, present and future. On the right side, or growing point, of the emergent system is egoic man, working or playing in his world of space plus clocks. On the left or central side is the deep center of the system, "I" as the central point of expanding CONSCIOUSNESS. And in between is subjective, experiential or relative, time. Together these make up the total personal time-continuum in a gestalt-of-three, which, although it may seem to be divided, can actually only be indivisible if we are ever to see, or be, our person, whole.

The Time-Track

In order to avoid confusion, it is better to grapple with paradox at this point, or we may find ourselves confronting contradiction in the end. Egoic man always "thinks" that wherever he is, light is. He therefore regards both his inner world (the Egyptians called this goddess "Amoun," but Freudians call it "the unconscious") as dark; and his central point being so far beyond his ken, he usually regards it as non-existent, or darker than dark. Thus egoic man projects his own darkness onto other areas which in themselves are relatively light (i.e. more conscious than he is) calling them "the unconscious," "the sub-conscious": or sometimes even "the super-conscious," if he acknowledges his central source at all.

Looking at it from the side, however, we can perhaps appreciate what was meant in the fifth verse of the first chapter of the Gospel of St John: "And the light shineth in darkness; and the darkness comprehendeth it not." The source of light is from the center, which is also the source of CONSCIOUSNESS, and of emergent TIME. "All things were made by HIM; and without HIM was not anything that was made."

I believe that this statement can and should be accepted as a true analogy of our personal experience of the time-track, from birth to now, and from now to our egoic death. We came into life at the source, on the left of our "continuum," and traveled from left to right, following the path of the sun across the sky, as light pressing forward into darkness.

Viewed in this sense, the time-track is seen to be the experiential movement from one moment "now" to the next, which proves the veritable spiritual nature of man. In fact, whether he knows it or not, even in his most egoic state of peripheral mind, man is a traveler through time who brings into lesser spaces the essence of his own eternal now.

The Time-Body and the Unconscious

Experiential time is like a sausage which extends from birth to death, made up of slices which are experience-now. The whole sausage can be called the time-body. Running through the center is the time-track along which "I" am advancing within the peripheral skin of my conditional circumstance. To this "I" am related, and it is this relationship with circumstance which produces my experience. This time-body is as real in its existence as my space-body; but, not being located in space, it is not apparent to the consciousness, or sensory apparatus, of egoic man. It is a serious mistake however for egoic man to deny altogether the existence of his time-body for this reason. If Freud could have recognized and made use of this concept, he could have eliminated from his "unconscious" much of the present confusion as to its content.

It would be as well, perhaps, to pause in order to review the contents of our time-body as it exists in terms of our actual experience. In this diagram I have only allowed a slice of time to occur once a year; but if there are sixty seconds every minute, it must be reckoned that our slice of time called "now" occurs more frequently than every second. Our experiential "sausage" is thus

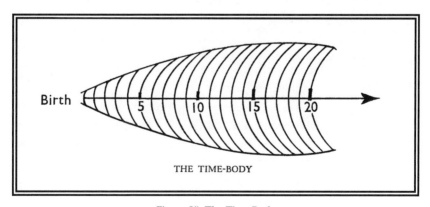

Birth

5   10   15   20

THE TIME-BODY

Figure 25 The Time-Body

319

made up of many "slices" and many slices may be comprised in our "experience." Normally, we pass through experience, or experience passes through us which is the same thing. At every moment of his experience our traveler is in the light, now, of his personal consciousness. His future is completely in the dark: or, as we say, he is completely in the dark as to what may happen next. Furthermore, every previous moment has slipped into the dark. Apart from the trace of memory which he can partially recollect, our traveler is as much in the dark about his own past as he is about his future. Being now unconscious of both of these, he is liable to describe them both as being parts of his own "unconscious."

Thus the anatomy of the time-body can become a very twisted, complicated and convoluted self-contradictory affair, full of dark tensions and unexploded depth charges which are apt to go off as unexpectedly as their occasions are inconvenient. These irrational outbursts from the past are called "unconscious motives."

They arise from dissociated energy in the time-body and are derived from actual experiences in infancy and childhood. The most important of these damaged areas occur in the first five years, and their influence may completely dominate our so called conscious minds subsequently, causing anxiety, compulsive activity, delinquency, mental ill-health, marriage problems and behavior disorders, even including the major insanities or psychoses.

Psychotherapy aims to liberate and resolve such undigested pressure points. Once they can be dissolved, with a consequent change of the images involved, energy which has been tied up or misused can come into play again, with restoration of more total health.

The Importance of Suffering

The Son of Man upon the cross, eternity suffering in time, is a familiar Christian concept of the experience of suffering being rejected by the self-defensive complacency of egoic man. The Buddhists were concerned with the same problem, which is that of enlightenment. In any place, at any time, it is always the custom of darkness (egoic man) to reject the light, as being altogether too disturbing for the convenience of his established world.

The Buddhists called our world of experience "dukkha," and the world of egoic man MAYA ("illusion"). They were concerned with the transition from resistance to acceptance, from attachment to detachment, from selection of either "this or that," into the realization of the existential reality of the "middle way" between them. This, without being in any sense a compromise, transcends the tension of the pairs in opposition, resolving this into a new light (illumination) or a new life (re-birth). In either case, the change requires its due measure of the antecedent "death."

In this predicament, man is in his usual dilemma. Like the corn between the millstones which turn in opposite directions and so churn him all about, he is apt to choose this one or that (but it always seems better, of course, for egoic man, to choose the one above rather than the one below). The possibility of being all messed up in the middle is never an inviting one: but how else is corn to be processed from hard indigestible lumps, into the flour which makes our bread? However, egoic man is not likely to let himself get into that invidious position without a struggle. If he can find someone else to make his bread, he certainly will. But the illuminating fact is that into this median, BETWEEN position, there advances another dimension, working a miracle of change. Life, illumination, conversion, call it what we will, it is the same experience of change, or "change of heart," which is described in another symbolism as the change from water into wine. It is the magical transition from more compulsive existence, to the freedom of more abundant LIFE.

Suffering is the total task of the time-body, in the sense of digesting experience by accepting it. But it is a fact that children can accept, digest or suffer, very much less than is generally expected of them by their anxious ignorant or ambitious adults. Suffering requires time, more time than is usually allowed for it in assimilating any lesson. Suffering is a process, not an action, and needs patience: which again is time. The word patient comes to help us here, in both senses of its common use. Children require our patience, especially when young. With too much expected of them too often and too soon, they will inevitably "suffer" from what they have been unable to suffer. They may become bored and fed up, indifferent to everything. They may become seekers for something or anything to make life worth living, such as money or the pools, drugs, sex, religion, tobacco or alcohol. Or they may become our patients seeking in our consulting rooms and hospitals, but rarely finding there, the help they need to make their lives worth living.

Father Time

Before going on to study some other aspects of our experience of time, it might be as well to emphasize again the source of it. As spirit enters into matter in the incarnation, so TIME enters into space, and we have the wedding, meeting or mating, of our two great archetypal parents, FATHER TIME and mother-space (measurement); or HEAVEN and earth. As the Kingdom of HEAVEN is said to be (and indeed can readily be experienced to be) within us, so ETERNITY dwells at our deep center, where "I" am centrally deposited within the energy working within the complex machinery which comprises "me," or egoic man. From this source all that is has emerged and, in all that has emerged, this central source can be seen to be reflected.

Physical Time

From FATHER TIME at source, we can proceed to study by contrast time-in-the-body, or time as it is experienced in physical life. In our bodies we are clocks, all of which can teach us a lesson, as they keep their own time and also keep time and tune with one another. Surely to preserve such perfect harmony and order, there must somewhere prove to be a MASTER clock? But meanwhile hearts beat, bones mend, lungs breathe, babies gestate, germs breed, and illnesses heal themselves—all in a matter of time.

Three words are helpful here to enable us to see the togetherness of our marvelously complicated, but apparently unconducted, orchestra. These are Tune, Tide and Time, which each provide examples of our bodies' physical use of rhythm. Our bodies work to the beat of their conductor; and music, especially with emphatic beat, deeply affects us all, as our bodies jig and dance to it. Tides flow, to and fro, rhythmically in time. In our bodies also time and tide should not be expected either to wait or hurry for the sake of obedience to any man's behest. (But egoic man has not yet learnt the lesson that King Canute was at such pains to teach his courtiers.) It was Heraclitus who, before things came to be regarded as existing by themselves, stated that "All things flow." He might have added that the flow of life, persons and things is always somehow both TIDAL and TIMELY.

Female (Cyclical) Time

Women are more original and personally realistic than men can usually be. Perhaps it is to conceal their own inadequacy by rejecting it that men have so often projected it onto women? In their own way, women are more creative, too; but this only applies to making homes and babies, while men are busy making other things.

In spite of her reputation for frequent unpunctuality, Time is a woman's world, in which she is in closest private consultation with her FATHER. Being of one nature with Time itself, women resent egoic man's dependence upon the machinery of clocks. Egoic man's laws must always be outside himself, reasonably declared, steadfastly maintained and scientifically proven to be correct. But woman's laws are in her special field of cyclical time, which is within herself. Hers is a field of experience, in which Time is not only linked with her FATHER through her heart, but also with the egoic world of man through her body. Woman has rhythm built-in, whereas for man it must be learnt and studied, until her play becomes his work, which sometimes seems to spoil her play for her.

Women today are made to feel particularly uncomfortable in a man's world in which there is no time. But man has really no time for women anyway. He is too impatient with them, and too busy with the importance of his own affairs, to study their cyclical realities. For him, the highest goal is the space-race, and the glittering prizes at the top. But for her the moon and the mysterious rhythms of the tides, which we are told "wait for no man," much to his annoyance.

To know that a woman's sense of time is realistic, personal, subjective, experiential and cyclical leaves us by contrast the opportunity to describe egoic, or masculine, time, as abstracted, dissociated, objective, impersonal and serial. It is thanks to egoic man's
perverted view of time that he is so unrealistic, so unrelated and so
blindly incapable of appreciating the supreme importance of such
a reality as love, which he cannot see. Therefore he prefers sex.
Egoic man is compelled to work for progress in the future instead
of enjoying life in the present; and having no time to spare, he is
always in a hurry to arrive somewhere else, although he has no
idea what he is going to do when he gets there.

Egoic, Masculine or "Serial" Time

Female and male, hearts and heads, wholesome and partisan-
abstracted, time for egoic man must be a copy of his own design
and limitations. Concerned as he is with making something better
of his mother's world, he has no time for FATHER. He is his own
authority apart from the time of his innumerable clocks which
must be beaten if he can.

His world of three dimensions, plus the appearance of time as
being divided into past, present and future, leaves him no option
as to what he ought to do about it, while he continues to believe
that the particular reality of his egoic world is the only one. Surely
he ought to improve it for himself and those who are joined with
him by love or for any other reason; and the sooner the better?
Egoic man therefore has a triple motivation, all impatiently urgent:
(1) to avoid the past as a bad thing to be left behind and forgotten
as soon as possible, (2) to avoid the present as a waste of time,
standing idly as it always does between himself and what he has
planned for the future, (3) to attain this objective, which looked
at in the future appears to him to be admirable in every way, as
soon as possible. All delay is frustrating, and time spent in getting
anywhere should be cut to a minimum. Arrival speedily is all that
matters nowadays.

"Images determine behavior," as has been said before. Quite simply, egoic man's image of time is of a one-way irreversible process, moving in a forward direction, as is shown here:

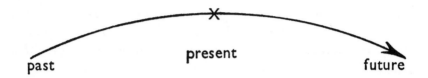

Woman's image of time, on the other hand, is not serial, but cyclical. We can draw her image either ⟳ or ⟨⟩ as long as both arrows complement one another, reciprocally to complete a circle or cycle, such as tides, day and night, the seasons of the year; and even that ultimate completion which is egoic man's anathema, the greater sleep of death which rounds off life's fulfilllment.

It is in this sense that woman's sense of life and time can be claimed to be more realistic than is man's. It is whole, not partial; inclusive, not exclusive. And what her reality includes, and his excludes, is the healing role of time.

A Child's Time Is Now

Having dealt with the FATHER and mother of time, or male and female time, we can now see how the child of time can fit into his place.

To the child, whose experience is for the first time, all things come new. A child's attitude to life as experience is therefore, in the first place until all becomes commonplace by repetition, one of wonder and joy. His life is only now, and in this present moment he is wholly concentrated, rapt in complete absorption of himself into his experience. How alien therefore is the world of his experience to that of his parents, who see life as compulsively divided into bits and pieces, now here, now there, according to their clock-bound needs.

As he grows up, the child must all too soon conform to the untimely laws of an egoic world, losing his innocence, his way of wonder and his joy in being joined to the object of his experience, for the sake of learning in another world. Paradise proceeds to Paradise lost, Innocence to much learning, wonder to knowing too much, as joy in the present is lost in man's more mature (?) anxiety about the future. But must this human trafficking in obedient slaves of the establishment only be a one-way stream, or can we ever hope to become as children again?

A child's time is now, and this can be true of any age. Even old men can wonder and live, now. One is never too old, in fact, to learn to live now, as long as one's ego can learn to become small enough no longer to stand in the eternal light. In fact, now is the child of TIME, eternally incarnate in its allotted space. Enjoyed so much by all of us as children, but for so short a time, the eternal now is not only the privilege of a few especial mystics. It is the birthright of us all, and to be enjoyed simply in the way of ordinary life.

Future Time

Foresight and synchronicity must appear to be grotesque oddities to the world of serial time of egoic man, because they belong to the other, inner, and too often lost, world of cyclical time. Egoic man at a point NOW on the periphery of experience in three-dimensional consciousness cannot see ahead. What he thinks may lay ahead bears no relation to what will actually occur, other than what he may perhaps be able to infer by deduction from his study of the law of averages. But in his dreams, he is no longer egoic man. In his dreams he often sees ahead, even though it is usually only in a partial and confused manner. If he is a stockbroker and "lucky," he may find himself knowing a little more even in daylight than his rivals do, thanks to what his "hunches" tell him. Some may prefer to resort for good advice to fortune-tellers, the stars, or the cards; but on the whole, egoic man is conspicuously unable to foresee his future. Nevertheless, he is mostly living for it, hopefully, instead of in his present moment Now.

But cyclical time and the continuum offer the clue to everything that serial time cannot understand. The viewpoint from within the circle, or rather spiral, from a point down the radius and nearer to the center, offers a different condition from which to realize a different state of experience from that of egoic man. It is this state of "consciousness" which operates in dreams, and those other more inward psychic states, such as trance. From this interior viewpoint, a different experience of time occurs, in which forward aspects of reality may sometimes be foreseen. Egoic man then wonders if the future has been fore-ordained for him by some dark power called "fate." But cyclical time sees no one else in the experiment of my life except myself, as I engage my choice of attitude within my various relationships. So, except for "me's" peculiar struggles and animadversions, I and my fate are one and indivisible. In the end, as in the beginning, "I" am the only fate for "me" to find. And the most constant enemy that "I" shall ever find will be my anxious and egoic "me."

Ripeness Is All

This applies to cheese and fruit, and it is certainly hard to find either of them at that critical moment which proves their perfection. This critical moment of the process of growth which is presenting "now" is the essence of cyclical time, but it is of this aspect of reality that egoic man has no inkling. Unless he has had his lesson forced on him by his experience of adversity, egoic man thinks (and so behaves) as if any time will do, as long as it suits his own convenience. He behaves as if he believes that the invisible clocks of life can be twiddled this way and that, backwards and forwards, to suit his every will and whim.

But children especially are made like clocks. Each one moves and grows, individually different, in his own mysterious time. This happens from the moment they are born, until external pressures interfere. First the domestic pressures of nursery and home, and then the still more complicated and aggressive pressures of the school, take over the mastery of many clocks to make them beat as one. Up to a point this is a good thing, because children cannot be left indefinitely to go their own way, in their own time. But it should also be remembered that time is an experience of relationship, so that in any group, given time, it is possible for them to find a common time within which all individual clocks can function, or else be moved to another, more suitable, experience of group-time. But only too often our educators are apt to force the pace of learning, with too much, too often and too soon.

The stage of the theatre is more respectful of the facts of time than is the stage of life. Here, timing is all-important. It is recognized to be the essence of relationship, especially in ballet, which combines the rhythm of movement and of sound, and in music hall, where the ill-timed joke is not a jest at all. Surely the same is true for life itself, especially in all our more intimate human relationships. It is not the WORD (logos) that matters, but the timing of it upon the sensory flesh. Love is neither a word nor a deed. It is an exact expression of a personal relationship in time. (Parents and lovers please note.)

Time the Healer

To egoic man, time seems mostly to have nuisance value. It gets in the way of his plans. To our more wholesome selves, however, who are interested in patient healing rather than impatient cure, TIME is our healer.

As a psychotherapist, I am sometimes asked, "If you do not use either knives or drugs, what do you do for your patients that justifies your charging fees?" My answer is a very simple one. It is, "I give them TIME."

Perhaps I ought to say I sell them my time? If that is what you are thinking, it is not what I mean. True, I am giving them more of my time than they have ever been given by anyone in their lives before. I am giving them, for the first time in their lives, the Time which they needed as children, but were never allowed to have. Whether we call our disorders psychological, emotional or mental, they are all disturbances of the function of relationship, which is time. Children need time, and if they do not get it when they need it, they will suffer subsequently from disturbances of relationship. These disorders will in their turn need more time if the bridges that were broken are to be mended. Our work in this sense is architecturally and anatomically real. If the original bridges are not actually repaired at the time and on the very site of their occurrence, the relationship disorder of today will remain impaired, unhealed.

But the point which is more strictly of importance is that the therapist, in giving (or selling) his own time (with a small t) is giving (and in this case not selling) the patient his own TIME, which is his source of PERSONAL healing within himself. The therapist in person is the outward and visible sign or representative of the patient's own invisible SOURCE of PERSONAL healing. The therapist in this case is the catalyst, enabling the process of healing to take place. It is the HEALER (SOURCE, PERSON, TIME, "I") who does the healing job, in time.

But the patient may well cry out in despair, "How long, O HEALER, how long are you going to keep me hanging about in my distress?" This problem is a most important one, because I believe that both therapist and patient do actually waste much time. What we really want to know is how to waste as little time as possible.

The clearest advice that I can give is by saying that FATHER heals, but mother wastes time. Besides being TIME THE HEALER, FATHER is also the proper source of COURAGE and of HOPE. "Mother" fusses around offering the patient advice which is unnecessary, certainly untimely and probably wrong. She also spreads around an aura of encouragement and hope in small letters, which should have been lost and given up a long time ago, so that our proper experience from source in capitals can arrive.

The other comfort I can offer to an impatient patient is to say that every illness knows its own good time, and is doing its proper best, obedient to the wisdom of its own rules. Every illness is wise in its own way. Precipitate healing does more harm than good and leaves us worse off, not better. Illness being so detailed in its living anatomy, it is useless to interfere with it in bits and pieces which can only do more harm than good. It is usually better to allow more time than less: so my advice is to be a patient patient.

It would be impossible to end this chapter without referring to the last of the healers, which is death. To egoic man death is "the last enemy," but to the whole man death can never be a disadvantage. As the other half of life, it has in its own way always been with us—and blessed us—ever since we began life at birth. If we are to live in this present now, we need to die from every yesterday as utterly as possible. And as for our egoic selves, it is only when they are truly dead that we can begin to enjoy our full inheritance.

Indeed, this is what bothers egoic man and causes him so much anxiety. In his heart, he knows that he must go, because he stands between us and our proper death just as much as between us and our proper life. Indeed, his case is hopeless; but this seems to make egoic man only more unwilling to abandon it.

PART V

Patterns of Avoidance

CHAPTER 24

Hysteria:
The Great Reversal

Not Confined to Women and Weaklings

A young man of twenty-five came to see me in hospital, because he had been discharged from the South African Navy on medical grounds. He suffered from fainting attacks: sudden "blackouts" which might affect him anywhere and any time, sometimes twice in a day. He would "come to" on the ground after a few minutes, feeling shattered and exhausted. He was intelligent and well developed: to all appearances, a very fine type of young man, but obviously with a shadow over him. He did not look happy, although he was happily married and was now in good employment.

My diagnosis was, of course, "hysteria," or I should not be using him as my introduction to this chapter. I do so in order to disabuse the reader of any idea he may entertain that hysteria is a feminine complaint, especially prevalent in disappointed housemaids, who laugh and cry in uncontrollable fashion, and are best treated by a slap in the face or a bucket of cold water, whichever may come handier. This young man had always been a "nervy" subject, for reasons which I will explain. Yet he had joined the Mercantile Marine at the beginning of World War II, and been trained as a gunner. Amongst other misadventures, he had been bombed and sunk in the Mediterranean, and on being landed in Greece he was bombed again. From Greece he was evacuated with the army, when he was bombed, sunk and rescued a third time. After a short period in hospital in Alexandria, he volunteered for the Navy, and soon found himself back in the Mediterranean again. This time he was a member of a crew of a fast motor-whaler, smaller than a

---

From *Invisible Anatomy: A Study of "Nerves," Hysteria and Sex*

corvette, which was in regular service running supplies into Tobruk. He was chief gunner and had a very busy time, making the journey into Tobruk about twelve times in all under all sorts of impossible conditions. The fainting attacks, from which he had previously suffered occasionally, became more severe. He said, "I was always perfectly all right at the time. In fact, I thoroughly enjoyed a good scrap while it was on; I can tell you we had some, and plenty. But I felt pretty rough before and after. My stomach would suddenly go all funny, as if I had something cold and wriggling inside my tummy, which was falling to pieces. Sometimes I would vomit and tremble all over so that I could not stop myself. Sometimes I would get a sudden blackout and fall down in a faint. Actually, I was never so bad when I was in the Service as I have been since I came out." We can see, I think, that this man was no coward: I believed him when he said that he would rather be back in the war again, and felt bad about being in "civvies." He was not the type to show off, make a fuss or find an excuse, consciously or otherwise, for making his honorable escape. Quite the reverse, he had fought his disability for eighteen months, ignoring it and making the best he could of it. His "nerves" had been with him from the beginning, but they had only got the better of him in the end, when he had been forced to leave the Services against his will.

And why these "nerves"? There always is a story and this was his. He had only seen his father twice in his life: his mother had broken her unmarried bonds when he was a year old, taking him and his sister, aged four, to face life together. She worked and drank: she left the children alone by day to care for themselves, and left them too at night, unless she came home drunk, when she was often violent and beat them. He had no other relatives, and was brought up by his sister, who was his only guardian when she was four and he was only one. It was no use being afraid: they faced their life together and their mother's absences and storms; they grew up as best they could, fending for themselves and each other. At the age of fourteen the boy ran away from home and went to sea, preferring its uncertainties to the drunken vagaries of his mother, whom he never saw again. His "nerves" were never good, but he was used to that. He had never taken any notice of his fears, and so, when the war came, he was well trained to face the enemy, which he very bravely did. But my diagnosis was—Hysteria.

The Erring Womb

Apparently, the Greeks were first to have a word for it, which they derived from ὑστέρα, meaning "a womb." Suffering in the womb, it seemed to them, caused those distressing symptoms of a hysterical kind. Some even went further and suggested that the womb had somehow slipped, so that it was floating, unattached, at large in the sufferer's distressed anatomy. I remember being told in my student days that this was of course a very foolish idea; we know much better nowadays! How could a womb be such an uncertain traveler: in fact, how could hysteria have anything to do with wombs at all, since men suffered from it too, without a womb to suffer with? It only went to prove how ignorant the ancients were and how much wiser we had become with our better knowledge of anatomy. So my teachers implied.

But are we so much wiser than the ancients were? They had poetry and insight, where we have greater surface knowledge and more literal exactitude. We have gained in science, but we have lost something in imagination thereby. Our anatomy is "visible"— and therefore obvious. But the ancient mind was never so literal: it spoke "as if," and implied inverted commas everywhere. Perhaps they never meant the womb as we know it in our *visible* anatomy, but spoke as poets or as children might, when they described the "womb" as if it were some mysterious "traveler"? The addition of those inverted commas is important, as we saw in the chapter "The War of Nerves." They mean that we must translate from metaphor to meaning, as we do in dreams, which must seem meaningless to us unless we can translate their metaphors.

For instance, I remember that as a child I was familiar with certain "lions" that used to frequent the stairs of our old three-storied house. They lurked round corners in the dark, prepared to pounce: and the further up the stairs I went, the further from my base in fact, the more invisibly multiplied these lions became in their ferocity. There were certain curtains on the top landing, beside my bedroom door, that were a veritable den of lions, past which I used to rush, narrowly avoiding their predatory claws. Of course that was very silly of me, but I was very young. I did not realize that these "lions" were in inverted commas and not real lions. In fact, they were an expression of my own invisible anatomy, or projected forms of my own inward fears. My fears were real and, as I regard them now, I see them with more sympathy. I even put the stairs themselves, and curtains too, all into inverted commas— which means that I myself am those inverted commas, and that "stairs," "curtains," "landings" and "lions" are all in fact *in me*. It is as if I am a house, a psychic house, in which the mysterious and often frightened traveler, who is also myself, moves up and down amidst mysterious furnishings, behind which lurk my many hidden fears. They are more familiar now and much less frightening. You may say, if you like, that I was hysterical—but I was just a child. I kept these deep impressions to myself and no one knew when or how I faced my ordeals of the darkened stairs. Why? Because I knew that people would only say that I was silly. Lions, indeed— they would not understand! So many scientific grownups have forgotten what inverted commas mean.

Freud and Sex

In our time, Freud was the first to study hysteria in a scientific way, as seriously and objectively as any other more tangible disease, and then our knowledge of the mind began to make a great advance. He realized the frequency with which hysteria was associated with sexual difficulty and came to the conclusion that it was a sexual disorder, due to unconscious sex repression and an emotional attachment to the parent of the opposite sex. Instead of floating free, the poor old womb was fixed, repressed and tied into a knot with mother's apron strings. With the term "mother-fixation" as an almost abusive epithet, both mother and child suffered some disparagement in themselves, for what was in fact a wrong relationship between them. The child retained its hold upon the mother as the mother played her counterpart by hanging on to the child. The womb was shut: and the child was still inside. So sex became repressed, and hence—according to this theory—hysteria.

From Freud's pioneer work, psychoanalysis spread over Europe and America both as a method of treatment and an instrument of research, and a vast literature arose. Of course, everyone was not convinced of the truth and wisdom of Freud's sexual theories, and some rejected them for a variety of reasons, good and bad. In this country, his views were usually somewhat modified and diluted by those of Jung and Adler, with a sound backing of neurology and orthodox psychiatry. Nevertheless, the Freudian theories still occupy today the highest rank in psychiatric orthodoxy.

I was not satisfied in my own mind, however, either by Freudian theory or practice. However far the meaning of the word was stretched, I never could regard sex as being as all-important as Freud claimed. Behind all behavior there is something more than unconscious motive: there is energy. That is where I wanted to begin, and to extend my framework of experience to include religion and art, as well as what I regarded as our less important biological drives. Perhaps it is a matter of individual preference, but sex did not always seem to be the cause-all, be-all and end-all of my patients' lives, any more than of my own. For instance, my "nervy" sailor with hysterical faints and fits whom I have just described, was happily married, as far as I could tell. Of course, it can be argued that "sex" in Freudian terminology covers a multitude of impulses and emotions not ordinarily associated with the word in common usage, and thus becomes a synonym for the whole content of life. But to give any word so wide a meaning is to make it almost meaningless. Besides, the Freudian method of psychoanalysis was quite impracticable from the point of view of hospital outpatients, who could not possibly afford the time for five interviews a week for years. Nor could I. And then again I had read in veterinary books that dogs and horses also suffered from this polymorphous and obscure complaint. Did they suffer from mother-fixation, too? If so, we must surely strain our use even of inverted commas, and assume that they are only suffering from "hysteria" (meaning something so far unknown) and not from true hysteria. Certainly these animals did not laugh or cry: but they did behave as if their balance of energy was disturbed, between two extremes of inaction and excessive activity. Some "traveler" had strayed and needed to be restored to proper place again. And I remembered that before my father died, in the last days of his old age he had wept and talked a little nonsense: and how the doctor had said that was only "hysteria." Actually, it was cerebral anemia and the nervous exhaustion of a dying man. And so it seemed to me that the term "hysteria" covered a multitude of the doctors' sins of partial understanding. Nevertheless, the fact of true hysteria remains; and through its various factual forms I now propose to study its invisible anatomy, as a doctor might who did not despise a poet's mind.

A Negative Disease

My basic structure for our invisible anatomy is always the turning spiral or, more simply, the breathing sphere. The jellyfish is one of nature's simpler patterns in this form. He breathes along, his circle quartered and ringed with arteries and nerves, his streaming tail behind within his watery element. He sets our pattern, and sometimes, I think, when things go wrong within his watery world, perhaps he too may suffer from hysteria? He is a simple fish and struggles through his simple problems with simplicity. If he got caught within the protective meshwork of his fear in sudden spasm ("tied into a knot"), then I think that he too might become hysterical.

As is the case in all our "nervous" disorder, so, too, in hysteria a *protective spasm* is the root and basis of this whole disease. It is due to an excess of negative nervous energy; the hysteric has a *negative attitude* to life. Our conduct is predetermined by the patterns of our energy, as all effect must be predetermined by its proper cause. All our attempts at cure must therefore be directed at the causal root. It is no use complaining or interfering on the superficial level of symptoms or effects. In fact, such a negative and impatient attitude towards the problems of hysteria is typical of the compulsive habits of hysteria itself.

Fundamentally, in our deepest and oldest level of the autonomic nervous system, we are not very different from the jellyfish. There, in our bellies, swims the "fish": and there, invisible within the pelvis, anatomically spaced, dwells the first protective wisdom of the "ancient one." Arrangements there are automatically marvelous in their protective complexity: hearts beat, lungs breathe, stomachs digest and kidneys excrete, with no attention from above and no interference with our outward lives. But the primary law here in case of danger is the old instinctive one of self-defense: *contract, withdraw, escape*. The body and its functions must be preserved by fight or flight according to the oldest jungle law, with no reference at all to the higher considerations of our personal or social requirements, which may necessitate a greater sacrifice. Thus we are placed in our specially human dilemma: having these two opposite natures of automatic self-defense and willing sacrifice, what are we to do? What do we do?

We cannot do other than as we are within ourselves. That is the law and penalty of incarnation. We are the victims of our own complex simplicity and we can only express in the forms of our outward conduct the various patterns of our invisible anatomy. Hysteria, therefore, expresses the tyranny of this lower aspect of our nervous system, which is functioning protectively on its negative side. Instinctively, in self-defense, the impulse comes: "Contract: escape. There is danger ahead: go back!" So speaks our jellyfish, and so the word goes forth, to work its way through our invisible anatomy. The whole intricate affair that is the "self" *contracts actively, expressing negative energy in self-defense.* Our psychic house becomes hysterical and "squeezes the tenant." And so the man whose troubles I described at the beginning of this chapter used to dream that he was enclosed by crushing walls from which he could not, but always must, escape. That is the living nightmare of hysteria. The body of our invisible anatomy has clutched us in its fearful grip and somehow we must get out of it. In various ways we do, and the symptoms of hysteria follow in their complex consequence.

Male and Female Psyche

In discussing the development of nervous disorder in general (see Chapter 6), I described the two aspects of the psychic breath of life as alternating between inner and outer, dark and light, passive and active, or unconscious and conscious phases. I suggested that these two poles of our reciprocal rhythm could be described as "female" and "male", respectively. That is to say, the characteristics of the female psyche may be considered as those related to the original source or seed, the "root" of the spiral, prior to its extension in three-dimensional space and time. The female psyche is therefore interior, occult, central, dark, unconscious and passive, like a cave or womb. The male psyche, on the other hand, stands for extension and activity in the world of form: it is therefore exterior, superficial, peripheral, light, conscious and active. Furthermore, the energy of the female psyche is "positive," latent and expansive, with diminishing tension: but the energy of the male psyche is "negative," dynamic and contracting, with increasing tension. Between these two extremes, energy normally ebbs and flows.

Here are two definitions which are conveniently simple: *the female psyche is concerned with the capacity to experience change: but the male psyche is concerned with the power to change experience.* The female psyche dominates the unconscious and the emotional life: some of its symbols are the seed, the egg, the womb, the cave and the cup. It is the *interior mother* from which we all must spring, to enter into the framework and overcome the resistance of the space-time world. The male psyche dominates our relationships in regard to that exterior world and is our *interior father.* His symbol is the sword or phallus, which stand for active penetration. The two together need to be wedded in right relationship in order to give birth and rebirth to the *interior child.* Together, they comprise our interior family of which we are all composed. We are each one of us, therefore, both male and female; we are not only bisexual, but also a complete family, with living problems of interior relationships. In the female sex, the female psyche is predominant, as in the male sex the male psyche is predominant: but in each the other is also latent and to be reckoned with, especially in so far as it is presented to us in the exterior world by our opposite number (male or female partner, mate or "beloved") in our exterior relationships, who mysteriously (and sometimes hatefully) reflect this other aspect of our selves.

In hysteria, we have a fault of interior relationships between our male and female psyche, which is characterized by an unconscious or compulsive rejection of the female psyche. In effect, we refuse to experience change and choose instead to wield the male sword and thus to change experience. With energy let loose and sword drawn from the scabbard of its proper opposite, hysteria is an attack upon the self, and also upon that with which the self may have become identified.

The Hysterical Attack

Hysteria—like "nerves"—is an "attack." This is a very significant word and it operates on different levels, in different ways. The first "attack" that happens is that we feel as if we are menaced by some event outside. "It," whatever it may be, is after us, and we are afraid of this attack and so we run away. (We will not suffer it, or experience change.) But watch what mirrors we are liable to be of our exterior experience: if we merely react, instinctively, we shall then attack ourselves. We shall contract, withdrawing with a jerk when the door slams—making a fist within ourselves, as it were, catching our breath, gritting our teeth, closing our eyes, gripping our muscles in an intensity of apprehension. This is the second level of the hysterical attack. The third level is where energy tends to be released in some way on the negative side. We think, perhaps, what can I do? Then mind also joins instinctively in the attack: it is thrown into a protective spasm of useless, ineffective, worrying energy. The fourth level of this same attack is in the hysterical outburst, which is now striking back again at the offensive exterior world: a scream or epileptiform fit: laughter or tears: a cruel remark, a blow, or some more practical effort at improving the situation, all express in some way the need to release this flood of our protective protopathic energy. The world which first attacked us has now been met with our attack: as we were slapped, so we have slapped it back. (I have shown these four levels of instinctive response in figure 9, "Triangulation," on p. 147.)

One important characteristic of our response to danger on this instinctive level is that it is what is called "protopathic" or "all or nothing." It is completely massive, total and undifferentiated. There is no selection in our behavior. Reacting automatically, we react *en bloc*, as it were, and the whole system is thrown uncontrollably into its behavior of compulsive "fight or flight." For this

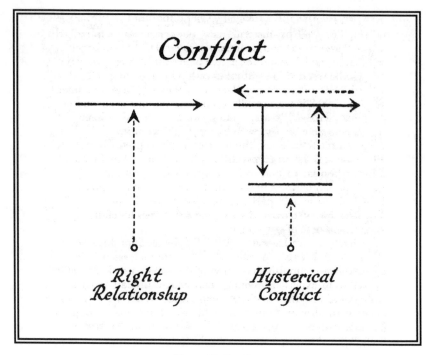

Conflict

*Right
Relationship*

*Hysterical
Conflict*

Figure 26 Conflict

reason it might be expected that the function of consciousness, within the higher head, would not become involved, because its job is to differentiate exactly, to distinguish appropriate detail in the exterior situation and to decide upon our best response. But here we come upon a most awkward verbal confusion, which is due entirely to our unfortunate misuse of words. The fact is that we are often quite unconscious in the way we use our faculty of consciousness. Confusing as that may seem, we can perhaps understand its meaning and its truth better, if we say that the way in which we use our "heads" is often predetermined by the way in which our "hearts" have decided to escape. Much argument and many opinions derive their motives from such unconscious sources: all ineffective worrying, all obsessions and fixed ideas, and all unreasonable behavior, are unconscious in their origin, in spite of their emergence into, and activity within, the realm of so-called consciousness. Actually, although it may sound absurdly paradoxical, our human development of this faculty of consciousness is as yet only very slightly conscious of itself. The difficulty is verbal: but it is important to realize that the hysteric is *always* in a very unconscious state of consciousness.

Conflict

The characteristic of hysteria is that energy is divided against itself. It does not function normally, breathing to and fro in a reciprocating rhythm, but abnormally, attacking itself, with negative forces morbidly superimposed upon the positive urge for self-expression. Thus willpower becomes won't-power, or obstinacy: the attitude to life is predominantly negative: and satisfaction becomes morbidly limited to the enjoyment of a state of pain (masochism). The hysteric cannot help being unhappy: everything tends to go wrong and to lead to a negative or unfortunate result. Avoiding pain, the paradox of hysteria is that it can only suffer pain.

The conflict of hysteria is illustrated in figure 26, "Conflict" (opposite), where every motive is shown divided against itself. This double motive leads to what is called "ambivalence," which is a double attitude of both love and hate experienced, either alternately or at the same time, towards a single object. Thus the hysteric may feel ambivalently towards parent, wife or husband: the result is negative satisfaction in either case, because the hysteric always wants what is not there and does not want what is.

From what I have said already about the defensive spasmodic nature of energy in hysteria, it will be readily appreciated that it is, in various ways, a very repressive and repressed condition. This fact becomes obvious if we realize the four levels of the attack which hysteria is experiencing. At each level, its object is the *dismissal of the offender*. It is trying to get rid of something, even of itself, as a means of escape from its fearful situation. Its fundamental prepositions, when it is "in" danger, are to get "out" (flight) or "at" (fight). If we cannot eliminate or obliterate (i.e. repress) "it," then we proceed in roundabout fashion to eliminate or obliterate "me," on various levels and in various ways. Thus *repression* is the protective process of the whole hysterical mechanism. Its method is surgical (without intending to be rude to surgeons); quite simply, hysteria means to *cut it out*. Within the law of its own being, according to the nature of its invisible anatomy, that is all that hysteria can do. It does it variously, and so creates a multitude of symptoms in many ways and places.

The effect of the hysterical response to danger, real or imaginary, is that it always joins the enemy. That is to say, seeing that it must attack itself it is *on the side of the attacker. It becomes protectively identified with the exterior world which was its enemy.* David, hysterically, is now Goliath; so David, having ceased to exist, has no problem whatever on Goliath's account, which is a neat solution of the problem. Unfortunately, however, in David's life there are many Goliaths: and by the time he has identified himself with all of them and all their many warring voices, there is very little of poor David left, except a mass of contradictions. The way of the hysteric is hard and complicated, in spite of instinct's unconscious efforts to make it soft and simple by escape from danger.

I have said that the protective purpose of hysteria is the dismissal of the offender. But who is the offender and what is the offence? The answer is that the specific purpose of hysteria is the *rejection of the limiting principle.* This "limiting principle" is the ring, whatever that may be, by which all life must be bounded. In the first instance, it is the Mother, in whose womb the child was once confined. There the first pattern is dramatically established of the "self" within the "ring," the positive expanding forces caught within the prison bars of the negative contracting force. The child is born and changes a lesser for a larger ring. He is now bounded visibly within the body, and less visibly within the boundary of the domestic circle. His body's ring expands, and yet the ring remains. His environment expands, through school and office, courtship or marriage ties—and yet the ring remains. For all of us, as long as we live, there always is a ring. That is the impossible offence, to which the hysteric reacts so abnormally, and compulsively declaims, "I must get out of here!"

What happens then? We get at once a false and timeless weaning; the child so suddenly cut off from its security, must as suddenly be balanced back again. The first effect is a *dissociation,* which means that there is no real communication possible between child and mother or self and ring. They experience no more love, which is the evidence of a true relationship. The second effect is an *identification* by means of which the child is now exactly one with the offending mother, or the self with the intolerable ring. To remain balanced, nothing else is possible: but now, all is possible, because if you are the limiting principle, there is no limiting principle to bother you, apart from yourself. If there is one, you become identified with it, and that is simply that.

But watch the consequent confusion. Firstly, you are now become what you cannot bear: you are not yourself any more, because to be yourself would necessitate acceptance of the limiting principle. Secondly, since you have dismissed your mother, your only role now is to become your own father: you must be male authority and your power must be unlimited. Thirdly, there must be *only* power, for to love at all is to be betrayed into the ring of the limiting principle of the beloved. Fourthly, you are bound to be "ambivalent," by which is meant that there are always two opposite feelings experienced towards the same object. The mother or ring which was dismissed ("hated") is now yourself, and deeply held inside yourself. The law must be obeyed: there must be two: now these are both in you, and you have become deeply divided against yourself. Hence the insoluble nature of the hysteric conflict. Fifthly, the process is "compulsive": it is far below the level of knowledge or free choice. It is a mechanical event, blindly driven by invisible energies. Claustrophobia is a very simple version of this most complicated and self-contradictory affair, in which by many and various ways the "child" must dismiss either the "(m)other" or the "self," by an act of timeless aggression. It is this process which sets up the hard core of hysteria, as an indomitably negative power-principle. In different ways, hysteria attempts to reject every limitation and to exploit its position of unlimited power.

Perhaps this discussion of the mechanism of hysteria has enabled us to understand better what Freud has described as the Oedipus (or Electra) Complex, in which the child dismisses the parent of the same sex and unites with the opposite one. I suggest that both the Grecian myth and human psychopathology owe their existence to the same source, which lies in the pattern of our invisible anatomy. The conflict of our energies emerges dramatized in our behavior, which is its outward evidence. Historically, although there may have been problems between the parent and the child, they cannot really be the cause of our hysteria. Events in the exterior world, however unfortunate they may have been, can never solely be the cause of our interior development. They can precipitate disaster, as secondary factors, *but they are never more than that.* The cause, as well as the only hope of final cure, is thus deeply laid in pattern in ourselves. When once we realize that, we can take the first essential step within the ring of fact and common sense again, but to blame external scapegoats in our personal history is to remain hysterical. To seek for cause for blame by working back to some event or early situation (reductive analysis) is not enough, if it only finds another scapegoat to bear the brunt of our intolerant attack. Finally, there must be no blame at all, and we must realize that the problem of hysteria's cause and cure is here and now, in me, and all within my ring. To believe in any outward evidence of other cause as being *primary,* is to be deceived that truth is on the other side of a mirror. It is not. Once and for all, let us realize that we do not live in any perfect world. We all must be allowed to make mistakes. The mistake that anyone has ever made is not enough to justify our bitterness. All that must be forgiven: and more too, if there is more to come. Yes, there have been mistakes, great mistakes, in all our lives. The great mistake of hysteria is that it cannot let mistakes occur. The proper attitude to our unjust experience is well described in the following Zen poem:

> *Out of the blue comes the insult*
> *Insufferable, like a smack in the face.*
> *Retiring from the Presence we make bows,*
> *The Master has been really much too kind!*

The Great Reversal

We can now consider the problem of hysteria's great reversal in more detail. The pattern is drawn in figure 27, "Hysteria—the Great Reversal" (on p. 349). The "inferior" positive energy of the hysteric slackens: in self-defense, the negative protective mechanism comes into operation: and the effect is that the attacked has now become his own attacker, thus reinforcing his enemy at his own expense. That is why the boy who is bullied by his father himself often becomes a bully, or bullies himself with his own self-directed sadistic phantasies. That is why the girl who is jilted decides that she hates all men and *tries to become one*. That is why the hysteric in general spends his life in feeding his hated audience, which he has himself become. That is why I call hysteria "the great reversal." It is the disease which, denying the paradox of incarnate life, becomes itself a paradox. There must be one and no other: therefore there are many, but there is no one. The hysteric is self-centered, but he has destroyed his real self.

Normally, growth occurs gradually and continuously; but not in hysteria, which proceeds by leaps and bounds, jumping to conclusions because it cannot bear to be confined. Normally, energy extends itself in time according to the laws inherent in its invisible anatomy; but not in hysteria, which grasps what seems to be a good and safe result, before it has been grown. Normally, energy is balanced within the ring of circumstance and self-imposed discipline; but not in hysteria, which must always balance itself by its exterior activities and, when that is no longer possible, by the development of symptoms of various kinds.

In hysteria, growth comes to a certain point and stops: this is a fixation point (see figure 27, p. 349). The impassable barrier may be set up by some single event or shock, such as would shatter the feeling of security; it may be set up by a spoiling mother who insists on keeping her child within her power, unweaned; or by a terrifying father who, standing to represent the exterior world, makes it seem impossibly threatening and insecure; or, in some cases, the tendency may be inborn to behave according to the pattern of hysteria, refusing growth and insisting upon the unweaned and unlimited privileges of infancy instead. From whatever cause, growth ceases to find its way across the bridge of life and jumps, instead, to become identified with some more advantageous position in the exterior world. Then, instead of the effort to express and achieve, adventurous and positive, the effort becomes reversed, to retain and avoid losing all that has been grasped; with a consequent negative attitude towards experience. The self has become identified protectively with circumstance, inner with outer, female with male, child with adult: and the peaceful preposition IN becomes the aggressive AT. The tree, which has been sketched in lightly in the background of the picture to stand for simplest growth, is broken in the stem; the roots are neglected, the fruits of life plucked greedily before they can be ripe. When the bridge of goodwill has thus been broken, the traveler can no longer return to find his peace within himself, unless he is willing to be "born again," by re-experiencing the problem that he first rejected, this time more positively. A nervous breakdown may, however, be the means of rediscovering those inward, long neglected roots, as we return to reenter the very problems which we insisted on leaving behind. We can be born again, but this must be the price: acceptance of all that was rejected in the past.

In hysteria the most important "loop" or "throw-over" is from the positive aspect of "heart" to the negative aspect of "head," which now must bear the brunt of life's attacks. "Hearts" are out of suit and only "clubs" are trumps, aggressively. But here is the point: the mind thus used by our hysteria becomes a self-defeated organ. Its purpose is not positive but negative; it will always try to shut the door it seems to want to open, and produce defeat in place of the victory which it seems to desire. Negative in its protective purpose, hysteria at every point can only achieve negative results. That is its problem and its penalty.

The especial activities of hysteria in the mind are concerned with anxiety, obsessions, forgetfulness, phantasies and the "querulous" state which gets nowhere. The hysteric is profoundly impressed with the importance of his own ideas, as if by thinking that reality is other than it is, he can thus change reality. All such thinking, however, is tinged with the conflicting forces of emotional anxiety. Even in thought, the hysteric is facing both ways. Nothing is simple or direct, everything is double. Conflict and self-contradiction are everywhere. There is no respect for facts at all, because they are too limiting. Ideas are compulsive: that is to say, they are reinforced by an ulterior or opposite motive. Ambivalence reigns in self-disappointing control. This is the cause of that anxious worrying, which is the common evidence of instinctive and self-protective

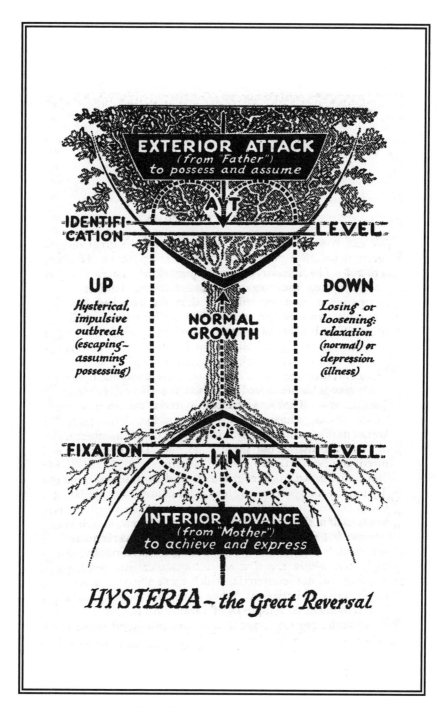

Figure 27 Hysteria—the Great Reversal

thought. The hysteric uses his imagination as if it pictured a real world and gives it an importance it cannot possibly deserve, endowing it with the magic properties which belong by rights to deeper levels of the creative self. To the hysteric, mere thinking makes a thing so, for better or for worse. Imagined fears are the only "real" dangers: imagined phantasies are the only "real" gains. Thus the mental level assumes a spurious importance and on to it are projected all the deeper emotional conflicts. The mind, which should be an objective instrument of measured, timely accuracy, becomes a subjective source of inflated and intemperate violence. To say, however, to a hysteric that an experience is "only imaginary," though true, yet does it less than justice, because to him it must be more than real.

It must be emphasized, I think, that the hysteric himself has no means of telling the reversed direction which has taken place. He does not know that he is "at" a job, rather than "in" it, because there are in fact no compass points to signify direction. The difference can usually be detected, however, by careful observation, and it is still more obvious when viewed from the standpoint of results. Even in reading a book the hysteric will consume it compulsively with greedy appetite, with forehead tense and purpose only to reach the end. All work will be attacked compulsively and probably not completed: or else a sense of duty will so bind him to the job that all may be destroyed to get it done. Hysterics do not go kindly about either work or play. Their sense of timing is bad and their relationships, like everything else that concerns them, are matters of extremes. A little creation may be achieved, but only at the expense of much destruction. Their way is littered with accidents, misfortunes, bad luck and illness: and it should be added that these unfortunate consequences do not by any means only fall upon themselves.

Inferiority and Over-Compensation

According to the pattern of hysteria, a state or feeling of weakness, being intolerable, tends either to withdrawal from danger altogether, or else to express itself in over-activity. This is called over-compensation. It is not done deliberately. It is always unconsciously mechanical in its defensive purpose. In practice, however, it is as dangerous as it would be to declare your weakest suit as trumps, if you wished to win the game.

Examples of overcompensation are innumerable and they all tend to lead to insoluble situations of weakness involved beyond its strength. Thus the small man may choose to marry a woman who is larger than himself in all respects: small men in general are liable for this reason to assume too much and to make too great a claim for themselves. A man who feels afraid of his own cowardice may unconsciously set himself most dangerous tasks to prove his bravery: another, fearing his incapacity in sex, may overdrive his sexual life to great extremes. A woman, who is excelled at home by her socially more brilliant sister, may strive to beat her with her brain, becoming a compulsive highbrow: another, who feels doubtful of her declining charm with passing years, may be led to act with over-youthful foolishness. It is as if a state of poverty leads naturally to a spendthrift policy.

A physical weakness may also lead unconsciously to the same extravagant display of power. Early invalidism in a child may foster compensatory phantasies of power that become dangerous standards for subsequent experience: a boy who is laid low by infantile paralysis may daydream of his prowess on the football field or on the pirate ship. The hunchback has a well-known tendency to exploit his power in various ways. In fact, any weakness in any organ, whether it is real or imaginary, tends to lead unconsciously to an overcompensation, so that the weakness may be covered and protected by a bluff of strength. Up to a point, of course, this might be a useful defense mechanism and lead to some achievement of success: but there is a dangerous weakness in the invisible anatomy of such a person, because of the tendency to break down under strain. They must do what they cannot do, because they feel they cannot do it. They are therefore intolerant of any criticism and cannot learn, as others do, by their mistakes. Nor can they ever easily surrender to defeat, which we must all face sometimes when the facts of life are set too heavily against us. Normally, we fall with grace and decency, to rise in time and try again. But the overcompensated personality can only break, because it cannot bear to fall. Worst of all, they find it hard to surrender to their experience of love, which is what they most need to give them the confidence they lack. They are so busy building up and supporting their facade, that they must be self-centered in their attitude to life. They cannot love because they cannot bear to lose themselves or surrender their facade. Intolerant of weakness, which is love's necessary price, they can only exploit power instead and thus they must destroy the beloved in the end and so prove themselves hysterical.

The hysterical mechanism of overcompensation is not always obvious, nor does it always lead to a nervous breakdown. Sometimes it shows itself as misuse of power and privilege in our daily lives; but sometimes it may play a quite unconscious part, even in such important matters as our choice of a profession. In any case, it leads to petty tyranny, to lack of consideration for others and to the introduction of the ulterior motive of *escape from inferiority*, which can only interfere with our working efficiency, whatever our work may be. We cannot serve our task so well, if we are even partly trying to conceal our weakness from the world and from ourselves, or trying to gain some personal advantage.

Hysteria and Pain

Why is pain so often self-sought and self-inflicted in hysteria? The answer to this important question is that it is a necessary consequence of the hysterical pattern of destructive self-centeredness that it should be so. To the hysteric it may seem optional, as so much of his behavior seems to be, but, in so far as the reversal mechanism operates, our behavior is compulsive and is not determined by our own free will.

Here are some examples of self-inflicted pain in hysteria. "I feel as if I am a cask bound round by iron bands: if only I could burst!" and the patient strikes himself violently with his hands or wishes to bang his head against a wall. Self-mutilation may persist in some specialized form, such as inflicting fresh wounds or opening up an old one; it must be done in secret, half-unconsciously but wholly under that compulsion from within which is stronger than the will to stop such foolish practices. It may also lead to a proneness to accident, or physical bad luck. All these are physical examples, but the same mechanism also operates on the mental level in which a destructive morbidity of conscience or tendency to self-depreciation is a common evidence of hysteria. Phantasies of beating and being beaten effectively portray and dramatize the hysterical conflict and the negative state. Imaginary terrors and anxieties may have the same effect of constantly self-inflicted torture. Indeed, the hysteric can use anything and everything destructively, and very often does, in order to achieve the unenviable state of negative satisfaction. Some innocent remark, or simple attempt at instruction, may seem to the hysterical patient to be a sign of our destructive purpose, for which he turns against us as the scapegoat and cause of all the trouble. Or else he takes our little word that seemed so unimportant when we said it, and uses it as a fiery sword on which to fling himself in tortured agony of self-disparagement.

Such persons cannot endure suspense and therefore jump to negative conclusions, imagining the worst for fear that something undesirable may happen. Often we hear them say: "I am afraid to be happy in case it may not last," and sometimes such a pessimistic attitude to life is speciously philosophized. Yet, rational as their argument may seem to be, it is not rational at all, because it is only a projection in the mind of their compulsively inverted state.

Dramatization and Conversion

Hysteria is emotional, imaginative and powerful, and it is often remarked that hysterics dramatize themselves, in order the better to produce an effect upon their audience. A problem of relationship, instead of being solved by more reasonable methods, is therefore dramatized and thus played out upon an inconvenient stage. In its simplest form, the hysteric "plays up" to produce thereby some outward change: to draw attention to himself, or perhaps to obtain revenge. No means are then to be despised, if he can thereby attain the desired end, for hysteria can be utterly unscrupulous. Apparently sincere and meaning it at the time, the hysteric may set the stage for suicide, in order to excite pity and punish the offender with remorse ("look what you have done to me, how you have made me suffer!"); he usually takes care, however, not to come to any real harm. Or, in a domestic quarrel, a woman will sincerely convince herself that her husband has been unfaithful, in order the better to belabor him with having caused some great disaster. The situation is intensified to bursting point, in order to produce the desired effect of uncontrollable explosion. Then words are weapons which have no bearing on the truth, for they are only chosen by the emotional spur for the sake of their destructive power. When an hysterical person becomes involved in such amateur dramatics, the purpose is not to give either entertainment or pleasure, but a maximum amount of pain to the person who is emotionally most important at the time.

Hysteria also shows its dramatic tendencies in quite another way, by turning its energy into the development of a symptom which conveniently solves the problem. This process is called "conversion," and distinguishes *conversion hysteria*, in which the problem is dramatized in the form of a symptom which effectively removes the urgent problem, from *anxiety hysteria*, in which the anxiety is free and therefore provides the main symptom. Loss of memory, hearing or speech, functional blindness or paralysis (which are called "functional" disorders because they are not due to an organic injury) are examples of such "conversion." They all have the effect of concealing the true nature of the problem, while temporarily solving it. To the trained eye of the psychiatric observer, however, the nature of the symptom which has been unconsciously selected may be a clear guide to the nature of the underlying problem. The following cases are simple examples of conversion.

A timid but ambitious man felt incompetent to do his work, but bitterly resented having a junior put in authority over him. It was frosty at the time and he had to walk cautiously to get to the office. This was sufficient to set up a phobia or conversion symptom that he could not walk, which lasted several months. He was afraid of falling down and therefore he had to stay at home.

A boy apprentice at a factory was very unhappy at his work: his young colleague received a minor injury to his eye which necessitated his staying away: the boy saw a film in which the hero was blinded, and the following day he was unable to go to work because he could not see. Functional paralysis is perhaps the most common conversion symptom of soldiers at the front, who find that the combination of exhaustion, anxiety and shock provides an intolerable conflict with their sense of duty. In one way or another, the symptom solves the problem temporarily, but at the price of developing a disability which, being unconsciously produced, is quite beyond the patient's power to control. Such symptoms can neither be acquired nor cured by an effort of the will, in which they are entirely different from malingering.

In dreams, in symptoms and in dramatized behavior, unconscious energy displays its deep creative power, according to its inward pattern and design. All such conversion symptoms are evidence of our deep unconscious will to solve the problems by which we are beset. But, being unconsciously devised, their plan is no better than escaping from the problem, on the ancient grounds of safety first. They therefore leave us with an added problem of a symptom to be cured, while the original problem must still be faced at some time.

Exhibitionisms and Depersonalization

Being so bent on the limitless privilege of exploiting power, hysteria must always be using power "over" and power "at": hence the importance of the audience, which is the material in regard to which the hysteric must be enforcing change. Because of this importance of the audience, which represents the outer world with which they are protectively identified, the hysteric must always seem to be something of an exhibitionist. But if you are compelled to be continually "blowing off steam," you might easily be accused of showing off, when that is not really your intention. Actually, hysterics are not quite so bothered about the audience as is sometimes suggested. They do have their fits and faints and spasms when there is nobody about. They do not care about their audience as such to any great extent, because nothing is so important to them as to externalize their problems as best they can. The problem must be got out and got rid of: hence the importance of an audience, but that is secondary. The hysteric's first importance is himself, because he is of necessity, in the pattern as it were, self-centered—and yet at loggerheads with self. Then the whole system is projected outwards, and, while identified with the audience, the hysteric must also be at loggerheads with that. It is all a matter of pattern: in hysteria, rejecting its confinement, energy is the more compulsively confined.

The most important significance of the audience is that, being self-centered, the hysteric is always looking at himself from someone else's point of view. Instead of looking out of himself (out into the world), his arrows of direction for both interest and energy are back into himself. "What are they thinking of me?" seems therefore to be a question of primary importance, as if, without that exterior approval, one cannot exist at all. "What am I thinking of myself?" puts conscience on a similar pedestal, and in hysteria the conscience is, like everything else, exteriorized, inflated and exploited as a source of power. The importance of these loud exterior voices of authority or of conscience may either be fiercely rejected or compulsively respected, but this is part of the general ambivalence of hysteria.

Full blown hysterics are like flowers identified with bees, but busier. They are beside themselves, outside themselves, in every way that they can be. Eventually, in certain extreme cases, this accounts for what is known as "depersonalization." The process of "externalization" has grown to such extremes that they are, as regards their invisible anatomy, inside out. They may then become like timid, pale and empty ghosts, whose feet hardly seem to touch the floor because they are so physically light. Everything feels to them unreal, because indeed their feelings are unreal. Reality depends upon how you feel about it: if you feel unreal, then reality must feel unreal to you. If feelings have been denied, repressed or displaced: if they have been distorted and interfered with and never trained: if these hysterics live only within a world of their own vain imagining: how can reality to them seem real? The great escape has gone so far in self-defense that not even the world in which they live is real.

Such a patient described her state as follows: "I can't do a thing for myself now. I have an empty helpless feeling inside me, as if I am worn out and dead. I feel I have no depth and can't get hold of myself. Everything seems flat, like looking in a mirror. I live ahead of myself all the time, as if there will always be something better round the next corner or tomorrow. I feel all screwed up, hedged in by my anxiety. I must find something to use me up, but I am terrified of hitching myself in desperation to something which has no ground." She dreamt various portrayals of her empty state: that she was only a head and neck, with no body below the level of her shoulders: that she was in a room open on two sides to the air with no ceiling: that she was in frantic flight pursued by some terrible unknown evil power. She was in fact what she felt herself to be, an empty shell, whose only hope of life was to be as firmly attached to someone else's world as a limpet to its rock.

Definition

Hysteria is a disturbance of the normal relationship which exists between the female (inner, positive) and male (outer, negative) aspects of the psyche. As we saw before, the female psyche is concerned with the capacity to experience change. The male psyche is concerned with the power to change experience. Hysteria is a negative and destructive disorder of relationship on various levels, which, refusing to experience change and insisting upon changing experience, is characterized by an unconscious compulsive rejection of the female psyche and a compensatory exploitation of the male psyche. In its purpose, the hysterical process is a protective protest against inferiority or frustration. In its effect, it produces a blind reversal from the expansive energy of the female psyche to the contracting energy of the male psyche, with consequent symptoms of dissociation, repression, dramatization and loss of function on various levels. In brief, hysteria is a negative protest against negative conditions, with negative satisfaction and negative results.

Symptoms

Of course, no single case can show all the symptoms of hysteria, which Freud described as a "polymorphous perverse" complaint. The variety of its complex perversities is unlimited, and we are variously afflicted. Some more, some less, it is doubtful whether any of us are entirely free from symptoms of hysteria. We are all to some extent the objects of our own attack. We all have our phantasies that swell and sometimes burst, making us look very silly to our knowing friends. We all have our over-conscientious morbid moods of self-analysis. We all have our mysterious aches and pains that mislead us, as red herrings do, from the real problems that we do not want to face. When the mind wanders, we have our little tricks, like biting nails or picking spots. We all have our anger, jealousy and even a little malice perhaps sometimes; and we repress it too, as being too inconvenient to our facade to be expressed. We all have our superstitious fears, and we forget, conveniently, what is too painful to remember. We all pick and choose our willful way through life, imposing our prettier pictures on our audience, hoping that they will believe that we are being frank about ourselves. We all think our thoughts are reasonably true. We are all sometimes negative, protective, and vulnerable to attack. In fact, we are all somewhat hysterical. It is only a matter of degree.

Before discussing symptoms in detail, I would like to stress one important characteristic of hysteria, which is the patients' attitude towards their symptoms. Intolerance of all frustration causes the symptoms, which are then new examples of intolerable frustration: hence, they must be dismissed at once, as if by the instantaneous use of magic power. The hysteric patient is a most impatient patient. The condition is catching and the doctor may become infected by the same impatience, but he cannot cure the condition if he has it himself. However urgently the patient may require the doctor to give a pleasing sign of his omnipotence, it must be clearly understood that such burdens cannot be removed so simply. Instantaneous dismissal of the problem is one of the chief symptoms of hysteria and therefore it never can effect its cure.

Here are three typical examples of hysteria in action as a "reversal." A girl of twenty was most anxious to be pleasing to her fiancé, because he was bringing her the engagement ring. Before she knew what was happening she had precipitated a quarrel about nothing that nearly caused him to break off the engagement. A business man of forty left me after an interview in some distress. He said he felt like crying, but instead, to his amazement and confusion, he laughed out loud as he walked down Harley Street and could not stop himself. A woman of thirty-five wished to get to Oxford Circus after leaving my consulting room to meet a friend. She therefore needed to turn to the left at my door. Instead, she felt compelled to turn right towards Marylebone Road and then go down Portland Place. But no, she must now turn left out of Marylebone Road. Whichever way she wanted to turn, she felt compelled to go in the opposite direction. By this devious process she nearly got to Paddington, and finally decided to take a taxi.

On the *level of energy*, hysteria implies a heavy preponderance of the negative, protective side, which is constraining the disintegrating forces of an oversensitive, explosive mixture on the inner or positive side. It is "as if" (but indeed I think it may also be truly and exactly so within the pattern of our invisible energy) a wheel or vortex spins: and spinning, throws out its centrifugal force in large unwieldy lumps of flame, more violent than sparks: in order to balance this unbalanced rush of energy, the surface of the wheel or vortex hardens and thrusts back towards the center, until the energy of the wheel itself becomes, as it were, concentrated in its own rim.

On the *level of the autonomic system*, we have a condition of acute nervous and emotional instability, in which the positive (parasympathetic) impulses are relatively overwhelmed by the negative (sympathetic) impulses, with resultant symptoms of anxiety. The effect on the *organic level* is to set up a series of contractions or spasms in all those muscles which can respond to the sympathetic impulses: in the heart, the spasmodic contractions set up acceleration (palpitation), in the lungs the spasms produce shortness of breath and the feeling of a lump in the throat, in the stomach anorexia, nausea, vomiting, in the bowel diarrhea and in the skin, gooseflesh, coldness, and pallor.

The selection of the site of the hysterical symptom on the organic level is a matter of some interest. Why is a certain part chosen for the symptom-expression and not another? There are several answers. In general, pain is a condition of *local pressure*. Pain may therefore be experienced wherever the pressure is, or in the area associated with that nerve supply. (This is called *referred pain*.)

Secondly, the symptom may be focused on the weakest link in the organic chain. Wherever there is a minimal organic defense against illness, the hysterical problem may fix on that point for a maximum demonstration. Very commonly there is, therefore, a comparatively minor organic basis for a major hysterical distress. Thirdly, there may be a history of some old injury to the part affected. Having suffered once, it is more prone, as it were, to experience suffering again. This may serve to remind us of *tissue memory*. Often, in hysterical disorders, there is a notable tendency to celebrate "birthdays," repeating the event, possibly even to the exact time, a month or a year afterwards. For instance, the man whose story I told at the beginning of this chapter told me that he usually experienced his "attacks" on Saturdays. He would wake feeling bad, depressed, as if he had no legs to stand on, and as if something awful was going to happen. Why on Saturdays? The question had never occurred to him, but when asked he gave a direct answer. As a child, Saturday was his bad day. Although he wanted to enjoy some freedom with his friends, his mother had decided otherwise. She told him he must be home at three o'clock when she returned, to run her shopping errands for her. Sometimes he stopped at home, wasting his time until she arrived. Even then, he usually got a beating for doing something wrong. Sometimes he went off to join his pals and then he always got a beating. Anyway, it was a bad day. Fifteen years after, his body was still remembering what his mind had been glad to forget.

There is another important cause, however, for the selection of the site of the hysterical complaint. This is called *organ jargon*, by which we mean that the body too can talk after its fashion, each organ having a meaning in the body's poetry. Problems of appetite, desire and greed, frustrated or repressed, tend to pick out the digestive system for their disturbances. Problems of the "heart," i.e. the affections, tend to be reflected in the physiological organ of that name. Anxieties on the mental level tend to affect the lungs. Slang is a useful guide. "I can't swallow that" brings lumps in the throat. "You make me sick" tends to nausea and vomiting. "You give me a pain in the neck"—well, perhaps you do, and it really isn't rheumatism. This is all organ jargon, and it is impossible to say how much the hysterical factor may not be at the back of our "organic" complaints and disturbances. More than we know, it must be, because there is always so much that we do not want to know. In general, where there is emotional repression ("let's forget it"), the problem is inclined to be expressed on the physical level in terms of the body's organ jargon. Repressed pain on the emotional level is thus expressed on the level of the body's pain, and the real problem is thus bypassed or laid off.

Repressed or dissociated on the emotional level, the hysterical problem is liable to be pushed down into the physical level, and it is here that it sets up its most remarkable variety of bodily symptoms. Energy thus applied against the physical body can grow disease as surely as it might have grown bridges, books or children if it had been more wisely applied to its material. Gastric ulcers, heart trouble (disordered action of the heart) and epileptic fits (these may be indistinguishable from the real thing or dramatically simulated), fainting attacks, tremors or paralysis (but this is always massive and never on neurological lines); blindness, deafness and dumbness; anesthesia, pain, headaches and various mysteriously flitting sensations; there is no end to what hysteria can do to upset the balance of the body's health.

On the *endocrine level*, the adrenal system is thrown into a state of over-activity, which reinforces the "fight or flight" reaction, with symptoms of restlessness, irritability and anxiety.

On the *emotional level*, there is a compulsive tendency to fly out, or break out centrifugally. "I must get out of here" is a general tendency on every level: Jack (or Jill) must jump out of the box, and the "box" may be any condition of frustration anywhere. But, thus leaping out, energy sets up its own counteracting resistance to nonplus itself: the door must slam back against energy's release and the energy goes into the door. Thus the hysteric would jump out of any ring, at the same time that he sets up the tension in the ring which is his own resistance. Out of the body ("my heart jumped out of my mouth"); out of the cinema (claustrophobia): out of temper (emotional violence): out of the room, out of the house, and temporarily out of mind (fainting, unconsciousness, collapse) are all examples of this negative attack.

The special problem of the hysteric is the always difficult one of *relationships*. There is no acceptance of duality, no trinity and no respect for individual integrity, because the hysteric cannot tolerate the space (or time, which in this case is the same thing) that is between. The hysteric must ever be indissolubly one with the desired object: one and the same, indivisibly united. Thus the wife must be one with the husband. The parent must be one with the child, and vice versa. Any threat of difference or separation sets up intolerable anxiety. In terms of appetite, if I can't have all of it when I want it (which is now), then I don't want any of it at all, ever. The hysteric is always protopathic, all or nothing, and knows no middle way. Neither the patient nor the doctor nor anyone nor anything may have a separate existence. The urge for interference is compulsively acute.

Hysteria is a twisted, sorrow-making, contradictory complaint, because of its unhappy knack of turning against the beloved if all is not immediately well. If the beloved object won't behave exactly as desired, then love must turn to hate and the beloved promptly becomes the best hated object. This accounts for the great list of hysterical reversals: the beloved object was not good, and so it must be bad and must be hated. A homosexual woman hated all sight and mention of the female breast, as she hated the physical evidence of her own emotional development. When she was seven she remembered having a very well-developed schoolmistress and thinking how she would love to stick a knife into her breast. Why? Her mother had had no physical affection for her children and never fed them as babies from her skinny figure. Her mother always said she hated children, too. The patient readily admitted that her hate was due to disappointment, and said that she could never bear to wait for what she wanted. It was quite simple if she hated it, instead of having to put up with the unbearable suspense and anxiety of wanting what she could not have. This hating of the beloved object leads to *ambivalence*, or having two opposite feelings towards the same thing. It is a consequence of the hysterical state of interior conflict and that in itself results from the hysterical refusal to accept duality or frustration.

There is a great intensity, or passionate inflation, about all hysterical emotion, which causes the unlimited enlargement and importance of everything on which its attention is focused. It is no ordinary degree of feeling or sentiment that the hysteric experiences, and it appears quite final in its absolute importance. There is no sense of time or likelihood of change: to the hysteric, at the moment of the "attack," this is all, this is the end. There never was a yesterday, there can be no tomorrow: everything is centered in one all-important moment, now. If the object of interest is a pain, it grows to an unimaginable extent; because so much energy and interest is poured into it that it must expand. It is as if we were painting a picture or writing a book *within ourselves*: the thing must grow, with so much energy behind to drive it on. Similarly, if the object of interest is some matter of argument between husband and wife or parent and child, the most trivial incident becomes exaggerated to the dimensions of a "cause célèbre." It is inflated to gigantic size and becomes a matter of life or death. Such arguments never can be solved on reasonable lines, because they are not reasonable. The eruption is volcanic and ends in an explosion: tears are perhaps the best solution, and screams may show that "flashpoint" has been reached; the crisis may come with violent blows if the attack is "extraverted" (turned outwards), or with a blackout of collapse or fainting if the attack is "introverted" (turned inwards). When it has reached the limit of intensity, the pressure must and will be resolved by an "attack." The pressure is then eased, but of course the problem itself, about which the discussion started, will not have been altered in the least.

The hysteric always has several of these foci of intolerable tenderness, where some repressed experience or fear has been concealed. (*Complexes* they are called; they live and grow, invisibly nourished by self-centered energy.) These are the dissociated elements of past experience, which have been partly or wholly forgotten because they were not good to remember or easy to assimilate. They poison the system and, by the conflicts which they generate, they absorb the vital energy which could be better used in other ways. Like abscesses, these septic spots require to be drained by exposure to the healing light of consciousness.

The hysteric is always being "squeezed" by the compulsive drive of negative protective energy: and, extraverted as he usually is (i.e. directed against the exterior world), he is inclined to put on a "squeeze" against someone or something in his exterior conditions. Hysterics cannot rest: they nag and drive compulsively. They are always using power to do the work that only love should do. They drive their household dust before their brooms: they drive their husbands or their children on to do the things that they want done, endlessly, timelessly, without a space or pause.

Intuitives have a special tendency towards hysteria, because they feel that they possess a certain knowledge of perfection all complete. They are the timeless ones who find it very hard to grow, because for them the end can always precede the beginning. In no time at all, they know: so why go through all the pains of growing? The end is readymade in the preconceived idea, so why realize it in external actuality? So it is all done in a rush in the beginning and never properly finished. This is a regular pattern in the problem of hysteria. The intuitive is also caught in yet another of hysteria's traps. Having the inner knowledge of perfection, beauty, goodness, truth, the whole, he has an endless yardstick with which to beat himself and all that is imperfect. The smallness of a growing child, the instant moment now, a teaspoonful of food, none of these can be enough, they simply aren't worth anything compared with the timeless vision of the whole. And so they are destroyed, in shame and guilt, by a tyrant conscience which is identified with some dimly imagined state of absolute perfection. Such is the practice of the negative mystics, who live in a grey and dreary world because they have a negative and aggressive attitude towards their inner light.

On the *psychic level* there is also a special problem. I am using the word "psychic" here to indicate those hyper-sensitives who are mediumistic, or have an exceptional degree of awareness of events beyond themselves. They know what is going on with an inner X-ray aptitude, as if their living world is clothed in cellophane. They see behind the scenes without being fully conscious of what is happening to them. Their psychic powers may become negative turning against them to destroy them. This condition is called *negative psychism*. Such uncomfortably gifted ones are more easily hurt than those who are created of sterner stuff and therefore they may be more liable to rely on instinctive measures with which to protect themselves. Their easiest way is through the assumed unselfishness of minding everybody else's business but their own. They can feel so much suffering in others that they may spend their lives in trying to abolish it in those with whom they are identified. This kind of unselfish interference may seem praiseworthy and benevolent, but actually it is dangerous for all concerned. It is inclined to spoil those whom it seeks to protect, while itself suffering from the inevitable exhaustion of its own unlimited but unaided efforts. We must learn to be ourselves and to mind our own business. Even ethically that is enough, if we know what our own business is.

On the *psychological level*, hysteria is indeed a "flying womb" or "flying woman." That part of self which should be central, quiet and still (the female psyche) flies off the handle, out—only to be thrust back by that very ring or womb which the hysteric must create. Essentially, the hysteric must recreate another womb within which to be confined. All serves this end: "You must be my mother, all-in-all, now and always." That is to say, hysteria is a revulsion against deprivation, and a compulsive creation of the child-in-the-mother state. That is the protective purpose of the negative ring, or womb, within which the hysteric is self-confined. "I must have my mother." But watch the awkward and uncomfortable paradox, the insuperable problem of the ambivalent conflict: "I will not be confined." The freedom of the child within the womb, identified with the mother, *cannot* be repeated in the post-birth state. Both time and space imply a state of difference, conflict, friction and suspense, that hysteria feels it cannot bear. The conflict is the more intense because it is insoluble.

Hysteria denotes the woman's denial of her own female sexuality; resenting the male, she at the same time identifies herself with him, his rights and powers, and so sets up to be her own destroyer. In terms of the ancient sexual symbolism of "sword" and "cup," hysteria is a restless agitation of the sword against the cup's unbreakability. She refuses to submit to him, and then attacks her own unwillingness. She is a man, a mother or a child, and each must be omnipotent in unbroken power, but she cannot, will not, must not be a woman. (Remembering that men also have their female psyche, the same distressing conflict also applies to them, but in a different degree.)

On the *level of consciousness*, the conflict recurs with varying intensity. All must be known, apprehended, understood. Hence the compulsive, querulous, seeking, studious mind, which must have all the answers, now. This may work out with encyclopaedic accuracy, but the conflict is still there. The compulsive and protective mind is really not a womb; it cannot be a mother, protecting us from life, danger, ignorance, mystery, suspense. Yet this field is large enough for some to feel that they are free and unconfined, in imagination's vast expansiveness and within the scope of what they think they know. But, thus compulsively ploughed, the field is sterile, because it has no darkness and no depth.

Amnesia (loss of memory) and *multiple personality* afford other examples of the "pocketing" which repression and dissociation can achieve. Amnesia may be total or partial: it may be selective to the most exact degree. For instance, if some person has intolerably offended, and every exercise of power has failed, then everything in any way associated with that person may be protectively blacked out, forgotten: the person's appearance and very existence, the person's gifts and every single detail connected with the problem is cut out as by a magic knife. Such a violent degree of repression, however, cannot be successfully achieved without some pain, and the headache and other evidences of somatic disturbance may be severe. This is an amazing piece of protective mental surgery, which appears to be beyond all human control. Yet it may have its own mechanical clock, and in one case the patient recovered her lost memory exactly four weeks to the day after she had received the intolerable shock. In another case, a patient arrived at my door not knowing who he was. After ten minutes' light hypnosis on the couch he burst into tears and said; "Why did you make me remember? I only wanted to forget!" He had done something he was ashamed of and, in order to forget it, he had forgotten who he was!

We all have to some extent our "Jekyll and Hyde" dual personalities: we show one face to ourselves and present another to our friends: we are one person at home (hen-pecked, perhaps) and quite a different one at the office, where we have a reputation as a slave-driver. The hysteric can carry these interior differences to a greater degree, with complete separation of different personalities within the sealed bulkheads of watertight compartments. Sometimes one comes out into the light of day, to be replaced at another time by a quite different and often very opposite one.

The hysteric overdoes this buildup in phantasy rather than in fact, as he is inclined to exaggerate everything. Imagination grows luxuriously when it is fed by otherwise inhibited desire. The pockets of the mind are limitless in their extent, when they are cut off from all reasonable bounds and factual restrictions. There is room for "all-or-nothing" here, and wealth may be thus inwardly acquired without effort or opposition. The hysteric has always to face this inner problem of a stolen wealth. This may and often does lead to lying and to stealing, which both have the same meaning and intention as this easy life of phantasy, viz. enjoyment of something which has not been given or earned, but only snatched at. If it goes too far, phantasy may lead to mental breakdown, or to the adoption of some other personality. The trouble is that phantasy must ever be at war with fact. Hence the need for hysteria's instantaneous attack.

On the *economic level*, property may become overvalued. It then means more than it should, because the self in its exterior course has become identified with it, and also dependent on it. At the same time, there is the same resentment active against the very prison walls which we build around ourselves by our attachment to our property, so even that is comfortless.

On the *social level*, the craving for power and influence over others is paramount. A spurious unselfishness disguises the fact of a dangerous identification: "Let me please you" may mean "You must be me." There is thus a gross tendency to interfere, "unselfishly," with other people's lives, with acute outbursts of emotion at any display of independence on the part of the beloved. "We are all one" is a compulsive, hysterical philosophy of the unweaned, who are aggressively up in arms the moment they detect potential difference. There is much that is hysterical in any autocratic or totalitarian political philosophy, wherein our simpler hopes may be exploited. Leadership may offer to do all our work for us as Providence, Fuehrer, State or Mother-in-disguise: the freedom for which we fight may be mere escapism from reality (freedom from):

the peace we hope for may be a sterile phantasy that never can come true, unless we face the facts of conflict and of difference, which are the measure of the work that must be done in time against resistance: the unity and brotherhood that binds all men together is merely an illusion and a negative destroyer of our highest hopes, unless we solve the problem of relationship and treat each other with respect. Hysteria ranks very high in politics. Only in a real democracy can there be no hysteria, because in it everyone is encouraged to be his own man, although he plays his part within his team.

On the *industrial level*, hysteria accounts for endless and immeasurable ills, from rheumatism to digestive disturbances. Wherever pressure is hard and security unsure, the tendency is to find automatic and unconscious refuge in some bodily illness. Hysteria is a partial factor in a large proportion of so-called organic ill-health. It accounts for hundreds of thousands of wasted working hours, and cash equivalent. Worse than that, however, is the amount of human suffering. There is no measuring the price we pay for our hysteria.

There is a condition called *accident proneness* which is also hysterical in origin. Some are more liable to accidents than others, and we need to watch these "unlucky" ones, who have an unconscious purpose of escape in their seemingly most unwanted accidents.

On the *level of the crowd*, hysteria is again a mass-reaction, "all-or-nothing," protopathic. Here energy is at the disposal of the least common denominator, instinctive, emotional, timeless, urgent, and inevitably destructive. Hysteria is by its nature, in one or all, a state of hyper-suggestibility, which may be either negative or positive. Hysteria is catching and spreads like wildfire; mob rule is a destructive eruption of subhuman energy let loose, at the direction of the most unscrupulous, loudest leader of the low. Crowd hysteria is therefore the easiest prey of all unscrupulous demagogues, who have enough hysteria themselves to be able to sway others where they will with their emotional and unreasoned oratory. With untamed energies let loose, the behavior of a mob can fall to the lowest levels of human conduct, expressing its will to wantonness by fire, and its destructiveness in lynching and the like.

On the *religious level,* hysteria finds its escape easiest of all into unlimited phantasy. "God is my Mother, and I am His beloved Child." Symbolically this may be true; but it cannot be entrusted to hysteria without the certainty of its being misused as a state of special privilege. All the subdivided schisms of religious intolerance go to prove religion's unreality when it is compelled by the hysterical driving force. Like all hysteria, being negative in intent, it must be negative in action. Like all hysteria, being determined to avoid conflict, it creates it all the more. Much of our religion, as of our politics, is hysterical—but not all. True religion is founded on FAITH: but hysteria has none of that. Hysteria must have its own self-chosen "facts" and a dependable and definite BELIEF, with POWER at call, immediately. Hysteria has no quiet interior principle of cohesion and synthesis. It depends utterly on external forms possessed of magical powers. Hence the external nature of the hysteric God: hence his ambivalent tyranny: and hence the deterioration of all religions based on such a false, negative, compulsive and destructive motive.

Hysteria on every level is a negative tyranny, which binds the creative element of life as it would bind a slave, or a dangerous criminal. It is a clamp, an iron band, a vice within which we are prisoners. In hysteria, the material principle in which we are incarnate is petrified against the expanding forces of the spirit's light. Therefore, where the forces of hysteria are active in religion, we may find that evil is moralized as good: and in the form of our negative and self-destructive morbid conscience, we are both driven by it and deceived.

Hysteria and Sex

Here, again, the characteristics are (1) negativeness; (2) lack of emotional development; (3) dramatization or symbolization; (4) reversal; (5) exploitation of power. In general, the nature of the female psyche is refused. It is not only that we cannot give and must take: the complication is that we must pretend to give when we can only take.

By *negativeness* I mean, fundamentally, *unwillingness.* The door is shut: the more we want to open it, the more it shuts. There is muscular, emotional and mental *rigidity*. There is no access or ease of entry: the passage is refused. The hysteric is ringed round with an iron girdle of compulsive chastity. The house is locked and the tenant not at home. Hence, frigidity, rigidity, anxiety and fear.

By *lack of emotional development,* I mean that the emotional condition is that of a child still identified with the mother. There is no proper sexual "polarization," by which the one has accepted weaning from the other, so as to be set over against the inevitable opposite, to dance there willingly with rhythmic reciprocity. Both must still be one, unsexed or asexual, because still undivided, unopposed. Hence mother-fixation (mother-love), masturbation (self-love, self-centered and self-satisfied), and homosexuality (self-identified with similar, in undivided ecstasy). The emotional nature is like a hard, unbroken, massive and undifferentiated lump, instead of being made up of myriad fine tentacles of separated aesthetic appreciation.

By *symbolization or dramatization,* I mean a tendency to transfer to various associated objects an emotional value which is not their own. This is the basis of all *fetishism,* and it is an abnormal extension of a normal process. The worth of the beloved is normally extended in some degree to her hair, her hands, her clothes or her handkerchief, which are all regarded as part of, or extensions of, herself. In hysteria, however, the process becomes abnormal, because she herself is dissociated or repressed, whereas the object takes all her value to itself. Thus certain objects stand out alone as having themselves become the beloved, "dissociated": e.g. hair, shoes, underwear, a certain kind of material such as velvet, or something once associated with the beloved, such as spectacles.

By *reversal,* I mean that an emotion, e.g. affection, becomes inverted to its opposite, e.g. hatred. This is the origin of *sadism,* which is not a direct derivative or extension of power, but an inversion of power, looped back or attacking against the beloved. Similarly, *masochism,* which is the opposite of sadism, is not an extension of normal weakness, but a kink, twist or reversal of it. Neither of these is a normal derivative of aggressiveness: they are typical hysterical reversals. They are always proof of an underlying condition of repression and dissociation.

In the female, the hysterical state makes for a better mother than it does a wife. As a mother, the undifferentiated emotional state can become identified protectively with the child, on the instinctive level. She may be identified with the child's welfare, which is good up to a point—but she cannot be weaned from it without excessive protest. She cannot let the child go, or grow up, because the hysterical mother is herself a child who has never quite grown up. She can therefore be a mother or a child or both; but she cannot be wife or independent adult in a mature, emotionally separated way. She can be her husband's mother and protect him: or his child and be protected by him: but that is not the same as being his wife or mate, which requires her to have a certain separate existence and a reciprocal relationship, both with her husband and her children. There is therefore a lack of sexual polarity and a state of sexual frigidity.

In the male, the hysterical state lends itself to a certain general negativeness of attitude and a consequent lack of staying power. Hysteria is always somewhat destructive and overcritical; besides being unbalanced, it also lacks continuous creative drive. In the male, it may cut out emotional desire altogether, becoming merely negatively "reasonable" and therefore compulsively (protectively) "thoughtful." It is therefore inclined to lead to anxiety, to swift outbursts of sexual desire without staying power (*ejaculatio praecox*), or actual impotence. In some cases, the experience of orgasm is only painful, shattering and deeply exhausting (negative orgasm). The proper polarization of sexual energy is "plus" from the belly and "minus" from the head. Therefore to diminish the unconscious emotional drives and to exaggerate the conscious critical faculty, as our civilization is inclined to do, must have a tendency to diminish sexual potency, both in certain over-intellectualized individuals (highbrows) in particular, and as a general tendency in both sexes, consequent upon present educational methods. Thus, as a consequence of our "civilization," we find the problems of a proper sexual reciprocity becoming increasingly difficult. As the timing of the woman becomes slower, so the male rhythm is inclined to advance in speed. Hence the difficulty of a satisfactory harmony of their opposed relationship in sexual life, and a tendency towards diminishing fertility.

In both sexes, there is a tendency towards emotional dissociation, or a splitting off of the emotional from the sensational aspect of sexual experience. When sex is no longer energized by love it becomes lust, and the body lives unto itself alone, as if it never had a heart. It is especially a male habit to avoid the danger of being involved or caught emotionally. There is a typical hysterical "throw-over" from love (which is emotionally dangerous, because you may get hurt), to lust (in which the affections are not involved at all). The habit of hopping into bed with comparative strangers is not evidence of virility, but of hysterical anxiety. In this case, also, over-activity is usually the proof of weakness and not of strength (over-compensation). Where desire cannot be sustained in deep content and hearts are not involved, the mere giving of the body slips the state of tension and for this relief need only pay an empty price. Sexual intercourse on these terms is an empty, worthless, foolish act, which can only lead to disappointment in the end.

At their worst, the unconscious motives of hysteria lead to the *exploitation of power over the woman*, with (disguised or repressed) the *intention to destroy her*. Womanhood is always in danger where hysteria is concerned.

Hysteria and the Family

A patient remarked: "Why are things always made to seem so much more important than people?" and followed up her cogent query with the following trivial story. Her father, an elderly and irascible clergyman, was about to drive his car out of the garage. Her relations with him had always been strained, but on this occasion she was anxious to help him, so she proceeded to open the garage door; but the bolt was down and scratched an arc in the smooth surface of the gravel. "You clumsy fool, look what you have done!" he said. She felt devastated and wondered which her father loved the more, his daughter or his gravel? The gravel had been "hurt," of course, but it was surely not as sensitive to pain as were his daughter's feelings?

In the prevention of hysteria, the most important thing to avoid is the negative attitude. "Don't be silly!" is enough to provoke a hysterical response *because it is itself a hysterical attack*. In order to illustrate my point, I will make a hysterical remark myself, by way of preventive advice: *Don't be negative.* That is a very simple thing to say and perhaps you understand what I mean, but it is the wrong approach. Put the other way round, however, *Be positive,* its meaning does not seem to be so clear. Destruction is easy: and destructive advice is easy to understand. It is so instantaneously simple. The creative act, on the other hand, by which things and people may be encouraged to grow, is mysteriously dark. It is not at all simple and requires time. Yet this positive, expansive attitude of respect and encouragement is the very essence of hysteria's prevention, as it is also of its cure.

People must be valued above any things whatever, and amongst "things" must be included people's conduct. It is not what they do, or what they have—it is what they are that needs encouragement. Some households have a negative atmosphere of protective rigidity, where exterior forms are valued more than the interior truth of growing life. The furniture must not be spoiled: the clothes must not be dirty: the manners must always be good: the forms and ceremonies must be rigidly observed: "Don't do that, it's dirty!" "Don't do that, it's dangerous!" "Don't". . . is the operative word, and it is the negative breeding ground for hysteria's subsequent development.

I do not mean to imply, however, that children (or adults, either), should be allowed to do as they please. That is "spoiling," and the spoiled child is the child who most easily becomes hysterical. In fact, there are two equally sure ways of making hysteria: the first is the unbalanced negative, the second is the unbalanced positive, where no restrictions are imposed at all. Either makes hysteria, which is an unbalanced condition trying to balance itself. A balanced life is needed for the child. Encouragement, yes: but discipline, also. Even discipline can be positively administered, by setting tasks that are within the compass of the child, yet not too easy. Hard enough to stretch and try the temper, but not so hard or dull as to destroy the interested will. This is the "breaking in" of the will that is required for all good discipline. We must be trained for life, from our self-will to willingness, with sympathy for other people all the time.

Hysteria is an illness which is largely due to over-stimulation and over-excitement. In terms of food, like indigestion, it is due to overnourishment. Therefore it is important to keep our children in a ring, to be nourished quietly, not too much and not too soon. Regularity and rhythm show the way of growth into a regular, rhythmic way of life.

Hysteria is a very negative complaint and all the oft-repeated verbal "Don'ts" imply some degree of identification in the relationship between the parent and the child. Of course, identification is not always wrong: it is good in so far as it adds to sympathy and understanding: it is only wrong in so far as it is compulsively protective of the state of fixation, refusing to the child the freedom of a separate individuality. Unweaned love on the part of the parent protests at every sign of difference or mark of growth, and tries to pull the child back again towards the mother's all-embracing, all-inclusive arms. Thus love itself may operate in reverse, denying the growth of which it might have been the strongest nourishment. Such unweaned love is negatively exploiting power.

It is more positive, unselfishly creative love that is the willing spirit's nourishment. This is the food on which human life grows. It is a continuous ring around the child that never keeps the child its prisoner. It says "Yes, go on: go forth and try it for yourself," and yet the ring of love remains intact, encouraging. It is a timely, differentiated, proper and appropriate love that knows the food that any child requires at any time. It is not negative and does not try to prevent anything—no, not even hysteria.

The variety of individual temperaments will lead to different reactions on the part of children to the same home conditions. In general, however, it may be said that the healthy, happy home makes the healthy, happy child. The wholeness of the home makes for the wholeness of the child. The balanced home, where father and mother each play the proper role, helps to create the balanced child. Egocentric parents make egocentric children; quarrelsome parents tend to produce quarrelsome children or—which may be worse—to cause aggressiveness to be repressed; broken homes make a break in the child's even line of growth; destructiveness or negativeness in the parents leads to destructiveness in the children. Naughty children were probably first trained in naughtiness by their naughty parents. Therefore, with all their children's problems, parents should first look to and correct themselves, before trying to eliminate their children's errors. The pattern of the home can make or mar the pattern of the child.

One of the ways in which the pattern of the home affects the pattern of the child's development is by the child's place in, and the number of, the family. The one-child family is a problem, because with only one there is no other to effect its proper balancing. The youngest child is also liable to show, to some extent, the problems of the only child, because there was no one to come after to help it to be weaned from its mother. The oldest child may be forced to undertake premature responsibility, with consequent overdevelopment of the male psyche, and deficiency or immaturity on the side of the female psyche. Where there are two boys, the older dull, the younger more brilliant, there may be unfair competition and assumed advantages. A boy amongst a family of girls, or a girl amongst a family of boys, will tend towards development of one side of the character at the expense of the other. Where father is weak and mother strong, the sexual roles of male and female psyche may follow suit and also become reversed. In some families, there are psychologically two fathers and no mother: in others, two mothers and no father. All these factors must affect, to some extent, the child's development, because we are most susceptible to influence and example at an early age. The unwanted child suffers an indelible wrong that can only lead subsequently to compulsive attempts to "get its own back," with the possible development of antisocial or criminal behavior. Similarly, for a parent to desire a child to be of the other sex may lead to a hysterical reversal, because the power of such contentious but discontented love is very strong. To be uncertain of their parentage, as some children are, again makes the relationship between interior and exterior world more difficult, and adopted children have problems all their own.

Hysteria and Insanity

"You are sure she is not going mental, doctor?" Thus anxious relatives inquire. No, I am sure she is not: reassurance is valid every time, as far as the pure condition of hysteria is concerned. It is a nervous-emotional disorder, to which the unkinder diagnosis "mental" does not apply. In fact, hysteria is the very opposite of a mental disorder, in that specialized sense. The hysteric is bound too tightly within the restrictive self-protective ring. The hysteric needs to go a little mad, to "let go," in order to achieve the balanced state of sanity. But here a difficult point arises: do we mean that the hysteric is to be encouraged to be unrestrained, to scream, weep, show off, to get excited and to behave in general exactly as she (or he) pleases? No, indeed I do not, because the hysteric has to learn a certain discipline. If you understand the nature of this disease, you will understand my point. Hysteria has to change from negative to positive: from exterior to interior: from "male" to "female": from tension to relaxation: from repression to expression, before it can be cured. Therefore it is necessary to let this inner life come forth, unfolding with encouragement from the mysterious darkness of its womb. There is a little madness within our potential mysterious divinity that causes us to fear and sometimes to escape from it, in panic flight. Nevertheless, we must be brave enough to see it through, to let it come as it evolves—and then to let it go. Hysteria denies the mother whom it then compulsively pursues. Hysteria must learn to let life spring from whence it comes mysteriously—and then to let it depart upon its way, as go it must.

There is always a certain measure of overlapping in our diagnosis of these various mental-emotional-nervous disorders, but the following classification may perhaps help the reader to make some distinction in his mind, by which to separate different abnormal conditions. Imagine a three-dimensional cross, of three lines each passing through the same center at right angles to one another. *Normal growth* evolves equally in three dimensions: it is all-round, balanced, wholesome, hale and hearty. *Depression* is due to an attachment to the upper end of the vertical dimension where values are measured selectively in terms of "better" (above) and "worse" (below): such a system is top-heavy and therefore tends to fall. *Hysteria* is an error of the lateral horizontal dimension, although it occurs on the others also: it prefers "power" to "love," "male" to "female" and "right" to "wrong." It is a compulsive protective throwover on the "right" or "male" side of the psychic structure. *Dementia praecox* (schizophrenia, a true insanity) is a fault on the antero-posterior horizontal dimension: it is biased backwards, against the forward-moving stream of life. It always wants to go back home, regressively, and cannot grow at all. All true *insanity* is a deteriorating, disintegrating condition, wherein the psychic unity is lost by falling into its separate, undeveloped and unrelated, constituent parts. Hysteria is too tightly bound up in itself for that. It has to learn the virtues of an open space, an empty time, a looser, losing touch. A little madness is its needed purgative, because space is the spirit's living-room.

Hysteria and Society

All illness, social and individual, can only be a modification of our normal structures and our normal laws. There is no illness of the human psyche which has not its social counterpart, and this is particularly true of hysteria. Society and the world in which we live show many signs of suffering from hysteria, of which I will enumerate some of the more important: (1) *overactivity* and the compulsive lure of speed and still more speed; (2) *peripheral stimulation* of the senses without any corresponding depth of feeling; (3) *deterioration of spiritual values* and religious significance; (4) *deterioration of the creative arts* (craftsmanship) with spread of mechanization and mass production; (5) *the tyranny of ideas*, with compulsive interference in regard to those who differ; (6) *conflict* and *scapegoats*; (7) *dissociation* or a lack of creative unity in education, with over-stimulation of the brain in certain limited directions and neglect of heart and spirit, which can see and make life whole; (8) *diminution of personal responsibility* and deterioration of the individual will; (9) *resort to phantasy*, wishful thinking, superstitions and ideologies, to cover a lack of real relationship with life; (10) *resort to the phantasy mother*, the mother-who-will-always-love-and-protect-us, who is now called the "State," and whose bounteous arms are overflowing with the promising blueprints of her all-embracing plans.

Prevention and Cure

There is a price for Life. The price is Death, which means our willingness to give ourselves—all we have, all we love and all we are, for Life. Death is the open door of our initiation into Life; this fact is spiritually true. The cause of our hysteria was *refusal of suffering,* which is "experience of change." Death, in this simple, living and symbolic sense, is the one full healer of hysteria, because it is the final proof of our willingness to experience change.

Fear of death in this widest sense is the problem of hysteria and the "nervy" man: many are his twists and turns, his achievements and activities, by which he hopes to escape from the suffering that he fears. Yet Death claims all and in the end we all are claimed. Death and Time are the destructive twins, before whose sickle every human stem must fall. It is no wonder then that we should be hysterical. At first, it must be so: but can we learn in time a different attitude to Death, accepting it as part of our inevitable change? Only as Old Adam dies, can the New Man arise. The real and simple price of all new birth is—Death.

Ultimately, the prevention and cure of all hysteria, individual and social, is that we should be thus willing to suffer, to die and to be born again. Ultimately, there is no escape from this. The point is, can we, each one of us, face his own responsibility now, to experience such change as may befall, with willingness and with intelligence, that thus we may be initiated into a new and better way of Life? That would be the beginning of a New Order.

CHAPTER 25

The Spoiled Child

As I have defined it, the quality of heaven is particularly present in babies, mystics, intuitives, women, drunkards, and in the states of love and sleep. It is most important for our consideration here, because it is the *sine qua non*, the "must-have," of the spoiled child. The aim and goal of the spoiled child is a state of perpetual bliss, where there is neither time nor tension, division nor conflict, between what is and what is wanted. If everything and everyone were under my control, and all were content to be one with me—ah me, that would be heaven indeed! Yet for me to insist on that for myself in any earthly state must surely make of earth a horrid hell for someone else, which in itself it does not need to be.

The earth on which we have to live has been made unnecessarily hellish of recent years, from which we should suspect that somewhere there are spoiled children who have been claiming too much heaven for themselves. If we are to understand human nature and our problems of relationship, then we must allow for the reality of heaven as a determining factor and a kind of moral yardstick in the quality of our personal experience.

The Hell of a Temper

We shall not go far wrong in our understanding of common meanings if we use words as they are commonly used. Sometimes the spoiled child has a hell of a temper and this is one way of recognizing him. I do not want to blame him, for he gets enough of that. I only want to see what this particular verbal association of "hell" and "temper" implies.

From *Mysterious Marriage: A Study of the Morality of Personal Relationships and Individual Obsessions*

379

I have said that the heavenly state is one in which there is no separation, no time, no space and perfect control over the other, who does not exist except as part of the one indivisible self. This is the state of perfect happiness, bliss, to which the spoiled child feels entitled. His moral assumption is very simple: heaven is his by right, and it must therefore be someone else's fault if he does not get it. Someone is always to blame for not restoring peace immediately. The spoiled child's protests can only be untimely, timeless or ill-tempered: they can only be directed against someone else, whose fault it is: and they can only be disposed to regain absolute control of his world again, immediately and by force.

The aggression of the spoiled child is therefore something special. It is not the aggression of growth in time, nor of willing effort in a studied world of inevitable resistances. It is not necessarily the wild panic aggression of the state of acute anxiety, which, in its blind distress, can do most unreasonable harm, either to someone else or to one's self. The aggression of the spoiled child has the combined quality of a foul temper and an incontrovertible morality.

It is often found (but rarely recognized for what it is) in parents, school masters and politicians.

Down to Earth or Not?

If it were possible for us to decide once and for all in which direction we ought to be moving in life, I think it would prove a great help in simplifying our general morality and solving many of our social, economic and political problems. We are not likely to experience other than confusion while some cry: Forward! and some: Back! some: Hold tight! and yet others: Let go! Would it be possible, I wonder, to have a clear idea of what we are about, of where we are going—or at least of what we want?

Granted the reality of heaven and its superiority (by definition) to the earthly state of tension and conflict, is the heavenly state really to be our aim and goal? Is it that *status quo ante* which we want to restore? If so, our direction must be away from the here and now, off upwards and backwards in our heavenly flight to rejoin the angels, even while we are down here on earth. Or alternatively, if we are determined to find heaven here on earth (which is not the same as bringing heaven down to earth, in the act and experience of incarnation), then our attitude to what we find here will be most aggressively acquisitive of what seems good, while we are impatiently dismissive of the bad. We shall come like Lucifer, torch in hand, to put this world to rights, because we know that it is wrong—as indeed it always must be, even by definition.

Whatever our answers may be to the questions: *What do you want? Where are you going?* questions to which we shall be returning in the last chapter, the spoiled child has his own answer and we should know what it is in case we may decide to differ from it, especially when we realize its appalling consequences. The answer of the spoiled child is, however, still the answer of the great majority of us, and especially of our leaders. The answer of the spoiled child always begins: I want MORE . . . more of what I want . . . especially more POWER over the others . . . fixed, secure . . . and to get rid of all that stands in my way, anything, anyone, including time itself . . . I want to enjoy contentment, happiness, peace at last . . . all that I ought to have, in fact, all that is good for me . . . and I want to know that I am right and good, and to know that you know that I am right and good . . . I want the best of both worlds, now and always . . . I want HEAVEN . . . or else! . . .

The Two Mothers

In the beginning, mother and child were one: and also in the beginning, the body and "I" are one. There is no consciousness possible until separation occurs, and then there are two of us. It is separation which makes consciousness possible; and it is consciousness which makes possible the experience of relationship.

In the beginning, to be one-with-the-other is to be good. Forever after, *guilt* is the claim to be restored at once to goodness and to unity. Separation implies being "other," apart, with opposing possibilities for good and evil, right and wrong. As soon as the child is born, for the child there are immediately two mothers, the good one and the bad one. Similarly, as soon as the child is self-conscious, there are two children, the good one and the bad one. Again, the urgent question is asked, Which way shall I go? Back to the good mother, or on to separate more completely my independent "I"?

Back to the collective, submerged in which I can feel good, or on to find out for myself? It takes great courage and self-confidence to sustain the weight of separation and of inevitable sin, and it is really not to be wondered at that most of us should prefer to find good cover by submerging ourselves in a powerful group, whose freedom from guilt we can comfortably share, while knowing that all those ignorant others who differ from us must be wrong.

At first, in the very beginning, enjoying her role of absolute Providence, the mother is very good indeed, as the child's every need is met even before it is asked for. But very soon the child must come up against the "bad" mother, the one who will not obey its call, the one who does not provide on demand, the one who is not there. In a certain way, as the child is gradually weaned to its more independent growth, it is obvious that the mother must get worse and worse, as she is less and less obedient to the child's every beck and call.

In the same way, the child is also getting worse and worse as it is becoming increasingly independent and therefore, to some extent, out of parental control. But it should be very plain, I think, that it is the words "good" and "bad" which have ceased to serve us at this point, because they have led us into this incredible confusion: that the mother is "good" for giving way to the child and "bad" because she encourages the child to be independent; and that the child is "good" in so far as he behaves as part of his mother, completely under her control, and "bad" as soon as he claims a right to his own identity. In fact, we are using the words "good" and "bad" with the meaning that the spoiled child gives them, and not with the significance of any more robust or far-seeing morality.

Yet it is true that there are two mothers, two fathers and, of every child, two opposite versions. The spoiled child wants to retain the better and dismiss the other, thus cutting off one horn of every dilemma, or one end of every piece of string. The spoiled child wants the best of both worlds, both to have good and to be good, and to dismiss the inevitable pain and punishment by blaming someone else. The spoiled child cannot stand suspense or uncertainty, but wants his answer now. Above all, the spoiled child wants to do good and to improve everything and everyone as soon as possible (with short cuts always preferred). Whatever is wrong (and that is many things and most people), it must be put right at once, because it ought to be.

But are we not all—more or less—like that? And what, as we are granted choice, is our alternative?

Duality and Ambivalence

The spoiled child's attitude to the problem of choice is to select the better and ignore or destroy the worse. On the horns of a dilemma, the spoiled child grasps one and rejects the other. Presented with the dual aspect of his mother or his father, the members of his family or himself, he wants to have their good side permanently present, and their bad side gone for good. The spoiled child divides, selects, and then destroys, if he can, what he cannot otherwise control.

If we are not to be spoiled children, what is the alternative attitude to experience? A more mature attitude would certainly require of us the ability to hold the tension of opposing forces, of change and uncertainty, without getting flustered or upset. We need to be able to accept the changing moods of parents, children, friends and enemies, even as we have to accept changes in weather or season. We have to hold the horns of the dilemma resolutely, experiencing patiently the strain, conflict, tension in ourselves. This is surely what is meant by "suffering" and reminds us of another fact about the spoiled child: they cannot, must not, "suffer" in the sense of *allowing, accepting* or *letting be.* "It" must always be changed and you must do something about it; or perhaps it is you who must change. But do not ask the spoiled child to live in an imperfect world amongst imperfect people! That is too much, and he can always point to the fact that the existent imperfections are obviously wrong, so surely something ought to be done to change them, now? But where and who does the spoiled child think he is, with his heavenly standards of perfection?

Meanwhile, by putting more patient folk so constantly in the wrong, he raises very difficult moral problems for those who are not so anxious as he is to improve and control the world.

Wise Mothering

Let us remind ourselves of the way in which life moves on, and how one after another, the mysterious umbilical cords that join us to the comforts of the past are cut. Forgetting heaven's initial brightness, increasing darkness falls upon us, as separation from our origin becomes ever more complete. But growing life provides another light. Increasing appetite with developing teeth enables the child to grow, until with maturity it can seek and forage, digest and assimilate, strive and win its independence for itself. And so another Soul is born, a man or woman, earth-bound but adequate to strive.

The role of mother, therefore, is to represent heaven until the child is ready in due time to be fully born, separate, independent and mature. Her role is, therefore, *constantly diminishing*. She supplies all at first, then less and less, as the ripening growth of childhood enables it to become increasingly able to fend and forage for itself. Heaven departs as we arrive on earth. Mother's importance goes as the child grows towards maturity. Our claim on heaven must diminish as our earthly needs are more completely satisfied.

If she is not to spoil her child, the role of the mother is to receive the gift of life as the ground receives the seed, nourishing it, but her role is only transient. She is life's guardian only until it is strong enough to hold its own. She is the child's temporary lodging until its proper home is built. Hers is the promise which he must never find fulfilled in her, but only in his own ultimate and uttermost endeavor. Herself comprised of both worlds, she is the living bridge between the two real but opposing worlds of heaven and earth. Indeed, she "earths" life's lightning flash of urgent energy, directing and harnessing it into its daily work in the world. The role of the mother is to show the way into the world, to introduce the child to its own world situation, which is to be its new "mother," through which it is to be perpetually born and reborn again, until it finally dies out of this world, to be born again into another. Meanwhile, it is the child's responsibility in his maturity to care for the mother, wherever she may appear, as she has cared for him; in his own parent, his body or the body of another, and in the situation in which he finds himself in the world.

If mother plays her self-diminishing part and knows her sacrificial role, then all is well. If mother gives enough yet not too much, nor for too long, the child's appetite is strengthened, as it is gradually diverted to other, outward and more awkward, food. If security is provided when security is due—in the beginning, but diminishing—the heart is strengthened to endure the inevitable insecurity which must come in the end. If heaven is realized for long enough its loss can be accepted, and the fall to earth can be experienced with the resilience that it requires. Having been gladly given what was needed as a child, maturity can gladly give, in its turn, to others what it once received, thus turning in time to fulfill the rhythmic way of sacrifice.

The rhythm of life is heaven first—and then earth; receive first—then give; rise first—then fall; security first—then danger. The order cannot be reversed, broken or in any part omitted, without the spoiling of the work of art, the Creator's masterpiece, the child. To give or to withhold too much; to deny either heaven or earth; to break the timely rhythm of the dance of life is to spoil the child, who then "must-have" what cannot then be truly given. The spoiled child is spoiled because its rhythm has been broken and its motive power reversed.

Mechanism of the Spoiled Child

The purpose of the mechanism is to reduce a duality to a unity, by dismissing either one of two. Confronted by any duality, such as beginning and end, pain and pleasure, yours and mine, worse and better, the spoiled child assumes the one preferred, rejecting the other, thus obtaining a fixed, "good" conclusion which is completely under his control. The spoiled child must-have-now the preferred "good," which is assumed, grabbed; at the same time, the rejected other, the "bad," must be expelled or utterly destroyed. There must be no problem, no uncertainty, no suspense, no tension, no alternative and no "bad." The situation must be under complete control, closed, fixed and finished. The "other" must be continuously destroyed until this end is sure. The effect of this mechanical attack upon the living, balanced, *process* of personal experience in space and time varies according to whether it is successful or not. If successful, everything and everyone is split in two, so that the good may be assumed and the bad rejected. The split occurs at the point of balance, "communication" or "articulation," between the two opposite poles or forces. (This is the "C"-point in our experience of relationship, see p. 84.) There is then a shift to one end or other of the two extremes, with *identification* at that end and *dissociation* from the other. This is inevitably counteracted by a resulting pursuit or pressure on the part of the rejected other, in order to obtain its return and so restore the normal balance and reciprocal rhythm of the opposing forces. Any tendency to return to this state of vital equilibrium must, however, be constantly and violently resisted by the spoiled child. For success, the bad enemy must be totally and finally eliminated so that he can be forgotten.

If this does not occur, "operation spoiled child" is not successful and anxiety occurs. The aim of anxiety is the same, but now intensified, namely, to get rid of the offending other, absolutely. Failing this, it may be possible to achieve some measure of success by at least obliterating the anxiety.

The effect of the prolonged operation of this mechanism can only produce progressively either an *inertia*, which is morbid and deadly, although it is not, and does not lead to, death. It is negative stagnation, lifelessness. Or else, it produces a state of tension and *restlessness* which, although apparently engaged in pursuit of some lofty moral purpose, is essentially destructive and unhealthy. The way of life of the spoiled child, therefore, produces either a state of inertia, in which there is no desire, no pain, no energy and no growth; or else a reversal of the vital current, which flows backwards instead of *on*, and inwards (self-centered) instead of *out*.

The collapse which must finally ensue in either case should not be regarded as only a disaster, or even as preferably to be avoided. It is an opportunity for change and a means of recovering a more healthy (and obedient) attitude to life, which is not present until the breakdown has occurred.

The Spoiled Child

The spoiled child is compelled to reject earth for heaven's sake, demanding heaven as right and due, without decrease. The spoiled child must turn B into A, part into whole, less into greater, worse into better, in one way or another, immediately. There must be no loss, no sacrifice—except for the benefit of the spoiled child. Life must be whole, complete, fulfilled, ecstatic, heavenly, now and all the time—or else there must be some satisfactory substitute to take its place—or else tears, depression, bitterness—or else anger, destruction of the enemy and war's revenge.

The spoiled child is an angel who will not, cannot, fall—an angry disappointed Lucifer, self-righteous, self-centered and self-willed. His aim in life is all for one purpose, to regain or retain that heavenly state of unbroken unity, in which subject and object, self and other, are securely and indivisibly one, as once they were. Refusing the hard way of accepting its diminished state and making the best of it which willing incarnation must imply, the spoiled child refuses duality and insists instead upon a pristine unity. Thereby the spoiled child offends against the very law of life by which it is offended. Demanding peace, rejecting conflict, it must make war to satisfy its peaceful aim. Demanding pleasure and rejecting pain, it must make torment of inevitable suffering. Demanding whole, rejecting part, it risks its own disintegration. Demanding heaven, rejecting earth, it must make life itself a state of hell-on-earth, which is but heaven's opposite and need never be true unless some unwilling and discarnate "devil" makes it so.

The spoiled child of any age or guise is gripped in the vice of paradox and pursued by the rejected enemies of its own making. Choosing only one of any two extremes, and rejecting all but the best even of that one, the spoiled child must find himself always inevitably confronted by his own contradiction, haunted by the shadow of his disappointed hopes and pursued by his discarded enemies.

To some extent and in varying degrees we are all of us spoiled children. There are "devils" in each one of us which need to be identified and clearly realized as the spoiled, unhappy children that they are. However, I am not for a moment complaining about that. I do not suggest that you or I ought to change ourselves, or to be changed in any way because of this diagnosis of our imperfection. Indeed, it is just such an impatient and untimely criticism as that which is characteristic of all spoiled children in their attitude towards one another. On the other hand, all that I mean is that we should admit the diagnosis if true, recognizing our faults for what they are, how they have come about and the way in which they work. I only go so far as to say, "Let's see what we have here, and why?" And then perhaps, one day—who knows?—we may possibly be able to experience change. But meanwhile, it is the self-deception, the unnecessary misunderstanding, the blind ignorance and moral damage that he does, which make the spoiled child such a peril to the peace of the world. He always thinks that he is right, that someone else is wrong and that they can (must, ought to) change immediately.

Causes

Admitting the generalization for what it is worth, that we are all—indeed that we must all be—to some extent spoiled children, then we must first look for a general cause which is of universal application. I suggest that this explanation is to be found in the very nature of our incarnation: we are earth-bound, earth-conscious and earth-identified.

The earth has three general levels of application to our enthralled spirits; firstly, in the body of the mother, which is the child's first home and prison; secondly, in the physical (including emotional and mental) body itself, which is another home and prison; and thirdly, in the world in which we live, which is our third home and prison. Within each one of these we are born; and also with each one we have become identified. This thing, this part, this place, this person, it seems to *me*, is me: this seems to be my *self*. Wherever I am, whatever I am "in," seems to be more than a part of me. It seems to be my very self, so that if you hurt it you hurt me, and if you take it away from me, it is like amputating a limb and threatens my destruction. This is the experience of incarnation which we prove to be true every day of our lives, as we ourselves become possessed by the grasping power of our possessions, progressively encrusted by these accumulated ideas in which the fluid forces of the mind have become cast, and attached to our hopes and fears, or to what we have said or done. We are like tortoises inside a shell, but we believe and behave as if the shell were the tortoise. It is the habit of the body, which is our shell or earth-crust, to crave for its own increase, even as it tries to forget that on which it depends for its life and welfare.

Yes, we are well incarnate in this world. Too well, perhaps? So well are we in it that we are identified with it, A with B, "I" with "me," spirit with matter, so that "A," "I" and Spirit are denied and forgotten, while "B," "me" and matter assume the causal role and place of primacy, becoming progressively inflated, accumulated and idolized. The spoiled child in our world today is like a thickened shell, who lives at all only by the grace of what he must deny; but even so he uses it to gain an end which can only bring him nearer to ultimate disaster. When threatened by disaster, the spoiled child uses all he has of power, knowledge and accumulated wealth to fend it off. (We are still being too successful in our aim of avoiding the real issue. We are still hoping that someone, something, will save us from self-caused disaster. This relentless and unscrupulous hope is characteristic of the spoiled child.)

Are some children born spoiled, or must they all have been spoiled by bad environment? If we are prepared to allow for inborn differences at all, then I think we must certainly admit that some children are born more "difficult" than others. Their difficulty in adaptation is shown by some degree of unbalance, or disturbance of the rhythms of normal infancy. Such children need coaxing before they will eat, sleep or conform to the normal standards of nursery requirements. From the very start, some children show signs of not being adaptable even to the simplest situations. Relationships, even of the most normal, simple kind, are confronted with difficulty and avoided if possible. Such children are all too easily upset. They therefore require, and obtain, more attention. They may be given in to, in order to avoid the situation becoming still further out of control. It is an unfortunate fact that a child born with a tendency to emotional instability (i.e. a difficulty in establishing normal relationships) is almost certain to be still further spoiled subsequently, if only for the very practical necessity of safe-guarding the time necessary for getting on with the innumerable other tasks of the home.

Too much or too little attention spoils the child, because either will disturb the balanced and regular rhythm which is required for normal growth. Illness, especially if prolonged, of necessity draws too much attention to children, so that even if they recover fully from their physical ill-health, they may never recover emotionally from the effects of the spoiling which of necessity they received during the illness. They continue to crave attention, and may find it easiest to obtain it by being ill again.

Normal life is balanced, breathing, rhythmical. The mother spoils the child by exceeding in either direction, whether by giving too much or too little, by being too gentle or too hard, too affectionate or too withdrawn. She spoils the child and fails to play her part as guardian and guide, if she errs too far on one side or the other of the middle way. Protection, nourishment and encouragement are what every child needs, but always in moderation: enough, and for long enough, but not too little or too much, and not to end either too late or too soon. The proper discipline of time and timing are all-important in preventing the most troublesome complaint of childhood, being spoiled.

The spoiled child finds relationships difficult, assuming identifications and dissociations instead. In other words, the spoiled child is still unweaned. It is not yet separated from the good object, the mother, but is still identified with her. The difficulty of obtaining separation between mother and child, i.e. of establishing a true relationship between one and the other, is, of course, doubled when the mother is herself unweaned from, and identified with, the child. Unfortunately, the difficulty is doubled again by the fact that the unweaned identification is always moralized on either side: namely, that it is a good arrangement to be thus united in one another's love, and separation (out of control!) would be a very bad thing. But the inevitable shock and clash that follows the discovery that such love can only be destructive of a separate personal existence can only add further to the confusion and bewilderment which the spoiled child is so anxious to avoid.

By far the commonest cause of the spoiled child, therefore, is the spoiled (or unweaned) parent. Unable to make a relationship with the child, the unweaned parent proceeds by one or other of the two extremes of identification or dissociation. In effect, identification leads to a state of mutual parasitism, with *too much, too often, too easy and too long*; while dissociation separates the need from the supply, making the contact *too little, too seldom, too difficult and too short.* So the balance is upset, and either half is left needing and hating its own opposite. These conditions set up an intense feeling of need, an unconscious compulsion towards satisfying that need, and an intolerable anxiety in case the need should not be satisfied. From these are developed the symptomatic conduct of the spoiled child.

Too much, too easy, too often and too long: When the mother remains identified with the child, she tries to make the state of heaven last forever and so sets up a *fixation*. In this state there is no relationship, because there is no separation of persons; there is no time for growth, because there is no urge that is not granted immediate satisfaction; there is no striving, because the desired object is already given; and there is no loss, because that would be intolerable. Such is the case, at least, if heavenly aspirations are wholly satisfied, but in a hard world that is impossible. The course is set then against the tide of life; not on, but back; not out, but in; not progress, but regression; not relationship, but identification or dissociation.

Too little, too hard, too seldom and too short: When the mother is dissociated from the child and the mother-child relationship is broken too soon, the urgent need is left unsatisfied, so that the child must somehow mend the broken bridge in order to find in some way the security and nourishment which it requires. The effect of too little, too hard and for too short a time, is exactly the same as was the case with too much, too easy and too long: the child cannot do without it, it cannot lose or fall, and so it cannot grow and come to terms with life. It cannot accept new experience, because it must obey the urgent and compulsive need to find and satisfy that first starvation, and to gain security in swiftest possible exchange for intolerable insecurity. Thus the spoiled child must always live in the past, avoiding life and loss, for heaven's sake. Too easy or too hard: too much or too little: too long or too short, the effect is the same. Regression, fixation, identification and dissociation becomes the compulsive habit of the spoiled child.

If mother died or left the child to its own devices while she enjoyed her freedom; if she was ill, with no sufficient substitute to take her place; if her husband was an invalid, who needed the time which must be taken from the child; if the mother had to work to keep the family and so had no leisure in which to enjoy them; or if any of the many wants which may recur happened to come between the mother and the child to effect their premature separation, then the result is to set up that backward and regressive urge, that compulsive search for the beloved object, which characterizes the unhappy state of the spoiled child. The child must have mother, but mother is no longer there. So what can take her place? To understand the variety of mother-substitutes by which the child is surrounded, we must now discuss the meaning of the term "Collective."

The Collective

The Collective is that common ground from which each one of us is (or should be?) now engaged in separating himself. It is what mother was, the earth in which our seed was sown, and all that "Mother" stands for as the source from which we each have separately sprung. It is the undifferentiated mass of the unconsciously coordinated many. It is the time-bound physical body left to us from the past as our unwilled inheritance, with all its nervous tricks and aptitudes. It starts with the family group, and spreads from the small nucleus through village and factory, to the nation, or even that complex whole we call humanity. The Collective is the protopathic pool or unconscious jungle of the instinctive and emotional life. Or it may be custom, convention or taboo, the accepted morality of what the neighbors think, or what the papers say, or what we learnt at school or mother's knee. The Collective is what each one has been given in common with the rest, before he has made anything out of it or done anything with it for himself. Like "heaven" or "mother," the Collective is a starting point, but like them also, to the spoiled child it is his goal.

Growth is away from the Collective towards the differentiated; away from heaven, down to earth; away from the mother, out into the world; away from the herd, towards the individual; away from the unconscious, towards the development of consciousness. But the way of the spoiled child is against the way of life. It is back towards the goal of the Collective, in which it seeks again to merge itself, thus losing its identity and feeling of personal responsibility.

The Collective is the mother-substitute of the spoiled child and assumes various disguises. Normally, it is the earth from which we spring, the root from which we draw our nourishment, and the background and beginning from which we gain the security and courage with which to meet the demands and perils of our experience. Abnormally, that is to say to the spoiled child, the Collective is not a beginning but an end, not a starting point but a goal, not a source of emergence, but a vacuum inviting mergence. It is a negative pull which reverses the vital current, pulling it back instead of pushing it on. It is, therefore, a vampire which sucks blood back into itself, an octopus with retentive, strangling tentacles, and a destroyer, instead of a nourisher, of life.

The power of the Collective is dangerously paradoxical. Rightly used, it is the power of life itself, emergent, creative for those who are willing and able to accept the fall of birth and weaning, the tension of separation and loss, suffering and travail, life and death. For those who grapple and strive for their personal independence, the Collective is a brave and willing servant who is both useful and obedient. But for those who seek to exploit or possess it as a means of avoiding suffering and loss, it becomes in the end their tyrant and destroyer. Thus the spoiled child is always defeated by the force of paradox; those who would avoid destruction must become destroyed, whereas those who are willing to brave the loss of the beloved can inherit the rewards of more than mortal life.

Consciousness Can be Exploited, Too

The spoiled child flies from one extreme to the other and plays equal havoc at either end. The one thing the spoiled child cannot do is to stay BETWEEN the two extremes, accepting the suspense of uncertainty which that razor's edge implies. Wherever it looks good, wherever there is something to grab and to collect, you may be sure he is off like lightning, to have and to hold it and if possible to collect more of it, to be added to his other tokens of security.

It is particularly in his attitude to consciousness that the spoiled child shows his morbid characteristics of fixation, identification, rejection and dissociation. The mental world is an easy, tempting one in which to exploit the advantages of gain. Knowledge is power and the attitude of authority is always to encourage more of it. Here is freedom to expand, unlimited, an endless meal to be consumed, a store cupboard that can be stuffed full and yet find room for more. The greedy mind is honored more, the more it can acquire.

By living sufficiently in the mind it is almost possible to avoid life's difficulties altogether. The mind can fulfill the spoiled child's highest ambition to have privilege without responsibility. If he can but know enough, he is sure to be admired and he can be certain of always being right. If he can but think enough, he can always avoid responsibility by telling others what to do. Believing in the power and rightness of his knowledge, he can be safely buttressed against the need to experience anything for himself afresh. His knowledge of life can all be acquired from books and he can live in safety at second-hand, passing on again to someone else what he has just acquired from someone else, and so on, endlessly. The mind can become an impenetrable shell, perfectly safe, immaculate, privileged, rewarded and respectable. It can become a haven and a heaven to the spoiled child, from which exalted height he can afford to expel all those who happen to disagree with him.

The mind thus used for self-satisfaction has endless possibilities. It is the perfect corner for little Jack Horner to sit in, where he can be utterly self-indulgent and morally impregnable. The most modern and insidious aspect of the death-trap of the Collective is in this invasion of consciousness by the unconscious principle. It leads to a perversion of consciousness of the most deadly kind.

The proper role of consciousness is to be illuminative. It is not dynamic in itself. Its function is to use power, not to generate it. That is to say, consciousness is like a lighthouse, not a lifeboat. It is a torch, but it is not a cozy fire with a pair of fur-lined slippers warm beside it. It is a watchful and suspicious eye, and not a larder crammed from floor to ceiling with a great reserve of goods. It is a means of communication, not of domination, a razor's edge and not a resting place. In fact, it is a means to an end that never comes, which is perhaps why we are so inclined to make it an end in itself.

Selfishness, Unselfishness and Self-Centeredness

The trouble which the spoiled child causes in our world is not so simple as we sometimes claim. It is not due to selfishness. In fact, if we examine our own experience and that of those whom we know most intimately, we shall find that most of the trouble has been caused by unselfishness, and not by the more common scapegoat, selfishness. This is a very difficult problem for us to sort out, in discussion and cold print. But it is an impossible one for the child who is brought up in the thick fog and flagrant contradictions of the moral claims of the lavatory, the bedroom and the dining room, in which goodness in another often seems to him to be at least as painful as badness in himself.

Therefore I propose to start off with an apparently most immoral and unusual statement: "*Selfishness is all right.* Go on, be selfish, as selfish as you like. Make up your mind what you want and go and get it. When you've got it, enjoy it to the full and share it with your friends. Enjoy yourselves, have fun! If you are the cautious type, who looks forward to the rainy day, then fill your cupboards with all you want when you have enough of it to spare." So far, surely, there is nothing very wrong in that? But now I would like to go further, and complement my first assertion: *Unselfishness is not all right.* I mean, please do not feel guilty about your full cupboards and groaning board! Please do not press me to accept from you what I should derive both more pleasure and benefit by winning in due course by my own efforts. You keep what you have and enjoy it. I would like to do the same. (And if, dear mother, you really like the breast of chicken, as I know you do, would you please keep some for yourself and not embarrass—or spoil!—me by always giving me the best, with none left for yourself?)

Of course, most unselfishness is so miscalled and so misunderstood. Actually, especially when judged by results, it is acquisitive, greedy and fixed, in its deliberate intention of obtaining what it wants, even at someone else's expense. What it happens to want is power over another, the satisfaction of giving, the pleasure of self-sacrifice, or an accumulation of self-righteousness. If we could only call this spade a spade, it would do much to save children from the moral destruction and confusion of their capacity for correct judgment, which must follow upon living amongst lies. Again, the harm is not in the greed, nor in the selfishness, even if satisfaction is obtained at someone else's expense. The harm comes from calling it something which it is not, and claiming virtue for what is in fact a vice. This is not love, except on the level of instinctive acquisitiveness. This is not unselfishness, but self-righteousness, and they are not the same. We shall at least clear the ground for simple moral judgment if we call a spade a spade, even if it hurt's mother's feelings to do so. (Having seen the results, in my opinion it is quite time that some mothers' feelings were hurt.)

But the point I want to make most clearly is that, putting on one side altogether the moral claims of selfishness and unselfishness, our real problem here is SELF-CENTEREDNESS. The forward arrow of direction ⟶ has been turned backwards, so ⟵. It is no longer directed at the world, out there, it is pointing back at me, in here. I am become my own object. I am no longer interested in obtaining or doing that-out-there, except in so far as it affects me-in-here. Everything out there is a means to the end of giving me a build-up. Everything I do has an ulterior motive—How will it affect me?

When SELFISHNESS is infected by FEAR to arouse ANXIETY, it sets up SELF-CENTERDNESS. Because I am not sure of myself, therefore, I cannot forget myself. Because I cannot forget myself, therefore, I find myself in between myself and what I am doing. I get in my own light, and find myself always in my own way. (I am rather shy, which spoils a lot of fun, not only for myself.)

Now there is no doubt that the best work (and play) is done when I can forget myself altogether, paying attention only to the object in hand, with no question of how the result will react on me. This simple subject-object relationship (I want it, I love you) which has "this over here" completely set apart from "that over there," is the healthy, normal, ideal relationship. Now we know where we are, you and I. I am over here, and you are over there. So far, so good. Now let's get on with it. Are you ready to meet me now, undefendedly, inoffensively?

But with self-centeredness all has gone askew, and I don't know where I am, except that I feel most uncomfortable. The only thing that seems to be of paramount importance to me is that I should cease to feel uncomfortable. Of course, that most urgent and compulsive prior claim must have its own effect upon my choice of what I do myself, or let you do to me.

Morals and the Spoiled Child

There is nothing wicked about the spoiled child, unless that has been super-added, which of course it may be. The spoiled child, however, is not wicked yet. The extent of its crimes are mischief, naughtiness, getting its own back, self-centeredness and self-righteousness. But these are enough to cause a considerable fraction of this world's troubles.

Mischief and naughtiness are the inevitable results of the clash between impulse and opportunity. The child feels frustrated and, learning by experiment, is trying to see how far he can go. Mischief and naughtiness are within the privilege of every normal child, but we should remember they are largely induced by the adult's foolish attempts at correcting them by more frustration. The negative adult (Don't do that!) must, in time and tears, produce the negative child (I won't!). Irregularities of frustration and concession are the breeding ground of irregularities in any child's behavior.

Getting its own back is responsible for many an "accident," from upset cups on the table to upset prams with baby sister in the ditch, and from stealing and lying to religious conversion and the comforts of self-righteousness.

Self-centeredness is the beginning of all psychological and emotional disorder, and sets up the most complicated disturbances of mind and body in its train. It is, therefore, a doctor's job to sort it out, but it is the task of parents and teachers to avoid its occurrence. It is not improved by treating it as a crime, or indeed as if it were anything other than it is, which is a morbid state, or a reversal of the living stream.

Self-righteousness is the most crying problem of the spoiled child, and the one that interests us most, who are considering the harm it does. The spoiled child must have his cake, and eat it too, and be assured of human and divine approval. Although this feat of moral and material gymnastics may seem at first sight to be no mean achievement, it cannot really be so difficult, as most of us manage the trick with some success most of the time.

The spoiled child is either identified with, or dissociated from, the conventional morality of the herd of collective majority. The spoiled child does not derive his morality from his own experience. He does not prove by experiment, nor learn at first hand from life. His answers are not worked out in course of time, because he does not approach any experience as an open question. Everything is approached with a moral cliché that makes it good or bad, according to whether it fits the spoiled child's moods and claims or not. For the spoiled child is not living in a real world, a world as it is. Instead, he is living either in a world-as-it-ought-to-be, or in a world-as-it-ought-not-to-be. In either case, others are always to be blamed, for whatever goes wrong it must be someone's fault. If the spoiled child does consider himself to blame, he has no sense of sin, but only a feeling of intolerable guilt, that must be immediately expunged.

The spoiled child must then find a savior, who is probably already suffering from delusions of grandeur and the idea that he has been personally chosen as the (all-too-human) savior of the world.

Religion and the Spoiled Child

Collective religion, which is the conventional belief of others, morally codified by church and state, stamped with the hallmark of authority and hallowed by time, is indubitably good: surely, it must be. It is, therefore, the natural victim of the spoiled child, who must also become its victim in a mutually destructive parasitism, in which it is hardly possible to distinguish the would-be-mother from the would-be-child.

The spoiled child must have a God and He must be good. He must be benevolent and omnipotent, with the clearest possible ideas of right and wrong. He must be on my side. I must be quite sure of that, or the whole scheme is utterly useless, and there might as well not be any God at all. Like all the other good things, He must be in my control. (If not, He is not good.) The purpose of prayer is to prove that I can have what I want when I want it (or what on earth is the use of prayer?). I must have Him on the end of a string (or is it really an uncut umbilical cord?), so that if I want Him, I only have to pull the cord and He will come.

But the spoiled child is still unborn. He is not yet out of his covers. He is not incarnate in this world. Nor is his God yet incarnate either. He is an Outsider, as any cover-principle must always be. His purpose, to the spoiled child, is to keep him safe forever in his womb, undisturbed, privileged and comfortable. His womb is, of course, the Church. To the spoiled child, the Church is the womb from whom birth (separation, guilt, individuality) is to be avoided at all costs.

It is to be noted that the spoiled child is always in danger of getting his values exactly reversed. He never seems to be quite sure whether he is coming or going. Somehow he cannot tell the difference. Is the best above or below? He does not seem to know. Ought he to rise or fall? He does not seem to know. Is heaven in front or behind? He does not seem to know—yet know for certainty he always must; which accounts for the discordant clamor of differing theological opinions.

Some spoiled children do know God very intimately. They are the intuitives, the sensitives, the mystics, whose early experiences of good or ill, pleasure or pain, may have set up so great a state of intolerable tension and anxiety that their discomfort claims urgent appeasement, whether by identification or distraction. There is nothing wrong with the divine intoxication which is called mysticism. But, as ever, the spoiled child spoils all he touches by his aggressive, anxious importunity. For, if the spoiled child knows anything of the state of mystic exaltation, as he may well do, then that of course is also his by right. Heaven is always his especial property and his aim is always heaven-wards. His life is Godwards, avoiding all the plagues of earth for heaven's sake. His arguments sound all right, and his virtues are made sufficiently obvious to be almost convincing. Yet which way is he going and why? Many of the most religious folk are activated by this simple motive, which is why we more ordinary mortals have found them so very hard to live with. They have been traveling, as spoiled children always do, in this negative and reversed direction. Too much religion in the world is of this morbid kind.

But for the spoiled child there must always be two of everything, the good and the bad, the one I want to grab and the one I want to get rid of. So there must be two Gods, a good one and a bad one; and two children, a white one and a black one; then the good God and the nice white child can be cozily wrapped up together, and all will be well as long as it is possible to get rid of that bad child and his particularly attentive Devil. But history and personal experience are at one in proving the extreme difficulty of getting rid of bad elements, either by destroying, forgetting or appeasing them.

Religion becomes of more practical importance when it is no longer preached either by, or to, the spoiled child.

Lack of Relationship with Others

In their relationship with other people, spoiled children must always cause discomfort, because they are in fact incapable of relationship. That is to say, relationship implies the capacity to accept separation and to build a slender bridge over an actual chasm. This is communication, one person with another, across a gulf. But to the spoiled child there must be no gulf, and separation is simply not allowed to occur. It is always either identification or dissociation: you are either in or you are out. If you are good, you are in: if you are bad, you must either come in and be good or get out. There is no relationship because "we" are collectively "I." Thus the Many are made into One, by eliminating separation, difference, tension and all that stands in the way. Where the tyrant can successfully dominate the slaves and eliminate the scapegoats, the rule of the collective is restored and the Kingdom of Heaven has come

400

to earth with a vengeance. But it is all in vain, because it is the wrong way round, as Hitler demonstrated so convincingly in Germany. All spoiled children, however, are not tyrants. They occur all over the world. But all tyrants were spoiled children.

To the spoiled child, the other person must be good or bad. If good, then the other is required protectively, and as a privilege, to restore and reproduce the child-mother, heavenly-collective state again. If the other is not good, he or she must either be made good—or else dismissed. Where there is this inherent incapacity for relationship, in case of any difficulty arising, either you go or I do! There must be no tension. Hence these tears, protests, quarrels, fights. They are all designed to restore a state of peace again. But it is all backwards, into the past, discarnate, morbid, sickly and against the way of life. It is not always easy, however, to avoid deception, because the wayward habits of the spoiled child lurk concealed in various ways within us all.

Enforced collectivization, backed by moral theories exclusively applied, is the compulsive habit of the spoiled child. It is our present-day disease that threatens to destroy us. It is the enemy of real growth, personal integrity, right relationship and the ultimate development of a true community.

The Spoiled Child in Love

Love for the spoiled child is cupboard-love: it is given in exchange for the goods received, conditionally. Moreover, the spoiled child has a rooted certainty that he is owed the goods, that he ought to receive them on demand, and that, if they are not forthcoming, love must be withdrawn from the beloved, who must forthwith be punished in order to learn never to do such a thing again. (In this sense, many of us have been brought up by spoiled children, because such an attitude is typical, of course, of much of our domestic authority.)

By definition, the spoiled child is entitled to the best of everything, now. If that is not forthcoming, then, by assumption and according to first principles, it is someone else's fault, who must therefore bear the blame for disturbing the peace and withholding the goods. The spoiled child's entry into love, therefore, is probably ecstatic: for here, at last, is the fulfillment of all life's promises, all mine, now. The great danger to the beloved is that, at least in the beginning, love willingly gives all. And the spoiled child takes all, too willingly. This is liable to set up one-way traffic, a tyrant-slave relationship, and a willing martyrdom on which the spoiled child swells parasitically, but alas! grows not at all, except in nuisance value.

The spoiled child regards the other as an extension of himself, and as much under control as one of his own limbs. The spoiled child regards the other as a thing, and not a person: as a thing to be used and enjoyed as long as may be, and then as a thing to be thrown away or destroyed. The spoiled child splits the other in two, taking the best and rejecting the rest.

The spoiled child does not live in a real world and is not interested in real people. His world contains himself alone, which all must serve, at his convenience. He only loves those who serve his will—or whim. The rest are out. The spoiled child, therefore—of any age—can only use his love as a destroyer, not only of the beloved, but also of the real and the true. Therefore, beloved, beware!

The Spoiled Child's Attitude to His Situation

When disappointed or at any loss, the spoiled child does not grieve. Instead, he has a grievance. The situation must be changed at once and a scapegoat sacrificed.

The unborn child-in-heaven, unweaned from the collective state, is securely privileged within a magic ring, through which no harm can pass. To keep the ring of privilege securely intact is the ceaseless aim of the spoiled child. There are many ways open to him, and many things will do it. For some, money and property provide the shell around the unborn chick, thickening as wealth increases. For some, an "unselfish" relative, mother, husband or wife, will do the trick and keep the victim safe. For some, it is a habit of wishful thinking in irresolute dreams. For some, a habit of scientific or philosophic thought, an ideology or "-ism," preserves an impenetrable barrier by which to avoid all personally real relationships. For some, it is by hero worship, by identification with others more fortunately or adventurously placed, even characters in some novel, play or film. For some, it may be the artificial aid of alcohol that brings and sustains the roseate hues of heavenly dawn, and provides the impenetrable barriers that exclude a harsh and cold reality. For others, a tame or terrifying Deity and a sufficiently exclusive religion may provide the deepest satisfaction. For all, the purpose is the same, to fulfill the same demand: I must have what I want, secured, increasingly. There must not be—*there ought not to be!*—pain, loss or death. Please keep me safe from life and death, unborn, intact. The magic ring of mother-love must not be broken, and the chicken must never be asked to emerge from its shell. The spoiled child is still incarnate in the wrong ring and is not yet willing to exchange it for the one which circumstance provides.

That is not to say, however, that the spoiled child is not inactive. He is very busy indeed improving the situation, accumulating goods, increasing power, and multiplying his securities. Instead, the situation is treated rather like a dugout planned to stand a siege at the time of an invasion. The utmost must be extracted, purchased, stored and then sustained in safety.

But even that is too inactive a picture by which to describe the ceaseless endeavors of our little moralists to ensure that their society enjoys its proper improvements with safety. The spoiled child is not only working for himself: he is helping others, too. So all persons of goodwill must join him to build his material Jerusalem, his planned Utopia, his heaven on earth. Meanwhile, our enemies are numerous and time is short. But if we all put our shoulders to the wheel and man the machine . . . and vote for democracy . . . and obey the politicians . . . and allow the psychologists to choose what is good for us . . . and if we go on hoping, hoping, hoping . . . and working, working, working . . . and fighting to destroy our enemies utterly. . . .

And is all this urgent crying for a better world only to avoid being born again—indeed, to avoid really being born at all? Is the betterness that we are asking for always a *wrong request?*

The Normal Attitude to the Spoiled Child

The normal attitude to the spoiled child is to behave in an exactly similar fashion towards him, to mirror him back to himself. The normal behavior of the adult to the spoiled child is the behavior of the spoiled adult.

Of course, the spoiled child is not always a tedious or annoying type. He can be an exceedingly pleasant fellow, flatteringly glad to please us or appease us, or ardently unselfish in his (or her) efforts to give us what we want. When he (or she) has his own way, when all is well, no one can be a better companion than the spoiled child. While he wants to please and appease us, his flattering opinions can be most gratifyingly welcome. His unselfishness, if tactfully directed, can be very well received. Dear spoiled child, he is really a charming fellow (what a darling she can be!) and how nice we can be in return. There is not a cloud in the sky, everything in the garden is lovely; this is heaven indeed! Here is no difference of opinion that matters, no emotional tension, no frustration, no disappointment, and no fear. We all have what we want, here and now. What nice people we all are!

But the spoiled child does not always want what we want when we want it, or to give up what we want when we want him to do so. Then the trouble begins. "Don't be silly! Little nuisance! Go away! Can't you ever leave me alone for five minutes, always barging in! You are a selfish little beast! Yes, certainly, I'll give you anything you want if you will only go away and not bother me now! Oh, blast you, that's finished it! This is the end! Get the hell out of here! Bang, bang: take that and that! . . . I only want a little peace!"

So the spoiled child receives back, but multiplied, what he or she first offers to the world: love for love, hate for hate, anger for anger, praise for praise, kindness for kindness, and blow for blow. He sees himself reflected in his experience, like a monkey in a mirror. As he changes his mood, so his experience seems to change. And as his experience changes, so he changes his mood. It is so obvious to the spoiled child that only someone or something else can make him happy or unhappy. Indeed, he proves it to be so, every moment, every day. If only . . . if only you were different and there was more of this and less of that, how happy I should be! Cannot you see that it must be your fault and that you ought to do something about it? It would be so simple, if only . . .

Cure

(a) *In one's self.* Perhaps this is an illness of which the doctor must always be prepared to admit himself diseased, and only treat himself?

Treatment is plain as soon as the diagnosis is clearly made. Confronted by any two, the illness reduced those two to one (and that one mine, for me). The treatment, therefore, must change the way of life, so that, when confronted by that same duality, no tension, no suspense, no loss and no conflict can be regarded as intolerable. The rule for us, who treat ourselves, is plain: *With any two, go on to three, not back to one.* It is the relationship that counts.

If the attitude to life prescribed by the illness is determined to dismiss the unpleasant (especially the illness, fault or weakness) the treatment is first to admit the illness, and to confess the fault or weakness: "Yes, I am ill: I am wrong: I am weak: I am behaving like a spoiled child, because indeed I am a spoiled child." Can I hold that fact in place, regarding it steadily for long enough to feel that it is true and to *understand what it means?* If I really understand, shall I not have to admit that I shall probably always be a bit spoiled, in the sense that I shall always somewhat exploit and take advantage of what I have been given? Shall I not always in some degree exploit the weakness and the love of others? Of course, I know I shall. There is no end to it. But if I know that, consciously, I may perhaps be able in time, with practice, to be a little less fat-headed?

On the positive side, there is the constant opportunity for the study of relationships with others *without assuming anything about them.* Meeting others—meeting other persons—"I" to "I" through me, in spite of me—understanding people, things, symbols, words, Life itself, in *depth,* is a lifelong exercise.

There is no end to that, either.

(b) *In others.* Why should you want to put another right? Why do you have to mind any other person's business?

It may be very inconvenient, unfair and most disappointing, but you may as well be warned and face it, here and now: even supposing that you do take yourself seriously (but not, I hope, too seriously) in hand, you will not find that others will always reflect back to you your more considerate attention for them. Rather they will take advantage of your kindness and exploit your patience: they will misunderstand your meaning and malign your motives: they will bite the hand that feeds them and hate you for your goodness or your guts.

So many people cannot bear anyone else to have what they have not; but neither can they bear to receive from another what they want, however much they want it, because they have an *inferiority complex*. It is impossible for them to receive what they need most, because they cannot bear to admit that they need anything at all. They are compelled not only to refuse your gift, but to hate you as the potential giver.

I have already said that I believe in "evil," as the deliberate intention to refuse and destroy "good." The inferiority complex also refuses and destroys the good, but it does not do so deliberately, nor for evil ends. Yet blindly and mechanically, pitifully and constantly, it is compelled to destroy the good, which includes the happy and the healthy.

Evil and the inferiority complex can, and often do, form an insidious partnership in destructive combination, but I believe that the inferiority complex works more harm in the world today than deliberate evil does. The inferiority complex, being an unconscious defense mechanism, is a psychological or emotional disorder, disease or sickness of the personality. It is not a sin or moral fault, although it is normally treated as such, especially by those who suffer from the same complaint. The differential diagnosis is a very important one for each of us to make in our world today, as it is trembling, unbalanced, on the brink of its destruction.

CHAPTER 26

The Inferiority Complex

It is the purpose of this chapter to indicate at least part of the reason why we so often manage to lose our lives without finding them, and why we find it so hard and uncongenial to experience the process of renewal, of being born again, preferring instead a flattened existence beneath this protective accumulation of hard crust, rather than the present gift of a renewing life.

The "word" in this case is an unhappy choice, being a fragment of psychological jargon that has penetrated through the pages of journalism into common use, where it has become flattened out until everyone thinks they know all about it. The label for our study in this chapter is an "inferiority complex," for which, I am afraid, there is no equivalent in either basic or biblical English. Unpleasant as the words "inferiority complex" sound, as there is no alternative, we must continue to use and make the best of them, meanwhile infusing them with such light of meaning as we can.

Why All This Fuss?

I once heard an inferiority complex defined as the feeling certain people have of *not liking to be what they are.* The speaker implied that this feeling of resentment about their inadequacy only applied to people who were in some way especially lacking, either in brains, beauty or hard cash, and that the solution of their problem was either to admit they were no good and stop annoying their betters, or else to go out and get whatever they wanted if they could. Émile Coué, New Thought and Christian Science have improved the prospect of all those who in the past have been disappointed by their recurrent failures and incurable deficiencies, by advising them to assert that there is no such thing, and that we can all have

From *Mysterious Marriage: A Study of the Morality of
Personal Relationships and Individual Obsessions*

what we want by simply assuming that we possess it already. But that simple remedy, unfortunately, does not always seem to work.

Granted that some have less and others more; that those who have less want more; and that those who have once had more find it very difficult thereafter to do with less; then we have to admit that everyone is in some degree confronted by a problem of inadequacy, of wanting something and not having it, and of wanting to improve his situation. But I suggest that we shall never really understand the human problem of values, if we look at it only from this side and in material terms. I want to judge the human problem of worth—how much am I worth?—from the very bottom and the first beginning. And I do not mean that we are to begin at the mother's breast, or in her womb. The bottom and the beginning, the core and center of the problem of value, is in the nature of life itself.

So let me state the basic fact, "I am!" Then what am I experiencing? There is no need to ask the poet or the mystic to describe to us his special experience-in-depth of here-and-now. The materialist, the sensualist, the practical person with no nonsense about him whatever, will do admirably for my purpose. In fact, he is just the man I want, because he knows exactly what it means to experience heaven and to feel like God. He knows about bliss and ecstasy as well as I do; and he knows—I hope!—full well how to enjoy himself to the utmost satisfaction. He knows what the glory, the wonder and the comfort of experience can mean. He also knows the feeling of splendor that follows successful achievement after sustained effort. (God, that's grand!) There are certain moments in our lives when we each experience either our own "divinity," or, as when we are in love, the divinity of another. Oh, yes, she is divine enough for my purpose, which is to establish the fact that for me to experience lack of such exceeding joy, when once I have known it, is enough to make that lack seem utterly intolerable. I know that there are heights and depths in me that I can splendidly achieve and desperately plumb. Surely the depth must be made to seem deeper by contrast with that experience of height? Surely the fall must be more painful, if once we have known that timeless joy?

Yes, of course, you have known those heavenly moments, reader, and not even rarely. Perhaps more often when you were younger than now, when you are more invested with the accumulated wealth of mounting years? Perhaps the joys of adolescence or even early infancy were more complete, as they were even then unutterable? Perhaps the first love, the careless rapture of our most inexperienced years, the ravishing of innocence by life's first close embrace, is best? Perhaps as we grow older, life must present us with a falling curve, a declining value, for the quality of experience?

Perhaps, for some; but not, I think, for all. Some find more joy later than before. But what I do claim for all is that, whatever heights they climbed to find the peak of ecstasy that is life's very heart and core, they fell! That peak, timeless in itself, cannot be sustained in time. It cannot last. The fall, the loss, the empty place, the haunting memory, is all that can remain. Such, in the long run, is the tragic core of all experience.

The human problem is haunted by hope that the fall, the loss, the weakness can be avoided, or that it is not true; that this one will give me what that one took away; that this one will save me from what that one made me suffer; that this will do instead to make up for the loss of that—if only I can have enough of this, and always keep it safe, forever mine! Our lives are haunted by this desperate hang-over of hope, as if the normal state that we should all expect is the spoiled child's heaven of happiness, unbroken, undisturbed.

The roots of the inferiority complex are not here, in this familiar world, but there in eternity, where are also the roots of the human problem. But, of course, eternity is not only there; it is also here, now, and in me. And so am I.

Surely it is just this close relation of the more with the less, the whole with the part, that-other-ground with this-familiar-field, eternity with space-time, then with now, I with me, which is the nature of the human problem and the measure of the inferiority complex?

Yes, I fell; and fall, again and again. I fell from heaven to earth; from there to here; from then to now; from all to so very little; from security to constant change; from loving arms to life's perpetual hope deferred in disappointment. How can I get back to my beloved, back whence I came, to get back all I ought to have, all that I am owed?

But that is easy, too. Surely there are many ways to regain our paradise, when paradise is lost. Let's go back; let's go forward; let's pretend; let's sublimate; let's keep moving, somewhere, anywhere; let's blame someone else and punish him. Let's keep this hangover of hope; let's keep looking for a savior; surely somewhere, sometime, someone must restore to us what we have lost?

Must they? But who will be my savior, and when will he come to me? Meanwhile, let me see what I can do for myself, now, with the help of my inferiority complex.

What Is an Inferiority Complex?

To some extent, some more, some less, we all suffer from this fell complaint. For the damage that it does unwittingly, I would not hesitate to claim that it is the greatest single cause of sickness, inefficiency and unhappiness in the human race, especially nowadays. It is a cancer which gnaws its sickening way unseen, undiagnosed, unrealized, while it sucks away our blood, destroys our very roots, and spoils our spiritual heritage. It is the enemy of personal growth, as it is of social relations. It is the height of folly, as it is the poison of all true wisdom, kindness and goodwill. In fact, it destroys the best that is in us and between us. As an enemy, it is worth our serious consideration.

Definition. "An inferiority complex is an unconscious defense mechanism, the purpose of which is to promote such activity as will protect the subject (whether organ, individual or group) from a condition or feeling of intolerable inferiority (inadequacy or insecurity), by the immediate assumption of a relative (compensatory) condition or feeling of superiority."

The essence of an inferiority complex is therefore not in the feeling of inferiority itself. It is not the same as a mere lack of self-confidence. Its essence is in the fact that this feeling is experienced as *intolerable,* so that an unconscious protective reaction of *immediate avoidance* is brought into operation, the purpose of which is to reverse the position to one of superiority. The unconscious defense mechanism is protective against a feeling of intolerable insecurity, and belongs to the instinctive or unconscious modes of

410

biological self-defense by fight or flight. It is an atavistic "hang-over" from earlier conditions of life in the jungle that has no place whatever in the ordering of human behavior. Yet it still persists in our everyday life, with disastrous results that are the more insidious and harmful to our personal and social welfare, because they are both unconscious in origin, and morally rationalized and justified by our conscious minds. The resultant behavior therefore appears to be not only inevitable, but also unarguably right.

Let us now consider our definition in detail.

Unconscious defense mechanism. There are certain basic reactions to common situations which are called "instinctive." These are set patterns or habits of behavior which we have inherited from our animal forebears, in common with our physical bodies and the nervous systems which form part of them. It is part of the price of our evolution that we are thus rooted in the past, and it is our human task to integrate and use such instincts as are adaptable to our present level of requirements, to modify such as require to be changed, and to outgrow those others, which are completely out of date. The appetitive and procreative instincts are capable of integration and modification. The instinct of self-defense, however, which is latent in the unconscious part of the nervous system, requires to be outgrown. It is not adaptable to modern requirements. It is no use nowadays running away unconsciously from danger. To use our heads will serve us better, whether the danger be in the form of a charging omnibus, a financial disaster, a falling bomb, a domestic quarrel, a threat of war, or any other mortal peril whatsoever. Yet the unconscious defense mechanisms still persist, to dominate and determine our behavior, especially in any crisis. Their influence is always wrong, tyrannical, untimely, anti-social, ineffective and harmful to all concerned. The indictment is not less than total. That such mechanisms should not only still persist, but also be regarded as morally right, is therefore a very serious and important problem for humanity, especially as we are today confronted by the prospect of imminent and complete disaster.

To promote activity. The instinctive remedy is always towards action, either evasive or aggressive, and either within the self or in the outer world. The cry is not so much in question form, "What can be done?" as rather, "Something should and must be done immediately!" But, surely, too much has been done already, as is evidenced by the fever of anxiety, the rapid pulse, the cold sweat, the aggressive mien and the general state of tension. All this is proof that instinct is already involved in action, and is seeking for a further outlet, either in fight or flight.

A common instinctive activity which is not sufficiently recognized as being unconsciously compelled is the activity of thought: the racing mind, the whirling wheels of cerebral activity that are involved in all states of worry and anxiety. This is perhaps our commonest form of instinctive defensive—aggressive activity, and it is to be recommended least of all as a practical means to the solution of any problem.

Protect the subject. It was all very well to protect the subject in the jungle, where instinctive requirements and dangerous conditions were comparatively simple and straightforward. Either your enemy got you or you him, or you got away. In the jungle the instinct of self-defense, fight or flight, was paramount, but even so it was never so effective as our added brains could make it.

But the instinctive habits of fight or flight will not work today, either in the complex political and economic structures of a civilized community, or in the simpler relations of the home and family. Instinct considers the safety of the "skin," the material part, the animal side of human nature. It will always sacrifice the whole for the part, the many for the sake of the one. It has no idea of self-sacrifice, self-giving, self-surrender, patience, or accepted suffering. All these are utterly unfamiliar, and indeed impossible, to the instinctive, unconscious way of life which is concerned only with the safety of itself and its immediate own. Instinct can safeguard things, but not relationships. Instinct is too short-sighted. Whenever instinct operates unchecked, it does so in a way that is destructive to the welfare either of the whole person or of the whole social group. Instinct destroys the subtle fabric of the whole system of relationships.

The sanction that is sometimes claimed for conduct that, because it is natural, therefore it is either inevitable or good, must be recognized to be quite inadmissible. The natural level of conduct, being instinctive, is both socially and personally impracticable and immoral. And, by itself, like all the rest of our lower nature, it is destructive even of the very life from which it springs.

Whenever instinct operates, it does so at the expense of all those actions that go to comprise the wholeness, the health and the holiness of the person or of the social group. Having grown up a little with the passing of the centuries and learnt that to give is more in harmony with advancing years than to keep on grabbing, we must also learn to forgo our ancient habits of aggression, or we shall not be men and women adapted to serve in our day and generation.

Organ, individual or group. Whenever an organ in the body is invaded by a foreign or noxious element, it proceeds instinctively (naturally) to deal with it by one of three methods, each of which illustrates different aspects of our personal and social conduct under similar conditions of "invasion." The first is by *absorption.* For instance, in the blood stream, the white cells of the blood eat and absorb the "enemy," so that the best of him, if any, can be made use of, and the rest discharged as waste matter. This is called "phagocytosis." It is similar to what happens in digestion, where the useful elements in food are absorbed and built in to various parts of the body, the remainder being excreted and dismissed. We deal in the same way (or should do!) with the nourishment of ideas provided for us by our education. (The Latin verb educare means to nourish.) Similarly, with the flow of experience constantly approaching us and knocking at our door, we absorb what we can as it flows through us, and evacuate the rest. (In either case, we do not need much for our sufficiency of nourishment.)

On the physical level, when the invader is more than can be thus absorbed, he is *made harmless by a protective capsule of fibrous tissue.* He is, as it were, thrown into a concentration camp, to be dealt with later perhaps, or left to languish in his prison. On the psychological level, this is called "repression." It is concealment or avoidance by convenient forgetting.

It is the third protective reaction, however, which is particularly characteristic of the instinctive mechanism of the inferiority complex. This is *immediate expulsion of the intruder.* Confronted by an enemy too large to be absorbed or digested, i.e. being put in a position of relative weakness, the whole instinctive protective effort of the organism (or individual or society) is called forth in an act of expulsion. On the physical level, the enemy is thrown out by coughing, sneezing, vomiting or diarrhea. On the level of personal relationships, there is an aggressive-dismissive explosion of indignation, impatience, anger, or active violence. Politically and in mass relationships, there is resort to war.

Condition or feeling. The experience may be real or imaginary, but in either case what the subject experiences is an intolerable feeling of inadequacy.

This feeling of inferiority may be a true judgment, but more often than not it is a reaction to an imaginary situation, and then the inadequacy is also only imaginary. However this may be, it makes no difference to the unconscious defense mechanism, which reacts just as viciously to mental apparitions and hypothetical possibilities in the mind, as to the real objective conditions. To the instinctive life and its reflex operations, the imaginary world is at least as real as the world of objective reality.

Intolerable inferiority (*inadequacy or insecurity*). The emphasis here is entirely on the word "intolerable." It means "I cannot bear it!" Although all of us must occasionally find ourselves in the inferior position, or at least on the lower slopes, we shall not find our position intolerable unless we have an inferiority complex. The situation of intolerable inferiority may be specific, i.e, a certain kind of situation: or it may be general, applying more or less to all kinds of inferior positions. The process which makes the judgment of inferiority is unconscious, and the protective mechanism which sets evasive action in operation is also unconscious.

Immediate assumption. The defense reaction which is set going is timeless and must therefore be untimely. In this reaction to experience, there is no time allowed for growth or change. The desired goal or end result must be assumed, immediately. There is no beginning, no process of becoming, only the final result. All the emphasis of security is placed on the fact that the goal has been achieved and therefore must be retained. Hence much anxiety is experienced in case it is not so, and much effort is spent in proving that it is.

Relative (*compensatory*). The goal is one of relative superiority, i.e. relative to the condition which has imposed the inferiority feeling. I must get my own back: I must get on top of *That* or *Them*. Unfortunately, however, the compensatory process may not stop here. It is usually overcompensatory, more than enough. The victory must be total, final, absolute. I must, therefore, be on top of everything, everyone, always. This is obviously a most exacting requirement and leads again to much anxiety, fear of failure and further insecurity, which sets up an endless spiral of further unconscious overcompensatory defense mechanisms, in a perpetually increasing vicious circle of anxiety and escape.

Condition or feeling of superiority. The state of superiority may again be real or imaginary, but again it must be fixed. It cannot bear criticism, for obvious reasons. Once achieved, it must be held, it must be right and there must be no doubt about it. For this reason the victims of an inferiority complex are always "touchy" folk. Always on guard against an injury, they are nevertheless constantly feeling intolerably hurt. They are not open to argument. They cannot be reasonable. In spite of the fact that they always have their reasons, and may appear to take delight in argument, the result of any discussion is always a foregone conclusion. It must end in their own verbal victory, or else war must be declared immediately to restore the balance in their favor. Their compulsive adoption of the faculty of reason as a defensive-aggressive unconscious defense mechanism leads to much subsequent discomfort and misunderstanding with their fellows, for whom reason is a more sensitive instrument and words are not synonymous with blows.

Mechanism and Reversed Mechanism

Confronted by any situation of relative deficiency, whether real or imaginary (e.g. fatigue, doubt, suspense, loss, or suspected inadequacy), the victim of the inferiority complex is unconsciously compelled to set in motion such activity as will obtain an immediate reversal of the situation, so that a state of fixed absolute superiority of some kind can be assumed and retained. The effect of the operation of this mechanism is to destroy the real values in any situation (which would change in time and might even improve), and

415

to impose instead a more desirable situation, the arbitrarily selected values of which must be sustained by force.

When this becomes too difficult, as it eventually must, or in the case of the less active and courageous types, the reversed mechanism comes into operation. Since the result of this operation needs to be successful with certainty, it is obviously easier to be sure of nothing than something, of pain than pleasure, and of defeat than victory. Hence the easier "choice" of a fixed absolute inferiority, in which the victim is to be found in a state of protective inertia at the lowest possible level.

Such false humility and compulsive abstinence has no desire to change nor ability to benefit. It must refuse any offered gift of what it so resolutely lacks. Such a state of total loss, being in fact total gain held in reverse, must feel that to receive anything, whether much or little, would imply not any gain at all, but only a reminder of the intolerable deficiency. These hungry, frightened, love-starved children who have swallowed "mother" whole, must live perpetually unsatisfied, dependent for their satisfaction on their self-induced and self-annihilating pain.

Causes

The inferiority complex is derived from a state of extreme and unbalanced contrast, the better aspect of which makes the worse intolerable by comparison. The defense mechanism is then set up unconsciously to make the worse state immediately as good or better than the other. This process can obviously occur both in general as well as in particular. It can be due to factors inherent in human nature or in temperament, as well as being acquired subsequently from conditions of upbringing and circumstance.

Human nature. If the Kingdom of Heaven is indeed within us and if our nature is thus dual, compounded of earth and heaven, we have in human nature itself the most profound basis for an inferiority complex, in which our earthly side will strive to surpass its heavenly counterpart. Bound in time and frustrated in circumstance, imprisoned in perpetual suspense, it would be but natural for man to make attempts to improve his lot by other and more urgent means than patient growth in space and time. Indeed, seen in their full contrast side by side, as best and worst, highest and lowest, ideal and real, we cannot but agree that the fate of man, to be thus suspended on the horns of a perpetual dilemma, is indeed an intolerable one. It is not to be wondered at that he should take matters into his own hands and set about doing something to provide, if not a solution, at least an improvement in his lot. With accumulated means to improve his position in the world at his disposal, it is not only pride or cupidity that induces him to take care of himself and to create a better world according to his own improved designs. The impelling motive is much more likely to be his fear of insecurity. It is typical, indeed, of the inferiority complex, that we should thus leap to blame one another or ourselves, for having committed some culpable "sin." But if we could first diagnose and separate the sick, whom we can treat, from the sinners whom we cannot, I believe we should discover that much of our so-called human "sin" is, in fact, actually a state of illness on the medical or psychological level, where an unconscious defense process of a morbid kind has been mechanically activated by a state of intolerable anxiety.

I believe that mankind in general is sick with this as yet unrecognized disease, for which we have no other name at present than the inferiority complex. I believe that most of our troubles in the world today, which are accumulating to the danger-point of ultimate disaster, are due to this disease, and not to ill-will or evil intent. And I believe that it is this unconsciously protective thrust of the inferiority complex, working to set us off our true balance at every level, in every time and place, which is the main root and cause of our human distress. When that heart-sickness has been recognized and treated, it will be time enough to talk of sin and wickedness. But it is quite certain that the deep-seated disease of the inferiority complex will never respond successfully to moral blame or to the untimely surgery of war. That is its symptom and its cause. It can never be its cure.

Temperament. Those who suffer most from difficulties of temperament are the more gifted, not the less. They are the superior, not the inferior, types. The sensitive, the quick, the subtle, the original, the new, are all likely to suffer more by contrast, at the critical and impatient hands of busy parent, fussy nurse, stupid aunt, arrogant school master or dogmatic priest. These sensitive ones are more easily moved by those lesser external stimuli, that others less sensitive might not even notice. To change the metaphor again, it is as if the notes of their piano move to a lighter touch, and they have octaves of experience beyond the reach of tougher folk. Thin-skinned, they cannot so easily keep the invaders out. They are therefore more easily disturbed, more deeply hurt, more liable to be confused by the many discords and rough contacts of their earthly world. Nevertheless, they are the salt of the earth, because their sense of values transcends the material comfort of their earthly needs. The tragedy is that these are the ones most liable to develop an inferiority complex, which can only have disastrous results upon their creative potentialities.

Inherently gifted beyond their immediate powers and opportunities, they therefore find it difficult to incarnate their gifts in earthly time. This makes them feel frustrated, handicapped and inferior to those who, less gifted but more tough, can get on better in this world. Hence they are the richest soil in which the seeds of the inferiority complex can be sown by the destructive influences or lack of encouragement present in their environment.

It is most unfortunate for the progress of the human race that the effect of the callous pressure of the world should bear most heavily upon the tender and more sensitive, the children, women, and creative artists, who may be forced in self-defense to cover their so-called deficiencies by becoming tough guys or tomboys, petty tyrants, school marms, civil servants or plain business men. Despising that which is superior and yet afraid of it, we raise that which is inferior above it, inducing by every insidious pressure those who know better to worship false gods.

There is no time in this world for the wisdom of the heart to grow to its maturity. The hazards which are set against it are utterly unfair, where moral values have been destroyed by the insidious machinations of the inferiority complex.

The inferior function. Why this taboo on tenderness, this inability to experience loss or suffering, this disinclination to feel anything at all? The answer is because anything which is associated with

418

weakness is instinctively associated with intolerable inferiority. We must do something immediately to reassert our pride of place, and to regain our lost control over the situation.

Instinctively the passive state of "feeling" (sensitivity, receptivity) is inclined, for obvious reasons, to develop an inferiority complex. The defense mechanism then operates by dissociating or repressing feeling as the inferior function, overcompensating instead in the direction of an aggressive self-assertion, either on the emotional or intellectual level, the purpose of which is to regain a satisfactory state of superiority. Thus the faculty of consciousness may become over-developed and overactive, as a defensive mechanism for the exploitation of an inferiority complex. The head takes over command of the exterior situation from which the heart has been withdrawn. The head advances as the heart retires. This is obviously extremely bad for human balance, but it has happened in some degree to us all, both individually and collectively. Education as a whole ignores the heart and over-stimulates the head, thus nourishing, not the person, but the inferiority complex. We think the more, as real understanding, which is a matter of the heart, deteriorates. We do the more, because we are less capable of understanding what needs to be done.

It is accepted in our world today that the "inner" faculties of intuition and feeling are inferior functions. It is not so generally recognized that the physical world of sensation is also denied its proper status. There is only one worthy function, only one certain way of being superior and making the world safe for yourself and democracy. Today, we must think about everything.

When thinking is thus misused, it becomes an end in itself instead of a means to an end. The mind becomes another womb for our protected safety, superiority and privilege without responsibility.

Many of us have thus become enslaved by the tyranny of a mind from which the living seed has flown away. It is a state of mind in which the world of his experience has been made safe for the thinker, because, now that he knows all about it, he need not experience it any more. He thinks and talks at second-hand, instead.

Sex inferiority. For obvious reasons women are liable, as the so-called "weaker sex," to develop an inferiority complex vis-a-vis the insufferable domination of the male. The danger of this is so great and the consequences so disastrous for all concerned, that it is impossible to pay too much attention to the problem.

The general tendency is for women to lose the essential pride in their womanhood, in their competitive efforts to become as good as men. The social trend in education is to bring up girls as boys, and to give them a similar education, in order that they may compete on equal terms with men in the industrial and professional markets. Where women have an inferiority complex, they strive to beat men at their own game, in order not to feel their sex inferiority. Thus their real contribution and their proper role is neglected. They become assertive and aggressive, restless and over-active pseudo-extraverts or compulsive intellectuals. When they attain positions of responsibility, they are liable to behave as petty tyrants, causing the development of further inferiority complexes in their "inferiors." So the vicious circle goes on.

In the field of sexual experience the feeling of intolerable inferiority may lead either to sex repression (frigidity), or to sexual promiscuity with moralized immorality acting as a protective over-compensation. (Sexual intercourse is good for you: you ought not to miss it: it is too bad to be left out of anything.) With an intolerable feeling of inferiority or anxiety in regard to sex, the behavior may tend in either of those directions.

The harassed, house-proud, overactive and aggressive mother, organizing her children's lives without allowing them either privacy or freedom to choose for themselves, shows how little joy her own womanhood has brought her, as she does her utmost to ensure that her children also will experience the same needless disappointment.

Upbringing. The outward factors which contribute to the development of an inferiority complex are, of course, mainly due to errors in upbringing on the part of the child's immediate authorities, either at home or school. Personal errors of this kind do far more harm than those shocks, misfortunes, and misadventures which we may meet at the less personal hands of life itself. In gen-

420

eral, the trouble is caused by interfering with the normal process of timely growth, which may be either over-stimulated, impeded or impoverished. Anything in the child's environment which sets up, whether it be sudden or prolonged, an excess of feeling of any kind whatsoever, is likely to produce an inferiority complex, through arousing an intolerable feeling of insecurity.

Excessive experience of fear, guilt, inferiority and frustration are in varying degrees the common lot of far too many children. The general situation of inferiority and insecurity may, however, be suddenly dramatized in a moment of experience that is the turning point from which the development of the inferiority complex took place. I remember the dream of a woman of fifty-five which brought to light an acutely traumatic episode of nearly fifty years before, the importance of which she had not realized either at the time or since. The dream was of a child of about six lying flat on a gravestone. The body of the child then disappeared and the gravestone was strewn with masses of pink roses. I asked the patient whether perhaps she had not died when she was about six? ("I died of shame.") Her recollection of the following episode was immediate. "I was going to South Africa with my family when I was about six. The first day out we had games for the children, as there were many on board. We had a potato race, the rules of which I did not understand. I rushed to the finishing post, to arrive alone. I was first, I had really won something at last, and for a fraction of a second I felt immensely proud, expectant of applause. But I looked round to find the other children still rushing up and down with their potatoes and everyone was roaring with laughter at me. I think I died of shame. Anyway, I know I never attempted to compete again in any way after that."

Such apparently trivial things matter so much to small children, because of the excess of feeling which is aroused. The stability of their fragile emotional world is so easily shattered by the sudden swing of feeling from one extreme to the other, as the height of expectation may experience the ruthless shock of an opposite realization. It is the relative feeling that is aroused which is the real measure and meaning of such an experience. The feeling which we have about it is the truth of our own experience for us. For fifty years this child's ordinary physical capacity for enjoying her body had been put away beneath a stone, and she had covered herself instead with pink roses—so sweet, so sentimental, so spiritual and so very uncompetitive.

Excess of feeling. At a tender age, any experience which overstimulates emotional development is liable to overstrain the inner workings of the system of affective relationships (the "heart"), with the subsequent development of a protective habit of withdrawal and consequent feeling of inferiority about such relationships. Demonstrations of excessive affection, coupled with effusive demands for love, are as dangerous as they are undesirable. (This is one of the special problems of the only child.)

Deprivation of affection. Lack of demonstration of affection by the parents is, however, another cause of developing excess of feeling in the child. Being always treated coldly, the child will feel the greater need for love and warmth. Deprived of proper comfort and protection, and forced too early into independence, weaned, in fact, too soon, the child is compelled to do something to correct the balance. The feeling of loss is intolerable, and it is the task of the inferiority complex to fill the awful gap. Either the feeling of loss is repressed, with the development of some overcompensating alternative, such as the lust for power over others; or, perhaps, phantasy will fill in the spaces which fact has left so painfully empty. But in either case the child is left forever unable to accept the love that was once longed for so intolerably. The space has been filled and the door has been shut. So intolerable disappointment must become perpetual.

Insecurity. Children need security. If parents do not provide it the inferiority complex will. Children must have a sufficient feeling of security. It is the purpose of the inferiority complex to make the intolerable tolerable, by filling up the gap.

Inferiority or inadequacy (insecurity) is the source of fear. It is good to feel a little fear sometimes, because fear is one of life's most vitalizing spurs; but it is not good for a child to experience excessive fear, whether it be too much, too soon or too often. In any case, life must be fearful to a child and the best circumstances of childhood's protection are quite fearful enough. To be one amongst many, small amongst great, is very frightening. An overdose of fear, either constantly applied or coming as a sudden shock, will do the trick and develop an inferiority complex which will last a lifetime.

The position in the family is a potent source of trouble. Examples at random are the only child who is expected to live up to grown-up standards; the slower-minded child who is easily surpassed at home and school by the quicker skill of a younger brother; and the girl who has two or three elder brothers above her, with whom she is expected to compete successfully.

What is commonly referred to as the "broken home" is now more fully appreciated as the danger which it is to the child's necessary feeling of security. Deprivation by death or illness of one or both parents may have a similar effect, but such a natural event is not usually so harmful in its results, because the child can be more conscious of the reason for its loss. It is always easier to adapt emotionally to a deficiency of things, rather than of people. But bad behavior on the part of people may lead to overcompensation in regard to things, so that a craving for power over more and more things may make up for the loss of security in personal relationships. It then seems safer to treat persons as if they are only things, and so controllable.

Invalidism in childhood, due to any cause, is a bad start for subsequent emotional and psychological development. Weakness at any point, if stressed too much, may lead to overcompensatory development of power, either in the same direction or another. I have known several cases of minor disability through infantile paralysis, in which the strain imposed upon the will, although it had successfully conquered the weakness at the time, led in later years through its overcompensatory effects to a serious nervous breakdown.

Physical weakness may be either general or particular. There may be either a feeling of not being up to the same standard of physical stamina as others (such as a girl might feel amongst her brothers, or the physically weaker type of boy at a strenuous school where success at games was all-important); or some particular defect or even difference, such as defective eyesight, a stammer, excessive fat, or the notorious power-lust of the hunchback. The critical comments of the gang upon its weaker members can be cruel in the extreme, and it is for this reason that any experience of being different at school can be so dangerous. Those of us who are blessed with good physical health can hardly be sufficiently aware of our good fortune, nor of the degree to which our self-confidence is derived from our unconscious habit of reliance upon such good physical foundations.

The attitude of others. Perhaps the commonest cause of the inferiority complex is that it spreads from infection by others, whose attitude of compulsive superiority must always make it intolerable for someone else to be in the inferior position. One or both parents may have it; other members of the family, or the other children at school; school-masters and mistresses usually have it to an exceptional degree; and where any or all have it the rest must catch the infection of it, so that life becomes a scramble for the top, from which secure position we can afford to despise—and keep excluded—the weaker brethren.

The operation of the inferiority complex may appear to be done in the kindest manner, because the accumulation of virtue and the goodwill of others is one of the most-favored means of establishing superiority. Minding other peoples' business, helping lame dogs over stiles, and in general being charitably disposed towards those less fortunate than ourselves, may be a sign of genuine goodwill; but, on the other hand, it may be evidence of the operation of an inferiority complex. Similarly, the choice of a profession such as medicine or nursing, and especially the practice of psychology, may be the answer to a vocation, the call to serve either the cause of science or the community, or even a means of earning a fair income in reward for interesting work. If any of these motives is the operative one, the object, end or goal of the effort is to obtain knowledge, cash or the benefit of other people: that is to say, the object is outside the person who makes the effort. But unfortunately this is not always the case; where the motive is that of the inferiority complex, the purpose is to establish the superiority of the one who is doing the work. It is not in the successful issue of the work itself. To the casual observer it may look as if the patient benefits by the "unselfish" efforts of doctor or of nurse, but even that may be only a means to the end of the other's feeling of superiority, which is the paramount motive.

As long as the patient gets better, the pupil is taught, or the country is governed, does it really matter whether doctor, nurse, teacher or politician has an inferiority complex or not? It is all a question of the price which is paid in the long run. Yes, the patient gets better, the pupil is taught and the country is governed—but to what end? The end pursued will be the end attained; and the end attained, whether we like it or not, will be the end which we have pursued. The inferiority complex may look benevolent on the surface, but its true character is always destructive, in spite of any mask it wears. Unfortunately, it is not always recognized as the devastating sickness it is. Too often our elders and betters encourage its operation in us as evidence of success and proof of our—and their—superiority.

To be successful the inferiority complex depends on two factors:

First, to be able to have and to hold the superior position, and second, to be able to prove that others are inferior, weaker and wrong. A successful inferiority complex enjoys the uneasy victory, not only of always being right, but also of criticizing others in the variety of their faults. To remain successful, however, it is necessary to go on proving that it is true by always being in control, by always doing good to those who are on your side, by always being able to prove that others are wrong and by always being able to disregard those who are not willing for you to put them on the right path, which is, of course, your own.

These are the people who feel that they are the heaven-sent, divinely appointed, leaders. They are chosen and therefore they are responsible. They get their feeling of superiority by telling other people how they are wrong and what they ought to do about it. Being unable (because unwilling) to feel their own inadequacy, guilt or inferiority, they must point out to others how very wrong they are. This they do interminably, self-assured of their own self-righteousness. Nothing and no one is allowed to be what it is, or to grow into what it is becoming. The only cause of change is force, verbal or otherwise. There is no faith in life, no acceptance of the facts of experience and very little willingness. Instead, I feel that I must show you what you ought to do—and I feel that I am right in driving you in the direction which you ought to take.

But the motive of the inferiority complex is always ulterior; I am not really interested in your welfare, but in my own superiority. It is that and nothing else which is of paramount importance. My apparent benevolence towards you is really spurious, as is too often proved in fact by the disastrous course of the events which follow. All that really matters is that I should be and remain on top. You, who are probably hoping that I am your loving savior, are really my scapegoat, my stooge and the necessary means to the end of my self-glorification.

Is that, in fact, too hard an interpretation of the motive behind at least some of the activities of some parents, doctors, nurses, teachers and politicians? I do not claim that it is present all the time, even in those who are most infected by this disease. But I do claim that it is present in all of us, part of the time: in some of us more than in others, but in all of us it is the more damaging because it is not yet recognized for the destructive force it is.

If the spiritual rights of the person mean anything, then it is essential that we should be able to recognize and debunk the pseudo-moral operations of the inferiority complex, because its effect is precisely opposite to the benevolent intentions by which it is disguised.

Other effects. The general effect of the inferiority complex may be expressed simply as a reversal. It turns everything upside down and leads to precisely the opposite result to the one intended. It loses inevitably what it sets out to gain, and is after all a poor, foolish, tragic mode of life.

It destroys the freedom of the Spirit, because it operates by unconscious compulsion rather than by the higher integrative faculties of conscious choice, persistent goodwill and the inclusive tolerance of the other's faults which we know as love.

Aggressive, tyrannical, impatient and dismissive, the inferiority complex is the enemy of all good relationships, because it leads to the dismissal or destruction of the other, the lesser, the weak and the supposedly wrong. It is negative not positive, and does not know how to offer encouragement or nourishment to its weaker brother. It is unscientific and pseudo-moralistic in its approach to every problem, because it is concerned only with what ought, and never with what is, to be.

It leads inevitably to war, because or in spite of its purpose, which is to abolish conflict. It cannot bear the inferior position and must always assert its strength to dismiss the problem, to overwhelm the other. It can consider no one and nothing except the achievement of its own ends. Its only purpose is to be on top of a defeated enemy, but what defeated enemy will ever support their vanquisher? The inferiority complex demands peace compulsively by tyranny and so makes war inevitable. In victory it attempts to keep its enemy in submission or pretends that he exists no longer, and so in the end it makes its own defeat inevitable.

The inferiority complex is the exact opposite to the scientific method, the integrative principle of intelligent goodwill, common sense, good humor, Christianity and the way of proved efficiency.

As a deceptive ever-present plague it is the very Devil: and yet it is not evil in itself. But if evil were to need a tool always at hand, an instrument perfectly adapted to its evil purpose of exploiting, deceiving and destroying good, then I believe it can find all that it could ever hope for in the unconscious defense mechanisms of the inferiority complex.

Examples

Worry and anxiety. The commonest effect of fatigue is restlessness: of weakness, overactivity: and of impotence, compulsive attempts to obtain control over either the unruly problem or some innocuous substitute for it. Feeling that suspense is intolerable and the outcome uncertain, we are thrown into a state of nervous tension in which all the whirring wheels of body and mind are set in motion, especially if nothing can be done. Muscles and blood vessels, stomach, lungs, bladder or heart, any or all, may feel this active grip, this compulsive urge towards aggressive action, fight or flight. *We must do something about it*; so, with overcompensated energy and a useless compulsive effort, we rush round doing things which are more or less irrelevant to the real problem which prompts our feeling of inadequacy. The squirrel of anxious thought pursues the endless rigmarole of unpleasant possibilities which are neither here nor now, but out of reach of everything except this frantic squirrel in the mind which goes on and on, round and round, moralizing about what ought not to be.

Of course, if it is possible to find someone else, whether child, husband, doctor or politician, who will take steps for us to pursue and destroy the cause of the problem; and if it is also possible to find the cause, the scapegoat to take the blame, then the squirrel really has something—or someone!—to get his teeth into. Protective and dismissive activities can be spread over a very wide front indeed, with doctors and nurses, parsons and lawyers, teachers and politicians, government departments and their hordes of civil servants, all organized in the most efficient manner possible in order to plan the sickness out of the patient, the sin out of the sinner, the ignorance out of the child, and the enemy out of the world.

Stupidity is something special, thanks to the inferiority complex. It is not merely a negative state of not knowing, of ignorance. It is a *refusal* to admit the possibility of ignorance and the *assumption* of knowledge, all complete, instead. "Oh, yes, I know; or if not, I'll very soon find out. I understand, perfectly!" So the pupil cannot listen to the teacher, because he already knows all the answers; so the workman pays no attention to what the foreman says because he knows better how the job should be done; so the young girl, facing her adolescent entry into the vigorous drama of her life, heeds no warning because she knows there are no dangers that are not under her control; so the politician plans his blueprint world; so the scientific humanist proceeds on the assumption that all will one day be known, measured, ordered and controlled; and so man always hopes either to save himself, or to find a savior who will save him from himself. (At present, hope in this well-meaning but fruitless endeavor is centered upon the psychologist.)

Meanwhile, the hallmark of stupidity is that everything must be shown, known, dragged out of its discreet hiding-place and publicly talked about. Stupidity, in its anxiety to prove itself superior, does so by the destruction of all values whatsoever. Everything is dragged out and down to the level of the commonplace, where it can be discussed even by those who, knowing nothing about it, can always prove that this is only that, which is something so much less and so familiar, that we need not be afraid of it.

The stupid person must always know all the answers. There must never be a silent, empty space: and so the stupid person drags every detail to the fore in endless discussion of trivialities. What a bore he (more often she?) is! How we hate her and avoid her if we can, thus adding to her (in this case, perhaps, very proper?) feeling of inferiority, because she is indeed unwanted. But the more we avoid her, the more she is unconsciously compelled to find an appreciative listener. Yes, she is everybody's problem. But so is the inferiority complex.

In a previous generation the stupid people used to be inexpert maiden aunts and unemployed retired military types. They were harmless enough. But nowadays it is fashionable to find too many stupid people in the highest offices of government, and holding the most responsible seats of learning. They know everything; and, what is even more dangerous, they can always find someone to do everything with masterly efficiency.

In fact, the inferiority complex has now become organized and approved in a very big way indeed. It aims to rule the world and there seems to be a strong probability that it will do so, with results that can only be disastrous.

Some Everyday Results of the Inferiority Complex

These are innumerable, and I need hardly remind the reader of the overcompensations to which the small weak person of either sex is apt to resort—the greed, the self-advertisement, the bullying, the criticism, the lack of consideration for others whether in business or at home, the sexual irregularities, the bossiness, the unnecessary accumulation of wealth and this world's goods, the display of encyclopedic knowledge, the grasping and the pushing, the impatience and the restlessness, the moral tyranny and the resistance to change, which all add up to comprise the immeasurable burden of needless effort and counter-effort which we all must carry, even while we meet the problems which are proper to our daily lives. Together they add up to a colossal dead-weight upon life's grace, sweetness and goodwill, an immeasurable incubus to disturb our rest and rob us of our joy and peace.

Man's Spiritual Heritage

Wherever the spiritual quality of man is most sensitively exposed, it is at that point that the inferiority complex is most inclined to operate destructively. The spiritual quality of love in action is essentially an unknown quantity, unguarded, self-giving, weak, and it is therefore preeminently exposed to wanton destruction by this mechanically aggressive process.

Man's spiritual heritage is placed at an immediate disadvantage when confronted by the accumulated factors of opposition and resistance, which are characteristic of our world. The lamb is confronted by the lion, and David by Goliath. The intuitive or "psychic" types, the imaginative, sensitive and artistic types, are born tender. They are born undefended, easily strained, shocked and spoiled. They are relatively weak and that weakness can so easily be made relatively intolerable for them. They are the most fitting targets for the inferiority complex of others to work upon. They are therefore, particularly liable to develop the inferiority complex themselves, in self-defense, discarding the weakness of A and grasping at the strength of B, as they forsake "That other ground" for the sake of the accumulated protections of "This familiar field."

What we are "given" is a way of living in the spirit, so that it may be interpreted in the letter, and of living in the word, so that it may be made flesh. But when we are confronted by the resultant problem of weakness versus strength, love versus power, life versus the destruction of life; then if we are moved by the instinctive motive of self-defense, naturally and automatically, our way must be the way of the inferiority complex; namely, less of the spirit, more of the letter; less of the word, more of the flesh; less of love, more of power; less of life, more—no, not of death—but of mechanical movement. The preference over against death is for a state of mechanical inertia, for to the victim of the inferiority complex death is at least as intolerable as life.

The Jilted Child

The jilted child presents a similar response to the shock of love's withdrawal as does the jilted lover. Love is gentle, tender and forgiving; but the moment those qualities of love are intolerably hurt, offended, shocked, then they can only be withdrawn, their place being taken by their opposites in terms of power. These are a defensive-aggressive determination not to be hurt any more, but to hurt someone else instead, and thereby "get one's own back."

To want or need something, to experience hunger or desire, implies the admission that I have not what I want. If this admission of lack or weakness is felt to be intolerable, then, for our better self-defense upon this instinctive level, it seems that there must be no more desire. *I must never admit that I want anything.* Desire is the driving force of all creative life, but the jilted child must not admit desire. The jilted child must always feel as if she has everything she wants, and therefore can only behave as if she is afraid of losing it.

"I wanted mother, but she went away. I could not bear it." Automatically the defensive mechanism of the inferiority complex solves this problem. "I don't feel anything. I have all I want, so I don't want mother any more. But I will pay her out if I get the chance!" In phantasy, back of the mind somewhere, or concealed in the most secret chamber of the heart, the jilted child is utterly possessed of a phantasy-mother, as an unassailable secret possession. Therefore the jilted child cannot bear to be offered love: she cannot bear to be given anything, because she cannot bear to admit that she has not everything she wants already. To do so would be to lose control again, and that would be intolerable. So the jilted child must to the very end deny herself the love she needs so much, while at the same time she destroys the willing one who tries to feed her.

Alternatively, the jilted child may unconsciously elect to identify herself with her phantasy-mother and so give to others that which she wished another to have given her. Thus she becomes everyone's mother, and like a morbid but benevolent vacuum she collects a stream of ever-changing (but always unfaithful) neurotics, spendthrifts, drunkards and ne'er-do-wells, who each in turn exploit her compulsive generosity, giving little or nothing in return and gaining no deep advantage either. This is a case of grasping by unconscious substitution, and it brings no peace or lasting benefit, because its motive is always ulterior and self-centered. It is often confused with sublimation, but that word should imply the opposite motive, being rightly based on accept-ance of the loss, and willingness to do without the beloved object or person. Sublimation accepts the weakness and the loss: but the inferiority complex is based on the rejection of any such possibil-ity, and the rearrangement of the situation in such a way as to make its recurrence impossible. Sublimation and the inferiority complex are completely opposite to one another.

One such intolerably disappointed jilted child (aged forty-five) who was determined not to like or want anything ever again said, "I don't like raspberries. They have maggots in them." She also said, "I hate men. They are always horrid!" They had maggots in them, too. And all this needless rejection of possible enjoyment was because her mother was the disappointing maggot in her infancy, and not the juicy fruit, secure, to be enjoyed.

Adolescence

Adolescence is like a second birth as new ways open outwards into life. The spirit abounds, producing such unstable darts of light-ning to and fro, such tender ecstasies and such illimitable depths of dark depression. Here is much weakness confronted by great power, power confronted by frustration, and all mixed up with hope, fear and confusion. It is the perfect occasion, with some help from others who also possess it, for the development of an inferiority complex. But, say our guides, of course we know all the right answers to your questions, we will tell you all you ought to know! There are all the prizes, up at the top! There is the ladder, climb! Getting on all right? Successful? Well, there is plenty more ahead. Go higher yet. Just keep on keeping on, collecting more. This really is worth while! This is security!

So the adolescent's shy mysterious breath is soon changed for our synthetic, more successful, reconditioned air. So the adolescent's dark mysterious spaces are soon filled with good ideas and "knowl-edge" of the "facts" of "life." So adolescent fears are hurriedly soothed away, and all made safe and smooth, with the way marked miles ahead with tapes and milestones, where all the rest have plodded on before.

But why not pause, uncertain and afraid, upon the threshold of this mystery of life? Why not savour the essential terrifying fact that I am only one, so terribly alone, and they are many? Why not realize a little the dangerous beauty of experience, as we sample the magic of this sweet new air? Why be in such a hurry to catch these fledgling spiritual giants in some puny, ready-made, conventional trap? More frightened than their pupils are of life, some teachers seem to want to trap them into early graves.

But surely you and I are—or might be—adolescent, too? And we are living in an adolescent world, which is both self-destroying and resurgent with new life. It is a world in which no one has yet reached maturity. Meanwhile, as it always is in adolescence, our situation is indeed most difficult and uncertain. But we need to remind ourselves that we are not asked, here and now, to solve a problem in any final way. We are not asked to save ourselves or others from disaster. However clever we may be, however strong in battle or agile in escape, that way cannot provide the answer which we seek. All that is required is that we should experience our lot in space and time, experimentally. Each one can then provide his own solution, as he is involved in his own experience. It cannot be the only one. It cannot be the end. It need not even be successful, so long as we live and learn, as adolescents should.

Illness

The trouble with the inferiority complex is that it can never face all the facts; or, if it does so, there is an ulterior motive somewhere. In many ways it adds needless suffering to illness.

Firstly, it may influence the doctor's or nurse's choice of their profession. The career of medicine or nursing is one that offers power, and there are some who are drawn to it for that reason. It also offers knowledge, which is not only power over the other, but a means of seeing into the other: it satisfies curiosity. At their best, these motives may serve science and the community. But the motives of the inferiority complex are never at their best. They seek to remedy some past inadequacy rather than to effect a result in the present, and to benefit primarily the one who is most in need of help, the sufferer from the inferiority complex. The unconscious motive, however deeply it may be disguised, is to *get your own back by obtaining control over the other.* It may lead to much hard work and to the acquisition of great skill: it may appear as unselfish devotion; but it is not good for the patient, because the patient is not the primary object of consideration.

Secondly, it influences the doctor's attitude towards illness. It induces a habit of doing too much, of trying too hard and of assuming too much responsibility. Actually, the practice of medicine is an art and a mystery. But the inferiority complex will turn it into an opportunity to exercise power and show skill, albeit in the most scientific manner. It is always curious and instructive to watch the moral compulsions of these pseudo-scientific zealots in medicine. There *ought* to be a cause for the disease, the doctor *ought* to find it and the patient *ought* to be cured. In this pedantic pursuit of some hypothetical "cause" of a physical nature, the patient is in danger of being stretched upon a rack of "scientific" procedure, until the enemy has been located and drastically dismissed. Meanwhile, various innocent parts of his body may be offered up in sacrifice, under suspicion of being to blame for causing the condition. Having found a cause, science is satisfied, but too often the patient is sent home to suffer in exactly the same conditions which have been responsible, whether in whole or part, for developing the illness. Causes are nearly always many and rarely one. The patient is usually a responsible factor, but the inferiority complex will never treat him as such. And the doctor also is somewhat to blame for giving the impression that, unlike God, he can save the sufferer from himself. The only certain beneficiary is the chemical industry, which provides the immense quantities of drugs all good patients are ready to swallow in the cause of "science."

Thirdly, it influences the patient's attitude towards the doctor, who is mysteriously "deified," being given powers that belong to life itself and only secondarily to its servants. But it is intolerable for an inferiority complex to find itself in the grip of such an unknown process. Therefore, the illness must be brought under control and the doctor must do it. ("My doctor is so clever!") On the side of the patient, the inferiority complex thus exaggerates both phantasy and irresponsibility.

Fourthly, it influences the patient's attitude towards the illness itself, which he either ignores for too long, or else dramatically plunges into in a frantic effort to get attention and be rescued from the risk of imminent disaster. The patient is either unwilling to admit illness at all, because it would be an admission of intolerable weakness (this makes early treatment impossible) or else, having no faith in life and his own natural recuperative powers, and no knowledge whatever of how to take care of himself, he demands immediate "rescue," with or without appropriate sacrifice.

Illness is not an "act of God" and the doctor is no "savior." Medicine is not a debased mumbo jumbo, which would shame an African medicine-man. The cause of the trouble is almost certainly multiple, including many intangible personal factors of relationship. And healing is not by a magical use of power, but by a cooperative relationship and how they may be corrected.

Treatment

Prevention is easier than cure and something can be done to cause or cure an inferiority complex at almost every meeting. Naturally, we are disposed to put another person down in any way we can, as the easiest way to prove our own superiority. Such instinctive trends are more deeply rooted than we wish to realize, and slip out unawares.

There are two guiding principles in the prevention of an inferiority complex which may be called ACCEPTANCE and NOURISHMENT, or, when put together, "feed my lambs." By acceptance I mean taking the other as you find the other, without prejudice, and offering yourself to meet the other as you are, without frills; meeting the other on the level, in fact, as a person, respectfully, whether the other be child or employee, wife or patient. This means paying attention to the other, looking and listening and giving the other time to come through the resistances as a person. Like the other if you can, respect the other if you cannot, love the other if you do, hate the other if you must: but keep an eye on your own ulterior motives so that you at least know something about your own bias. The nourishment goes over to the other in the flow of your interest, attention and affection, as long as the motive is not only self-interest and self-love, which are bad nourishment, however disguised. (Of course, they usually are disguised, but we can judge the quality of the nourishment in the relationship by its results.) A good sense of humor—or a sense of good humor—will do more to establish a nourishing relationship than much piety and unselfish goodwill.

Children, especially, need encouragement with opportunity, and to have as little explained as possible, in order that they may find out for themselves. ("Let me do it!" "No, darling, let Mummy do it, you take such a long time!") It is to be remembered that in the world of levels, higher and lower, older and younger, children are always in the weaker position and that they can easily be made intolerably uncomfortable by an adult who has (and most adults have) an inferiority complex. For those in authority over children, "Let them down lightly" is a good motto to remind us that they are experiencing their fall.

Perhaps the most important single factor in avoiding the inferiority complex in children is by reversing the usual attitude to faults and failures, from the negative one of bad marks and threats of punishment to the positive one, "Let's see what we can learn from that." Faults and failures are either to be feared and avoided (or covered up) as being a cause of deprivation of affection and approval; or else they are to be sought out, studied and used as stepping-stones to deeper understanding. Our mistakes and disappointments are kindly teachers if we are wise, but an intolerable threat if we are over-sensitive to correction. (The same applies to any illness: it is not something bad to be got rid of, but a teacher— if we are wise!)

We are all children in the sense that we find life hard and need to learn. We all need respect and straightforward encouragement from our fellows. If we could encourage one another more, life would be much easier, happier, and even healthier, too.

In *women* the problem of weakness is especially constant. They need an ever-flowing stream of nourishment. Therefore, husbands, praise your wives and say it with flowers more often than you do! Women are realists who feel the strain of life in a way that men can never know. They need a build-up all the time. Their proper nourishment, of course, is love, but they will not take that for granted. They want continual evidence and repeated proof to reassure their failing confidence.

Today a woman's greatest difficulty is to avoid fatigue. It is fatigue which gets her intolerably down, and then it is too often only her inferiority complex which gets her up again, but in such a way as to waste more energy and cause more fatigue, in increasingly vicious circles.

Curing ourselves. The commonly advocated way of cure for an inferiority complex is as negative and futile as the disease itself. It is particularly popular in America, where hope still thrives undismayed along with every kind of religious cult that offers the Promised Land Now. "There is no problem and there is no pain. Only believe and you shall receive. Knock and enter. All is yours." Yes, that is true up to a point. But we have inherited too much history, both our own and other people's, to find life so cozy now. In more than one way we are the children of the fall, but what we are suffering from is no far-off divine event. Our inheritance and present problem is the fruit of man's inferiority complex, so tortuously repeated, so willfully moralized and so disastrously misunderstood. To escape into compensatory phantasies of omnipotence is to repeat our usual gramophone record of refusal to be what and where we are, according to the usual rules of the inferiority complex.

The pertinent question for each to ask himself now is, "Can I, or can I not, save myself?" The answer is diagnostic: if I believe that I can save myself then I have an inferiority complex because I cannot bear to admit the truth, which is that I can do no such thing.

I suggest that we need to strike a much less optimistic note and to say something like this, in so far as it is true now: "I am weak and sick, confused, muddle-headed, and wrong-willed. I have done wrong and caused great trouble. I cannot save myself and yet I am confronted by the urgent threat of ever-pressing disaster."

I believe it would be better for us all if we could stop rushing about, saving ourselves and other people, and sit still for a moment to consider this situation. So let me gather myself into this chair, into this skin of mine, into my place in this world situation, *concentratedly*, single-pointedly, centrally. *Now I am in here*, reincarnate in my problem-situation, born again, as weak as ever, dependent on so many for so much.

(Now don't grumble that there is not enough time, or that you have an important appointment elsewhere. Stay where you are and pay attention. And please note that nothing could be more modern or scientific than that I should ask you to pay attention, to every factor in your situation, avoiding none, seen or unseen.)

This is called *detachment* (also called "acceptance") and requires *patience* (also called "suffering"). It requires *courage* (also called "love" and "goodwill"). The next step is your *personal interpretation*, what it all means to you now, in the light of past experience and future purpose (this is also called "understanding"). The next step is *what you can do about it*; but that needs a pause for further consideration before you make your plunge.

But do you think that you know all about it, so that you feel sure you can do exactly what you want? Have you got it all taped so that the result is a foregone conclusion? Are you completely in control of the situation, assured of success, as hopeful as can be? Because, if so, your inferiority complex is still with you, and therefore in every crisis you will behave accordingly.

It is *not* true: you do *not* know; you are *not* in control: you can *not* be sure. There is an uncertain factor in life and persons, which is not present in the world of things which you can control. It is this third mysterious factor which I have called the "C" factor, which is in the quality of the relationship itself. It is something that happens between you and your work or between you and the other. It is something given. Sometimes it is called "luck" and sometimes "accident," but it is "real" and "true," and therefore part of the whole picture for our scientific matter-of-fact friends to consider. And it is something more, something added, over and above the contributed effort of either partner in the struggle. It is the "moral" factor.

When once this new dimension of experience is gained, a curious reversal of values is discovered, in which the highest becomes lowest and the lowest highest: and in which the highest is discovered in the lowest and the lowest in the highest. Values turn topsy-turvy and appear to be interchangeable, during a process of demoralization which precedes a new remoralization. This is what has been called "conversion."

The effect is wholesome, but it sets a problem. It is sad but true that those without this fell disease, or who have been cured of it, are apparently at the mercy of the victims of it. They seem to offer a perpetual temptation to be exploited by those in whom the anxiety of the power-lust is still paramount. It looks as if there is no peace for any until there is peace for all. It behooves those without an inferiority complex to see what can be done for those who are thus infected, because if they are not saved from themselves they may yet destroy our world.

Curing others is perhaps largely covered already by what has been said under the heading of "prevention." In general, it comes under the heading of "education," especially when that is understood as "nourishment." It is our job to nourish one another. But it is also our job, I think, to see that we are not consumed, exploited, or destroyed by parasites who, in their over-anxiety to stick to a good thing, are quite prepared to take advantage of our indifference to power.

It is certainly very unfortunate that the inferiority complex should be especially rampant in those who are in high places and in authority over us. It is obvious why it should be so, but what can we do, if not for them (their case is usually hopeless!) at least to spare ourselves? I can only suggest some principles of bare advice. At least, diagnose their illness, but do not pity them, because they do not need it. Then stick to your real task, whatever that may be. Pursue your main objective with concentrated will and right relationship, and do not be put off by blundering critics who try to interfere. Trust yourself and take praise where you can earn it. If blame is due, accept it willingly and learn from your mistakes. If blame is not due, but comes from someone else's inferiority complex, let it flow like water off a duck's back. It does not hurt you unless you hurt yourself by trying to avoid it. And sometimes it pays effectively to play at jujitsu. When blamed for a little do not defend yourself, but accept a great deal more. Of course, you are the greatest sinner in the world—and laugh it off! Never resist an inferiority complex in another: it only makes it worse. But do not let it get you down. Stand up for yourself.

Nations are notoriously touchy in matters appertaining to their honor. They all seem to have an inferiority complex in varying degrees, especially in any particularly difficult situation. How should we proceed? Of course, it is nothing to do with us, really. We are only the people, the voters. We do not count. Or do we? We are inferior people, common people, ordinary people, just people. Do we count—or not? We are many and we shall count the more if we can count as one.

Which one? Certainly not this one, or that one, if they are you or me, one nation or another, or even East or West. Certainly not if we are bound to any "ism" whatsoever, for they are, each and every one, all born and nourished out of an inferiority complex. All factions and cults, even when they are as large as nations, are stiff with a false moral superiority. This is even true of the great world religions.

The only truly international power is the power of THAT OTHER in us, which is the power of the Spirit. It is not yours, not mine, nor any man's, especially. It is neither black nor white. It is the common birthright, the source and seed, the light and life itself, of all mankind. It functions in every relationship, and its outcome cannot be bound or foretold, although it can be destroyed.

There is no hope for the inferiority complex of mankind unless it puts its trust in THAT.

CHAPTER 27

Compulsion Neurosis

The Ploughman and the Child

Look at this great field. Fortunately, the ploughman is a patient man. His horses must have great endurance, too, as they pull their plough up and down the seemingly endless furrows, from early morning until their long day's work is done. In time, the field is ploughed, but then the seed must be sown, which is another tedious operation. Time passes. The seeds sprout and grow until the harvest ripens, when it is cut and gathered. Nature cannot he hurried or deceived and, from beginning to end, the long processes of ripening require time. The ploughman is aware of Nature's law, and does not flog his slowly plodding team. Slow step by step, gradually and continuously, the work is done until the job is honestly completed. Such is the living law of Nature's invisible clock, according to the moving hands of which we have to learn to be in Time. Such is the law which wise men follow, as they care for the heart of the field. In turn, they know that it will care for them, if only they are obedient and patient. In time, so much is given: more, indeed, than we have any right to expect in return for our labor, however great and deserving that may have been.

Such patient plodding on in rich expectancy is all very well for the ploughman, who is gently rooted and nourished in the comfort of his native soil. But what of the child, whose horses are untamed, whose field is steep, stony, and apparently unbounded, and whose every moment is beset by impatient interference and unwise advice? Confronted by a rock in the path of his too slowly moving team, yet urged to carry on, what is the child to do? He sees others far ahead and is told that he is bad to lag so far behind; and yet he is stuck there, confronted by his impotence to move

From *Mysterious Marriage: A Study of the Morality of Personal Relationships and Individual Obsessions*

that rock. He feels a sense of overwhelming insecurity. He fears lest approval, which is his proof of love, will be withdrawn. He sees the distant end in the far corner of the field and thinks he would be safer there. And so he leaves the place in time where he belongs. He leaves his horses and his plough behind the rock, to run as swiftly as he can to reach the distant end, where safety and approval seem to be. And there he sits, immovable, without his horses and plough, his task completed although it has hardly been begun. But he is split in two, divided between his premature advancement and his retreated self. He is related neither to himself, nor to his proper place in space and time. Obsessed by anxiety and the burden of his unfinished task, he feels he must do something to occupy his restlessness and ease his pricking conscience. So he spends his time removing innumerable stones from the endless furrows of his mind.

The continuity of that child's stream of experience has been destroyed, because he was confronted too soon by an insurmountable obstacle. His libido has become "fixated," as we say, behind that rock; and he is fixated, too, by his "identification" with the "good object" of having reached his end. He is "dissociated" or split off from the driving force within himself, as he is also separated irreparably from his companions in the field of life. He is "obsessed" with his insoluble problem and is compelled unconsciously to solve it over and over again, in his own mind, although he is no longer in touch with his reality. His will is split. Escaping time for good he has become its prisoner, condemned to the ceaseless treadmill of compulsively reiterative acts.

This is compulsion neurosis. There are many such broken and dissociated lives, varying in the degree of their compulsive behavior and yet overwhelmed by their unsolved, unconscious, problems. They cannot get on with the job now, because the continuous stream of their experience was interrupted then, early in their infancy. For the rest of their lives, some more, some less, they are compulsively engaged in trying to solve the very problem which they have always been determined to avoid. With their lives thus irrelevantly absorbed, the exercise of their compulsion does not leave them much energy for living.

Growth, Time, and the Process of Becoming

It is never possible to understand a deviation from the normal, except by contrast with the normal process itself. We should realize, of course, that we shall never fully understand the meaning of such words as life, time and growth, but there are certain features of these processes of which we need to remind ourselves, because they differ when we come to consider the abnormal state of compulsion neurosis. The living process of growth in time is flowing, continuous and rhythmical; but the condition of the sufferer from compulsion neurosis is fixed, interrupted and split. The normal process of growth is effortless, whereas the life of the obsessional is a constant conflict of effort, in which no important problem can be solved. And finally, whereas in normal life a man can freely choose, at least within certain limits, what he will do, in compulsion neurosis, as the name implies, the sufferer is perpetually driven to perform reiterative acts which, even if he thinks that he was free to choose, were in fact unconsciously motivated and beyond his capacity to refuse.

In order to bring before the reader's eye the two contrasted pictures of the normal process of living and the abnormal condition of compulsion neurosis, I have drawn figure 28, on p. 444, called "In Between." In the normal process of becoming, the rhythmical continuity of growth in time is uninterrupted. The rise and fall, the outward flow and inward return of activity and rest, of waking and sleeping, follow one another, easily and naturally, like breathing. In the diagram, I have suggested that the life of action, with its unconscious choice in the exterior world at B, is derived from, and related to, deeper levels of desire and awareness, through which, like pools, the stream of life ("libido") mysteriously flows. Then, out of the pool of awareness of which I AM is the center (A), there springs, through the range of differentiated feelings (C), the energetic Will, which makes its selective impact on the outer world with its appropriate action (B) on the conscious level. The flow of experience passes back as the feelings are again stirred and it is on this intermediate level (C) that the meaning of the experience is realized, and the continuity of purpose sustained. (In terms of the "tree of life," the roots of I AM are watered by the

443

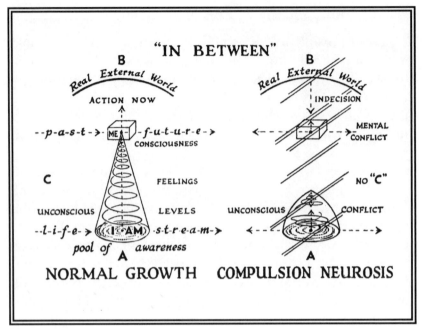

Figure 28 "In Between"

concurrent streams of the libido, the stem of the tree is sustained by the will, and the growing point or "shoot" is the action which materializes in the "real external" world.) Thus the activity of our behavior is generated on two planes: on the one hand by our relationships and needs in the exterior (objective) world and, on the other, by our nature and feelings in the interior (subjective) world.

In compulsion neurosis, the field of force (C) is broken, and the state of vital tension is split between two extremes, each of which has become fixated and therefore must be compulsively repeated. It is as if the intermediate field C, which is the level of our *experience of the relationship,* is missing. Instead, there is a fixation on the world of exterior good objects ("identification") and another fixation at a regressive (unconscious) level, with further identifications on good "images." The "timing" and the "meaning" of experience are destroyed, and a split ("dissociation") occurs on each of the three levels, A, C and B. There is "identification" and "dissociation," but there is no relationship. The bridge is broken and the field of experience is irrevocably split.

Normal development, or growth in time, is a process of being born and born again, ever onwards, as we move along life's time-track. We move forward constantly and continuously, as we experience a gradual change in situation, passing through ring after ring of circumstance, like a train through a tunnel. In this sense, we are always experiencing our new conditions as if we were still children enwombed within our mother, but born onwards through our changing circumstances within which we have our limited freedom to choose and move.

By contrast, the state of compulsion neurosis is completely earthbound or "mother-fixated," with destruction or non-existence of the father-principle of the emergent will. There is no trinity, no time, and no relationship. A state of unity with the other is absolute, final and compulsive. There is no rhythmical blending of A, B and C in the dance of life-and-death. There is A alone: or B alone: or C alone, but each one, although cut off from the other, must also be identified with, and enjoy the fullest benefit of complete possession of, the other.

Energy, instead of flowing gently through its needed circles and cycles of resistances and relationships, is unbound and uninhibited. It must therefore be checked (repressed) as violently as it is in danger of being released. Similarly, the emotions of sufferers from this unhappy state are not like normally balanced feelings which experience gradual flow and change. Emotions in compulsion neurosis are always final, absolute, all or nothing, moving with violence, untimely, or as violently fixed. Thus "love" is an infinite possessiveness, an absolute identification with the other; and "fear" is not a pleasant trembling in the pit of the stomach. It is a final state of devastation and annihilation, an utter and intolerable panic from which a certain reiterated compulsive activity is the needed—and only—relief.

Compulsion Neurosis

Definition: Compulsion neurosis occurs as an *unconscious defensive reaction* against extreme insecurity, unendurable conflict or excessive strain. Its purpose is to provide an immediate solution by escape (regression), to prevent the experience recurring, and to obtain instead a state of absolute and fixed security. Its method is to destroy the normal affective system of relationship, and get rid of the "bad object" (dissociation) and to obtain instead a state of permanent attachment (fixation). Feelings become attached to good and bad objects by identification, which therefore become obsessions. The effect is to set up certain compulsive reiterative habits, which are unconsciously determined for their ritual or symbolic value, and not related to the real or conscious situation. Frustration of such unconscious impulses causes extreme and increasing anxiety and guilt, until this can be alleviated by performing the necessary compulsive activities.

Certain characteristics of the compulsive process require our special attention. Force takes the place of freedom of relationship, because both good and bad objects must be completely under control. The normal, gentler energy of gradual growth gives place to the instantaneous tyranny of compulsive aggression. Energy, instead of being a spontaneous natural flow, must be forced. This leads to fatigue, which is a common and inevitable symptom of compulsion neurosis.

As I have already remarked, true relationship is impossible in compulsion neurosis. Identification is not a true relationship, because there can be no subject-object relationship, if the subject is identified with the object. For instance, the verbal statement "I want it" denotes a normal subject-object relationship, where the verb represents the dynamic bridge across the space between the two. Where there is no space, there can be no bridge. Where there is no verb, there can be no dynamic, no movement and no "life." Where subject and object are identified, there can only be fixation. Where suspense and uncertainty are intolerable, there can be no enjoyment of the "flow" of life. Nor can there be any experience of the Spirit as a relationship, because its fruits of love, peace and joy can never be won by the compulsive means of identification and fixation. Faith is therefore impossible: even if it be called faith, it cannot be other than a fixed, compulsively unshakable belief (fanaticism).

There must always be unsolved conflicts and inherent instability in the mechanical process of compulsion neurosis. It cannot provide a true solution for any problem, because it is only an attempt to provide escape from an intolerable situation by finally dismissing it. Identification always implies dissociation, and there can never be one without the other. The attempt at dismissal of the bad object therefore implies, to put the matter in its crudest, simplest terms, either murder or suicide: it is "murder" if the bad object is outside, "suicide" if it is inside, the self. But such an aggressive-dismissive attitude is in itself regarded as a "bad object," so that it also must be dismissed or repressed, to provide a state of absolutely proven and inviolable innocence. The subject of compulsion neurosis is therefore constantly trying to cut off— compulsively—one-half of every dilemma, or one-half of every vicious circle, thereby making it more vicious still, in an infinite regress of compulsively reiterative, protective-dismissive activities. The state of intolerable suspense or "conflict" is brought to a conclusion, therefore, not so much by the simple process of declaring war, as by a final attempt (in the most modern fashion!) at an instantaneous total destruction of the enemy, which must at the same time be as complete as it is final, and as morally approved as it is inevitably ordained.

Indeed, it is the essential nature of compulsive neurosis that, although the activities are compulsive, being mechanically and unconsciously motivated, they must always be rationalized as right, moralized as good, and brought to an immediate conclusion as inevitable.

Mechanism

Confronted by a situation of intolerable shock or strain, the victim of compulsion neurosis experiences a split or "fracture" in the system of affective relationships. It is as if the hyphen of his subject-object relation snaps, so that the bridge of his previous means of communication rotates, to become an impassable barrier, a closed door. The tension is eased, but it is at the expense of the life of the organism, which has been dropped to a lower level, or dimension, of experience. As a result of this fracture, his energy has been split into two unrelated systems, part becoming identified with the outer (objective) and part with the inner (subjective) world. The same split is repeated on all levels, with the dual purpose of obtaining, at

447

one and the same time (immediately), both a state of identification with the "good," and of dissociation from the "bad," object.

The effect of this condition of unrelatedness (i.e. split or fracture) is to eliminate the spontaneous and gentle flow of energy in its normal growth through patient time-relations, substituting compulsion by interference of exterior force for the normal process of experience. Compulsion neurosis compels its victims to jump to conclusions, to fix the possession of good objects, to provide a stop-gap for every space, an answer for every question (if possible, before it can be asked), a scapegoat to be blamed for every failure (it must never be my fault), an enemy to be utterly destroyed, and a moral mantle to be cast over all, in order to provide absolution and justification for all such actually "immoral" (because unrelated) behavior.

The incentive in this condition is supplied by exterior *compulsion*; desired objects must be obtained instantly by force, instead of gradually by growth (this type of *aggression* is pathological and must be violent); relationships are destroyed (*dissociation*); escape into safety is provided (*regression*); approval is assured (*freedom from guilt and anxiety* must be obtained with absolute certainty); all movement ceases (*fixation*); the values and meanings of inner and outer (subjective-objective, unconscious-conscious) worlds become confused (*projection*), while possession of "good" objects (*identification*) is secured with complete moral justification (*rationalization*).

Compulsion neurosis affects groups and nations as well as individuals, with similar results. In different individuals, the system of affective relationships (feelings, or degree of psychic sensitivity, or being what parents sometimes call "highly-strung") possesses a variable quality of elasticity. So also in larger groups, the same unconsciously protective, aggressive dismissive, habits of irrational, but consciously rationalized, conduct occur. The larger and less coherent the group which is required to be sustained in the relationship, the less is their integrity and the more "touchy" they become, i.e. the more susceptible to the development of compulsion neurosis. On the international level, also, we must be right and they must be wrong. The elasticity of international relationships is so terribly sensitive and unstable that resort to war, in spite of its apparent madness, still seems to those engaged in it, on either side, always to be right, always to be inevitable, and always to be the will of God.

In its paradoxical attempt to dismiss the cause of conflict, war is the most classic of all symptoms of compulsion neurosis, whether within the individual or between nations. It will continue to deceive us, until the symptoms of compulsion neurosis on every level are clearly recognized as those of an insidiously destructive disease, which is fatal not only to every human virtue, but even to Life itself.

Causes

Earth-bound: There would not be much point in my offering a somewhat detailed clinical study of this illness to the general reader unless we were all to some extent infected by it. It is my belief that a tendency to compulsion neurosis is part of our human heritage. To be born at all, as separate individuals, is to be born both bound and blind, however normal we may seem to be. Discovery of our self-bound limitations comes later, if it comes at all, when we may be "born again."

If it is a true surmise that man is incarnate spirit, so that we are indeed composed of THAT in this-here-now, then it is not to be wondered at that, having made so good a job of our incarnation and become completely identified with our earth-bound state, we should have forgotten whence we came. Here now, it seems, THAT is only this; and I am only what I seem to be to myself. This false simplicity, this erroneous unification, is further proved for us by the way in which we make use of the so-called scientific or objective method of consciousness, which has neither the means nor the will to recognize the reality of the mysterious, immeasurable, indwelling factor, "A." It is suggested, therefore, that the diagram on p. 444 is not only a picture contrasting freedom from this illness with its occurrence. It is also a picture of us all in our fallen, broken state, in which we have lost contact with the life-giving influence of that original other state, from which we are descended.

Identified with earth, we now behave as if we were its only competent rulers. We attempt to control all things, and persons, too, as if we all must depend on man, and man's initiative, without any other intervening factor. In our world, there is not much respect for the spacious, patient Trinity of gently growing and mysterious relationships. In our world, the compulsion of an impatient tyranny rules instead, proudly enforcing its moralized conclusions against the unrecognized opposition of its ignored opponent, which is life.

But however this dubious question of our human origins may be answered, we are surely obsessed (identified) with our earthboundness in another, and very important, way. I refer to our relationship with our own past experience. During our lives, it is inevitable that we should become time-encrusted. Like tortoises, we acquire something of a shell, derived from past experiences, to protect us from the discomforts of our uncertain future. It is the penalty of increasing age that we should thus have more past in store, but less future in reserve; and therefore a more negative, less positive, approach to life. Both birth and age, therefore, bear their share of the responsibility for our infection with this sickness of the soul itself, which it is our responsibility in these pages to reveal, discuss and perhaps to find some relief from, by better understanding it.

For the first nine months of life, that is to say up to the age of weaning, there is no actual separation between mother and child other than the physical one. As far as the child is concerned, the mother is still regarded as an extension of itself. At first, therefore, these two are indeed identified with one another, and to this extent, compulsion neurosis may be regarded as the normal state of earliest infancy. As soon as the infant recognizes its own separate identity, however ("hullo, monkey"), it moves into a higher dimension of experience, in which relationship first becomes possible. It moves from its first condition of requiring attention, to being able to pay attention, both to itself and its surrounding world. If the craving for attention persists after this earliest phase of normal identification with the mother, as it so often does, it is evidence of the existence, to some degree, of the condition of compulsion neurosis. Such a child (at any age) has not reached the self-reflective stage of self-awareness, and is therefore unable either to bear, or experience, objective criticism. To be criticized at all means disapproval and that love has been withdrawn, which is intolerable.

Heredity. Apart from such general considerations, a tendency towards this illness may be undoubtedly inherent. Characteristically, it occurs in its severest forms where the family history is bad, i.e. where there have been sufferers from "mental" and "nervous" disorders, or instability of character amongst the members of previous generations. It is particularly likely to occur in the children of families in which there is a history of prolonged alcoholism in either of the parents. Careful inquiry about the parents and their forebears will prove that the obsessional trend can usually be discovered running back from generation to generation. It is as if the child is born with an inherent lack of vital elasticity, a lack of, or broken "spring," a tendency to clutch and clamor, to feel excessive anxiety and to attach himself too firmly to persons and objects in his immediate environment. Instead of *flowing* out and on, the life of such a one will tend to *stick*: either forwards on some grown-up virtuous goal, or backwards in a mood of regressive dependence, or both.

Such hereditary tendencies are, of course, further strengthened by the fact that the child must also experience, from an early age, the obsessional trends of the persons in his environment. Environment thus reinforces the preexistent inclinations of heredity.

Acquire. Compulsion neurosis occurs most readily, of course, in those who are both predisposed to it, and where circumstances also impose too great a strain upon a child's development. Combined, the two factors together cause a split in the vital energy, which falls back from the challenge of experience at the same time that it clutches at the outward evidence of safety and approval. Compulsion neurosis is a consequence of unbalance, excessive strain and impossible contrast in a child's early experience. It is a proof of an excessive burden having been imposed on immature shoulders, with insufficient support.

Its incidence may be either gradual and hardly noticeable, or sudden, when it is due to some extreme shock. If gradual, the child's system of affective relationships ("feelings") is split by an unbridgeable chasm between two variably repeated extremes: e.g. a soft mother and stern father, the thunder of whose voice and presence perhaps claimed unneeded reinforcement from divine authority; a mother who was exceedingly fond at times, but whose moods varied through cold indifference to calculated cruelty; or a mother who hated her husband and poured her compensatory affection on the child, who, however, also loved her father. Indeed, any situation in a child's life which is not capable of being emotionally spanned, must set up an insoluble conflict, due to the impossible ambivalence of the feelings which has been generated.

Sudden shock, however, acts like a fracture on a bone: the structure of an invisible anatomy is split, or torn open, as the feelings are sundered. In such a case, in a most literal sense, the "heart" (in inverted commas, meaning the affective system, which is different from, but surely as real as, the physical organ of the same name) is broken. The vital elastic, subject to too great a strain, snaps in the middle and springs back to its attachments at either end. Such shocks may be the obvious ones of extreme disaster and sudden death, or the inexpressible terror of a child when her drunken father chased her mother round the kitchen with a knife in his hand. But such shocking domestic dramas, serious as they may be, are on the adult level of tragedy. To a child, tragedy of an even more shocking kind may lurk in an event which an adult would pass by as if nothing untoward had happened. Adults are curiously insensitive about the deeper meanings and feelings of childhood, when sensitive antennae are first exploring moral values in a deeply confusing world. A sudden clash of contrast, a contemptuous laugh where loving approval was expected, indifference about some little gift, a lack of feeling in regard to some object deeply beloved by the child but obviously worthless in itself, may cause a minor or major fracture in these subtle springs of sensitivity.

Briefly, the causes most frequently found are intolerable insecurity and sudden shocks to self-esteem. The moment of fracture, when the strain was too great to bear any longer, is sometimes experienced as a definite sensation of a "click" in the brain.

Symptoms

In severe cases, the symptoms may be so all-absorbing as to make attention to the normal requirements of life impossible. Hours at a time may be taken up in such reiterative behavior as compulsive handwashing, finger or face picking, touching or avoiding certain objects, fear of contamination by germs, worrying whether something has or has not been done, endlessly repeating the same act, doubting whether the gas was turned off or on, counting, or repeating certain phrases. There is always an unconscious compulsion that must be obeyed. Some protective course of behavior must be repeated again and again without apparent reason, or else the patient experiences intolerable anxiety and guilt, with an agony of impending disaster, which may be accompanied sometimes by symptoms of acute physical discomfort, until the unconscious requirements have been satisfied. The state of satisfaction does not last for long and then the whole performance must be gone through again. When the compulsion is perpetual, the disability may be complete.

It is important to emphasize that the peculiar characteristic of all symptoms in the compulsion neurosis is the same. It is, in fact, the primary characteristic of the disease itself, namely unrelatedness. There is therefore no spontaneity, no flow and no natural timing; there is no natural selection of an inevitably right action, but instead a compulsive reiteration of some irrelevant activity. There is no sense of proportion and no sense of humor. The mind is therefore filled, to the exclusion of all else, with a certain dissociated idea, an idea cut off from other related ideas, an idea that stands utterly and absolutely alone. Such an idea is called an obsession. (Hence the term obsessional neurosis, which is an alternative description of this illness.) Obsessions are inevitably compulsions, as they are bound to achieve good objects, and to dismiss bad objects. (These are called respectively fetishisms and phobias, which are again always objects dissociated from their proper context, or unrelated parts by themselves and therefore out of all context and proportion.)

The hidden significance of such reiterative acts may or may not be of importance in the psychotherapeutic treatment of the case. For instance, handwashing is generally associated with an unconsciously derived sense of guilt, as in the classic case of Lady Macbeth. But to point this out to the patient does not in itself have any beneficial effect in enabling him to control the obsessional activity, because the compulsive behavior is always unconsciously, not consciously, motivated.

We must therefore consider the problems of unconscious motivation and subconscious meaning.

Symbolism and Unconscious Motivation

Indeed, symbolism is at the very root of our problem of understanding, not only the illness of compulsion neurosis, but ourselves. It may appear strange at first that the word symbol, meaning a conventional sign, should come from two Greek words which mean "to throw together." Perhaps its origin in far-distant time sprang from the reading of runes and oracles. Meaning was then derived from the magical significance of the way objects lay in relation to one another, such as lines in writing, patterns in sand, or the flight of birds in the sky. Be that as it may, it is certain that all language has sprung from this way of capturing and repeating the agreed meaning of a certain pattern, or "thrown-togetherness." A relationship of simpler parts to form more complex relations, amongst themselves or with other groups, is the basis of all language. So meaning is devised, and so we are accustomed to express ourselves, both in the spoken and the written word. A certain thrown-togetherness, it is agreed, means something. What it means to us is what we "feel" about it. And what we feel about it determines what we are going to do about it. Thus certain objects such as national flags, religious symbols such as the crucifix, or magical symbols such as the cup and the sword, have an agreed common affective value which is of great power in evoking emotion and subsequent mass-action. All poetry depends upon this power of evoking latent meaning, to touch and move us with its mystery.

But in its ordinary everyday use, if meaning is to be valid in any civilized community and in a socially possible sense, symbolism must obviously depend upon its thrown-togetherness, or relationship, within its social context. It must link us with other meanings, which may be associated with other people's sense of different values, with our own history yesterday and our needs tomorrow. Other nations have other flags. Other religions have other codes and customs. Other times have other manners, other magic. It is by our capacity to span these gulfs of time, place and meaning, that we prove not only our intelligence, but our capacity to live with, as we are thrown together with, our neighbors near and far.

But in compulsion neurosis the bridge is broken, the articulation is extinct, the tenuous thread of living relationship has snapped. The parts are no longer thrown together, integratively and positively. They are thrown apart, disintegratively and negatively. From this fact, the meaning of many words must change, if we are to understand the inwardness of this disease.

Hatred, Guilt, and Panic

The vital force, having thus relapsed disintegratively, compels some reiterative activity. The unreasonable habit of constantly repeated handwashing is typical of such an unconsciously motivated activity. The patient is sunk, lost and smothered, in an act and a value that has no relationship either with his own life or with his past experience. His compulsive behavior has gripped him in a vice, and he is like a prisoner immured in the cement of his unconscious motive.

During treatment, the analytical interpretation of the patient's earliest experiences in childhood and infancy may disclose mother-fixation, father-fear and subjective loads of incalculable guilt. The relationship of such childish levels of experience to adult consciousness may in some cases be liberative and beneficial, even to the degree of successfully releasing the patient from the compulsive pressure of his repeated acts. But unfortunately for our therapeutic endeavors so patiently pursued, this need not be so. Indeed, it is not usually so successful; for the whole system of the patient's early affective experiences may be only a secondary effect of his own innate predisposition, and not a primary cause. The compulsive trend may itself be the primary cause. The mother-fixation and the father-fear, the guilt and the anxiety, the identifications and dissociations, may all be but evidence of the patient's primary obsessional disposition. Then, after all our analytical efforts, we are still left with that. Indeed, we should expect our problem to begin on that level, if our treatment is ever to be effective.

As we change in ourselves, so meanings change for us. It is no use looking up the meaning of words such as hatred, guilt or panic in the dictionary, if we ever hope to understand the nature of this complaint, from the standpoint of those who suffer from it. In compulsion neurosis, we are not dealing with normal hatred, guilt and panic, but with what each word means to its victim in his fractured (dissociated) state.

Hatred is of the very essence of compulsion neurosis. But whereas hatred normally allows good and bad to exist in one ring, as it were, within the normal swing of the pendulum, in the diseased condition of compulsive neurosis, the purpose is to cut the ring itself in two, to fix the pendulum so that it can never swing back, and then to get rid of the other forever, so that they may never be "thrown together" again. There is thus no bridge and the communicating gate has closed. This is dissociation. Behind that shut door, we are identified with the good, the beloved object. But there is no relationship.

So far, so good. But it is extremely difficult to sustain any such situation for long, for various self-evident reasons, but mainly because it can never be true. For life is not like that, with black and white so clearly, so absolutely and eternally divided. Besides, to feel hateful is intolerable. The feeling of hatred is itself a "bad object," and must therefore be dealt with, as all "bad objects" are, by dissociation.

Guilt. It is clearly to be understood that the whole point and purpose of this illness is to prove that the patient is, and must be, "good."

The obsessional attitude to guilt is therefore quite peculiar and most unnatural. Indeed, naturally, I am guilty, in the sense that I am separated from perfection by my imperfection. In that sense I can freely admit that I am a sinner. Quite honestly, I can see no possibility of ever becoming a saint, not even in a thousand years at the rate of progress which I have shown so far. But, in any case, was there ever a true saint who did not see his sin as sorrowfully inevitable? Thus good humor sees tolerantly not only its own faults, but those of others, too. Good humor measures up from below, and, not expecting too much, is surprised by the amount of good which it finds lurking in the shadowed heart of man. Good humor encourages slow growth from darkness into light, from less to more, from part to whole. Good humor has a wholesome way of life which watches pendulums swing and hands go round the clock, seasonably.

But the obsessional attitude to guilt is not like that. *I must not be guilty: you must take away my guilt immediately: I must be good, now.* Thus both the guilt to be dismissed and the good to be achieved are dissociated, guilt and good. They are thrown apart, not thrown together. They are utterly and totally opposed in principle and practice, therefore, not only from common sense and all good humor, but also from Christ's teaching. Yet they have become most insidiously prevalent in the conventional preaching and practice of the Christian religion.

Panic. In this condition, panic is not fear magnified. It is fear in a vacuum, in a state of infinite regress. It is fear avoided endlessly in an eternal, spaceless void. It is a fact of experience for those who suffer from it, but it is not a fact in any positive sense. It is a consequence of a denial which has been negatively denied, because the experience of panic is intolerable and must therefore be dismissed as a bad object. If hell exists, then this state of panic agony must be worse than hell, because it is a state of utter non-existence.

Yet it is the common characteristic of the compulsive mood and behavior. It explains why those sufferers must return again and again to their compulsive acts. This rising power of panic to the nth degree, which is not ordinary fear, is the driving force behind them.

I hope that what I have said about hatred, guilt and panic may have helped the reader to experience some sympathy and understanding for those recurrent "accidents" which are sometimes reported in the daily Press, where mothers kill their babies, or husbands their wives. These are not crimes in the ordinary sense, but the law has not yet entirely risen above its own contamination with an obsessional attitude towards guilt and punishment. Too often, the dismissive habits of the law still aim at the dissociation of the alleged culprit from society, and the extortion of retribution by punishment.

Before ending this section, I would like to say something to those readers of this book who suffer from this disease, especially those who fear their own compulsive urges to injure others whom they truly love. If they will bring that which they fear within the ring of that which they love, throwing and keeping them together, then they will find the power which doctors also find, with which to mend these broken bones. There is no primary hatred. It is a derivative of disappointed love. In the beginning, Love. So go back to the beginning, which is always here, given, now. In any case, seek help where it can be given. It can be given, but only if you do not try to save yourself from yourself by yourself. Do not keep the problem to yourself, but bring it into right relationship with someone who will help you to understand it.

The Obsessional in Love

Compulsion neurosis is obviously the opposite to love in any real sense. Love is a capacity for relationship, which compulsion neurosis most certainly is not. The subjects of this complaint are invariably bad lovers, yet they can never admit it. The boot must ever be upon the other leg, but the words "faithless tyrant" describe their attitude only too well. They have no "faith" in the other, but must have proof of their affection constantly at hand; and the other must be an obedient puppet, forever on a string, responsive immediately to every jerk.

They are not only always identified with the beloved object or person; more than that, they are also identified with the idea or ideal of their own perfection and blamelessness, *especially as lovers*. They are for these reasons exceptionally hard to live with, especially when married. It is as if the mate must first be swallowed whole, with identity lost in identification. In the first glorious confusion of having fallen in love, such transports of affection may seem to be utterly unselfish, but in fact this magnificent obsessional attachment is only possessive and soon proves itself to be completely destructive of any personal rights whatever. Then if the beloved does cause any disagreement or disturbance ("indigestion") in the matrimonial stomach, the offender may find herself as suddenly flung out, "vomited" as it were, to become in an instant the dissociated scapegoat, who can never be right. The compulsive mechanism can be very shattering to matrimonial harmony and usually comes as a great shock of surprise to those who are not previously aware of its dangers.

Identification with the other may appear to be a beneficial kind of relationship, but it is not in fact a true relationship at all, because the separate existence, or spiritual integrity, of the other, is neither recognized nor permitted. Two people in such a relationship to one another may be justly considered as "unweaned," because it is as if the one is still held contained in the womb of the other. Intuitives, for whom the principle "All are one" is a fundamental axiom, are very liable to be thus unweaned in their protective attachment to others whom they "love." Their state of being in love keeps them so closely bound to one another that they can only live in each other's pockets, as it were, with no allowance made for difference of feeling, life or point of view. These two are one, identified, but with their own identities submerged, confused in one another. They can hardly even breathe apart, and must not differ at any point. But the strain of such a persistent and profound attachment cannot last for long; and yet, when the break comes, it can only seem intolerable. When difference (or indifference) occurs, as sooner or later it must, then it must be dismissed, eliminated ("dissociated") immediately. In the ordinary course of events, a lovers' quarrel is a matrimonial commonplace, and does no harm at all, unless one of the parties is seriously obsessional. Then the breach is irremediable, the collapse of all love's hopes is final, and the scapegoat outcast, unforgiven and unforgivable. "Either you must agree with me, or else you or I must go." This is the cruel alternative, and such lovers can behave to one another with appalling cruelty. The love of years may be shattered in an instant, its place being taken by the most callous indifference and exclusion. The lack of true relationship in the previous state of identification is thus proved by the disaster of a rupture as complete as it may be surprising.

Another characteristic of the obsessional attachment to objects of affection is that it may light upon apparently quite irrelevant aspects or parts of a person, which thereupon come to represent the whole person. This accounts for the fetishistic attachment of obsessionals in their sex relations. Indeed, they do not love persons, because they cannot be related to them. They prefer to have control over things, which take the place of persons. The sex act may in itself be such a dissociated event, from which the partner is completely dissociated as a person.

We are all somewhat obsessional in our attitude to sex: but less so, the more we are actually related-in-love to the personal reality of the other.

The characteristics of the obsessional towards the beloved, whether person or thing, are therefore (1) the person is regarded as something which can be utterly possessed and controlled; (2) in case of disapproval, the other ought to be either changed or dismissed immediately; (3) certain "good" aspects of the other are abstracted, split off from the whole: or alternatively, certain other "bad" aspects must be ignored and forgotten (dissociated).

Such obsessional behavior does not only occur between "lovers," whether married or otherwise. It also occurs between parents (especially mothers) and their children. It often occurs between employer and employee, frequently between doctor and patient, and sometimes between master and pupil. In each case the other is treated as if he or she belongs to a possessor, who has the right to compel obedience by force.

Sadism and masochism are typical derivatives of compulsion neurosis. They are not rightly to be regarded as normal modifications of the masculine and feminine attitudes towards the enjoyment of power. They are both essentially morbid and abnormal, because they are always compulsive and obsessional. The normal attitude between the sexes is one of relationship. The normal attitude to power is one of relationship. In sadism and masochism there is no relationship with the other: there is only identification and dissociation, so that these two extremes are always found to be inextricably and compulsively intertwined. They are always to be regarded as being evidence of a state of disease—namely, compulsion neurosis.

Time and the Door

In compulsion neurosis there are no bridges, which are the sign of a relationship; instead there are walls, which are the sign of a proprietary fixation, a division of property, perhaps a prison or a tomb. There is no *process* in the sense of a beginning, a middle and an end, with an extension of growth in time; instead, there is a jumping to conclusions, an immediate identification with a good (or, if reversed, a bad) end result, and a perpetual "stop-gap" state of fixation.

This is essentially a disease in which time is out of order. The patient cannot fit in to time. Time in itself may sound a very metaphysical problem, a philosophic abstraction of no importance to children, patients, or ourselves. Actually, however, nothing could be more real, more present and more urgent. Consider, for instance, the child behind the closed door—locked out, alone. Such a situation might occur many times a day in any ordinary household. Perhaps mother is working in the kitchen, or resting on her bed, or there are important visitors in the drawing-room. If the child has a sense of time as flowing, what does it matter? The visitors will flow out, the child will flow in, and mother will flow back again. But in compulsion neurosis there is no flow. To be outside the door now is to be outcast forever, because there is no difference. A mere gesture of bored dismissal, "Go away now, I am busy," is interpreted by this unhappy mood as being an utter, final rejection, signifying a total withdrawal of love.

The rhythm of life, the flow of energy, the rise and fall of the living sap of interest and affection, passes through doorways (technically called "synapses" in the nervous system) which open and shut, to the regulate flow. They jam. Time stops. So does the patient.

The Larder and the Lavatory

As I have already remarked, it is characteristic of this disease that dissociated objects should take on an exaggerated, sometimes a "fetishistic," value. The world of good objects is viewed as morally mine, or "owed" to me. ("I ought to have what I want.") It is the common error of this condition, observable in various degrees, to project value into objects, thus making them good-in-themselves, to attach objects to persons, confusing one with the other, and then to attempt to control both object and person. The operative words are: OUGHT, MINE, MORE GAIN, LESS PAIN. The incentive is compulsive, from outside, by force: *You Must!* The purpose is to obtain more "goods," and to fix them in a safe place. The larder shelves, whether of mind or bank, must be loaded with securities. Thus the principle of circulation is impeded, if not totally destroyed, by an alternative principle of acquisitiveness, of puddles, pools and dams, by means of which the "goods" can become the "securities" of anxious persons, whose purpose is to accumulate more than is required for mere storage against the possibility of short supply or a rainy day. A surplus must be acquired for its own sake, and accumulation has become an end in itself, instead of a means to an end of supplying a need or making something work.

This is the cause of economic constipation both in social and personal relationships. The child's first sense of "goods," or of being "good," is referred to the constantly repeated praise—and blame—for what it does, and does not do, in its little pot. Thus the lavatory is liable to become our first moral forcing house, in which goodness is achieved and guilt assuaged. The early oft-repeated injunctions of the nursery must sink deep into the affective background of the impressionable child, to recur subsequently with obsessional force.

Our patient, however, has door trouble again. The door will not open, the goods do not pass. I do not mean to imply that physical constipation is an invariable symptom of compulsion neurosis. It is not, although it may be so. What I do suggest, however, is that an acquisitive, retentive, miserly, aggressive tendency to keep good things behind closed doors, and to prevent them passing into free circulation, is as characteristic of the compulsive patient, as it is in fact of our society.

A complication arises, however, in the fact that our compulsive society (or patient) must also be right, good and morally approved, which means that we must be kind and generous on suitable occasions to the right people. This is not impossible. It is not even difficult. In fact, we all manage to do it so frequently that it never occurs to us that much of the fabric of our lives and social habits is composed of such compulsive rationalizations.

Meanwhile, we are tied fearfully to the past, encrusted, earthbound. It is as if we also are actually identified with our own excreta, hoarding it jealously against potential loss. We also are obsessed with the magical value of things, and feel that our lives depend on their collection and control. So does the obsessional patient.

The Fallacy of Self-Control

Within myself, where is my leader? Who is my interior personal boss, and where may I find him? I am told to control myself, to pull myself together, and in general to be a good little boy. But where do I find the mysterious power with which to effect these instantaneous improvements?

Before attempting to answer such a difficult question, let us examine for a moment the motive and intentions of my moral instructor, who is attempting by force to change me from outside. *You must . . .* ! he says, *or else . . .* ! he says, with threats more or less disguised by his soft words and promises. ("Come now, be reasonable, darling, and mummy will explain. . . . " The underlying threat is there, the force, the exterior control, in spite of those soft words.) And so our outward would-be tyrant (though in the name of love, of course, and what is good for *me*) is showing every characteristic of compulsion neurosis in expecting me to become a willing party to her anxious tyranny. ("You will do it to please me, won't you? You would not want to hurt dear Mother!" Or would you?)

In fact, to be quite frank about it, there is no such interior function entitled to exercise supreme authority. The human being has no one in charge, and no one in control, unless some self-righteous and self-assertive part jumps up and assumes the responsibilities and privileges of leadership, for its own partial ends and to the ultimate misfortune of all those other parts and functions which go to make up the whole person.

But, you say, you do know who your leader is, you do know how to keep yourself in perfect self-control? (Perhaps you know, too, how to pull yourself to heaven by your own ears?) Come on, then, tell us where you have found your master principle. "I am." Is it really so simple? But who on earth do you mean by "I"? Do you mean that point of light in consciousness, which stands above and yet related to two meaningful oceans of great darkness, the field of unconscious forces, feelings and motives on the one hand, and your central self, your core, your soul, THAT I AM, on the other? Why, you cannot even control your liver, heart, or lungs. Don't make your dreamer laugh. (He does not try to control you, does he? Yet he also has his influential part to play.)

But, you may ask, what about this conscience that we hear so much about? Surely that can be in control, or what is the use of having one? Yes, I agree. If your conscience is strong enough, it can terrify you into cowering obedience. But if that is what you mean, do you really advocate encouraging so cruel a tyrant? That is, in fact, exactly what I mean by compulsion neurosis: that is an obsessional conscience, and its system of control is as morbid and destructive as tyranny must always be.

Although it is often such a noisy imposter, I do not mean that "conscience" is always wrong. Of course, there is another kind of conscience, which is no tyrant. To be in touch with love is to be visited sometimes by a little gentle voice, whispering into the empty spaces of your mind. Sometimes you can hardly hear it: sometimes it may give you a good shaking, if it catches you unawares and off your guard. But never could you call such a mysterious influence a controlling factor, when, if it is heard at all, it can be so easily forgotten.

As a matter of fact, a person is a true democracy, the parts of which, by reason of their right relationship alone, can work as one. Some parts of a person are known; some are unknown, but knowable; some are unknown, and will forever remain unknowable, at least to mortal mind.

The healthy kind of self-control is not one for which "I" can hold myself responsible. It is a consequence of subtle harmonies between balanced and opposing forces. It is what I have called a "C" factor, an effect of synthesis between known and unknown parts, mysteriously thrown together. If it is less than that, it is not a wholesome kind of self-control. It may be self-restraint or self-suppression. It may even be self-destruction. But to attempt self-control by violence ("stiff upper lip") is dangerously like the unconscious dissociative and destructive habits of compulsion neurosis.

It is as false to think that you can, or should, control me, as that I can, or should, control you: it is also false to think that you or I can, or should, control ourselves. All these bosses, benevolent or otherwise, are obsessional inventions of a sick compulsive mentality. It is that same state of mind that invents a tyrant conscience and a tyrant God.

Empirically, it is quite certain that God shows no mortal evidence of wishing, or trying, to control us. On the contrary, He sets us free to travel on our own, alone, amongst strangers who are as much alone as we are. We can be in touch with Him if we will, as He will always be in touch with us. Would that not be enough? Or must we try so ambitiously to control our world, each other, ourselves— and Him as well?

Upbringing and Education

Judged by results, the manners and methods of upbringing and education are either good or bad. They either succeed or fail, to the degree in which they develop personal character, creative ability and responsible citizenship. Judging by the results apparent in our world today, we should feel profoundly dissatisfied and may all wonder where, with so much expenditure of money, effort and goodwill, we have gone so far wrong. I believe that it is particularly in this field that we can learn, from our study of compulsion neurosis, at least where some of our efforts have been misdirected. The avowed aim of compulsion neurosis is always to arrive at the best possible results in the shortest possible time. Its actual results are always disappointing, however, because of its total ignorance and avoidance of the vital factors of time, the process of growth and the experience of relationships.

The characteristics of the compulsive attitude on the part of authority, as it is expressed in upbringing and education, are: (1) insistence on having power over the other, the ideal being to have complete control over the other, who is then regarded as being "good"; (2) disregard for time, the process of growth and the experience of relationships, supplying the initiative instead by force from outside; (3) a habit of dealing with everything by itself, separately, under control; (4) exact separation (dissociation) of the good from the bad, collecting and multiplying the good, but dismissing and punishing the bad; (5) reverence for knowledge as an end in itself; (6) reverence for tradition and fear of change, preferring the past to the present and the authority of another to proving by experience; (7) in general, fear of the unknown, the new and the mysterious, which springs unbidden from our experience of the vital factor revealed in our relationships.

It should be borne in mind that all our earliest learning is necessarily somewhat obsessional in character, as it is deeply buried beneath the accumulated crust of subsequent experience. We are identified with what we learnt at "mother's knee," and may never develop that mature attitude of self-critical detachment and reflection, which brings freedom from the compulsive force of our deeply acquired first impressions. Thus a patient said: "I learnt all that I know of life at my mother's hands," but what she learnt was *fear.* The hands that might have meant peace, comfort, security, warmth, nourishment and love seemed, as she looked back over thirty anxious, disappointed years, either to have let her drop unwanted in some corner of the floor, or else to have come prodding, poking, peering into her private places, when she had wanted to be quiet and alone. Her mother was a busy, booming, interfering type of woman, who regarded children as things to be efficiently controlled. Oh yes, they ought to be loved and so she loved them. They ought to be fed and cared for, and so she cared for them, most thoroughly. They ought to be hardened off from any sentimentality, and so they were always left to cry. She had theories (most modern, therefore best) and she exactly practiced them. She managed the home, her husband, the children and herself efficiently. She was morally most virtuous, but totally insensitive to her children's real needs. And she left a memory, at least on this one child, of sheer abhorrence. "I feel now, as I felt then, that I simply cannot bear her to touch me."

Surely, it was not her mother's touch that she had objected to, but her lack of it: either the hands were not there when she needed them, or, if they were, they pushed and prodded, poked and pried, until she could not call any part of herself her own, and did not even want to. This patient had turned for support, as many anxious and unhappy people do, to higher education. For knowledge is power, power is control, and control is safe. And knowledge is approved. Development of the mind became for her an over-compensation for the intolerable lack of the loving touch that was missing in her childhood; but not all the power that words can give, can ever take the place of what one woman's loving hands could do.

There are, of course, many reasons, or we should say ulterior motives, for the sufferer from compulsion neurosis to indulge in over-development of the mind. As I have already said, a good education assures approval and may become a means to that self-centered end. Education is a "good thing" to be acquired, posses-sively, and put in the larder, where it can be accumulatively hoarded as an end in itself. But the faculty of consciousness is dangerous, for it is both *exterior* and *dissociative*; it considers objects from outside, one at a time, by themselves, in dissociated detail. It takes away the cement of relationship, removing the unknowable intermediate (and therefore frightening) factor, thereby more easily reducing the higher to the lower term, by the derogatory process of perceiv-ing that "this is only that." It provides a facile conceptual approach, a well-worn rut, by means of which it is possible for the anxious and impatient student to approach every unknown (or unknowable) object with a preconceived idea of what to expect, or what ought to be. Values are thus ready-made, meanings forecast, possibilities pre-judged and mysteries made safe for anxious minds, who seek the privilege of knowing without the responsibility of experiencing, the safety of arrival without the danger of traveling, and the assurance of approval without the risk of being found different.

It is as if a dangerous dimension of mystery, an unknown and interfering element which might upset our earnest calculations, can, with a certain care, be abstracted (or is it castrated?) from the sum total of our human lot, so that what is left can be made smooth, safe and certain, for timid feet to tread. They can even feel approved into the bargain, for being so extraordinarily clever to know so much about so little. Being so quick to understand, these clever ones need never ask the questions, because the answer has already leapt to fill the impatient gap.

Of course, those who are most experienced in education know that the true function of education is not the training of the mind to pass examinations, nor is it only a means of ensuring material success within the limits of our present compulsive economic system. Its aim should be the development of the full compass of the whole man or woman, within the field of opportunity. Education should be a living, growing process, in which the student is encouraged, under the watchful eye of his teacher, to develop his own judgment from his own experience of how meanings and values change on every level with changes of relationship. The aim of education should be the integration of the many into one, by means of developing the relationships between the one and the many. The fieldwork of education is in the study of relationships, and in the progressive development of the C-factor.

The questions, therefore, for education to study are: who are our relatives, what are our possible relationships with one another, and how can our experience of relationships be made more fruitful? What is the most fruitful relationship between soul and body, God and man, female and male, religion and science, history and geography, mathematics and philosophy, or man and his speech? Nor do I mean that these questions are to be answered in such terms as the teacher may dictate, such as that "The answer is so and so, and so you must believe." The C-factor is not a tyranny, but a personally considered experience which develops freely of itself in time, when the opportunity for the relationship is provided.

It may seem easier for teachers to use the rubber-stamp method of impression, "Take that, it is right!", applying it in turn to each dissociated subject in the school curriculum. It may be an effective method for passing examinations. It may be a short cut to acquiring knowledge. It may even lead to individual success, by the successful adoption of a tyranny amongst tyrants in a tyrannical society. But it is not good for the development of personal integrity, nor for the welfare of society as a whole. That can only come from learning right relationships, which is the wisdom of life acquired from experience.

Magic works: So does Science. So does tyranny. It is quite possible to control our world, and each other, up to a point. It is even desirable, up to a point. But what happens then?

Money and Machines

All that we make must pass through our hands, to pass out of our hands into circulation. This applies to children, money and machines, all of which are in different ways modified hands, or means adapted to a certain end.

Money and machines especially have become the tyrannical instruments of compulsion neurosis, because of the opportunity for power which they afford. They provide for the attainment of the good object and thereby enable us to control the world of objects, to our material advantage. They provide security and privilege, so that "goods" are "cheap," and may be endlessly multiplied.

Of course, there is no harm in either money or machines in themselves. There is no harm in having cheap "goods." The harm is in the motive of compulsion neurosis, which makes of both a tempting playground for spoiled children with an inferiority complex. Then power is exploited, goods are acquired beyond our needs, money becomes God and the machine becomes the master—and all to escape from the problems of relationship, by giving us material security and opportunity to control the lives of others who are less fortunate (or less acquisitive?) than ourselves.

Money, in fact, is only a *medium*, a C-factor. It is a means of communication. It is a bridge between persons and between societies. It fulfills the function in society that blood serves in the human body. But in compulsion neurosis there is no "between," means become ends, and circulation is not allowed. So money has become an end in itself, to be increased as a "good object" for its own sake, and to be used as an instrument for controlling and compelling service from others.

Money, in fact, is a token, a sign; it is like a word which stands for a meaning. Or it is like a convenient boat, which is itself valueless, except for the fact that it can carry valuable passengers and cargo. But in compulsion neurosis the value is transferred from the meaning to the object which stands for the meaning. The "passengers" are ignored, while the "boat" is worshipped, as master or God. So money is no longer a token. It does not stand for anything. It has become something good (or bad?) in itself, a monstrous tyrant, a false God.

Money and machines were once to be calculated amongst our possessions, which we might freely use. In compulsion neurosis there is no freedom and we have no possessions. Being identified with them, they possess us. As we accumulate more of them, so they grow at our expense.

So money and machines become industrial monsters, whose growth is increasingly parasitic upon persons, and destructive of the essential spiritual values of mankind. It has indeed become very obvious, today, that we are increasingly in danger of being destroyed by the products of our own hands.

Religion

All religions have tortoise trouble. That is to say, not only the Church, which is religion's "body," but its beliefs also, tend to thicken and petrify, as passing time precipitates an ever-increasing accumulation of dead and decaying matter over the heart and substance of its living truth. Religion, like us all, suffers in its ageing from arteriosclerosis, or a thickening of those channels which supply its blood.

Yet that is not the most serious part of the problem. The real trouble lies in this: that *the thickened wall takes to itself the worth of the blood which it obstructs*, and the intrinsic values are transferred from cause to effect, from there to here, from THAT to this, from spirit to material form and from the future to the time-encrusted, hallowed, past. Thus every Church, of every creed and denomination, must progressively deny her Lord, unless she is prepared to ensure her constant renewal by her willingness to die, and die again, for Him. Compulsion neurosis has always operated with insidious regularity in the history of every Church, whose constant problem is that of the renewal of its present life.

The questions are many, the answer is one. Compulsion neurosis runs riot in politics. It is even more rampant there, if that were possible, than it is in religion.

In all its moral and pseudo-benevolent disguises (I will take care of you, if you will only give me your vote—and your soul!) compulsion neurosis not only leads to war, but to war against the spirit, which is far worse.

I will only make this general statement, which is as far as my special theme will allow me to go. Compulsion neurosis always tends to destroy the father, and to set up the son in a privileged relationship with the mother. Exploiting her, he usurps his father's place. This applies inevitably in some degree to every one of us. Without particularizing any one religion, it applies to all. Embodied and time-bound as we are, we dearly love to fortify our life-resistant shells.

Compulsion neurosis divides and sets apart in all things, with quarrelsome efforts to gain superiority, to acquire prestige, and to avoid guilt and inferiority by transferring them to others. Compulsion neurosis extols war, and moralizes the killings which it causes. Religion, on the other hand, as the word itself implies, "binds together" all those whom it joins in a common enjoyment of the fruits of the spirit. Religion—and I mean any religion whatsoever which is true to the laws of the spirit—enters into no arguments of higher or lower, more or less, better or worse, because it humbly sees the truth that all must be sinners now, to whom so much more is given than we can either rightly use or generously enjoy. No religion which was not deeply infected by compulsion neurosis could ever regard war as other than the crudest mixture of sin and sickness that it is.

Compulsion neurosis has no "faith" whatever, but much "belief," with which all faith has been confused and utterly destroyed. Similarly, it has no sensitivity, no touch with the spirit, no little voice speaking in silence and in space: instead, there is only a bolstered blasphemy that shouts terrifyingly: *You must now, at once . . . or else . . . .*

Compulsion neurosis is crudely literal, and cannot recognize the dream-like, poetic quality of life. Most profoundly guilty of the crime against the spirit, it must project its guilt upon others who are more innocent, exacting from them the price of punishment. From this source springs our recurrent, topsy-turvy tragedy of embittered fanaticism.

Fanaticism is never the good thing which it always seems to be to its adherents. It is the result of the combined operations of the unconscious motives of the spoiled child, the inferiority complex and compulsion neurosis.

Life and Death

Splitting all things and setting them apart, we have even destroyed the existent link between life and death, as if the one is to be desired and the other shunned. Yet if our philosophy of "That in this" is true, then death is in life and life in death, and you and I are even now, whether we know it or not, in constant touch with both. Part of our healing from the morbid grip of compulsion neurosis is that we should learn to make a better bridge of love with death.

In compulsion neurosis we live between our pin-up pictures on the one hand, which represent the best we hope for and most zealously uphold, while on the other, as keenly to be avoided and concealed, are our skeletons in their cupboards. We are determined that these two worlds of the chosen and the rejected must be held apart so that they never meet. Some of us are successful all the time, or at least until death brings deeper knowledge. But some of us are only partly successful, and then our failure may bring us in confusion to the psychologist's consulting room for much-needed aid.

What the psychologist does is to help pull out the pins so that the pictures fall to the ground, while he encourages the skeletons one by one to emerge from the confinement of their cupboards. He shines the light of common sense and the cool detachment of experience upon the resulting melee. The long process of sorting out may be very painful in its readjustment of values, but in the end the mills grind small and the wheat is garnered from the chaff. The over-all loyalty to the truth as it is and as it has been supersedes those lesser loyalties to which we have clung so tightly, and in the end the healing is given and we are whole enough to go upon our way, enjoying life again. But first so much must die.

Now I do not claim to know much of what happens after death, and yet I believe that we can perhaps here obtain a glimpse of it. The Buddhists speak of experience after death as being spent in the "bardo," amidst the shadows of our self-made realities, all co-existent in a confusing dream-like continuum, through which we pass until the real "self" is sorted out. The Christians call this state of suffering, the confusion of our own reality, "purgatory." In either case, the idea of being confronted by our own errors and absurdities, of facing our own facts, of meeting again both our hidden skeletons and our pin-up pictures, as they are revealed to us by contrast with a more glorious light, is the same.

It seems quite reasonable that just after death it should be so, as we prepare to venture forth upon a further journey, a little wiser than we were before. If it be so, I like to think that psychotherapy may have saved some peoples' time and trouble on the other side, in the long run of life and death.

Medicine and Surgery

Compulsion neurosis typically falls back into more archaic modes of rendering meaning and effecting change. Identifying names and images with the objects which they represent, it has a primitive, magical attitude towards experience, as if the outer world is all inside the self and part of the experiencer, to be controlled and changed by inward spoken formulae. It is a curious but important fact that this most ancient practice should persist in modern scientific man. Particularly in his role of healer, the ancient "medicine man" is with us still, although his spells and incantations are carefully concealed beneath the most scientific dress.

Correct diagnosis must always play an honorable and essential part in the healing work, but it is not enough, because it begs every question of the relationship between the doctor and the patient, and both with the disease. There are some doctors who use diagnosis as if it conferred upon them magical powers, as if, by pronouncing some long Latin name, they could thereby exorcise the evil force which is causing the disease. This may give some relief to the doctor, but it affords little, if any, to the patient.

Doctors are notoriously bad philosophers. They are too busy to consider first principles. Besides, philosophy is not scientific, and they are practical men, who are taught not to believe in anything unless they can see it, measure it, and prove it to be true. We cannot see or measure an idea, and therefore the presuppositions which lurk unseen behind the immensely complex structure of orthodox medical teaching are ignored. Yet many of them are archaic, magical, contradictory and false. They are concealed in the background, unconscious, unrecognized and therefore uncriticized, to insinuate themselves compulsively through the whole fabric of the art of medicine, to the misfortune of the doctor as well as the patient. Such ideas are typical of compulsion neurosis. They differ from the true wisdom of teaching and practicing the art of medicine, as any conglomeration of magic, nonsense, benevolence and mere pragmatism must differ from a more profound understanding and practice of the principles of sound and wholesome living.

Implicit but unstated, one such presupposition is that illness is *bad*, but that health is *good*: and that either drugs or knives will so drive out, eliminate or otherwise destroy the bad, that the good may rise triumphant. There is so much of this primitive magical exorcism prevalent in medical practice today that it is time we were invited to reconsider our first principles, and to see in what it is that we can really put our faith.

Is the power of healing in the knife and the drugs? Or is it in the patient as a person, and the life which is in him? Is it in the doctor, or is it in the mysterious *vis medicatrix naturae*? Is the doctor the principal, or only the agent or assistant of the healing force? If so, what is that healing force, how does it do its beneficial work, how does the doctor play his part and of what use and purpose are his drugs and knife?

The answer to all such questions depends upon our answer to an earlier, deeper and most important question: Is health the result of eliminating disease? (Is A obtained in its purity by getting rid of B?) Or is health a C-factor, dependent on a right relationship between balanced and opposing factors, A and B? Our practice of medicine and surgery will depend upon our philosophy.

Surgery, which is based upon the theory that it is possible to eliminate the bad by cutting out the part which is at fault, may be regarded as a very rare example of the success of compulsion neurosis in action. If it is, then it is a notable exception to a more general result of disappointed hopes and false promises. But, of course, there is more in surgery than the skilful execution of a dismissive operation. The whole art of surgery—and, like medicine, at its best it always is an art and not a science—depends upon the strictest observation and utilization of the principles of right relationship. When the surgeon is as careful about his relationship with the patient, and the patient with his sickness and his other problems, as he is meticulous about the details within his field of operation, then and only then is he a really good surgeon. Efficiency without respect for the intelligent cooperation of the patient is not only reactionary. It is Fascism.

I claim that we cannot get rid of disease by merely getting rid of the germs, any more than we can cure the plague-spots of the world by defeating one or another country. Although compulsion neurosis continues to deceive us with its specious claim that we can solve the problem by destroying the enemy, life answers otherwise. The more we try to overcome our enemy by force, dismissively, the more widely and variously will he rise against us, to pursue and finally vanquish us. Neither appeasement nor victory, neither fight nor flight, neither wishful thinking nor compulsive activity, will save us in this battle, which is life itself. Surely the solution of the problem is again in the common sense way, by accepting the opposing forces, by including the different parts, and by their eventual integration by right relationship into the inclusive whole?

Such a philosophy and practice of healing require more time and more attention to individual cases. It means that the doctor must take the patient into his confidence; it means discovering all the relevant facts in the relationship, not only the material ones; and that we should then all, doctors and patients alike, become partners with the mysterious healing force of life, waiting as patiently as ever on what is wrought in time by THAT. There is nothing new about it. In fact, it is no other than the art of healing has always been.

But would not this attitude of right relationship between patient and doctor, and between both and their common problems, diminish the number of spoiled children, inferiority complexes, compulsive neurotics, petty tyrants, moral exhortationists and clever exhibitionists amongst the ranks of both patients and doctors?

Psychology

The argument of this book, here as elsewhere, depends upon the philosophy that *right relationship is the basis of all healing*, personal as well as social, emotional and spiritual as well as physical, and that wrong relationship is the basis of all disease. In healing, our aim is the integration of the dissociated parts within the framework of the whole. Our method is to replace dissociation and identification by right relationship, and to loosen the fixations, so that the healing flow of life is able to do its integrative and creative work in mobile freedom. With good psychological technique there is no interference, no moral compulsion and no tyranny whatsoever. We sort out the parts (analysis): we lay bare and clean the wound (recollection of past unhappy experience, retrospection): we purge the channels of the heart and soul (catharsis, self-expression and dream-interpretation). We are like midwives at the birth of life, comforting and encouraging; but we do not interfere. We have our faith in a healing that is not our own. We have our faith in life, the spirit or the person, call it what you will. But most of all, for practical purposes, we put our faith in right relationships, and so the healing happens.

I do not wish to imply, however, that psychology knows all the answers, or that all psychologists are therefore saints. This is far from true! Apart from other faults, we have our symptoms, too, of compulsion neurosis. We are in a like dilemma with all the others, and need to know the dangers of our chosen alliance with psychology.

Psychology has its limitations. The structure of "scientific" psychology is only a matter of form, an abstraction from a limiting point of view. However accurate it may be, psychology does not reveal to us the whole truth about the person of the patient. In fact, it must obscure it, unless we can see through psychology to the spiritual problem. We have to learn to see through psychology, as we must learn to see through all words to find their latent meanings, and through the labels on the bottles, to discover by experience what they actually contain. Illness, whether mental or physical, is not a label, and diagnosis is not enough. Illness is maladjustment in relationships occurring to a person. *It is not the person.* The illness is obscuring the person. It is preventing him from seeing through himself, and being seen. To identify the person with his disease, or life with psychology, is again to be the victim of compulsion neurosis.

476

But present day psychology, as a matter of form or structure, is not even good form. Freud, Jung, Adler and the rest have not yet developed a sound, complete and wholesome structure of their findings and beliefs. Psychology is a clumsy, contradictory jargon. It is patchy, partial and incomplete. Yet there are many psychologists today who are identified with the particular teaching of their own approved Master, often exceeding him in their zealous over-emphasis on certain articles of his all-too-rigid "faith."

In this matter, psychologists need to be reminded that they are now behaving as the Churches did before them. Psychologists thought that they had seen through the compulsive schizophrenia of the Churches. Yet they have themselves fallen victims to the same disruptive and schismatic disease of disagreeably competing partial-"isms," each seeking to be recognized as not only right, but best.

There is therefore much evidence of compulsive identification and dissociation amongst psychologists. They claim that psychology is "true," and their own particular brand of it is the only one that can be "right." Thus they also worship false Gods, exclusively. For psychology is only a way of looking at the True. It is a means to that end, and not an end in itself. Misused, as it too often is, it is a trap and a pitfall. It is no longer a bridge but becomes a barrier. Psychology is the study of life as it is humanly experienced. The person is at least in part spiritual. Therefore psychology must be spiritual also, at least in part. The spirit is the inclusive or C-factor. Psychology is therefore a means (and not the only means) to the discovery of the spirit. If it is less than that, it betrays itself to be the victim of its own undiagnosed disease of compulsion neurosis.

Dreams

A dramatic illustration of the nature, cause and effect of compulsion neurosis is given in the following dream which was recurrent between the ages of six and ten. (The patient suffered from obsessional anxiety.) *I was sitting on a fence, with a road between me and the canal. Along the road came trundling a steamroller. I knew that I must fling myself underneath, because only when I was fully flattened out would the danger be past.*

In this dream we find the familiar reference to "sitting on the fence," or protective indecision, which is a common symptom of compulsion neurosis. It is an attempt to fix the intermediate C-factor, to keep the relationship in control, which would be lost if we came to a decision one way or the other. The same idea is expressed in the canal, which is not naturally flowing water ("feelings"), but stationary, artificial, locked and dammed, so that again it is under control. The same controlling influence is represented by the steamroller (authority, conscience) whose function it is to flatten out the road, and keep all safe by eliminating the mysterious dimension, the vertical, in which we rise and fall. The theme of the dream is, therefore, that there must be no movement and especially no rise and fall.

I will quote two other typical dreams of this compulsive state of mind. *A nurse's hand was directing a hypodermic needle into my skin, which was exceedingly tough. So I put my hand round behind hers to direct the needle and help push, but it still would not go in.*

Hypodermic needles are notoriously liable, like anesthetics, to arouse the compulsive protest and provoke resistance. I would remind the reader of our basic pattern which could represent the impact of the needle-point upon the skin. It signifies the problem of the "mysterious influence," the touch of the other who is beyond control, and must therefore be resisted. But not only resisted, because in this case the patient is giving the nurse a helping hand. Thus, in order the better to control it, we are liable to ease the pain in self-defense by identifying ourselves with the cause of it. The split of motive is evident in the resistance on the one hand, and the reinforcement of the stimulus on the other. (It might be said, or "dreamed," that the victim of compulsion neurosis is only willing to bat to his own bowling.)

I was riding a pony. On my left side there was an enormous brick wall. Whichever way I tried to turn his head, he always turned towards the wall.

Was that pony wise or not, we may wonder? The wall on the left is, of course, the resistance to the other side, which is protectively cut off. The pony is the instinctive life, the animal side of human nature, which is probably the one that has been cut off. This patient was in process of meeting her shadow, represented by the

478

pony whom she could not control. But she was on his back, which is our right relationship with the instinctive underworld; and the pony was determined that his rider should not lose touch with what was the other side of the wall.

As we might expect, there is much concern in the dreams of compulsion neurosis with problems of heights and the vertical dimension, with great difficulty in descent: roofs and attics occur with broken stairs, cliffs with a perpendicular fall to rocks below, airplanes that fall and crash. Bridges high in the air lead from nothing to nowhere, and danger greets our aerial traveler at every turn. The insoluble time problem is illustrated by missing trains, always being late, and the very common dream experience of not being able to get the luggage packed.

Water, representing the feeling or "affective" ("between") level, may be conspicuous by its absence. Or it may be contained neatly in a swimming bath or a canal, to show that feelings are always artificially conditioned, limited, and so kept under control. Or it may assume the most threatening proportions of an overwhelming flood, showing with how much fear its dangers are regarded.

Pursuit is common, with panic flight ("but I could not move a limb!"). The "bad object" may be a wild beast, a burglar or a giant, or an indescribable unknown horror. It is, of course, always another aspect ("shadow") of the self.

Early problems of relationship are commonly dramatized, with parents, brothers and sisters, and nursery authorities cast in various appropriate parts, so that "good" and "evil" are often as clear cut as figures in a fairy tale.

In general, the dreams of compulsion neurosis may be said to have much in common with the drawings and paintings of the same type of patient. The tendency is towards an over-complication of reiterated detail, an over-emphasis upon authority, negativeness and lack of life, and the absence of originality, feeling and warmth.

Summary

As an undiagnosed disease, compulsion neurosis may yet be responsible for the death of our society. It is the radical sickness of one and of all, since it attacks by disintegration at the level of relationships, where integration would normally occur. It infects every aspect of our lives, destroying our goodwill, corrupting our behavior, and deceiving our minds. It is particularly the enemy of the Spirit which it must supplant. Where compulsion neurosis is, there can be neither love, nor peace, nor joy.

Its motives are compounded of fear, pride and ignorance. Grasping only for the best, in the end it must produce the opposite effect to the one aimed at. Seeking for profit, it finds loss: for success, it finds failure: for security, it finds collapse: for approval, it finds rejection: for happiness, it finds sorrow: and for health, it finds disease. Without the humility to make a proper start, it can only find its unwanted end in its refused beginning. Confusing means with ends, it sacrifices the real world for the sake of an idea, or an "ideal." It exchanges the natural order of growth-in-time for a man-planned tyranny. Instead of growth being from within outwards, movement is forced by blatant moral pressure from outside.

In its insidious extension into consciousness of the morbid unconscious motives which are the polluted springs of human conduct, compulsion neurosis is the logical development of the moral fallacies of the spoiled child and the inferiority complex. In varying degrees and in a multitude of ways, but always with a strong flavor of unselfishness and self-righteousness, our compulsive planners, whether parents, politicians, or ourselves, are undermining the very structure of the society which they are apparently seeking to serve and striving to sustain.

Open or concealed, the underlying attitude to life in compulsion neurosis may be summarized as bad-tempered and backward. The restless, noisy and ceaseless activities of mind and body to which it compels us are as socially and personally valuable as the buzzing of a bee in a bottle.

The Patient's Attitude to Cure

Unfortunately, as a disease, compulsion neurosis is particularly hard to cure for several reasons. First, it is to be remembered that the patient must always be morally and unshakably sure that he is right. Second, it is the nature of the disease that the patient is embedded, if not immured, in it. Third, there is probably a basic fault in the faculty of relationships itself, a lack of elasticity, bounce or "spring" in the make-up. (Another way of saying the same thing is that the patient lacks a sense of humor, but this disaster may be disguised by a heavy overcompensation.) Fourth, the patient's attitude towards the doctor is one of complete unreality. He is seen only in divine disguise. The slave is to be dragged well by the tyrant, the good child is to be sat immediately on the mother-God's knee, and my doctor will save me, specially, I know he will. The ambivalent extremes of good and evil, God and Devil, are not allowed to swing. The worst is too bad, the best is too good, and the patient finds it extremely difficult, if not impossible, to sustain any real relationship either with the doctor or himself and his problems. Fifth, as it is impossible to ask a question, to admit a doubt or to recognize a misunderstanding, the patient will always be jumping to conclusions and assuming that he understands, when he does not. Sixth, the patient can so take refuge in the jargon of psychology that, knowing more about it even than the doctor, he is quite unable to see its limitations, or to stop talking in psychological terms about himself. Seventh, the patient will attempt to identify himself with his doctor, to be just like him, which can only have the worst effect on the patient's progress. And finally, there still remains the greatest cause of difficulty, which is that the patient who suffers from this disease can only behave according to his type. Avoiding the proper means, he must always try to identify himself with the "good object," which is "cure." His one idea is to get rid of the disease and to have the health, immediately, with anxious questions as to how long it will be before he can enter into the "promised land."

It is inevitable that the patient should approach the doctor with the symptoms of the disease upon him. It is inevitable that the patient-doctor relationship should reveal the basic nature of the disease. It is to be hoped that the doctor is not also a victim of the same complaint.

Treatment

In treating this disease, we need to remember that if an answer is provided too readily to the question, "Whatever shall I do?" the remedy may be as compulsive as the disease it hopes to cure.

Gradually, the patient may be brought to learn that where there are two alternatives, neither must be eliminated. He needs to become consciously instructed in the principle of right relationships and in the respect which is due to his own, and other people's, feelings.

If he can realize that compulsion is his disease, and, therefore, can never be his cure; if he can wait on his disease until he does recognize it; and if he can realize that this is his sickness and be a patient patient; then he will be at least half-way towards being cured. But that is a great deal to expect of any impatient sufferer from this compulsive complaint.

A proper diagnosis will always make plain the proper cure. The disease is untimely, so the cure must take time. The disease is exclusive, so the cure must be inclusive. The disease destroys relationships, so the cure must mend them. The disease is fixed, or moved by force, and so the cure must gently flow, as feelings grow.

The sufferer from this disease has experienced a fracture in his system of relationships. Something, somewhere, has been broken off. It is this broken bone which needs to be mended. Or, to put his trouble in another way, the sufferer is like a bee in a bottle, buzzing frantically in an ineffective attempt to find freedom and a way out. As this affects us all, to some extent at least, we may consider how to treat, first the broken bone, and then the bee in the bottle.

The Broken Bone

Broken bones require for mending that *the wound should be cleared of irrelevancies, the parts should be held in alignment* in such a way that they can be kept quite still, and then, that *sufficient time* should be allowed in this *resting phase* for the *healing to be given*. It will be seen that, rightly understood, the one who undertakes a healing work must be satisfied to play a secondary, passive and waiting role, while the healing darkly and obscurely happens.

The broken bone implies a lost or fractured relation with the "other." But who is the "other"? It is necessary to emphasize that the patient will expect it to be what he has lost, what he has always longed for, what he has never had but thinks he ought to have had, what he feels is due to him and what he cannot do without. It is also necessary to say at once that this is not the solution. The "other" is in fact exactly the opposite to this. It is what the patient was given in the first place, but rejected at the time. The "other" is the intolerable, the *rejected* other, and no less than that.

The patient usually pleads, "But I am not ready yet. Later, perhaps, I shall be able to face it. But I must have what I want first." This plea is half-true, half-false. Yes, we can provide comfort, attention, sympathy, security and a sufficient time in which to rest. Yet it is not by satisfying such natural desires for peace and plenty that healing comes. However much we may be able to give of "good mothering," there will be no experience of being born again until this child is wholly willing both to go *forth* and *go without*. Remembering with what retentive hooks our compulsive selves are fitted, it is important to bear in mind the utterly ruthless end towards which our care and comfort, both for ourselves and others in like cases, must always be directed. Facing that rejected other, which we have spent our lives in avoiding with more or less success, we must accept the relation with that, exactly, if we are to mend this broken bone and become articulate again.

Now, who or what is this rejected other? Specifically, it may be some childhood's experience of shock, strain or disappointment; a cruel parent, a misguided nurse, a foolish aunt, a stupid schoolmaster, or one of the many self-centered and obsessional types by whom our childhood was beset. Therefore it is necessary to reenter our past experience, to reenter our feelings about this person or situation, and to stay in that awkward and painful womb long enough to realize our actual relief from it by our rebirth. In such a release there is a "period of gestation," a time factor which is as unknown as it is all-important, which must not be planned, forced or hurried. In time, release will come and the healing of rebirth will be given. Then, and only then, will this bone have been mended.

In general, the "other" is to be sought and found wherever we are, and with whomever we may be living and meeting in our daily lives. Here and now, we meet our habits of rejection, falsification and escape. Here and now, we need to practice clearing away the irrelevancies, so that we can indeed meet one another simply, and with careless rectitude.

In particular, it is necessary to meet our own rejected selves, our shadow side, the parts which we have been anxious to lose sight of, because we did not like the look or feel of them. It always takes the external presence of another, however, whether psychologist or priest, relative, friend or enemy, truly to introduce us to our more wayward, shy and disappearing, shadow selves. Alone, our habits of self-deception are too deeply laid for us ever to be able truly to meet our other selves.

And then, of course, there is always "THAT" other, the mysterious one, the Dreamer, the Hound of Heaven, the visitor from the Most High. THAT is also another end of our personal bone. In my experience, it is a mistake to expect THAT to appear always in kindly or benevolent guise. More often than not, THAT's appearance is sufficiently distressing to account for THAT's rejection. But, in my opinion, THAT is always right: THAT has a perfect sense of humor: and THAT is impelled by nothing but true love for the other end of the bone that has so willfully rejected Him.

The Bee in the Bottle

Then there is the poor bee, caught in his bottle, buzzing frantically. What can be done for us poor buzzing bees who have neither time, means, nor inclination to resort to the dubious advantage of a psychologist's care? What can we do for ourselves? Again, we must diagnose the disease and accept our sickness for what it is: a proof that we need to make a radical readjustment in our values, and a proper admission of our just dependency upon factors which are beyond our own control.

And then? *When the bee goes to sleep peacefully in his bottle, then the stream of life will mysteriously flow again.* When we cease our urgent ordering of life's events, then time and tide are restored to their secret supremacy. Then life flows on and we can play our part in the emergent stream of our experience, taking it as it comes, enjoying or enduring as may be.

Our body is like a boat, floating on a stream. There are sails which flap to catch an idle breeze, according to the way we want to go. There is a motor, too, in case we want to go upstream, against the tide. (But why?) With hand upon the tiller, our touch need be only finger-light. Our traveling is almost effortless. ("However shall I get through the day?" But you need not worry, for, whether you like it or not, the day will get through you.) Of course, the traveler upon life's stream-in-time has certain things to learn and do, but that should not disturb his enjoyment of the constantly changing process of his traveling. Yes, he can choose—at any time—what he will do, where he will go, whom he will meet. (For choice, like air, is free.) He can turn his craft which way he will (but why upstream against the tide?). He can travel fast or slow (but what's the hurry?), alone or with his friends (but why the crowd?). He can work or play, or even enjoy an empty space of leisured contemplation for a while. (Even that is not wrong.) He need not provide the motive power, nor assume the whole responsibility for carrying the world upon his back. I do not believe that he is called upon to save the world or his friend, or his children, or even himself. (At least, not yet.) Traveling takes time. He has a whole lifetime for his journey, so why blindly hasten on?

This is no idle dream. It is the way to explore with others life's perpetually fruitful, mysterious adventure.

CHAPTER 28

Depression

Depression is a disease of poverty amongst riches, due to false leadership, wrong attachments and a poor circulation. It is a fault in our experience of the vertical dimension, on which our values are established. Although we have fallen to the bottom, it is because we were too attached to the top. (Yes, "pride comes before a fall.") The symptoms are low enough in all conscience (pay particular attention to that conscience!), but the cause is to be found much higher up.

For depression to occur, we have got wrong in our relationship with God. The depressed patient insists that God does not love him any more. He feels deserted, valueless, of no account. The communication cord is broken and Life itself seems dead. He is submerged beneath the slowly turning wheels of deep engrossed unhappiness. He is dispirited and life has got him down.

"Life got him down?" That is not true. It was not life, but "it," some THING in his experience that got him down, some outward happening. The "IT" was greater than the "I," and the spirit of the "I" succumbed to "IT." I have already emphasized the importance of getting down to "it," and getting into "it," and getting on with "it." But if "it" gets "me" down, then the cart is before the horse, and though I have arrived at the bottom of the hill, the cart is on top of me. I am its useless victim, underneath.

Get *you* down to *it*, but don't *let* it get *you* down! Between these two phrases lies the difference of the right and wrong place of the spirit in regard to its external instruments and conditions. If the spirit is in it, willingly, then the spirit is the master, as it should be. But if the spirit is caught against its will, with the mechanical instrument on top, then the spirit has been defeated, and the case

---

From *The Triumphant Spirit: A Study of Depression*

487

must become ill. The health and the wealth of the community, as of the individual, depend upon this willingness on the part of the spirit to serve in low places and tight corners. If the spirit objects and tries to run away: or if it defends itself with violence: or, worse still, if it betrays its side and joins the enemy: then "it," the material side, has for the time being established itself as the master of "you," who are relatively a spirit, and "it" has got "you" down. You are the slave of your mechanism, which possesses you. You may possess the world, or large imposing lumps of it, but you have lost your central self, your soul, your "I." Whether you know it now or not, you soon will, for *it* has got *you* down.

Real and Imaginary Causes

We vary in all things, and certainly not least in our capacity to stand up to difficulties. When illness comes, some doctors and some patients are inclined to give or claim an "alibi," by means of which we can avoid all blame for our disasters. It is as if they say, like bashful schoolboys shirking responsibility for their misdeeds, "Please sir, no sir, it wasn't me sir, I wasn't there, sir!" Thus they "pass the baby," and the guilty party or scapegoat who holds the blame instead, is either the event itself, which proves to be overwhelming ("I can't bear it!"), or else there is an oversensitive nervous system, or perhaps some glandular defect ("and so it wasn't my fault!"). High or low blood pressure, illness or fatigue, may all be brought into the picture as the appropriate cause or wicked actor in the otherwise innocent drama. Up to a point, I agree. I believe in multiple causality, and I would not wish to belittle any or all of these possible causes. Here and now, before I go any further, let me at once admit that amongst the many physical "causes" of depression you may find *fatigue* (overwork), *toxemia* (e.g. dental sepsis), *influenza* (that does get us down and the extra day in bed is well repaid!) and *glandular disturbances* (as in childbirth and the "menopause" or change of life). These are not all and none is all to blame. To blame some fault within our box of instruments is to do the very thing which I deplore, namely to put the cart before the horse, and plead a spiritual alibi. The spirit, myself, must be there, and must be made to be there, taking its rightful place at the heart of the trouble, ultimately responsible. "Yes, it was I, and I am here to learn!"

I feel, most strongly, that the policy of evading personal responsibility by finding scapegoats is a dangerous one. I believe that if we are to make of life what we can make of it, we must *within ourselves* assume responsibility for all our ills, and also find therein the healer. "Within ourselves," I emphasize again. Responsibility is not to be laid upon the surface of the self, in what we called "thinking" in category 2 of the Psychic Compass. There is no proper leader there, nor healer either. The responsible authority is not in the mind we know as human consciousness, nor is the healer so glibly capable of winning the victory of "mind over matter" as we are apt to think. If mind can conquer matter, it is not from the second category of the psychic compass, but from the first. It is the spirit that can rule, and should, and will, if we do but realize the nature of that force and use it as it can be used. If the spirit is enduring and indomitable, how can we be dispirited? Life cannot get us down if only we can keep our spirits up.

I do not wish to imply, however, that I have any means of making this an easy trick. It is no use exhorting one who is dispirited to be high-spirited, and it is no use telling a person who has no faith that he must have faith. Words are not so powerful as to be able to work such easy miracles on their own, unless they are exceptionally inspired. The problem of healing depression, therefore, is how to regain inspiration, and how to reinstate the spirit in its true supremacy?

The Pattern

It is easy to put depression into a pattern, because it is a disturbance of our normal rhythmic life. Life is a breathing process a rhythmic up and down, or give and take, in which we alternate as travelers in two worlds. One foot in either world, we are the bridge between them both. And so in figure 29, "Normal 'Breathing'", on p. 491, I illustrate the normal breathing and the broken breath. In normal "breathing," we travel willingly from one world to the other, keeping time and neither pushing on nor hanging back. The upstroke is measured by the down: we rise and fall, and wake and sleep alternately.

Between the two worlds A and B of the circle and the square, emerging life evolves and takes its middle, balanced way.

But of course most of us are somewhat unwilling travelers, subject to preference and the uneasy victims of desires and fears. We prefer the high places and some of us would, if possible, be permanently fixed on an unmoving eminence. We like to know where we are and what we have and keep it all in order, safe and in control. In fact, we know the 2/4 side of life, and with thought and sense and well-intentioned action we propose, quite rightly as we think, to rule it and to make a decent job of it. What is this mysterious nonsense about an unseen world? Leave that to women's intuition and childish fairy tales! We will be realists! We are. And then? What are the penalties of such a broken breath?

It all depends on our experience and how well we are balanced in our inward selves. Some are born unbalanced, and some have their wobbles thrust upon them by their wobbly homes or still more wobbly parents. Some are like gyroscopes that always right themselves, no matter how often they are buffeted by adversity. Some are sensitive and some tough: some have more A and some more B: some have "give" and some have "take," and some have "bounce" and some have "guts." On the whole, most of us have enough of the opposites within ourselves to keep a fairly steady course, by reason of our inward contradictions. We breathe and bump along the road without too many bruises. But others fly apart more easily: some seem to fall for falling's sake, as if they liked it: and some have a lumpy, hard, unteachable consistency that simply asks for trouble at the kicking heels of life.

In any case, we are ourselves. For better or for worse we have our instruments. They can be improved somewhat by practice and an intelligent understanding of their limitations: but they cannot be changed in discontent or abandoned with impunity. We are ourselves and we must learn in time to make the best of it. Meanwhile, it is not enough to claim an alibi, blaming the sensitiveness of the nervous system, or weakness of our glands, when really it is at least partly owing to our attitude towards life that we must owe our downfall. There are limits to the powers that we can claim to interfere successfully with all Life's various adventures. For

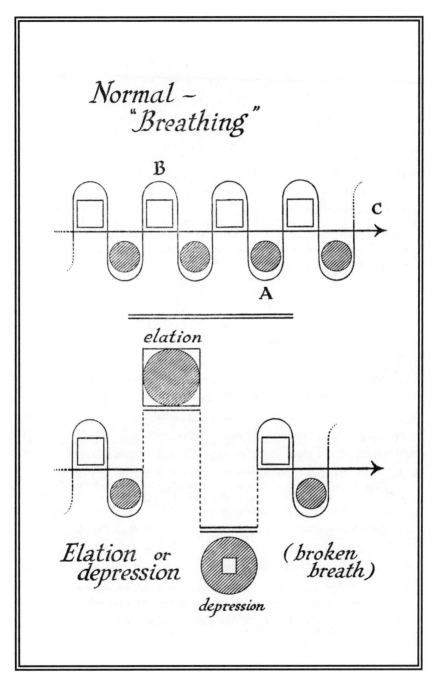

Figure 29 Normal "Breathing"

instance, if I were to insist that mosquitoes must not buzz, or that a fly has not the liberty to perform its antics in my neighborhood, the strain imposed upon my will power, if I pursued my will to victory, might be enough to break the will of Hercules himself. There are many weak backs carrying such impossible burdens which they have imposed upon themselves, because of certain ideas which are fixed only in their imagination. However true such ideas may be to them, they are not true in fact, and the real scapegoat for all our disasters is our ignorance. We can treat experience with more respect than we usually do, and an attitude of non-resistance to reality, or positive acceptance of it *as it is now* is at least half the trick of normal living. The other half is always to retain our contact with that bright star within ourselves from which shines out our sure enduring will.

As soon as our prejudices, of which we are not even aware because we are so close to them, come up against the kind of experience which threatens them, we are at first irritated, then aggravated, and finally overwhelmed. But let us not forget that the real scapegoat was the fixation itself. For instance, we speak of the "weight" of a depression. What made it weigh so heavy? And why does the same thing weigh so differently to different people? The answer to these questions involves relativity, but it is nevertheless a very simple one. We make the weight ourselves by what we do. If I strike my head against a brick wall, the force with which the wall hits me and hurts me will be equal to the force with which I strike against it. Similarly, the weight of a depression will be determined by the force of my resistance against it. Life cannot get us down unless we insist on rising up or staying up. The point about which we must be quite clear is as to what belongs at the top and what belongs at the bottom. That point I illustrated in my story of the Holy Mountain, and made at least my own opinion plain, that the place of spirit was at the top, but the place of the personal self was at the bottom, in all humility. We get into trouble when we reverse the process. If we raise the value of the personal elements we shall lose the spiritual ones, and be turned upside down. It is better, I maintain, for our efficiency and for our happiness, to descend the Holy Mountain willingly, and to pay the price which Life demands.

The Mechanism

The mechanism which sets up the state and symptoms of depression is essentially a simple and instinctive one. Its purpose is the ancient one of self-defense and safety first: fight or flight. The choice within ourselves is always bounded by two opposites, but there are many such double-edged alternatives. Stop or go? And if we stop, is the flag up or down? And if we go, do we go as cowards do, or do we withdraw to fight again another day on better ground? We are always faced by such alternatives; but the most important of them all is this: When danger is near, which matters most—to save our skins, or keep our soul's integrity?

Let us consider how the instinctive nature reacts to the threat of danger. Of the two alternatives of open and shut, it shuts: of advance or retire, it retires: of expand or contract, it contracts. In fact, we behave inside ourselves in much the same simple protopathic and protective way as hedgehogs, or sea anemones, or those sensitive plants in the greenhouse which contract and withdraw from the finger's alien approach. Such is nature's instinctive protective habit of defense by escape. It closes down until the danger is passed. We are the same and still behave inside like little furry animals who find their safety by simply folding up in a protective gesture of natural recoil.

Imagine yourself in the very height of comfort, dozing and relaxed after a good meal, seated at your fireside with just the right companion. You have expanded inwardly in all your three dimensions and you glow with the mysterious comfort of your inward warmth and well-being. Life is good! Then suddenly, without warning, Bang! The bomb drops, or the door slams, or you remember that someone has his knife into you and is twisting it—it is all the same. Self-defense! The limpet contracts on the rock, the oyster shuts on the pearl, the hedgehog rolls into a ball. *And so do you, inside.* Just behind your navel, you shrivel and turn cold: you lose your appetite and your heart goes off at a gallop, as you would do yourself if you could. For a moment you are paralyzed with fright. If it is a false alarm, you settle down to sleep again. But if you were to stay like that, then you would feel depressed and you would experience all the symptoms of depression.

The little arrows of attentive interest which were idly occupied, enjoying pleasant objects, would be violently and suddenly reversed. Self-centered, energy would run for home. The sap, instead of feeding petals full with life, would go petering backwards down the stem to find its home in earth again, and the petals would wilt and fade and fall. You might be petrified, paralyzed and still as death: or writhing in impotent agitation: but with those arrows seeking self and selfish safety, your state would be depressed. Yours would be the instinctive reaction of the "natural" man, whose center of gravity was no higher than his body's safety, comfort and pleasure, here below. But there is another man, a higher Adam, whose center is up above, although his job is down below. He is not so easily put off by disturbance here upon the contumacious earth. He is integrated at an altogether higher and more complex level than is the natural, or instinctive, man. He is linked with others than himself, in working out a common plan. He is affected by yesterday's memories and tomorrow's hopes, as well as today's fears. He knows that the flesh is but a pleasant and efficient group of instruments for him to use while the instruments remain. If they are shot to bits, well it's a pity, but the worker and the work goes on. He cannot be depressed, because his contact with his upper end remains intact. But if he loses that higher incentive and falls into the lower nature of his old Adam, becoming dominated by the deep-laid plots for his material defense which have been prepared through the ages by his autonomic nervous system—then he will be depressed! The cord broken and the soul cut off, with no connecting link, the body and the mind which speaks for it are pitiable things indeed.

"When the light goes out, the lantern trembles." This somewhat cryptic description is the best means I have of conveying the cause of the trembling that accompanies shock and collapse. "Bombed out," the "tenant" has left the "house," and what we notice then is that the house cannot stand up alone without the inward presence of the tenant. Deserted and unoccupied, it trembles and it may collapse. The negative energy of the framework, when unsupported by the positive energy of the spirit, is unbalanced and shows itself to be the secondary and dependent structure that it is. When the lower instinct of self-defense dictates the flight of the higher man from danger, then shock has done a shocking thing and we are rightly shocked.

"When the light returns to the lantern, the house is founded on a rock." Cryptic again, I mean to state that never should the spirit flee, because it never need. The tenant must never be "bombed out," and the "I" must hold the fort of the more objective "me" with willingness, endurance and goodwill. There is no need to go, if only we can learn a trick or two and practice them. If we are blown out against our wills, then we must be willing to return, at once or the sooner the better. So the fallen rider must remount his horse, and the airman start to fly again—at once, if possible, or else resistance hardens. It is as if the house contracts, doors jam and windows stick, to make it harder as time passes for the spirit to recover mastery. It must be remembered that it is the nature of the "house", or "B" stuff, to be of a resentful and resistant texture. Once out, we can return more easily *if we return at once*. But delay means redoubled resistance on the part of B, and it may mean months and months before the tenant can return. Even then he may find his house shrunken, distorted and to some extent beyond repair. This war will show again, I think, as did the last, that the shell-shocked patients who did best were the ones who were put under treatment and returned to work with least delay. Delay is dangerous treatment here, and more active treatment pays in order to let the spirit in, the sooner to regain its right supremacy.

First Aid

And how? First, relax. "Pull yourself together" approaches the problem from the wrong side. It will not do, because it adds to strain and tension in the house. It pulls it to pieces instead of putting it together. Second, enter into the heart of the problem, face up to it and do not run away. Stay in, stay put and hold the fort. Let nothing you dismay. Your courage is the thing. Third, deep easy breathing helps, especially if it is done intelligently, i.e. knowing that the breath is balancing, and so are you. Fourth, get back on your horse, or better perhaps, get back into your harness and your shafts and pull your cart. "It" must not get "you" down, and will not if you get down to it. Now use your will and use it with goodwill.

Words and Meanings

Let us get down to a more detailed study of our subject. Words tell us much by their "feel." "Depression." This word feels heavy, and the dictionary says: "*a state of reduced vitality*: dejection." Pushed down, thrown down, sat on by a great weight: trapped, caught, submerged and near to, yet not released by, death. Life is worthless, empty; to be depressed is to feel condemned, the guilty culprit of some unknown crime. How does it come about, this fall? And is there any link between this fall and that other one dear to theologians which I also have been trying to describe, the "fall of man"? In depression, too, we have the direst sense of sin's conviction, "original" because it is not externally imposed.

I shall be discussing in more detail presently the more serious states of depression, but in its upper levels and less lasting states, depression is something which all of us must know in some degree. "I feel depressed! I do feel so depressed!" Let us think back and catch the point when it occurred. Stop the unfolding picture on the screen of your life's cinema, and hold it in the focus of your attentive eye. Where did you, when did you, why did you, feel depressed?

Where did you? In your tummy, heavy as lead, somewhere below your diaphragm, between your abdominal wall and your backbone, you can locate physically what is nevertheless a feeling —cold, frozen fear, as if the clammy hand of Death itself was placed upon your heart (or solar plexus), dragging it slowly down, suffocated, submerged, with your will powerless to interfere.

When did you feel depressed? Disappointment, frustrations, those are the words. And why? Desire—"I wanted to and I couldn't because. . . ." Back to childhood, back to the beginning, when desire meant so much of life, and disappointment seemed so final. Loss: loss even worse, more poignant still, because we never possessed the beloved, but only hoped that one day, perhaps, we might. And now hope and beloved, both are lost. Alas, we are depressed!

But is this such a simple matter of cause and effect as at first it seems? Because I loved and lost my beloved, therefore I am sad, cast down, depressed. Are our moods so irrevocably connected with the inconstant changing external world, that if a cloud passed over that external sun, therefore a cloud must pass also over our internal sun, so that our internal brightness also must become overcast? If he is angry with me, must I be angry too with him or else against myself? And if she dislikes me, must I always dislike her? Are we so tied to the world outside ourselves that we must act simply as reflectors of its inconstant state?

We often do, it's true: and yet we need not let our moods reflect our outward state. Our human dignity is such that we are just by some fractional margin capable of behaving as something more than mere automatic reflectors. "The day is wet, and I wanted it to be fine!" Then shall we weep, and be depressed? "My beloved passed me by and loves me not at all!" So what? Can we not rise a little out of the instinctive rut of animal conditions and their reflexes? Can we not rise above the protective self-indulgent habits of the lower Adam, and realize the potentialities which exist in Man? Can we not experience the spirit's victory over these earthly tricks? We can, but we have not traveled far as yet upon the road of higher consciousness that separates us from our old ancestral background of a jungle life.

"I am disappointed." Well, what are you going to do about that? Here are some alternatives for your consideration. (1) *Sulk*: after all, if that is the treatment that you are going to get, it isn't fair. What you wanted was perfectly reasonable—of course, you ought to have it—and if you don't get it, it isn't worth playing in the game at all. (2) *Protest*: be angry: get it out of your system, and kick someone or pull the place down. That is much better—for you, if not for someone else. (3) *"I don't care, I didn't really want it anyway!"*: That is really very clever, incredibly subtle for an instinctive cover on the spur of the moment. You never really wanted it at all, so it doesn't hurt when you don't get it? You're never going to want anything any more, so that you can never be hurt by anybody again? Well, you certainly have discovered the perfect anodyne! No desire, no feeling, no disappointment, no pain. It seems too good to be true, and actually it is. The prospect is depressing! (4) *Lump it*: stick it: endure: keep smiling! So very simple, it's just what Nursie said, and Mummie too. That way the hero walks; as long as he forgets his righteousness. And only in that way is he certain to be free of depression. Trained suffering, experienced sensitiveness, enduring desire: these are the living keys to life without the clammy hand of death pawing at our miserable and cowardly vitals: The first alternative, sulking, is halfway to depression already: the second, anger, passes it on to someone else ("when the father is angry, the child becomes depressed"), although it is good cathartic medicine for constipated souls. The third, apathy or anesthesia, is much more common, than we realize, and is the most dangerous because it is the most deadly. Desire and feeling are the very meaning and point of personal life and to stab them dead from fear of being hurt is to invite death by suicide. They are the color in the picture and the variety and spice of life. (It should be growing increasingly plain that I am not one of those more pessimistic mystics who advocate "Kill out desire! Annihilate the self!" I do not regard a negative state of unselfishness as a virtue, because it has so often been found to be the maiden aunt's prim and private path into depression.)

Dangerous Corner

Now let us pull out the Psychic Compass, and see what that can tell about depression. Depression means that there is trouble in the third corner. In liquid terms (for this is the liquid corner), we are "in the soup." Here, as the doorway of all appetite, is the mouth of our personal stomach, the filter of our private experience, into which Life is poured, invisibly. But watch us twist and squirm! How we resist and pretend! With what success our vaunted freedom of the will attacks and defends, resists and runs away! This is where the price of suffering is paid or refused; and this is where we had best be quite clear as to what is to be our philosophy of life. Can we take it (the beloved) with us? If we cannot take it with us, "can we take it?" Are we to struggle like spoiled children on the floor (how depressing!) or are we willing to let go and jump for it, plunged in, swimming naked in this tide of life?

It is as simple, I believe, to see this matter clearly, as it is to see by his or her behavior whether a child is spoiled or not. In their adversity, how do they behave? In the same way, a dog is trained to obey its master's voice and respect its master's wishes. Colts must be broken to the saddle and the shafts. So let us decide quite clearly in our minds; when we are disappointed, how shall we behave? We can be "natural," of course. The instinctive sanction for our conduct will then permit behavior which is no whit better than that of spoiled children and unbroken colts. Surely, there is no depression there, yet. *But there is as soon as instinctive conduct is repressed,* which it must be, for other people will always see to that. Let it out, kick, curse and cry, destroy your disappointing world—you'll never be depressed. But turned in against yourself, all this energy sets up a state of bitterness. Sour in life's stomach, rejected experience sets up a state of indigestion. To be embittered is to be well on the way to becoming depressed.

Intuitives Can Be So Impatient!

There is one especial problem of the intuitives that leads directly to depression, and that is ANGER. Obviously, they are an angry crew, because they cannot get from us the rewards they feel so sure that they are owed. But more than any of us the intuitive "knows" the unity and brotherhood of all mankind. *We are All One!* Therefore anger must not be, it cannot be allowed. With most cause for anger, the intuitive has least heart for it. He therefore has two alternatives. Either he must find a scapegoat and vent all his God-sent wrath on that: or else his anger must become repressed, smothered and bottled up within himself. In the first case, someone else will soon become cast down, in order to uphold the intuitive and his chosen people. This is extraverted sadism. In the second case, he may have fits, as anger overflows in protopathic waves against himself. This is self-directed sadism. Or he may fall into a state of depression, with the protopathic forces congealed in a state of apathetic negativism. This is repressed sadism. The war lets out our repressed and introverted anger, and releases by its encouragement the pent-up fires within our constipated souls. And so perhaps "shock" also does its healing work. But both are blind forces leading blind forces and they do not lead towards a lasting light. For that we need intelligence patiently applied in detail to our ignorance.

If anger and resentment strike outwardly in words or otherwise, even though someone else may be injured, the striker's health benefits. That is one of the reasons for the war's good effect on many of us; it has given us a needed scapegoat, and something to be angry about. But even the longest wars do not go on forever, and when the flow of anger ceases, depression and bitterness will set in again like a returning tide. The aftermath of war, amongst many other problems, will have to face the problem of depression. Truth has been "pegged" for propaganda's sake. It will be no use being angry then, when we are face to face with simpler facts again.

We can be sure, I believe, that a person who is depressed has had some falseness in his attitude towards reality. Desire was too firmly fixed, too fully demanded, too impatiently attacked. It was as if we could not accept less than some perfection that we knew of and hoped for: we must have it all in its perfection, at once, now. This is unweaned desire, because it has not learnt its proper attitude towards reality. It cannot lose, surrender or let go the object which it loves. Instead, desire turns aside and invents in some way the full satisfaction that it demands. It feeds on phantasy, when fact is not so good. It builds in phantasy, and finds increasing satisfaction there. Desire loses contact with the real working world, preferring self-indulgence on the higher inward planes. It turns its back more and more upon reality, escaping into easier and less obstructive fields. Negative itself, depression is the outcome of a negative attitude towards life. It is the unwilling expression of unwillingness. Those who lack the willingness to suffer and go on, become increasingly negative in the first and third categories of the psychic compass. They therefore become increasingly dependent on the world of external objects. They look to conditions to satisfy them, and try to influence the external world in such a way as to be satisfied by it. As the left-hand side of the psychic compass becomes increasingly negative and deflated, so the right-hand side of the psychic compass (that which is related to the external world) becomes increasingly inflated and important. Such an unbalanced person, however, has not a proper attitude towards reality. He does not see it as it is, but as he wants it to be, and in imagination he tries to rule the world in such a way as to satisfy his wishes. This is Phantasy, the motive of which is the double one of escape from pain on the one hand, and the achieving of unreal pleasure on the other. We can see, I think, how full of holes the floor of such a person's life must be. He is living in the air, fixed only by his own self-will to hopes that life cannot fulfill, with the constant fear of falling from such giddy heights into the awful, black and smoking abyss that yawns beneath him. Many of us achieve this gymnastic feat successfully. Some of us do not even realize that it is a gymnastic feat. Some are terrified, and some are thrown into the abyss when life gets difficult. Although they do not realize it at the time, the latter are probably better off, if only they can learn from their experience.

There are many ways, however, in which the gymnastic feat can be made to seem safer, and the danger forgotten. By identification with a good person, such as an anthropomorphic conception of the deity, or some hero figure; or with some good object, such as wealth; or with a good quality, such as fame or virtue, many people are able, like Little Jack Horner, both to hold tight and to feel good. With any luck they will find a coterie of friends and admirers to inflate their prestige. They will find books written to honor them, and parsons and teachers ready to praise them for their good works. Although they are selfish, these successful exalted ones, their real selves are curiously absent, because of their protective identification with the external shell of measurable good things. It is as if with more and more of "it," there is less and less of "me;" as matter becomes more and more important, so the spiritual side, which is the creative side of the self, becomes more and more atrophied. The back gets weaker and the burden gets heavier, which is dangerous to those who hope that their grip will never relax and the burden never fall. When the light fails, we may find ourselves deserted in a waterless desert.

Morbidity

The trouble seems to rise because of our "morbidity," or lack of "vitality." We can be disappointed, but we need not be morbid about it. What then is this condition of morbidity that has not sorrow's solvent quality, but sits instead wringing its hands, in end-less ineffective grief? Disappointment: *I cannot bear it*: that is the fault. And so defensively, to save a state of pain, we join the enemy and become depressed. "You would push me down? Then I will fall! You would hurt me? You cannot hurt me more than I have hurt myself already!" Thus morbidly we allow the pain of suffering to take the place, as actual substitute, of the pleasure that we have been denied, and enjoy it as if it were indeed itself the beloved. Thus we make capital for self-indulgence out of depression's protective pur-pose. If we break the communication cord that joins us to our higher will, and jump into despair, it is true enough—we cannot be hurt! But we cannot be anything else worth while, either.

As I have said, in the first instance depression has an instinc-tive protective function. In an "all-or-nothing" blindly protopathic way, it withdraws the sufferer within himself, away from pain. By breaking the mainspring of the emotional life, its purpose is to dis-miss the pain of the external break by this inward act of sabotage. The person, who is predisposed, therefore, to experience the mor-bidity of depression rather than more solvent sorrow under the shock of disappointment, is the one who has previously permitted himself to live under the protective aegis of his instinctive nervous system. If he has evaded proper suffering on the emotional level: if he has said, "I cannot bear it" and failed to face unpleasant facts: if he has invented a pleasing fantasy as substitute instead: or if he has indulged himself before in pain's inverted joys, and become the self-indulgent victim of self-pity: then he is predisposed by these "morbidities" to suffer depression when the strain is great. If our path is always upwards and to the right, seeking only success in pleasant places, then we dig for ourselves a bottomless pit, below, behind us, and to the left. Our unstable house is already leaning over, when "Bang!" goes the bomb, and down we go—into the pit which we have dug for ourselves by our own unwillingness to be pushed down. The depressed person says, "I feel a weight inside me trying to drag me down. It will not yield, it will not give way;" but he does not realize that the mysterious sinister hand that is clutching his vitals, giving nothing away, is no other than his own. He was like that: he was a clutching hand, pulling at life. Now his past unwillingness has got him down. He would not give before, but now he must both give and forgive, or stay depressed until the inward clock releases him from torture's wheel.

"When the bough breaks, the cradle will fall; and down will come baby and cradle and all." To speak to a person in depression one could hardly imagine that there was any deliberate volitional tendency behind or within so great a personal disaster. Certainly there is no conscious volitional tendency to provoke the downfall of such Babel's towers; and yet there are certain elements in the psyche which are profoundly dissatisfied with its own false arrangements. If the spirit is alive to its own welfare, it is wise for it to will the defeat of that part of the self which is behaving so strangely and unwisely. If there is an "unconscious" part of the self that has been so long neglected, we can understand the existence of a downward pull which, though not deliberate in the conscious sense, is nevertheless dynamic and volitional. It is even possible to recognize in some cases a certain tired defeatism in these self-willed mental monarchies, which willingly grasps at the prospect of giving up the burden and escaping from the battle. It is not, perhaps, that such people actively want to be depressed, but that after a time they begin to feel they want to take a back seat, they want to give it up. They want to fall and fail. All things grow, and this applies to burdens too; and when they get top-heavy, well, let's be depressed!

More Gain, Less Pain

In this preliminary survey of the psychological causes of depression, we may summarize them as "self-centered self-indulgent exclusiveness." The angle on life is essentially "What do I get out of it? How can I get more and pay less?" The attitude to life is one of grabbing gain, avoiding loss. It is instinctive, protopathic, undeveloped, and unweaned. This may sound more rude and uncomplimentary than I intend, yet I do insist that depression is, at least on the psychological side, founded on a moral error. *There is a fault in our attitude to life.* Our philosophy assumes that we ought to be happy, growing easily upwards, gaining all the way. Facts which prove the case to be different can be easily ignored. The external world is treated as if it is there for the self to plunder and to profit by. We become increasingly dependent upon it, and more and more at the mercy of its vagaries and disappointments. When things go wrong and we lose the beloved, that is more than we can bear and so we become depressed. But depression too is one of the things we cannot bear, and so a vicious circle is set up as we become depressed at being depressed.

Self-centeredness is primarily a matter of direction. It is bad for health and bad for others, too. Everything in life is considered as it affects "me" personally, in so far as it is good for my feelings, my advantage and my unbroken gain. Even my apparent concern with outward matters, such as my children, my home, or my country, may be entirely self-centered, if I have entirely identified myself with them. The appearance of such unselfishness is often very hard to prove to be as selfish as it is, except by those who have the mis-fortune to live with it. Of course, selfishness may be self-centered (inflowing arrows) or object-centered (out-flowing arrows). It is only morbid, if the flow is always inwards. The same applies to introspection. It is an excellent thing to look at your secret places, and to see where and how they are. It is an extremely bad thing, however, to set about them with a surgical rudeness because you do not approve of what you find. The rule should be "Do not touch the works or interfere with the exhibits."

Conscience Can Be Wrong

One of the most obvious characteristics of depression is the extraor-dinary weight and vigor of that force within ourselves which we know as conscience. It is always there to show us how we have failed, and how low we have fallen, and how wicked we must be, and how utterly terrible it all is. In depression we see the uttermost extreme of conscience's most gross morbidity. This is that same conscience which makes cowards of us all, inflated to the utmost and showing itself as the crazy fiction that it is. When we lose the pinnacle of self-righteousness that vanity had appointed as our own, pride becomes inverted. All is now lost, nothing remains, and best is turned to worst. We are outsiders then, and know it. We are cast out, useless and unwanted, and feel as if we are turned on by the herd and spurned as if we had the plague. Perhaps we have. But the fact is that we always were outsiders, because we were concerned only with the outside of things. We lived in our external selves, externally. To live exclusively in that external 2/4 world is to invite depression. When the wells run dry, fertile fields become sandy and barren deserts. When the candle is burned at both ends, the wick smokes and the oil of life runs dry. Depression was not an act of God, but an inevitable—we might almost say mathematical—consequence of the balance, or lack of it, of our internal forces.

So down we go, willy-nilly, to taste of the abyss until we are sick of it. We become submerged and swallowed up in all that was repugnant in ourselves. Being the sort of people that we are, we have at last something to be depressed about—our own depression. We alway tried to rid ourselves of what we did not like, and so, our attitude towards depression is what it always was towards life. We are trying to get out of it, but this time we are caught and cannot get away.

Conscience and constipation should be considered together because they are never far apart. "Stuck-up" is a phrase that neatly applies to both, and of the two I believe that constipation is in fact by far the more innocent and less harmful condition. The tyranny of conscience is responsible for far more harm than ever constipation did. Constipation only harms the physical health, whereas a tyrannous self-righteous conscience can mar the very soul. On different levels, they mean the same unwillingness: unwillingness to live and unwillingness to lose. Both are essentially vicious, because neither can let go.

We may say that depression is the effect of a negative attitude towards a negative condition. It is the very opposite to willingness, where willingness is not a lovely dream, but a complete acceptance of every aspect of the experienced fact.

If experience is taken on every level and fully absorbed and digested (i.e. accepted), there can be no bitterness and no disappointment; and no surprise, because there was no escaping, no prejudice, no unwillingness and no fixed attachment to beloved objects in the external world. When the emotional life has been aesthetically and athletically trained to be willing to surrender to experience, to be personally accurate, and to endure without any argument and without any limit, the spirit simply cannot experience depression. The energy of life is then within, centralized, restrained, reserved—and ready for spontaneous release as required to meet all experience intelligently and willingly. Thus poised, an emotional system could face physical factors such as fatigue and toxemia with a certainty of the least disturbance of emotional balance, and the swiftest recovery of normality.

From Negative to Positive

When the balance has been irrevocably upset, and the patient is depressed, what can be done about it? It must be said at once that because the degree of depression and the force of external factors are so infinitely variable, it is a very expert, and often even then a very uncertain, matter to foretell the future in any particular case. It is too much to ask the sufferer to accept the situation, for that is what he never could do. But if he cannot accept it, perhaps we can? Having faced the fact that the patient is depressed and that depression is like that, there are two things in depression that may make us a little more contented. Depression is an attempt at cure, an attempt at self-cure; and it is a necessary phase in the patient's recovery. That is to say, it is not simply a bad thing. It is a real thing and has a real purpose. It is the expression of a real need. Negative as it may seem to be, the patient has not only been brought face to face with his effective instrument at "three," but pushed right under and overwhelmed by it. He is, as it were, swimming around in his own unconscious depths. He needs holding to it, keeping there; and that may prove difficult, because a negative attitude towards life finds itself intensified during depression into the will to suicide or ultimate escape from every unbearable problem. First and foremost the patient must be protected from himself and kept alive, because however low he feels himself to be, the hands of the clock will one day bring him up and round again. How long that time will be we cannot tell, but—and this is the second cause for our encouragement—it is a characteristic of depression that it is a temporary phase followed in course of time by its conclusion. Depression, like any other disease, is like a clock. It may be fast or slow, but the hands are always moving.

Unfortunately, if we merely leave the cure to the evolution of such natural cycles, the patient may be thrown up in course of time to where he was before, or even higher still. The Buddhists set themselves the problem of release from these rotating wheels of life, and they speak of the "Middle Way" as the path of real efficiency. It is wrong, I think, to imagine their philosophy as crying for escape from life itself. Like the doctor of today, they only wished to master the Law of the Wheel, so that they may not be bound in blindness to it. Like the doctor with the depressed or elated patient, the aim of our philosophy and "cure" must be not only to escape from illness, but also to achieve the middle balanced way of health, that will avoid recurrence of disaster.

How is that to be done? It must be a job of work for the patient if he is to counteract or rebalance the forces in himself. A great deal of inertia must be overcome, and there must be a persistent and enduring will if freedom from these unconscious battles is to prevail. Putting this item of the persistent and enduring will first and foremost, I would put as the next most important arm for battle—"Consciousness." By this I mean a willingness to look and see; no more, no less. Consciousness, in the sense in which I am using it as a healer, is not in itself an effort to change anything or to escape from it. It is simply an act of vision or "contemplation;" it combines a gesture of surrender with accurate and objective observation. This process probably needs the help of some person other than the patient with whom it can be shared, so that together they can study the phenomena as they appear. Such details include everyday conduct and dreams, past and present experience, hopes and fears and all imagination. The point is that they must be examined in detail, for depression is an undifferentiated continuum that must be sorted out, and each part related in its proper place to the other parts and to the whole.

Seen from this point of view, the cure of depression provides an opportunity for paying for such tickets as in life the patient had not yet bought. He has to pay his debts to life in full. He has to face again the jumps that he has refused to take, and meet the situations from which he has previously escaped. The process of healing is a kind of recapitulation of life's previous events that permits a second chance and provides the opportunity for an actual new birth. We can redeem the past if we accept responsibility for it.

Of course, there are all degrees of depression, and some are ultimately beyond the hope of cure. There are very many, however, which are not so severe and which can be dealt with either by the patient taking himself in hand or by the assistance of someone close to him, who must be willing meanwhile to share the price in suffering. What is bad for depression is that it should be surrounded by an atmosphere of depression or agitation. Being so dark, it needs to be lightly treated; but of course I do not mean causally or with indifference. It is one of those serious matters that most requires good humor, good manners, and goodwill, for the very reason that the condition possesses none of these itself. If the depressed person feels that here is an atmosphere of sympathetic insight and encouragement combined with patience and willingness to suffer, then at least the magic circle has been drawn, within which a miracle can be done. Efficiency will not do the trick, nor even common sense, unless it be lit by these qualities which belong to the left-hand side of the psychic compass in categories one and three. These are the healers, and we must use them if we are to help the healing process on its way.

Although I do not wish to go into too much detail for the general reader, it may perhaps be useful to attempt a classification of the various types of mental illness in which depression occurs. I suggest the following:

Depression

(1) *Normal:* a passing mood related to present experience.

(2) *Hysterical:* the mood is relatively of longer duration than present experience would justify, and is part of a negative and unbalanced emotional state.

(3) *Schizophrenic:* the mood is only a minor part of a deeper regressive and possibly deteriorating mental disorder.

(4) *Cyclothymic:* the mood is a deep excessive exaggeration of the normal rhythmic emotional swing, sometimes recurrent and sometimes alternating with an opposite phase of elation.

(5) *Melancholic*: a fixed "involutional" emotional condition only partially attributable to recent experience, usually found in later life.

It should be noticed that only in the first case is the mood of depression actually to be described as "caused" by a proper reaction to an external incident. In all the other cases, the incidence of depression is effected not so much by the external episode itself, as by the inner factors within the psychic life, the emotional "build-up" as it were. In all these cases, from least to greatest degree, the personality shows to some extent signs of being "double" in different ways. In change of mood, we change our personality: but in the more pathological instances such as are found in (3), (4) and (5), we can well speak of the patient having become "quite a different person." Also, in varying degree, all of these types show a similar tendency to lose their emotional balance, to fall suddenly through a hole in their psychic structure, and to be immersed and lost, out of their depth in deep waters. One of the most interesting points from the medical point of view is that depression tends to be self-limiting, i.e. to come to an end automatically when it has lasted a certain time and run a certain course. That is to say, it behaves as other diseases in regard to time, in that they have to take time to work themselves out. But unlike some, there is no telling how long a time will be required. Meanwhile, doctor, patient and relatives, all must wait until the wheels are rightly set for recovery to take place, assured in all but the most serious cases that it certainly will. In the first two types, "normal" and "hysterical," there is usually a sufficient "reason" to account for the breakdown: in (3), (4) and (5) however, the cause lies deeper than any recent event or outward disappointment. The cause is in the self, built up within the psychic structure by the attitude to past experience.

I do not propose to go into the symptoms of depression in each of these types in too great detail, except in so far as the main features illustrate the problem of the patient's attitude to life. I will therefore discuss the symptoms briefly in what I call "normal" depression, and then more fully as they are shown in "pathological" depression.

Normal Depression

Although I have used the word "normal" in this classification, I do not mean to imply that I think that depression is, ideally speaking, a normal reaction. I do not think it is, nor is it necessary if we suffer sorrow willingly, accepting and absorbing in our hearts and spirits the burden and pain of the beloved's loss. We suffer sorrow then and, even in our utmost grief, we need not be depressed. That word implies, in my use of it, a degree of abnormality. Something has gone wrong, because the poisoned arrow has missed its proper target. But, since we are the kind of people whom we are, it is normal at times for all of us to be somewhat depressed. We shall quite soon, however, in the normal course of events, get out of it.

For this "normal" degree of everyday depression, desire has experienced disappointment. The normal subject-object relationship has been broken by a disappointment in regard to the object, resulting in a regressive and negative condition of self-attention. Interest which was previously directed towards and centered in an object, has now "snapped back," like taut elastic, upon the subject. The patient has, be it noticed, "given-up" or "given it up," but morbidly, unwillingly. If the surrender had been made, since it must be made, willingly, the condition of depression could not occur.

The person is "up against it," "down and out," "crushed by the burden." All these phrases express exactly what has occurred. "Downcast," "outcast"; unloved, unloving, unwanted; empty, lifeless, worthless and dispirited. Restless, irritable, at loggerheads with one and all, he is wanting affection but unable to give or to receive it. Tears or anger may put the matter right, by releasing pent-up energy towards a resumed subject-object relationship. But meanwhile the condition of the depressed person is fixed, low, deflated: an empty shell. The symptoms are the outward signs or manifestations of an inward condition. It is therefore no use arguing with the symptoms. What has to be effected is a change in the inward condition. This is actually effected when a new subject-object relationship (a new form of interest) is established. In its own mysterious way, Time is the greatest healer.

Tears are an interesting example of our natural dramatic symbolism, or the way in which the body talks its own poetry. Tears are solvent; it is as if they say, "When life is hard and things are dead and dry, take more water with it!" We do dissolve in tears and wash our lumps away. These are good tears, the ones we mean when we recommend having a "good" cry. But even tears are good, bad, and indifferent. Like champagne or religion, they are not always good. They can be very morbid useless things, if we enjoy wallowing in them as if they have become an alternative satisfaction for the beloved that we have lost.

Abnormal Depression

The evidences of this condition repeat themselves with the invariable monotony of a gramophone record. There is very little originality in mental disorders, because we are actually dealing with something very similar to gramophone records. The turning wheels within the self cause outward patterns of behavior, unrelated to the various external causes which are so often brought in to provide a ready explanation. The cause is within: the pattern is deeply operative: the wheels rotate, and the conduct and expression is as unchangeable as it is mechanical. It is emerging from within, with inexorable precision and determination.

Elated or depressed, the wheel is no longer in contact with the road. Up in the air, elation goes in for rapid action and the wheels fly round unimpeded by reality. Reality is represented by a scapegoat, who includes all those others who do not understand. Not being equally elated, they are obstructions in the way and so must be swept on one side. All things seem possible, all wealth possessed and all moral obligations absolutely clear. "I am God; I know I can, I must, I will," sings the deceptive "daemon" through the unguarded door.

Fast—slow, elated—depressed, up—down, the pendulum has swung. So worthless and so low, the only scapegoat he can find now is himself. His judgment of himself in this affair, however, is completely warped. It is of the "all or nothing" kind, which shows its protopathic origin. He is in fact quite overwhelmed by the unweaned, undifferentiated mass of protopathic stuff. Caught, imprisoned, trapped within the deadweight darkness of the body's world, without the saving grace of any light, the patient can only judge in terms of utter hopelessness. All limited (epicritic) measurements being thus judged by unlimited (protopathic) standards, the answers can only come out with mathematical certainty as a minus quantity. It may be possible, too, that there is actually less experience of real pain than sometimes seems to be the case to the outward observer, owing to this total immersion in a protopathic state. The experience of pain depends upon a state of measurable change. With no change and no relationship by which to measure it, one wonders how in fact there can be pain. The protest of it is certainly excessive, and I do not think we are far wrong in believing that the affective state of the depressed patient is not actually as bad inwardly to himself as it sounds outwardly to the sympathetic listener. There is some blessed anodyne within this stony grief. It proves again that we are usually wrong when we judge others by what we feel ourselves.

Technically, depression is a paroxysmal attack associated with deficiency of vitality, inhibition at the highest level, and more or less complete paralysis of the will. It is characterized by lowered excitability of the nervous system as a whole, with paralysis of all effective thought, feeling and action. With communications broken, nothing is coming through, and even the bowel itself tells the same constipated tale of obstruction and paralysis. The patient lives in a grey and weary world of his own morbid imagination, dissociated equally from Will on the one hand and from Action on the other, as he is dissociated from his real inward Self, and his customary outward relationships.

Symptoms

The other chief points about depression are:

(1) *Self-centeredness*: the patient is in a state of protective self-withdrawal, facing inwards and backwards, in what can be described as an "involutionary" phase, contrasted with the normal outward-looking, onward-moving, "evolutionary" phase. At the same time there may be a strong feeling of hatred, a turning against those who were previously best loved. There may be a state of restless agitation, with no peace of mind anywhere. But the most outstanding characteristic of the depressed state is its extreme self-centeredness. The flow of life, such as it is, is inwards all the time. The

depressed person has no interest whatever available for outward things: they might as well not be there for all the attention he can pay. He cannot enter into anything, nor give anything out. The field of interest has contracted until it has ceased to exist, and all that matters is the grinding out of the same old grim tale, like the slow rotation of a cracked gramophone record. "Worthless—sin—no money—ought to die—burden to everyone—fraud," the same pitiable story is repeated by them all, be they comedians or kings, persons of no understanding or even psychologists who thought they knew all the answers. These deepest ruts within the self are fraught with patterns quite unvarying. They speak of darkness because they have no light.

(2) *Retardation,* or fixation of all the normally moving parts, is apparent. Nothing flows except the sluggish means of physical life and that has almost stopped. Physically constipated, incapable of effort or interest, unable to read or write, time hardly hangs for time has almost stopped. The wheels of life are barely turning round and the patient is more incapable of emotion even than of motion. He lives in petrified eternity, or in constant frozen fear.

(3) *Guilt* is perhaps the most remarkable thing about depression. Always his sense of sin has caught him up, and hardly ever is there more than a subnormal justification for it. The most unimportant peccadilloes are dug up from the past to justify the sense of guilt and to take the place of scapegoat. There is a sense of unbearable isolation, intolerable sin. The burden of responsibility is the more severe because it feels to the depressed person as if something must be done to solve the problem immediately, although he is equally certain that nothing can be done about it, ever. He must be made perfect, now—but he is hopeless, worthless, not worth saving, utterly condemned to all eternity.

Certain points are of especial interest, and I believe that the depressed patient can confirm certain theological conclusions, while throwing doubt on others. If "sin" is to be defined as "separation from God," and guilt as our sense of that separation, then the depressed patient has traveled all the way. He is in fact utterly separate, utterly cut off: the bridge is broken and the light is out. This is his fact, but not his fault; and he interprets it, in the only way he can, as guilt, sin and worthlessness. He is not wanted any more, at least for the duration of his own especial Hell. But where I believe that the doctors are sometimes in advance of the parsons in general, is that we regard the conscience of such a one as being a sick and morbid thing. He is wrong in thinking that he should be "one with God." Health is not a sinless state. To be born at all is our Original Sin; not, thank God, because our parents were of opposite sex and proved it, but because to be born at all is to be born a separated Being. Therefore we are born into Sin; and such was God's intention, apparently. He wants us separate. The depressed person, however, feels deeply, deadly, otherwise. He is suffering from the backward look. He has tried before to make good his escape and put himself on the right hand side of his Father in Heaven at the top of the Holy Mountain. That is just his trouble. He would not come down to earth and get on with it. He could not bear to sin. He was fearfully and obsessionally good. In fact, *his conscience was his greatest sin*, and that is why the illness of depression is especially the lot that falls on so many "good" people. My contention is, however, that it cannot possibly fall upon those who have faced life truly. For health's sake, in body or in mind, the Truth is a stronger and a braver healer than the good. The good, being unbalanced, must always bring an opposite of evil somewhere in its train. But truth is all there now, circle and square. It cannot fall or fail; neither can we if we attend it whole and properly. (It is also worth noting the great similarity that exists between the conflicting parties, both within the self under the dictatorship of Conscience, and externally between societies under their moral dictatorships. War in either case is energy unweaned, without intelligence; and yet its motive force is always moralized, owing to the innate worth of the source from which it emanates. In either case, it claims divine authority. In either case, judge it by its works. It is the destroyer. It is madness. It is the tyranny of death. In either case, those in high places who ought to know better are most easily fooled.)

(4) *Worthlessness*, hopelessness, emptiness, nothingness: only this urgent bleak besetting sense of sin.

514

(5) *Insomnia.* Of all the things that make depression hardest to bear, this is the worst of all. With time stopped, everything gone wrong and nothing to look forward to, it might still be not too bad a prospect if we could forget it all in sleep. But no, never. This is depression's constant bugbear and most unwelcome companion: sleeplessness. Cast out, thrown down from Heaven, unwanted, constipated, guilty, on the brink of doom—and cannot even sleep. What experienced torturer devised this ultimate doom?

If insomnia is such an integral part of the symptom complex of depression, we can be sure that it is fundamentally connected with the same root cause. Sleep, like the 1/3 side of the psychic compass, lies the other side of the psychic rubicon, and, the bridge *has broken down.* There is now no way across, and the traveler is wandering in a waterless desert, dead with fatigue yet unable to rest. We have all experienced a similar condition on occasions when we have been either mentally or physically overactive, i.e. over-exerted on the 2/4 side. The life that we have evoked will not be laid to rest again: we are possessed by the demons of our own activity and they will not let us rest. The wheels continue to drive round mechanically and all the faster, because there is no real external work for them to do. The world of "B" is buzzing with impotent excitement and the returning road to "A" is barred. This is the common basis both of insomnia and of depression.

The question is often asked as to whether the depressed patient, who has no desire to go out or indeed to stir a finger, would not sleep better if he could be made thoroughly exhausted by long walks or some other form of exercise? The answer is No. Only in the very slightest cases will depression respond beneficially to either exhortation or exercise. It must be remembered that depression is already a deeply depleted and exhausted state. It has long passed the pleasant state of fatigue that leads to sleep. The patient is instead already too tired to sleep. In general, in spite of all the evidence of inertia, the proper treatment is rest, with great patience on all sides. In spite of constant pleas that something must be done, the kindest condition for this insufferable complaint is that it should be suffered willingly. Rest is what it needs and cheerful, but not bland or callous, acceptance.

(6) *Suicide.* This is the last characteristic of depression that I will mention, as it is indeed too often the last point about such a case that there is to mention. Of all the cases of suicide, we can safely assume that nearly all of them occur while the subject is in a state of pathological depression. Without being unduly scared by such a possibility, it is the more unwelcome because, in the great majority of cases, the patient would have completely recovered in the course of time, with a return of all his normal interests and faculties. Depression tends towards its own recovery, but the way to death through suicide is an irreversible step for which no cure is known.

There are two motives for this self-sought death, as there are for any other journey. If you travel from Birmingham to London, it may be either because you wish to leave Birmingham or because you wish to arrive at London. It is the same with Life and Death. You may wish to leave Life because it is difficult, or to find Death because it seems more attractive. Life at any time is bad for some. Life when we are depressed is Hell on Earth, and that in itself is surely reason enough for wanting to get out of it. But there is more to suicide than that. Suicide is a symptom and like all symptoms it has a protective healing purpose. It seeks the way to cure by finding source again, so that the body's deadweight may be cast off and the healing presence of the spirit rediscovered. This is the deep unconscious pull drawing the depressed person across the boundaries of death's Rubicon. Like other short cuts, it is not to be recommended, although it is not to be too sternly judged. It is one of the many follies of good intentions and is usually strongly backed by the vehement demands of a morbid conscience. Like other false steps, even if in the right direction, suicide leaves the dispirited and spirit-hungry traveler too literally "in the air."

Escapism

The habit of escaping from reality grows from little short cuts and innocent evasions to bigger ones; from little make-believes to larger fantasies and greater disappointments, until depression finds its last escape in suicide.

Escapism is the wrong way round the spiral course of Life. It is backwards, widdershins, black magic and indubitably, insidiously wrong. It is true that fear and loss, "blood, sweat and tears," bar the way if we face the enemy. But the spirit can take it if the spirit undertakes it as a job of work. Fear faced is fear diminished, but fear fled is fear redoubled. Burdens tackled are burdens halved, but burdens shirked are twice as heavy. Walk on, patiently. That is the way that works and pays. It proves so much the easier in the end. But it is not *natural*: at least, it is not natural to the lower, coarser Adam. It needs the higher man to bring the higher zest and the more important motive than the welfare of his private skin. One way or the other, right or wrong, we are building up the structure and the substance of our lives. It behooves us to build well, if we are to avoid having our houses falling round our ears.

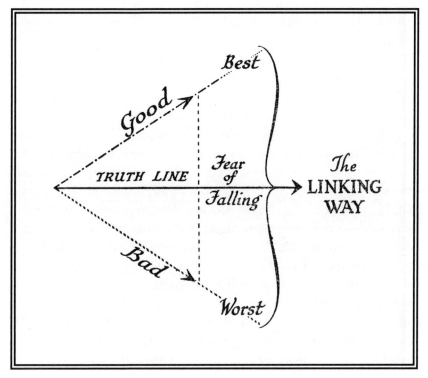

Figure 30 The Linking Way

We are like tops and need our balancing. In fact, balanced we are and balanced we must be. We never can be otherwise, and that is why we have to fall about as we do in order to complete our balancing.

As I see life, it is always arranged in terms of balanced forces, and I often draw the pattern (in figure 30) to illustrate the principle of equals and opposites. The middle line is Truth, by which I mean Reality, or experience as our instruments record experience, if they can be unbiased. The upward tilt is what we do when we prefer the "good" to the "true." (Of course, we usually do, if we mean by good what we regard as good for us!) Thus we create its opposite and the most desirable and Heavenly "best" is balanced high above the bottomless pit of most horrific Hell below. Thus is fear relative, not to life itself, but to that inward reality that we have made of it, within ourselves. The upper flees from the lower, but the lower pulls and pulls and pulls—until we are depressed, brought low, yet balanced up. There is no need to conceive of a demon torturer, when our own best intentions are capable of doing so much harm!

It is characteristic of depression that the patient is trying to move in a certain direction *opposite to normal*, and for two reasons. Out there is trouble, so he will escape from it: but back in here and somewhere behind him where he came from, there is Heaven, Peace, Love, Ecstasy, Unity, Home, God, Mother—what a list! With so much to tempt behind, and so much to threaten him in front, why not go back? Why not reenter the womb and replace the chicken in the shell? Why should not emerging life get back again within the seed? The reason why not, amongst others, is that the path of such return is so arranged that it is completely barred for the depressed person. The bridge across is broken and the way is barred. He cannot return, he cannot escape, he cannot even sleep or rest. This is indeed a dreadful demon to possess a man, and we are well advised to keep our faces front, our feet on earth, and make the best of it. God: Mother: womb: egg: seed: source: and Heaven's mysterious ecstasy are not for us, who have been sent the other way. Your conscience pricks you? Original sinner, go and sin some more!

I conceive of the inner process as a spiral movement, evolving, emerging, unfolding as A enters into B, or 1/3 into 2/4. Normally, B owes its life and nourishment to A, and not alone to earthly foods. We are born of the spirit, and by the spirit's grace we dwell, alive and well, within a material world, all of which is upheld by that same spirit's grace. In depression, the grace does not arrive: the current is reversed, and we fall down, dispirited. This I have drawn, spiral fashion, in figure 31, p. 520. The bridge that links the two worlds has crashed: the chasm is open, with no passengers crossing. Why?

I believe the most important point about the answer is to realize that it is because of something that we did ourselves, deliberately and morally of good intent. As we have lived before, so we have built for ourselves a certain constitution, and so next time we shall behave again. By the way in which we are living now, so are we conditioning our future lives. As we have sown, so we must reap. There is a great inertia withstanding change. "I have been here before?" Yes, and you will probably pass this way again, and for no better reason than that mere repetition is always the easiest course. We broke the bridge. We caused the depression. Depression is always self-caused. Depression must therefore be self-cured. But how?

The bridge was broken by two means, each with one purpose. If we treat B as if A did not exist, pretending that B is all we really need, we break the bridge, because we do not go back to A. And similarly, if we treat A as if B did not exist, pretending that A is all we need, we break the bridge because we do not go back to B. In either case, we are demanding from either A or B a complete contact, a satisfactory wish fulfillment, a gratification of desire; and we do not accept the frustration that the other opposite implies. And so, denying either pillar, we break the bridge. Thus lamed we must in time become depressed. From this point of view, there is nothing to choose between would-be saint and would-be sinner, A or B. They are both equally damned if they would escape from reality by getting rid of the other half.

If this scheme is right, the cure is plain, and effective treatment can follow right diagnosis. At least we can concentrate our intelligence upon prevention, which is sometimes worth more than cure. We must concentrate on the bridgework and keep the traffic going over the bridge: not A or B, but A and B, and C, where C is the living link between two worlds, the symbol of relationship. At this

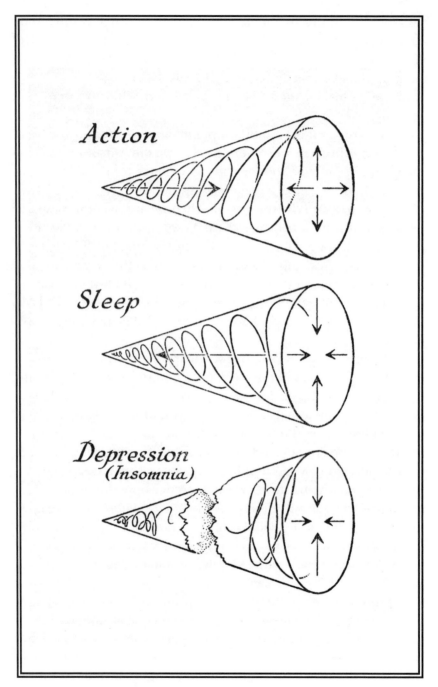

Figure 31 Action—Sleep—Depression

point we enter a new orthodoxy for our encouragement. This business of right relationships has always been Christ's job. It was also known, in Buddha's day, as the Middle Way. He worked at it, as well. If the upper and the lower way must cause depression's curse, then the middle way must cure it. (We may refer this dialectical solution also with advantage to the social problem and the class war.) If the upper man and the lower man are having trouble with one another, then let the "Christ" do His bridgework. If old and new are at loggerheads, then let intelligence set to work, for it has been well defined as "the capacity to see relationships." Where two alternatives are in conflict, neither can ever win finally without the healing presence of a third.

The day of our uneasy identification with good objects should be over, or at least we should be less easily deceived after our experience of war. Good intentions without intelligence have done harm enough. Let depression teach us the lesson of becoming willing to accept both sides and of turning our backs on the heavenly places, while we go forth to fight for the King and for the Kingdom, in the one and only War that is worth while for men.

Mending Broken Bridges Means Greater Willingness

The solution of the problem of depression is the solution of the problem of life. It is the solution of the individual and the social problem. We must adopt a different philosophy of life, if we are not again to court disaster, depression and breakdown. To continue to believe in rising gain, fixed good and other scapegoats than ourselves, is to set the whole bad system on the road again. The other alternative is to be born again, as life is born again, unhampered, fresh, alone—but finding right relationships.

To regain our right relationship with each other and with life, we must sometimes be willing to be depressed. We must be broken down, experiencing a needed suffering as our lumps are dissolved and our stuff prepared and our instruments made good. Sometimes we must fall, lose, die willingly and be dissolved, to be born again. Actually, although it may sound high-faluting, it is not really, because it is simply the way life works. It is the way that we also must learn to work, intelligently. It only means that if A is different from B and you intend to travel from A to B, then you cannot take what belongs to A with you to B. Therefore it is important, in order to avoid confusion and disappointment, to know exactly what belongs to A, and what does not, and also exactly what you can expect from B.

Life has evolved by many different means and by many different paths. These means, these paths, these forms and patterns that they make, are just so many facts. The fact that we exist with all our differences, should be enough to ensure a right respect from others who are different from ourselves. It is so easy to assume superiority, but so hard to prove it. Death wins all wars, and victors and vanquished must all be joined one day upon the other side. Depressing thought, if we believe that that can be the end! On this side, death wins all and scoops the stakes. But if we assume that we are indeed the children of duality, then what must happen upon the other side of death? Perhaps life itself is simply our depression and we shall find in death release, rebirth—and rise again! This is no false hope nor wishful thinking for those who can face all the facts and understand the darkly breathing pattern of the whole.

Breathing, we live: breathing, we need never feel depressed in spirit while the spirit breathes, or while we breathe the spirit. Death itself is but the other half of the living spirit's breath. Knowing this, our lives are changed and we can wait more patiently and work more willingly. But if we are blind to this, the deepest fact of all, we shall either be depressed ourselves, or else project depression into others' lives.

Like breathing, Life is a giving and a taking business. It is not always more blessed to give than to receive, because experience is sometimes very hard to take and very rude to give. Respect for fact is a great and sometimes grievous discipline. Our fellow men are facts: they are our discipline, especially if they cause us grief and disappointment. It is right that they should sometimes do so, simply because they must if they are ever to become themselves. There is never just cause for our depression in the simple and indubitable fact that others may cause our suffering. Their will is theirs: ours is our own. They have their spirits' light and we have ours. Not Death itself need put us out.

CHAPTER 29

Hysteric or Schizoid?

Unacceptable Impulses

The spiritual nature of man confronts him with special problems in regard to resolving his primary state of personal omnipotence in everyday experience. The word "togetherness" seemed to describe his constant temptation to regress to the comfort of non-duality, rather than to advance into the dangerous uncertainty of experience in the field of personal relationships. Behavior determined by the good image of togetherness could be considered to be normal. There is much behavior, however, which derives from the admission of the basic spiritual nature of man and belongs to the psychopathology of abnormal behavior. This can best be classified under the states of illness known as hysteric and schizoid.

The word which best expresses our human problem in this regard is *indivisibility*. It is another aspect of *togetherness*, but whereas the latter word has a meaning of outwardness, the former implies an inward state which is related to the diamond hardness of the spiritual core of the psyche. If we are considering the pairs of opposites which stretch across the psychic balance of the whole man, then we can see that Heaven/earth, fire/water and diamond/blood must set a tremendous problem of intra-psychic tension and potential imbalance. No single word as soft and pliable as "love" will serve to represent this terrifying aspect of our human problem. In fact, although it is one of egoic man's favorite "good" words, love is so misleading a temptation to egoic man's soft-heartedness that in the end it may even lead to his destruction, through his refusing to face the truth of his more implacable reality.

From *Cure or Heal? A Study of Therapeutic Experience*

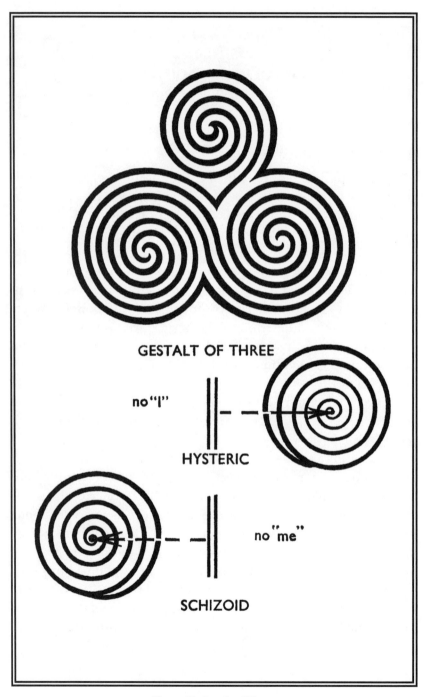

GESTALT OF THREE

no "I" HYSTERIC

SCHIZOID no "me"

Figure 32 Gestalt of Three

If our energy is to be polarized in these vast terms we realize its potential violence, unless it is very carefully caught and housed in an image which must be strong enough to hold it. Primarily, man himself is just such an image. Holding the opposing infinities of inner and outer worlds, of expanding and contracting space, between his very hands, he contains them constellated within the measured places of his images within his mind and brain. It is as if man's task on earth is taming energy, not only in the world of natural forces outside himself, but also in that inner psychic world within himself. Normally, he does this by constellating and relating images, in a balanced field of opponent forces. He gets into trouble, however, if he interferes with what is true, preferring only what seems to be convenient to his egoic welfare. Egoic man's preferential selections lead to abstractions, dissociation and imbalance, from which his psychopathology of unbalanced behavior must follow.

The unit of energy described as a "chakram" and illustrated on p. 106 depends for its operation on its *divisibility*, i.e. the essential hard core of the positive pole at A is given out or poured forth in streams of energy which may be very large or very small, but all of which need to be used in some way in ordinary life. The hard core itself is energy in the raw, ruthless violence, because at this stage it is uncaptured by a suitable image, unconstellated and unrelated. It is only when the chakra are related to one another by "dying into one another," so forming larger and subtler constellations, that the whole psyche can operate as a unified experiential field of effective activity.

Energy needs to be employed by wedding it in relationship to opportunity. In this way it becomes neutralized and harmless. If energy is not used owing to frustration or dissociation, it remains dangerous as potential violence. It is the energy of such *unacceptable impulses* which then motivates the psychopathology of our unbalanced behavior. Egoic man, in his Christian aspect, has chosen to abhor violence and prefer love. His problem of violence remains therefore unresolved and threatens his existence.

It was not always so. Before the Great Divide of history (300-400 BC), since which the influence of Christianity has played so great a part, the wrath of the Gods, the punishment of Fate, the vengeance of the Furies, were all accepted as part of our total psychic field of experience. The natural elements of fire, air, water and earth, were known to be the untamed threats to human safety which they have always proved when off the human leash. The sap in the tree, the blood in the heart of a man, the violence of a woman, the claws of a cat, the roar of a lion and even the bite of a mosquito were known to be capable of unmitigated savagery. The spirit of Dionysus entered his Bacchae and, if frustrated in their madness, these women tore their own children limb from limb. We seem to have forgotten that the whole of man contains each of every pair of opposites in rhythmic balance. As Euripides stated in his play, *The Bacchae* (400 B.C.) "hold the balance and stay whole. If you can do that you are a wise man." But the Christians found another way of dealing with their unacceptable impulses. They dissociated them, so that they remain with us today as our unsolved problem, and the cause of much of our disease.

What Is Normal Life?

The world of experience has been already defined as a gestalt-of-three, "I-experience-it," and the basic brick of life from which our psychic house is built in its almost infinite complexity, has been seen to be a relationship of subject and object, joined by the middle term of X for experience:

$$I \longrightarrow X \longrightarrow it$$

More specifically. X may refer to the fact that I-see-it, I-want-it, I-know-it, or I-love-it, but it is from this gestalt-of-three, subject-verb-object, that we build up the reality of our experiential world.

So far, X may not be "good," but X will be true, and we can remain loyal and faithful to the component elements of our experiential world. If this can be called "normal" in the sense that deviation from the truth has not yet occurred, we can build up our view of a normal world of experience-in-time, as a time-stream, or time-track, of Xs: - - X - - - X - - - X - - to denote this experience of continuity-in-time in our experiential world, and indeed of our real Selves.

This may be figured as a relationship between two worlds, such as inner and outer, subjective and objective, male and female, with X to denote the specific quality of the experience between them:

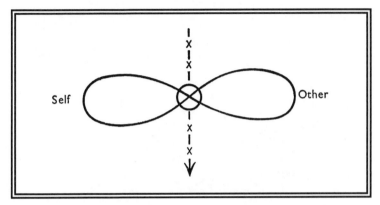

Figure 33 Opposites Joined

So can any pair of opposites be joined, linked, hinged or wedded in their particular mode of meeting (mating). To bring our two related worlds to life, we can spin them on their axes, each in its own orbit, while each remains in true relationship with the other.

Our illustration can now be compared with the Celtic diagram at the top of figure 32, or with the dynamic system of the relationship between the worlds of the father and mother which allow for the creation of the child, whose experiential reality is now, upon the time-track.

So the banks of the river have formed a stream, which will henceforth wander upon its devious but unrelenting course towards the open sea. As a result of such a creative partnership between a pair of opposites, a process has been set in being, the consequence of which no one can foretell. And such indeed is life: ordinary life, as it makes its mysterious way through the perpetual partnership of the invisible and the visible, the inner and the outer worlds.

Here then is our way of experiencing balanced living. We are suspended between female and male, darkness and light, unknowable and known, sickness and health, death and life. We are each indivisibly mated to our other opposite, with the regulated rhythm of systole and diastole at the very heart of our relationship. Here is the truth about normality, reality, personality, experience,

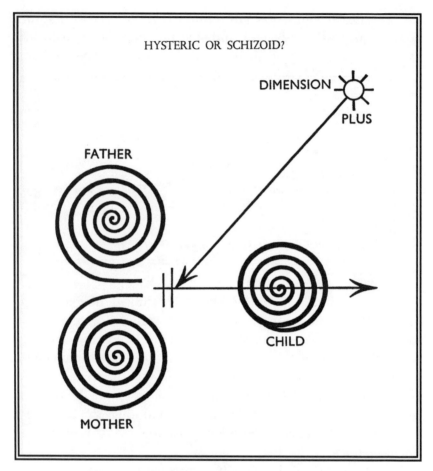

Figure 34 Father—Mother—Child

health, life—and death. This is what and where we "really" are, whether at work or play. Whether we know it or not this is the TRUTH, which is at the heart of all of us and of everything, always.

This is what the Buddha saw in his enlightenment. He called it the "Middle Way." This is the TAO of Lao-Tzu, whose man-of-experience walked the middle of the road, turning neither to this side nor that. The same teaching turned up again when the Bodhidarma arrived in Japan about 600 A.D. as the founder of Zen Buddhism, with its stick on the back, claiming the indubitable reality of experience-now, and no thinking about it, either. To make our diagram relevant to the Hebrew realization of the activating

528

presence of the Shekinah, and its Christian continuation in the visitation of the Dove of the Holy Spirit, it is only necessary to emphasize the in-coming or "incarnation" of another dimension at the point of meeting. As the Jewish tradition has it, the place of meeting is in the "marriage bed." In the Christian tradition the Divine visitor joins with us at the communion table, or the more ordinary eating place of all of us in every home.

There are those both in the church and outside it today who believe that such ideas as the Virgin Birth, Incarnation and Holy Spirit, are dispensable as being unsuited to the modern, scientific mind of secular man. And yet every attempt in any religion to describe the TRUTH OF ULTIMATE REALITY has found that it is just these ideas which are indispensable. In this symbolic picture of mother and child, woman is shown in her crucial, mediate role, between the FATHERHOOD-OF-GOD on the one hand, and the son-ship-of-the-child on the other. Thus she holds the bridge between spirit and matter, eternity and time, past and future, inner and outer worlds. She is the living symbol of the spirit of man and of our ultimate reality, as the child in her arms is the symbol of our growing point, pressing ever outward and onward, now.

The role of Joseph is important enough, but he stands to one side. He is never the central figure of the cross. His role is catalytic, and his position is that of the caretaker of mother and child, as he is also husband-man to the earth which he must till. His authority is not his own but representative. As the father he is "standing in" for the FATHER. As watcher or witness, he stands in awe, silent and inactive, at the birthplace of the miracle of life. This is the role of the psychotherapist.

So much for our attempt to describe truth, self and normality, as they exist in reality. That they are so rarely found is not surprising, seeing that the "true" must usually fall so far short of what seems either "good" or "best." If we are to be confronted with any choice between the alternatives of "very good mother" and "not so good mother," or "very bad mother," or "no mother at all," are we not wise to insist on only the very best mother, fixed and forever? Humanly speaking it is obviously worth trying, so we will now consider the three different ways of interfering with experiential reality.

Three Different Ways of
Interfering with Experiential Reality

In our gestalt-of-three, consisting of I-experience-it, we can interfere either with the first factor "I," the middle term "experience," or the objective aspect, "it."

(a) *Interference with "I"*: There is good reason for doing this, and different ways of doing it. The sometime Christian ambition of "I crossed out" in order to achieve unselfishness, is one way of avoiding all personal responsibility by virtue of an identification with the good (best possible) other. This would seem to be due to a common misunderstanding of Christian principles by egoic man, who is always inclined to see what is really inside himself as outside, and what is truly spiritual (symbolic) as only materially, or historically, true.

In the outward direction, "I" can therefore be identified with good images, from ideas to prestige symbols, such as motor cars or washing machines. (This will be referred to later as the hysteric trend.) In the inward direction, "I" can be withdrawn partially or altogether, reversing the normal direction of the flow of life from Heaven to Earth to send it backwards from Earth to Heaven again. If it chooses to do so, the Will can achieve even this. Indeed, it has often been recommended as a good thing to do, both by Christian and Hindu teachers. (This will be referred to, however, as the schizoid trend.)

(b) *Interference with experience*, or X the unknown: Egoic man abhors uncertainty and often prefers to believe the worst rather than be in any doubt. In any case, this middle term of experience is man's capacity for suffering, or what the Buddhists term DUKKHA. If egoic man could stop suffering, would he not do so in himself? In fact, he can do so in various ways. He can stop himself from feeling altogether if he chooses to do so, by "hardening his heart" as many doctors and nurses learn to do in order to protect them from the repeated, meaningless and intolerable pain of others. He can dissociate from fact and choose his flight to phantasy or daydream instead. He can so easily close his eyes to what he does not want to see.

But the most serious and common damage to this area occurs in shock when, either temporarily or permanently, it shuts down altogether. Too much, too often and too soon of any stimulus from the outside world, whether painful, pleasant or only neutral, causes exhaustion in this instrument of suffering. It takes time to develop its strength to endure. Children, having very little capacity for suffering, may be put into shock very early in their lives, subsequently complaining of a feeling of unreality, or depersonalization, which is due to their inability to "feel" experience, or experience feeling.

Psychopaths, who are defined as emotionally defective, or unable to learn from experience, are either born or conditioned to be deficient in their capacity to experience feeling, i.e. to endure the tension of the "middle term" of suffering.

(c) *Interference with "it."* From what has been said already, it should be understood that by his very nature, egoic man has already interfered with the objective reality of "it," by reason of the necessary limitation of his three-dimensional state of mind towards it. "It," as it appears to egoic man, is egoic man's abstraction from reality, conforming to his own egoic limitations.

Apart from this, egoic man can project his own ideas upon it, "wishful thinking" as we say. So when he is in love, he hallucinates her out of her reality into his world of phantasy, which she may find a pleasant dream on a honeymoon, but very hard to live up to during later more humdrum life.

Although "it" is there for all to see, egoic man can see nothing that he does not want to. By closing his mental eyes he can become as one blind; and by using his mental projector of images he can see only what he wishes. But interference with reality in this way is only successful as long as it succeeds. When it works no longer, egoic man needs to seek truth for truth's sake passionately, because madness is the threat he most fears who suffers disillusion.

Egoic man, whether he knows it or not, is in a very fearful position. He is afraid of the unlimited immensity of "I," of the uncertainty of experience as well as the sometime certainty of suffering loss or death, and of the enmity of both "they" and "it." He is afraid of being and of not-being, of feeling and of not-feeling, of what he knows and of what he does not know. He is afraid of being alone and of meeting an other, of holding on and of letting go, of making a decision and of remaining undecided. No wonder egoic man takes care of himself as best he can by moving this way or that:

towards an inner indivisibility (the schizoid alternative) or towards an outward togetherness (the hysteric variation). These represent respectively the refuge of the son by identifying himself with the FATHER, "I," or with the mother, in the egoic world of "me." Between these two alternatives he wonders: if he were to be his experiential self and live just for one moment, NOW, how could he bear it? Would his identity not be dispersed utterly? Egoic man is reasonable man, and it is most unreasonable to expect him to stay in such a dangerously indeterminate situation as here-and-now presents, unless he must. But there is no compelling him. Whether it be consciously or not, egoic man is free to choose and choose he does, one way or the other, "hysteric" or "schizoid."

It is not the purpose of this book to set out to be a psychiatric treatise, but a brief study of the contrasting images and behavior in the hysteric and schizoid states should now be of interest, and prove how much we are all involved in both these deeply rooted psychic maladies.

Definitions

(N.B. The following definitions are to be considered valid only in the context of the ideas expressed within this book.)

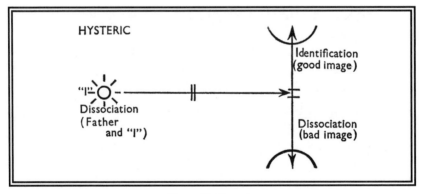

Figure 35 Hysteric

Definition:
The hysteric trend is a motivated tendency towards

(a) *identification* with a good (mother) image in the outer, egoic world, and

(b) *dissociation* from the opposite bad (mother or father) image as well as from the inner, centrally motivating source of "I" (FATHER).

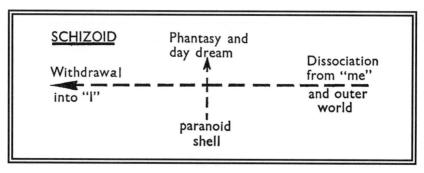

Figure 36 Schizoid

Definition:

The schizoid trend is a motivated tendency towards an essential inward indivisibility or unbornness, contrary in direction to life's normal outward flow. It is a regressive identification with inward older sources of energy, producing a negative attitude towards, and withdrawal from, a normal life of personal and other object relationships.

Let us now consider these two trends in turn in some detail. (It should be noted that we are not discussing the formulated diagnosis of the mental illnesses of HYSTERIA AND SCHIZOPHRENIA, but only the common tendencies of motivation which we all share to some degree in the hysteric and schizoid directions.)

The Right Turn: Hysterical Variation

Egoic man has become an abstraction from his total SELF, as well as from REALITY. Our present task is to see one way in which he has done so, which we will call the "hysterical variation," and then show it in contrast with the opposite alternative, the "schizoid variation."

Given the two alternatives of inner and outer worlds and of their point of relationship, the hysterical alternative denies and dissociates the inner world of *qualitative* or personal experience, and values only the outer *quantitative* world of "power over things." The inner, personal, subjective world, if it is to be successfully excluded from our conscious reckoning, must be totally dissociated. Therefore, am not to be my SELF, except in so far as I can control my

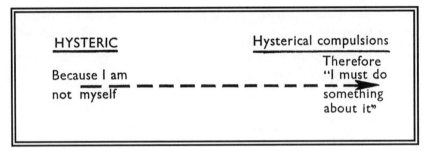

Figure 37 Hysterical Compulsions

"self" and have power over my thinking, so that I can exercise further (nearly always benevolent or at least well-intentioned) control over all that matters in a quantitative, objective and exterior world.

In fact, it is my (very Western) intention to make of it a "better world," both for myself and for those on my side who agree with me as to what I mean by "good." We will together then be able to make it ultimately into a "better and better" one, until eventually it is the best of all possible worlds, including Utopia and the Kingdom of Heaven rolled into one—tomorrow if not today.

If we can recognize the "shadow," or "bogeyman," in this woodpile, we shall the better be able to see how contradictions occur to confuse and upset us in so many aspects of our human enterprise. Because we have elected to live in one world only, which is the "right" one, we can expect trouble from the one which has been cut out, or left behind. We shall need a scapegoat, or "other," to take the blame for causing so much trouble, and so preventing us from carrying out our simple plan to our success and satisfaction.

The characteristic of this way of life is its *reversibility*. Claiming to be only objective, its reverse side is very subjective. In being scientific, it conceals a vigorous morality. In being religious, it finds itself pursuing materialistic goals. In being educational, it must block the very way of learning, by its compulsive efforts to grasp at too many ways of thinking about things. And finally, to be consistent, it must forever be threatened by the return of all it has excluded.

The hysteric trend being towards togetherness, either with mother or other, it is fascinating to discover the many ways in which our Western civilization, with its predominantly Christian ideology, even up to and including the industrial revolution and the final product of our evolutionary process, scientific man, has aimed at being and producing bigger and better "mothers," who are constantly offering more comfort, more security and more of the things that are good for us.

The state of mind of modern man, subject to the contradictory rules of paradox, is predominantly motherly, in that monstrous way that mothers have who are not conscious of why they want to do us so much good. Our state of mind is one in which the inner world, which is the inclusive belly-mind, has wrongly taken to itself a very different outer-world discipline of methodical exclusion and differentiation. The outer, or quantitative mind, should be concerned only with seeing things apart from one another, without interfering with them. But no, the modern state of mind is more concerned with "ought" than "is," with "do" than "be," with "good" than "true," and with swallowing great masses of undigested knowledge rather than experiencing any event meaningfully. All is smothered in a monstrous womb of unassimilated similarity and undifferentiated togetherness.

Thus all is now prepared in industry, science and medicine for the amorphous and ubiquitous monster of the Welfare State, in which we live, as "me" or "we," but not as "I." We think alike, we act alike, in groups of mass-produced mentalities. Meanwhile, we have no idea how brainwashed we have become as a result of the mass media of mass-education, mass-information and mass-entertainment.

But I would not wish to oversimplify my picture of civilization exclusively situated on the right bank of the stream of life. It is humming with conflict and anxiety, full of paradox and contradiction, exhausted, restless and constantly hoaxed by another promise of false hope. When things get too impossible on the right bank of the river, society can always go to war with its opposite number, in order finally and rightly to get rid of it. Everyone in this society will always think this is a VERY GOOD THING, on whichever side of the battle they may be so unfortunate as to find themselves.

No, not everyone; for there are many who contract out of it, choosing the other bank of the stream of life. For them it is not right, because they do not believe that it makes sense. It is not good enough. There is another alternative, which is even better than the best. This is the opposite or schizoid variation, which we will now consider.

The Schizoid Variation

Like the hysteric, the schizoid is determined to live in one world only, without an "other." But unlike the hysteric, who is identified with his mother-world in get-togetherness, the schizoid is dissociated from it, having withdrawn negatively and indivisibly in the opposite direction "out of this world," towards FATHER. In doing so, however, he has reversed the principle of incarnation. His arrow of direction is turned from earth to HEAVEN, instead of from HEAVEN to earth.

Dissociation always either diminishes or destroys that which is unrelated. It is therefore important to realize that the nature of any X in its relationship with Y is different from the nature of the same X when dissociated from Y. This applies, of course, to Y also. Deprived of relationship with X, Y cannot be more than a semblance, or shell, of Y-ness. This should be worked out in detail, where X stands, for instance, for SPIRIT, HEAVEN, FATHER, father, husband or man: and Y for that to which each N needs to be wedded, but always in the direction of $X \longrightarrow Y$; namely, matter, earth, mother, wife and woman.

Whereas for the hysteric the SELF was unselfishly denied, except as the "other" with which it was identified, for the schizoid the SELF remains omnipotent, and any principle of limitation is denied. The SELF of the schizoid is therefore required to aim at, if not actually to attain, perfection. It is not only unweaned from its early "clouds of glory"; it is wrapped up in them, and so remains fixed in a static perfection which must be better than the best, and indivisible.

Actually, and even short of lunacy, this state of mind is not so impossible to obtain as might be expected. In the good old days when Kings were Kings and enjoyed divine rights without responsibility, this is surely what they enjoyed. Even nowadays some dictators can enjoy the same sort of fun, although usually it does not last for long. It is only necessary to feel absolutely superior, with total power over others. This state of mind *can* be achieved with varying success by some exhibitionists, Narcissans, and psychopaths. The difficulty is to keep it up without becoming actively paranoid, because all such persons are inviting everyone to turn against them, which they eventually must.

It is as a religious phenomenon that this state of mind can be of special interest to us. It is certainly not true that all religion is schizoid, because apart from what is "true," much so-called religious experience belongs to what has been described as "hysterical." The latter includes all those who choose to escape from personal responsibility by identification with the Establishment, which may of course be of any denomination.

That schisms (the word comes from the same root as schizoid) occur has been proven all too often in the course of Christian history. Religious people in general and Christians in particular, are usually not the easiest persons to live with, especially if they are obsessionally intolerant of difference and "unco guid."

All religions are inclined to run a schizoid heresy, as a counter-balance to the hysterical one. The schizoid heresy praises the virtues of those who escape from life, from hermits wearing hair shirts in the desert, to a more general encouragement towards a too premature association with the communion of saints. The Vedanta movement of Hinduism, with the ashram so beloved of American tourists, tends to discover the Divine Ground securely out of this world, from which, however, it still continues to derive its comforts and material supplies. Modern Buddhists, with their encouragement to renounce the world at a very early age in order to follow the path of enlightenment, may find thereby their own experience of Nirvana, but it is more than doubtful if this was ever either the experience, or the intention, of their founder.

In religion, as in ordinary persons living out their private lives, schizoids are usually more interesting than hysterics. (Incidentally, it is perhaps interesting to notice that you will never insult a psychiatrist by calling him schizoid. He will rather like it, because he knows these are the superior people. He will equally and rightly resent being called an hysteric.) Actually, probably all the second-best psychiatrists are schizoid. Their hardest job is to learn to become normal "middle-of-the-road" people, who will always prove in fact to be the best psychiatrists.

In our psychological classification in terms of the four elements of "fire," "air," "earth," and "water," it is the intuitives who belong under the great spiritual symbol of "fire." They are born closer to Heaven and often find it hard to forget the fact, which they must do if they are to travel earthwards on their prodigal journey. "Knowledge of certainty not derived from experience" is their common lot. They KNOW and therefore do not require to be taught, which they usually bitterly resent. They also resent all little things and small places, and do not suffer fools gladly. Priest-Kings by nature, they prefer being leaders to being led. They may therefore become priests and parsons, by direct "vocation": or psychiatrists, who occupy this role in the fashions of today. But certainly our teachers are apt to have an undue proportion of this heady and impatient mixture. With EXCELSIOR their motto, the danger with all such is that they may lead their anxious and impatient pupils still further up the garden path of Eden, Heaven-bent for positions of authority which are still further designed to keep them "out of this world."

Also in this connection, an awkward sign of the Zodiac to be born under is Aquarius (January 20th–February 18th) because these people are inclined to similar dangers as the intuitives. They know what is good for other people, and so mind everybody's business but their own. All signs of the Zodiac have their awkward aspects as well as their compensatory advantages, but the sign of Aquarius is said by those who claim to know such things to be the one into which our state of consciousness is currently moving.

If we are to be what we are, be it intuitive or Aquarian, schizoid or hysteric, it is surely a good thing at least to know what we are, in order that in course of time we may become wedded to our opposite, and thus enabled to experience change.

Depersonalization

Particularly in regard to what is called "depersonalization," schizophrenia provides a useful background, or frame of reference, against which to consider our personal experience of reality.

The characteristics of the schizoid state, which may rarely increase in degree until it ultimately develops into a deteriorating state of chronic schizophrenia, are: withdrawal into a state of intellectual abstraction and mental phantasy, with ego-inflation: absence of sustained affection, extreme emotional instability varying from apathy to violence: absence of experience of any kind, or "feeling of unreality": depersonalization, experience of "not being here," of non-existence: and finally, but perhaps not so easily recognized, the withdrawn and still omnipotently inaccessible "I," which is absolutely and often incredibly truthful in its capacity for criticism and judgment, but utterly incapable of the saving grace of bending to insincerity, as most of us obligingly do in order to adapt ourselves more easily to the requirements of this world.

The term "schizoid" means split, and is sometimes confused with the dual personality of hysteria, but the split occurs on quite a different level. The split in the schizoid state occurs between inner and outer worlds, between "I" and "me," between spirit and matter, between experience of FATHER and experience of father/mother. The split in the hysteric state is on the level of emotion, i.e. it is between "heart" and "head," or ego and shadow, or father and mother, or between that aspect of self with which we are identified and that from which we are dissociated.

The important task of making a differential diagnosis between schizoid and hysteric has in the past been mainly empirical. It has been made more difficult theoretically because no psychological system has yet recognized the spiritual category, or been based on the assumption of the spiritual nature of man. It is my belief that any psychological system must be unsatisfactory and misleading, both in theory and practice, until it does admit our essentially spiritual nature.

The schizogenic and the hysterogenic family patterns differ, as do their requirements for treatment. In the *schizogenic family*, the "I" is denied or alienated, the emotional life is taken over by one or both of the parents, and the ego is inflated, over-intellectualized and prematurely developed. The parents themselves are unrelated to one another, and also to the actual personality of the child. There is indeed only one indivisible world, and this is dissociated from all but itself. There is no meeting or mixing, but only worlds apart. In consequence, the schizoid is a bad mixer, who cannot meet anyone or anything on his own level. He has to "think about" it: which is why most of us are somewhat schizoid.

The *hysterogenic family* pattern, however, is sharply divided from the schizogenic. As between any pair of opposites such as good and bad, or black and white, there is a clear compulsion towards *identification* with the better and *dissociation* from the worse. Hysteria is therefore very much an emotional illness, protopathically dominated and epicritically deficient. Hysteria is emotionally unbalanced, all or nothing, with emotions here today and gone tomorrow, sometimes intense but never deep. It is the exact opposite of the schizoid, where emotions are either absent or violent. In the hysteric, emotion is always dominant, even, or perhaps especially, when it is dissociated.

In this respect the schizoid may be termed relatively "masculine" and the hysteric "feminine"; which again declares the two states to be comparatively opposite to one another. Relationships in a hysterogenic family are emotionally highly charged, with rights and viands clearly delineated. There are always two worlds in a hysterical situation: ours and theirs, yours and mine, which the hysteric attempts, morally rightly, to reduce to one by exterminating, dissociating or blandly refusing to recognize, the other. In the schizogenic family there is only one world and no other is possible; it is ours and therefore mine.

The treatment of the two states needs to be as different as are the states themselves. Hysteria is eminently suited for treatment by psychoanalysis and all deep analytic forms of therapy, which aim at setting apart what has become joined together, and joining together what has been set apart. Through the experience of transference in the consulting room, the relationship of father, mother and child, which had become as jumbled and confused as the bits in a kaleidoscope, can be restored to a more matter-of-fact pattern and proportion. In this process the analyst or therapist can afford to be detached, and the less he is involved in the operation the better.

The requirements of the schizoid, however, are quite different. His need is to be met personally, and his illness is severe just in proportion to the intensity with which he refuses what he needs. He is unable to "suffer," or experience, what is between any two worlds, such as yours and mine. His world is complete in itself, and can by no means be broken into by the requirements of a relationship with another. In fact, any infringement of his omnipotence can only lead to intensified withdrawal. This is why institutional treatment of the schizoid is usually likely to lead to an increasing development of schizophrenia.

The psychotherapist should be warned before undertaking treatment of a schizoid: "Here your self-protective analytic detachment will do your patient no good whatever." There is no reason why the analyst's detachment should make his patient better, because it is to be hoped that the schizoid patient is even more schizoid than his analyst.

What the schizoid needs above all is to be *met, personally*; not to be "analyzed," nor even "treated," but to be *lived with in spite of* his particular refusal to permit just that. The patient's refusal to suffer therefore transfers to his therapist the need to suffer him personally, to allow him to regress completely, to be as violent as he feels sometimes, and to meet him at all times on all levels.

The outstanding characteristic of the schizoid being his absolute if unrelated integrity, he may play every trick upon his therapist in order to disprove him, but his ultimate loyalty to himself is final and abiding. If his therapist can last the course, and give him time enough, "meeting" and "living with" him to the end may sometimes supply the therapeutic need.

But at present the opportunity for study and treatment of this all-important psychological disorder is sporadic and neglected. It is to be hoped that adequate provision will be made before long for the training of the therapists they need, and for the treatment of such patients in the especial conditions which they require. For this we need a great deal of money, but the label "schizophrenia" does not act as a pocket-opener for those who have too much. In fact, it seems to have an effect similar to its own nature, of causing withdrawal, dissociation and indivisibility.

Forgiveness

I would like to insert this word in this context because I believe it to be the most important therapeutic factor when confronting the human dilemma of not choosing horns, but riding in between them. Life needs courage above all other virtues; but perhaps the greatest example of all human courage is forgiveness. That is to say, providing this word is not too glibly misunderstood, which it usually is.

Forgiveness is an experience of suffering in time; it may require very great suffering and for a very long time. In fact, all that egoic man may cherish most dearly of his images may need to go, forever. And this giving must happen in advance, before any reason can be found for it, in faith, and in the absence of any evidence of success or reward. In fact, in all probability, the evidence will only prove that, on the contrary, all is hopeless. Yet in spite of all the evidence to the contrary, LIFE is indestructible. In the end all can be, because in fact it has already been, forgiven.

Meditation

Definition (again specific to the context of this book): "A state of primary or axial CONSCIOUSNESS, the characteristics of which are a complete absence of images of any kind, a total loss of personal identity and a state of rock-like calm."

The aim of such meditation is to correct SELF-dissipating centrifugal (hysterical) forces of our world by setting up a practice of more centripetal trend. Meditation is not necessarily motivated by any schizoid intention, because of the will to return to the world again, as diastole follows systole, refreshed.

There are many methods of meditation, but the best are completely lacking in self-righteousness. Plotinus said, "Any aim which contains the self is a bad aim." The SELF is SEEKER and should not be sought: it is subject, not object. The aim of a successful meditation is therefore to experience SELF as not-self, in order the better to return to our right incarnation in egoic self again.

CHAPTER 30

Schizophrenia

Schizophrenics, and to a lesser degree those called "schizoid," are "out of this world." They are not "all here" and so, by implication, they are mostly somewhere else. They are withdrawn, negative, un-cooperative, unrelated, dissociated. We may well ask, where are they, and why?

Hysteria and Schizophrenia

Hysteria is the commonest emotional disorder, to which we are all somewhat prone, especially if we occupy positions of authority. It is characterized by a state of mind seeking by power over the other to diminish or demolish the other. Instead of a rhythmic victory over "tock," good over bad or Jekyll over Hyde—until they experience a reversal. Both hysteric and schizophrenic suffers from the "splits," but on different dimensions and seeking different goals. Hysteria is an emotional disorder, seeking a return to the maternal heaven (haven) of safety-in-possession. But schizophrenia is a more serious spiritual disorder, which, in the absence of sufficient "charisma," or vital energy, is subject to fragmentation, while greedily but unsuccessfully seeking it, especially by seeking to return to the paternal Heaven of original omnipotence, "out of this world" and therefore totally ungetable. Unfettered in both cases by the frustrating demands of reality, both conditions suffer from dissociation, wishful-thinking, exhibitionism (showing off) and identification with things, including the habit of verbalising by naming and labeling. A tendency to blame any other than themselves for their own self-created ills (projection) and a convenient condition of sugestibility, including fixed clichés rather than showing any responsibility for personal judgment, includes a comprehensive

From *Cure or Heal? A Study of Therapeutic Experience* and
Consciousness: A Western Treatment of Tibetan Yoga

indictment that involves most of us, in our varying degrees of complacent, emotionally dependent irresponsibility.

Of recent years, much attention, both psychological and physiological, has been devoted to the subject of schizophrenia. In an earlier book I wrote many years ago, I said, "Psychiatry has more to learn from schizophrenia than schizophrenia has from psychiatry," by which I meant to claim that the schizophrenic still has something which the psychiatrist has lost. (You may well say that it is better lost, but let us first see if we can find out what this "it" is.)

I would say that the schizophrenic is still possessed of the "diamond," but that he is without a "bus fare;" and, rightly or wrongly, that he is not willing to exchange the one for the other. Like the just-born infant, he is still *omnipotent*, and is unable or unwilling to break down his energy to meet the lesser tasks of living. He is *absolutely*, in the sense that he is not *relatively*, addicted to the truth, and the sincerity with which he approaches life is incorruptible. Met by a nonsense, a humbug, or a confusion, he will *not* give in. So he is withdrawn, refusing to accept so much less than he has already in himself.

The reason why the schizophrenic is so important to our studies of human experience is that, because he is incapable of, and therefore withdrawn from, relationship, he points to and reinforces the importance of what he has not got and cannot do. Above all, the schizophrenic tells us what relationship means, simply because, having been denied it, he is incapable of experiencing it. Because we did not "play" with him originally, he will not "play" with us, now or ever. Better death by madness, perhaps, than lower the flag of his ideals? But nowadays we do not blame him. In fact, in his own way and after his fashion, we think that maybe he is right.

The usual watershed of divided opinion appertains to schizophrenia, as to everything else. Such funds as are received for research nearly all go to the "respectable" aspect of schizophrenia, which claims that it is a physical disease, with physiological changes ultimately susceptible to physical treatment.

Certainly it has been shown that chronic schizophrenics have certain demonstrable changes in blood plasma or cerebrospinal fluid, and it has been suggested that these may be the cause of the disease. But surely, if schizophrenia is a condition of a-polarity, i.e. of unrelatedness, it is to be expected that changes are likely to ensue on the physical level, which depends just as much upon relatedness and polarity, as do those levels which are responsible for our psychological and emotional behavior. In short, therefore, we may suspect that these physical changes are an effect rather than a cause of the disease.

It should be realized, also, that such a disorder of unrelatedness as schizophrenia would necessarily appear as a result of a disordered and unrelated social system. A dissociated society, of maximum verbalization but minimum communication, is the perfect hot-bed for the breeding of schizophrenia in its individual members. The experience of no-meeting but much-talking, of over-stimulation without attention, of loving without allowing for "being," is what has become known as the typical schizogenic family background.

Perhaps it may be only the best of us who have the courage and integrity to become schizophrenics. Others are better endowed with insincerity and adaptability than with integrity. They can cut all their corners and get away with it, without ever needing to become ill. But alas, the truth must in the end be served. However successful we may be at dodging the real problem, by living on borrowed capital and getting by in our invented worlds, even sometimes with credit, the more must others pay and suffer instead of us. Schizophrenics, and their lesser colleagues, the schizoids, are a vicarious sacrifice for our socially successful insincerity and humbug.

If the whole truth is to be told, it must be further admitted that the disease called schizophrenia, which has originally been developed by the well-intended confusions and suppressed conflicts of society and our parents and teachers, is further complicated and intensified by the present system of medical diagnosis, treatment and institutional care.

It is true that when he is brought to the doctor's consulting room, the schizophrenic patient may be out of the familiar world of the doctor who is examining him. Hence, all the symptoms which the doctor can describe will necessarily confirm his diagnosis of insanity, and the need for treatment within an institution. Here a dissociated patient will find himself still further dissociated, by being cut off altogether from his family and friends. His insanity is pinned on him as a label, indicating that he is socially outcast and a failure. He is thus still further confirmed in his guilt, in which he is already too deeply self-convicted. And finally, being already dissociated, his self-expressive outbursts of violence must necessarily be stopped by force, i.e. by strongly sedative drugs. Under these conditions, it is no wonder that schizophrenia has for too long been regarded as a necessarily deteriorating condition, which has been inclined to respond negatively to the circumstances of hospitalization, by the patient becoming increasingly withdrawn and inaccessible. It would seem, however, that such aggressive and anti-social behavior is still defensively motivated and protective of the original PERSON. We have been born into a world in which our homes do not make sense, and in which our parents have confused and misled us; while society speaks of peace, it threatens our ultimate destruction by atom-bombs; where the priest invents our sins to oppress us with a further sense of guilt; until the doctor puts the final touch to our protecting need for being met, by certifying us as insane. In sending us to hospital, he puts us finally out of this world. We now realize, however, that insanity, as an ultimate refuge, is a motivated protective attempt on the part of our defensive devices to find asylum.

It is surely towards the study and solution of these psychological problems that the available funds for research into the causes of schizophrenia should be applied. It is ourselves and our society, our problems of relationship and the infinite variety of our escapes from them, which require examination.

Prevention Is Better than Cure

A breakthrough is, however, taking place both in this and other countries, in the medical attitude towards insanity. At present the pioneers may be few, but I believe that we are now beginning to discover the proper direction for psychological and psychiatric development.

The difference is in the attitude of the doctor to the patient, who is now regarded as a real person living in a real world, albeit of his own, but one to be studied and respected. Whereas the previous medical orthodoxy was (1) examination, (2) diagnosis, (3) appropriate treatment to stop the disorder or diseased condition, the new attitude is quite a different one.

(1) *Unprejudiced enquiry*, without preconception, takes the place of the old way of examination, which implied, "I'm the doctor, you are the patient. Therefore I know and you do not. Therefore I am right, and you are wrong." Whereas the previous doctor-patient relationship (or lack of it) was an ↕ up and down one, the new relationship, as every true relationship must be, is ←→ on the level. This really means meeting the patient in his own world and on his own terms, using his own "language." It obviously requires more time than the old way of "doing the right thing now."

(2) *Diagnosis* needs to be carefully avoided, both in the mind of the doctor and of the patient. Of course the trained psychiatrist who is working in this way knows that his patient is, for example, a schizophrenic: but he also knows that knowing this does not matter. It is merely a necessary handicap, to be made light of, particularly in the mind of the patient.

(3) *The appropriate treatment* of schizophrenia is meeting, meeting, meeting, on all occasions, by all persons associated with a schizophrenic's care, and on all levels. It requires great experience and enormous patience. In fact, anyone who is accustomed to being efficient, either as nurse or doctor, at "doing the right thing at the right moment," is unlikely to be able to so reduce themselves to being NO-THING and NO-BODY, so as to be able to operate this method successfully. It is meeting, PERSON to PERSON, SPACE to SPACE; and realizing that now anything can happen, come what may, within the reasonable requirements of the ultimate safety of both parties, without the necessity of stopping the development of the shared "experience."

The essence of all successful methods of psychotherapy lies in the development of this ability *to meet the other as the other is to the other, and not as the other seems to be to the therapist.* This is what is meant by insight. To have a little to start with is a gift, but the faculty of insight can be greatly developed by experience, especially in the study and treatment of the symptoms, dreams and drawings of the schizophrenic.

Insight was the first thing required of the patient by the doctor of the old school, and of course he did not find it. "No insight" was what he wrote in his casebook. But in the new medical attitude, it is of the doctor that we require the insight, because we believe that even the most insane patient has a point of light within his seeming darkness, where he still knows what he is about, and why: which is something effectively lacking in the doctor who examines him.

PART VI

The Therapeutic Process

CHAPTER 31

What Does THAT
Mean for Psychiatry?

In 1949 Erich Neumann, who had studied under C. G. Jung, published a book entitled *The Origins and History of Consciousness*. But, like Dr. Jung himself, he did not specifically believe in THAT, so that his studies refer only to the development of "little c," which is still dependent on "the unconsciousness," and not on the NON-DUALITY of original CONSCIOUSNESS. In fact, no book has yet been written for doctors and psychologists on the importance of THAT.

Of course, in our scientific age, THAT does not come up to our scientific requirements, which require experiments that can be repeated exactly under specific conditions. But experience is another matter. It is individual and unique. It can neither be accurately defined nor indubitably proven. Experience, therefore, whether of THAT or anything else, never can be proven, scientifically.

In his statistically measured world of spatial relationships, little c can be as scientific as he likes, as long as he sticks to quantity and does not intrude upon values of quality. Quantity is scientific, but quality is not. The scientific world of little c can only be an abstraction, with every experience of value left out.

The scientific psychologists of little c overcame this difficulty by postulating "the unconscious," which contained everything otherwise left out. From their superior viewpoint on the eminence of little c, "the unconscious" had only to be made "conscious" for everything to be all right. But behind the duality of unconscious/conscious, there was absolutely nothing.

From *She and Me: A New Statement of an Old Problem*

Our statement of man's wholeness is in three parts, not in two: and the most important aspect of his total reality is that he is emergent, in all his states of consciousness, from THAT, which is original CONSCIOUSNESS, in the beginning. This is THAT I AM, which enters into and inspires "me," however scientifically forgetful "me" may prove to be of his unusual origin. His consciousness is therefore everywhere, running all through his various parts and instruments, including his very specialized and clever brain. His every "state of mind" is functionally limited by the instrument it uses. All instruments operate as mediators, between origin and periphery, which may be expressed in the simple statement: I – X – "it," or "me." Orthodox psychology is limited to the "X" and the "me," ignoring the origin of both in "I," as being too unscientific to merit their concern. Here, therefore, are our two different IDEAS, each of which will determine our different actions.

IDEAS are spiritually exciting. Images are emotionally stimulating. Concepts are exact in meaning and are definable in any dictionary. But all ideas and images must finally accept the measured framework of disciplined thought, as they are brought down to earth in a world of timely action, with consciousness clearly expressed in an acceptable communication. Such is the necessary descent from REALITY to reality. Our danger, however, is that the last stage of the operation may destroy the first and second, so that our subjective enthusiasm may be fitted into the scientific process of objective reason like a straitjacket. Then the originality of the creative process of experience is overwhelmed by the collective repetition of proven experiments, and our scientific progress can put our individual lives at risk more dangerously than by the atom bomb.

The development of our scientific skills expresses the development of consciousness, and is all to be encouraged as evidence of our proper growth in time and space. Research of every kind is all to the good, especially in the field of human relationships; but this is only true insofar as experiment does not take the place of *experience*, quantitative measurement replacing qualitative judgment, and repetitive collective thinking ousting individual responsibility.

There is always the danger that egoic self-inflation will take place, as the seeking mind takes too much upon itself, losing its larger context with its inner source and more mysterious origin. Quantity may be measured scientifically, but quality is still beyond the ability of the most complex computer. Compulsion can be applied negatively to thwart free will, but who can tell the extent by which men can be irrationally inspired, to risk even death, for the sake of an IDEA or an ideal?

Sex, as a meaningless abstraction, can be taught casually at school by leaving out all the danger of its dramatic power, for better or for worse. But what psychologist can speak of "love" and make any sense of it? The infinite drama of living must always be beyond the description of poets, and surely still more so, of scientists. Psychologists, who are usually neither, must make the best they can of their jobs, but in effect the result has been both over- and under-rated. Like doctors, as long as they do not try too hard, they are on the winning side, because the infinite adaptability of THAT will always give us a healing ace up our sleeves, for which the doctor can claim the credit.

Such words as spirit, soul, faith, hope and love can never be scientifically measured or defined, and therefore as concepts they must be excluded by our scientists in favor of more statistical and behavioristic conjectures, such as "sex" and "unconscious motivation." Even so, it is difficult in practice to exclude the entry of certain moral pressures even amongst the scientists: such as that, if the self is divisible into "conscious" and "unconscious," then the latter *ought* to become the former, as ignorance *ought* to become knowledge and darkness *ought* to become light.

Even such apparently innocent concepts as health or wholeness, progress, maturity or integration appear to press on egoic man the idea that illness or weakness *ought* to be replaced by health and strength, and that he is the one (albeit with the doctor's help) who *ought* to be able to do something about it. But in effect, this is too much like the patient's already overanxious determination to pull himself up to Heaven by his own bootstraps. Unfortunately, however, it is part and parcel of a scientific psychology which must see all things done, and all progress made, as a result of the successful exercise by someone of some sort of power-over-the-other. In scientific psychology, the idea of power-over-the-other operates by and large, so that it is still the doctor who is expected to push or pull his patients into betterness.

Our scheme for the psychology of the whole man is bound, however, by no such scientific limitations, although we are still bound by the scientific method of observation and classification in context. Basically, we have our unit-of-wholeness, or "gestalt," including the BEYOND, the "between" and the egoic agent, as I – X – "me," with the implication that the only ultimate solution for "me's" many and real anxieties is "I." Then all "me's" growth of any kind is through the mediator X, who provides for every kind of loss and death, paradox and reversal, simply by his willingness to "accept" it. In the end, the false hopes and blind beliefs of "me," who has so often been misled by those more successfully blinder than himself, can best be resolved by the *experience of despair,* supported by that HOPE which springs from his eternal verity. Although this may seem to be a religious matter, as it can be a personal experience independent of any religious belief, it should be included in this psychiatric section.

Experientially, I AM at the center of my varied world, looking out upon what is over there through the various instruments which "me" provides, such as blood and bone, muscle and skin, sense, heart and brain. What "I" experience is determined by three factors: who I AM, and what my intentions are: what particular instrument or instruments "I" am using: and what is happening "objectively" over there where "it" and "they" are signaling some sort of message to me. Out of this very complicated situation of relationship and communication, consciousness is able to make some sort of sense, image or experience, which then determines my behavior in response, if any.

The human dilemma is indeed an exceptionally dangerous one and we need great courage if we are to bear with it. Between two worlds, as bridge between them both, which world is more dangerous, the inner or the outer? Which is more threatening to our security; that our small light should be swamped and flooded by our inner energies, or eliminated, whether deliberately or accidentally, by our outward enemies? Fortunately, THAT is on our side, or the human lot would indeed be too perilous to endure.

Naturally (which is to be instinctively "neurotic"), we are disposed to refuse to recognize our inner problem, forgetting all that if we can, except by projecting it outwardly, where we can more suitably dispose of it. We are then "free" (albeit compulsively) to devote our whole attention to our outward problems, solving them to our best advantage, optimistically believing that they will stay so and that we shall therefore (one day in the future) have nothing to worry about. And, also naturally, our good doctor or psychiatrist is disposed by all his clinical training, to diagnose our "disease" and do something to get rid of it for us. (This is also what the patient has come for.) But there is another approach to the patient, which is to ask him in effect "Who are you ?" and—but much later—"What have you been up to ?" It is not the descriptive label which is important (this has been called "denigration by diagnosis") but the person in himself. Behind all the complex of his conditioning, there is concealed the real, the unconditional SELF. Can we see him, contact him and communicate with HIM, in spite of our own conditioning, as well as his? It may take a long time and much discovery before we can both get down to this level of reality, but this is where THAT can work its miracle of healing and where the TRUTH will set us free.

Apart from sheer fatigue and exhaustion, the commonest state from which we all suffer is *anxiety*, which is a state of mind that is compulsively attempting to improve either itself or its situation— or someone else's. Anxiety, in fact, is our attempt to "strangle the struggle": it is the greatest cause of excessive tension and fatigue. Instinctively, it is motivated by the natural desire to avoid suffering. So what should we do about it? Stop it by tranquilizers? Or relieve the tension in some other way, by gradually changing the negative state of mind from that of *compulsive avoidance* to one of more *positive acceptance*, i.e. willingness to "suffer all these little devils to come into me"?

The belief that suffering or anxiety is wrong, and so to be avoided, is only true in a world ruled by "mother" and the "old women" who support her. In truth, in the "son of man's" world, relationship is meeting, is experience of change, is holding the strain, is containing the tension, is anxiety accepted as such, is suffering. (The experience of anxiety accepted is of course totally different from that of anxiety rejected. To "give in" or relax to pain, but not to wallow in it by identification, is to minimise it; but to struggle against it raises it to a maximum.)

Thus the attempt to get rid of anxiety in our relationships, both inner and outer, upsets all our natural rhythm and reciprocal harmony, setting up conflict and compulsion instead. Furthermore, the role of woman as the real mediator of suffering is eliminated, as the role of the omnipotent phantasy-mother is put in her place. The freedom which is our right then becomes the compulsion which we owe to the establishment for keeping us all safe and sound, both in this world and the next.

The desire for power over the other is certainly "natural." In the same way that the mother wants to have control over her baby, so the baby also wants to have control over his mother. All psychologists recognize this potential inborn omnipotence of "his majesty the baby." We are born inwardly potentially omnipotent, but outwardly actually impotent. As we grow in our ability to use our instruments as opportunities offer, we acquire "know-how," and normally the situation becomes reversed in time. The monster of our central consciousness THAT I AM plays his self-diminishing part, while she-the-enabler ($-X-$) plays hers, and so we grow. But it is not always so, and "high spirits" are sometimes not so easily humbled. Residual omnipotence can be expressed in impatience, bad-temper or delinquency: it can be projected on to others, either in this world or the next, such as doctors, political leaders or God, (this is convenient because it absolves me of all my responsibility). It can be used as "power over the other," mainly by the misuse of money, such as by affluence or influence: or we can withdraw from the pains and pressures of this world altogether, because we are plainly too good for it and it is not good enough for us. Self-righteousness, which causes so much of our schizophrenia, has much in common with it.

The proof of the presence of the indwelling spirit, big C, THAT I AM, is in the way it works in our experience. It is not always healthy, although it always seems to be to our advantage. Undue optimism, magical thinking and the excessive charm of children who never grow up, may lead to the diagnosis of "*psychopath*," or unteachability, because of an inability to "suffer." The need to keep pace outwardly with one's inward euphoria, in order to sustain the feeling of well-being, may lead to *alcoholism. Mania,* in which we feel too "high" with too much anti-gravitational "light," may swing into and out of *depression,* where there is not enough of it. In everyday life, we normally project onto the "beloved," be she mother or motor car, sweetheart or plans for the future, far more than mortal light, so that they are endowed with magical qualities quite other than their own. But the "Ghost" is only "Holy" when it has died upon the cross, and the spirit is only to be trusted when it has suffered all that is humanly required of it. *Animism* is not enough, for all life must learn the lesson from its opponent death, before it can be humanly endured in a viable society.

In all our experience of health and ill-health, the influence of the family constellation is basic, because it is not only "out there." It is also "in here." It is not only immanent, it is also transcendent. As light and darkness are our primal parents, so also are "Heaven" and "earth," "spirit" and "matter." Our outward and immediate family are participants from whom we derive our conditioning in instant relationship and communication with our inward and invisible "relatives." To ignore the inward facts of experience in favor of the outward ones, is to court disaster, even as the scientific point of view of little c is sometimes inclined to do.

If our inner and outward worlds are not originally reciprocally balanced, and in harmony with one another, the balance must somehow be restored subsequently by force: either by errors of behavior or, very often, by the incidence of illness.

For better or for worse, in health or sickness, it is the image of our "relatives" which determines our behavior. It is in this connection that the take-over bid by mother has been bad for us. By upsetting our balanced harmony, which is good health, and superimposing an outward authority instead, attention has been directed towards getting rid of all sickness, and such other naughtiness as by rocking the boat might cause us "suffering." The preservation of our good mother image has in the past determined too much of our "good" behavior. But Life-in-itself cannot be so mocked. It will exact the necessary balance of the rejected opposite to the last grain, until the measure has been set right again. Such are the requirements of our "therapy" for our true "salvation," that we shall need to suffer many "deaths" upon the way, if we are ever to arrive back home where we belong.

In medicine and law, in politics and education, the social pressures which are sometimes referred to as "big brother," after George Orwell, are actually derived from our projected and inflated *maternal* images. We must not be deceived by seeing men as men only. Men make excellent mothers; often, in fact, much better than they do fathers. Hitler, Mussolini and Stalin were all "mother figures," desperately blind to their own ambivalence, and nourished by the magical thinking of those who were so willingly deceived.

To set the family pattern in its balanced form, we can use the too often rejected as unreasonable image of the Virgin Birth, to put all members of the human family in their proper places; for we are finally dependent not on mother, but upon FATHER and the woman whom he uses as his "instrument of suffering." The members of the family can then be seen as representing different levels of consciousness, which, constellated in dynamic relationship, constitute the state of the whole self in health or balanced harmony.

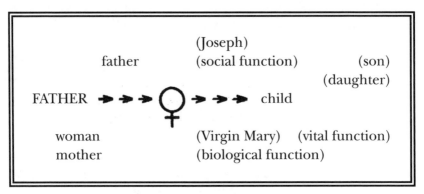

Figure 38 The Holy Family

Thus the child of life, the "little wriggler," is seen as being in a primary, direct, or immediate relationship with his FATHER; but only in a secondary, indirect or mediate relationship with his earthly parents, who are his temporary guardians or "enablers," until he can discover for himself his FATHER'S WILL for him, through the mediating function of his own heart (which is his inmost woman or "Virgin Mary").

We are at present experiencing a reaction against too much "mothering" and "big brothering" in the past, with the pendulum swinging, on the part of the rising generation, away from acceptance of authority and against taking the previously accepted views of morality for granted. Schizophrenia, "drop-out kids," flower children, experiments with L.S.D. and other drugs, and the cult of "transcendental meditation," all share a common rejection of that which has in the past been socially acceptable and unquestioned. There is a strong swing away from authority of every kind, in religion, politics, industry, at school and home. For better or worse, we are now witnessing a break-away, if not tear-away, generation. Our society may be in the throes of a break-through or a break-down; but perhaps the latter state must precede the former?

In the past, "they" have wanted to be too responsible for us, and now we want to be responsible only for ourselves. But some of us want only to be irresponsible and not to be responsible at all for anybody else. The median position, of course, is for each one to be responsible for himself, and to encourage a similar opportunity for everyone else. There are the individual trees, and there is the forest, and both need care.

It should be realized that irresponsibility, with or without drug-taking, is an addiction, and that violence is an infectious disease. Drugs do not lead to an expansion of consciousness in the proper meaning of the term. Like alcohol, they diminish responsibility by lowering cerebral control. What may then be let loose can be anything, but it will be worthless because it is outside the necessary framework of "I," "X" and "me." In this way, the very value of experience is diminished, as the whole creative strength of the conscious process is destroyed. "Dropping out" is all very well as long as we can drop back again, but that never proves so easy. It is as painful as trying to put a swollen foot back into a shoe that is too small for it. To be permanently "ex-carnated" is a kind of hell. This is technically called "depersonalisation," and is characterized by a feeling of unreality. Reality may be defined as *wholly responsible experience*.

CHAPTER 32

What Is the Therapeutic Process?

1. The word "analysis" in psychoanalysis is the right word to describe the effective beginning of the therapeutic process. The aim of wholeness, or healing, requires relationship; but this is not possible until the parts have first been set apart from one another by analysis. The process of synthesis is automatic. The process of analysis comprises the work, which can be very exhausting.

We are identified with so much (including even with egoic man himself) and blind to so much (for egoic man is blind) that the material with which we need to become related is quantitatively and qualitatively vast.

2. *The truth will set us free,* but must be personally realized as our own and experienced as such. "The true is better than the good" is a therapeutic axiom. In fact, we cannot afford to be fussy about any of the pairs of opposites when we are in therapy because we are all of them. But this applies especially to the good/bad, better/worse categories.

3. *The therapeutic process* aims at the great liberation of "I" from me, and the eventual discovery, not of "total man" who is a hypothetical and moralized image, but of the experiential Self. All moral terms which image a state of "betterness" are best omitted, and this includes integration, individuation and maturity. (This accords exactly with the Buddhist philosophy of ANATTA, which means NOT-SELF, but is easily misunderstood. Also with Zen, but again only if this is understood in conjunction with ANATTA.)

"I" am the witness, the experiencer. I am responsible. I am the HEALER, but I am not me. I am the point of the whole therapeutic process, but I need a great deal of work done on "me," before me will allow I to stand firm in my relationship with me.

From *Cure or Heal? A Study of Therapeutic Experience*

4. *The presence of the analyst* is necessary as he represents every "other" in relationship, including I who AM the HEALER. The analyst is not himself the healer but works as a *catalyst* through *transference*. A *catalyst* enables change to take place without taking any active part in it. *Transference* is that process which translates to the person of the analyst those unsolved problems of relationship which are either internal or external, past or present. Therefore in the person of the analyst, both worlds, inner and outer, past and present, are held securely within the four walls of the consulting room.

5. *The therapeutic process* operates mainly through *negative transference*, i.e. through hate rather than through love. "Mine is the best doctor in the world and I am getting on fine" is a feeling that belongs only with the honeymoon phase of therapy. It is only when we begin to experience the impossible, to suffer the insufferable and to digest the undigested that the work of therapy becomes effective. Then it becomes too clearly obvious that all the patient's troubles are due to the therapist's fault. In fact, in saying so the patient may be right, because even the best analysts do make mistakes, but some of their errors are thrust upon them by the pressure of the patient's necessity.

This stage may be very acute and almost unbearable. It is now that the whole treatment is thrown into jeopardy by the jealousy of parent, husband, wife, friend or G.P. "Well, I always told you that you were wasting your time, didn't I? What do you expect? You ought to stop before he takes away from you such sanity or self-respect as you have left."

To break off treatment at this point, even if it is only to transfer to another therapist, can only be very dangerous to the ultimate success of the therapeutic operation.

6. *The therapeutic process proceeds* by systole and diastole. The first stage is to get it out of the system, vomiting the undigested residues as it were. The second stage is to take new images back into the psyche, where they can become positively reconstellated. This is a process of digestion of experience, sometimes called ingestion. (This is not the same as "introjection," when we are identified with outer images such as parent figures which we swallow whole.)

This systole and diastole between patient and therapist requires meticulous articulations, i.e. fitting the parts of experience together in appropriate speech. It is a dialectic process.

7. *The therapeutic process* involves a change both of the images themselves and of our relationship with them. A dissociated past experience (e.g. I hate cats, or women, or being poor) may act as a chip on the patient's shoulder to motivate a whole life-time of behavior. It is necessary to see the image for what it is and then to reconstellate a different image, which can be positively accepted and used. It is usually not difficult in analysis to set free the general (e.g. I hate all women) from the particular (e.g. I hated my mother, but was afraid to admit it).

8. *Dreams* were described by Freud as the "via regia to the unconscious." They are the royal road to the whole psyche and every part of it.

Dreams are not for interpretation, i.e. for reducing to the terms of egoic man's ability to grasp their meaning. Dreams are larger than life and state the truth more exactly and more dramatically than does any other means of communication. They therefore need to be related to experience, as best we can; to be lived with, for as long as they require; and to be learnt from, as a communication or direct message from the HEALER.

9. The aim of therapy is not the same aim that brought the patient to the therapist. The only thing that ever brings a patient to a doctor is a pain he wants to get rid of or a need for something he hopes to get, which he usually expresses as "better." In fact, the reasons why patients come for analysis are usually highly fantastic and out of this world; such as at last being able to justify their claims to be superior beings or to find someone to love them. Unfortunately many analyzes have gone on for years before either therapist or patient realized the hopeless nature of this quest.

The aim of therapy can only be to become your Self, viable in your situation, able to enjoy yourself and to encourage others to do the same. Let there be no false idea of superiority, such as becoming your SELF or THAT I AM. Our object is to leave all THAT behind, forgetting it in our simple act of incarnation, now.

10. The therapeutic relationship of persons is not only face-to-face and heart-to-heart. It is also SPACE-TO-SPACE. It therefore requires a willingness and ability to sacrifice all possessive attachments on any "bodily" level: or at least, since such must to some extent persist, that we should recognize that they do so, and accept the fact that they must damage the possibility of a full personal relationship.

However much two egoic personalities may be in love with one another, and willing to help and do good to one another, we should realize that this can never in itself be a truly therapeutic relationship. It is more likely to be a benevolent attempt to cure distress by saving from suffering. (Be it noted that neither grumbling on the one hand, nor "Don't cry, darling" on the other, are therapeutic. They are only waste of time, therapeutically considered.)

Therefore, if we are limiting the word "therapeutic" to a true healing of persons, and not merely to a curing of "things" by concealing or otherwise getting rid of them, then we have to admit that both general hospital and mental hospital methods, and indeed most doctor-patient relationships, are not therapeutic in the wider sense in which we are using this term. They are intended to cure and not to heal, as simply, as quickly, and as cheaply, as possible. They are operating benevolently but blindly, within the limited consciousness and intentions of the egoic personality, which is all we are entitled to expect.

A therapeutic relationship, however, is concerned with persons willing to meet in a whole context. This must include their own admitted weaknesses, and especially the fact that no two people can ever fully understand one another. How can a space understand a space except in emptiness? Acceptance of the unknowable, as well as the undesirable, is the very essence of a therapeutic relationship.

For the development of a truly therapeutic relationship we need to pay attention, to love and let be, to suffer the other as part of myself, and my self as part of the other. Above all, we are not entitled to interfere, even or perhaps especially if we are in a position of power over the other, because we can never entirely know what is good for them, except in our egoic personality, which by definition can only make the illness which it cannot cure. It may be hard to realize that this is so, but time and the great benevolence are working day and night to find our way of wholeness, if we do not interfere, prematurely by rescuing ourselves, or by finding someone else to rescue us yet once again, from the ills we only need to suffer if we are to be healed.

The therapeutic process is therefore only proved, or worked through, by the meeting (wedding or mating), of the opposites. In the state of tension which this entails, it is to the credit of our modern therapists that they have realized the supreme importance of serving the needs and holding the strain of what has been called "negative transference." Indeed, our healing work is done more through our acceptance of hate, both in ourselves and in our patients, than by virtue of our previously much lauded love. In the security of the therapeutic relationship, whether this be in the nursery at home, in the asylum of the hospital, or the sanctum of the doctor's consulting room, anything, even the worst, can be allowed and even encouraged to happen, as long as it is held in its proper total context, which is on Holy ground. This includes a most intimate and responsible personal relationship with the therapist. In this total context, the satanic mills can darkly turn, and the repressed devils can gradually be loosed to do their evil wills, within the total ambience of the ultimate benevolence. But this can only be trusted to occur if the rules which I have already indicated are faithfully and courageously obeyed.

It is clear, therefore, that it does not serve the therapeutic relationship for the therapist to be only detached, objective, scientific and inaccessible to the other. On the contrary, I believe that the therapist should be willing to meet his patient in the consulting room personally, space to space, to face the danger and challenges by which he and his patient are constantly confronted, in an often anxious experience and ever changing anxiety of detail. But not, I would hasten to add, outside the limits of the consulting room. The healing work in hand, which is surely complicated enough, should not be allowed to become entangled in the unresolved problems of unanalyzed egoic man.

11. The healing process is autonomous in TIME. It happens from within, in course of time. The efforts of the therapist can delay the process by over-anxiety and interfering too much, as mothers often

do. But Healing is strictly FATHER'S business. We can clean up the wound, set straight the bones and bandage all secure. Then all is left to HIM.

The critical problem for me has always been the relationship between healing and time. I have seen "faith healers" working in public almost instantaneously, to effect apparent change. Usually, it was a disabled joint that could be made more mobile than it was before, but I have never seen what I would call a real, serious or personal problem changed instantaneously before a wonder-seeking crowd of ardent hopers.

I have heard Christian priests speak of their direct means of obtaining divine intervention to heal the sick through the act of prayer, but I have never seen the proof of it. I know the power of suggestion and self-hallucination, both towards sickness and towards health. I have seen many who pray themselves sick, but none who prayed themselves well. I have studied the Christian Scientists, and know that it is possible to dissociate a person from a state of illness, so that there is apparently no possibility for it to exist. Yet there it is, for someone else to bear, perhaps, if not the one to whom the truth of sickness should in fact belong.

I have known a woman take her eighteen-year-old daughter to a psychoanalyst for professional advice. He diagnosed schizophrenia, and told the mother that it would take eight years of continuous psychoanalysis, five days a week, to see her through and put her right. But surely eight years is long enough for anything to happen, even a miracle? In this case, the promise of eight years or eight minutes would not impress me that the miracle of healing was finding its mysterious way from darkness into light by this particular means.

I believe that we, as egoic men, are on the fringe, between the healing forces of light on the inner side, and the curing powers of darkness on the other. I believe profoundly in the powers of darkness. Their advantages are sufficiently obvious to impress, if not actually finally to convince, us all. They work, because they have power over the other. There is no harm in that, and great is their power to cure us of our ills. But I am still interested to distinguish between cure and heal, which I believe involves a vital difference, both in our state of mind and in our methods of procedure.

To cure, one does it through one's power over one thing and another; and what is so done had best be done efficiently. To heal, on the other hand, one straightens the limb, cleans and bandages the wound, but leaves the work of healing to a mysterious, and yet effective, other.

The healing process is to relate, meet, wed, the opposites and to hold them together in a relationship such as wrestlers endure, but without a referee. But how long, how long, how long, must we endure before we are relieved by a benevolence of healing, or by that final change which we call death?

The point is that a great mystery exists between the essential light that "I am," and the relative darkness, which is egoic "me." From this unknown between state we derive all our energy for life, as well as all our resistance against the privilege of living. From it we derive all our healing as well as all our resistance against being healed, and our persistence in preferring to remain ill.

The light enters the darkness in which we are, and we reject its healing powers, for excellent reasons, as well as for old and virtuous habits. As long as the determining images of our illness continue to exist, our illness will remain. Therefore even the question "How long will healing take?" must depend in the end upon one or other aspect of our selves.

N.B. One of the most difficult puzzles for the therapist to solve is the anxious question of so many relatives: Is she (or he) being naughty or being sick? After over thirty-five years of psychotherapy, I can only say that to me we all seem sick, which includes all the relatives and all the doctors, too.

CHAPTER 33

What Makes a Good Therapist?

1. Unpopular as this may seem, I believe that it should be stated clearly that the best therapists are born not made. Some are born with a greater degree of intuition, insight, compassion and concern: they have a greater quickness of imagination and intelligence: and a more ready sense of humor, which need never be used as an escape by means of which to "laugh it off," or gain one-upmanship.

2. The reason why all therapists must be analyzed is that they need to be themselves as they really are; that is to say, without "one-upmanship," or "one-downmanship" or—and this perhaps especially—"one-out-manship." The attempt on the part of the therapist to leave himself out of the therapeutic operation must be regarded as being somewhat outmoded and ridiculous, because it is impossible. The more he thinks he is not there, the more obstinately intrusive his "shadow" must become. It is therefore much better to accept the problem of the relationship ("counter-transference") between analyst and analysand in the first place, keeping it under observation throughout the operation.

3. The successful therapist needs to be an expert at his own SELF-EMPTYING. He is required to disabuse himself of any idea of the exclusive rightness of his own opinion, experience or training.

4. The successful therapist needs to be able to PAY ATTENTION with meticulous discrimination to the experience of his patient, both past and present, as it is meaningful to the patient, and not as it is meaningful to the therapist.

5. TIMING: As in all art the element of timing, or fitting into context, is most important for the successful therapeutic relationship. It is not wrong for the therapist to intervene, but of course it is wrong to intervene at the wrong time or in the wrong way, thus

From *Cure or Heal? A Study of Therapeutic Experience*

causing a wrong result or missing a right one. Intervention, to be therapeutic, should be regarded as tentative or provocative, rather than instructive.

6. ENCOURAGEMENT, if it is to be effective, need not necessarily be verbal. The therapist is required to be in constant concern with the patient as a person, who may be suffering the most acute anxiety. Patients show amazing courage in their willingness to undergo the most intense degree of suffering, which has always been too great to bear or they would not have needed to come to us.

Detachment is needed, but never an attitude of cold indifference, with the analyst leaning against his chair "waiting for Godot." The therapeutic process may prove to be long, but an attitude of indifference on the part of the therapist makes it needlessly so, and indeed may make the whole therapeutic process ineffective.

7. FREQUENCY OF INTERVIEWS: The degree of anxiety experienced by the patient should determine the frequency of interviews. Although gaps may in themselves be therapeutic, successful therapy requires that a gradual process of building up should not be allowed to lapse owing to too long intervals between the interviews, or it will be destroyed by the accumulated egoic-defensive forces of the illness. Some patients can manage with weekly or even fortnightly interviews; others may require three or even five interviews a week, their needs varying from time to time.

8. INSIGHT: This would seem to be the word most descriptive of the greatest asset for the successful therapist. Some are born with more than others, but all can learn to acquire more than they have, particularly by study of their own and their patients' dreams. This should be regarded, however, as only a small part of the study of the significance of symbolism as the mediator of all experiences. Furthermore, insight is deepened by the general use of the dialectic method. Instead of pursuing one path only, the dialectic method proceeds by arranging for the impact (or "wedding") of the opposites, part to part and part to whole. Insight into the meaning of experience is the product of our studies of such relationships.

9. EXERIENCE: On the part of the therapist is important, but may easily become a danger to therapeutic success. Experience needs to be digested and forgotten ("self-emptying"), or else it may form a defensive crust between therapist and patient, thus preventing the former from ever appreciating the present reality of a new, always different and ever changing, personal situation. For the same reason, people of great intellect or much academic success are handicapped as psychotherapists, because they have so much the more to lose.

10. FAITH: The successful therapist needs to have a simple faith in the purpose, power and presence of the Healer in the whole man, when patient and therapist are together engaged in, and committed to, the mystery of the therapeutic process in this personal relationship. In this sense, our therapeutic faith has no connection with our religious belief, or lack of one.

PART VII

The Way of the Spirit

CHAPTER 34

The Meaning of Growth

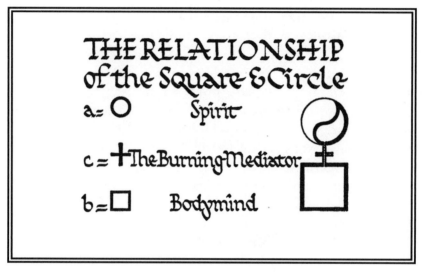

Figure 39 Square and Circle

I wish to return to our central concept of the meaning of growth, which is that progress round the spiral including both the positive and the negative, and all the parts within the whole. To compress the meaning of growth into a definition, I would first divide it under two heads, material growth and spiritual growth. I would then define material growth as "the movement of life through matter in time" and spiritual growth as "the expansion of wisdom through the assimilation of experience." Material growth and spiritual growth are different, and yet at the same time they are also in one respect essentially the same. For both, growth is weaning, which is a form of burning; but from the point of view of our material self-defense, it feels as if the real nature of spiritual

From *Time and the Child: A Study of Morality and Reality* and
I and Me: A Study of the Self

growth is something very like decay. We feel as if this way of burning is going to lose us something, and yet it is the essence of spiritual growth. From the material point of view it feels exactly as if we are asked voluntarily to surrender something that we value and to make a sacrifice.

Now the immediate definition of this word "sacrifice" that comes into our minds, the feeling that it conveys, is that somebody is asking us to give up to them something that we want to keep for ourselves. That is what sacrifice means from the point of view of material comfort; but it is not what sacrifice really means, for literally the word means "making holy." So the real meaning of the word is that we are not having something taken away from us, but that we are having something added to us to make us whole. From the point of view of spiritual growth it is a gain, but from the point of view of material value, of course it is a loss.

And then again, in another form of words, when we are asked to "renounce" something, who wants to do that? As I have said before, we are all business-like at heart. Some of us sometimes feel that material gain is all that matters and some of us see the essential wisdom not only of material gain but also of spiritual growth. These last are just as much out to "gain," but they are growing on a larger scale. So let us examine the meaning of this word "renunciation." Is it also something which we have to give up? Not a bit, according to the dictionary or at any rate according to the original meaning in the dictionary if we take the word to pieces. Look it up and you will find interesting links; nuncio, tell, tally, count: and so we have the meaning of re-count or re-value. This business of renunciation is certainly a re-valuation, but that does not necessarily mean that we are any the worse off for it.

Then there are the three good old words "whole," "holy," and "hale." They are in origin the same words, coming from the same Anglo-Saxon root, halig. "Hale and hearty" is nothing to be ashamed of, and nothing to lose, and such words should have no association with the idea of deprivation. In fact they are all gaining words. Yet in our material civilization, and in the mind of the community at large, the word "holy," at least, has developed this atmosphere of our being asked to lose something for somebody else's benefit, instead of being given something to gain for our own. It is not instinct that can choose the method of our gain for us, but wisdom, where the only sin is ignorance.

Burning is not merely poetic symbolism nor esoteric mystery. It is hard-bitten scientific fact. Our body is burning all the time, burning like a candle, and we are sometimes told that we are inclined to burn it at both ends. We breathe oxygen, and the blood vessels act as our wicks, so that every cell may have the light of life to burn. Each cell is like a lantern, burning the oil of life, and the whole body is a veritable "Body of Light." Through this process of burning ourselves up we are re-creating all the time a new body. In this way, even materially, we can gain new lamps for old by burning them. It is curious that instinctively we should be so anxious not to burn, when burning is the very nature of the law of life. We feel that we ought not to burn: and then having refused to burn, we feel we ought, and must devise a red-hot Hell for our own punishment.

This burning is not merely poetic imagery. It is not only the religious privilege of holy men. It is a fact of life that we all must burn. For we all do burn, whether we like it or not. That the hard lines about burning sometimes get harder, so that they are too much to bear, is only a matter of speed. If we are asked to burn too fast it hurts too much and we say, "Not so fast, I cannot bear it!" Although religion is inclined to take this privilege of burning as its own particular prerogative, it is most important that it should not be allowed to make this exclusive assumption, unless it is prepared to regard itself as a way of life and not as something to be separated from life. The way of life is itself the way of burning, and we require no Theology to complicate our understanding.

The experience of Abraham and Isaac is not to be regarded as a religious privilege for unusual people; it is the experience of every parent in relation to every child. It is not a "religious" matter in any separate sense, for it is a matter of everyday fact and individual experience. Sacrifice is not mystical, nor is it an illusion: it is the essence of reality as it is also the essence of all art. With the scientist it is the burning of oxygen in the body, through the medium of the thyroid gland; for the artist it is the burning of his own feelings on the altar of his canvas, through the medium of his paint and brush. Art is the incarnation of eternity, the definition of the infinite, the very act of crucifixion of spirit upon a material cross. Life is the ritual of burning, and it is not in any sense to be regarded as a mysterious religious privilege, unless religion is the way of life for all. Life is a miracle: but then not even miracles are to be regarded as religious favors, for although we all are born, we yet remain ignorant of how and why. Birth, like life itself, is still a miracle. The scientist cannot be more than the servant of the mysteries which he sees, observes and compares, and he must himself be prepared to accept the way of burning upon the altar of life. He is presented, as indeed we all are, with the problem of experience. Can we do more than hope to understand, accepting the hopelessness of finality?

CHAPTER 35

The Spirit

Whatis the "Spirit"? Mothers know it and all babies have it: lovers and mystics know it (oh, ecstasy!): writers and musicians know it, and know that it is sometimes only fairy gold: priests and professors know it, as they burn their incense or their midnight oil: drunkards and sinners know it as the very sweetness of their sin: even stockbrokers know it, after a good "deal," or a good dinner. How then could we forget it, when we all knew it so well? It is hardest to notice the simplest, most familiar, things. So much a part of us, yet so little acknowledged, we used the spirit even if we knew it not. Basic in fact and yet insensible: omnipresent but immeasurable: the spirit is the heart of mind and memory, the substance of Life as well as Death.

Of course, there must always be a catch in any attempt to describe the working of the "Spirit." Its best description will ever be, perhaps, that it is indescribable: its best definition, that it is indefinable. But these are somewhat negative statements with which to commence our study of one of the commonest and most important facts of life. Yet the very fact that we must be negative about it tells us something important. In the same way, "I" must be in part negative about "you," because "I" am *not* "you": and "you" must be negative about "me," for the same reason that you are not "me." We must be in part negative about spirit, because we are not only spirit. We are earthly bodies, containing spirits within a material mesh or prison—and we are personally much more identified with our earthly than with our heavenly sides. We are more familiar with our 2/4's than with our 1/3's, because we are on the job of living in the "here" and "now," with which our 2/4's are primarily concerned.

From *The Triumphant Spirit: A Study of Depression*

I have already said that I am a firm believer in the principle of "incarnation." I believe that "spirit" is incarnate in "flesh," as a light is embodied in the lantern that protects it. I believe that "spirit" and "flesh" are representative of two worlds that are rightly and inevitably in conflict with one another, because they are opposites in every sense. And finally, to complete my introductory "credo," I believe that it is the job of the spirit to enter into, dwell in, and inspire with light and life, this opposite material world. That is to say, I believe that the spirit is always "up against it," and that it is also always "getting down to it," if it is doing its job properly.

Before going further, I would like to clear up one point of paradox, that shows how difficult it is to be "logical" about the "Logos." I have said already that the spirit is analogous to light and fire: and yet I have said that the spirit is on the dark (1 / 3) side of the Psychic Compass. Both are true, but the contradiction shows us something very important. The side that we are on always seems to us to be the "light" (and the "right"?) one. Because we are not, as 2/4 beings, on the 1/3 side, therefore the 1/3 side seems dark to us. But to 1/3 beings on the 1/3 side, the opposite is true, and the 2/4 side seems to be the one that is dark. The best way to get over the difficulty, I think, is to learn to recognize the opposites from both sides, realizing how they seem to change at we enter and depart from them. Meanwhile, the "light" of 2/4 should be regarded as secondary or reflected light, busy manifesting the primary source of light, which is veiled in the encompassing darkness of I.

Clearly, as a doctor, I do not regard the study of the spirit as a separate religious matter; because I believe that the spirit is the Healer and the source of health, it is of course for me, a medical matter. It is the source of life and health, in body and in mind, in action and in repose. It is a double tragedy, therefore, and the cause of much ill-health and misunderstanding, that whereas the doctors have chosen to ignore it altogether (except for occasional reference to the *vis medicatrix naturae*), the priests, on the other hand, have taken it off with them into some obscure corner of their Church and there hidden it, to its subsequent disrepute in the scientific world.

The trouble with religion has been that it long ago became divorced from life. But it is not, in fact, a thing apart. It never was and never should be so. Religion is the spirit of the matter, and these two are inseparable. Gradually, spirit is emerging through the medium of matter, into which it entered of its own free will. Gradually, matter is becoming differentiated and refined by the indwelling spirit, as new powers emerge. The spiritual power is now most evident in human consciousness, but this is where the "son" has turned most violently upon his "father." Being invested with so much power through his detachment and capacity to store and use his knowledge in human consciousness, man has become indeed as God: and he has gone off on his own for a while, to show what he can do without God. Truly, man has done much. But it must be all to his own undoing, until the "son" can again become obedient to the "father," taking his place once more as a willing cooperator in the general team.

Figure 40 It's Quite Impossible!

Meanwhile, it seems to me to be of paramount importance to get the spirit back to the place in which it rightfully belongs. "The greatness of a nation is in the spirit of its people. So it has ever been: so it shall be with us." So said the King, in one of his Christmas talks to his people. The spirit belongs to the people, and upon the every-day working out of the spirit, the everyday health of the people must depend. The tasks of tomorrow, when we must clear up the after-math of war, may very well seem to be, and prove to be, impossible. But that is no odds to the spirit, if we approach the matter in the right spirit. The spirit loves impossibilities: it simply thrives on them. Impossibility activates it with miraculous energy. The spirit then gets down to it, gets into it, and gets on with it. (See figure 40, "It's Quite Impossible," p. 581.) The miracle of life is quite impossible; and yet it happens, everywhere, every day.

It is interesting to discover the number of different ways in which we make use of the word spirit in our everyday speech. "The spirit of our troops is excellent." Thus, in wartime, words pay trib-ute to a fact that peace more easily forgot. Contradictory as it may sound, yet it is always true that it is the spirit that matters; for the spirit is the source of meaning, as well as of value. Yet, since the decay of religion, the spirit has lost most of its importance in reli-gious teaching; its existence is not recognized at all by orthodox psychology; nor does it hold the paramount place that it should in our philosophy.

SPIRIT is one of the big words, and its meaning well repays attention. The Oxford English Dictionary derives it from the Latin verb *spirare*—to "breathe"—and gives to the noun the meaning of "the breath of life," the animating, or vital, principle. The word also signifies the quality of ardor, courage, or vivacity. It is there-fore a very warlike word, although, as Shakespeare uses it in *Henry IV*—"as full of spirit as the month of May"—we see that it has its peacetime usage too. In peace or war, the "spirit" is the breath of life, and it is quite certain that we shall not get far without it.

The various changes that have come about in the form of the word "spirit" are also interesting. For instance, we have the word *sprightly*, meaning cheerful, gay, brisk or vigorous. Then there are also two other words, each slightly modified forms of the same word "spirit." These are: *spirt*—meaning a jet of fire, or slender spout of water; and *spurt*—meaning a short spell of rapid movement.

In common language, we recognize again the importance of the spirit when we say that, being in low spirits, we are "dis-spirited."

That is a poor and wretched state. On the other hand, we can be in "high spirits," and then we are "inspired." We have "aspirations," too, that link us with the goal we long for, or to play our part in the ultimate victory of goodwill over the evil powers by which the frail fabric of goodness is ever threatened. From the point of view of any war, the spirit is the core and kernel of morale. It is the "stuffing" and the "guts" of the people. And yet, how vague a thing it is—how little understood, how much neglected! How do we lose it, and how nourish it? Having lost it, how do we regain it? Once upon a time it was religion's task to care for it and keep it in the forefront of its teaching. But since religion lost its hold upon us, in spite of our material gains, I think there is no doubt that some of the importance of the spirit has faded from our lives, leaving us worse off, dis-spirited.

I do not wish to discuss the spirit from the theological point of view, because I am not in any way qualified to do so. Nor do I wish to consider it as an abstract, metaphysical theory, only of interest to philosophers because of its ancient historical associations. But I do wish to be a realist; and because I know the profound importance of the spirit in our lives, I wish to treat the spirit from the medical angle, and to consider it in relation to our health. It seems to me to be a doctor's job, especially if he be a psychologist, to keep his patients in good spirits, because they so often come to him depressed and dispirited. And also, since we now facing the results of war, it is a problem of immediate importance, because nothing but the right spirit can see us through the darkness and dangers of the war and its inevitable aftermath. There will be so much work then to be done, for which the inexhaustible energies of the spirit will be required.

For the spirit is, above all else, a living source of energy, a veritable powerhouse for all the jobs of life. But some of us seem to have an attitude towards life that tries to do without the spirit together. We live as if we must make the wheels turn round ourselves, or else we seem to think that they might stop. We not only take upon ourselves the responsibility of being the director of the machine, steering it where we think it ought to go, we also try to become the driving force inside it. We have lost whatever faith we ever had in God and so must be like God ourselves, creating life as and when we please. So we plan our lives and choose according to our pleasures and our ideas, steering our mechanical systems this way and that, shoving them along by the effort of our own wills, avoiding hills wherever possible and hoping to be able to stop in some delightful place of our own choosing in which to spend the evening of our days. And so, with furrowed brow, clenched fist and straining eyes, we take upon our shoulders the burden of the world in which we live—and it is not surprising, perhaps, that we often find ourselves exhausted. Even so, we cannot rest, because excessive fatigue is a very restless state. The more fatigued we become, the more restless we are, racing round in the last stages of exhaustion like a decapitated hen.

Is it not strange that we should take more liberties with life than we should ever dare to take with our banker? Our respect for him is such that we always try to keep our income slightly greater than our expenditure, or else we know that we shall be in trouble. If we spend too much, we shall be facing an overdraft, with demands for the handing over of securities. In life, although the banker is quite invisible, he is no less real. The laws of life are not simply to be beaten with impunity; they are as rigid as the laws of mathematics. Yet we behave as if there are no laws at all, and no banker either; but only an unlimited influx of the miraculous stream of wealth and health, with our almighty selves to choose just how and when they are to be spent. When we come to the end of our tether, and the miraculous supply shows signs of becoming exhausted, we complain bitterly and send for the doctor. We groan about our "tiredness," about feeling "run down" and "out of sorts," and hope that a pill or two will help us to pull ourselves together. That is indeed a childish faith in powers greater than our own! Actually, of course, our symptoms are simply a sign that we are temporarily overdrawn, and must restore our credit at the bank of life. Normally, if we have not gone too far and set turning the vicious circle of restlessness, we can go to sleep and experience the blessed and recurrent miracle of having our spirits restored, through time spent in no more arduous activity than rest. Let it be said in all simplicity, that sleep restores our spirits and thus revives and revitalizes us. From lesser "naps" and "forty winks" to those long nights of deep oblivion, sleep is our healer and restorer. Sleep, with nothing paid for it, repays into the bank of life the income which we spend either in working or in playing during the day.

With nothing paid for it? That is not true. The price we pay for this natural restorative is nothing less than all we have. Sleep means surrender: complete surrender. To enter into sleep at all, we must surrender not only ourselves, but all our fond attachments, too. This nightly journey which we so lightly undertake seems to me to be the greatest essay in adventure of our lives. What faith it would require, if it were not a habit, to allow ourselves to be parted from ourselves and all we have, to enter this unknown abyss of sleep, not knowing whither we may be going, nor how we may return! It is as if each night we die, but miraculously our consciousness returns upon the flowing tide of morning, with all the energy of life renewed. The secret of the mystery is still unknown to us, and yet from birth to death we experience it, and most of us need hardly ever know the want of it. But this much of the secret we can understand: the doorway of the spirit opens up as we can give up, give in, give out. It does not work for constipated, apprehensive lives.

The spirit may be either good or evil in itself, but in general we shall not go far wrong if we regard it as the great unlimited. Given to us as a gift, it needs to be given away, and it is to this release we refer when we say "Let yourself go." Words are sometimes so full of paradox and contradiction that we have to stand upon our heads or spin before we can sense their meaning, and this is a case in point. "Blessed are the poor in spirit" is very hard to understand, but it is true. This indwelling spirit is core, diamond-hard (from one point of view, as shown by the mean, unwilling spirit) and seed-like in potentiality. It is far more than a million pounds and yet is worthless in that state. We need small change: sixpences and shillings to be given away here and there, and sometimes more and sometimes all. The more we give, the more will come to take its place. As it goes out, so it comes in: in fact, it flows through us as an endless sea flows through a tidal channel.

Therefore, we cannot be too generous with this spirit stuff. The order of its economy is, priceless though it be, get rid of it, give it away—but never lose touch with the source from which it comes. Spend it with divine extravagance, and ask no questions why or how! As men we are rich when we are poor as gods: as gods we are poor when we are rich as men. There is a great waste within the spirit world, because it is unlimited. It is Niagara and we are teaspoons: catch it if you can. Therefore I submit that "Waste not, want not" is a depressing slogan for men in good spirits. It suggests meanness and miserliness, congestion and constipation, when what the healthy life requires is a steady flow. It protests a false economy of life. In life, I think, we need the "party spirit," which must never be too close in counting up the cost. And for a lovely party, there is great virtue in a little waste.

Although it is possible to make a moral analysis of the spirit, in itself it is quite amoral. The spirit is like energy; it is a force that may be used for good or ill, but in itself it is neither. It enters the first of the four levels of the psyche, and proceeds to activate the whole. But whether this activity be good or ill depends on what we do with it. If it is encompassed at each level, ringed round within its proper instrument, caught within its proper channels and disciplined and harnessed like an unbroken colt, all will be well. We shall have a "good" spirit. In fact, in spite of necessary discipline, through acceptance of Life's burdens without trying to get rid of them, we shall be "in good spirits." But if the spirit enters into Life unwillingly and refuses to surrender to this living coffin which is our earthly prison; and if, instead, it strives like Lucifer to put all things to rights, untimely, instantly, by the simple process of getting rid of them; then we shall have another Hitler, driving, driven, demon-possessed.

It is seldom wise to insist on the full measure of spiritual power: and it is seldom wise to insist on all our desires being gratified. It is longing, emptiness and continual frustration, which make the wheels go round. Victory is fatal to the spirit. A state of ultimate satisfaction, with goal completely realized, is its very end. The spirit is a fighting force, which will ever seek for fresh foes, further afield. It cannot rest victorious, but must always desert the victor for the vanquished. It must seek again until it can find another impossible task, where it is again up against resistance, embattled in crisis and in tragedy.

Yet that sounds as if the spirit works with the same kind of mechanical power that we are accustomed to see externally applied to move resistances within the material world. But that is not its way. Although the peak of spiritual power is to achieve the impossible, it does it by a precisely opposite way to that which mechanical power would use. In fact, the way of the spirit is not only effortless. It somehow dwindles, getting less and less. Its mysterious trick is a sort of "jujitsu" method of making use of the resistance, without opposing it. Thus only can the camel get through the needle's eye, by getting down to it, and becoming as one-pointed as a ray of light. Then, effortless and silently, it is through to the other side. But there was none of the panoply of power, no big guns, and no golden crowns or academic honors. The spirit has an empty, open hand. "Blessed are the poor in spirit." And if they know how to be poorer than they are, then let them give away even what they have. Falling: empty: open: those are important words for the opening of the door through which the spirit may pass. This is not a visible traveler, nor can his path be traced. He slides down the fourth dimension, and remains hidden round the corner of a mysterious right angle. That is why the spirit cannot be caught within the clenched grasp of mortal hands. Only with open hands and open door by which he may come and go, can the visit of the spirit be enjoyed. However, fortunately for us, there is no need to deny ourselves any of the earthly fun, as long as we do not try to clasp it tight, or falsify its clocks, or run away from something else that is coming.

The difference between the mechanical and the vital is that in every mechanical system force is applied externally. By whatever sort of contraption energy is confined, at the point where it is released to do its work, it is always getting at the job from outside. But that is just where life is different. It is always getting to work from inside, invisibly, silently and at the proper time. The mechanical external (2/4) world must be mechanically timed with mechanical clocks. But in the living (1/3) world, "time" is actually self-manifesting, and does not need to be introduced at all. All living things are alive "in time," in their own time. Therefore it is always a bad policy to try to make living people obedient to other time-systems, rather than to the ordered evolutions of their own inward clocks. "Don't interfere with the clocks" is very good advice, because then they will not interfere with you.

How does the spirit work within our living incarnation, in the peculiar pattern of our own real selves? It is as if a certain quantum of amoral energy enters into different incarnations, to form different people, and to become manifest through varying personalities. That is to say, each one of us is a spirit, in so far as we are speaking in spiritual sense, or *has* a spirit, if we are speaking in material terms. The distinction is important, because, without understanding the difference, we may make a mistake. I have repeated more than once the paramount importance of personality. I would advise everyone: "Be yourself and find out for yourself." It is important, therefore, that any relationship with the "spirit" should be a highly responsible, personal and serious one. It is not enough to assume that we have a spiritual guide or guardian angel, and then to ask him to direct us. Important as spiritual guidance is, it must come wholly through the various psychic levels, from first to fourth, so that it is finally experienced wholly within our own personality. That is to say, the spirit must come down and visit us; but it is not to be regarded as a desirable human privilege that we should have a tame and powerful "spook," or slave of the lamp, on whom we can call whenever we are in difficulties. To be a spiritual man is to realize that we have a higher nature, whose normal task it is to enter into and redeem our lower, instinctive, animal nature, creating out of this dual relationship a child, or third, with added powers.

It is our responsibility as individuals, therefore, to aid the spirit's entry into such places as may be most lacking in it, most unready for it, and therefore most inclined to resist it. In Chapter 7, "The Holy Mountain," each traveler was sent forth with the message, "Go forth and *be* my light!" Not, be it noted, "Go forth and bear my light." The spirit is not something that we are to have to guide us: it is something that we are to *be*, within ourselves—especially in the absence of any guide whatever. But being ourselves is a most enduring business; and against all things the spirit is so designed that it can, it should, indeed it must, endure. Yet we so easily become identified with other things and with other people: things we want, or people we admire: things we have, or people whom we love. But then the spirit is in danger of being subordinated to material things. It is one thing to be a willing prisoner, but it is quite another for the prisoner to have become so enslaved by his prison as not to recognize that he is a prisoner at all.

Against all things the spirit must endure. It is no use our saying we are in the wrong place, or that we will do it another time, or that we would like to be somebody else. *We are ourselves.* We cannot be anybody else, and therefore it is always wrong to copy or pretend. We must preserve our own integrity and, above all, retain the supremacy of our indwelling spirit at the core and center of our being. Without excuse, without evasion and without protest let us be ourselves, shining the light we have within ourselves into whatever darkness we may find. "I AM" is a spiritual statement of our responsibility to manifest our particular "quantum" of the spirit within the resistant medium of our earthly lives.

The spirit is the continuation of the "unlimited continuum" within the framework of the "limited abstraction." It is the representative of the unlimited principle within the limited world of our three-dimensional creation. On the other side of the Rubicon, where it is at home in the world of the "wheel" or "circle," it is of the most tenuous, diaphanous and insensible texture. In fact, it is so refined that it has no texture at all, as we would be able to understand texture. It is finer than the very finest mist. But, paradoxically enough, as it comes over here it seems to effect a remarkable change. It behaves with cataclysmic violence and so requires harnessing, training and much discipline, before it can be safely used for our advantage. It behaves as something so obstinately solid, so impregnably hard, that not all the granite in the mountains can be more resistant to change. From being the very essence of all penetrability, it now becomes the representative of obstinate resistance—unless it has been properly incarnate in its living task.

Discarnate Unlimited

It accounts for that stubbornness we sometimes meet in people (a "stubborn" spirit) or rebelliousness (a "rebel" spirit) or just plain awkwardness (for there are "clumsy" spirits, too). *The spirit is always of itself unlimited*, for better or for worse. It is for the better if the spirit is properly incarnate and disciplined in time, but for the worse if the spirit is resenting its enforced imprisonment, kicking against the pricks, and destroying all that threatens it with limitation. *And the spirit is always experienced as the source of value.* Where the spirit is, there is elation, euphoria, happiness, well-being, vitality—call it what you will. Other sources of wealth may assume reflected worth, but they cannot provide life. If we believe they can, we deceive ourselves, and soon find out the contrary. Food: clothes: money: friends: comfort: safety: honor: those are all fine things and worthy of much praise, but they cannot create life. They can only support it, as they are themselves supported by it. They owe their worth to the presence of the indwelling spirit, as we owe our worth also to the same. Without the spirit, if a man is dispirited, what then is the worth of anything?

The spirit is the source of wealth, but it is not therefore "good." Nothing is good in itself—not even spirit. It is up to us to make it "good" or "bad" by what we do with it, and by the use we make of it. It is just so much stuff, material for use—but a different sort of stuff from the matter that encloses and encompasses it. It needs a lot of managing and mastering, this spirit stuff. We must wrestle with it through long nights and many days if we are to subdue it to a manageable state, under the mastery of conscious Will.

Therefore, those who are more spiritually gifted, those who are as it were "nearer to God," must always have their own especial problem. They feel alight with life and may therefore burn away too freely, perhaps causing other conflagrations as they pass. They feel so sure of the rightness of their inner knowledge, and may therefore be impatient with those who differ from them in opinion. They are so quick that they hardly need to start, because the end is already close at hand. They feel that they are "special" in some way: specially gifted, specially good, specially clever or specially responsible for taking care of others less fortunate than themselves. Each for their different unbounded reasons, they feel they ought, they must, they are simply bound to interfere for someone else's good. So these "chosen people," or unweaned children as they really are, not only deceive themselves but many others too. For we are very easily deceived as yet, especially by all that claims (but how erroneously!) to do us good.

The special problem of the spiritually gifted ones is to overcome the resistance which seems to forbid them to enter into the conflict of the world. I emphasize those words enter into, because Heaven knows that they are often quick enough to cause a conflict or to start a row. What they are unwilling to do as a rule is to take part in it on equal terms, to get down to it and be just ordinary folk They feel that they must be different from the rest. Saviors or missionaries, they find it easier to teach and to lead than to live a simple life themselves. They are not better than the rest, and many bus drivers and charladies are doing a better job of work more "advanced" in every way that matters for the spiritual life. They really have got down to it. They are in "being," in the job and living in it. They have forgotten what the problem is all about, some of them, but that does not matter. One day they will remember whence they came and whither they are bound. But meanwhile it is important that they should not be fooled by leaders who have not half the wit or decency they have themselves. These ordinary folk have proved the spirit that inspires them, with all the selfless speechless decency of which they are capable. The spirit is in us all, and the best leaders are the ones most competent at minding their own business, while constantly encouraging and teaching others how to do the same.

We are all faced with the same problem of frustration and obstruction. How do we react? How do we treat the ever-present wall across our path? I have suggested my view of the answer in "The Holy Mountain." I believe that the way of Christ is the way of incarnation, the way of life, the way of all good manners in human affairs, and ultimately the way of best efficiency. It is the way of willingness, the way of gentleness, the way of endurance and the way of a passionate will-to-live to the utmost, in spite of every obstacle and temptation to the contrary. It is the heroic way, and yet the most ordinary everyday way of life. The "Son of God" showed us the principle of accepted limitation, where He entered into the earthly frame and paid the earthly sacrifice for the Spirit's sake. By this mysterious adventure both sides become redeemed, which is a desirable result that neither could achieve without the presence and resistance of the other.

That is why to my mind the Christian Church has been right in regarding animism or pantheism as dangerous deceptions. Religions they both are, but they are not Christian. The babyhood of all religions sees God in everything, and gives to all things a resident spirit as its guardian overlord. This is primitive animism, and it is at the root of all religions. It is their common mystic stock, but it is not enough. Pantheism recognizes the unity of all lesser gods and spirits in one superlative overlord, and gets much satisfaction from admiring and communing with God through the mirror of his created works. So far so good, but it is still not Christianity. It is still only paganism at heart, though less to be despised perhaps than some of the nonsense that many Christians have made of their religion. Buddhism knows that and more. Indeed, it seems to me that Buddhism has a more fully developed body of knowledge, or intellectual side, than Christianity. But Christianity has something the others have not. It is as if the other religions have not yet quite grown up, although they would and will in time. But what Christianity has is not something narrow or private for Christians. The Christian knows (or should know!) exactly how to get a camel through the eye of a needle, and a rich man into his real kingdom.

As with all gifted ones, the special problem of the Christian is his pride. That is the rub, that is the very Devil: pride! It breaks the Church into innumerable schisms, inflates the parsons, and sets all the congregations quarrelling amongst themselves. Pride is not only the problem of the religious and the mystic. It is, for the same reason, the especial problem of the leader in every other walk of life, be he atheist, agnostic, or some especial brand of religious devotee. They have all got something, these men and women. But what are they doing with it? Something unselfish, something for our good? Perish the thought that anyone should talk such nonsense or think such foolishness! It is impossible. No man can do another good, without the one who reaps the advantage being placed in a state of even greater obligation, that cannot be paid in terms of cash. *All merit must be spiritually earned,* by paying a proper price *yourself.* To think or act in terms of expected saviors who can do good things for others at no cost to themselves is to encourage lunacy and to achieve disease. Christ was no Savior in that sense. His was a different way. It brought salvation, but not to those who do not walk that way, or pay the proper prices for it.

This same essential pride is the problem also of the intuitive. Some are born with these faculties so fully to the fore that they always seem to have an inward knowledge denied to others and to be walking in their simplest ways in the very presence of God. There is something so big, so utterly and overwhelmingly important, in this knowledge of the Living Presence, that the things which others regard as important in the outside world seem to them relatively to be so much rubbish, fit only to be spurned or changed, burned or born again at the behest of the inner light. But let them be warned, these Warrior-Babes! Their time has not yet come, because they have not yet been quite born. They are still victims of the most illusory mother-stuff. They are inmates of that undifferentiated and unlimited asylum of the spirit from which they require to be discharged. Like drug addicts they are doped, and need to wake, coming down to earth amongst these other ordinary folk. They have much to learn from them!

I do not want to be misunderstood about mystics. I do not want them to be persecuted or interfered with or even in the least disparaged. If they are refugees from life, there are many others who have the same intent in other ways. If they are self-indulgent seekers after the privileges of private Heavens, there are many others who are like them in that respect. All that I am concerned with is that we should not be deceived by them. We must not let their inflated consciences infect ours. They may be different, but they are not therefore better folk. If we must compete in our moralities, then my money is on a charwoman or a bus driver every time for the Perfection Stakes.

I do most strongly believe that our task is not to train ourselves for the life of the spirit, as Gerald Heard has suggested. It is on the other hand, if my contention is correct, to train the spirit for Life! The proper movement is not towards the spirit, but away from it, earthward, into ordinary natural things and amidst ordinary natural people. The merit of the spirit is to be measured by the extent of its travel and incarnation in our ordinary everyday three-dimensional world.

The doctors are somewhat to blame for having led people to expect something for nothing. We are our own bodies' keepers. Our bodies are in simplest fact the temples of the Holy Ghost. They need treating with care and with respect. They should not be passed over to other hands without retaining an inward bond of our own responsibility. The doctor is not God, nor a medicine man, nor a magician, nor a carpenter, nor an upholsterer! We are not savages nor slaves. The average doctor is an honest man who knows his job; he also knows the limitations of his materials, his instruments and himself. He knows that this powerful energy of Life, or Spirit, is running through us all ("vis medicatrix naturae" he calls it) and he makes use of it. He clears the rubbish away, cuts out dead wood, cleans up the wound, prescribes a rest, and thus performs—a miracle! The patient should know, however, the part that the spirit plays, and give honor where honor is due.

This leads to consideration of "spiritual" healing. The spirit is always the healer. There is no other. The spirit as healer is unlimited—but time is not! The spirit could heal all diseases *if space or time were unlimited*. But they are not, and so we must accept our limitations, which include disease, at times incurable, and at last Death, which is a healer, too. The instruments alone cannot heal, but they can prepare for healing and assist the healer. Through the various means of surgery and medicine, psychology or sun, it is first and last the spirit that does the healing work. The doctor provides the channel and the instrument. The doctor cleans the wound and bandages it. The doctor knows the limits and the laws, and can advise how to reduce discomfort and avoid recurrence. The doctor has an immense amount of knowledge and an increasingly various range of instruments to assist him. He is an honest hardworking man who loves his work better than himself and pours his life into it. But he is apt to forget—and certainly his teachers do not make it plain enough to him in his student days—that he is only an assistant at the operating table and the bedside. He does the donkey work. Life alone can perform the miracle of healing—Life or Death.

Although doctors sometimes forgot the primacy of the spirit in their healing work, others remembered it. Because doctors left it out, others brought it back, and called themselves "spiritual healers." Without knowledge and other qualifications, but with an unlimited (protopathic!) faith, the spiritual healer claimed to do the doctor's work, with due reference and sometimes even some deference to the Divine Will. I do not deny that these "spiritual" efforts may sometimes have met with some success. I do deny utterly, however, that such endeavors are comparable in their results with the success accomplished every day of their lives by the most ordinary doctors. The spirit plus technical skill and experience will far outmatch the spirit employed in faith by itself. Of course, there are highly refined techniques of spiritual healing, but those require so great a knowledge of the background of the mind and so great a degree of personal austerity, that they are not in use today. Rightly carried out, these require as much knowledge and skill as surgery or medicine and they are not therefore to be compared with the vague endeavors of spiritual healers "on the loose."

I do not deny the claims of what is called "Magnetic healing" or laying on of hands. I believe that certain people have these powers to a greater degree than others and that we all have them to some extent. I do deny that these are any very special or important gifts that now require development. Rather I believe that this is all early, undeveloped, protopathic stuff. It is undifferentiated healing, medicine in its infancy, which we have far outgrown in knowledge and in general efficiency. When we can go back again more humbly over our lost ground, then perhaps we shall be able to learn again and extract still further wealth from this unlimited store of earlier wisdom. But as a cult by itself, or as a superior method of healing—no, I do not believe in it. It belongs to the past, not to the present or the future.

It is most unfortunate that divorce should ever have come about between "healing" and "spiritual healing," or between "life" and religion. The proper place for the spirit is in the very heart of all healing, as a light caged within the limits of a lantern. The proper place for religion is in the very heart of life, manifest thence in appropriate action duly related to the real external word of space and time. Religion and the spirit, they are not things apart, to be considered separately from everyday experience. They are the very heart of it. When they come back where they belong we shall have learnt a thing or two. We shall have learnt that for health and wholeness, whether in ourselves or in our community, we cannot do without them. We shall have learnt to recognize the master power on which we draw and upon which we depend. And we shall then begin to learn the proper way to manage these great forces, so that we can use them without either destroying ourselves or each other. Then we shall be upon the Middle Way, the proper Christian path. Although this way of life is never new in history, it will seem very new to us. No Church can walk it for us. The time has come for us to walk it for ourselves.

The problem of right relationship between the opposing elements of our two worlds may perhaps become plainer and less confused if we "analyze" it in our minds, setting out two separate and opposite categories, called "positive energy" and "negative energy" respectively. Here are some pairs of corresponding opposites:

Energy

positive	negative
chaos	order
darkness	light
total	abstracted part
protopathic	epicritic
immeasurable	measurable
eternity	space time
four dimensional	three dimensional
spiritual	material
"wheel"	material
psychic	psychological
tidal	focal
will	knowledge
healer	destroyer
good	evil

Each word should be kept "up against" its opposite, to see what emerges from the conflict. But what I want to emphasize is that there is a certain "right relationship" which exists between the two.

When this is present, all is well, and evil is redeemed by good. It is only when it is "off on its own," or "attacking its Father," that the negative principle can properly be stigmatized as evil.

The right relationship is brought about by bringing the positive element into the very center of the negative element; the light into the middle of the lantern and the lantern into the heart of darkness; the healer into the very core of the sickness, so that the spirit may in truth be said to be "crucified" in the three dimensional meshwork of the material world. This implies both a very strong pull exerted between the two worlds, and also a very strong counter-push, or resistance. It is no use expecting an easy passage for the spirit, or an easy job. It has to be quite humbly crucified, because that is the way it works. It is in this sense that the Christ story is a very accurate and "scientific" statement. The Christ-life dramatized the central truth of Life itself, and showed the way Life always works and how it grows. That is all. We are Life's children, conspirators with Christ. And we too must learn as best we can the way Life works, so that we can cooperate, too, and not be permanently confused by the conflict of our dual nature. But meanwhile, it is no use A complaining because A must suffer: or, indeed, because B must suffer, either. Both must suffer, all must suffer, if the work is to be done. The work is to get down to it, to get into it, and to get on with it, manifesting the light in spite of the resistance which light's opposite must always offer to the light. The "littlest one" must be enthroned at the heart of earthly pomp and power, in spite of earth's resistance. But the price of that advance requires much suffering for all, with none for long having the privilege of being spared.

The twin forces of Light and Darkness, or Christ and Anti-Christ, or Healer and Destroyer, or love and power, or vital and mechanical, or female and male are interdependent, in proper relation with each other, or else . . . the fat is in the fire. We must not get the two too far apart or the wrong way round. If Light is in the heart of Darkness, and Yin in Yang, and the vital in the mechanical, and the spirit in the matter, and the 1/3 in the 2/4, the inner emerging through the outer, all will be well. But if 2/4 gets proud and goes off by itself; if power excels and has no use for love and sacrifice; if matter becomes independent, and the Son attacks the Father, then the crash must come.

But only the sick can feel the need of getting well again. How then are we to treat our state of spiritual deficiency when it occurs? Once dispirited, how to regain the contact with the source of life that we have lost? We must know first that it exists, and then we must discover where to look for it. For it is always there, ready and inexhaustible. The only trouble is within ourselves: We are not always easy to maneuver into the right position to receive all that we need from the everlasting pump, because we have our own resistances, and time is long!

The order of these requirements may not be important, but here are some of them: (1) a clear sense of what is, as it is, and a clear picture of what might be, as it is desired; (2) a state of relaxation, emptying, giving up and letting go; (3) an attitude of acceptance or willingness that if necessary all must be exactly as it is (don't kick against the pricks); (4) entering into the heart of the problem in the right spirit: not mechanically, from outside by force, but vitally, from inside; (5) making a hollow, or partial vacuum, of oneself: being "poor in spirit," sucking gently like a baby (but don't be impatient!); (6) accept the will of God, or earthly accident; (7) use your spiritual will if you can: vibrate, with a peculiar intensity, the high bright will: lift up your heart: call: knock; (8) use the power of words (in prayer, perhaps), ardently, eagerly, but not aggressively. Life is a prayer, and praying is the trick of it. But don't forget that prayer is only one of Life's essential tricks. Prayer is the heart of Life itself, and there is nothing special about it, except our use of it. Life works that way, and if we know the way Life works (the way Christ taught, in fact), we too can share in its advantage. But it is a dubious privilege, with much to suffer and much to sacrifice. In fact, it is a way of working better in the cause of Life, but not of gaining privilege, or escaping pain or loss.

The trouble with many of us is that we want the best of both worlds. We treat the material world as if it ought to be like the spiritual one, and then blame someone, or lose our faith in "God," because things do not work out that way. It is our mistake, not God's, that is the cause of our trouble. To make the Kingdom of

Heaven on Earth ("Thy Kingdom come") will require an enormous concentration of the Will, and an appalling amount of creative, and not merely wasted, suffering. It is no use simply praying for it, or going upstairs to enjoy it in solemn privacy. We must bring it down to earth by being it ourselves. Meanwhile, lazy people like to get others to do the work for them, and many of us use powers that are our "evil spirits," just as witches used to do. Money, today, is the commonest of the "evil spirits" who work for us, and in exchange for our possessing it, of course it then possesses us. Unless, that is, we know how to spend ourselves, instead of spending or hoarding money for the sake of the power that it brings. For money itself is not evil. It is only our misuse of it that makes it wrong.

Beware of an empty house. There is danger in unselfishness. A negative attitude towards responsibility, a tendency to retreat upstairs, leaves too much empty space below. If this space is not rightly occupied, it will be wrongly occupied. If we fill our lives with our goodwill, within such limits as our lives present, it is as if we make the mysterious sign of the cross within our psychic compass. There is no room for alien entrance there. But if we leave even so much as a corner of ourselves unfilled, then into that evacuated space may come an evil visitor. Or if some corner of ourselves contains not light and air, but dust and damp and dirt, then we can be fairly sure of the kind of spirit that will find himself a home. He is bound to be an evil one, because where dirt and darkness, are the evil one can feel at home. A lazy tenant of a house, of course, may feel disposed to let such evil forces do their work for him, and so in time he may surrender his whole integrity, hoping to use the evil spirit for his ultimate advantage. Such cheap witchcraft, however, works the other way, and evil spirits soon attain the mastery, until what is left of the tenant is enslaved by them to do their bidding as they will. In this sense, also, crime doesn't pay and it is better for each one of us to mind his own business, however small and unimportant that may seem to be. We should fill our houses with the spirit's light.

The Holy Spirit is in different case, and I use these words intentionally. The Holy Spirit works in a special way and has the

utmost willingness to accept whatever pain or temporal imprisonment he may find. Willingly he enters in and silently he speaks.
Each one in turn, he willingly forgoes the highest powers, to enter
the lowest places. Wherever Darkness is, he takes his Light. No
matter what the form may be, he goes where he is needed most; he
is, of course, most, needed where most darkness and most evil is.
Although the word "willingness" probably conveys most of the
characteristic meaning of the Holy Spirit, other words may also be
used with which to catch some aspect of this very subtle quality.
The Holy Spirit is effortless and as invisible as air itself. We cannot
see it move or work, because we have no "sense" with which to
measure it. That is to say, it does not taste, it does not smell, it does
not sound. It cannot be seen or heard. It cannot be described. Its
existence can only be proved by the negative evidence of our experience when we lack it. The Holy Spirit makes no demands, it
exacts no price, and it gives no account of itself. It is always "poor"
and if it could be poorer, so it would be. I hesitate to use the word
love to express its quality, but if love could be purified in its meaning, then this word would serve the Holy Spirit well.

But love as we know it best is more a matter of the heart. It is,
as it were, a reflection on the earthly plane of that Spirit which is
itself not an earthly thing at all, but a heavenly one. Our earthly
love is like the reflection in water (not so clear!) of a heavenly star.
The impact of the ray from the star upon the surface of the water
is like the impact of the Holy Spirit in our lives, except that the former is more visible. That same quality of endurance which belongs
to the spirit must be reflected also in our earthly lives. To become
disheartened is more temporary than to become dispirited, and
yet it is bad enough. The work which the heart is designed to do
in the third corner of the psychic compass, is to act as the focus-
point or filter through which the spirit can enter into matter in the
fourth corner of the psychic compass. To expect of our personal
hearts so much endurance as the spirit requires is to expect too
much. We need, perhaps, some clearer statement as to what this
responsibility involves.

Though the physiologists may say that they have never seen a
broken heart, and the anatomist may deny the possibility of such

an occurrence, yet we know that the phrase "a broken heart" means something. Hearts can break, and it is possible to say when and why they do so. I have said before that the journey from heaven to earth is a heart-breaking business for the very simple reason that the heart was broken before the journey commenced. That is why I told the story of the broken coin. The heart that knows its business accepts this fundamental principle, which has been expressed with simple tragedy in the traditional phrase "The Lamb slain since the beginning of the World." There is no limit to the sufferings which humanity may be called upon to endure for the spirit's sake. As men and women working in the spirit's cause, we have no rights whatsoever, and no reserves or privileges. It is only in so far as we lay claim to such rights, reserves and limitations, that our hearts may be "broken." Only the unbroken heart can experience the shock of being broken, when it feels that its claims have been improperly ignored. But "a broken and a contrite heart" can never break, nor be broken, for the simple reason that it has been broken once already—and has accepted it.

How can such calamities as a sickness of the spirit or an unbearable broken heart be remedied? By recognizing the Truth, I think, and by understanding things better than we do. The heart must first be healed before the spirit is set free again. Errors must be corrected and Truth stand in its place, before some of these puzzles of experience can be solved, and tragedies healed and shared. The first mistake to correct is that of thinking of our bodies and minds as the rightful owners of our spirits. They are not. They are the house, but they are not the householder. Our bodies are held by the spiritual tenant on a short lease that can be terminated at any moment without warning. Meanwhile, we are the trustees of certain instruments which it is our responsibility to keep in good order.

The spirit is a gift, but it is not our own or entirely for our private using. It is "of God;" which may mean, at any rate, that it is not "for me," but "for Him," or someone else but me. Similarly, all the instruments which belong at different corners of the psychic compass, including the framework of the body as a whole, are instruments of which we are but the temporary masters, yet servants ourselves of a higher and a deeper Law. The measure of our earthly pain is the measure of our resistance to the spiritual law; though, being human, we must resist, and so must suffer sometimes, too.

Make the Bells Ring

Yes, we are like bells. We are dependent things, slung from somewhere up above ourselves, to ring in time or out, cracked, true or silently. Each one is like a bell, a living flower to flow with beauty's sound and thus shine forth the voice of an emerging life, which is the music of God's Word. Our skin itself is made of many bells that can all tingle with the thrill of life. Each single cell is like a little bell and every pulsing movement of its heart is like a note that sounds in silence, rung by the inward hammer of the spirit, in living harmony with the myriad other bells that all make up our single symphony. This is our joy in Life: to play within our bells and make them ring. Each one of us is like a human carillon of many bells, on which some great Musician plays the music of the spheres. Especially, the bells of Christmastide remind us of good news, as the willing spirit enters incarnate into the dark, cold earth again. Yet bells ring all the year and joy lasts all the time, if we can learn to play our parts within this greater symphony.

When the last bell tolls that points the body's end, it only marks the finish of a phrase. To Life itself there is no end, as the traveler journeys on through working days, as well as sleepy nights. With the rising sun, he wakes refreshed again, to find and face another day, with some enjoyment and the usual work to do. With rise and fall of tone, with silence interlaced with sound, the bells ring on with their uncertain intervals. The round of Life-in-death cannot be broken by the fact of death-in-Life. The willing spirit can still ring true, as it lets its worn-out bodies die, becoming freed at last from their familiar grasp, to rise again, with faith, love, courage— the spirit's gifts with which to face a new adventure in individual responsibility. So each can ring his bell for joy in more abundant life. When space provides the silence of itself, let us make the bells ring. And, when the last bell tolls, let the bells ring!

From *Invisible Anatomy: A Study of "Nerves," Hysteria and Sex*

ENDNOTES

1. David Michael Kleinberg-Levin, *The Listening Self: Personal Growth, Social Change, and the Closure of Metaphysics* (New York: Routledge, 1989), back cover.

2. It should be noted that Howe's "I" and "me" predate and are of a completely different order than the "I," or *je*, and the "me," or *moi*, of Lacanian psycho-analysis, both of which Howe would view as different aspects of "me," the egoic self.

3. John Heaton, personal communication, December 13, 2011.

4. Endorsement by Jeffrey Kripal, on back cover of *The Knee Of Listening* (Middle-town, CA: The Dawn Horse Press, 2004), .

5. Ian C. Edwards, *Truth as Relationship: The Psychology of E. Graham Howe* (Pittsburgh: Duquesne University, 2006), 199–209.

6. Sung Bae Park, *Buddhist Faith and Sudden Enlightenment* (Albany: Suny Press, 1983), 125.

7. In practice, however, this proves to be grammatically inconvenient, unless it is done with due warning. But with their more perfect sensitiveness, "the Greeks had a word for it", and it may one day be possible to establish the words "Ego" and "Emauton"—there is no nominative, but neither should there be—as the orthodox and convenient verbal messengers of this distinction.

8. "Let each one do the best for himself in his own line of business, but let not one man interfere in that of another." *The Dictionary of Phrase and Fable, Brewer* (Wordsworth, Herfortdshire, 1993), 1018.

EDITOR'S ACKNOWLEDGMENTS

It has been nearly a quarter of a century since I first met E. Graham Howe's daughter and literary executor, Carolyn Whitaker, at her literary agency in London to propose that I might write a biography of her father or perhaps prepare an anthology of his writings. Despite my conspicuous lack of either credentials or experience as an editor, she embraced my enthusiasm for her father's work and generously entrusted me with his papers. Throughout the many ensuing years in which she has had to await my creation of DharmaCafé Books and then getting this book into print, Ms. Whitaker has shown me unfailingly patient support and good humor. I thank her very much for these.

I also offer my deepest thanks to my dear friend Markell Brooks, who quickly recognized the value of bringing Dr. Howe's spiritual psychology back into print and ultimately made it possible for me to do so.

It has taken me much longer to bring this book to press than I anticipated, and I am grateful for the steady support of both Richard Grossinger and Douglas Reil at my copublisher, North Atlantic Books. Hisae Matsuda, my able and gracious editorial counterpart there, has consistently provided the most thoughtful and timely assistance throughout the long editorial process.

This book could not have been delivered to the printer on its assigned date were it not for the extraordinary team who generously sacrificed portions of their December holiday time to render their assistance. They are Matt Barna, who has once again done his usual excellent job of design and layout; Megan Anderson, my unfailingly perspicacious copyeditor; Mary Harper, who produced her excellent index in record time; and Rose Young, who brought her eagle eye and keen intelligence to a very unusual text. I would also like to thank Steve Alexander, the cover designer, for yet another delightful collaboration.

I would buy any book endorsed by as gifted and diverse a group of writers on psychotherapy as Nathan Schwartz-Salant, M. Guy Thompson, Michael Eigen, and John Heaton. I thank them again for taking the time they took to review the manuscript and for lending their names in its support. I also greatly appreciate Andrew Harvey for graciously alerting spiritual aspirants to the value of Howe's work.

John Heaton very kindly shared with me his recollections about his time with Dr. Howe and his thoughts on the process of therapy from Howe's point of view.

I owe a special debt to M. Guy Thompson, a close student of R. D. Laing, whose own writings on a truly phenomenological psychotherapy have long since established him at the forefront of those carrying on Laing's work. Mr. Thompson not only contributed an engaging and illuminating foreword to this book but gave me sage advice that improved my own introduction. I also thank my longtime friend and colleague Eliot Hurwitz for his reflections on that introduction.

My dear intimate partner, Kouraleen MacKenzie, is the unseen presence behind the preparation of this book. The labor required to produce a work such as this inevitably requires the sacrifice of shared resources of time, attention, and money, a burden she has long borne willingly and without complaint. Her good humored relinquishment of our entire holiday season to the effort of completing this project, and her tender care of me during its most demanding moments, makes the publication of *The Druid of Harley Street* our joint gift to the world.

My deepest and most enduring debt, however, is to my beloved Spiritual Master and Eternal Heart-Companion, His Divine Presence, Avatar Adi Da Samraj. It is only because of Adi Da's perfect non-dual Teachings, which address and illuminate the complete spectrum of human growth and spiritual transcendence—and His Blessing-Transmission of the Truth those Teachings proclaim—that I was able to appreciate what a unique resource we have in the writings of E. Graham Howe. Once Adi Da's consummate Revelation about self-contraction and Divine Happiness become universally acknowledged, the world will look back upon the writings of Dr. Howe and see what a prophet he was.

Index

Page numbers in italics refer to figures.

Goethe, 317
ground (that other ground), 75, 76–79
groups and compulsion neurosis, 448
guilt, 286–289, 453–454, 455–458,
 513–514
guts, use of term, 17–18, 182, 192, 583

hand open/closed, simile of, 14–15,
 37, 119, 192, 235, 341, 584
hands, as instruments of relationship,
 111–113
handwashing, compulsive, 453–454, 455
hatred, 283, 456
hay fever, 150–151
headache, 151
Heard, Gerald, 593
Heaton, John, ix–x, 10–11
Heidegger, Martin, 51
Heraclitus, 49, 323
heredity, 451
Hinduism
 chakra system, 104–107, 137–138,
 150, 525
 interference with "I," 530
 Krishna, quotation of, 41
 and schizoid trend, 537
 Shiva/Shakti, 205, 278
 Yoga, 189, 218, 280
Hippocratic oath, 65
Hitler, 558, 586
holy, use of term, 576–577
the Holy Family, 273–330
 and balance, 558–559, *558*
 consciousness, 275–280
 man/male/father principle, 290–291,
 294, 298–299, 305–307, 558–559, *558*
 marriage, 308–314
 sexuality, 281–289
 Time, 315–330
 woman/feminine/mother principle,
 290–304
the Holy Mountain, 161–169, *162*, 492
 See also spirit
Home, Daniel D., 15
homosexuality, 29
hope and wishful thinking, 44–45, 66,
 264, 531, 554
Howe, Caroline, 27

Howe, Doris, 34, 35
Howe, E. Graham
 "The Autobiography of an Unwanted
 Man," 27
 biography of, 27–35
 clinical portraiture by, 4
 *Consciousness: A Western Treatment of
 Tibetan Yoga,* 35
 *Cure or Heal? A Study of Therapeutic
 Experience,* 6, 23, 35
 foreword by M.G. Thompson, viii–xi
 Heaton on, 10–11
 I and Me: A Study of the Self, 22
 influences on, 22–24
 introduction by W. Stranger, 1–25
 *Invisible Anatomy: A Study of "Nerves,"
 Hysteria and Sex,* 33
 and Laing, ix–x, 35
 meaning of relationship, 7–13
 The Mind of the Druid, 35
 Motives and Mechanisms of the Mind,
 x, 2–3, 6, 32
 Mysterious Marriage, 4, 34
 photograph of, 62
 relevance to spiritual practitioners,
 20–21
 scientism, critique of, 4–6
 *She and Me: A New Statement of an Old
 Problem,* 2, 35
 *The Triumphant Spirit: A Study of
 Depression,* 33
 *War Dance: A Study in the Psychology of
 War,* 33
 Where This War Hits You, 33
Howe, John Foster, 27
Howe, Norah (Blaxill), 31–32, 34
human consciousness, use of term, 178
human development, 214–217
humanism, 25, 155
human will. *See* Will; willpowers
humiliation, 232
humor, 259, 456–457
Husserl, Edmund, 7
hysteria, 333–378
 attacks of, 341–343
 and conflict, *342,* 343–346
 definition of, 357, 376
 dramatization of, 353–355

spirit *(continued)*
impact of force on, 112
incarnation, anatomy of, 159–169
It's Quite Impossible illustration,
581, 582
meaning of growth, 575–578
mechanical force vs., 586–588
positive vs. negative energy, 596–597
square and circle illustration, *575*
as that other ground, 78–79
use of term, 582–583
and wheel-and-road relationship,
200
and whole self, 61–63
See also headings at incarnation;
the Holy Mountain; psychic
compass
spiritual body, 161
spiritual practitioners, Howe's
relevance to, 20–21
the spoiled child, 379–406
and aggression, 379–380
causes of, 388–392
and the Collective, 392–393
consciousness, attitude toward,
393–394
cure and treatment, 405–406
duality and ambivalence, 383
explanation of, 385–388
and hysteria, 373
and love, 401–402
and morality, 397–398
relations with others, 400–401
and religion, 398–400
and right mothering, 384–385
selfishness, 395–397
situation, attitude toward, 402–403
and spoiled adult behavior, 391,
404–405
two mothers of, 381–383
and wise mothering, 390
Stalin, 558
Steiner, Rudolf, 3, 125, 213
Stranger, William, introduction, 1–25
stupidity, 428–429
suffering
in Buddhism, 528

explanation of, 555–557
and the spoiled child, 383
and Time, 320–322
suicide, 65, 516, 522
Sung, Bae Park, 21
superiority, feeling of, 415, 423–426
surgery, 474–475
Suzuki, D.T., 34
symbolism, origins of term, 454
sympathetic nervous system, 19, 146,
148–150, 152
sympatheticotonia, 150
"Synchronicity: An Acausal Connecting
Principle" (Jung), 15

Taoism, 16, 22–23, 41, 49, 168, 528
Tavistock Clinic, ix–x, 16–17, 32, 33
That, 2, 551–554
Thera, Nyanoponika, 34
therapeutic process, 551–571
cure vs. heal, 566–567
encouragement, 570
explanation of, 561–567
frequency of interviews, 570
Heaton on, 10–11
and meaning of relationship, 7–13
and psychiatry, 551–559
within relationships, 564–565
stages of, 562–563
therapists, characteristics of, 562,
565, 569–571
and Time, 565–566
See also psychotherapy
therapists, characteristics of, 562, 565,
569–571
thinking mind, 18, 179
See also imagination/thinking
Thompson, M. Guy, foreword, viii–ix
thrill, use of term, 164–167
Time
and aggressiveness, 249–254
and children, 325–326, 327
egoic/masculine serial time,
324–325
Father Time, 322
female/cyclical time, 323–324, 325,
326–327